College & University
Food Service Manual

COLLEGE & UNIVERSITY FOOD service manual

PAUL FAIRBROOK

With a Chapter on Vending by John Milano.

Colman Publishers
1147 Elmwood
Stockton, California 95204

Printed in the United States of America
by Vanguard Press, Stockton, California.

ISBN Number: 0-9602456-0-X

Library of Congress Catalog Card No.: 79-50956

Cover Design:
Kirk Beebe, Stockton, California

TABLE OF CONTENTS

APPENDIXES

EXHIBITS

FOREWORD

If you are a young college or university food service manager eager to learn more about your profession and hopeful that some day soon you too will be in charge of the food services for an entire campus, then this book is for you. If you are a not-so-young food service manager who feels perhaps a little bit "in a rut", then this book is for you also. Finally, even if you are a successful head of a college or university food service, this book can serve as a "refresher course" and remind you of all the things you did once, wanted to do, or should be doing to be more effective in your job.

When I became Director of Food Services at Northern Illinois University in 1954, the only real qualification that I had to offer was boundless enthusiasm, a liking for people, food cost control training, and a reference from Michigan State University. As a result, all of my early experiences, from the first food riot to the floods in the dining room, to the head cook quitting without notice, had to be solved by intuition without any real knowledge, and without anyone to guide me or to stop me from making a mistake. The purpose of this book is to prevent this from happening to you. It is intended as a working manual -- a blueprint for action -- and a guide to your problem-solving. When you start on a new job, for instance, and everyone is watching to see what you're going to do -- what should you do first? How do you get your image across so that everyone understands just who you are and what you stand for? How do you handle the many eager salesmen, ready to pounce on you the minute you arrive on campus? What do you say to the president's wife, who wants an intimate dinner for twelve, gourmet-style, served the following Wednesday? What about the "chef", who gives you an ultimatum before you've even put down your briefcase? What about your boss, who has been waiting with plans for the new kitchen until you arrived, and who wants your opinion right then and there? How do you handle the Faculty Dames, whose Renaissance Christmas Party just "can't wait" and who insist on a price from you before September 15?

Answers to these and many other questions are readily found in this book. Read it once, perhaps a second time, and then continue to use it as a reference guide as various problems come up. The appendixes are samples for you to use as you see fit: adopt them, change them, or improve them. Discard them if you want to, but let them give you your own, fresh solutions to the problems that will beset you in your job.

A food service manager's job on a college campus is an exciting and rewarding one: you meet interesting people; you feel creative in making others happy; you have freedom to use your imagination and inventiveness; you work in a supportive atmosphere; and you find each day full of new and interesting challenges. All this is doubly so if you feel that you are on top of things, that you have the solutions to your campus's food service problems. Let this book be one of your tools.

Throughout the book, reference is made to the food service director as "he." **Needless to say, this is done only for the sake of convenience.** Some parts of the book are aimed specifically at the food service *director* -- i.e., the person responsible for all the food operations on a campus. Most of the book, however, is aimed at *all* food service managers and supervisors in colleges and universities.

If you read this book from cover to cover, you will read something about most, though not all, of the matters which concern a college or university food service manager in the performance of his job. There are some subjects, important to you, which have been intentionally left out. The question of whether or not a college food service should be run by the school itself or by an outside caterer; the problems of energy conservation in food service; sample purchasing specifications, and specific quantity recipes are examples. In each instance it was felt that the subject either went beyond the scope of this book, or was available elsewhere in greater detail than would have been possible here.

This book is intended to help you in two ways: One, in the way that you will use it as you read it -- as a general manual, intended to acquaint you with the profession of college food service director in general, and with the daily problems that must be dealt with in particular. The other purpose for the book is to serve as a reference book, which you can keep at your fingertips and use as specific problems arise. Because a number of highly qualified food service directors have read, criticized, and contributed to the book, the solutions to problems are generally applicable, and do not represent only one person's individual approach.

I take pleasure in acknowledging the many professionals who have reviewed and criticized either the whole, or portions of this manuscript. My particular thanks are given to the following four friends and colleagues who served as readers of the entire manuscript, and whose many helpful suggestions and valuable advice is reflected in these pages:

Maxine Anderson, Director of Food Service
    Stanford University, Palo Alto, California
Terry Adams, Director of Food Service
    K-State Union, Kansas State University, Manhattan, Kansas
Donald M. Jacobs, Director of Dining Services
    University of Pennsylvania, Philadelphia, Pennsylvania
Douglas H. Richie, General Manager, Forty-Niner Shops
    California State University, Long Beach, Long Beach, California

Others whose help is gratefully acknowledged are Larry Brehm, Al del Prete, Mary Heacock, John Milano, Ross Moriarty, Doyle Minden, Gerald Ramsey, Agnes Bierwagen, the late Dr. Alan Morrison, Charlotte Schwyn and my niece, Jean Vogt. Lew Herbst and Sam Huff were the readers for the chapter on vending. Jim Bratcher and Ted Cole gave valuable technical advice concerning the printing of this book. To Stanley E. McCaffrey, President and to Robert R. Winterberg, Financial Vice President, of the University of the Pacific go special thanks for making available the time and the funds needed for a project of this kind, and to my boss, Bob McMaster, for his constant support. I am also deeply grateful to Susan Gage and Linda Dillard for their enthusiasm and skill in typing and typesetting the manuscript, and to my friend Dr. Roger Mueller for serving as editor and advisor in this project. Finally, I want to pay a special tribute to my wife Peig, who knew how much the publication of this book meant to me and who encouraged me every step of the way.

Paul Fairbrook
February 1979

I. PROFILE OF THE MODERN FOOD SERVICE DIRECTOR

The single most important factor in the success or failure of a food service on a college campus is You, the food service director. If you are the *right* person for the job, everything else will fall into place. Let's take a look and see just what it takes to be a successful food service director on a college campus today:

Enthusiasm

Serving others can be drudgery or it can be a joy, depending on the rapport that exists between the server and those who are being served. A college community takes its cue about food service from the director and his attitude. It is reassuring for the students to see their food service director proud and happy about the food being served; the faculty and staff are relieved when they see that food service, so often a problem on campuses, is in the hands of a director who obviously likes his job, likes his school, and is self-confident and joyful in the performance of his duties.

Empathy

The ability to understand others, and to try to "get behind" the superficial facade that people put up is terribly important for the food service director. Students' reactions about the food being served are seldom caused exclusively by the quality of the food itself. The needs of the college student go beyond housing, food, and academic knowledge. A yearning to be independent, to discover one's potential, to develop one's own identity, in other words the need "to find one's self," lies at the root of every student's words and actions. Somber feelings such as loneliness, homesickness, rebelliousness, disenchantment or ambivalence toward family and friends, insecurity, and frustration do constant battle with the more positive expressions of a young spirit such as curiosity, pride, receptiveness, and a constant willingness to love and to be loved.

Food and drink, therefore, actually hold a minor rank in the value scale of today's college student: only inasmuch as these are subjects used to express some other feelings do they really matter to the average student (unless the food is *really* bad, in which case students might riot). The food service director understands this, and tries to get behind the words and actions of his student-clientele. The ability to meet the students' real needs with empathy and affection thus becomes a major requirement for success.

Dedication

Successful service on a college campus is more closely akin to serving in the ministry than to working for a large corporation; it is a commitment rather than a job. Most often, those who decide to work at a college are somewhat idealistic: they like to work with young people; they enjoy their employees, the academic environment, the intellectual stimulation of the faculty; they believe in the goals and ideals of the institution which they serve; and they are determined to help in achieving these goals. These are not abstract concepts, rather they are essential prerequisites for the food service manager who truly wants to be part of the team.

Ethics

Ethical behavior is an obvious requirement for any successful career, not just one at a college or university. A college or university career, however, requires a degree of integrity and honesty not normally found, nor necessarily asked for, in business and industry. The kind of honesty we deal with here is more than that normally understood; it is dealing with others in complete candor and openness which comes from a fundamental recognition that problems must be shared in order to be solved, and that members of the college community must be trusted if they are expected to be supportive of one's actions. The temptation to treat students differently than faculty and staff, to regard them as merely a part of a transient wave, is one experienced by every college administrator, especially when some students seem to thrive on complicating the life of administrators. Nevertheless, to be successful means to resist such temptations, and to live in accordance with one's ideals. If anything, students need to be treated more tenderly, and with greater understanding, as they are younger.

Quality

A young food service director in the Midwest has the following slogan hanging above his office desk: "Nothing Counts But Quality!" With that slogan he has captured the essence of his operational goals and, at the same time, has announced to everyone else just what he stands for as a food service executive. An unflinching commitment to quality is not merely good for public relations, it is an invaluable aid in the solution of most everyday problems. If quality is truly the primary objective, then the conflicting claims of time, finances, etc. must take second place. It is in the self-interest of the food service director to opt for quality before settling for expediency. The person who gets fired for spending too much money usually gets fired for not also doing a first-rate, quality-conscious job. It is better not to serve an item than to serve one of poor quality; it is better not to accept a catering function, than to do it poorly. If you put on a special dinner, make sure it is really exceptional. Most important, perhaps, is the feeling within the food service manager himself that everything he has planned and done has been to provide a first-class, high-quality food service operation for the benefit of the campus community.

Outgoing Personality

There are some jobs in which a quiet, demure, introverted personality is well suited: researcher and librarian are two that come to mind. That of food service director, however, is not one of them. While it may not be necessary to dance up and down with joy in the dining room, the good food service director must reach out to all of his students, even to those who are shy, distant, or otherwise unapproachable. He must be a naturally pleasant person, and his cheerfulness should be contagious. You cannot imagine how much this means on a college campus. A long line of anxious students waiting to eat can be calmed down just by a friendly world of explanation by the forthright food service manager who admits to some goof-up or another in the kitchen. A lonely, brooding student can suddenly feel a part of everything if the manager just takes the trouble to talk to him.

Leadership Ability

The higher a person gets in his profession, the more important become his leadership and his human relations skills, and the less important become his technical skills. A good food service director can inspire his staff to accomplishments that even they were unaware of; since many food service employees are students, the degree to which he can direct his staff has an especially important bearing not only on how these students will work for him, but also on how they will support his food service with the rest of the student body. The regular kitchen staff needs a food service director who will lead them, teach them, and who will set their standard for them. The ability to "steer the ship through often-stormy waters" is of paramount importance to a successful food service manager.

Food Service Knowledge

Everyone looks to the food service director for guidance in matters involving the serving of food and beverages, and generally he is expected to speak from personal knowledge and experience in giving advice or making decisions. While a solid academic background, in whatever field of study, may be helpful in dealing with the faculty and students in general terms, there is no real substitute for the specific knowledge that comes from having studied restaurant or institutional management and nutrition in college, or from having a solid background of good supervisory and production food service experience. A qualified food service manager knows just what to do when someone complains of (possible) food poisoning, when the cafeteria line runs out of food, when the dish-machine goes on the blink, or when half of the help doesn't show up for work. Everyone on campus is also aware that he knows his job. His word, therefore, in areas of food service, is accepted without question and he can concentrate on getting the job done without interference from others who know less than he does. While it is not absolutely essential that he know every job in the kitchen, it would be helpful if he could at least familiarize himself with every job; pitching in as cashier, cook, dishwasher, and pantry worker is a smart idea, and the successful manager is one who has done that type of work frequently.

Business Knowledge

A good food service manager must be able to not only maintain his credibility with those working as his subordinates but, equally important, he must do so with his superiors. Whether he reports to a business manager or to a dean -- in both cases he is expected to achieve the financial objectives of his institution and to do so in a manner consistent with good business practice. While a "unit manager," (the person in charge of one residence hall dining room, or one eating area, or one kitchen) can be expected to understand basic cost control practices, to take and control inventories, and to prepare and interpret simple periodic operating reports, the food service director must be able to do much more. He is, after all, ultimately responsible for the management of a business with a volume of several hundred thousand dollars annually. He is therefore expected not only to understand and analyze financial statements, but he should also possess a good grasp of accounting. He should be familiar with the ways in which computer services can help his operations, and be able to see clearly how the food service operations mesh with the overall financial picture.

Close Liaison with Other Food Service Professionals

One of the problems besetting many food service directors is that there is no one on campus who can be considered his peer. Since he is the top food service officer of his school, he has little opportunity to be evaluated by others who know his profession as well as he does. Satisfied students, good profit and loss statements, and relative calm on the campus are significant goals to accomplish. Somewhere, though, each manager should test his ideas, and his operations, against the impartial judgment of others who are qualified to judge. Frequent close contact with professional equals is intellectually stimulating, provides an incentive to try out new and novel ideas, and gives the manager a feeling that he is developing professionally even though he may have been in the same job for some time. For all these reasons, and many others (good public relations, social stimulation, etc.) the good food service director makes it a point to maintain the closest liaison possible with his peers in regional and national organizations (e.g. the *National Association of College and University Food Services*), to attend local, state, and national conventions and trade shows, as well as workshops and seminars pertaining to his daily work.

Awareness of and Dedication to Good Nutrition

Good nutrition is not only of tremendous importance to the health and well-being of your students, it is also a subject which is more and more coming to the fore in public consciousness. Students are not always as aware of good nutrition principles and practices as they should be. It is an essential part of the food service director's job, not only as the students' friend, but also as their advisor and teacher, to fill this void. Whether he does it himself, or sees that nutrition education is handled by one of the dietitians is immaterial: a deep and abiding commitment to nutrition education and good nutrition practices in the dining room is an absolute necessity if he wants to be truly a modern food service professional.

II. SETTING UP A FOOD SERVICE ORGANIZATION

Whenever a new food service director takes over on a college or university campus, he is inheriting someone else's organization. It must be clear right from the outset that the new director cannot, and should not, be burdened with the past, or be expected to follow exactly in his predecessor's footsteps. A new director is never identical to his predecessor. From the day he arrives, the campus food service is his responsibility, be it bad, good, or indifferent. It is essential, therefore, that the new director sets up *his own* food service operation as quickly as possible -- one that reflects his thinking, his philosophy of operations, his standards of quality, and his special way of doing things. The sooner this is done, the better it is! The "honeymoon" never lasts very long, neither for new presidents, nor for new food service directors. The following chapters list, in order of *chronological priority,* the various steps that need to be taken to organize (or re-organize) a food service operation.

III. BUILDING YOUR IMAGE ON CAMPUS

The first question that everyone asks whenever any new, important person arrives on campus is, of course: "What's he like?" In your case, it is especially critical that the answer to this crucial question is provided *quickly* and *accurately*. Since you will not only represent, but in fact personify, the entire food service organization, the campus community must find out right away who you are, what you have done, what you know. Even more important, they should know what you believe, what you stand for, and what you aim to accomplish in your new job. You cannot permit yourself to "settle in" slowly, and let the campus come to you; like a new restaurant owner, you must sell yourself to your clients from the moment you arrive. Remember that those who gave you the job are not necessarily the ones who will enable you to keep it: it is the students, the faculty, and the staff of the college who will be your clients, your judges, and hopefully, your enthusiastic supporters. There are several steps you can take immediately upon arrival:

Personal Visit to All Department Heads
Ask your new boss to take you around personally, to meet all department heads, both in the faculty and administration. Be sure to include the heads of the student government, maintenance, security, building and grounds, public relations, personnel, accounting, academic senate, student activities and all other major departments on campus.

Personal Visit Through All Dining Areas
Start making contacts with all the students immediately upon arrival; if it is summer, meet the summer students (there are always some who will be there in September!). If freshmen arrive for orientation, ask for the chance to speak to them. Important Hint: Do *not* give them a whole lot of information at this point; *no one is listening anyway.* What others are doing is merely "sizing you up", so try to project yourself as you really are, and save the "facts" for later.

Personal Visit with Each Food Service Employee
In addition to the general introduction made for you by your new boss, the people in the kitchen must have a chance to meet you personally, directly, and without long delays. Remember that they are full of *anxiety* ("I wonder if he'll fire me?"), *self-importance* ("There are a few things about this place you ought to know. . ."), *pride* ("I set up the breakfast line every morning, all by myself.") and *special items of information* ("The former director promised me. . ."). You must arrange, therefore, to give them this opportunity -- either through extended visits with each one in the dining room (between meal periods), or else through personal interviews in your office. In the latter case, you want to make certain, of course, that all employees know it's just a "social visit", and don't worry unnecessarily prior to coming to see you. In colleges where the food service staff is unionized, some extra discretion is advisable.

Publicity Releases

First, ask your boss how he intends to publicize your arrival. If he has no specific plans, and is willing to leave it up to you, contact the director of public relations and work out, with him, a suitable news release that can be mailed out by his department to the local news media, as well as to alumni and other college organizations. Such a release should tell not only of your arrival, but also of your personal and professional background, your family, your goals and expectations, and why you are pleased to become a part of the college community. Make sure that this news release is also sent to every regional and national profesional organization to which you may belong, or which you may wish to join in the near future (e.g., the National Association of College and University Food Services (NACUFS), the Association of College and University Housing Officers (ACUHO), the National Association of College Auxiliary Services (NACAS), and the Food Service Executives Association (FSEA).)

Story in School Newspaper

The college newspaper can be many things to many people: some regard it as a handicap, others as an aid, others as a dispenser of vital information, and still others as a gossip sheet full of slander and misinformation. During your career on the campus, you will at times regard the student newspaper as all of these; if you are wise, however, the paper can become one of your staunchest supporters. It all depends upon whether or not you appear to the cautious, often-skeptical, and usually inexperienced newspaper staff as a sincere, enthusiastic, and knowledgeable person. An interview with the editor, who will probably arrive on campus just before the school year starts, is essential: this will usually result in your being interviewed by a student reporter. These are often young, nervous, and totally inexperienced freshmen, and your ability to get them to write an accurate story, one which properly reflects your point of view, will be crucial. Complete candor on your part, mixed with an honest enthusiasm and a willingness to really "open up" with your student reporter, is the best prescription for such an interview.

Memos to Students, Staff, or Faculty

Part of your image has to be a feeling on the part of the campus community that you're a person who "gets things done." Shortly after your arrival, you will note certain policies or practices that require an immediate change. After checking signals with your boss, a good idea, especially during the first few months on a new job, is to issue memos announcing such changes. Whether these deal with improved sanitation, food preparation practices in the kitchen, extended serving hours or additional choices in the dining room, or revised billing procedures for the faculty -- doesn't really matter. What does matter is your image as an able, decisive, competent and forceful administrator, who is dedicated to making improvements.

Staff Meetings with Supervisors

As a modern, imaginative, and idealistic food service director, you will surely be committed to a policy of "participative management". This means that all of your supervisory assistants will be encouraged to make suggestions, criticisms, or modifications in the existing procedures, and that you will look to them to help you accomplish your objectives. This can only be done if you conduct *regular* staff meetings, and if you begin these almost immediately upon arrival on campus. Some food service managers believe that they are having "staff meetings" when they merely sit down to have lunch with their supervisors, but this, obviously, is not the same as a regular meeting, in a more formal setting like an office or private room, where notes are taken and an agenda, however informal, is followed.

Town-and-Gown Relations

As soon as possible, you should make an effort to get to know segments of the community which could affect your work on campus or your reputation. One such group is the private caterers, who will regard you as a possible competitor. If you make a special effort they may come to regard you as a friend and colleague, who may occasionally be in a position to steer catering business to them, to help them with special problems, and to call on them for help if needed. One area of concern to private caterers is always that of unfair price competition, and you will need to give them some assurance on this point as soon as possible. Another influential group consists of the service clubs in town; an indication of your willingness to address then at an upcoming luncheon meeting, preferably on a subject connected with your work at the college, would be a wise move. Remember that colorful slides of interesting food items are always popular and remember also, that you must make your talk brief. Finally, an important group to contact is the campus ministry; the various ministers, priests and rabbis should receive your pledge of support and interested assistance (e.g. serving fish during Lent, matzoh during Passover, and an alternate choice for pork products whenever these are served).

IV. DEVELOPING A MASTER PLAN FOR FOOD SERVICE

In trying to decide just what you should do first when starting your new job as food service director, consider yourself an architect; instead of building a house, you are building a food service operation. If the "house" is already standing, you're planning a major renovation. In either case, you need a *blueprint,* that's your first step. The following will tell you how to proceed.

SUPERVISION

Type of Manager

Your first, key move is to decide on the type of supervision you need to run the entire food service. Please note that we are talking about the "type" of supervision, and not about the individuals. You cannot probably judge fairly and adequately immediately upon arriving at your new location, which of your assistants is qualified, which is loyal, and which has growth potential. Of course, if there is an *obvious* problem with one or another individual, make the necessary changes as soon as possible. It becomes harder the longer you stay there, and on some campuses, it is almost impossible! Make absolutely certain that you have the whole-hearted support of your superior, or else you begin to erode the confidence he placed in you at a dangerously early stage of your new employment.

A clear decision that you must make is just what *style* of supervision you want to establish. There are basically three types of college food service supervisors (The term "supervisor" is used interchangeably with "manager" throughout this book; no difference in position is intended in the use of either term): the professionally trained food service supervisor, the chef or head cook, and the student manager. Each has something unique to offer:

The Professional Unit Manager -- Most colleges and universities utilize a professionally-trained person to run the various food service units on a campus. This is true both of food service management companies and institutions which operate their own food service. The term "professionally-trained" is, of course, subject to various interpretations. Normally, it describes a person who has a college degree and several years of experience in college food service work, of which some was spent in a supervisory capacity. This could be a young man or woman who had worked as a student manager while going through college and decided to continue in this field of work. It could also be a highly qualified dietitian, whose experience could include internships and residency work in a hospital, but whose college food service experience might be limited. It might describe someone without college training, who has worked himself up through the ranks into a supervisory position.

It must be clear already that, even within this category, the backgrounds and talents of the individuals will vary tremendously, and your deciding to work with such a type of supervisor will not, in itself, guarantee you a good management team.

The young ex-student can be a marvelous person in the dining room, and an absolute failure in the kitchen; the dietitian could, conceivably, be great on menus and nutrition, and a dismal failure in kitchen production and management; the supervisor from the ranks is probably a great cook or salad maker, but might not know how to communicate properly with the students, and might be completely lost when it comes to food cost control and other types of accounting work. Nevertheless, if you decide on this type of manager, then you are, at least in theory, raising the level of your food service operation to that of all other departments in your institution, including the instructional ones, and you can count on a reasonably effective level of communication, not only between yourself and your immediate subordinates, but also between your supervisors and the rest of the campus community. *While there are many, many exceptions,* it is often true that students and faculty respond better to a food service supervisor who has gone to college, than to one who has not. The reason is obvious: there are many areas of shared experiences that bring such a supervisor closer to his campus clients, and conversations need not be limited only to what's on the menu and how good the food tastes.

The Chef or Head Cook -- Very seldom can a college or university find or afford to employ a real chef in the true sense of the word. Such an individual, usually trained in Europe or apprenticed to a European chef to learn the finest standards of food preparation and classical cuisine, demands a salary that can be afforded only by the finest hotels and restaurants; furthermore, his skills are often beyond those needed, or even wanted, to satisfy the rather conservative tastes of the students. A chef would be a tremendous asset to any large catering operation, and the college food service director who has managed to attract and keep a trained chef on his staff has a tremendous advantage when it comes to the preparation of special dinners or other catering events. In any case, often the term "chef" is given to persons who are, in reality, only head cooks; they have probably been at the college or university for a very long time, they know the operation thoroughly, and they are supervising the entire kitchen staff, under the direction of the food service director. There are some cases where such an arrangement works well: in a kitchen, where the food preparation functions are totally separated from the serving of food, and where the latter is handled either by student managers or else by a separate service supervisor. It can also work in a very small college, where the chef knows most of the campus community, where his lack of a college education and, possibly, lack of management skills are outweighed by his friendly personality and familiarity with his institution. Usually, however, it is very risky to utilize a chef or a head cook as a food service manager. His abilities to communicate on an equal level with faculty and students are seriously hampered not only by his own educational limitations but, perhaps even more, by the way others perceive him in the scheme of things: title or not, he is always considered a cook and, in America, this title unfortunately does not rank very high. Furthermore, you might have difficulty in getting across to him your new ideas: many of these involve delicate balancing between costs and profits on one hand and the achievement of subtle objectives such as helping students to overcome homesickness on the other. It helps to be dealing with those who can understand what you are trying to accomplish.

The Student Manager -- The use of students as supervisors in a college food service operation is in many ways the most challenging and also the most rewarding experience of all. It is challenging because the stakes are very high: in case of success, your food service can quickly become a highly popular operation. In case of failure, you pay not only in terms of poor food quality and poor morale on the part of your staff, but also in terms of the attitude of the rest of the students, whose normal instinct is to defend the student manager. Furthermore, the campus community as a whole is not really interested in your problems with student supervisors, but rather in the final products of quality food and service. Successful use of student managers, however, is most rewarding. There is a good feeling on the part of the students, who respond much better to their peers, on the part of the regular staff, (the kitchen women tend to "mother" a popular student manager), and on the part of the faculty, who like the idea of a student getting an early advancement. The good student manager can also help you create good communications between the students and food service, and can act as a valuable liaison between the students and yourself.

There are, also, however, some problems with hiring a student as manager:

The job goes to his head -- The job demands unusual maturity for a young person placed in a position of authority and responsibility. Some students who are given such authority may try to make up for their lack of supervisory experience and self-confidence by being bossy and argumentative. If this is the case, then you have created problems for yourself that are difficult to overcome.

He does not take the job seriously -- For most students, a job on a college campus is generally only a means to an end, not the end itself. You may expect from your student manager a degree of devotion to the job that he is simply not willing to give. His main objective, remember, is not to work in food service, it is to get a degree, make new social contacts, mature, and learn to live away from home -- sometimes, of course, a student becomes really "turned on" by his food service job, and perhaps even decides on a food service career, and then your choice will prove to be fortuitous.

He shows favoritism to friends -- This is an obvious problem, and one not easily solved by warnings and promises; the pressures of peer friendships are too great to allow for a simple solution to a basic problem.

He leaves you just when you have him trained -- Normally your student managers are juniors, seniors, or graduate students. This means that you have use of them for two or three years at most. Your best managers will often be those who have worked with you for a number of years and thoroughly understand what you are trying to accomplish. Unless a student manager, therefore, decides to stay with you upon graduation, you have lost a large investment in management training as soon as he leaves college.

You cannot terminate him easily -- While terminating your employees should not be a major objective in your planning, the ability to make personnel changes as needed is crucial to your success. Try to dismiss the popular student manager! If the cause is serious you probably cannot divulge it; if it is less serious, no one would agree with you. All the students really understand is that you, the administrator, are firing one of them, a student, and this is enough to make matters complicated.

In spite of these drawbacks, students, carefully selected, are an excellent management source, and should be utilized whenever possible.

Staff Meetings

Obviously, if drastic changes need to be made in the area of supervision, you won't be able to do this immediately. What you *can* do right away, however, is to form your management team, and work with it to accomplish your objectives. It is essential that your managers get to know you, not only as a person but also as a department head. They should know what you stand for, how you operate, what you expect from them, and how you want them to do their job. One of the best ways to accomplish this is through *regular weekly staff meetings.* (At the Kansas State University Union, staff meetings are held daily, but for no more than 30 minutes).

A good staff meeting lasts no more than two hours, is a happy medium between an informal luncheon discussion and a formal committee meeting, has an agenda that is both planned as well as open-ended, and, most important of all, allows a *free interchange of ideas between all of the participants.* It is here, in the staff meetings, that "participative management" is put to the real test. Your willingness to accept input, criticism, and constructive suggestions, plus your ability to conduct these meetings on a high level and to turn them into learning experiences for your management staff, will make the difference between success and failure. Be sure to appoint someone to take brief but accurate minutes of each meeting, and then distribute typed copies to each participant as well as to your own supervisor, so that he, too, knows what is going on in food service, and knows the reasons for the decisions you have taken. A sample set of minutes is found in Exhibit IV-1.

Weekend Supervision

Since you are being held responsible for everything that goes on in your operation from the moment you arrive, it is essential that you cover all your bases quickly. One of these is the problem of weekend supervision. Because so many students go home on weekends, and because all the campus offices are closed, there is a great temptation on the part of many administrators on college campuses to let the weekends take care of themselves. Why anyone should think that merely because the numbers are cut in half, the kitchens and dining halls need little or no supervision is not quite clear, but that is often the feeling on many campuses, a feeling no doubt encouraged by the fact that the food service manager would like the weekend off. Obviously, if there is insufficient supervisory staff to cover the operation seven days a week you have to make some arrangements for days off. Your own effectiveness is at stake if you work too many days in a row and, of course, you are expected to be working on campus during weekday office hours. The solution is to delegate some of the responsibility to other employees (e.g. a head salad person, a head cook, and a student manager for the serving line) and if necessary have a manager come in just for the crucial serving period during the dinner meal. If there is any kind of important catering function, however, supervisors have to cover it regardless of days

EXHIBIT IV-1

UNIVERSITY OF THE PACIFIC
Food Service Staff Meeting Minutes
March 2, 1978

Joyce Smith
Bob asked if Joyce could be made head porter at Grace Covell, even though he is temporarily at the Bake Shop. This would be a raise from $3.65/hr. to $3.95/hr. Mary Heacock okayed the raise. Bob will fill out a change of status form.

Good Nutrition Week
Paul Fairbrook would like the week to be light-hearted and a happy week. We want to share with them our knowledge and information on the subject. Sheri is in charge of the week's program. Whatever is done at Quad should be done at Grace Covell also. Some comments (menu) have already been received by students. P.F. and Sheri went to a meeting in San Jose on nutrition. Obesity for teenagers is mostly caused by lack of exercise, not necessarily eating too much. P.F. would like to know the cholesterol level of the current liquid shortening we are using, also a cost comparison between the current shortening and safflower oil.

Sack Lunches
On Friday, March 17, 1978, M.H. would like the residence halls to have a going home sack lunch table. Grace Covell closes after lunch Friday, March 17, and Quad after dinner Friday, March 17. Grace Covell will re-open Monday, March 27, 1978.

Students Serving on Lines
M.H. and P.F. are concerned with too many students serving on the line and not the full-time staff. We should be saving money but utilizing our full-time staff more. P.F. feels that the full-time staff is finding other jobs to do instead of serving on the line and making sure that our service is as good as it should be. We have to guide and supervise our full-time staff so that they will reach their full potential of being a good, loyal employee of the University.

Catering
M.H. went through the catering for this weekend. Sheri is on, so have a good one m'lady!

Objectives and Requirements for Food Service Supervisors
P.F. discussed these objectives and requirements. P.F. and M.H. will be evaluating the supervisors using Personnel's new evaluation forms. Evaluation is a two-way street and they will expect to be evaluated by the supervisors. P.F. has decided to write the objectives and requirements. He would like our modifications and ideas so that he can use these two documents. Whenever he or Mary have perceptions about an employee, he or she will write the supervisors about that employee. That comment will be filed in the employee's file. If the supervisors do not agree, then that disagreement should be noted.

Merit Raises
P.F. will dedicate one staff meeting to merit raises. Mr. Case will be invited to this meeting.

off. Perhaps the easiest way to explain this all to your staff is to state, right from the outset, that you will not necessarily be bound by their desire to have two days off each week, and that there will be quite a number of weeks during the school year when this is simply impossible. Obviously, the Christmas and Easter recesses are when you can make up for some of these "lost" days.

Shift Work for Supervisors

In some larger operations, food supervisors are often scheduled to take either the morning shift or the evening shift. It is crucial that you don't let your staff back you into a corner. For example, some manager may think that he has been hired primarily for the morning shift. If you suddenly need his services on another shift, you have a problem. During the school year at least, a manager has to be willing to work anytime from 7 a.m. through 7 p.m. or late, including some weekends. Anyone who cannot or is not willing to do that, is not a good candidate for you. Make this clear from the outset.

QUALITY CONTROL

Earlier, this book referred to the following motto: "Nothing Counts But Quality!" It summarizes exactly what each food service director should strive for. Convenience, finances, and popularity all come later. Establishing a quality food service operation is not easy. It requires, first, that you know what constitutes a quality food service operation. There are many throughout the country: one notable operation is at Brigham Young University in Provo, Utah, where the same Food Service Director, Wells Cloward, has been in charge for many years, and has honed his operation to the fine edge of perfection. In such a good operation, you will immediately note the following:

a.   All the food is served either very *hot* or very *cold* and the dinner plates are heated. Covers are used with steam table pans, as are overhead infrared lights.

b.   All the food is decorated. On a cafeteria line the food pans are decorated; all banquet platters have colorful garnishes, individual salads or desserts have some little extra touches (e.g. croutons on the salads, slivered almonds on the pudding) to add something "extra" to the dish.

c.   Everyone is in uniform -- regular as well as student employees. All with long hair wear hairnets without exception.

d.   The beverage and salad counters in the dining rooms are constantly wiped up and kept in spotless condition throughout the meal.

e.   The kitchen itself is immaculate. Not only are the floors kept clean throughout the day, but there is little or no trash such as cardboard boxes, towels, books, etc. lying on top of refrigerators, range shelves, or dishtables. Each department has easy and quick access to a broom and a mop, and each person cleans up after himself.

f. The cooks have a standardized recipe in front of them when they cook, carefully protected in a plastic cover.

g. The pot room and dishroom are clean and sterile, and little or no excess water spills on the floor. The trash cans in the kitchens are all lined with plastic liners. None are overflowing, and all have covers on them.

h. The cafeteria servers are all cheerful, and give each customer individual attention. Servings are either pre-proportioned, or else the servers use designated spoons or ladles. A list of portion sizes is prominently displayed at each serving line.

i. All griddle items are prepared progressively, and the customer has the opportunity to order even a hamburger rare or well-done if he so chooses.

j. Certain food accompaniments, such as apple sauce with pork, cranberry sauce with turkey, tartar sauce with fried fish, and mint jelly with lamb are *automatically* served with the dish and placed on the condiment table.

k. The manager is clearly and prominently "in charge" and is visible not only in the kitchen, but also in the dining room.

l. The rest rooms in the kitchen are always kept in immaculate shape.

m. The storeroom door is locked at all times -- except while someone is working there.

n. The receiving dock is clean, smells sanitary, and is free from flies. All trash and garbage is covered. A steam hose is ready and the driveway also is kept clean. A fly fan covers the entrance door to the kitchen.

o. Saucers are always available next to the coffee cups. Ice is available next to the punch and soft drinks, and lemon slices for the tea drinkers.

p. The week's menu is prominently posted not only at each station in the kitchen, but also in the dining rooms.

q. The roasts for the dinner meal are not placed in the ovens until after lunch, and the oven temperatures do not exceed 325° Fahrenheit. The ovens are checked monthly for accuracy.

r. Each day's menu is written with nutrition and eye appeal considered every bit as important as cost and popularity.

s. All food in the walk-in refrigerators and freezers is covered with plastic wrap or aluminum foil.

t. The cashiers are friendly and interested in customers and call them by name. So does the manager, as he visits with the students on the serving line or in the dining room.

u. The food has little indicators that someone cares: the fruit cocktail has some fresh fruit in it; there is always steaming hot gravy available whenever roast or mashed potatoes are being served; the peas might have some mushrooms or small onions mixed in; one can taste wine in the gravy; the baked chicken might be basted with orange sauce, or the ham covered with mustard and cloves and garnished with pineapples. The stew might be served in individual casseroles and be garnished with a mashed potato topping applied with a pastry tube; the broccoli or asparagus will be topped with buttered breadcrumbs, and dinner rolls will be warm and soft.

If you are quality conscious, then your main problem is how to transmit this knowledge to those who work for you. The answer is, of course, that you do it in *any* and *every* way possible. You start out by personally reviewing the process of food preparation and service as soon as you arrive on campus, and -- where you are sure of being right -- insisting that procedures be changed to suit your wishes. You also review ways of raising quality at staff meetings and solicit suggestions on how this can be best accomplished with the available staff. Finally, you start issuing a series of policy memos which describe your standards and your objectives. Several examples are shown in Exhibits IV-2 and IV-3.

SERVING HOURS AND SERVING LOCATIONS

One of the most effective ways of cutting operating costs without affecting food quality is to coordinate, combine, and amalgamate your food service operations in such a way that you will get optimum productivity from each employee, will operate as few locations as possible -- and will do so only during the serving hours that are actually needed. This is not as easy as it sounds. If you are operating a number of residence hall kitchens, it is not easy to get the students from one hall to walk over, voluntarily, to the dining hall of another. Neither is it easy to tell the campus secretaries that the snack bar will be closed on Friday afternoons at 3:30, when they normally take their coffee break at 4:00. Furthermore, in addition to the students, you must contend with the student personnel deans, with the faculty and staff, and, in fact, with anyone who might get annoyed at your reduction of services through either limitation of hours or the closing up of dining rooms at certain periods. Nevertheless, it is vital that you start planning in this direction as soon as you arrive, even if the actual implementation of such budget-cutting plans might take a little longer. If, for instance, you operate one dining hall for only 200 students, when another one, feeding 1,000 is just a block away, then, during the first semester, you could try closing the smaller one just on weekends. The following semester, you could close it during the dinner meals also. Finally, after a year's experimentation, you then could make the move and close the smaller kitchen altogether. Clearly, you must keep the students fully informed of each step along the way so that they know why you are doing it and can support you in your efforts.

First and Last Meals During Recess Periods

A related decision you must make deals with the first and last meals to be served to residence hall students before or after vacations. Although you will probably inherit an existing policy, it may not be a policy you can live with. One foolish policy, for example, stipulates that the first meal to be served is the breakfast meal on the day classes start. Most students return in the afternoon, or early evening of the day before. Are you right in making them pay for that evening's meal, when they have paid to be fed during the entire school term? The most logical solution is to serve the first meal right after the residence halls open to receive students. The last meal should be the meal following the last official examination period. For many years,

EXHIBIT IV-2

UNIVERSITY OF THE PACIFIC

DEPARTMENT OF HOUSING AND FOOD SERVICE
FROM: Paul Fairbrook, Director
TO: Food Service Employees
SUBJECT: Paul's Pet Peeves

March 30, 1978

* Uncovered Food in Refrigerators

* Lukewarm Gravy and Lukewarm Coffee

* Dirty Mops in Dirty Water

* Lettuce on the Floor

* Running out of Food on Serving Line While More is Available Elsewhere

* Serving (more) Food that is Not Wanted by the Customer

* Dirty Tables and Messy Salad Tables

* Wet Trays - Napkins on the Floor

* Dirty Wash Rooms and Dirty Hand Sinks

* Starting to Cook Dinner Too Early

* Roasting Meat at High Temperatures

* Serving Food Without Utensils

* Evening Cooks Not Helping with Lunch

* Salad Women Not Helping with Lunch

* Cold Dinner Plates

* Cutting Cake Early and Letting It Dry Out

* Unfriendly Serving Personnel

* Food Service Employees Eating Special Food

* Employees Who Get Sick Regularly One Day Each Month

* Overpreparation of Food

EXHIBIT IV-3

UNIVERSITY OF THE PACIFIC

DEPARTMENT OF HOUSING AND FOOD SERVICE
FROM: Paul Fairbrook, Director
TO: All Cafeteria Line Personnel
SUBJECT: Dishing up food in advance

The practice of dishing up food in advance is BAD for two reasons:

1. It is IMPERSONAL -- Part of your job is to be pleasant to our students, and to be interested in *what* they would like and *how much* they would like of an item. When you dish up food in advance you are acting like a machine, and not like a warm, interested human being.

2. The food gets COLD -- No matter how fast the students go through the line, there is always someone who has to take the last of the dishes you have set up in advance -- and the last one is doomed to get a cold meal, or a cold "hot cereal," etc. There is NO EXCUSE for serving cold food.

This matter is so important that I expect everyone to discontinue this practice immediately -- permanently -- and without exception.

UNIVERSITY OF THE PACIFIC

DEPARTMENT OF HOUSING AND FOOD SERVICE
FROM: Paul Fairbrook, Director
TO: Food Supervisors
SUBJECT: Condiments, Garnishes, Relishes, etc.

Last evening, one of the halls served spinach, but neglected to serve vinegar, lemon slices, or some other suitable condiment with it. Last Friday, one of the halls served deep fried fish sticks, but there was no catsup on the condiment table.

Serving such items as tartar sauce and catsup with fried fish, lemon slices with most other types of fish (or vinegar, if you prefer), pickles with hamburgers and most meat sandwiches, etc. should become a matter of *routine.* Neglecting to serve them can ruin an otherwise perfectly good meal -- and yet it's only a matter of supervision.

Please try to make sure that you review in your own mind before each meal what condiments and garnishes are required, and make sure that they are served.

colleges and universities closed their residence halls to students during Thanksgiving, thus literally forcing students to sleep and eat away from campus during the Thanksgiving weekend. Such a policy completely overlooked the possiblity that some students perhaps didn't want to go home over Thanksgiving, couldn't afford it or, in the case of foreign students especially, simply couldn't do it even if they wanted to. The same applied to the few days between quarters or semesters. Now most colleges permit the students to stay in their dorm rooms during these few days, and many even keep one food service unit open for those few who stay throughout the recess period.

Weekend Food Service in Residence Halls

Almost every college has its own plan for serving meals on weekends. Some serve three meals daily, others just two (brunch and dinner), some only the main meal, and others no meals at all. There is no ideal answer, and much depends on the location of the school, the habits of its students, and many other factors. One of the most popular arrangements is the following:

8:30 a.m. - 10:00 a.m. Continental Breakfast
11:30 a.m. - 1:00 p.m. Brunch
5:00 p.m. - 6:30 p.m. Dinner

The continental breakfast consists of hot and cold cereal, orange juice, toast, donuts or sweet rolls, and beverages. It can be handled with one regular, and perhaps one or two student employees. The midday brunch consists of such breakfast items as pancakes, French toast, or eggs together with bacon, ham, or sausages and hash brown potatoes. In addition, a salad bar containing various green, potato, and meat salads, relishes, and cottage cheese, will satisfy those who already had the earlier continental breakfast and are ready for something more substantial. The evening meal is then normal in all respects, except that Saturday evenings are especially suitable for such popular, inexpensive items as spaghetti and meatballs, while the Sunday dinner is normally a fancier dinner, with roast meats, etc. Weekends are also often an ideal time for outside barbecues during the warm weather.

Satellite Food Service

A vital part of your master plan involves analyzing the unprofitable or inefficient food services which you inherit, and devising a plan to solve the problem. In most instances it is difficult, if not impossible, to discontinue a food service operation on a college campus merely because it is inefficient. Pressures from deans, students, or the administration normally work against such a solution, and as a new food service director, it is risky to immediately reduce services. In such an instance, consider the possibility of converting the "problem" operation into a "satellite food service." Most residence hall food services serving fewer than 300 students are ideally suited for such satellite operations -- and sometimes even larger units (feeding anywhere from 300 to 500 students daily) can be effectively converted. Basically, the term is used to denote a food service operation in which the food is prepared in a main kitchen, trucked in heated and cooled containers to the satellite location, and served there by student employees, supervised and assisted by one or two regular employees. Depending on the individual situation, "satelliting" allows for many variations. At the University of Oregon, for example, the baked items and the entrees for the entire residence hall system of several thousand students have, for years, been prepared in a central kitchen and then trucked to the various residence halls, where desserts and salads would be prepared on location. The University of the Pacific for a number of years successfully operated a 100% satellite food service for a fraternity and a sorority, each housing about 50 students and each staffed with one full time employee. Breakfasts, however, were not included in the plan and were served in another dining hall. With careful planning and attention to details, satellite food services can be operated easily, efficiently, and with no significant loss in the quality of food served.

In planning a satellite operation, it is important not to get locked in to one fixed method of operation. For instance, it is not necessary that every food item be prepared in the central kitchen. If possible, such short order items as hamburgers and eggs can be prepared at the satellite location, while all other food items are prepared centrally.

Serving Hours in Cash Operations

One of the special problems in managing cash operations on a college campus is the necessity to remain open during unprofitable serving hours. Saturdays, Sundays, and the early evening hours are often such problem hours. When first taking over a new operation, you cannot afford to antagonize the entire college community by arbitrarily closing down your cash operations whenever you feel them to be unprofitable. The decision about whether or not to remain open must be made carefully; it must be backed with solid facts about the number of sales and customers during the period in question, and it must be done with some regard to what other facilities may be available to the students on campus. Above all, as a new food service director, you should not make such decisions alone. First check with your immediate superior and with the dean of students. In the long run the matter of serving hours will be crucial in your cash operations, but it is not one of the problems to be solved immediately, especially if doing so would create early resentment and ill will.

Campus Food Service During the Summer

In spite of valiant attempts to operate in the black during the summer (through workshops, conferences, special summer programs, etc.) many colleges and universities lose money in their food service operation during those three months. Ideally, your college or university should employ a conference manager who would find enough conference business to make each summer profitable, thus making special economies during the summer unnecessary. But few do. Not only are the kitchens operating below capacity, but few food service directors are able to pare down their staffs sufficiently to keep productivity and expenses in line with summer income. If you add the cost of vacations it is very possible that the summer months on your campus may turn out to be a losing proposition. What can you do about it?

The first step is to make a complete schedule of all your summer conferences and workshops, so that you and everyone else have a comprehensive overview of how many meals will be served every day of the summer (See Exhibit IV-4). Next, analyze this schedule to see if several groups can be served in one dining hall or, better yet, if several kitchens can actually be closed. Remember at this point, that reducing food services during the summer as an economy measure is *much more acceptable* to the college administration than doing the same during the school year. Also, you can probably argue that, with your reduced staff, *you can do a better job* by concentrating your food services in as few kitchens and dining rooms as possible.

You must also distinguish between the first and second summer sessions (most colleges and universities which operate on the semester system have two 5-week summer sessions) or, in the case of schools which are on the quarter system, you must allow for the "down periods" before and after the summer quarter. Be especially firm about closing down or reducing your evening and weekend operations during the summer months. These are often costly luxuries and serve only a small number of students.

RESIDENCE HALL FOOD SERVICE

On most campuses which have a substantial residence hall population, the food service in these halls is by far the largest, and thus, to the campus food service director, the primary operation. While the various cash operations are also important and deserve your careful attention, you must get the residence halls in order before you start streamlining and changing your student union or snack bar food service. If you are fortunate enough to start your new job sometime in the middle of the summer, you will just have enough time to prepare a food service handbook prior to school opening. (Some schools, like the University of Pennsylvania, issue a series of pamphlets and posters in lieu of one comprehensive handbook.) Such a booklet is *crucial* to you, since it is an excellent policy guide and reference manual, even if most of the students only read parts of the booklet.

Suggested Outline for Food Service Booklet

1. Welcome to Campus
2. Introduction of Food Service Managers
3. Statement of Food Service Objectives
4. Residence Hall Food Service
   a. Meal Hours
   b. Menus (patterns, seconds, special diets, sack lunches, weekends)
   c. Special Dinners and Steak Nights
   d. Meal Tickets (type used, loss, transferability, places where used)
   e. Guests, Parents, Faculty Guests
   f. Self-Bussing
   g. Waste
   h. Dining Room Behavior; Smoking; Dress Regulations (if any)
   i. Communications, Food Committees, etc.

EXHIBIT IV-4

UNIVERSITY OF THE PACIFIC
Food Service
Summer Conference & Program Schedule 1978

Dates	First Meal	Last Meal	Group	Coordinator or Office	Age Group	No.	Residence
Mon. Apr. 26 / Sat. July 31	Mon B	Fri L	Pharmacy - 3rd Term	School of Pharmacy	C	50	Phi Delta Chi (McConchie) Apartments
Sat. May 22 / Sun. May 23	Sat L	Sun B	Half Century Club	Alumni	A	25	East Wing - Grace Covell
Fri. May 28 / Sat. June 25	Fri B	Mon D	HEP Program	School of Education	HS	35	Phi Kappa Tau
Mon. June 7 / Wed. June 9	Mon D	Wed L	Burrough's Executive Seminar	Computer Services	A	55	Holiday Inn
Sun. June 13 / Tues. June 15	Sun D	Tues L	Orientation I	Student Advising Office	C	150	South/West Complex Jessie Ball (Parents)
Mon. June 14 / Fri. July 16	Mon B	Fri D	Special Summer Session	All Univ. Programs	C	30	Werner House
Mon. June 14 / Fri. July 16	Mon B	Fri D	Summer Session I (5 weeks)	All Univ. Program	C	150	Apartments Manor Hall
Wed. June 16 / Fri. June 18	Wed D	Fri L	Placement Conference	Placement Center	A	80	John Ballantyne
Thur. June 17 / Sat. June 19	Thur D	Sat L	Orientation II	Student Advising Office	C	150	South/West Jessie Ball (Parents)
Sun. June 20 / Fri. June 25	Sun D	Fri B	B'nai B'rith Youth Organization	Housing Office	HC	200	Price, Farley, Ritter Wemyss

B - Breakfast   L - Lunch   D - Dinner   A - Adult   C - College   HS - High School

    5. Cash Operations
       a. List, Description, Locations
       b. Hours of Operation
       c. Menus and Prices; Price Policy
       d. Use of Residence Hall Meal Tickets (if any)
       e. Check Cashing Policy
    6. Student Employment
       a. Where to Apply
       b. Hiring Priority
       c. Pay Scale; Advancements
       d. Types of Jobs
       e. Working Hours; Time Cards; Tax Forms; Social Security Number
       f. Job Attendance and Substitutes
       g. Uniforms
       h. Personal Hygiene and Sanitation

Much of the material you will want to put in your handbook is covered in succeeding chapters of this book. Chances are that your first handbook will not be anywhere as complete, or as polished, as your revised handbook the year after. No matter. The main thing is that you get it out quickly, in time for school opening. Sample pages from a student food service handbook are shown in Appendix 1.

In preparing your master plan, there are some decisions, however, which you cannot postpone. One of these deals with residence hall menus.

Menus and Menu Cycles

Your main cost control tool in residence hall food service is the menu. If it is well written, has a good blend of "solid meat" entrees (roasts, chops, chicken, etc.), extender items (spaghetti and meat balls, stews, meatloaf, etc.), and vegetarian dishes, with fish at least once weekly, both sandwiches and casserole dishes for lunch, and a well-balanced mixture of eggs, pancakes, French toast, and breakfast meats, then a large part of your cost control will have been accomplished. If it is carelessly put together, then you will either be making frantic changes shortly after the school year starts, or else you may be spending too much on food without finding out about it until it is too late.

First, decide who will write the menus. If your various unit managers are all well-qualified, then you might assign each one responsibility for one week of menus. The initial set is reviewed and modified each time the cycle is completed, but the changes remain the responsibility of the one who originally wrote the menu. Most food service managers will agree that the ideal length of a residence hall menu cycle is five weeks during the school year and three weeks during the summer. Many college food service directors have discovered that a three or even four-week menu is repeated too often (the average semester has 16-17 weeks), and that a popular six or even eight-week menu is difficult to construct. Obviously, much coordination must take place between the menu-writing managers, since each week's menu must flow smoothly into the next, so that you don't have, say, a Jewish student telling you: "Did you know that you had pork three days in a row?" If you discover that your unit managers are not uniformly qualified, imaginative, and anxious to build *excitement* into the menu, then you might let your dietitian or other qualified staff member write the menus -- with input solicited and requested by you from every supervisor. Regardless who writes the menus, you are the final reviewing authority; you are ultimately responsible, therefore you have the power to veto or modify any item on the menu. This must be made clear from the outset. The students hold YOU responsible for their menu, and therefore, you must approve and believe in it.

The following are basic principles to be followed when writing residence hall menus:

Food cost -- Each week's menus must be costed out to make certain that they are in balance with the overall budgeted food cost; expensive items should be intermingled with less expensive items, and current market prices should be kept in mind. Some think of current prices to an excessive degree, others not enough. Obviously you use apples in the fall, oranges in the winter, strawberries in May, and peaches in the summer. On the other hand, merely because beef prices go up in early summer is no reason to leave beef off the menu.

Nutrition and color -- You have a tremendous responsibility toward the parents and the college administration to see to it that your food offerings are nutritionally sound. Furthermore, you have an obligation to educate your students (at least to the extent that they are willing to learn) about basic nutrition principles. Your menus should reflect your concern about nutrition, and should be full of fresh fruits and vegetables. They should also be attractive from a color standpoint, and you should visualize the appearance of each dinner plate when reviewing the menu (too often we see bland-looking plates of chicken with gravy, potatoes, and corn).

Popularity -- There is no point in being a "food missionary" on a college campus. If the students haven't learned to like certain dishes before they get to your school, don't waste your time and money. While it is perfectly all right to experiment with new items, caution and good sense are required. It is better to modify proven, popular items (there are dozens of ways to fix chicken) than to try and serve Oysters Rockefeller in a residence hall. Furthermore, if you have a "new" item, make sure the students know what it is, and what is so special or new about it. Explanations of new menu items are crucial to their acceptance.

Production capability -- It is easy to write a menu without thinking of the cooks. Even cooks fall into this trap. If you have pizza as one of the dinner entrees, for example, you cannot tie up the ovens with baked potatoes and roast beef as well. If you serve flank steak, which requires your cooks to slice it throughout the meal period, make sure the other entrees come out of the ovens ready-to-serve and don't require additional work by the cooks. If you serve bacon, lettuce, and tomato sandwiches for lunch (all hand-work) make sure the other item is a casserole dish.

School calendar -- It helps to keep in mind the dates covered by your menus. During the first week of school, for instance, when numbers are usually much larger than expected, have a flexible item (like hamburger steak, roast beef, etc.) so that you can feed variable numbers. On the last day prior to Christmas recess, again make sure you serve items that will allow you to serve an unexpectedly small number of students, without incurring leftovers.

Menu pattern -- In order to be certain that your menus are relatively uniform from the standpoint of cost, quality, and variety from week to week, it is wise to establish a "menu pattern" in which you instruct your staff on the basic features that a menu should include. Such a menu pattern would include data like the number of times you want to serve meat for breakfast, the number of different salad varieties to be offered at lunch and dinner, and the type and number of hot entrees, baked desserts, etc.

Once the menus are written, make certain that everybody (yes, everybody on campus) has access to them well in advance of the actual date. All student deans, all dorm directors, each kitchen, your bread men and milk men, in fact, all of your purveyors should get a copy of your menu. To the campus community, your menu is a vital piece of information and may help them to decide whether or not to eat on campus on any particular day. To your purveyors, it is a check against the orders received. Make certain, therefore, that it is rapidly and effectively distributed. Ideally, get it printed weekly in the student newspaper, even if you have to pay a small set-up charge to get this accomplished. (See Exhibit IV-5.)

Cash Prices

Establishing cash prices in residence halls is not as easy as it may appear. In fact, it is much more difficult than it is in cash operations, where there are three basic criteria which determine the selling price:
- The food and labor cost
- What others, in similar operations, are charging
- What the customer is will to pay

In setting a price for the residence halls, there are two additional factors to keep in mind:
- The relationship of the cash price to the amount paid by the meal ticket holder.
- Your desire (space permitting) to have as many off-campus students as possible eat in the residence halls.

With regard to the first point, any cash price should be at least 12%-15% higher than the meal ticket value for such a meal. The meal ticket holder should be aware that his meal ticket is less expensive than meals purchased for cash. He should know that the reason for this price difference is that he has signed a year's contract, which is based on an average number of meals per year and on the probability that he will miss a certain number of meals during the year. If you have a shortage of dining spaces, you may question the statement that it is desirable to have as many off-

EXHIBIT IV-5

Paul's Menu

Paul's Menu, compiled by Paul Fairbrook and the food service staff, is a special service offered by the *Pacifican* for those students eating in the various campus dining halls. Fairbrook is Director of Auxiliary Services and in charge of campus food service.

TODAY

Lunch
Cr. of Tomato
Minnesota Swiss
  Cheese
Ragout
Green Beans Deluxe
Cherry Nut Salad
Creamy Lime Salad
Pecan Crispie

Dinner
Sole Summer Style
Swedish Meatballs
But. Rice
Corn Cobbette
Green Veg.

TOMORROW

Breakfast
Apricots
Cold Cereal
Cake & Raised Donuts

Lunch
Frozen Mix Fruit
Grilled French Toast
Bacon Strips
Scrambled Eggs
Apple Country Cof.
  Cake

Dinner
Hamburger Patty
F. F. Shrimp
Baked Potato
Sour Cream
Onion Rings
Cole Slaw

SUNDAY

Breakfast
Applesauce
Cold Cereal
Apricot Kuchen

Lunch
Melon Sliver
Eggs Benedict
English Muffin
(Ham)
Fruit Snails

Dinner
Chicken-Cr. Ch.
Baked Chicken
Whipped Potatoes
Cream Gravy
But. Broccoli
Green Noodle Salad
White Cake/Banana

MONDAY

Breakfast
Cream of Wheat
Pancakes
Sausage Links
Syrup
Donuts

Lunch
Minnestrone
BLT Sandwich
Shrimp Creole
Sliced Roast Beef
Broccoli Crown
Cardinal Pear
P.A. Gelatin Mold
Fresh Fruit

Dinner
Beef Stew/Biscuits
Mush/Cheese Omelet
Wild & White Rice
Tomato Slices
Glazed Sweet
  Spanish Onions
Cukes/Sour Cream
Orange Trifle

TUESDAY

Breakfast
Ralston
Waffles/Syrup
Bacon
Bran Muffin

Lunch
Cr. of Mushroom
Grilled Ham & Cheese
Eggplant Casserole
Cheese Slices
Peas
Cherry Cola Mold
Frosty Fruit Mold
M & M Cookie

Dinner
Rt. Turkey/Dressing
Frank-K-Bobs
Giblet Gravy
Whipped Potatoes
Fr. Cut Green Beans
Gingerman Salad

WEDNESDAY

Breakfast
Grapefruit Sections
Oatmeal
Fried Eggs
Hash Browns
Cinnamon Twist
Donuts

Lunch
French Onion Soup
British Burger
Plain Patty
Macaloni Con Chorizo
Celery Almondine
Crown Jewel Mold
Man. Or/Or Mold
Fresh Fruit

Dinner
London Broil
Quiche Lorraine
Yorkshire Pudding
Carrots
Citrus/Avocado Sal.
Berry Yogurt

THURSDAY

Breakfast
Applesauce
Malt-O-Meal
French Toast/Syrup
Linguica Sausage
Sour Cr. Coffee Cake

Lunch
Green Cheese Soup
Fun Food Sandwich
Hot Chicken Salad
Tomato Slice
Pear Half/Lime
Hawaiian Eyeful
Chocolate Cookie

Dinner
Spaghetti/Meat Sauce
Hot Ham/Bun
Hamburger Patty
Baked Zucchini/Corn
Canlis Salad
Banana Splits

campus students eat in the residence halls as possible. You may, in fact, prefer to have all these students eat in your cash operation (student union, snack bars, etc.). Hopefully, you will not feel that way. The ideal is to make all your food service operations so flexible that students on your campus can eat wherever they want to, regardless of whether they pay cash, with a meal ticket, or in some other manner. You are more than merely a food vendor: you are the campus food service director. This gives you a very special responsibility, the responsibility to see to it that the students at your college or university eat nutritious meals, get enough to eat, and are happy with their food. Your off-campus students are important. Make residence hall food service so attractive for them, so competitive with outside fast-food places, that *all* your students will want to eat your food. Judiciously low prices will help in this respect, and your recommendations should reflect this.

In addition to cash prices for your own students, you may be called on to set special prices for visiting high school students (i.e. prospective students). The admissions office will be most anxious to keep prices especially low since they want to make a good impression on these visitors. The solution? Prepare a simple, special menu (e.g. hamburgers, potato salad, salad, milk and fresh fruit), charge very little, and serve it at a convenient time or on a separate serving line.

An additional problem is the one concerning the faculty and staff: should you charge them less or more than you charge the students who purchase meals in the residence halls? You can argue either way, and be right and wrong in each case. You can make a persuasive agrument for charging faculty less money, in order to encourage them to eat with the students and thus enhance the quality of the dining room experience. Quite a number of schools have a special discount for faculty and staff. You can also reason that they should pay more than the students. Many feel that the best solution is to make no differentiation at all: once you set the cash price, all pay the same regardless of who they are.

Sack Lunches

While a sack lunch sounds like a very simple, uncomplicated item, it is one to which you must give some careful thought. You have three separate areas of concern: (1) quality, (2) price, (3) distribution.

To meet your quality standards, decide what basic ingredients you want in a sack lunch (e.g. one or two sandwiches, meat or cheese, fruit, cookie or cake, milk or fruit juice), and then set a selling price *at least double* that of your raw food cost. You may also establish a more expensive sack lunch for athletes (e.g. three sandwiches, an extra drink, perhaps potato chips) and a special box lunch for catering functions. The latter should be merchandised in a special box, possibly imprinted with the school's emblem, and every item in it should be wrapped in plastic wrap or otherwise be made sanitary and attractive.

Your decision on who is entitled to a sack lunch and when, depends much on how permissive you are in your overall food service policies, and whether or not a liberal sack lunch policy would significantly increase your costs. Ideally, all students with a meal ticket should have the option of a sack lunch whenever they want it, provided that they give sufficient advance notice. As an alternative, they should be given a chance to make lunches for themselves. This is arranged very simply by placing all the various ingredients for a sack lunch (bread, mayonnaise, mustard, cold cuts, pickles, etc.) on a separate table in the cafeteria out of the main traffic stream, and letting the students make their own sack lunches right there. The only problem may arise when a too-liberal policy results either in hundreds of students wanting you to make lunches for their trip home at recess periods (an unlikely event), or when sack lunches given to students upon request (without any special reason such as field trip) cause unusual operational difficulties. A sample of a policy memo on sack lunches is shown in Exhibit IV-6.

Special Diets

One of the first problem letters that you will receive will be from some doctor whose patient (often his son or daughter) requires a special diet. The typical letter will contain some phrases like these:

> "Our daughter has a complicated problem of obesity.
> . . .Her problem is not psychological, but rather physiological,
> based on a sluggish metabolic rate and body chemistry imbalance. . .
> We understand that you employ a dietitian who will supervise
> and prepare special diets for students who require them. . .We will
> be happy to pay any added costs required."

Variations on this letter will include such ailments as hypoglycemia, diabetes, and innumerable others. As legitimate as these various ailments may be, and as distressing as they may be for the students and their parents, there is a definite limitation on how much responsibility you can personally assume in solving these problems.

Students with serious diet problems may be better off living off-campus and taking care of their own diets. If your school has on-campus living requirements for freshmen, it is usually wiser to make exceptions to students with special and unique dietary problems, or give them permission to move off-campus.

On the other hand, there are many special dietary needs that a college food service director can handle, usually without significant or cumbersome changes in menus or serving patterns. Most students with mild problems of blood sugar can watch their diets and eat from your regular menu with care. It is easy for you to write some special permission slips for students who need some extra meat or extra fruit in place of some other food items. The serving of yogurt for dieting students at lunch is a good idea in any case; students with temporary diet problems, like the football player with the broken jaw who needs a liquid diet until his jaw heals, are not a nuisance but a real challenge: you and your food service can be of real service if you rise to the occasion and take special care of such short-term needs. The basic guidelines lie in the answers to these two questions:

(1) Am I involving the college in a legal obligation by promising to provide a special diet to a sick student?

(2) Will such a special diet cause disproportionate disruptions in the kitchens?

If the answer is "yes" to either question, don't do it; if "no," do it cheerfully. For more information on special diets, see Chapter IX.

EXHIBIT IV-6

UNIVERSITY OF THE PACIFIC

DEPARTMENT OF HOUSING AND FOOD SERVICE
FROM: Paul Fairbrook, Director
TO: Food Service Supervisors
SUBJECT: Charges for Sack Lunches

The following is our policy regarding prices for sack lunches taken out:

A) Regular sack lunch -- consists of 1 meat sandwich, 1 non-meat sandwich (cheese, egg salad, etc.) 1 fruit, 1 cookie, 1 half-pint milk (on special request only).

B) Special (or "athlete's") sack lunch -- consists of 2 meat sandwiches, 1 bag of potato chips, 1 half-pint of milk, 1 fruit juice, 1 fruit, 2 cookies.

C) Box lunch -- As per request of client:

Whenever an individual meal ticket holder requests a sack lunch for a valid reason, he will get Type "A"; whenever an organized group requests sack lunches, the meal ticket holders will get either "A" or "B" depending on the wishes of the group's leader. If sack lunches are made for non-meal ticket holders the charge for Type "A" lunch is $2.00 and the charge for Type "B" is $2.50. The charge for box lunches is $2.50 and up.

If the group is organized in such a manner that the lunches can be distributed under supervision, it is better to supply the food in bulk (i.e. sandwiches in a cardboard box lined with foil, drinks in wood boxes, etc.) so that no food is wasted (this is also easier for the kitchen). Only if the person in charge asks for individual sack lunches do we bag everything in sacks.

In any case, however, it is important that you make a special effort to talk with the student personally. There is simply no substitute for an honest, interested conversation with the student about his or her needs and your ability to meet them.

One final word should be said here about weight-reduction diets. You may assume that at least one third of your women student customers are seriously interested in either reducing or maintaining their present weight and a number of your male students are interested in gaining weight. You should do everything possible to encourage healthy, intelligent, and moderate food intake for these people. Some schools, like the University of Maine, set up special serving lines for dieters, where calorically calculated meals are served; others list the caloric value of each dish on the daily menu. Some have a more formal weight reduction program, supervised by a college dietitian; still others serve a modified diet entree item whenever the regular entrees are too high in fat content. Any of these steps is recommended. The good feelings created and the great personal satisfaction that you gain make the extra efforts in this area worthwhile. For a sample residence hall menu, footnoted for dieters, see Appendix 2.

Vegetarian Food

Another decision that you must make is whether or not you plan to serve a special vegetarian menu and, if so, how elaborate it should be. While vegetarianism, as a campus fad, may have reached its heights during the late Sixties, it has still many serious adherents -- especially among the young people.

There are many types of vegetarian programs on American college campuses today. They range from a dedicated program such as the one at the University of California in Santa Cruz, where organic foods are actually being grown for the program, to token programs where vegetarians are merely given an extra serving of vegetables. In between, there are schools which have special serving lines for vegetarians or feature a special entree item for vegetarians, and some which merely offer cheese, fruit, or yogurt substitutes. It is difficult to lay down a fixed rule, or even make a firm suggestion on how you should handle this problem at your school: the number of vegetarians, the intensity of their commitment, and the vegetarian offerings on your regular menu are all factors which contribute to your final decision. For more on vegetarianism, see Chapter IX.

Portion Sizes

Portion control, a vital ingredient in an effective food cost control system, is more difficult in a residence hall food service than in a cash operation. Difficult, not because it is any harder to set up the controls, but because it is a much more complicated issue when you feed customers two or three meals daily and try to convince them that your food is as good and as satisfying "as Mother used to make. . ." Well, Mother certainly never weighed three ounces of turkey on patty paper at Thanksgiving, or refused to serve a second helping of roast beef if it was available, or limited her children to two slices of bacon if there was enough for three. On the other hand, Mother knew how much each of her children could eat and normally dished up the food in servings appropriate to each child. In the same manner, the food service director must determine *appropriate* servings, just as Mother did. However, the issue is complicated by the fact that, unlike Mother, he has to deal in averages, and the food is being served in the dining halls either by students or by regular kitchen workers -- neither of whom are as concerned about preventing the waste of food as are Mother and the director. Cafeteria servers fall into four types:

1. *The smiling, charming, friendly student.* He is determined to make life better for everyone, and his aim is to please. Whatever you want, you can have it.

2. *The super-loyal, super-efficient, self-appointed student manager.* He is so worried about the cost of food and following the rules that even reasonable requests for more food are refused.

3. *The conscientious but inflexible kitchen worker.* He usually wants to do everything just right. He will follow your instructions to the letter -- and tell everyone exactly what they can, and cannot have. When asked "why?" he replies, "I'm just following orders."

4. *The server who never looks up.* On every cafeteria line you will occasionally find a server who is so fascinated with the food in the pans that he actually forgets to look up when dishing up the food. Consequently the 90 lb. sorority girl will get the same portion as the 200 lb. football player, and usually the serving is geared to the latter. Worse yet, he is so efficient that the plate is filled even before the student has a chance to say: "No potatoes, please."

With such a staff to back you up and with the friendly image you are trying to portray, is there any point in setting up a portion control system in your master plan? There certainly is. Choosing appropriate portion sizes is a key factor in avoiding waste. Without portion control, a budget becomes meaningless and the waste of food left over on the plates soars sky-high. You cannot, and should not try to, replace Mother's home-cooking. You are cooking for hundreds. Certain basic formulas (e.g. average servings of 4 oz. of cooked roast beef give you an overall yield of 2½ servings per raw pound, if cooked at proper, low temperatures) are essential for your purchasing and budgeting activities. Furthermore, if you have an "unlimited seconds" policy, it is vital that your first serving is not too large, so that the student who does come back for a second helping can actually eat it. While it is not appropriate at a fancy buffet or other special occasion, students do not resent preweighed portions of sliced meat separated by patty paper or a specified number of scoops of potatoes and vegetables. Your cafeteria servers need training; they need to be told what the proper portion sizes should be and *why* they were set up as they were. Tell them that the average student will not normally eat more than 3 oz. of vegetables, if, indeed, that much. Pre-determined yields for pies and cakes not only are good for food cost control purposes, but also assure everyone a similar-sized portion. Good portion control also gives you the assurance that every student gets a fair serving of everything. Without such control, the servers have a tendency, especially at the end of the meal period, to "stretch" an item by reducing portion sizes so that they don't run out. For a sample list of portion specifications, see Exhibit IV-7.

Food For Field Trips

Before the semester is even four weeks old, you will be contacted by at least one geology professor who is planning a class trip to the mountains, a philosophy professor or a campus minister organizing a retreat, a biology teacher planning a trip to the beach, or a representative from your Associated Students who is sponsoring a "fun-filled weekend to the lake or the woods." All of these will have one thing in common: they want you to furnish the food. Since each will plead a convincing case, and since each request will differ somewhat from the rest, you need to be prepared by developing a clear-cut policy about the furnishing of food for such events before the requests start to overwhelm you. There are certain obvious and defensible criteria that will help you in establishing a reasonable policy:

Sanitation -- Since you are responsible for any food that comes from your kitchens, you have a right to make reasonably certain that such food will be handled correctly after it leaves your premises and will not spoil before it is consumed. You can also assume that your clients will not be as aware of or as cautious about food poisoning as you are, and that you have a duty, therefore, to set up whatever rules are necessary to protect them from food-borne illnesses. Immediately eliminated from consideration, then, are all perishable foods, except, perhaps, food that is consumed within two or three hours after it leaves the kitchens. Even then you should eliminate such risky foods as mayonnaise, cream-filled dishes, poultry, fish, and pork items. Whatever promises are made to you ("We'll put the hamburger into the refrigerator as soon as we reach the cabin. . .") you simply cannot risk the chance that some of your students might get sick.

Cost considerations -- While it is reasonable for the contract meal ticket holder to expect food when he is away on a legitimate field trip, it is equally reasonable that such food should not cost you more than if he were eating in your dining halls. Since your labor and overhead expenses continue whether or not the field trip participants are on campus, you will normally have to limit the value of your food contribution to the actual value of the *cost of food* saved. Most students have difficulty understanding this at first. They cannot understand why, if they pay $3.00 per day for meals, you can only credit them with about $1.25 worth of food and must charge them the balance. In fact, this is so hard to explain that you will often be tempted to just give them all the food they need at no extra charge. If such trips occur only rarely, and if you set up sufficient restrictions so that not every little "outing" becomes an officially sanctioned field trip, then this matter should pose no special problem for you. Some schools prefer to give cash rebates to the extent of the value of the raw food instead of sending food. This, too, is a good solution, and most students will be happy with such an arrangement.

There are other considerations, however: How do you know that the food you send will be eaten only by those with meal tickets? Chances are more than half of the field trip participants have never paid you anything for food service. How do you handle a request for, let us say, 100 hamburgers, if the applicant admits that only 50 of the participants have meal tickets, but pledges that the other 50 will contribute

EXHIBIT IV-7

University of the Pacific Food Service

Recommended Portion Sizes

Meats
Sliced meats: 3½-4 oz., cooked meat (Beef, Pork, Ham, etc.)
Ground meats: 4 oz., cooked meat (meatloaf, meatballs)
Pork Chops: 6 oz., raw
Cutlets, Liver: 4 oz., raw
Cubed Steaks: 5 oz., raw
Hamburger patties: 5 per raw lb.
Hamburger Steaks: 7 oz., raw
Stews, Goulashes: 8 cooked oz. in casserole (50% meat concentration)
Creamed dishes, Chop Suey, etc.: 6 oz. ladle
Chicken (2½ lb. bird): ¼, 10 oz., raw
Hot sandwiches: 2-2½ oz., cooked meat

Soups
Bowl: 6 oz. ladle

Potatoes
Baked: 6-8 oz.
Boiled: 4-5 oz. (medium)
Scalloped: 3 fl. oz.
Creamed: 3 fl. oz.
Hash Browns, American Fried, French Fried: 2½ oz.
Whipped: #12 scoop

Vegetables
Fresh, frozen, canned: 2½ oz. per serving

Salads
Fruit, loose: 4 fl. oz.
Fruit, packed, gelatin: 28 servings per jello pan

Desserts
Pies: 8 cuts to 10" tin
Puddings: 4 fl. oz.
Jello: 4 fl. oz.
Ice Cream: #16 scoop

Our Policy: We want all of our students to get enough to eat. On the other hand, we want to avoid waste. The first serving for each student will be limited to the above portion sizes. The only exceptions to this is a lunch, if the student asks for a side order of the casserole dish along with his sandwich.

Students may have "seconds" on everything except steak and desserts, insofar as there is enough available. If there may not be enough for seconds on an item, students have the choice of taking the "#2" item, or waiting until the end of the serving period - at which time they can have all they want.

other foods such as the buns or the drinks needed to round out the meal? Generally, take the students at their word and agree to any arrangement that is fair to both the students and food service.

Definition of a field trip -- The problem seems simple: since it is always possible to send a sack lunch for those who miss *just one meal,* you can define a "field trip" as one which, organized and participated in by a member of the faculty, involves food requirements *for more than one meal.* As soon as you have done that, however, the student government leader will come in with his planned weekend camping trip and then what will you do? While you have every right to be arbitrary in matters concerning sanitation and health, your campus expects you to be flexible and understanding in all other matters. If you try to extend the field trip privilege to, let us say, any organized group of meal ticket holders numbering at least four students or more, then within months, you'll be manning the barricades against the onslaught of those who feel that you should supply food to any four students who decide to go skiing together. Where do you draw the line?

There is no categorical answer. You do have the right, in a contract food service operation, to benefit from the absenteeism of students who, by their own choice, and for purely personal (i.e. non-academic) reasons choose to absent themselves from your campus. Your contract is to feed them *on campus,* and nowhere else. On the other hand, the continued good will of your students is vital to your success on campus, and the categorical refusal to be of help to students seems unwise. The solution is to establish a firm policy which adequately protects your institution against frequent and unreasonable demands, and then modify or soften your stand in the specific instances. Remember, a student will be pleased and appreciative if, in spite of the existing policies, you decide to donate some doughnuts and soft drinks to the expedition. For a sample policy on food for field trips see Exhibit IV-8.

Meal Ticket Control

One of the continuing and unenviable jobs of a college food service director is to constantly devise new ways of preventing students who have no meal tickets from eating in the dining halls, or to prevent meal ticket holders from "ripping off food." While you may legitimately feel that "ripping off" is merely a euphemism for "stealing," many students have no such moral scruples: ripping off food is considered a "sport."

In Chapter VI you will find a detailed discussion of the various types of meal ticket controls available to you, together with an evaluation of the advantages and disadvantages of each system. It may be wise, if you are not absolutely certain which one to adopt, if you go along with the existing system for one year. Don't plan on changing it in the middle of the school year; the effort is not worth all the uproar it will cause. Change at the beginning of your second year. In any case, when setting up your master plan, review the existing system of internal controls and decide whether or not it needs some immediate corrective action or whether this can wait a while until you have "settled in." It normally takes students several months to figure out ways of beating the system; at that point, it will be wise to take some steps either to tighten up the controls or, if absolutely necessary, to change to a new plan altogether.

EXHIBIT IV-8

UNIVERSITY OF THE PACIFIC
Stockton, California 95211

POLICY ON FIELD TRIPS

Definition:
A field trip is any official University function organized and supervised by members of the faculty which involves food requirements for more than one meal. In addition, occasional trips involving *at least fifteen (15) students* with meal tickets, organized by ASUOP, student personnel officers, or by the Director of the University Center may qualify as a field trip, if approved by Mary Heacock or Paul Fairbrook.

Perishable Food:
The University food service does not furnish sack lunches, or any other perishable food *for more than one meal.*

Non-Perishable Food:
The following are the requirements for issuing non-perishable food for field trips:

    a. The group must include at least fifteen (15) meal ticket holders, *unless it is an educational field trip headed by a faculty member.*

    b. Advance notice of *at least 48 hours* is required.

    c. Meal ticket numbers must be turned in by 12:00 noon at least two (2) days before the event.

    d. A letter from the faculty or head resident sponsor is required.

    e. Each meal ticket holder is entitled to a value equivalent to that portion of their meal ticket which is normally spent on food (i.e. 40% of $5.89 = $2.35/day (21-Meal Plan) 40% of $5.52 = $2.20/day (15-Meal Plan)

    f. Any food sent in excess of the meal ticket values shown in (e.) above will be charged as a steward's sale (cost plus 15%).

    g. The supervisor on duty at the time the request is made must handle the order from start to finish.

    h. All items ordered must be *limited to items readily available.*

Cash Rebates:
Cash rebates are *not normally* allowed for meal ticket holders going on field trips. At the discretion of the Director of Food Service, however, cash reimbursement can be made *to individual meal ticket holders if one week advance notice* is provided by the instructor.

Reader please note: This policy is being re-evaluated at the time of publication and may be made more restrictive.

CASH OPERATIONS

The operation of snack bars, cafeterias, and other a la carte cash food service units on a college campus is a complicated task and one that is described in detail in Chapter XIII. In setting up your master plan, don't expect to solve all your food service problems at once, least of all those in your cash operations. The analysis of sales, the setting of prices, the proper staffing patterns for various time periods, all these take time, and even more, actual physical observation by you and your supervisors. In devising your master plan, however, there are a few basic questions that you must address:

Use of Meal Tickets in Cash Operations

Do you want your meal ticket holders to use these in your cash operations? If you can work it out without too much trouble, it is certainly a "plus" in your food service program. It means, however, that you must translate each meal on the meal ticket into cash value, and devise a means of controlling such sales (see Chapter VI). It also means you must consider the location of classrooms in relation to your cash operations and your residence hall dining room. On some campuses, where the residence halls are far away from the center of the campus, such a policy would create absolute havoc. The student center would be overwhelmed at noon, while the residence hall dining room is quiet as a morgue.

Duplication of Services

Do your cash operations represent a sufficient variety of services so that each one adds a new and different dimension to your overall operation? If not, and if each snack bar or lunch counter is merely an extension or copy of the other, should you try perhaps to change one of them before the beginning of school? Is one operation competing with another, so that both are unprofitable and inefficient?

Selling Prices

Even though you may not have time when you first arrive for a complete analysis of current selling prices in your cash operations, at least check the following: Are they generally in line with other similar operations, do they meet the campus community's needs, and will they yield the desired pre-budgeted food cost? Your master plan must consider a la carte selling prices in the cash operations and also know the prices in each type of food unit compare with selling prices in other units both on and off campus.

Blending Cash Operations with Residence Hall Food Service

Do you plan to blend the two types of operations together and run both as one, integrated food service, or is there an advantage for you in keeping the two systems separate, each one reporting to you through a separate chain of command? The answer depends very much on the circumstances; on the attitude of the campus administration, on the quality of the supervisory staff, and on the advantages and disadvantages of each approach on your particular campus.

CATERING

It is sad but true that some college or university administrators will judge your performance more by the quality of your catering services, which they have frequent opportunity to experience, than by the quality of your daily food service to the students, which concerns them only when there is a problem. It is essential, therefore, that in setting up your master plan you take a good look at the campus' current catering practices and make some initial moves to upgrade these if this seems called for.

Campus catering is a field all its own and is described in considerable detail in Chapter XIV. Much of the work involved in upgrading campus catering takes time, to train your regular staff, to educate your student waiters, and to acquire the necessary catering equipment. There are some decisions, however, that simply cannot wait:

Policy Regarding Private Functions

A private function is one which cannot be legitimately charged to your college's account because, although it may be sponsored by a member of the faculty or staff, it does not have any direct connection with college affairs. Different colleges and universities have different approaches to such functions. Most campus food services are ideally set up to do a first-class catering job and, in fact, encourage such business. Catering is certainly a major source of income for student unions and university centers everywhere, and making a distinction between university and private functions would only serve to reduce the potential catering business available. Thus it may be that your college has traditionally competed with private caterers in this lucrative field, and you will be expected to continue this practice.

On the other hand, there are some schools, particularly the smaller ones whose facilities are limited, which frown on catering private functions. They are reluctant to antagonize and compete with the private caterers in town who may resent the fact that the college with its superior facilities and tax-exempt status is taking lucrative business away from them. There is also the question, in the case of smaller schools, of whether the food service director has the right to use his limited facilities and staff merely for making money. Students have a right to object (and they will!) if they are short-changed because you agree to feed the Rotary Club every Thursday noon or agree to cater wedding receptions in their lounges or dining rooms.

Even if your school should be one which restricts its catering to college-connected affairs you must have a rule that will allow exceptions. If the president wants to have a private dinner catered in his home, you must be able to do it. If an important civic group wants to have a special dinner on campus (e.g. the Junior Aid Society, or the city council) there should be some provision to make such an affair possible. In establishing or revising a catering policy for your campus, you should work closely with the school's director of public relations. Remember, the purpose of a catering policy is to help, not hinder you, and you must therefore retain the flexibility needed to make responsible decisions as situations arise.

Policy Regarding Catering Prices

In setting catering prices, just as in all other food service pricing, it is well to start with the three basic pricing considerations:

(a) The cost of the food and labor

(b) The cost of similar services elsewhere

(c) What the customer is willing to pay

Catering, however, has some special dimensions which affect your pricing structure. One of these is the special amount of effort that goes into a catering event, an effort that is not justly rewarded by a 10%, 20%, or even a 25% markup. The meetings or prior telephone conversations with the client, the preparation of the banquet room, the special table set-up, the hiring of extra staff, the time of your supervisory staff, all these are services for which you should be compensated. A 20% net profit on a $3.00 luncheon for 150 people yields $90.00 to your institution, barely enough to justify all the extra work involved. A more realistic profit objective is 30%-40% of all catering sales, including a mix of coffee hours, served luncheons and dinners, buffets, etc.

An additional consideration should be whether or not you wish to differentiate between university-connected functions and those being served to outside groups. One way to define a university-connected function is to stipulate that at least 50% of those attending must be members of the university community. Certainly you would not want to have students subsidize the dinner of an outside group because your price is too low to make a good profit. On the other hand, students will tolerate an outside function much more if they understand that the profit from such a function may help to keep down room and board prices in the coming year. A sample policy on banquet prices is shown in Exhibit IV-9.

Policy Regarding Banquet Menus

There are two points of view regarding writing and printing special menus for catering clients. There are those who swear by them, and those who absolutely reject them. Those who believe in giving the client a printed brochure which contains all pertinent catering information including a variety of sample menus for lunches and dinners do so in order to simplify the banquet scheduling process. They simply send their brochure to the client, the latter makes his selections, and any secretary or clerk can handle the booking from then on. Those who oppose such brochures feel that the personal input of the food service director (or catering manager) is important from a public relations standpoint, and may also facilitate the handling of catering events. Often the client will accept the entree recommendation of the catering manager, who may suggest an item that is being prepared anyway on that day, or one that will not interfere too much with the normal production in the kitchen. Beyond the matter of entree selection, the absence of a catering menu allows the catering manager more leeway in advising his client. He may suggest a buffet instead of a served meal, or perhaps encourage more nutritious menus instead of the one the customer originally had requested. Both points of view are valid. Which particular approach is most suitable in a given food service operation depends on the ability of those doing the catering scheduling, and on the flexibility of the kitchens. For a sample catering menu see Appendix 3.

EXHIBIT IV-9

UNIVERSITY OF THE PACIFIC

DEPARTMENT OF HOUSING AND FOOD SERVICE
FROM: Paul Fairbrook, Director
SUBJECT: Policy on Banquet Prices

The following are the prices now in effect for all University-sponsored served functions for the immediate future:

1. (a) Luncheons -- minimum price: $3.00. This type of function will be based on the line menu for that day or, at the discretion of the Catering Manager, the line menu from the night before.

   (b) Special Menu Luncheons -- minimum price: $3.50. These luncheons involve planning a special menu and the price of the luncheon will depend on the menu selection.

2. (a) Dinners -- minimum price: $5.00. This menu involves a line menu similar to the $3.00 luncheon above. It does generally involve a starting course, however, and minor changes in the menu are permitted at the discretion of the Catering Manager.

   (b) Special Menu Dinners -- $6.00 and up. These are similar to the $3.50 luncheons listed above.

Please note: The above listed prices are based on a minimum of 10 persons per function. On any function below 10, there will be a surcharge of $2.00 for breakfast and lunch, and $3.00 for dinner to help cover the cost of table service.

V. SETTING UP A PURCHASING SYSTEM

To the outsider, the purchasing of food and kitchen supplies seems like a complicated activity, requiring much technical knowhow and special skill. Chances are that your new boss will regard food purchasing in the same manner, and therefore urge you, as one of your first and most important priorities, to "check into," "change," or "re-vamp" your entire purchasing set-up. The thinking behind such a set of instructions is that your predecessor probably was not as good as you are in food purchasing, that "one never knows what went on under the table" and that any changes which you will institute will probably be changes for the better. Most of this is nonsense. Whether or not your predecessor was a better buyer than you are is problematical. Chances are that he was honest, for the days of crooked purchasing, kick-backs, and shady deals are long past, especially in colleges and universities where such practices are very much the exception to the rule. Changes which you may initiate are not necessarily changes for the better and, unless you know exactly what you are changing and why, could just as easily turn out to be for the worse.

Effective purchasing does not depend on how tough you are, how lengthy or detailed your specifications, or on the personality of the salesman who calls on you. It depends primarily on how desirable your business is to the purveyor, and on your ability to put your purchasing power to work in the most effective manner. Here is how you can make these two factors mesh:

Start out by establishing clear purchasing procedures. Some items should be purchased on a formal bid, others through informal price quotations, and others yet on a cost-plus basis through a direct order to a pre-selected purveyor. Your suppliers have a right to know in advance how you intend to purchase. Some buyers are not honest with their suppliers. They encourage competitive bids for the sake of appearances, without having any intention of selecting the low bidder. Every purveyor has a right to know just where he stands, what his chances are for getting some of the business, and what he must do to get it.

In addition to clear-cut purchasing procedures, you should make your purchases in the largest possible quantities. This does not necessarily mean that you should have all items delivered at one time, nor that you should pay for everything you buy at the time of purchase. Purveyors are businessmen. If they are guaranteed large sales, such as an annual contract for bread, they can reduce their overhead costs while giving you a better-than-average price. Their cost of transportation is high; if they can reduce the number of deliveries to your kitchens, they can afford a smaller mark-up. Therefore, if you can assure your supplier orders for a minimum quantity over a period of time, you can save yourself money. Volume sales and low delivery costs are more important to the average supplier than high markups. If he knows that you are interested in helping him reduce his overhead costs in serving you and that you are a careful buyer, he will probably pass on the savings to you in order to retain your business.

Another way to encourage low bids from your suppliers is to maintain an excellent credit rating. Most suppliers are not equipped, nor do they wish to, finance you for long periods of time. In fact, they allow 30 days in which to pay your bills only because usually they have thirty days to pay theirs. Some directors choose their purveyors because of the latters' willingness to be patient and wait for payment. This is one of the most expensive ways to get "financing." Going to a bank for a business loan is usually cheaper in the long run. If food service bills are paid in the business office, do whatever possible to get your purveyor's bills paid regularly and within the thirty days normally allowed.

Finally, organize your buying procedures efficiently. There is nothing complicated about planning your food requirements one or two weeks in advance and ordering accordingly. In fact, once you start ordering your meats, canned goods, and frozen foods on a weekly basis, and your produce and other perishables twice-weekly, you will find that it is actually more efficient than ordering daily and skipping from one crisis to the next. Part of an efficient buying procedure is to have the order ready for the salesman when he arrives. Your conversations with him should be short and to the point: explanations and instructions from you; market conditions, availability of certain items, and new product information from him. A salesman's call is neither an adversary proceeding (some young buyers, full of exaggerated self-importance, ruin any chance they may have had for a mutually constructive relationship by abusing the salesman unnecessarily), nor a social visit. He has come to find out if you need his products and if so, to get your order. The quicker this can be accomplished, the better for both of you.

RELATIONSHIP WITH YOUR PURCHASING DEPARTMENT

On most college campuses, the food service director enjoys a unique status when it comes to purchasing: he is given the authority to make food purchasing decisions without necessarily going through the regular purchasing channels. This authority is granted to him because the purchasing staff normally is not equipped to make decisions on food quality, specifications, and amounts required and also because much of the merchandise is perishable and must be available to the kitchens on relatively short notice. While the extent of this special authority will vary from campus to campus and from private colleges to state-supported universities, its existence is generally the rule rather than the exception. The reason purchasing on a college campus is usually channelled through the purchasing department is to eliminate the possibility of fraud, to maintain close budgetary control, and to take advantage of professional purchasing skills and procedures in order to yield the optimum price for a given product. *The food service director can never yield the important right to make the final determination as to the quality of food and service rendered by a supplier.* There should exist a general agreement between purchasing and food service as to the procedures followed, and shared responsibility for seeing that money spent on food purchasing is being spent in accordance with generally accepted business principles. The ideal relationship is one in which the purchasing agent freely yields certain purchasing prerogatives to the food service director, while the latter follows the same general rules and principles that are being followed by the purchasing agent.

Many of the larger universities operate central commissaries for all campus food services. Sometimes these operate independently from food service, and sometimes they are under the direct supervision of the food service director. Either system can work well, provided that the basic principle is never forgotten: the person who is responsible for the food service must also have the authority over the food he buys.

There is no clear-cut guideline that establishes when a school is large enough to operate its own food commissary. In times of inflation, even a modest warehouse can be a great help to the food buyer who wishes to protect his school from rising prices. A school that may not be able to justify having its own food commissary can at least institute a first step, i.e. central food purchasing, so that the institution can get full benefit from the expertise of its staff, and the accumulated quantity of its purchases.

FORMAL BID (CONTRACT) PURCHASING

Certain food items lend themselves ideally to purchasing by contract. These are items which are used in fairly large quantities, which normally have stable prices, which can be clearly described and specified, and for which there is competition in your area. While sharp price fluctuations in food commodities make long-term contract buying more difficult or impossible, the following items are generally bought under annual contract:

> Bread products (bread, rolls, buns)
> Bakery products (pies, cakes, doughnuts)
> Milk and dairy products
> Canned goods and staples
> Frozen foods
> Carbonated beverages (including paper cups)
> Non-carbonated beverages
> Paper supplies
> China
> Silverware
> Kitchen equipment

The above list includes almost every key food item except meat and produce. Both of these are perishable, and subject to great price fluctuations throughout the year. Therefore, it is wiser to purchase these in a different manner, as described later in this chapter. Coffee, orange juice, and linen are also exceptions to the rule, as will become clear later on.

The obvious advantage to be gained by contract purchasing is low price. Bidders, when assured of a firm quantity (or even when they are assured merely of selling and *estimated* quantity), are generally willing to make significant price concessions to gain the contract. If you have written the contract wisely, so that the successful bidder can also save in delivery and handling costs, then there may be a further price concession passed on to you.

One key requirement for a well-written request for bid is *careful preparation on your part*. When you are preparing a set of specifications covering a given food item, you must be sure to include every significant fact or feature that may be important to you or to the bidder. Each food item has some special peculiarities or conditions which must be considered. In your bakery bid, for instance, the matter of "pick-ups" (the pick-up of unused bread or buns at full or partial credit) must be clearly spelled out. The timing of the actual baking may be important to you for such products as French bread, where crisp freshness is of primary concern. In your ice cream bid, in addition to the obvious variations in butterfat content that exist among various dairies, there is the matter of flavor variety available, the choice of ice cream novelties, specialty ice cream items, and special services that may be important (e.g. packing products in dry ice for picnics and field trips). From your dairy, you may require such special services and items as yogurt in bulk, or half-pints of orange drink, or the use of their refrigerated trucks in connection with all-campus barbecues. Often the soft-drink vendor may be requested to lend, lease, or sell to the institution some of the vending or ice-making equipment used in connection with his drinks. The paper supplier may have to arrange for imprinting of his cups or place mats with the university (or student center) seal. Soap dispensing equipment will probably be furnished by the successful bidder on the soap contract. All these, and many more details, should be determined by you *prior* to the sending out of your bids.

As a matter of general policy, it is wise to check out your rough draft of any request for an annual bid with *at least* two of the potential bidders. Give them a chance to look over your rough draft, ask them for their advice, find out if you forgot some important item, and generally satisfy yourself that there is nothing in your draft which would unintentionally work in favor of one or another of the bidders. If you want to play it absolutely safe, send your draft to *every* bidder, with a request for suggestions. There are always some institutional buyers who disapprove of this procedure, however; their argument is that you should be able to develop your own specifications, independent of the bidders, and that soliciting advice prior to bid is, if not downright collusion, at least unprofessional. This is a matter of opinion. Generally, when carried on in an open, forthright manner, and especially when done in close collaboration with your purchasing agent -- your solicitation of input by the bidders will be constructive and will probably save you from future problems.

One key item of information that should be provided in every request for bid is the actual or estimated quantity to be purchased. Frequently this information is available, either within your own institution, or from the current supplier. Sometimes, however, it has to be compiled through a summary of previous invoices. It is important that you furnish this information as accurately as possible, and that you distinguish between a firm quantity to be purchased and an estimated quantity. Make certain that you do not accidentally commit your institution to the purchase of an amount larger than intended. Sometimes, in periods of inflation, you may have to take certain risks by buying ahead -- but such are intentional, calculated risks, and your probable consumption can normally be estimated fairly accurately.

Your college undoubtedly has its own forms for requesting formal bids, and these forms would include such paragraphs as instructions to bidders, general information, signature page, etc. It would be wise for you, however, to review these forms and compare them with those of food service bid forms from other colleges. You may discover that you require certain clauses or provisions that are not normally included in standard bid forms, and may have to add them to the standard bid form. An excellent reference work is Professor Lendal Kotschevar's *Quantity Food Purchasing** -- which provides all types of sample bid forms for food service managers.

Bread and Bakery Products

Regardless of whether or not you operate your own bakery on campus, chances are that sliced bread and hamburger or hot dog buns are items which you would do better to purchase from an outside bakery. While many colleges and universities operate their own bake shops and many even bake specialty breads and rolls for their students, few college bake shops can compete favorably with the large commercial bakeries when it comes to the above-listed items. A college account, on the other hand, is a most desirable piece of business for commercial bakeries. Not only is the volume considerable, thus helping to defray much of the bakery's overhead, but the delivery stops are also much more efficient and economical than those in a super market, where the driver has to merchandise his product on the shelves, rotate the stock, etc. In fact, a college account is a "prime account," and generally the senior drivers compete for it.

Unless you have an overwhelming reason to do otherwise, you should place your bread purchases through strictly competitive bids. Differences in quality of product between large commercial bakeries are more imagined than real, and more a salesman's tool than a food buyer's concern. Differences in service may be real enough, but in the absence of solid information to the contrary, you may assume that every bidder will give you excellent service. That leaves you with important, though not clearly related considerations, such as the extent to which each bidder supported the university's fund-raising efforts in the past, which of the bidders is a friend of one of the regents, and how much trouble it would be to teach a driver from a new company all the technicalities of serving your various kitchens. While each of these considerations must be dealt with, they should not be directly related to the purchasing function. Your job is to obtain the best price for the product you need, and obtain it at a level of service compatible with your operations. Once you have done that and other factors enter the decision-making process, get guidance from your superiors before making a decision.

Bakeries generally establish a wholesale price a few cents below the recommended retail price for supermarkets and other small restaurant clients. They also frequently quote a much lower price (often as much as 20%-30% lower on sliced bread and buns) when bidding on annual contracts. These contracts are frequently with the local school district. They are thus public documents, and a telephone call will give

*Kotschevar, Lendal, *Quantity Food Purchasing;* John Wiley and Sons; N.Y.; 1961; 619 pp.

you the information you need regarding currently prevailing contract prices on bread and hamburger or hot dog buns.

One important detail to be covered is the matter of returns. Your bakery will probably agree to accept a limited number of returns of white or whole wheat sliced bread and perhaps also hot dog and hamburger buns. This protects you from running out of a product during a meal and also enables the driver to leave an adequate amount with you each day. This concession is costly to the bakery, however, and normally does not apply to specialty items such as special breads, muffins, etc. The bidder's return policy should be clearly stated in the bid.

In order to provide your students with a truly large and imaginative variety of breads, you may have to give a contract to more than one bakery or else prevail upon the successful bidder to purchase some of these more unusual breads for you and deliver these with the regular order. This is a service which many large bakeries will perform and, while the discount to you is not nearly as formidable as the bakery's regular products, it might still be somewhat below prevailing wholesale prices. Some of these breads are listed in Chapter VIII.

One additional consideration, when preparing your bakery bid, is the problem of control over receiving and invoices. Most bakery drivers are responsible to the bakery for the amount of product on their trucks. They have a considerable amount of leeway on how and where they deliver and sell this bread as long as it is on their route. With returns and other refunds, the honesty of the driver *plus* the careful checking-in of the product becomes a major factor in bread supply. You should insist that all bakery statements are supported by signed invoices, with the signatures limited to your regular employees or pre-selected individuals.

Milk and Dairy Products

Certain states such as California have laws governing the price of milk and dairy products which effectively stifle competitive bidding for institutional accounts. Nevertheless, you should be aware that most dairies are extremely eager to land a college or university account, and depending on the state and on prevailing laws, you should turn this eagerness to your advantage. For example, a small college in the Midwest once paid 33% less for milk than was charged in the supermarkets. The college's milk, of course, was delivered in 6 gallon containers, while the supermarket sold it in gallon- or half-gallon bottles. Obviously the contract-buying of milk can be profitable.

Beyond that, however, are other considerations. Unlike bakeries, where there is no significant taste difference among the breads, dairies differ in the butterfat content of their milk; they differ in cleanliness and procedures, and there is often a tremendous difference in their products such as cottage cheese and ice cream. Another important aspect in choosing a dairy supplier is the level and quality of *service* he supplies. In times of emergencies, the good supplier makes a special delivery; on special all-campus barbecues, he supplies a refrigerated truck for dairy and ice cream products; on holidays, he comes up with different and interesting ice cream products. For these reasons, you should be very selective in your choice of bidders. Visit each of the dairies which are interested in bidding. Conduct product taste tests, and inquire from other institutions about each potential bidder.

An important factor is your own method of dispensing milk: whether you use gravity-type milk dispensers which use 6-gallon cardboard boxes, or pump-type dispensers which use 10-gallon metal cans, or 1-gallon or ½-gallon containers: all this must be spelled out in advance and each bidder's capability to handle your needs should be determined before the final bid list is approved. In this connection, remember that if a company is stricken from your bid list, you and the purchasing agent should be prepared to give your reasons to your superiors. Especially in state institutions, it is difficult to eliminate bidders from a bid list. Nevertheless, this is sometimes necessary if you are to obtain the product and the service you need. Remember, however, that it is always easier to eliminate potential bidders *before* sending out bids, than to send them a copy of your request for bids and then, when they are low bidders, disqualify them. This is not only immoral, but probably illegal. Once you send someone a bid form, it is assumed that the firm is acceptable to you if it bids low and meets all the other specifications.

The frequency of deliveries (two, three times weekly), the pick-up of leftover products during recess periods, the providing of special services such as dry ice and special products such as egg nog are all items that must be considered in your dairy bids. Another consideration is whether or not to prepare a separate bid for ice cream products. This depends a great deal on the type of competition available, on your own judgment, and on whether or not it would benefit your school to split the dairy business between two suppliers, one for milk and one for ice cream. Many school districts change dairies each semester as a matter of policy and thus have two suppliers during each school year. This is not ideal, however, and unnecessarily disrupts operations in the middle of the school year.

Canned Goods and Staple Items

The principal reason for sending such items as bread and dairy products out for competitive bid is that of price. It was noted earlier that while there is normally little quality difference among bread products of large commercial bakeries, there could be some difference among competitive dairy products. In both instances, however, the determination of quality is relatively simple and is handled by your decision as to who is qualified to be on your bid list. In the case of canned goods, however, the situation is very different. Here the quality of the product is determined not only by the integrity and ability of each supplier, but also by your own decisions regarding the desired quality for each product, and by your own ability to describe the desired product clearly and accurately.

It is easy to make mistakes in the buying of canned goods. Here are some:

Selecting one grade of product (e.g. "U.S. Fancy") for all your products -- This is poor buying, since you may not need such high quality for some items such as fruit cocktail, for example, which gets mixed with fresh fruit before being served as fruit salad.

Selecting on the basis of grades only -- While government grades are helpful, they should never be the only basis for your purchasing decisions. Actual can-cutting tests are still necessary. In a good year, for example, you may find many fruits which normally would qualify as "Fancy" packed in "Choice" cans. Thus, specifying "Choice in Heavy Syrup" may be more advantageous than insisting on the "U.S. Fancy" grade. For certain uses, standard or even ungraded merchandise may be very satisfactory provided you have opened samples and checked on the actual quality of the food in the can.

Copying someone else's specifications (e.g. those of the federal or state government, or of another institution) -- The canned goods specifications for most colleges and universities, except those which operate their own, large commissaries, should be simple, clear, and practical. The more *complicated* the specification, the more *cautious* the bidder, and the more *expensive* will be the bid price.

Writing specifications without consulting suppliers -- Your canned good suppliers (they need not necessarily be local, in fact you should solicit some out-of-town bids to help keep the local vendors in line) can be tremendous help in drafting your specifications. As you review each item with them, you will learn about their own operations, the products they carry, and the price difference among grades. The average food service director will be tempted to include *too much detail* in his specifications. Remember that this may be of little benefit and could easily work against you.

Insisting on taste tests for every item -- Some food service directors get a special thrill out of setting up a test kitchen. They point with pride at the special kitchen, complete with scales, sieves, and all sorts of fancy equipment; they state proudly that "everything we buy gets tested here first -- for drained weight, quality and appearance, etc." This impresses the visitor, perhaps, but not necessarily another professional food buyer. While products of canned good suppliers change from year to year, and while *continuous testing of food items is an important aspect of quality control,* it is not feasible to make valid test comparisons on every canned item each year and, in fact, it is not necessary. Selective testing, both of new items and of heavily-used items about which there may be some question, is a much more realistic approach.

Asking for too many free samples -- Another result of possible preoccupation with product testing could be that you are asking for too many free samples from the suppliers. Some food service buyers actually use this device to save money on food purchases! This is not only unethical, but actually foolish. Suppliers soon get wise to such a scheme, and you could ruin an otherwise good business relationship.

Asking for fixed prices in a period of inflation -- It is difficult, even under the best conditions, to ask a vendor to commit himself to a fixed price for a product which may be subject to severe price changes during the contract period. There are some periods of wildly changing price fluctuations, when buying on contract for extended periods of time may actually be *unwise*. You always have a choice of either asking for prices for a very limited period (e.g. 30 days), or else including an escalator clause, which allows for changes in prices during the contract period that are based on the supplier's own price changes, or on some other mutually acceptable standard, such as the U.S. Consumers' Price Index.

Asking for too-frequent deliveries -- Every delivery costs your supplier money. Under normal conditions, you should be able to manage each kitchen with once-a-week deliveries. Naturally, your supplier will expect a small number of "emergencies" and will gladly help you out with these.

Being unclear about quantities -- Whether you plan to purchase fixed amounts of canned goods and staple items at one time or whether you plan to order these items as needed, make it absolutely clear just what will be the basis of your award. You cannot in good conscience expect your suppliers to bid on an expected 200 cases of green beans and then feel free, at the same time, to take advantage of a special 100-case green bean bargain that may come your way from another supplier and reduce your bidder's order by that amount.

Frozen Foods

Frozen foods should be purchased on a formal bid basis in a manner similar to the purchasing of canned goods. If your operation is grossing several thousand dollars monthly, and is therefore large enough to justify buying from more than one supplier, try to select at least one who is located in your town. It is helpful to have your frozen food distributor nearby. If he is a good supplier, he will make occasional emergency deliveries on weekends, or let you store your frozen foods in his freezer if your compressor should break down.

An important requirement for a frozen food distributor is that he makes all his deliveries in refrigerated trucks. Even though this seems obvious, there are unfortunately many small distributors who have not made this investment, and who make their deliveries in regular panel trucks. Even if the local health authorities accept his argument that the food is never in his truck longer than 30 minutes, you should not. The matter is potentially too serious for you to be lenient, and you must have absolute assurance that your frozen food arrives in your kitchen in the solid frozen state in which it left the warehouse.

The reputation of your frozen food vendor in the industry is of special importance to you: if he has an excellent credit rating and a fine reputation, then there are few products that he cannot get and stock for you. If, on the other hand, his is not a first-class rating, then you will have to shop elsewhere for new and interesting products.

Another major requirement of a frozen food vendor is his enthusiasm for, and ability to discover, new and interesting products. You should be able to depend on your local supplier to tell you about such new products, and not have to rely only on manufacturers' representatives, on your annual visits to a restaurant show or on tips from colleagues to keep you up to date. Similarly, when you come across a new product, you have a right to expect your frozen food supplier to try and get this product for you, as long as you buy it in sufficient quantities to make it worth his while.

Carbonated Beverages

Because of the intense competition for carbonated beverage syrup sales in the college market, you would be wise to purchase your syrup (and CO_2) for non-carbonated beverages on a formal bid basis. Some companies, in fact, have set up a special pricing arrangement for colleges and sometimes the price quoted to colleges and universities from corporate sales offices is lower than if it were computed by your local bottler.

Ideally, you should not be dependent upon your beverage supplier for equipment. If you own your own dispensers and ice makers, you are free to choose whatever product you prefer and can be certain of getting the lowest price possible. In practice, however, this situation seldom exists. You are certainly justified in selecting the vendor who offers you the automatic icemaker which you cannot afford to purchase, but which you need desperately. Make certain, however, that in accepting such a deal, you are not paying for such equipment indirectly by paying a much-higher-than-normal price for syrup. Compare your price with those of other nearby colleges and you will know how well you did.

In requesting quotations, make sure you share with the vendor as much information as possible: the approximate amount of syrup you expect to purchase during the year, the frequency of deliveries expected, whether delivery is to be f.o.b. your campus, and the number of places to which tanks must be delivered. Some of the larger institutions such as the University of California at Berkeley have saved a few cents off the usual net price for syrup by accepting delivery of syrup in their central commissary, and by handling the delivery to their various units with their own commissary personnel. For the smaller schools such an arrangement is unwise; it is helpful to have the soft drink vendor send his salesman directly into your various units to exchange syrup tanks. Not only is this convenient, but the salesmen have technical knowledge which you will often need to discover why a certain dispenser is out of order, or to adjust the brix (strength of mix) on a certain dispenser head.

Although nutritionally valueless, your carbonated beverages are so popular with the students that a breakdown of dispensers in the middle of lunch or dinner can be troublesome. The good vendor will offer you 12- or 24-hour, seven-day service, and have radio-equipped trucks which can speed to your rescue when you're in trouble.

In some towns and cities, there may be a good soft drink bottler representing a lesser-known brand. If his quotation for syrup is cheaper than any of the most popular brands, you have a slight problem. The students' identification with the major brands is so strong, that you cannot lightly overlook it without being accused of serving poor quality drinks. It is not advisable to serve any type of carbonated beverage without also offering one of the major brands at the same time.

Non-Carbonated Beverages

Normally, your carbonated beverage dispenser will dispense at least one flavor of non-carbonated drink, usually an orange drink. As a wise food service manager, you should, however, offer at least one or two other flavors of non-carbonated drinks or punch as most of the students call it. A glass of punch is about half the price of a glass of a carbonated drink, but neither of course, is nutritious.

Tasting punch -- It is extremely difficult to taste the difference between one punch and another unless you taste both products at the same time, drink plain water in between, and have others tasting with you so that a consensus can be established. Some people, including the majority of the students, like a very sweet punch; others prefer punch a little more tart. When conducting a taste test, be sure that only the person who actually mixed and numbered the samples knows which product is which. It is very easy to be influenced by knowledge of a certain brand or product name.

Purchasing punch dispensers -- If at all possible, buy your own drink dispensers on a formal, competitive bid basis from your regular kitchen equipment suppliers. It saves you the time and trouble of figuring out how much you are really paying for the dispensers which are continually being offered to you (together with a specified number of cases of the beverage) as a "very special deal." If you keep in mind that the vendor has to finance the cost of the equipment just as you would need to do, then it becomes obvious that such a deal seldom produces real savings for your school. On the other hand, sometimes this method of purchasing is the only way in which you can bring a certain product to your campus. If so, there is nothing wrong with such an arrangement, provided that you know exactly what you are actually paying for the equipment and that you can extricate yourself from the purchasing arrangement at any time by paying for the unamortized value of the equipment.

Paper Supplies

Shortly after your arrival at your new job, you will be visited by a manufacturer's representative who will leave you sample sets of very attractive paperware, and make all kinds of interesting offers. Included among these will be the printing of your school's seal or mascot on the paperware at a nominal cost. Listen to everything -- and make no commitment. Not for a while, at least. It is generally unwise to buy from a salesman when a new product is first introduced. There is much information that you need to have about your institution, before you can make a long-term decision about paperware. Some of this is as follows:

- How strongly do your students, and you personally, feel about using styrofoam products, which are less expensive than paper, but are not bio-degradable?

- What is the quantity of the various paper items that you will use in one or two years?

- What is the best logo to use on your paperware? This decision should be made in collaboration with your public relations department, the student union, and any other interested parties. Is the small extra cost worth the quantity commitment that goes along with it?

- What types and sizes of paperware are best for you?

- How does the price of paper cups compare with the prices quoted you by your carbonated beverage supplier?

Once you have made up your mind, by all means purchase through the formal bid process. Even though your manufacturer's representative may have *his* favorite distributor, that is of no interest to you. Insist on the names of at least three area distributors, and then get competitive quotations from each.

China

China is another product about which many people have strong feelings. In the early days of residence hall food service, it was often the prerogative of the residence hall director (or the dean of women) to select the china for the women's residence hall. This turned out, usually, to be very expensive, often had its own special logo, and was appreciated largely by the deans and visiting parents. Early in the 1950's, restaurants and institutions were offered a new product -- dinnerware made out of glass. Slightly less expensive than most vitrified china, this new dinnerware was unusual in that it did not break as easily as conventional china, although when it did break, it would shatter into a thousand pieces. Both the regular institutional china as well as the new glassware had the disadvantage of being quite a bit thicker and heavier than the china used in the homes, a fact necessitated by the harder use and the processing through commercial dishmachines.

In the mid-sixties, several china manufacturers developed a new, thin, graceful china, with the same strength and qualities as regular commercial china. This new product is considerably more expensive, but also much more beautiful than regular china.

Another important fact about china purchasing is that special patterns take much longer to obtain and cost quite a bit more than stock patterns. In view of the fact that you will experience a tremendous china loss each year (many colleges and universities experience a turnover of from 75% to 100% yearly!), you may not be able to afford a school logo or school colors. This is especially true when you consider that your china will be stolen by students moving off-campus. Having school logos on the dishes will make such theft even more attractive. Even the selection of stock patterns requires some careful planning: the more complicated the pattern, the more costly it will be.

Delivery time and replacement of china are two other important factors. If you have a special pattern, your order for September should be in the hands of the successful bidder no later than April 15th. Your purchase order should read:

"Delivery must occur on or before August 15th, or else this
purchase order is automatically cancelled."

Even stock patterns, in the quantities you require, take a few months to process, so purchase your china well in advance of your needs.

Next to theft, your main reason for china loss is breakage. Although this may sound simple, breakage can be minimized if you are aware of the reasons why your kitchen crews break so many dishes. Here are some of them:

- Defective wheels on dish dollies.
- Obstructions, such as water and steam hoses, on the floor.

- Imperfect stacking of dishes. Don't ever mix two different patterns or shapes in the same pile or else the pile is likely to spill over.
- Careless handling at the dirty dish conveyor.
- Poorly designed dish dollies.

It will be very helpful if you have your maintenance people mount a sample of each dish on a large board with a friendly, but clear message to the dish crew to be careful in handling these dishes. The cost of each dish can also be shown under each of the samples attached to the board.

When purchasing china, be imaginative. Don't limit yourself to the normal selection of cups, saucers, butter and fruit dishes, and dinner plates. Buy some individual casserole or "au gratin" dishes (the 8-oz. ones are perfect for residence hall food service) so that you can use them for such items as pot pies, fish, and souffles. Remember that stew on a plate looks ordinary, but dished up in a casserole dish, with duchess potatoes piled on top, browned in the oven, it looks gorgeous.

For banquets and other special dinners, you might wish to invest in a different, more expensive china pattern. Since your college president probably likes to entertain and impress campus visitors, the china used for such special luncheons and dinners should be especially attractive. Furthermore, you may wish to purchase additional items just for banquet service, such as bouillon cups, creamers, sugar bowls, and gravy boats.

Silverware

There was a time, in the 1950's, when many residence halls actually used real silverplated dinnerware in their dining rooms. Those were the days when residence halls were still separated by sex, when visitors to the dining rooms were strictly limited, and when gracious dining was still something considered to be a vital element of a student's social-educational development. Those days, for better or worse, are gone forever. Today's food service director buys the cheapest stainless steel silverware he can get, knowing beforehand that he will have to buy more in the middle of the year, knowing that he cannot really control the wholesale theft of such silverware by students living off-campus, and cannot stop the less obvious, but equally damaging "borrowing" of silverware by students in the residence halls, where they use it to eat food and beverages prepared on prohibited hot plates and coffee pots. It is possible that you may decide to choose medium weight, rather than light-weight silverware for your school. There is some logic in that, since the lightweight spoons and forks are so easily bent that students like to play with them (when they get tired of playing with salt and pepper shakers), and bend them into interesting shapes.

When asking for quotations, make certain that you have clearly described the silverware you want. The imported stainless ware (from places like Taiwan and Hong Kong) is normally less expensive than similar products manufactured in the U.S.A.

Kitchen Equipment

As a general rule, kitchen equipment should *always* be purchased through formal, competitive bids. The reason for this is the tremendous variance in prices bid by different kitchen equipment dealers. The normal discount allowed them by the manufacturers varies from 20% to 50% off list price; some allow an additional 5% discount beyond that, and others have special discount arrangements for their major dealers. Equipment dealers have to add their freight costs (from 5% to 15%), their overhead and finance costs, and their profit. A normal price quotation for a major piece of kitchen equipment will be somewhere between 10% and 20% off list price. Some dealers, however, will quote the equipment at full list, especially if they believe that you will buy it directly from them without going to the trouble of asking for written quotations from others.

A piece of equipment bought from a dealer's showroom will cost you more than one which the dealer can order directly from the factory. In the former instance, his overhead is considerably higher, and you must expect to pay for the convenience of getting the item immediately, instead of having to wait for it for several weeks or months.

Try to get a copy of the manufacturer's catalog or else a copy of the specification sheet for the piece of equipment you want to buy, together with a list of accessories available. As with buying an automobile, many accessories are of vital importance, and improve either the usefulness or the appearance of the item purchased. When purchasing a mixer or food cutter for instance, you may decide to purchase the vegetable slicer attachment at the same time. In order to do so, you must select the various slicer and grater plates, all of which are listed and illustrated on the "spec sheet." As another example, consider the purchase of a restaurant range: not only are the griddle-burner combinations too numerous to mention, but the options of a stainless steel front, sides, and top shelf will make a tremendous difference in the appearance of this piece of equipment three years hence.

There are occasions when a genuine "deal" does come up: equipment dealers sometimes purchase a manufacturer's closeout or make other advantageous arrangements which can produce real savings. Hopefully, your school's purchasing policies allow for such unusual circumstances. If you trust the dealer, you have little to worry about. If you are not absolutely certain, check out the proposed deal carefully before making your decision.

Finally, there is the question of equipment warranties. Most motors and similar parts have a five-year part warranty directly from the manufacturer; in addition, the dealer will normally give you a 30-day full-service warranty. It is not wise to insist on a longer service warranty (such as a 1-year warranty). It forces the dealer to add a special mark-up to your price; since you probably have your own maintenance staff at the school, this additional warranty may well be an unnecessary expense.

INFORMAL BID PURCHASING

There are certain items purchased in a college food service operation which do not lend themselves well to formal bid purchasing. Whenever a formal request for bids is sent out, the institution announces, in fact, that it will select the lowest bidder who meets the required specifications. Even though the purchasing agent may insert some sort of disclaimer or "escape clause" (i.e. giving the school the right to select the successful bidder regardless of price), a school which often abuses the formal purchasing process in this manner will soon find itself without interested vendors. The items described in this chapter, however, differ from those discussed in the previous chapter: meat, because it is quoted weekly, and because the quality can vary greatly from one week to another, thus providing the buyer more discretion than is normally possible in formal bidding; coffee, orange juice, and dishmachine soaps, because the bidder must supply service together with the product, and the quality of this service is so important that you will want a freer hand in making your selection than is possible in formal bidding; kitchen supplies, such as small utensils, because you may need these frequently and quickly, and may wish to select these directly from a dealer's showroom; and linen, because the quality of the laundry and the range of services offered is more important than the cost.

The above does not mean that all college food service directors possess the freedom to engage in informal purchasing. Many state institutions, in fact, strictly prohibit such purchases, although most give some latitude to the buyers when it comes to meats. This book is intended, however, to suggest the ideal purchasing system. The reader must be flexible enough to make his own adjustments to a given situation.

Meat and Fowl

Meat purchases ("Meat," in this chapter, includes poultry, unless a specific distinction is made) represent 20%-30% of your total food purchases, and are the single most important item on your shopping list. Those who have never purchased meat in large quantities find it complicated and mysterious; those who have done it find it fairly easy. Because of constantly changing prices and because of the factors which affect the price of meat (grade, cut, age, trim), you must acquire some basic knowledge about meat purchasing, and, even more important, must follow a clear and constant set of procedures. The main ingredients to good meat and poultry purchasing are:

- Honest, reliable purveyors
- Clear and practical specifications
- Weekly price quotations
- Orders at least one week in advance
- Careful receiving procedures
- Frequent feedback to the purveyors

Honest, reliable purveyors -- Find and do business with those who are knowledgeable and honest in the wholesale meat and poultry trade. Fortunately, most meat purveyors serving the institutional market are. There are always some, however, who try to enlarge their profit at your expense. Such purveyors will underbid their competition, try to substitute ungraded, less expensive meat for U.S. graded meat, cheat just a little on the amount of fat left on the meat, weigh the meat after it is wrapped rather than before, change the fat or soybean content of your ground beef, or think up their own ingenious ways of increasing their profit.

Selecting the right meat purveyor is not a quick or easy process. At first, you will do well to continue doing business with those who have served your school in the past. Before doing so, however, call in their sales managers and explain your philosophy of operation, your specifications (see below) and make it absolutely clear that, regardless of how well or how poorly he may have served your institution in the past, his standing with you begins *right now*. Explain that you are not interested in special favors, in donations to the school's athletic fund, or gifts at Christmas time. Make it absolutely clear that what you expect from the meat purveyor is quality meat, meat that meets your specifications, meat that is cut and shipped in a sanitary manner. You also expect good and timely advice about prices and trends, suggestions regarding new products, timely and dependable deliveries, and a genuine interest on his part in your possible problems with meat or poultry items. Furthermore, make it understood that should you ever find clear proof that there has been an intentional violation of these basic rules which govern relations between meat purveyor and customer, you will drop his firm from your list of acceptable purveyors.

In smaller towns and cities, where there is only one, or perhaps no hotel and restaurant meat supplier, the local supermarket operator will sometimes try to fill this void. Sometimes this works well, but normally it does not. You must realize that hotel, restaurant, and institutional meat is sold through a distinct and separate channel of distribution. The local supermarket butcher cuts meat quite differently than does your meat purveyor; he also buys it differently. Young, new food service managers are often astounded to discover that many cuts of meats are *more expensive* when bought from their suppliers than when purchased from the local meat market. This is easy to explain: the local supermarket, for instance, may have two or three tenderloins which they can afford to sell at $3.50 per pound. This is a strictly limited supply. If, on the other hand, you need to purchase 200 filet mignons, your price, wholesale, may well be $4.75 per pound. Your wholesale meat purveyor, in order to supply you with this large amount of filets, had to cut his beef in such a way that he would get tenderloin steaks, rather than the more popular cuts of steak such as sirloin, T-bone, etc. If, however, a local butcher is your only local source of meat, purchasing from him may be a sound move. There are always emergencies when a local supplier will come in very handy. Just be aware of the fact that your *regular* supplier should be one who specializes in selling to hotels, restaurants, and institutions. Get a list of members from the National Association of Meat Purveyors, 252 W. Ina Road, Tucson, Arizona 85704.

Clear and practical specifications -- If you have ever seen specifications put out by a government agency, you may note that they are both excessively lengthy and unnecessarily confusing. Avoid that, if you can. One tool that will help you tremendously is the *Meat Buyers' Guide* published by the National Association of Meat Purveyors. This illustrated set of two booklets contains brief, clear specifications of the major wholesale cuts, as well as specifications for portion-cut meats. Each such specification has a number, so that you can refer to it easily without having to list without having to list the details. There may be instances in which you would like to modify the "M.B.G. Specs" as they are referred to, as in the following case:

> No. 1 TOP ROUND (INSIDE), cut in accordance with M.B.G. Specs No. 168, except that it is to be split and tied. Maximum fat cover: one-half inch. Weight range: 18-20 lbs. Minimum age: 10 days.

Some food service managers develop their own specifications by collecting a number of specifications from other institutions and extracting whatever is useful for their own purposes. This may be helpful for purposes of general orientation, but is not really the best way to write your own specifications. One very effective method is to get together with one or two of your meat purveyors and review with them the major items of purchase. Let them help you come up with language which is brief, clear, and to the point. After you have written the first draft, go over it with the other meat purveyors to make sure that everyone understands it, that there is no confusion, and no accidental phrasing which would favor one vendor over another. Finally, send out your completed draft to all your major vendors and ask them, in writing, for any changes or modifications they might wish to suggest. In this way you have bent over backward to be fair to all concerned, and everyone will know exactly what each of your specifications demands. Of further help to you is the *Meat Evaluation Handbook* published by the National Live Stock and Meat Board, 444 N. Michigan Avenue, Chicago, Illinois 60603. This book emphasizes *Retail Cuts.*

When you have completed your specifications, be sure to prepare a "cover page," which lists all the general terms and conditions which apply to your institution. This page includes instructions about how and when to quote, the period covered by each quotation, the amount of tolerance allowed for portion-cut meats, when meat may be delivered in the *frozen* state, and if necessary, the fact that all your purchases are to be graded *U.S. Choice* unless otherwise stated. Also include terms of delivery, whether or not it is to be pre-paid by the supplier and billed to you later. Sample pages of meat specifications, including cover page, are found in Appendix 4.

Order one week in advance -- Advance planning is one of the basic elements of good management. In purchasing, it will save you money. The more time that you give your meat purveyors, the more efficient they can be in filling your requirements. Even though you are an important customer, you are not the only one, and your meat purveyor must schedule his production in the same way that you do your kitchen work. On the other hand, meat prices fluctuate so frequently that ordering too far in advance is not practical either. The normal procedure is to place orders at the beginning of the week for the meat that is to be delivered starting with Monday of the following week. Obviously your purveyors will be glad to add to or delete from your order during the week, if your requirements change.

Weekly Quotation Sheet -- The meat purveyor's weekly quotations should be recorded by someone in the office on a printed form and then given to you (or to whoever does the buying) for final decision. Normally the buyer underlines or circles

EXHIBIT V-1

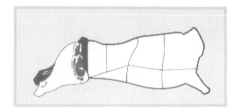

168 - Top (Inside) Round

The top round is the inside portion of Item No. 158 that is posterior to the round bone and is prepared as described in Item No. 163. When smaller roasts are specified, the top round shall be separated by not more than 2 lengthwise cuts and subsequent cuts, if necessary, shall be made girthwise. All cuts shall be made reasonably perpendicular to the outer skin surface.

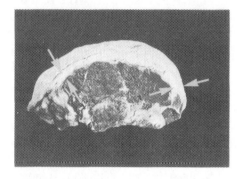

168 - Top (Inside) Round

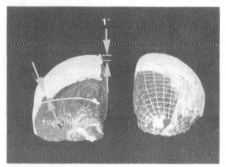

168 - Top (Inside) Round
Split, Tied and Netted

BEEF   27

that quotation which he deems in the best interest of his college. In those instances, when he is not selecting the low bidder, it is wise to make a written note at the bottom of the sheet, indicating his reasons for selecting the higher bid. The purpose of both the sheet and the notations is to provide you with a permanent record of how, from whom, and why you purchased as you did. Since meat expenditures are such a significant budget item, it is important that you can justify, even a year or two after the event, why you made the buying decisions you did. A sample of such a form is shown in Exhibit V-2.

Weekly meat purchasing summary -- Whenever meat purchases are done centrally for a number of campus units, it is necessary to summarize these for the information of the unit managers and their receiving clerks. This enables them to check the vendor's invoices against what was actually ordered, and tells them immediately if some item was forgotten or delivered in error. A sample sheet is shown in Exhibit V-3.

Careful receiving procedures -- None of your eloquent words to the meat purveyor will, in the long run, be as important as the steps that you take to back them up. Unless your vendors know that your staff is following tight, efficient receiving procedures, they may not take your specifications seriously. After all, why state that "all products shall be purchased at *net weight* only" if you don't even have a scale to weigh the meat when it comes in? Why should he worry about giving you only a maximum fat cover of one-half inch if he knows that no one at your place will bother to check it? True, the majority of vendors are honest, and will supply you properly regardless of whether or not you check up on them. It only takes one, however, to send your food costs up, and you want to know the reason why. Another important reason why careful receiving is essential is that *honest mistakes* are inevitable. If your purveyor knows that you and your staff check in the meat carefully when it arrives, he will usually take your word for any mistake that he may have made.

Frequent feedback to the purveyors -- Close and honest communications with your purveyors are essential to mutual trust and confidence. There is no way that your meat purveyor can know that his Swiss steak was tough unless you tell him. When you do, he might have some helpful solutions. He might, for example, suggest that you use a different cut of meat, or run the meat through a tenderizing machine. As you gain more experience in purchasing, you will discover that a great deal of information can be gained from your salesmen if you treat them in a cordial, professional manner and if you share your problems with them. Another good idea is an occasional visit to your meat purveyor's plant. You should be satisfied that it is clean and sanitary, and you should be able to see how your meat is being prepared. Better yet, take some of your cooks and some students with you, and let everyone see where you buy your meat for the college.

EXHIBIT V-2

FOOD SERVICE
WEEKLY MEAT & POULTRY QUOTATIONS

Revised October 31, 1971
Mr. Fairbrook
Phone No. 946-2533

DATES COVERED Jan 29 TO Feb 5, 1979
U.O.P.
SPEC. NO.

SPEC. NO.	ITEM	SWIFTS	LUCE	C & H	FREMONT	TED'S	SOUZA'S
1.	BOTTOM ROUND 1169R (Split)	1.61					1.55
2.	TOP ROUND 1168R (Split)	1.76		1.74		1.73	1.77
4.	CHUCK ROLL 1116R (Split)	1.86				1.85	1.75
7.	FLANK STEAK, SKINNED & DEFATTED 1½–2 # Average						
8.	CUBE STEAK, FROM FLANK, 5–5½ oz.						1.76
12a.	STEW MEAT, 1/8" Fat Max. 1195	1.69	1.89			1.79	1.73
16.	HAMBURGER PATTIES, 18% Fat Max. 5/1	1.30	1.14			1.28	1.26
17.	HAMBURGER STEAKS, 18% Fat Max. 7 oz. ea.	1.30	1.14			1.28	1.25
18.	GROUND BEEF, 18% Fat Max.	1.08	1.14			1.24	1.09
24.	FRANKFURTERS 8/lb	1.12	1.12			1.12	1.15 will go up next week
–	SAUSAGE LINKS	1.07	1.05			1.07	1.14
30.	HAM, SMOKED, BONELESS, ~~TAVERN STYLE~~ Deli Hams	1.66	1.56			1.49	1.62
–	HAM, BONED & TIED, Metal Tip ends, Ac Casing, rd.			1.92		1.98	1.89
31.	FRESH HAM ROLL, ½" Fat Max.			1.89		1.75	1.59
32.	~~CANADIAN PORK LOIN~~ Short Ribs	1.16					1.25
–	PORK TENDERLOINS, FROZEN, Approx. 2–3 # ea.						
34.	PORK STRIPS, ½" x ½" x 2"						1.65
36.	IMPORTED PICNIC			1.84		1.85	1.87
38.	BACON, CENTER CUT, 18-22#	1.41	1.28			1.31	1.34
39.	BOSTON BUTT STEAKS, BONE IN, #1406, 7 oz.						
50.	~~CHICKEN, FRESH, 2½-3# WHOLE~~ 6 oz. center cut Pork Chops	2.12	2.19			2.14	2.25
51.	CHICKEN, FRESH, 2½–3# Quartered						
53.	TURKEYS, Grade A, Double Breasted, 26–28#			.86		.93	.86
–	TURKEY ROLLS, COOKED, MIXED 60–40–Firm Specify Brand			1.19		1.29	1.37
–	BOLOGNA, ALL MEAT, 26" or 44" Size, (Specify Which)			1.12		1.11	1.06
–	SALAMI, COOKED, 12# Roll, AC Casing			1.16		1.32	1.12
–	SALAMI, ITALIAN, 3–4½#/Roll			1.96		2.05	1.97
–	CORNED BEEF			1.39		1.45	1.33

EXHIBIT V-3

UNIVERSITY OF THE PACIFIC

WEEKLY MEAT PURCHASING

UNIT Grace Covell   COVERING DATES Jan 15 TO Jan 21, 1979

ITEM		PURVEYOR	DELIVERY DATE	COST
Chipped Beef	10 lb	Luce	B - 1/15	
Bulk Sausage	10 lb	Luce	L - 1/15	
Ground Beef	10 lb	Luce	L - 1/15	
Ground Pork	on hand		L - 1/15	
Hamburger Patties	"	C+H	L - 1/15	
Turkey Roll		C+H	L - 1/15	
Ground Beef	40 lb	Luce	D - 1/15	
Ground Veal	10 lb	"	D - 1/15	
Ground Pork	10 lb	"	B - 1/15	
Canadian Bacon	3 sticks	Ted's	B - 1/16	
Cubed Beef (Stew)	10 lb	Luce	L - 1/16	
Top Round	on hand		L - 1/16	
Ground Beef	70 lb	Luce	D - 1/16	
Pullman Ham	on hand		D - 1/16	
Turkey Roll	2	C+H	D - 1/16	
Turkey Breast	on hand		D - 1/17	
Bacon	30 lb	C+H	B - 1/17	
Ground Beef	60 lb	Luce	L - 1/17	
Deli Ham	on hand	"	L - 1/17	
Hamburger Patties	"		D - 1/17	
Flat Meat (London Broil)	110 lb	Ted's	D - 1/17	
Bacon	15 lb	C+H	B - 1/18	

Coffee

If it were not for the fact that a coffee urn and other coffee dispensing equipment requires special servicing, and that coffee brewing needs special supervision if it is to be consistently good, you could purchase coffee from your wholesale grocer, along with all the other staple goods. Some national coffee brands are, in fact, distributed through wholesale grocery houses whose salesmen have been trained also to be coffee salesmen. The specialized coffee routeman has become a somewhat unique phenomenon in institutional food service: he delivers coffee, helps train your staff in proper coffee brewing methods, leaves training materials and visual aids. If coffee urns are used, he also leaves urn cleaners, brushes, faucets and gaskets and, in general, acts as a kind of special assistant to you, the manager, to make certain that proper coffee brewing methods are followed at all times. For a sample list of services that can be provided by a coffee salesman, see Exhibit V-4.

There are, of course, other effective ways of serving good coffee besides coffee brewed in an urn. Automatic dispensers using instant freeze-dried coffee, as well as dispensers using a liquid coffee extract are becoming more and more popular, both from a cost as well as maintenance standpoint.

You will find that institutional coffee prices are usually within a few cents of each other, and there seems little point in having such small price differences become a major determinant in the selection of your coffee. Your selection should depend first on taste and second on the quality of the specialized service that you expect from the purveyor.

While your objective should always be to serve the best cup of coffee possible, you are not expected to purchase the most expensive blend of Columbian coffee carried by your supplier. Most coffee houses carry three or four grades of institutional blends, and the second from the top of the line in price is often of excellent quality and the one carried by most commercial restaurants. A taste test, involving students as well as faculty and staff, is always helpful and also can be a lot of fun for everyone. You would, of course, announce such a test well in advance, serve complimentary doughnuts or cookies, let anyone interested participate and then, a few days later, announce the "winner": the coffee brand finally selected for your operation.

Even in periods of wildly fluctuating coffee prices, your coffee brand selection should be based primarily on the quality of the coffee itself and on the quality of service or the equipment used to dispense it. Another consideration in times of inflation should be the shelf life of the coffee. Vacuum packed cans can be an excellent hedge against rising coffee prices, whereas coffee packed in paper bags loses its flavor after several weeks in storage. Younger college students generally drink very little coffee. Older students and faculty members generally buy their coffee in the cash operations, where you can adjust selling prices in proportion to your costs and thus keep your overall food costs in line.

Orange Juice

Orange juice is a very competitive sales item in the commercial market. You have several choices available to you:

EXHIBIT V-4

UNIVERSITY OF THE PACIFIC

DEPARTMENT OF HOUSING AND FOOD SERVICE
FROM: Paul Fairbrook, Director
SUBJECT: List of Services Expected from Coffee Salesmen

Please note that we expect your driver to be more than merely a delivery person. We expect him to assist the unit managers in making certain that the coffee at the University is being properly prepared, that the urns are properly maintained, and that everything is being done to serve a good cup of coffee. Specifically, some of the steps a good coffee route salesman should take are as follows:

1.   Make sure that the coffee is prepared properly.

2.   Make sure that the coffee urn cleaning procedures are known by our staff, and followed.

3.   Leave ample supplies of complimentary urn cleaner and make sure they are being used.

4.   Supply us, at your regular price, with coffee urn brushes of all types, gaskets, sight gauges, faucets, etc.

5.   Conduct periodic (once a year perhaps) training sessions on how to make coffee.

6.   Assist our unit managers in getting maintenance or repair service from coffee urn manufacturers (e.g. deliming of urns, repair of burnt-out elements, etc.)

7.   Assist the University during its special occasions (about twice a year) when it needs additional "airvoids" on a busy weekend, by lending us some at no charge.

Frozen orange juice in automatic dispensers -- This is the most commonly used product. Sold under various trade names, it is normally a product of Florida Orange Juice. There is also a small amount of California juice available, but most California oranges are sold as fresh fruit. There are often two grades; one is slightly less costly, because the juice is squeezed from a mixed batch of oranges instead of a selected batch. Make a taste test, and if you *can* tell the difference, buy the number one grade.

The key to your decision as to whose product to buy is the quality of the *equipment and* degree of *service* offered. Normally, with orange juice, the equipment is furnished with the product, similar to non-carbonated beverages. The difference, however, is that an orange juice dispenser is slightly more complicated than a punch dispenser, and you will probably prefer to have the supplier maintain his equipment, rather than purchase your own.

Frozen orange juice mixed by kitchen staff -- It is possible that your frozen food distributor can sell you a good quality frozen orange juice at a lower price than the orange juice that is sold with equipment. Mixing the juice in the kitchen and dispensing it in vacuum cans is no big problem. Whether or not the savings to you is worth the extra work in the kitchen (especially at breakfast, when you have a minimum staff on duty) is questionable. You can make this decision, after weighing all the facts.

Reconstituted orange juice -- Your dairy supplier will be happy to quote you on orange juice reconstituted in his plant. While this is usually packed in quart containers, you might be able to convince him to pack it for you in 6-gallon milk cartons (as was done by Rutgers University in New Brunswick, N.J.). The cost of this product may be slightly less than frozen orange juice; whether or not it tastes as good as the aerated juice from the dispensers is for you to decide.

Canned orange juice -- Canned orange juice is ideal for picnics and sack lunches, but does not compare in quality to the frozen product. Consider it only under special circumstances. For more information about orange juice, see Chapter VIII.

Orange whip -- A drink that is growing in popularity is one made from an orange base, composed of about ⅔ orange juice and ⅓ low fat milk and other ingredients. This base is dispensed through a dispenser with a "whipper" attachment and thus comes out rich and foamy looking. Known under various trade names ("Orange Bang," "Orange Spa," "Orange Comet") this type of drink is gaining in popularity and is cheaper than pure 100% orange juice. *It is not really a legitimate substitute for orange juice,* but you could offer it as an alternative choice.

Dishmachine and Potwashing Detergents

Dishmachine detergent, like coffee, is another item which you should not be buying primarily on the basis of price. The companies from which you should buy such products have highly trained route salesmen, who are experts in dish and potwashing procedures. They probably possess more technical knowledge than anyone on your staff and can be of tremendous help to you in making sure that proper warewashing methods are used, that the equipment is operating properly, and that all vital sanitation measures are being observed. They, like the coffee salesmen, are extensions of your supervisorial staff: they notify you if there is anything wrong with the equipment or with the techniques used. If they are good, they will often correct the situation on the spot. They can detect a plugged up dishmachine nozzle, a detergent or wetting agent dispenser that is not working, or a spray arm that is not functioning. They will hook up a detergent dispenser to your pot sink or dishmachine, and make certain that your kitchen porters don't use an excessive amount.

On the other hand, they are not electricians or plumbers, and you cannot expect them to act in such a capacity. If you find the right type of detergent salesman in your area, then choose him and his company -- even if the price of his product may be slightly higher than several others available to you. Remember: If he can help you prevent food poisoning on your campus, then whatever premium you may have paid for his products will well have been worth the cost.

Linen and Uniforms

In a well-run institutional food service, every food service worker is in uniform while working. In college food service, this means that all student workers are issued shirts, jackets, smocks, or aprons when working, and all regular employees wear complete uniforms. There are a number of ways of handling the issuing and washing of all these uniforms. The most common method is to offer the women employees a choice: They can wear (and maintain) their own nylon uniforms which fit better and are more attractive, or else they can use the cotton uniforms supplied by the laundry in which case the college takes care of laundering them. Many schools purchase two uniforms yearly for their women employees, with the employee having the right to select the one that fits her best. Male employees normally opt for the cotton uniforms supplied by the laundry. Students, both men and women, will generally wear whatever is issued them. Since student workers normally work only 2-3 hours at a time, jackets, smocks, and aprons are really the most practical items to use for this purpose.

For banquet service, you require a variety of table cloths and napkins. If your local laundry is modern and progressive, it will give you a choice of several colors of table cloths and cloth napkins so that you can decorate your banquet rooms in different ways to suit the interior decor as well as the occaion. At Christmas, for instance, you could request red table cloths and gold napkins; on Valentine's Day, perhaps pink table cloths with red napkins; at other occasions, the combinations could be white and red, gold and red, green and white, or even, for an Italian dinner, red-checkered table cloths.

Your commercial laundry will work with you in many different ways. If you would like to introduce a new student smock, but do not wish to purchase the smocks yourself, chances are that the laundry will buy them provided that you agree to use these for at least three or more years. If, on the other hand, you wish to buy your own uniforms, the laundry will launder them for you at a slightly lower price.

Quite a few food service operations maintain their own washer and dryer somewhere near the kitchen area for the washing of kitchen towels. This is a good idea, not only because it saves you money (it is cheaper to buy and launder than to rent towels from a laundry) but also because you'll never run out of kitchen towels and your staff will never be reluctant to use as many as needed for cleaning and polishing.

Because your success, insofar as linen and uniforms are concerned, depends a great deal on the quality of the laundry and the range of items that they can offer, it is always best to select your laundry not strictly on the basis of price alone, but also on the services they can provide. Even with the very best laundry, however, it is always good to maintain some control over your costs by having someone in your organization do a preliminary count of the linen before it is picked up and another count of the linen when it arrives.

COMMISSION PURCHASING: PRODUCE

Perhaps the most variable product in food purchasing is produce. It varies not only because of the seasons or the supplier, but also because of the many different grades and descriptions, which tend to confuse all but the most experienced produce buyer. A "head" of celery, for example, can consist of beautiful large heads (24 to the pack) or of much smaller heads (30 per pack). Both oranges and apples are described by grades and sizes. Apples, for example, come 88, 100, and 125 to the case. There are packed No. 1 apples, loose No. 1 apples, plus "C" Grade apples which are different runs of apples packed loosely in a case. Potatoes come not only in several grades (No. 1 is without blemish, No. 2's are those which are cut or damaged), but also come by count in boxes (No. 80's are between 10 and 12 oz. each, 90's between 8 and 10 oz., and 100's between 6 and 8 oz.). They are also sold by weight (a 100 lb. No. 1 sack consists of a "field run" of potatoes of various sizes) and by size ("bakers" are specially selected large potatoes suitable for baking).

Produce buying, as you can see, is complex. Complex but not impossible. Once you have learned about the various grading and packing methods used for each type of produce, it is very feasible for you to purchase produce on an informal bid basis, once a week, as you do meat. In fact, many institutional food services do exactly that, and do it very successfully. All that is needed is a short, clear set of produce specifications and two or three good local produce purveyors who understand your specifications and are willing and able to supply accordingly.

If you purchase on the basis of competitive bids, however, remember that there is one aspect of produce buying which is different from buying other foods: not only is the dollar volume low, but the risk because of perishability is very high. *It is essential, therefore, that you make the order worthwhile* for the produce vendor. If you start to pick and choose and break up what would normally have been one good, large order into several smaller orders, you are hurting only yourself. Remember that the prices you receive are prices for the merchandise already purchased by the produce vendor *on speculation;* if he cannot sell his merchandise either to you or another customer, it will spoil and he will take a loss.

For the above reasons, many schools have developed a different system of purchasing produce. The larger universities, with thousands of students in residence halls, might send their own buyer to the market. The smaller colleges (especially when there are not many produce dealers in town) often turn to a commission purchasing arrangement. This is an arrangement whereby a selected produce vendor is "commissioned" to act as a produce buyer for the school. He has the produce order in his pocket *before* he goes to the market, buys produce in accordance with the general needs of the school, and then adds a predetermined markup for his services. Such a markup may vary from 10% to 15% depending on the volume, the items involved, and the local circumstances. There are several distinct advantages in such an arrangement:

There is no risk to the purveyor -- Since the produce purveyor has your exact order before he buys, he knows that whatever he buys, as long as it conforms to your specifications, will be sold, and his risk has thus been removed from the purchasing process.

He can save you money -- Since he is acting as your buyer, and since he knows your needs as well as the latitude that you have given him, he can act on your behalf when he gets to the market and save you money. He can decide, for example, to substitute one grade for another, if the price of the latter is unreasonably high on a given market day. He can take advantage of special sales knowing that you would be happy to avail yourself of such savings. He can also buy ahead, in order to protect you, if there is an especially fluctuating market.

He can help maintain your quality -- Under a commission purchase arrangement, the produce purveyor is, in fact, *your buyer*. Thus, he can help you achieve, and maintain, your quality standards, by simply refusing to purchase any produce that does not come up to your minimum standards. This is tremendously important when it comes to produce. In fact, top quality produce is usually the cheapest in the long run. Except for special applications (you don't need packed 88 apples for Waldorf salad, for example), it is almost always better to buy top quality produce, than to try and save money by buying second grades.

Proper handling of produce after receiving goes hand-in-hand with good produce purchasing. Here, too, your produce purveyor can be of great help to you. Ask him to come to your employee training session sometime, and to show to all your staff what happens when produce is not properly cared for. Let him demonstrate the importance of removing lettuce from the crates, of watering your produce periodically while in your walk-in refrigerators, of culling bad oranges from the case. Let him also show the difference between quality and second-grade merchandise.

Insofar as your control over prices is concerned, this, too, is no special problem under such an arrangement. Obviously, a considerable amount of mutual trust is required, if commission purchasing is to work in the first place. You must trust him to charge the right price, and he must know that you'll accept what he buys for you. Beyond that trust, however, your vendor must be willing to have you periodically audit the invoices which pertain to your merchandise. This does not imply that you can go down to his place and audit his books: it means that he is willing to show you his invoices for a given period demonstrating that his mark-up is in line with your standing agreement. Furthermore, he might be willing to give you information of the wholesale produce prices that applied during the period in question to other wholesale customers who were not on a commission plan. If so, you will be able to prove to your own superiors that, most of the time, your arrangment gives you better produce quality at a lower cost.

INVOLVEMENT OF STAFF IN THE PURCHASING PROCESS

There are some food service managers who consider the purchasing of food to be their own special prerogative, so special in fact, that they refuse to share it with anyone else. The result? A disinterested staff, poor morale, and poor controls. A progressive manager realizes that effective food purchasing is a cooperative effort: it depends on the interest, the knowledge, and the watchfulness of the entire kitchen staff, just as much as on the manager's own knowledge of what he must buy, why he needs it, and why he buys it from a specific supplier. The people in the kitchen should feel that, somehow, they have a "say" in what is being purchased. In the case of the salad worker, such input might be the right to complain if the quality of the produce is poor, in the knowledge that someone will listen and do something about it. The head of the salad department should, perhaps, have the authority to refuse or to return an unacceptable product. The cooks should be able to make suggestions which will be listened to by the manager. Student workers are often the most discerning and frequently have excellent purchasing suggestions. The most important person to involve in the purchasing process, however, is the manager of each individual unit. He is held responsible for the overall quality of the food, and the general satisfaction of the students. With such responsibility must come authority, and, in this case, "authority" means playing an active part in decisions regarding food purchases.

The ideal place for such a part is the weekly manager's staff meeting. That is the proper time to discuss or test new products, to talk about problems of delivery, and to answer questions about how, and why, and from whom certain items were purchased. In addition, the management staff must also be used in the receiving process whenever possible. Many small colleges do not have a special receiving person; this means that often anyone who happens to be near the back door may sign the purveyor's invoices. Too often, the bread man or the milk man shoves an invoice under the nose of some uninformed kitchen worker who, by signing his name, obligates the school for the accuracy of the delivery. If the supervisory staff of an institution is trained to become involved in this process, then good receiving becomes a natural and daily routine.

There is an important distinction, however, between having your managers do the receiving, and letting them phone the suppliers whenever they have a mind to do so. You will have to develop a clear and strict policy which calls for the coordination of all purveyor contacts from one central place, such as the food buyer's office, under normal circumstances, but allows for exceptions in emergencies.

Visiting with, and talking to salesmen is another important aspect of your purchasing process. At the beginning of your career in a new job it is essential that you get to know each salesman personally. It enables you to size him up, to evaluate his company and his product, and to take advantage of his knowledge about your school, about area conditions, etc. Ideally, you will reserve one or two days a week for interviewing salesmen, and your regular salesmen will make appointments rather than walk in whenever they like. As your responsibilities increase, you may decide to delegate this function to an assistant. Whatever you do, however, don't shut the salesman off. Your sales representative is a source of vital information, and potentially a great help to you. Market trends, price changes, new products: all this information is readily available to you from your salesmen, provided you recognize this and treat them with the courtesy and respect to which they are entitled.

Finally, be sure to develop good, sound, practical procedures for the testing of samples and new products. Taking a product and merely sampling it is not testing and, is usually a meaningless exercise. Most food products should be tested by comparison with another product so that the tester has a basis for his decision. Try to test each item against at least one, but preferably several, competitive items. Involve at least your managers and, if possible, other staff members and also students in the testing process. Be sure to remove all brand identification while testing, so that the testers do not know the name of the manufacturer, the price, or any other vital data, such as whether the sample is a convenience item or was cooked in your kitchens until *after* they have indicated their preference.

CASH PURCHASES

Regardless of the tightness of its controls or the efficiency of its purchasing system, every business needs to have a petty cash fund for small, incidental, and emergency purchases. In those institutions where this is either not permitted, or where petty cash purchases are made inordinately difficult, the problem is merely transferred to the individual department head, who solves the matter in one of several ways, none of which are good. He either advances the money out of his own pocket until such time that the purchases can be vouchered routinely, or else he takes the money out of the cash register, documents the withdrawal, and replaces it later when the voucher is processed. It is never a good idea for an employee to advance money from his own pocket for an institutional purchase. Taking money from sales is even worse, and possibly subjects the individual to very serious questioning by auditors, regardless of how well the instance was documented.

If there is no school policy on the handling of petty cash, it is up to you to establish such procedures which conform to the overall policies of your school and give you close controls over what is purchased. Following are some basic rules which will help you achieve this objective:

- All petty cash purchases must be documented by a cash register or other signed receipt.
- No petty cash purchases should exceed $X without specific, prior approval.
- The petty cash account is subject to the general rules of the institution and under the control of the bursar.
- Petty cash should be used only if the item purchased is small, if it is needed quickly, and if buying it through petty cash is the most efficient way of obtaining it.

In addition to the basic rules, you could adopt some additional ones, such as personally inspecting the petty cash slips, or making a list of the types of items that, in your judgment, are legitimate items for such purchases.

ETHICAL BEHAVIOR IN PURCHASING

Anyone charged with spending large amounts of money on behalf of his employer encounters temptations, large and small, which involve ethical decisions. Food service managers are no exception. This chapter attempts to discuss some of the temptations with which the food service buyer is often confronted, and to suggest possible courses of action. Obviously, not everyone follows the same path. In some institutions, for example, the acceptance of gifts of any kind, however small, is strictly forbidden. In others, small, token gifts are permitted. Following are some suggestions for a few of the decisions that you will have to make:

Gifts from Purveyors

When purveyors offer you gifts, their probable purpose is to influence your purchasing decision. Therefore, as a matter of basic principle, neither you, nor anyone else on your staff, nor anyone related to you or your staff, should be permitted to accept gifts from vendors. This rule should be so clear, that no one confuses its meaning. Gifts include anything that has a monetary value, and anything that, under normal circumstances, you would have to buy yourself. This includes meals, entertainment, rooms in resort hotels, club privileges, and material gifts. There are some specific, clear-cut exceptions to this rule however, which are generally, (not always!) accepted in business and industry:

Christmas gifts -- Some buyers make an absolute rule that no gifts of any kind, and in any amount, are accepted. Others set an arbitrary value, such as $10.00 and return any presents that exceed this amount. Still others accept any reasonable gift that does not appear to be excessive or intended to create an improper influence, while a few buyers accept anything that is given to them. None of the above procedures is necessarily unethical *per se*; the key, in every case is whether the procedure follows the policies of the employer and whether the gift could consciously or unconsciously influence a buyer's decision at a later time. If there is no rule against it, your acceptance of a *modest* gift from a vendor at Christmas time, whether it is a box of candy, a case of apples, a bottle of wine, a turkey, or a poinsettia plant is, by commonly accepted standards, quite appropriate. In fact, to refuse or to return such a small gift may be unnecessarily rude. In deciding upon your course of action, remember that this may be the vendor's only opportunity to thank you for any courtesies that you have extended to him and that he would probably be genuinely disappointed if you refused. Some buyers who have developed a genuine friendship with some of the vendors with whom they deal can use the occasion to return a small, personal gift of their own -- such as an embossed mug or ashtray from the college bookstore, a bud vase, etc.

Fortunately for everyone, the practice of giving gifts to institutional buyers has diminished during the past decade, so that your gifts will probably be few and appropriate.

It is wise, however, to keep clear and full record of such gifts by acknowledging the gift in a short thank-you note, which specifically lists the item given to you. A copy of the note should be kept permanently in your files.

Meals with Purveyors

There is a significant difference between having dinner with a salesman in a fancy night club, or having lunch with him in a restaurant during business hours. The business lunch is an accepted commercial practice, and it gives you and your purveyor an opportunity to visit together in leisure and away from the interruptions in your office. Most buyers do not particularly enjoy such lunches, but they find them helpful both in terms of exchanging useful information with the salesman, and also in cementing cordial business relationships. A good practice is sometimes to invite the vendor to eat with you, *as your guest,* in one of the campus dining halls. This is an informal and friendly way of expressing your independence.

An invitation to cocktails or dinner is another matter. You must distinguish between a friendly invitation such as "Let's have a drink," given by a vendor you meet at a convention, and an invitation given in your office such as, "Why don't we have some drinks together when you get through working?" The former is probably a casual and innocent gesture of friendship; the latter may well be a thinly disguised effort to influence your purchasing decisions.

Purchases from Purveyors

The opportunity to purchase products for personal use at wholesale prices exists always, is very tempting, and is practiced frequently by many. While state law often prohibits the use of state purchase orders for personal use, and many colleges and universities clearly prohibit any direct buying from vendors by members of the college staff, there are other private colleges and universities which use such buying opportunities as a recruiting tool and proudly point to this practice as a fringe benefit for their employees. Faculty members who can purchase their color television sets at $100 to $150 below retail prices will obviously take advantage of such opportunities.

No one expects you, as the person responsible for food purchasing, to punish yourself by refusing benefits available to other members of the college community. On the other hand, as the person responsible for the expenditure of hundreds of thousands of dollars, you must truly be "purer than Caesar's wife." A good rule to follow, in deciding whether or not you should take advantage of purchasing food or other items at wholesale prices is to ask yourself the following questions:

- Is the same opportunity available to other members of the faculty and staff?
- Is this purchase one that I might be ashamed of, or might regret having made sometime in the future?
- How would I feel if this were written up in the student newspaper?

If the answer is a clear "yes" to the first, and a clear "no" to the second and third questions, chances are that you can complete the purchase. But even then, because of your special, sensitive position as food buyer, make certain that you document the payment by insisting on an invoice, and by paying with a personal check.

A final comment on wholesale purchases: Whether these are of furniture, appliances, or 28 lb. turkeys, they should be kept to an absolute minimum, both for the faculty and staff as well as for yourself personally. Seasonal offers, such as taking orders for turkeys at Thanksgiving, or Valentine Day candy in February, are easily understood on a small campus, and your willingness to be of service is probably appreciated. On the other hand, don't let your college food service become a wholesale discount store, where faculty families do their shopping regularly. If you are even slightly in doubt about the propriety of a certain course of action, discuss the matter with your boss, and whenever it seems appropriate, put it in writing. An honest person has nothing to fear; when he documents his actions, he has even less to fear.

Giving Out Price Information

Whenever you solicit prices from vendors, guard this information as a sacred trust until the purchasing decision has been made. This is not always as easy as it sounds. In formal bid purchasing, where all the bids are in writing, sealed, and opened at the same time, this is no problem; in all other instances, however, you will be subject to pressures which you must be aware of, and must resist. Some of these pressures are as follows:

Favorite vendors -- It is human nature to like some person better than some other person, and you will, no doubt, deal with some vendors whom you will prefer over others. Your temptation, therefore, will be to give your favorites a slight advantage, either by actually giving them the competitor's price, or else making some small suggestion or hint on what it would take to get this order. *Don't do it!* First of all, it is highly unethical, since it violates the principle under which all your vendors are competing; that the one who submits the lowest bid for identical products or services gets the order. Second, it creates an unhealthy relationship between yourself and your favorite supplier; both of you feel uneasy with each other because neither has been completely above board in soliciting and getting business. Third, the other bidders will surely find out what is going on eventually, and when they do, they will not only stop submitting bids, but your credibility as a buyer will be shattered.

Obtaining lower prices -- Some inexperienced buyers believe that by dangling another vendor's price before a vendor, they can obtain a lower bid and thus serve their institution better. Nonsense! It's true that you can try to use the power of your office to pressure a vendor into shaving his bid, but doing this is not serving your employer well. Not only are such actions resented by the vendors, but if they can, they will certainly try to make up for their "lost" profit in some other way.

Some institutional buyers go too far in the other direction: they refuse to give out prices at any time, even after the purchasing decision has been made. This is unfair. Bidders have a legitimate right to know what the successful bid was, and you owe it to your bidders to give them this information when the bidding is over and you have made your decision.

Donations by Vendors

Of all the various pressures that tend to impinge upon the purchasing process, one of the toughest to resist is pressure from the top. Regents who are also vendors and who misuse their position through subtle or overt pressure can make your life miserable. If you must yield to such pressures, however, as a result of instructions from your superiors, at least the issue is clear: everyone knows that such actions are improper, and the responsibility for decision-making has passed from you to others.

The problem of vendors who make donations to your institution is slightly more difficult. First, you have no right to doubt their motives, and must assume that such donations are made selflessly, for the benefit of the institution. Your school's fund-raiser, in fact, will be the first to tell you, as he tells you about the amount of the donation just made, that "this should, in no way, influence your buying decisions," obviously he thinks that it should, and in fact it probably will. Anyone who tells you that donations by vendors can be completely disregarded in purchasing just has not faced the issue, particularly in private colleges and universities, which depend upon gifts and donations for a significant part of their operating budget.

The solution, in many cases, is to establish a policy which states that in cases where bids are alike, and all other factors are even, then and only then will a vendor's continuing interest and support in the institution be considered. This is a reasonable position to take, and one which will probably be fully sustained by your school's president. Once again it should be pointed out that in this type of situation, the difference between state-supported and private colleges is great: in a private college, the administration is almost forced to weigh the advantage of maintaining an open purchasing system against the benefits of large donations from vendor-friends.

Your job, in this sensitive area, is to be both professional and tactful. As a professional, you must present your superiors with the pros and cons of several alternatives; as a tactful person, you must be willing to accept a decision with which you disagree, and accept the possibility that, perhaps, you really do not see the overall picture as clearly as do some of your superiors.

VI. ESTABLISHING BUDGETS AND INTERNAL CONTROLS

The ability to establish budgets, and to set up and enforce workable cost controls is essential for a food service manager. Much of the knowledge required to accomplish this can be gained by taking courses in accounting. Such training is invaluable, since it helps you to organize your information properly, teaches you the value of comparative statistics, and familiarizes you with the use of operating percentages and other important tools for the control of costs.

If you were to conduct a survey of successful food service directors, you would find that they have at least one skill in common: they are all skilled in budgeting and have efficient systems for controlling their costs. A budget is more than merely a prediction, it is a proposed plan of action. Cost controls are the tools with which this plan will be accomplished. A budget that is carefully prepared constitutes a solemn promise by the food service manager: "Barring unforeseen circumstances, this is the financial path that we will follow." To accomplish this, he must make certain at all times that he is heading in the right direction, and that he is proceeding as planned. For this reason, current, accurate cost information is absolutely essential. Later in this chapter, you will read about the pros and cons of daily, weekly, or monthly cost reports. The key, at all times, is the answer to the question: "Are things going according to the plan? If not, why not?"

Normally, if you deviate from the budget, there are steps you can take to "get back on the track." Tightening up on overtime hours or enforcing better portion control are two examples of such steps. There are times, however, when things are beyond your control: a change in the number of students in the residence halls, for example, or an unexpected sharp increase in the cost of raw food, or a new labor contract that is unexpectedly costly. In such instances, your budget must be updated to reflect these changes, consequently, your overall plan also changes.

Operating costs fall into three basic categories: food costs, labor costs, and other costs. You will find that you can exercise a considerable degree of control over food and labor costs, and, to a much lesser extent, over many of the other costs, since this includes such items as utilities, depreciation, and telephone. In discussing the entire subject of costs, let's get one thing straight: your job as a good manager is to *control* costs, not necessarily to *reduce* costs. There is a tremendous difference. Some think that in order to be a good manager, one should always strive to reduce operating costs; this is a fallacy that can lead to tragic results. In times of inflation, especially, it is a sign of considerable skill if you can merely maintain costs at existing or predicted levels. Reducing operating costs without reducing quality is possible only where there is some waste (waste of food, waste of labor, waste of energy, etc.), and reducing quality is not what we are talking about.

The field of cost controls is not a mysterious one. Common sense tells you that if you have a lot of waste, theft in the kitchen, too many employees working for the amount of work, or excess overtime for work that should be done during regular working hours, then your food and labor costs will be too high. Common sense, experience, and training also will tell you, in most instances, what you should do to correct such problems. The control tools which we shall discuss in this chapter will help you primarily to spot the source of the problem and solve it before it can do you a lot of harm.

BUDGETS

If yours is a typical college, your budget for the following school year will be requested during October or November, about two months before you're ready to think about a budget, and just when you've caught your breath from the hustle and bustle of school opening. It's needed then because it will probably include your recommendations for board rates for the following year, recommendations which must be evaluated by your superiors, blended in with other possible increases in housing and tuition, passed on to the trustees and, finally, presented to the students whose perennial complaint will be: "Why didn't you tell us earlier?"

Preparing a budget is really not difficult. It takes time, patience, study of what happened in the past, and a careful guess as to what might happen in the future.

Comparison with Previous Years

Since a budget is the product of a set of well-informed predictions, you might as well start with the most accurate and current information available to you -- the operating statement of the previous school year. Every important item of income and expenditure should be listed there for you to see and study -- in dollars as well as in percentages. In fact, were it not for the constant changes from year to year, you could almost take last year's statement and convert it into your budget for next year. Be careful! This is a trap! Your budget will be much more than merely a copy of past years: it will reflect your ideas and those of your staff, and will be a result of your creativity and imagination; it will include some new ideas, perhaps some experiments with different meal plans or different serving hours, some new snack bars, or other exciting innovations.

Nevertheless, studying the profit and loss statements of the past several years and looking for trends, percentages, and unusual variations from year to year is certainly the right way to begin developing your new budget.

Analysis of Each Item of Income and Expenditures

Once you are thoroughly familiar with last year's operations, you must then study each individual item of income and expenditures and think about it for a while:

- Did something unusual occur last year which will not happen again next year?
- What am I planning for next year which will change particular items?
- Should I use the dollar amount from last year, or is it better to use the percentage figure to arrive at a budget projection?

For example, take an item such as "Income from Banquets and Catering." Suppose that for the past three years this item amounted always between $90,000 and $100,000 per year. Suppose, furthermore, that you increased catering prices by an average of 8% this *current* year and that you estimate that *next* year the increase will be about 5%. Does that mean that your budget for next year would be $113,000? Yes, unless you have some specific ideas of how to improve or increase your catering operations. Perhaps you are thinking of selling pizzas at night in the residence halls -- how will this affect your catering totals? Perhaps you have decided to turn one of your private dining halls into an extension of your residence hall dining room -- how many dollars in sales will you lose by doing that? Perhaps you were asked to take over your school's concessions operations, as part of your catering -- will that add to or deduct from next year's total? All these variables, plus the realization that you are really planning for *two* years ahead (the current one has just started, and you're already planning for next year) should enter into your budget calculations.

Synthesis of Information

A good budget is the result of many sources of information. It does not emerge fully grown, as did Minerva from the forehead of Jupiter! Your staff should have an opportunity to tell you what they think and what changes they would like to see in the food service operations. Perhaps that automatic floor scrubber which the porters have been asking for might get approved in this new budget? Why not see if you can squeeze it in? An important source of budget information is your salesman. He can tell you, probably better than anyone else, what wholesale price changes are anticipated in the trade. His information, when added to economic indictors, other campus information, and as well as your own knowledge of the situation, can then be synthesized into a final budget figure.

Documentation

When you are working on the budget, you are so thoroughly engrossed in it that you think you'll never forget any part of it. Four weeks later, when your boss asks you how you arrived at a certain figure, you will fret and fuss and stew but you'll never be able to remember. Don't depend on memory. Footnote or document in some other clear fashion every calculation and every factor that entered into your budget preparation.

Budget Summary

A typical budget consists of many different schedules. One, for example, might deal with the various types of income; another, with your calculations concerning labor costs; a third with food costs, etc. A schedule might have one or several appendixes. When calculating the total of your "Other Costs," you might have, as an appendix, notices from the local gas, electric, and water companies with information concerning utility rates, used to arrive at your estimate of these costs. On top of all these schedules, however, prepared in easy-to-understand format is a budget summary. In this summary, you should present a concise operating statement for the following year, complete with percentages and footnotes. Such a summary is illustrated in Exhibit VI-1.

Percentages

If you understand the purpose of percentages in cost analysis and budget preparation, and know how to use them, you should have little trouble preparing your budget. If you're not too sure, the following review will be helpful. Remember that a "percentage" is a figure which remains constant while other figures change: If your food cost, for example has been 42% of income during the past several years, this means that even if your income increased each year, your cost of food increased in exactly the same proportion. Remember also, that your percentage figure depends on what you use as the basis for the other figures: If you spent $50,000 on meat the previous year, and $200,000 on all food purchases, against an income of $500,000, then your percentage of meat cost to total food cost is 25%, but your percentage of meat cost to income is only 10%.

Elementary? Perhaps so. There are many food service managers, however, who don't really understand how to use percentages. Instead of comparing their own operation internally with previous months or previous years, they keep trying to compare themselves with other colleges. They will invariably ask another manager: "What is your food cost percentage?" and then volunteer: "Well, last year mine was so-and-so." Percentage comparisons from two different institutions mean very little unless those who do the comparing are thoroughly familiar with all the variables and differences between the two schools. If you have a food cost of say 40% of sales in a snack bar where the check average is $1.35, you might be much more efficient than someone else with a food cost percentage of 30% in a restaurant where the check average is $2.50. On the other hand, when you compare your own current percentages with those of last year, you can gain very helpful information. At least you can find the answer to the question: "Why the change?" If, for instance, your cost of food this year is running 3% - 4% higher than last year, your job is to discover the reason quickly, while you can still do something about it:

- Was your board increase sufficient to meet the rising cost of food?

- Which food category (meat, canned goods, dairy items, etc.) is causing the problem this year?

- Is the number of students less than last year? If so, is that the reason for the higher food cost percentage?

- Is someone stealing large amounts of food? If so, when and where?

The value of percentages in budget preparation is simply this: once you have worked out the percentage of total income that you will spend for each item of cost, your budget will almost write itself. Following are two tables, both showing an anticipated increase of $15,000 in next year's food costs. In the first table, each food group is shown as a *percentage of total food costs;* in the second each food group is shown as a *percentage of total income.* The latter is the approach most commonly used.

EXHIBIT VI-1

FOOD SERVICES AND HOUSING
Summary of Income and Expenditures
For the Fiscal Years Ended 1975 through 1979

	1975-76 Actual	1976-77 Actual	1977-78 Est. Actual	%	1978-79 Budget	%
INCOME						
Food Service	$1,467,900	$1,488,800	$1,694,600	60.3	$1,751,100	58.1
Housing	893,700	921,200	1,115,600	39.7	1,263,000	41.9
Total Income	**$2,361,600**	**$2,410,000**	**$2,810,200**	**100.0**	**$3,014,100**	**100.0**
EXPENDITURES						
Labor	$ 600,700	$ 609,000	$ 675,200	24.0	$ 747,700	24.8
Food and Staples	633,600	679,300	761,500	27.1	799,600	26.5
Other Expense	212,700	219,000	311,500	11.1	317,100	10.5
Allocations	578,900	578,900	619,600	22.0	716,200	23.8
Total Expenditures	**$2,025,900**	**$2,086,200**	**$2,367,800**	**84.2**	**$2,580,600**	**85.6**
AVAILABLE FOR DEBT SERVICE	**$ 335,700**	**$ 323,800**	**$ 442,400**	**15.8**	**$ 433,500**	**14.4**
DEBT SERVICE	340,400	340,400	503,000		503,000	
EXCESS OR (DEFICIT)	**$ (4,700)**	**$ (16,600)**	**$ (60,600)**		**$ (69,500)**	
OTHER INCOME:						
Student Fee	--	--	52,500	1.9	52,500	1.7
Bookstore Fee	--	--	17,000	.6	17,000	.6
Total Other Income			**69,500**	**2.5**	**69,500**	**2.3**
CONTINGENCY			$ 8,900		$ -0-	

NOTE:
OTHER EXPENSE - Includes laundry, detergent, chinaware replacement, normal equipment breakage, service contracts, furniture repair, window and door damage, payroll taxes, duplicating and printing, and painting.

ALLOCATIONS - Includes insurance, telephone, janitorial service, maintenance, electricity, gas, water, grounds care, security and business office support.

Table Showing How to Project Food Costs When Preparing Next Year's Budget Using % of Cost*

Cost of Food	Dollar Amount Last Year	% of Cost	Est'd Increase	Est'd Dollar Amount Next Year	% of Cost
Meat, Fish, Fowl	$ 50,000	25.0%	12%	$ 56,000	26.1%
Canned Goods and Staples	$ 60,000	30.0%	8%	$ 64,800	30.2%
Dairy Products	$ 20,000	10.0%	2%	$ 20,400	9.5%
Fruits and Vegetables	$ 30,000	15.0%	5%	$ 31,500	14.7%
All other food	$ 40,000	20.0%	5%	$ 42,000	19.5%
TOTAL	**$200,000**	**100.0%**		**$214,700**	**100.0%**

Table Showing How to Project Food Costs When Preparing Next Year's Budget Using % of Sales*

Cost of Food	Dollar Amount Last Year	% of Sales	Est'd Increase	Est'd Dollar Amount Next Year	% of Sales*
Meat, Fish, Fowl	$ 50,000	10.0%	12%	$ 56,000	11.2%
Canned Goods and Staples	$ 60,000	12.0%	8%	$ 64,800	13.0%
Dairy Products	$ 20,000	4.0%	2%	$ 20,400	4.0%
Fruits and Vegetables	$ 30,000	6.0%	5%	$ 31,500	6.3%
All Other Food	$ 40,000	8.0%	5%	$ 42,000	8.4%
TOTAL	**$200,000**	**40.0%**		**$214,700**	**42.9%**

*Sales, for *both* years, are estimated at $500,000.00

The above illustrations may be elementary. Nevertheless, many food service managers have difficulty with their budgets because they simply have not fully understood, nor fully utilized percentages as the valuable tool that they are.

Cost per Meal Served

Percentage comparisons are helpful primarily if the factors affecting the base figure (i.e. total food cost, or total sales) do not fluctuate; in times of inflation, when selling prices rise continuously, a percentage comparison becomes meaningless unless all price changes that occurred during the period involved are also considered. Fortunately, there is one statistic which is not so changeable: the *cost per meal served*. Although meals obviously differ from one another (breakfasts, lunches, dinners, snacks), the overall "mix" from meals of all types probably remains fairly constant from year to year. In a period of rising costs, it is helpful to have a statistical figure (i.e. meals) which remains constant. It gives you a fair idea of how much change you are experiencing from year to year. This can become the basis for your recommendation regarding board increases or it can act as a "double-check" on your other calculations. The following example will illustrate this: Suppose last year, when your food cost amounted to $200,000 (see preceding page) you served 225,000 meals. Next year, when your food cost is expected to rise to $212,800 (see preceding page) you again expect to serve 225,000 meals. How much more do you need to charge to cover the extra cost of next year's food? The answer, using cost-per-meal figures, is simple:

Food Cost per Meal-Last Year: $200,000 ÷ 225,000 = .89/meal
Food Cost per Meal-Next Year: $212,800 ÷ 225,000 = .95/meal

Now that you know the amount of food cost per meal, you can do the same with the cost of labor and other costs. Then, if you decide to offer a meal plan with fewer meals, for example, you know at least what, if any, potential savings you may experience and how much of the savings you can pass on to the students.

Cost-per-meal figures lend themselves much more easily to valid comparisons with another college. If the meals served in the other college are comparable to yours, and if the prices paid by each school for raw food are similar, then the cost of food per meal served should also be similar. Obviously such factors as the physical facilities, labor-saving equipment available, purchasing and storage will always cause some variations between two different institutions. *Please note:* It is vital to distinguish between *meals paid for* and *meals actually served*. A student having a full board contract may have paid for 21 meals per week; he actually may have eaten only 16 of those meals. It is the second, smaller figure that is used in calculating the *cost per meal served*.

Meals Served per Labor Hour

The ratio of meals served per labor hour worked is one of the most useful cost controls available. It is useful because changes in wage scales which affect labor cost percentages do not affect it. A "meal" in the broad definition used here is a fairly constant item; a "labor hour" always represents sixty minutes of work. Therefore, if the normal ratio of meals-per-labor-hour in a residence hall kitchen is 9, this means that for every hour of work in that kitchen, nine meals were produced. This ratio is arrived at as follows:

Meals per Labor Hours Calculation-Week Ending May 1st

Total labor hours*	2800 hours
Total meals served	25,200
Meals Served per Labor Hour	25,200 ÷ 2800 = 9

*All labor hours (supervision, regular, and student employees) should be included in the calculation.

Some colleges and universities, which have very efficient food service operations, serve as many as 12-14 meals per labor hour; the average in residence halls is probably closer to 8 or 9. A sample table, which shows how a daily record is kept, and how this ratio is calculated every week, is shown in Exhibit VI-2.

Another advantage of this ratio is that it lends itself better than most others to comparison with other, similar operations. If it may be assumed that the physical facilities are fairly equal, and that the meals served are similar, then the productivity in the two operations should probably also be similar. If one unit achieves only 7 meals per labor hour, while another does 10, you have a right to wonder why the latter is so much more efficient than the former. Often the answer lies in careless scheduling, unnecessary overtime, and similar, easy-to-resolve causes.

Projection of Income

Estimating income is much easier in colleges and university food services than in commercial establishments. When preparing your new budget, separate your income into the various main categories, such as: Meal Ticket Income, Banquets and Conferences, Cash Sales, Inter-Departmental Sales, etc. In each category, try to anticipate any changes in income from the previous year. These changes could be increases in your meal ticket rates, selling prices in cash operations, prices of served banquets, increases or decreases in volume due to student enrollment, additional conferences, etc. Following is one way to incorporate an increase in board rate in your income projections:

Table Showing Projected Board Income in Residence Halls Serving 2,900 Students and Offering 3 Different Meal Plans (please note: the figures used are arbitrary, and shown for purposes of illustration only).

Meal Ticket Plan	Est'd No. of M.T. Holders	Two-Year Increase in M.T. Rate	Total Increase in Dollars
21 Meals	1,400	$50.00	$ 70,000
14 Meals	1,000	$40.00	$ 40,000
10 Meals	500	$30.00	$ 15,000
			$125,000

Meal Ticket Plan	Meal Ticket Income Last Year	Budgeted Meal Ticket Income Next Year
21 Meals	$210,000	$280,000
14 Meals	$140,000	$180,000
10 Meals	$ 65,000	$ 80,000
	$415,000	$540,000

EXHIBIT VI-2

PRODUCTIVITY TABLE FOR FOOD SERVICE EMPLOYEES

DINING COMMONS   **NOVEMBER 1977**

Date	Mgmt. Hrs.	Salaried	Hourly	Student	Total Hrs.	Meals Served	Meals per Labor Hr.
Tues.	8	0	79	81	168	1772	10.54
Wed.	8	0	79	81	168	1785	10.52
Thur.	0	0	79	81	160	1695	10.60
Fri.	8	0	79	81	168	1413	8.41
Sat.	8	0	24	50	82	653	7.96
WK.	32	0	340	374	746	7819	9.81
Sun.	8	0	24	50	82	759	9.25
Mon.	6	0	71	81	158	1668	10.55
Tues.	8	0	87	81	176	1907	10.83
Wed.	8	0	75	82	165	1769	10.72
Thur.	8	0	79	81	168	1555	9.25
Fri.	0	0	79	89	168	1270	7.56
Sat.	8	0	24	50	82	645	7.87
WK.	46	0	1439	514	999	9573	9.58
Sun.	8	0	24	54	86	867	10.08
Mon.	8	0	79	81	168	1557	9.27
Tues.	8	0	79	81	168	1649	9.82
Wed.	8	0	79	81	168	1689	10.05
Thur.	8	0	79	81	168	1531	9.11
Fri.	0	0	79	81	160	1382	8.22
Sat.	0	0	24	62	86	700	8.13
WK.	40	0	443	521	1004	9375	9.33
Sun.	0	0	24	62	86	1040	12.09
Mon.	8	0	71	81	160	1784	11.15
Tues.	8	0	78	81	167	1525	9.13
Wed.	8	0	71	61	140	849	6.06
Thur.	off						
Fri.	off						
Sat.	off						
WK.	24	0	244	285	553	5198	9.39
Sun.	off						
Mon.	8	0	71	81	160	1602	10.01
Tues.	8	0	86	81	175	1599	9.13
Wed.	8	0	76	81	165	1619	9.81
WK.	24	0	233	243	500	4820	9.64
Month	166	0	1699	1937	3802	36785	9.67
Nov. 76							9.40

Projecting next year's income in cash operations (especially in student union food service units) is more difficult. Cash operations are subject to so many more fluctuations than residence halls, that normally all you can do is to look at each food unit individually and take an educated guess. If you have a clear idea of the number of people served in a year and of the average check, then you can estimate the effect that any price increases may have on the *check average,* and thus arrive at a sales figure. In the absence of such information, you can estimate next year's sales by using this year's totals as a base and superimposing any anticipated increase in selling prices on top of that figure. This assumes, of course, that your volume will remain constant and that your customers will not balk at the higher selling prices. Whether or not you will get strong customer objection to higher selling prices depends, to a large extent, on your own skills in selling the need for higher prices to your customers. A carefully planned public relations effort on your part, detailing your program for expected price increases and perhaps showing what services would need to be curtailed without an increase in selling prices, will prove most helpful. Sometimes it helps to tell the customers, by way of easy-to-read charts, how little your own selling prices have increased over the years in comparison to wholesale prices. Sometimes it may also be a good idea to soften the blow a little, by offering a special at the time of the new price announcement (e.g. when you raise coffee prices, serve the second cup free, or at a lower price, for one or two days.)

In addition to looking at this year's sales, you must also study next year's college calendar. Following are some changes in this calendar which can affect your sales projections:

- Number of weekdays classes are in session
- Number of Saturdays when classes are scheduled
- Weekends and holidays
- Recess and vacation periods
- Dates and total days of examination periods
- Summer school, summer conferences, special events
- Special orientation programs for students and parents
- Days and dates of pre-registration and registration
- Beginning and end of residence hall food service

Projection of Labor Costs

Once a sound labor pattern has been established in a food service operation, it is much easier to project the costs for the coming budget year. In theory, if you know exactly how many people will be working for you, and the total hours of labor scheduled, how much they are earning, then all you need to do is apply any projected raise to their present earning and there's the budget!

In practice, it is usually a bit more complicated. First, it takes years of experimentation and modification before you can state, with certainty, that your labor pattern is sound. Your staff will complain that they have too much work to do and need more help; your boss will wonder if you haven't hired too many people; you will waver back and forth because at times you agree with both. Second, the amount of wage increase is sometimes dependent on the rest of your budget -- so that often you may be *working backwards* to find out just how much of a raise you can afford to give to your staff. This is especially true if your board of regents has set the room and board rate without consulting you. Third, there are always variations in staffing (the addition of supervisors, creating of new jobs, closing of certain departments) which have to be considered in the overall labor cost budget.

In most college food services, the cost of labor is divided into four basic groupings:

1. Administration (the food service director, assistant, secretary, bookkeeper, etc.)
2. Supervision (your line supervisors)
3. Regular Employees (all kitchen workers who are not students at your school)
4. Student Employees

In addition to totalling the estimated wages for each group of employees, you must be sure to add *employee benefits* (fringe benefits) to your overall budget. These benefits, which are sometimes shown as part of labor costs and sometimes among other costs, vary from 15% to 25% of total payroll, depending on the individual school and the mix of student and regular employees. They include such items as employee meals, social security, retirement, state unemployment and disability taxes, health insurance, workmen's compensation, disability and life insurance.

The table in Exhibit VI-3 shows how you might project the budgeted wage increase for your regular employees. In the case of student employees, such great detail is probably not necessary. The student employment pattern is very fluid, and you do have more control over the amount of funds to be spent on student labor costs. If you have a satisfactory staffing procedure for student workers, then you need to take the total number of hours worked by students during the year, and add a reasonable amount for wage increases. Normally, each school has a set wage increase and incentive program for student workers so that each year they earn a little more. Since at least one third of your student workers will be freshmen, who come in at the starting wage, the amount of student increase is usually not a significant factor in proprotion to other cost increases.

Projection of Food Costs

In times of rising prices, projecting food prices 10-20 months into the future becomes an almost impossible task. No one can really do it with any kind of certainty. At the same time, the instructions from your boss are clear: "Whatever you come up with, that's going to be the board rate for next year. Don't come to me for mid-year increases, if the going gets rough!" Thus you are caught in a dilemma: if your estimate of board increases is too low, you'll get in trouble with your boss; if you make them too high, you will upset the students (they will probably make you prove your reasons with blood, sweat, and tears. . .), you might get fewer boarders, and you'll still be in trouble with your boss. Since this is obviously a game in which you cannot win, then at least take some chances, and if you lose, lose in style! The chances you take are your predictions about how much food prices will rise next year. There are certain techniques that will help you in this task:

EXHIBIT VI-3

SAMPLE PAGE FROM PAYROLL BUDGET

Name of Employee	Current Wage/hr.	Current Wage/mo.	No. Mos. per year.	Total Income per year	Amount of Increase/ hr.	Amount of Increase/ mo.	Projected Income per mo.	Projected Income per yr.
COOKS								
A. Adams	$4.50	$778.50	12	$9,342	$.25	$43.25	$821.75	$9,861.00
B. Bell	4.00	692.00	10	6,920	$.25	43.25	735.25	7,352.50
SALADMAKERS								
C. Cleaver	3.75	648.75	12	7,785	$.20	34.60	683.35	8,200.20
TOTAL LABOR COST EMPLOYEES ---			This year:	24,047	Next year:	25,413.70		
Add: Employee Benefits (20%)				4,809		5,082.74		
			This year:	28,856		30,496.44		

AMOUNT OF PROJECTED INCREASE: $1,640.44

Commodity groups -- In order that you may better control the costs of your various food items, organize the various foods you purchase by commodity groups. A typical breakdown might be as follows:

- Meats, poulty and seafood
- Fresh and frozen produce
- Dairy products
- Coffee, tea, hot chocolate
- Groceries and staples
- Bakery products

This organization will help you monitor the food cost changes of each commodity group individually and you will be able to step in when necessary to control it quickly and decisively. At budget time, you can evaluate the possible price changes for each group separately and thus make a better estimate than if you had to consider food prices in total.

Predictions by purveyors -- Your sales representatives, as mentioned earlier, are an excellent and normally very reliable source of price predictions. When they know that you are in the process of preparing next year's budget, they will go out of their way to assist you. Through their own companies, they have helpful sources of information and your own forecasts will be much more authoritative than if you merely estimated the increases by yourself.

Economic indicators -- Fortunately, you do not have to prepare your budget in a vacuum. As manager of a large food service operation, you may be expected to read such publications as the *Wall Street Journal, Time* or *Newsweek,* U.S. Government reports, and other respected publications which cover the state of our economy. It is appropriate to include the findings of American economists in your own predictions about next year's food prices.

Projection of Other Costs

The projection of costs other than food and labor is not difficult. Information about the anticipated increase in energy costs can be obtained from your local utility company. Allocations to overhead and debt service are normally constant. Equipment depreciation will be affected only if you plan to purchase large amounts of expensive equipment -- in which case you would be the first to know. Kitchen and dining room supplies increase, more or less, in proportion to the overall price increases in the economy. Such items as travel, taxes, and equipment maintenance are usually not significant. In each case, you should make an informed estimate as to the cost of the item next year, and show this in the budget as per previous illustrations. If you should make large investments in equipment which will be written off over a period of 3 to 5 years, be sure to document such purchases with a footnote. It will serve as a quick explanation to the reader that you have sacrificed some of your possible profits for equipment.

Missed Meal Factor

In calculating your anticipated food costs in residence halls, be sure to include the effect of the "missed meal factor." This factor, which represents the difference between meals paid for and meals actually eaten by the students, can make a great deal of difference in your actual cost of food. The following example will illustrate this:

Importance of the Missed Meal Factor

Example "A": No Missed Meals

Total Meals Paid For	1,000	100%
Total Meals Served	1,000	100%
Food Cost/Meal Served		$1.00
Total Food Cost		$1,000

Example "B": Missed Meal Factor - 18%

Total Meals Paid For	1,000	100%
Total Meals Served	820	82%
Food Cost/Meal Served		$1.00
Total Food Cost		$820.00

The missed meal factor varies from one college to another, depending upon the types of meal plans offered, the weekend activities of students, and the types of students themselves. Prior to the mid-1960's, missed meal factors in residence halls varied between 25% and 35% of total meals paid for. With 20 or 21 meal plans the only ones available, many students missed either breakfast or weekend meals, in other words, one fourth to one third of the meals paid for. Since the introduction of "no breakfast" plans (14 meals) and "no weekend" plans (10 meals), this factor has declined drastically and schools with such variable meal options are now experiencing missed meal factors of between 15% and 20%.

When budgeting your cost of food, therefore, it is essential that you take the missed meal factor into account, and your budget calculations should show any significant changes expected in this factor.

Distribution (Pro-rating) of Common Costs

In most multi-unit food operations, there are certain common costs which must be pro-rated among, and shared by all food service units on the campus. Such costs may be your own salary, that of your assistant and office staff, purchase of a food service truck, the cost of making photographic I.D. cards for all meal ticket holders, etc. Such common cost allocations are often done by the auditors as one of the closing entries at the end of the fiscal year. Make certain that you are familiar with these, so that you can include similar distributions in your budget for next year.

Clarity and Brevity in Budget Summaries

Perhaps the most difficult part in the entire process of budget preparation is your ability to summarize everything in such a way that others can read it quickly, easily, and can get your main point without much effort. If you keep in mind that yours is only one of a number of different budgets, which the financial vice president must combine into one overall budget, then you can understand why clarity is all-important. Although you can find an example of a budget summary in Exhibit VI-1, this doesn't mean that such a summary is necessarily suitable for your own use. In fact, it probably is not. When it comes to financial statements, each institution differs in what information it considers important, how it wants reports presented, etc. Follow the examples of others in your college or, if necessary, ask your boss if he has a preference for one type of budget presentation over another.

INVENTORIES

If you ask the person who has to take an inventory of food in the storeroom and walk-in refrigerators, he will urge you to have one taken as seldom as possible; ask an accountant, and he will want one every week. Inventories do take a lot of time, if done properly, and to the average kitchen worker they seem like a waste of time. Yet they are so vital to your cost control efforts, that you simply cannot manage without them. The reason can be shown in the following formula:

	Opening Inventory	$ 6,000
plus:	Purchases	10,000
	Subtotal	$16,000
less:	Closing Inventory	(7,000)
equals =	Cost of Food Used	$9,000

Simply stated, this means that there are two factors which determine how much food you have used up during a given period: One is the total amount of your purchases during the period, and the other is the change, if any, that occurred during this period in your food inventory. Since your purchases vary (sometimes you will obviously purchase enough to last for several weeks, and perhaps several months), you need both the total of your invoices and the difference between beginning and ending inventories to really tell you the value of food consumed.

Any food manager who wants a very tight system of food cost control and who is willing to pay the price in the labor it takes for weekly inventories will insist on them. Most food management companies, which have to control dozens, and even hundreds of different food operations from a central office, will insist on weekly inventories from their managers. Under ideal conditions, an inventory taken on a Friday afternoon will be on the manager's desk, extended and all added up, by Tuesday morning. The manager can then pinpoint the specific area of food cost problems and immediately take steps to remedy the situation.

Unfortunately, ideal conditions seldom prevail. In a residence hall kitchen feeding approximately 1,000 students, an inventory takes several hours and extending the figures at least another hour. Unless the school engages a full-time storeroom clerk whose job is to do exactly that, it is often difficult for the average manager to find the time to do an inventory every week. What is more, it often is of questionable value. Even a full-time storekeeper should only assist, but not take the inventory alone; inventories are a management responsibility, and a supervisor should always participate in taking inventories. This is particularly true in a food operation like a residence hall, where special dinners and other events tend to distort the food cost picture when viewed strictly on a week-to-week basis. Often a cumulative food cost figure, reviewed monthly, will be much more meaningful to the food service director.

The argument over whether it is better to take inventories once a week or once a month has been going on for many years and cannot be settled definitively in these pages. There are many highly knowledgeable food service directors who insist that a weekly inventory is an absolute necessity for close cost controls. There are others, equally knowledgeable, who feel that a weekly inventory is a waste of precious management time, making little real difference in terms of corrective measures that can be taken. More important, they feel such measures are always taken after the fact, and that a good manager can spot his problems even without such weekly data.

On balance, it seems that in *cash operations* (which fluctuate much more than residence halls) *a weekly inventory is advisable.* Many colleges now have the inventory extensions and additions done by computer, which makes the whole process much simpler. *In residence halls, a monthly inventory is adequate* for most colleges and universities. In either case, an accurate physical inventory of your food and kitchen supplies once a month is an absolute minimum! The manager's analysis of food and labor cost percentages which follow such an inventory is equally essential for good food service management.

Perpetual Inventories

It is customary in many businesses to rely on inventories through the use of the *perpetual inventory method.* This is a set of records, usually kept on cards, in which are recorded additions to the inventory through purchases, and reductions of the inventory through cooks' requisitions. Perpetual inventories work well in such a tightly controlled business as the bar business, where requisitions of bottles from the storeroom are easily recorded, but do not generally work well in college food operations. Relatively few colleges keep all of their food in a central storeroom or have a central commissary with a full-time storekeeper having the time to maintain such an inventory. Some schools, such as California State University in San Diego, maintain a perpetual inventory primarily as a guide in purchasing, and not as a strict cost control tool. For tight cost controls, only an actual count of the food actually in the kitchen, in the walk-ins, and in the storeroom will suffice.

Production Inventories

A production inventory is an inventory of those food items which have been taken out of the storeroom and are currently used by your cooks, bakers, and salad people in the ongoing preparation of food. It includes not only the food that is being cooked at the time, but also such items as half-empty boxes of spices, partially used cans of fat or oil, and any of the food that is presently in the kitchen rather than in the storeroom or walk-in refrigerator. It also includes leftover food, dining room condiments, etc.

Few operators will bother to take a careful count of their production inventory every time a major inventory is taken. Almost all will do so once a year, at the end of the institution's fiscal year. At other times, most food managers will select an *arbitrary sum* which more or less approximates the average value of the production inventory, and add it as "Production Inventory" to the inventory total. Naturally, if the fry cook has just requisitioned two 30 lb. cans of shortening minutes before the inventory is about to start, the person taking the inventory may well decide to add these two cans (or any other large dollar items) to the regular inventory. Again, the point is to take an inventory as *accurately* as possible, but not to get bogged down in time-consuming details which have no real value in the long run.

Equally important as accuracy is *consistency*. You must be consistent in *when* you take the inventory (e.g. every Friday afternoon) and also in *how* you take it. You cannot estimate the production inventory at, say $500 one week, and another week add up every item in production and come up with $700. If you do that, you lose the basis for comparison and analysis, which is the whole point of the inventory in the first place.

Inventory Formats

There are a number of different ways to set up inventory control. One, the perpetual inventory system, used individual cards for each item in stock. Another uses a book with 12 columns across. A third method is to type or print separate inventory pages which are then stapled together when the inventory is complete. This method enables you to delegate the inventory-taking to more than one person. The fourth method, one that is becoming more and more popular in the larger schools, is to take the inventory on computer forms, and then have the school's computer extend and add it up. Your choice of system depends upon what will work best in your school, and what will be most beneficial for you and your managers. For an example of a computerized inventory form, see Exhibit VI-4.

WEEKLY AND MONTHLY REPORTS

In large hotels, the food and beverage manager receives daily a complete report of all the activities in his department. This includes the total number of clients served in each of the hotel's restaurants, the numbers served at all banquets, and the total income from each separate food activity in the hotel. In addition, he will probably get a daily food cost summary, which will give him the food and labor cost, both in dollars and in percentage of sales, for each individual banquet, as well as for each separate kitchen. In some very large hotels, he will also get a comparison between his actual costs and his "pre-costed" costs, the latter being a budget figure calculated in advance by the cost accountant, which serves as a basis for staffing and for selling prices. In a complex, multi-million dollar food operation like a large hotel, this

EXHIBIT VI-4

UNIVERSITY OF THE PACIFIC
FOOD SERVICE DEPARTMENT
MONTHLY WORKSHEET
MONTH ENDING NOVEMBER 30, 1977

INVENTORY NUMBER	ON HAND	CATEGORY	ITEM	UNIT	UNIT PRICE	AMOUNT
23550	0	G	Rolls, Hotdog 12/	PKG	.33	
23575	0	G	Roll Mix Dinner 50#	BAG	16.63	
23600	24	G	Sauce, A-1 24 10 ½ OX BTL	BTL	.69	
23700	4	G	Sauce, Barbecue 4/gal.	GAL	4.40	
23800	8	G	Sauce Cheese 6/#10	GAL	6.13	
23850	0	G	Sauce Chili 6/#10 w/Beans	CAN	4.23	
23900	53	G	Sauce, Chili 6/#10 w/o Beans	CAN	4.61	
23950	18	G	Sauce, Chili Las Palmas 6/#10	CAN	2.50	
23955	0	G	Sauce, Hollandaise 12/1 lb.	CAN	2.21	
23960	2	G	Sauce, Lea & Perrin 12/10 oz	BTL	.84	
23975	48	G	Sauce, Meat 6/#10	CAN	2.88	
23980	2	G	Sauce, Melba	JAR	1.69	
23990	3	G	Sauce, Oyster 12/#5	CAN	6.38	
24000	2	G	Sauce, Soy Gal 4/1	GAL	1.92	

information is essential to the department head if he is to exercise any kind of control. Since he hires banquet waiters and waitresses on a daily basis, he must, of course, be able to tell instantly whether or not the hiring is being done in accordance with his actual needs. If the cost of food in one of his many kitchens is disproportionately high one day, he must immediately determine whether the cause is legitimate, or whether theft, waste, or other problems are the cause.

In a college or university, a daily food and labor cost report is seldom necessary. There are always exceptions to the rule. At the K-State Union, Kansas State University, the food service manager calculates a daily labor cost and adjusts his next day's staff accordingly. The results are reportedly promising, and well worth the effort. True, there are many schools with food operations totalling millions of dollars -- but the operations are not normally so complex or volatile as to require daily cost controls. *There is nothing worse than a cost control system that is not necessary or not utilized!* Nevertheless, the needs of the college food service manager are the same as those of a hotel's food and beverage manager: he must be able to tell, at all times, where he stands financially, what his income and expenditures are, how they differ from the budget, and if so, why. Furthermore, he must be able to predict where he is going, and what, if anything, needs to be done to change the direction. For all this, he needs, and must have, either weekly or monthly income-and-expense statements.

Daily Reports

If you are responsible for a "cash operation" (i.e. one in which food and drinks are sold for cash), you will need daily reports which give you at least the following basic information:

- Cash sales
- Charge sales
- Total sales
- Cash over (or short)

This information should be broken down by unit if there is more than one location, by cash register and, sometimes, by meal period (breakfast, lunch, or dinner). Managers who hire students or other part-time employees on the basis of the business they expect each day may want additional information on the daily report:

- Number of labor hours
- Sales per labor hour
- Meals (or customers) served per labor hour
- Check average
- Customer count

Suppose you drew up a form for such a daily report, *what would you do with the report once you received it?* That is really the basic question to be answered. You must plan to read it daily, and must plan to act on the information it contains. With the information shown above, you would be able to do the following:

1. Keep track of the sales in the various cash units, note whether or not certain special sales promotions are reflected in total sales, keep generally informed about

whether or not sales come up to budget expectations.

2. Train your cashiers well. Excessive overages or shortages could be signs of carelessness and even theft.

3. Adjust your temporary or part-time help, if your labor cost percentage gets too high, or your meals served per labor hour start to drop.

A sample form, Daily Report of Cash Operations, is shown in Exhibit VI-5.

Weekly Reports -- Cash Operations

Once a week, you must take stock. Where are you going? How are you doing? Are you operating at a loss? What corrective measures must you take before the next week starts to get back on the track? These questions are especially important in your cash operations, where the volume varies from week to week and where one slow week (perhaps the week of Thanksgiving or Easter recess) can play havoc with your profits. Can you really afford to stay open during Thanksgiving recess, merely because the football team is staying on campus? If so, how much should you charge for this period? How should you staff your cash operations to cause a minimum of loss during recess periods? Can you serve the staff of the college even if most of the students and faculty are gone, such as in early August, for instance?

Your weekly report on operations will give you the answers to most of these questions. Once a week, you must calculate how much you spent on food, on labor, on overhead expenses, and compare that with your total weekly income to find out whether you made money or lost it. To get your cost of food and supplies, take an inventory (see page 91); to get your cost of labor, total your time cards for hourly workers, and then add the cost of all monthly employees. For all other costs, use a pre-determined percentage of sales, unless you have a better way of determining this figure. Your sales must, of course, be broken down into the various income centers: snack bar sales, cafeteria sales, rathskeller sales, etc. Furthermore, the report should show the breakdown between cash sales, charge sales and meal ticket or food scrip sales. A sample weekly report form is shown in Exhibit VI-6.

To Date Figures

"To Date" is an accounting term which means "cumulative up to this date." It is an important concept and one that you must thoroughly understand when working with financial statements. Because of the fluctuations that occur from one week to the next, especially in colleges, with their frequent recess periods, winter terms, registration periods, and summer school, you must have some sure way of knowing how well you are doing *overall,* or up to that point of the year -- regardless of the performance of the current week. Therefore, in addition to a daily or weekly column, you must also have a "to date" column, which shows a cumulative record of all your income and expenditures from the first day of your fiscal year on. The value of this becomes apparent in the following, simple illustration:

EXHIBIT VI-5

DAILY REPORT OF CASH OPERATIONS

UOP FOOD SERVICE DAY: Thursday   DATE: 11/9/78

CASH RECONCILIATION:

REGISTER #1 MALL

			MEAL TICKETS	PUNCH CARDS(3)	SALES TAX ( )	DEPT. CHARGES	TOTAL(w/o tax)
Todays cash Read.	$ 9,391.33	CASH					
Yest. cash Read.	$ 9,085.49						
M.T. Cash (II)			81,416.03				
Taxable (IV)							
Non-Taxable (I)			81,338.08				
Todays Gross Cash Sales	$ 305.84		77.95 ↦ off 65				
LESS: Overrings&Voids	$ 3.93						
Net Cash Sales	$ 301.91						
Cash Deposit	$ 277.89	$ 297.89	$	$ 84.10	$ 6.56	$	$ 381.99
OVER/SHORT	$ 4:02						

REGISTER #2 HOF BRAU

Tax (9)	.16						
M.T. Cash (3)	.30						
Non-Taxable (1)	58.00						
Taxable (6)	2.70						
Total Cash per tape	$ 61.16						
LESS: Overrings &Voids	$ 1.55						
Net Cash Sales	$ 59.61						
Deposit	$ 58.01	$ 58.01	$	(2)$40.60 (4)$ .16 (9)$			$ 98.61
OVER/SHORT	$ 1.60						

REGISTER #3 BAR

After Cash Read.	$10,683.58						
Before Cash Read.	$10,641.88						
Total Cash per tape	$						
LESS: Overrings &Voids	$						
Net Cash Sales	$ 41.70						
Deposit	$ 40.90	$ 40.90	$	$ .60	$	$	$ 4a.90
OVER/SHORT	$ .80						

REGISTER #2 RATHSKELLER

M.T. Cash (3)	9.65						
Non-Taxable (1)	17.50						
Taxable (6)							
Total Cash per Tape	$ 27.15						
LESS: Overrings & Voids	$						
	$						
PLUS:Bar Cash sales (tape)		39.41					
Net Cash Sales	$						
Deposit	$ 27.95	$ 27.95	$	(2)$ 21.00 (4)$	(9)$		$ 88.41
OVER/SHORT	$ .80	67.41					

REGISTER #4 REDWOOD ROOM

TODAY'S CASH READ.	$80,109.74						
YEST. CASH READ.	$79,937.04						
Non-Taxable (I)							
M.T. Cash (II)							
Taxable (IV)							
Total Cash per tape	$ 172.70						
LESS: Overrings &Voids	$ 6.50						
Net Cash sales	$ 166.20						
Deposit	$ 166.17	$ 166.17	$	$ 56.15	$ 7.13	$ 20.50	$ 242.82
OVER/SHORT	$ .03						

TOTAL		$ 630.38	$	$ 201.85	$ 14.45	$ 20.50	$ 852.73

DAY Thurs   DATE 11-9-78

EXHIBIT VI-6

WEEKLY REPORT · CASH OPERATIONS

UNIVERSITY CENTER FOOD SERVICE
Operating Statement Week Ending _November 12, 1978_

	CASH	MEAL TICKET	FOOD SCRIP	DEPT. CHARGE	THIS WEEK Amount	THIS WEEK %	THIS YEAR TO DATE Amount	THIS YEAR TO DATE %	LAST YEAR TO DATE Amount	LAST YEAR TO DATE %
SALES										*11-13-77*
MALL (includes HOFBRAU)	234839	42890	69780	22 -	734409	45.4	6707392	48.8	5496761	44.7
REDWOOD ROOM	71433	30,55	22950	25980	155418	9.7	1430.690	10.4	137.7036	10.3
RATHSKELLAR	62374	344580	15420	34530	457252	28.5	3947724	28.8	3956,757	28.2
CATERING	—	—	—	263318	263318	16.4	1,1439999	17.0	2,123201	16.8
TOTAL SALES	373638	798.25	10.82.10	325928	1616401	100.0	17446206	100.0	12628757	100.0
EXPENSES										
COST OF FOOD *			629446			39.1	6258616	45.5	4428542	52.8
COST OF LABOR	hours	amount								
Adults	504	253420				15.7	2436735	17.7	2,141154	16.9
Students	900	174185				14.0	1891.194	13.8	1459152	11.5
TOTAL LABOR			474625			29.7	4327929	31.5	3600306	28.4
OTHER EXPENSES**			32720			20.0	2749364	20.0	2372720	20.0
TOTAL EXPENSES					1424321	88.8	13335946	97.0	12524604	97.2
NET OPERATING PROFIT (or LOSS)					180100	11.2	4108160	3.0	102153	.8

* Based on beginning inventory, plus purchases, less ending inventory
** Calculated at 20% of sales
*** 6,28474 ÷ 6,28476 = 6,054/14 × 74,657.8 (Food + Paper)
    250 portion × 290 portion cost to 97.6% to food cost

EXHIBIT VI-6 (continued)

WEEKLY REPORT - RESIDENCE HALL

Unit __Grace Covell Hall__

UNIVERSITY OF THE PACIFIC FOOD SERVICE
UNIT MANAGER'S REPORT

Week Ending:_____ 196 ____
No. of Contracts:_____

Day	ENTREE ITEM	Ordered		Left Over		Used		Time Out	Last Time		Date	Comments
		Lbs.	No.	Lbs.	No.	Lbs.	No.		Lbs.	No.		
Sat. L. 1												
2												
D. 1												
2												
Sun. L. 1												
2												
D. 1												
2												
Thurs. L. 1												
2												
D. 1												
2												
Fri. L. 1												
2												
D. 1												
2												

COST ANALYSIS

	This Week %	Last Week %
INCOME		
Estimated Contract Income (No. of M.T. x 7 days x $2.00)	$ 13,037.50	$ 13,037.50
Estimated Catering Income	354.26	659.65
Cash	174.65	198.25
TOTAL ESTIMATED INCOME	$ 13,566.41	$ 13,895.40

NO. OF MEALS SERVED   Contract Students __7534__
                      Employees __279__
                      Banquets etc.* __401__

TOTAL NUMBER OF MEALS SERVED	8214	8754

FOOD COST PER MEAL SERVED
Cost of Food Purchased** __8529.23__ : Total No. Meals ____8214____ = $ __1.04__ $ __.96__

MEALS SERVED PER MAN-HOUR
Regular Hours __612__
Student Hours __376__
TOTAL HOURS __988__ : Total No. of Meals ____8214____ = __8__   __9__

*Do not include coffee hours etc.   **Total of Week's Invoices

Table illustrating the importance of "to date" figures in operating statements

Sales	This Week	%	Year To date	%	Last Year To date	%
Cash	5,000		120,000		105,000	
Charges	3,000		65,000		52,000	
TOTAL SALES	8,000	100%	185,000	100%	157,000	100%
Cost of Labor						
Regular	2,700		32,000		29,440	
Students	800		10,200		9,900	
TOTAL LABOR	3,500	43.8%	42,200	22.8%	39,300	25.1%
Cost of Food	4,200	52.5%	65,400	35.3%	52,300	33.3%
Other Costs (15% of sales)	1,200	15.0%	27,750	15.0%	23,550	15.0%
TOTAL COSTS	8,900	111.3%	135,350	73.1%	115,150	73.3%
NET PROFIT or (LOSS)	$(900)	(11.3)	$ 49,650	26.9%	$ 41,850	26.6%

Please note that even though operations during the current week *lost* $900, the *overall operations are better* than the previous year. The cost of labor is 2.3% below last year, but the cost of food is 2% above last year. You can see clearly that, while weekly percentages tend to fluctuate widely, the to date percentages usually remain fairly constant.

Weekly or Monthly Reports - Residence Hall Operations

It was suggested earlier that food service operations in residence halls do not fluctuate as greatly as cash operations and, therefore, a daily, and perhaps even a weekly report, is not necessary. Note earlier in the chapter that there is no general agreement with this viewpoint, and that some directors insist on weekly statements! However, you should be just as concerned, just as much in control, and just as watchful of your residence hall units. Unless you have a tight grip on the hiring of part-time employees, unless you cost out your menus each week, unless your procedures for receiving, preparing, and serving food are clear and professional, you can have cost problems in residence halls just as you can in cash operations. The basic difference is that your cost controls are more permanent, more long-range rather than day-to-day. If you use a carefully-written, fully-costed 5-week menu cycle, for example, if your cooks use standard recipes, and if your servers serve standard portions, then, unless there are wild price fluctuations in the meantime, your cost of food should be fairly constant from month to month. Unless you suddenly hire more students, or approve unusual overtime, or suddenly give great wage increases to your staff, your labor cost also will remain more or less constant from one month to the next.

Nevertheless, you should satisfy yourself that all is running as well as possible. You should compare your financial condition at the end of each week or month with the same period last year, or with your budget. You should check your "cost per meal served" as well as your "meals served per labor hour" figures. If you can develop a system in which your meal ticket income is properly allocated to each month of the school year according to operating days in each month, you can develop monthly operating statements for your residence halls very easily, and thus be fairly sure whether or not you are operating within your budget. If possible, convince your computer services department to write a program that will give you a monthly operating statement. An excellent example of such a statement is shown in Exhibit VI-7 which contains a page from the monthly statement of Dickinson College in Carlisle, Pennsylvania.

Use of Financial Statements

One of the dangers of being a food service manager in an institution is that you can get into a rut, take things for granted, and become careless. This is especially true in the preparation, reading, and utilization of financial reports. Unless you are trained in accounting and enjoy the analysis of financial statements, you may regard these periodic statements as a necessary nuisance. You will probably read them, perhaps even check to see what caused any variance from the norm, and then file them away, ready to show them to your boss whenever he asks you about them.

Your operating statements should be *living documents* -- they should give you vital information about your operations, information to share with your supervisors and employees. By way of example, take the case of a student-managed Rathskeller at the University of the Pacific: during the first year of operation, this unit lost a considerable amount of money. In the second year, the student managers were brought into the picture: the budget, which called for a maximum of 30% labor cost and a 5% net, was explained to them. Each week, the food service manager reviewed with the student managers deviations from the budget. During the week, they made staffing adjustments to meet their cost objectives. At the end of the second year, the Rathskeller ended with a labor cost of 28% of sales, and a net profit of 3.5%!

Some bosses don't care to see interim operating statements. This may be especially true if your boss is student-personnel oriented, rather than business-oriented. Try to get him to read your statements anyway. Attach little notes or comments for his information. Do anything to keep him current and aware of any trends you are experiencing. The best way to lose a job as food service manager is to "surprise" your superiors with sudden deficits or unexpected financial crises.

A final word of caution: avoid either extreme. On one hand, make time in your schedule for preparation and analysis of financial statements; on the other, don't become a fanatic. You are too busy managing a food service operation to be spending all day on accounting. It is very easy to get involved in what some call "busy work," work which, upon close analysis, is really not very productive. As the Latin poet Horace said: "Travel the Golden Mean."

EXHIBIT VI-7

FOOD SERVICE - INCOME STATEMENT

Description	Curr-Month	Percent	Yr.-to-Date	Percent	Budget	Percent
Fall Semester		.0	556088.19-	42.1	565500.00	43.3
Spring Semester		.0	539705.41-	40.8	549900.00	42.1
First Session		.0	13202.82-	1.0	17000.00	1.3
Second Session		.0	10061.00-	.7	15000.00	1.1
Casual Meals		.0	15318.61-	1.1	12000.00	.9
Conferences		100.0	102883.83-	7.7	70000.00	5.3
Special Events		.0	77922.19-	5.9	72000.00	5.5
Miscellaneous		.0	4611.05-	.3	2000.00	.1
TOTAL INCOME		100.0	1319793.10-	100.0	1303400.00	100.0
Employee Wages		.0	226590.16	17.1	229180.00	17.5
Salaries		.0	51931.38	3.9	52270.00	4.0
Student Wages College		.0	91275.17	6.9	94390.00	7.2
Student Wages High School		.0	2376.83	.1	1290.00	.0
Retirement		.0	15256.33	1.1	15500.00	1.1
Social Security		.0	16598.91	1.2	15900.00	1.2
Life Insurance		.0	2263.51	.1	2630.00	.2
Unemployment Comp.		.0	1449.96	.1	1450.00	.1
Blue Cross		.0	5817.74	.4	6500.00	.1
Disability		.0	886.38	.0	980.00	.0
Major Medical		.0	614.31	.0	690.00	.0
Workmans Compensation		.0	883.33	.0	550.00	.0
SUB-TOTAL EXPENSE		.0	415944.01	31.5	421330.00	32.3
Meat		.0	177004.94	13.4	186400.00	14.3
Poultry		.0	37929.51	2.8	45600.00	3.4
Seafood		.0	26733.73	2.0	28700.00	2.2
Fruit Frozen, Canned		.0	26178.90	1.9	32580.00	2.4
Juices Vegetable, Fruit		.0	23076.56	1.7	23460.00	1.7
Vegetables Frozen, Canned		.0	62225.29	4.7	62560.00	4.7
Butter, Cheese, Oleo		.0	25756.70	1.9	23460.00	1.7
Eggs		.0	18623.61	1.4	18240.00	1.3
Milk, Cream, Yogurt		.0	45869.40	3.4	43000.00	3.2
Ice Cream		.0	17536.70	1.3	15640.00	1.1
Pastry, Baked Goods, Flour		.0	34264.21	2.5	32580.00	2.4
Oils, Shortening		.0	9131.54	.6	16940.00	1.2
Tea, Coffee, Cocoa		.0	8063.12	.6	7820.00	.5
Jams, Jellies, Preserves		.0	2464.11	.1	2600.00	.1
Sugar, Vinegar, Syrups		.0	24839.98	1.8	32580.00	2.4
Cereal		.0	8185.00	.6	6520.00	.5
Condiments and Spices		.0	16198.87	1.2	15640.00	1.1
Misc. Food Purchases		.0	9253.23	.7	5280.00	.4
Resale Items		.0	76.20	.0	.00	.0
SUB-TOTAL EXPENSE		.0	573411.66	43.4	599600.00	46.0

EXHIBIT VI-7 (continued)

Description	Curr-Month	Percent	Yr.-to-Date	Percent	Budget	Percent
Laundry		.0	5980.18	.4	5560.00	.4
Sanitation		.0	6997.54	.5	5500.00	.4
Paper		.0	13016.76	.9	15500.00	1.1
China, Flatware		.0	7122.88	.5	10500.00	.8
Telephone		.0	282.25	.0	600.00	.0
Printing		.0	1429.75	.1	1400.00	.1
Operating Supplies		.0	6077.90	.4	4000.00	.3
Equip. Purchases		.0	12879.09	.9	1100.00	.8
Equip. Service Contracts		.0	1795.26	.1	1600.00	.1
Equip. Repairs		.0	8373.25	.6	6100.00	.4
Travel Office		.0	130.53	.0	.00	.0
Professional Fees		.0	130.53	.0	.00	.0
Miscellaneous		.0	5870.00	.4	5300.00	.4
Subscriptions		.0	.00	.0	230.00	.0
Xerox		.0	78.06	.0	80.00	.0
Fuel		.0	2963.79	.2	2400.00	.1
Replacement		100.1	32000.00	2.4	20000.00	.1
Uniforms		.0	2626.61	.1	2700.00	.2
Trash Removal		.0	1882.50	.1	2500.00	.1
Travel Meetings		.0	750.00	.0	750.00	.0
SUB-TOTAL EXPENSE		100.1	110403.09	8.3	97220.00	7.4
From Business Office		.0	37646.40	2.8	37930.00	2.9
Overhead		.0	28753.06	2.1	31100.00	2.3
Debt Service		.0	12700.00	.9	12700.00	.9
SUB-TOTAL EXPENSE		.0	79099.46	5.9	81730.00	6.2
TOTAL EXPENSE		100.1	1178858.22	89.3	1199880.00	92.0

NET

Courtesy of Dickinson College, Carlisle, Pa. The above figures are furnished for purposes of illustration only.

CASH CONTROLS

In any business, tight control over cash is an absolute requirement. This is as true in colleges as in commercial operations. You must consider yourself personally responsible for the cash that flows through your operations, and must make absolutely certain that you have set up controls which will help to quickly identify any irregularity or dishonesty. The following chapter will guide you in these efforts.

Petty Cash

The subject of petty cash has already been covered in the chapter on Purchasing (see page 72). As was explained earlier, the setting of strict limits to petty cash purchases, insisting on proper receipts or other documentation, and frequent audits of the petty cash fund are the basic control tools. If your school has an internal auditor, it might be a good idea to ask him to check the petty cash accounts periodically, so that everyone knows that someone from outside food service is checking on the petty cash.

Cash Registers

In most large commercial establishments, each cashier has a cash drawer and is personally responsible for the accuracy of the cash. In addition to having a separate drawer for each cashier, there is also a separate register key assigned to each so that shortages can be directly traced to the cashier responsible. Furthermore, the cash register cannot be "cleared" by the cashiers; they can only take a reading of the totals, and the tape adds continuously to previous receipts. All transactions are also numbered consecutively. This prevents the cashier from removing the tape before the end of the working day, and keeping the remaining sales for himself. In modern, commercial cafeterias, the registers often have a separate set of keys with the main sale items marked on the keys, and with the prices pre-set in the machine, so that human error becomes difficult, if not impossible.

Amazingly, colleges and universities often do not follow the same strict procedures. With many student workers in food service, and most of them working only 2-3 hours per day, it is sometimes difficult to assign a separate cash drawer to everyone who is handling cash. In many residence dining halls, a cash register is not even used. A variety of reasons is given, none of them being valid: e.g. it would destroy the home-like atmosphere; the registers are too expensive for the small amount of cash collected; etc. In small snack bars, everyone working behind the counter also does cashiering, and assigning responsibility to a specific person thus becomes impossible.

Your job is to buy the most practical register for each operation and to establish the tightest controls possible. Because there are many different types of food service units, it is impossible here to tell you just what you need; your cash register salesman can do that much better. Whether the register is manual or electronic, whether it should be tied to a computer, how many separate totals are needed, and whether prices should be pre-set, these are all specifics that must be worked out locally.

Generally speaking, the purchase of a first-class register with many capabilities, is an excellent investment. If the machine adds automatically, you remove one chance of error. If it calculates the sales tax, you remove another. If the price of the item is pre-set, there is a third; and if, in a limited menu situation, you get an automatic count of the numbers of each item that you sell, then you have added a fourth important control feature.

Daily Cashier's Reports

Whether you use a fancy cash register or just a plain metal cash box, a written, signed report by each cashier at the end of the shift is necessary. While some managers ask the cashiers to make up their shortages, this is not generally advisable on a college campus. It is important, however, to have the cashiers indicate on their daily cash sheet every penny of shortage or overage, so that you can get an overall view of the accuracy of each cashier, and the total of all shortages. Insisting on proper cashier's reports, even from student cashiers, is good also from a psychological viewpoint. Most of your cashiers are honest; most students are honest. It is up to you to keep temptation away, through the use of detailed cashier's reports. These are then checked against the cash and the register tapes. A sample of a typical cashier's report is shown in Exhibit VI-8.

MEAL TICKETS

There are times, in the life of every college food service manager, when he wishes that meal tickets had never been invented. These times occur normally at the beginning of the school year (when the meal tickets are issued), three days later (when the meal tickets are lost), a month later (when students loaned meal tickets to somebody else), and every month thereafter (when students steal, sell, duplicate, falsify or, perhaps, simply decide to return the meal tickets). How much simpler life would be if you could just operate a commercial cafeteria, where anyone who wants to buy something simply pays the cashier at the end of the line!

On second thought, perhaps it might not be all that wonderful. If a customer in a commercial cafeteria is dissatisfied, he can simply go somewhere else. If it rains or storms, he simply stays home. Remember, on the day school starts, you have collected or have been assured of getting one third of your total income for the entire year. Remember also, that the students living in residence halls are a captive audience forced either by the rules of the college or by virtue of the distance from other eating places to eat your food. On balance, you will no doubt agree that the fellow who invented the college meal ticket was pretty smart.

For the student and his parents, meal tickets also provide some real advantages. Foremost among these is the assurance that, for a pre-determined sum of money, the student is *assured of getting an adequate, nutritious and well-balanced diet*. When one considers that the average college freshman is only 18 years old and has relatively little experience in budgeting and in handling money, such pre-planning by the college is usually a source of relief for both student and parent alike. Another

EXHIBIT VI-8

UNIVERSITY CENTER FOOD SERVICE
Cashiers Daily Tally Sheet

			Amount
Checks			$ 120.00
$20	120.00		120.00
$10	—		—
$5	65.00	5.00	60.00
$1	84.00	28.00	56.00
50¢	1.00	1	1.00
25¢	19.50	19.00	.50
10¢	11.10	11.00	.10
5¢	5.65	560	.05
1¢	1.40	140	—
	307.65	7000	
Total Deposit (Cash)			$ 237.65
+ Guest Meal Charges			3.50
		TOTAL	$ 241.15

Cashier's Daily Summary

I	Meal Ticket Cash		$ 4.10
II	Non-Taxable Sales		144.00
III	Taxable Sales		86.11
IV	Tax		5.06
		Subtotal	$ 239.27
Less:	Overrings and Refunds		- 1.62
CORRECTED GROSS SALES			237.65
TOTAL DEPOSIT			237.65
Over or (under)			0
TOTAL SCRIP			$ 69.40

REGISTER: Mall

DAY AND DATE: Tuesday 1.30.79

CASHIER: Coleman Thorpe

significant benefit is the *discount* which usually accompanies a meal ticket. Normally, this discount ranges from 10% to 15% of the regular cash price -- a discount made possible, in part, by the fact that the student will miss some of the meals included in his meal ticket plan, and that this "missed meal factor" (for more about this factor, see the sections on budgets earlier in this chapter) has been considered in the final price calculation. Yet another important advantage for the student is that the meal ticket, even though normally non-transferable, is *replaceable* when lost. Finally, for many college students, one of the fringe benefits of meal tickets is the fact that their *parents pay for it.*

At this point it may be in order to explain just what type of meal ticket is being discussed: This chapter deals with meal ticket plans for residence halls, and meal ticket plans for cash operations, but in order for you to decide which plan is best for you, a brief history of meal ticket plans in colleges and universities may be helpful.

History of Meal Ticket Plans on American Campuses

When residence halls were first constructed on the campuses of American colleges and universities, their dining halls were operated largely along the lines of those in fraternities and sororities, or in some cases, the "eating clubs" that had sprung up in some of the Ivy League schools. Everyone living in the residence hall was expected to eat all meals in the dining room while school was in session; meals were served at a specific time and in the case of women's halls especially, everyone waited in the lounge or living room until the residence hall director entered. What is more, no one sat down until the director took her seat. Students who lived off-campus had no meal ticket plan. In fact, in many cases, there was no campus cafeteria to serve them, only some sort of snack bar or "tea room."

In the mid-1950's, this changed. Feeling a responsibility toward off-campus students, school administrators built cash cafeterias and devised special "weekday meal tickets" to meet their needs. Students living in residence halls, however, still had only one option: a total meal package (usually 20 meals weekly, with only 2 meals served on Sundays), valid only in their own dining halls. If any student wished to eat with a friend, he had to arrange for a special pass at least two or three days in advance.

Ten years later, with the advent of the Free Speech Movement in Berkeley, and a general assertion of students' rights across the country, there came some significant changes. For years, students in residence halls had complained about being "ripped off" by their schools, since they felt that they were paying for meals which they did not eat. Breakfast was a prime example, as were meals on weekends. At this point, college food service directors came up with "variable meal plans." Instead of a 19 or 20-meal plan, students were offered a choice of 14-meal plans (2 meals daily, 7 days), 10-meal plans (2 meals daily, 5 days), 15-meal plans (3 meals daily, 5 days), and similar combinations. Some schools experimented with "made-to-order" plans, so that the students could purchase a plan tailor-made for their particular needs. Furthermore, the rules concerning transfers were gradually liberalized, and students could now eat in any residence hall dining room without special advance arrangement. Still, the "missed meal factor," though minimized by these various options, continued to rankle college students. In the late 1960's, several large universities experimented by dropping all obligatory meal ticket requirements for students living in residence halls. The results in some instances, were dramatic and disastrous: students deserted the residence hall dining services in droves, the food services affected lost hundred of thousands of dollars in revenue. Instead, the students flocked to nearby fast-food operations, where they could purchase items they really wanted, such as hamburgers, milk shakes, and French fried potatoes.

In response, college food service directors countered with two "revolutionary" solutions which helped to stem the tide, and stopped or reversed the students' flight from their dining halls. One was the establishment of "scrip" plans for residence hall students; the other was a plan permitting such students to use their meal tickets in cash operations as well as their own residence halls, thus giving them an almost limitless set of options as to when, what, and how they would eat. This flexible arrangement is called the "free flow" system.

The "scrip" or coupon plans, pioneered largely by the State University of New York/Cortland and by San Francisco State University, substituted scrip money (paper tickets used in place of cash) for meal tickets, and eliminated the "missed meal factor" as a problem. Students purchased a certain amount of coupons, and when these were used up, bought some more. The "free flow" system had two important results: first, the students loved it; many of their former complaints about meal monotony ceased. Second, the number of students using the residence hall dining rooms diminished. At Brandeis University, which was one of the early pioneers of this system, two residence hall dining rooms were able to accommodate the students instead of the three previously needed. The result was significant savings in labor costs and other operating costs.

Early in the 1970's, colleges throughout the United States experienced a significant drop in residence hall population. A few years later, as a result of more liberal college housing policies generally, and more flexible meal plan options specifically, students returned to the halls in large numbers. By the mid-1970's, most colleges were offering a choice of several meal plan options, some were using a variety of scrip plans, and an ever-increasing number (usually schools where the *entire* food service operation was concentrated in one department) were letting students use their meal tickets anywhere on campus. On some campuses, such as California State University/Chico, and the University of Pennsylvania in Philadelphia, where the residence halls are at the fringe of the campus and in the cash units in the center, this "free-flow" option is offered at breakfast and dinner only. If it were done at lunch, the centrally located food service units would be overwhelmed, while the others would be empty. The latest innovation in script plans has recently been instituted at Southern Oregon State College in Ashland, where students have the choice of a plan which gives them *unlimited choices* and *second portions* or a plan which provides for only *limited choices* and *no seconds* on food and beverages.

Factors Affecting Choice of Meal Ticket Plan

Proper selection of a suitable meal ticket plan is one of the most important decisions that you can make in college food service. Whatever plan you select, it should meet the following criteria:

- It should meet the needs of the students.
- It should stimulate sales.
- It should be relatively foolproof.
- It should be simple to understand.
- It should be simple to administer.

Whatever other reasons there may be for issuing meal tickets, one of the major ones is sales stimulation. In the residence halls, meal tickets are bought not only by those living in the halls, but in many schools also by off-campus student who can see the advantages of such a plan. Your plan should be so attractive and so well merchandised that at least 5%-10% of your off-campus students purchase regular boarding tickets. In addition to the multiple option plans, and discount feature, you can sell the special dinners, free-flow privileges, guest privileges, field trip privileges, and any others that will help convince students that a meal ticket at your school is simply a "good deal."

Students know what their needs are, perhaps better than you do. There is little point in saying, "You really need a 3-meal plan, because breakfast is the most important meal of the day," if the student to whom you are talking has a habit of sleeping late. No amount of persuasion on your part will get him to get up for breakfast for health reasons. Meal tickets should *conform* to the students' needs, not frustrate them.

Types of Meal Ticket Systems

There is no meal ticket plan in existence today that is 100% fool-proof. College students are just at the age when their minds are most inventive, and using other students' meal tickets is still considered a harmless prank. In spite of this, you should make a real effort to select a plan that is relatively cheat-proof. Following are some of the systems currently in use on American campuses:

Punch-type tickets -- A plain punch-type ticket without a photograph is not at all secure. It will take an imaginative student less than a day to find a printer who can duplicate it for him. Furthermore, punching is time-consuming and not always accurate. If a photograph is attached to the card and both are then plasticized so that both the card and the photo become non-separable, this plan works much better. When used in connection with a punch machine, which lights up if the card has been punched, then this system works quite well.

Numbered check-off sheets -- Some schools use a pre-numbered check-off sheet, with the student using his room key for purposes of identification. This system works well only if the students permitted in the dining hall are exclusively those living in that residence hall. Even then, you may expect problems with such a relatively loose system. Another problem with the use of pre-numbered sheets is that where several residence halls are involved and the school permits "free-flow" between dining halls, the sheets must be matched up after each day to see if anyone used his meal privilege more than once during a meal. This is always time-consuming and since the offending student has to be called in after the fact, it is also cumbersome and unnecessarily embarrassing.

I.D. cards with (non-removable) labels -- Stanford University pioneered the use of an I.D. card with a Polaroid photograph and a special sticky label, which cannot be removed from the card without being destroyed. The card itself is embossed for added security. The labels indicate the type of plan for which the student is eligible, the semester, year, etc.

Meal ticket booklets -- Brandeis University, and other schools are using a meal ticket book with individual stubs for each meal. This is particularly useful in a "free-flow" system where the students are allowed to use the cash operations. The stubs become a permanent record which forms the basis for inter-departmental charges for the various food service units. This booklet is good only if used in combination with a photograph for positive identification. San Jose State University in California is plasticizing the booklet with the photograph in one process. Some of the disadvantages are that when students lose the booklets, replacements become expensive. San Jose State will therefore switch to a plasticized card in 1979/80. If cashiers do not look closely at the photographs, unauthorized students can use these, especially in campus food service units where they are not known. Issuing the booklets once, or even twice a semester also involves a great deal of bookkeeping. A description of this plan is shown in Exhibit VI-9.

Scrip booklets -- The use of booklets with scrip in various denominations has been described earlier. In a typical scrip system, the scrip tickets are completely interchangeable, and anyone may use them. Thus individual identification is not so essential. One possible disadvantage, however, is the need for absolute honesty on the part of the cashiers. Where student cashiers are used, the temptation by an individual cashier to pull less than the required number of scrip tickets is sometimes irresistible. When you put such temptations in front of students, don't be surprised when they succumb. By the time you discover the "error," it may have cost you thousands of dollars in uncollected scrips.

Photo I.D. card with computer -- An increasingly popular control system uses plasticized I.D. cards with a magnetic tape containing basic meal plan information. This card is handed to the cashier, who places it into a card reader connected to the central computer (memory unit). This system is excellent, since the cashier can get an instantaneous reply concerning the student's meal ticket status. The ticket cannot be used twice, as an invalid ticket is immediately spotted. The main disadvantage is that the initial cost of the computer and terminals is quite costly in comparison to the other plans, a cost which the distributors claim is saved by more effective controls. This plan was originally called "Vali-Dine;" a description is shown in Exhibit VI-10.

Several other schools have adopted variations of the Vali-Dine plan, also using computers. Brown University in Providence and California State University/Berkeley both have a highly effective, though very expensive system using a central computer for meal ticket controls.

EXHIBIT VI-9

FOOD MANAGEMENT

By Paul Fairbrook

New Meal Plan Lets Students Take A Ticket to Lunch, Brunch or Munch

What can a food service director do in times of rising costs and a relatively limited ceiling on how much can be charged for food services — particularly when food service includes so much debt service which the student doesn't (or doesn't want to) understand? One solution is to close down unprofitable operations by extending student "free flow" to student centers for food service.

This idea was successfully implemented at Brandeis University by food service director Larry Jeffries. He issued little books of date-stamped tickets in which three tickets, worth $1, $1.25 and $1.75, constituted one food service day. The tickets could be used by the student in either the residence halls or the student union.

Using Brandeis' concept as a model, a new meal ticket plan was instituted at the University of the Pacific, Stockton, Calif., this year. All resident students are required to have a meal contract and off-campus students may also purchase them. To increase the flexibility of the contract system, the new meal ticket plan enables the student to obtain meals both at the snack bar and the residence dining halls.

At the beginning of both semesters, each student with a meal contract is given a coupon book with

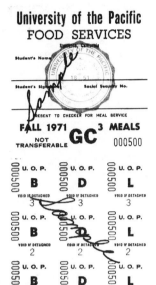

University of the Pacific
FOOD SERVICES

Coupons may be used only for the designated meal and day.

his or her name and social security number on it. The number of tickets in the book is dependent upon the type of meal contract for which the student has signed, and each coupon book contains enough tickets for one semester. Ticket books are not transferable from one student to another, and the student is requested to show his identification card when turning in a meal ticket.

Each ticket is marked B (breakfast), L (lunch) and D (dinner) and has a number on it. Each ticket is valid for one meal on a designated day and may not be used at any other time. Loose tickets are void, and a lost or mutilated coupon book must be replaced at minimal cost to the student.

If the student chooses to dine in

a residence hall, he presents his coupon book to a cashier at the entrance who removes the appropriate ticket from the book. Standard residence hall dining regulations are in effect: certain hours of operation and unlimited seconds.

If the student chooses to use his meal ticket in the snack bar, he may purchase items a la carte up to the cash value of the coupon. If his purchase exceeds the cash value of the coupon, he must pay the difference in cash; however, there is no cash refund if his total purchase is less than the cash value of the coupon. While unlimited free seconds are not available at the snack bar, the hours of operation are more flexible.

There are four distinct advantages to the new plan:

1. It gives the residence hall students an opportunity to eat in the snack bar at all hours, thus giving them more flexibility in arranging their lives to suit themselves.

2. The snack bar menu is such that students can always have such items as hot dogs, hamburgers and milk shakes, so that the popularity of the residence hall menu is not as significant as before.

3. By setting a cash value on the snack bar meal, a student can buy a certain amount of food and share it, if he wishes, with a guest who has no meal ticket. This is impossible in a residence hall dining room where there are unlimited seconds and where such a practice would lead to widespread abuse. Thus, the new plan encourages honesty.

4. By diverting a number of students from all residence dining rooms to the snack bar, any small or unprofitable dining halls that may exist on the campus can be closed, with significant savings to the university. □

PAUL FAIRBROOK is director of housing and food service at the University of the Pacific, Stockton, Calif., and is head of Paul Fairbrook Associates, Chicago, food service consultants specializing in operational studies and kitchen design for institutional clients. Mr. Fairbrook, a graduate of Brown University, served as food service consultant to EXPO '67, the world exposition in Canada.

For more facts circle 32 on reply card →

EXHIBIT VI-10

EXHIBIT VI-11

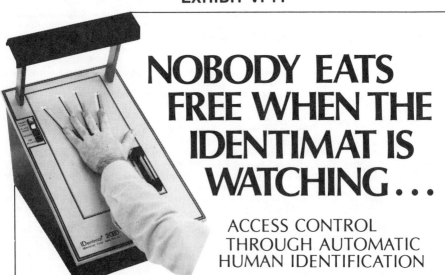

Handprints with computer -- A novel system, using student handprints for positive identification has recently been developed. Several schools, such as the University of Tennessee are claiming some success with the system which asks students to put their hands, palms down, on a plate which then photographs the hand prints and flashes the picture to the computer. Any irregularity is flashed back to the cashier in seconds. A description of this plan is shown in Exhibit VI-11.

There is no point in devising a system so complicated that only you and your staff can understand it. Students have other things on their minds besides meal tickets. One such example is a system using scrip money, with each meal or components thereof, converted into units: a sandwich is two units, milk is one, and perhaps fresh fruit is one-and-a-half. While students will undoubtedly master the mathematics, one wonders whether such complexity in meal ticket plans is really necessary.

Finally, a good meal ticket system is one that is relatively simple to administer. There is no point in your saving two or three thousand dollars yearly by having a secure system, if it costs you five thousand dollars or more in clerical time just to maintain the system.

Remember that your students are all basically honest. If you devise a system that is relatively fool-proof, fair, and easily understandable, your percentage of loss will be small. Students are also generally fair. If the plan you select is clearly explained, and the consequences of cheating spelled out in advance, then most students will accept such consequences stoically, and the student judiciary will support you in your efforts.

How to Handle Meal Ticket Problems

One of the less pleasant duties of a college food service manager is to handle minor disciplinary problems in the food service areas. While major problems of discipline are normally handled by student personnel officers, most deans will be happy to have you take care of any minor matters arising in connection with food service in your own way. We all like to be popular, and are loath, suddenly, to be cast in the role of the "villain." The key to this problem is to be *fair, firm,* and *friendly.* You must let the student know what the problem is as you see it, you must be firm in your resolve, and you must always control your own feelings and behavior in such a way that the student can leave your office with his self-respect intact. Remember at all times that *your job depends on your relations with the students.* No boss, no matter how kind and supportive he may be, can defend you against an avalanche of complaints from students concerning your personality or your behavior toward them. At the same time, you do represent the college or university for which you work, and must help to uphold its policies. Furthermore, you are, in effect, the trustee for the students' food service funds and as such, have a duty to prevent the unauthorized use of meal tickets or any other type of cheating that will ultimately be paid for out of the students' pockets.

One way of minimizing such problems is to establish certain routines and procedures for specific offenses, *before* they occur. Take the most common one, the unauthorized use of a non-transferable meal ticket by another student. From the student's standpoint, what he is doing is absolutely proper: "I paid for the meal, so why can't I give it to my friend if I want to?" After you have explained the theory of the "missed meal factor" a thousand times, and after seeing students shake their heads in disbelief a thousand times, you may begin to wonder if your reasons are really justified. Your argument, "If everyone did what you did, your meal ticket would cost at least 15% more," is theoretically sound, but both of you know that this would probably never happen. Therefore, decide in advance not to make too big a deal out of this relatively minor offense, at least not the first time it happens. Explain to the student why he did wrong, and then, perhaps, ask him not to do it again. Handled properly and casually, such an informal procedure will be very effective, and few students will violate your regulations a second time.

Much more serious, of course, is the case of a student caught selling his original meal ticket while obtaining a duplicate from college food services. Here is an instance of petty theft. Your responsibility is not only to the college but also, as a responsible educator, to the student himself. Unless you make a deep impression, he may miss his last chance to learn the difference between right and wrong before he learns it the hard way in later life. Since you need *absolute proof,* you must obtain either a signed affadavit by the student who purchased the meal ticket (usually easy to get, since the latter doesn't want to get involved) or a verbal confession from the student who sold the ticket. Such a confession is not as hard to get as it may seem. If you tell the student exactly what his penalty will be, and what alternatives he is facing, he will often opt for the lesser of two possibilities. For example:

> "I have every reason to believe, Jim, that you sold your meal ticket to John, and I think I can prove it. You have two choices: If you admit that you did this, and apologize for your behavior, we will charge you for the cost of the duplicate meals. We will also place a note of this incident in your file, to be destroyed within a year if there is no repetition of dishonest behavior. If you do not admit it, I shall turn your case over to the student personnel office, for forwarding to the student court. Take your choice."

Meal Ticket Plans - Residence Halls

The brief history of meal ticket plans outlined earlier in this chapter shows that there is a whole range of options open to you if the decision about meal ticket plans is yours to make. Briefly summarized, they are as follows:

No choice plan -- Students purchase one standard plan (either 19, 20, or 21 meals per week) and that's it. The advantages of this plan are that it maximizes your income, gives you the highest possible "missed meal factor" (probably as high as 35%-40%) and is very simple to administer. The disadvantages are that students will hate it, will feel "ripped off," and may not stay in the dorms if they don't have to.

Limited choice plan -- Students can purchase one of three or four basic plans, such as a 21, 14, and 10 meal option. Fortunately for you, common practice is to

reduce the lesser plans only to the extent of *actual savings* and not by the full value of the meals not served. In other words, if the value of a 21-meal plan is $1,500 per year, then a 14-meal plan may be reduced by only $80-$100, instead of the ⅓ reduction ($500) which one would normally expect. Your normal payroll and overhead expenses continue regardless of whether students purchase the 21-meal or the 14-meal plan. Even your food cost is affected by the fact that students with the lesser plans miss very few meals, and your "missed meal factor" drops down to less than 15%. Nevertheless, such limited-choice plans are common, not too complicated, and seem to satisfy the majority of students.

Multiple choice plan -- Students can purchase 20- or 14-meal plans (7 days weekly) or 15- and 10-meal plans (5 days weekly) or even 5- and 7-meal plans (one meal daily); in some cases, students can even get tailor-made plans, such as a 12-meal plan (which includes 2 meals on weekdays and one each on Saturday and Sunday). Several colleges (such as the University of California in Santa Barbara and the University of the Pacific) experimented with such plans for a number of years; both came to the conclusion that while the students liked the limitless options available to them, it was fairly complicated to administer and, in any event, most students chose the basic 10-, 15-, and 20-meal options.

Scrip plans -- Students can purchase a certain minimum amount of script (usually about 50% of the normal semester cost). They can sell this script, give it away, or use it up. It is usually non-refundable unless the student leaves the dorms, and if lost, no duplicates are issued. If students eat little, the original scrip package may last the whole term; if they eat a lot, they must buy additional scrip. The big advantage with this plan is that *students apparently like it.* They pay only for the meals actually eaten and a dieting person, for example, does not have the frustrating feeling that parents are paying a lot of money for food not wanted and not eaten. The disadvantage for many colleges is that this plan is difficult to put into effect if the food service has a high debt service obligation. "Debt service" is similar to the mortgage payment of an ordinary citizen. These funds must be included in the cost of the residence hall meal ticket, just as they are included in the room rate charged to students. Sometimes debt service amounts to several hundred dollars per student. With a scrip plan, this money would have to be included in the initial sale of scrip (which, as was stated earlier, may only be 50% of the normal semester cost). When the food service manager adds $300, $400, or even $500 of debt service to, let us say, $600 worth of food scrip, then the initial purchase of scrip may be too expensive and a whole-semester plan may be preferable. A description of a typical scrip plan is shown in Appendix 5.

No meal ticket plans -- There are some colleges which have lifted all meal ticket requirements for students. While they may make some sort of semester scrip books available, the basic idea is that the food service should "sell itself," and that if the food is really tasty and the service excellent, the students will purchase meals in the residence hall dining rooms anyway. This is a great idea, especially from the point of view of the good food service manager, who is proud of his meal service and sure of his ability to attract students. Unfortunately, it is also very risky. If you convince your superiors to lift the college's meal ticket requirements, and then find that your income is dropping 25%, you may be in serious trouble. The fact is that tasty food and friendly service are not the only factors which determine a student's choices. The ever-changing nocturnal study and eating habits of the modern college student are difficult to project. The pizza parlor downtown, which serves beer and is a social center for the campus in the late evening, may win handily over your pork chops with apple sauce at 6 p.m. Only in very special situations, where there are little or no debt service requirements, and where such a plan would enable you to close the dining services on weekends and at other quiet times is this approach advisable.

Meal Ticket Plans - Cash Operations

As stated earlier, in a residence hall, some sort of meal ticket plan is usually a necessity; in a cash operation, it is principally *a merchandising tool.* The off-campus students, especially men, will eat relatively few meals in their room or apartment. Yours is a logical place to eat; that's where all the other students are eating, that is the most familiar, the least expensive, and hopefully the best place to eat. Furthermore, it probably is the most convenient. Therefore, under normal conditions, the entire college community, except for those in residence halls, prefers to eat in the cash operations on campus. If your cash cafeteria or snack bar is an attractive place, serves nutritious, well prepared and popular food at competitive prices, has the variety expected by the various campus groups, and is not too crowded, noisy, or confused during the rush hours, you can count on getting the large share of all cash business available on campus. Nevertheless, there are always *some* who will leave the campus for other eating places, and usually for one of the following reasons:

- They just want to get away from campus.
- They want a change of atmosphere or menu.
- The campus operation is not open when they want to eat.
- They have no cash and must first cash a check or use their credit card.
- They want to be with someone who plans to eat off-campus.
- They have particular dietary wants.

A meal ticket plan, any plan at all, is an agreement between the buyer and the seller, whereby the buyer agrees to eat some or all meals at a given place, in exchange for some benefits. Therefore, if you are managing a cash operation, you must be able to devise some sort of plan which will be of clear-cut benefit to the buyer, in exchange for which he will probably eat more meals at your place then he would without such a plan. It's that simple. For this reason, you must be willing to make special concessions to the buyer, more than you would have to make to the student living in a residence hall. The latter, for instance, might be willing to pay for some missed meals during the course of a semester, but the off-campus students, the department secretaries, and the rest of the faculty and staff, will not. What are some of the benefits that will entice these people to eat more often than normal in your student union or cash cafeteria? Here are a few suggestions:

Special discounts -- Everybody loves a bargain, and if you can sell a $25.00 meal ticket book for $22.50, some people will buy it just for that reason. A cash discount is not always wise. If your total profit margin is less than 10% of sales, for example, then you can hardly afford to give another 10% discount to meal ticket purchasers.

Charge privileges -- If members of the campus community, and especially students and faculty, can charge meal tickets to their personal accounts, this will be a big factor for many of your customers. Students are often out of cash, and many parents will authorize charges to their personal accounts, as long as the charge is for food and beverages. Faculty also find a charge privilege a handy convenience, and will take advantage of it if offered.

Special merchandising gimmicks -- You can take a page out of the various merchandising and promotional efforts of other businesses: Dozens of clever promotions that can be tied in with your meal ticket sales. You can add some extra "bonus tickets" which entitle the buyer to free drinks, for example. Chances are, your local soft drink dealer will agree to share the cost of such a promotion. You can perhaps get other local businesses to offer their own specials in the back of your meal ticket booklet (e.g. discounts in movie houses, ski or boat rental places, etc.). Your campus grocery and campus bookstore are logical partners in such an enterprise. Even the cost of printing these meal tickets can be shared with some of these other "partners" in your promotional venture.

Special events -- Special festive dinners and other holiday events are one of the fringe benefits in a residence hall food service program. Why not latch on to this idea for your cash operations? If you can plan a series of festive occasions, which are free, or discounted, to meal ticket holders, you can add special excitement to such a meal ticket purchase. Once-a-month birthday parties, night-owl pizza feeds, ice cream socials, and special holiday meals are just as popular with off-campus students as those living on campus. Tie these in with your meal tickets in some imaginative way, to make them more popular.

Types of Meal Tickets - Cash Operations
Meal tickets can vary as much as the ideas which you incorporate in them, but two basic types are generally used on college campuses:

The punch type ticket is usually wallet-sized with amounts from $.05 to $1.00 printed around the edge of the ticket. It can be bought for cash or charged, in both cases for less than the face value of the ticket. There are some serious drawbacks to such a meal ticket, however:
- They can be duplicated by almost any printer.
- Student cashiers may not punch the proper amount when their friends are involved.

- Unless you have a special key on each cash register it is difficult to keep track of the amount of meal ticket sales at each location.
- It is difficult to incorporate special sales promotions.

The meal ticket booklet with scrips in various denominations, perhaps with advertising or other helpful information printed on the back of the scrip tickets, is very useful. It, too, can be printed in a convenient, small size. Additional sales promotions can be added at the back of each book, and it is difficult, though not impossible, to duplicate such booklets. Its disadvantage is the printing cost, which can be as high as $.25 to $.50 per book of tickets.

Other approaches can be used if these two are not satisfactory. There is nothing to stop you from corraling your cash customers in manners similar to those used in the residence halls. If you want to devise some special weekday, weekend, morning, lunch, or evening plans, special events or night-owl tickets, go ahead. If you want to use photo I.D. cards and set fixed maximums for each purchase, go ahead. If you want to collaborate with the residence halls in a novel and imaginative way, go ahead. Suppose, for example, your campus residence halls could actually close down on weekends, if you were willing to feed everyone in the cash operations. What a great solution that might be for everyone. You would save money and the students would mix in a different way, making new social contacts.

The possibilities for meal ticket promotions are limitless. So are the different ways in which you can make your students feel that they are "special." Where a significant number of customers are campus visitors, you might consider a two-tiered price approach: regular commercial prices for visitors and discounted prices for students, faculty, and staff.

CONTROL OF LABOR COSTS

The ability to control the cost of labor is one of the most important skills you bring to the job. If you are good at that, you are probably a fine manager in all other areas of food service management. Not only skills in budgeting, accounting, and production, but also human relations skills are needed, if you want to maintain proper control over labor costs without alienating your work force and seriously affecting its productivity. In the management of people, not everything can be learned. Not everything can be spelled out in this book. Much of what you do will have to be based on intuition, on a kind of "fingertip feeling" which tells you the right course of action. Management decisions are easy to make when they involve products or other inanimate subjects. They are difficult when they involve human beings. Have you ever fired someone, especially someone you liked? Have you ever had to tell someone he was being retired? Have you ever stood up for someone as a matter of principle, even if it could affect your own job? When you approach the subject of directing the lives of human beings, please approach it with the humility and the respect it deserves.

In general, the control of labor costs on a college campus involves three groups of people: supervisors, regular employees, and student employees. The same basic

areas concern your relationships with each group:
- Supervision
- Staffing
- Wage Determination
- Promotions
- Assessment of Productivity (Evaluation)
- Control of Overtime
- Maintenance of Flexibility
- Control Mechanisms

Supervisors

Some people use the word supervisor to indicate one level of management above that of a unit manager. No such meaning is intended in this book. The term is being used interchangeably with "manager" and is meant to designate anyone, man or woman*, with management responsibilities who reports to the food service director.

Supervision -- Since the end of World War II, behavioral scientists have espoused the cause of participative management; they have pointed out the value of each employee taking part in some decision-making, taking part in goal setting ("management of objectives") and believing that he too is part of management. If you disregard these relatively new theories of modern management you will be in trouble. Involving as many members of your staff as possible in the decision-making process is the best way to manage. Nevertheless, in spite of these new discoveries, it is still true that you cannot operate a food service without adequate supervision. No matter how loyal your employees, no matter how long they have been there, no matter how enthusiastic and intelligent your student workers, each and every one of them needs, wants, and is entitled to knowledgeable, intelligent, sensitive, and helpful supervision. A quality food service operation doesn't just happen, it is created as a result of painstaking planning and dedication on your part, faithful follow-through on the part of your supervisors, and loyal execution on the part of your employees.

Since supervisors are so important to your success, one of your first acts should be to decide just what type of supervisor you will need to help you (see Chapter IV). With reference to cost controls, you must also decide how much supervision you can afford. Your decision is crucial: if you hire too many supervisors, it will take you years to reduce the number; if you hire too few, you will not achieve your quality objectives. If you hire supervisors with excessive qualifications, your cost will be too high, and your turnover of supervisors will be great. If you hire relatively inexperienced supervisors, or promote excessively from within, your quality standards will suffer. What should you do?

Staffing -- Unless you are walking into a new operation which has never been staffed before chances are you will inherit a staff of supervisory people. These may be head cooks and head salad workers or assistant managers, or in some cases, even

See also explanation on page 1.

managers who were by-passed for your job. At first, don't make any changes at all. Be like the fourth grade teacher who, upon hearing that the new boy had been a disciplinary problem in his former school, said, "I don't want to see his records, I would rather find out for myself." Give every supervisor a chance, and wait to see what happens. On the other hand, you must have at least one or two persons on whom you can depend to help carry out your plans. If you feel surrounded by a staff which is incompetent, untrained, or even hostile, you need help from someone you trust, someone you can depend on. Thus it is quite legitimate, if you can justify the need for another supervisor, to hire someone from outside your institution. Someone with fresh and new ideas from somewhere else may be just what you need.

It is impossible, in a book, to provide specific answers about the number of supervisors you may need to help run your operation. A few suggestions may assist you, however, in making your decisions:

Let your supervision filter downward -- Whenever possible, appoint kitchen department heads (such as head cooks, head salad makers, head porters) from among your staff. This will be good for morale, good for efficiency, and may enable you to manage effectively with fewer full-time supervisors. The slight extra cost in wages is well worth the price.

Do not staff for "weekend relief" -- While you do need some sort of supervision on weekends, you probably should not hire a supervisor just for this purpose alone. Before you do, consider the possibilities, such as the use of student managers on weekends, the hiring of supervisory trainees, or perhaps both.

Assign each supervisor a special task -- In addition to regular assignments, each supervisor can be given an additional assignment that will help the entire food service operation. Humboldt State University in Arcata, California, has been experimenting very successfully with this system. Each supervisor has some campus-wide duties in addition to his daily tasks. One is responsible for all the food ordering, another for the hiring and scheduling of all student workers, a third handles the catering, etc.

Groom someone to be your principal assistant -- Remember that one sign of a good food service director is his ability to leave the campus for days at a time without any noticeable change in the efficiency of the operation.

Allow each supervisor sufficient time to visit with the students -- Spending time talking to the students, visiting in the dining room during meal time and in general getting to know students are vital functions of supervision. As you decide on your staffing pattern, allow enough time for this important activity.

Wage determination -- Some experts feel that the wages paid in the rest of the institution are an important guide, others use the cost of living as a basis for deciding salaries. Most generally, the prevailing average wage paid for specific positions by similar institutions and by the local restaurant industry in your region is the best basis for making salary decisions, since there is no position on campus that can be compared to that of a food supervisor. Cost of living may be an important factor in deciding raises, but not necessarily in deciding salary ranges. When you use the prevailing wage structure for similar positions in your region, then you will have a defensible policy. Where you feel that these wages are too low or too high is immaterial. You must, of course, offer competitive salaries in order to recruit successfully, but you cannot set salaries which are seriously out of line with those in nearby schools.

Promotions -- Colleges and universities are not operated like commercial restaurants. Employees should not have to ask for raises. Your institution should have a basic personnel policy regarding salary increases, and so should the food service. Once you yield to an employee's demand for a raise, your labor cost control goes out the window. When you hire your supervisors, make it clear from the outset that any increases in salary will be either annual increases, or increases due to reclassification to a higher position.

In addition to the problem of labor cost, promotions are difficult matters to decide for yet another reason: the famous "Peter Principle." You have heard the truism that people are often promoted to the level of their incompetence. Once you have promoted someone who is incompetent, it is very difficult to undo the damage. Sometimes it takes years, sometimes never. Be certain, therefore, that the person being promoted is really able to do the higher job, not only right now, but also in the future. If in doubt, wait a while, make the promotion temporary, or forget it.

Assessment of productivity -- How do you rate a supervisor? How do you decide whether or not he is doing his job? Can you develop quantitative, objective standards by which to evaluate your supervisors' performance? Admittedly, it is difficult. Many of the areas of performance cannot be objectively judged: how well does he get along with the employees, with the students, with the faculty? How effective is his production supervision? How dependable is he? How much does he contribute to the accomplishment of your goals? Yet these criteria are just as important as more objective ones such as: the food and labor costs in his operation, ability to follow a budget, and the existence of a performance plan.

Performance appraisal is as important in the case of your supervisors as it is with all other employees. You should sit down and prepare for your future use a list of questions to be asked, a performance appraisal form for your supervisors. Review this list with your supervisors when you have completed it, and modify it if you get some good suggestions. It is much more difficult to sit down with your supervisors and evaluate their performance if you have not formalized the process in advance. Performance appraisal need not be a difficult or painful experience; it can be something both of you look forward to, a positive, mutually rewarding and informative experience.

Sometimes, performance appraisal becomes a necessary first step to disciplinary action. Every new manager must face the problem of the non-producer whom he must either "shape up or ship out." Working closely with your school's personnel department, you should thoroughly document each case, starting with performance evaluations, then proceeding to letters which state improvement needs, written warning notices, and finally if necessary, a letter of dismissal.

Control of overtime -- Most states have an Industrial Welfare Commission which defines clearly what qualifies a person to be classified as a supervisor. In California a supervisor is defined as anyone who earns at least $720 per month, and is responsible for the work of at least two (2) other employees. Anyone in your organization who does not qualify as a supervisor in accordance with the laws of your state is probably entitled to overtime, at time-and-a-half of regular pay. Chances are the above definition applies only to your supervisory trainees, and you can arrange to keep track of their overtime when it occurs. Your regular supervisors should not expect, nor be paid overtime. They are hired as and compensated for being managers. Managers do not, as a rule, work a limited number of hours, even if they do normally work according to a regular schedule. During emergencies, the managers must manage. During strikes, the managers are the only ones you can count on to work. You and they are on the same team.

Obviously, you must not take unfair advantage of your supervisors. There are many ways in which you can compensate them for working extra hard: an afternoon off for some physical exercise, or other personal reasons, time off with pay during recess or vacation periods, or perhaps even time off during the regular school year, when you can spare someone for a day or two. Compensatory time, yes; overtime payments, no. That should be your basic approach to your supervisors. There is one occasion when you might want to compensate supervisors for overtime, however. If you have a large, unionized food service where lower-level supervisors receive overtime payments under the terms of the union contract, it may well be appropriate to compensate even the higher-level supervisors similarly for extra time worked.

Maintenance of flexibility -- When you have a flexible payroll, it is much easier to control labor costs. Unfortunately, in the case of supervisors, it is difficult to achieve. Not many food service managers have someone whom they can call on as a substitute, the way a school principal can call on substitute teachers. Few have a supervisor who may be retired, but who is willing to work one or two days in an emergency. As a result, you can do one of two things. You can either be slightly overstaffed in supervision to take care of emergencies and absenteeism or you can always be a little short-handed when one of your supervisors is off. This is where a supervisory training program comes in handy both in the training of regular full-time trainees, and in the training of student managers. If you keep your eyes open, you will always find some young man or woman, or perhaps even one not so young, who is interested in being trained for a career as a food supervisor. Since such a trainee can do some productive work (e.g. weekend supervision, relief supervision, catering functions, etc.), you can justify the payment of a modest salary, perhaps ⅔ or ¾ of the regular salary of a supervisor. The more flexibility you retain in staffing, the lower will be your labor cost.

Control mechanisms -- Food supervisors are professional employees and should, therefore, be treated in the same manner as teachers and other salaried employees. When hired at the beginning of the school year, there should be a written obligation on your part to employ a new supervisor for the duration of the school year (barring exceptional circumstances) and a written agreement on the part of the supervisor to stay for the entire school year. Under those circumstances, then the control of your supervisory payroll must occur *before* you do the hiring. Careful evaluation concerning the number of supervisory employees, the needed qualification (not everyone, after all, needs to have 5 years of previous experience in order to be a good supervisor!) and the period of their contract has to be done each year. You may not need every supervisor for a 12-month period, and many might prefer to be hired on a 10-month basis. The use of student supervisors to assist your professional staff is also one way of controlling supervisory costs.

Regular Employees

A note about union shops: The following principles concern the supervision of regular employees in any food service operation. Should you happen to be employed in a university with a labor union contract, all of the principles still apply, though they are modified by a collective bargaining agreement. Some managers confronted with a union use that fact to avoid following good management principles and abdicate their rights as managers.

A good manager understands the union contract thoroughly and uses his college personnel department for counsel and access to sound legal advice. Good management principles can often prevent a union shop from ever coming to a campus, but the important point is that principles apply equally in all situations.

The largest part of your payroll is spent on regular employees. The word "regular employees" is used in this book to denote a steady employee (either full-time or part-time), as distinguished from temporary or student employees, and from supervisors. More important than the payroll, regular employees are the ones who will make the difference between your success and failure. If you have a well-trained, loyal, and conscientious staff, you will probably run a high-quality and profitable food operation. Without such a staff, you can do nothing at all. In fine commercial restaurants, the professional skills of the kitchen staff are all-important. The head chef must be able to prepare a large variety of dishes, the pantry chef must be able to do fancy decorations and possess other special skills, the baker must be a pastry chef and bake all types of fancy desserts. If they possess these skills, the personal characteristics and behavior of the individuals may not be important to the restaurant owner. In colleges and universities it is the opposite. While cooking and salad making skills are important, these can be taught. Institutional cooking is not, after all, too complicated. What is more important, however, is the *character* and *personality* of each kitchen worker. If a chef in a hotel wants to swear or have temper tantrums or go on a rampage, that's between him and the hotel. No such behavior can ever be tolerated on a college campus: If a dishwasher in a restaurant goes on three-day binge every payday, and the restaurateur wants to permit it, that is his privilege. However, you, as a college food service manager cannot permit it. It is more important that your staff consists of intelligent, decent, hard-working, pleasant people, than that they possess superior culinary skills. As you review your kitchen staff, remember that your clients, the students, and staff, will judge you partly on the quality of your food, and partly on what they feel about your employees. If there is anyone working for you whom you would not trust to baby-sit with your small child, or whom you would be embarrassed to have visit in your home, then he or she is probably working in the wrong place. The time to discover this, ideally, is during the initial probation period, and not later on.

Supervision -- Good supervision is essential in any successful food service operation. Even the very best workers who in emergencies can do a superb job all by themselves, need the advice, the control, and the stimulation that a good supervisor provides. You cannot be everywhere at once. Your office work, in fact, will take up much more time than you are willing to give it, but it requires your presence, just the same. You can only effectively supervise a small number of people. Your "span of control" is limited and therefore your supervisors must represent you. There are some who think that good kitchen workers, especially those in colleges, can work without someone to tell them what to do; don't believe it. Since the productivity is one of the determinants of labor costs, your supervisors will assist you in getting high productivity from your regular staff. They do this not by threats or discipline, but rather by good advance planning, by friendly advice, by optimum scheduling and assignment of the kitchen help, and by constant training.

Careful planning for supervision over the work of your regular and student employees is an essential aspect of your efforts to control labor costs through high productivity.

Staffing -- One of the most difficult assignments facing a new manager is deciding on the size of his kitchen staff if the decision is his to make. Most likely, you will inherit an already existing staff and be told by your boss that you probably have more people than you need. If you ask your kitchen workers, they may tell you, "we are working our heads off and badly need additional help, but nobody in the front office is listening." Don't get discouraged, you won't have the right answer for at least six months. Food service does not have industry-wide standards like those of the automobile or hotel industry. A maid in an average hotel can make up 12-14 rooms per day, but how many salads should a salad maker make? You can use some statistical data such as "meals served per labor hour" (See page 83) but that alone won't give you the correct answer. The ideal college kitchen is staffed with a finely-honed combination of regular and student employees, and the exact mix depends very much on the individual school, the menus prepared, type and quality of supervision, and other related factors. Ideally, you should have two or three part-time students working an average of 10-12 hours per week for every full-time regular employee. Whether you have too many employees or too few will be discovered in times of emergencies. A flu epidemic in February, for instance, when 15%-20% of your staff is out sick, will quickly tell you what your minimum needs are.

There is no way for you to know in advance just what the right staffing pattern should be in your kitchens. You have to learn the answer by trial-and-error and you alone must make the final decision. Take a kitchen which prepares food for, let us say, 800 students. How many cooks are needed to prepare three meals daily for such a number of students? If you search long enough, you will find college kitchens employing two, three, four, and five cooks per day, and in each case you will be told that the number is "just right." Below, you will find a staffing schedule for a residence hall kitchen which prepares food for approximately 750 students, of whom about 33% eat breakfast, and 90% eat lunch and dinner. While the example is typical of many residence hall kitchens, you should try to do better and aim for a higher productivity through more efficient staffing.

Staffing Guide for Residence Hall Kitchen Serving 750 Students

Regular Employees

A.M. Shift	**P.M. Shift**
(5:00 a.m. - 2:30 p.m.)*	**(10:00 a.m. - 7:00 p.m.)**
1 Lead Cook	1 Lead Cook
1 Second Cook	1 Second Cook
2 Salad and Line Workers	1 Salad and Line Worker
1 Dishwasher	1 Dishwasher
1 Potwasher/Porter	1 Potwasher/Porter
1 Hostess/Cashier	
(7:30 a.m. - 4:00 p.m.)*	

*Regular employees are normally scheduled for a nine-hour period, which in residence halls, allows time for two 30 minute meal periods. Those working other shifts take only one 30 minute meal period.

Student Employees

Breakfast (7:30 - 9:30)	**Lunch (11:15 - 1:30)**	**Dinner (4:15 - 6:30)**
Dining Room Runner 1	Dining Room Runner 1	Dining Room Runner 1
Serving Line 1	Serving Lines (2) 4	Serving Lines (2) 4
Serving Line Runner 1	Serving Line Runners 2	Serving Line Runners 2
Dishroom 1	Dishroom 3	Dishroom 3
Total Hours: 8	Total Hours: 22½	Dining Room Porters 2
		Hostess/Cashier 1
		Total Hours: 29¼

Please note: The above-cited staffing example gives you a productivity of approximately ten (10) meals per labor hour:

> 750 students x 3 meals/day = 2,250 meals paid for per day
> less: 29% missed meals factor = 1,600 meals eaten per day

> Total hours worked: Regular Employees   96 per day
> Total hours worked: Student Employees   59¾ per day

> TOTAL 155¾ per day

Meals per Labor Hours: 1,600 ÷ 155¾ = 10.3

In addition to preparing staffing guides for each operation, it is essential that you post actual work schedules for every day of the week. On weekends, you will need fewer workers, perhaps you will use more students. Unless you have everyone's work schedule clearly posted, you cannot retain tight control over your labor costs. Sample work schedules are shown in Exhibit VI-12 and VI-13.

Retirement practices -- Since productivity and labor cost control are closely tied together, and since the productivity of older workers frequently drops with advancing age, it is essential that you face the problem of retirement of your older employees squarely and honestly. Some schools, of course, have a suggested retirement age of 65, in which case you have little freedom of action. There is nothing magic about the age of 65. Some of your workers start slowing down long before that, and others are still going strong at age 70. How should you handle retirement in an effective but gracious manner?

The most traumatic aspect of a forced retirement is usually the suddenness with which it occurs. Often the employee is simply called into the office and told flatly that his or her services are no longer needed. A much better approach is to give each employee a year or two to prepare for it, both mentally and financially. When one of your older employees is clearly losing his or her effectiveness, you are not the only one to know it; the employee knows it also. There is nothing wrong in calling him in for a counseling session to discuss with the employee whether he has given some thought about retirement "sometime in the future." At that time, too, you can bring up the subject of a partial retirement at first whereby the employee could still plan to work two or three days a week in your kitchens, or be available as a steady substitute on a call-in basis. Such partial employment, when added to Social Security benefits, is often enough to make partial retirement financially feasible, and actually offers the older employee a solution which he might not have thought of. It is also a gracious solution; as the employee gets older, the timing of complete retirement becomes almost a mutual decision, and all the trauma and pain have been removed from the process.

One thing you cannot do is overlook the problem. As people get older and their reflexes slower, they become a danger to themselves and others when working in a large institutional kitchen. The floors are often slippery, the equipment dangerous, and the chance of injury is great. The ultimate responsibility is yours, and therefore you must act.

Wage determination -- In most institutions, the decision on wages will not be yours to make. If it is a state college or university, there will be state-wide wage schedules for every position. If you have a unionized staff, the wages will be negotiated by others. Even if it is a private institution, the basic wage rates for non-classified workers have probably already been established. Nevertheless, you will be amazed how much important input you will eventually have on wage and salary determination in food service. Your bosses will look to you as the expert who knows what the appropriate wages should be. They will expect you to keep age levels within reasonable bounds or to fight for higher wages if present ones are unrealistically low.

EXHIBIT VI-12

NO.	JOB	NAME	HOURS	23 MON	24 TUES	25 WED	26 THURS	27 FRI	28 SAT	29 SUN	30 MON	31 TUES	1 WED	2 THURS	3 FRI	4 SAT	5 SUN
	Date Oct.23-Nov 5,1978																
1	MANAGER	Eddie Lang							off —								
2	BREAKFAST COOK	Abigael G.	6-3	6°°	6°°	6°°	6°°	off	10-7	off	off	6°°	6°°	6°°	6°°	off	off
3	COOK'S HELPER	Alba O.	10-7	10	10	6	off	6	10-7	10-7	6	10	off	off	10	9-2	off
4	HEAD SALAD	Catherine K.	6-3	6					off	off	6						
5		Rose D.	6-3	6				off	off	6					off	6-3	off
6		Thelma K.	10-7	10	10	off	off	10	10	off	10-7	10	10	off	10-7	10-7	10-7
7		Margaret B	10-7	10					off	10-7	off	10				off	off
8		Evelyn E.	10-7	off	off	10-7	10-7	6-3	10-7	off	10-7	off	6-3	10-7	6-3	10-7	10-7
9	Relief	Ella H.							10-7								
10	CASHIER	Pamela A.	10-7						off	off	10-7					off	off
11	HEAD PORTER	Jose A.	6-3						off	off						off	off
12	Porter	Arnel S.	12-9	12-9	12-9	off	12-9	12-9	11-8	11-8	12-9	off	off	11-9	12-9	12-9	off
13	AFTERNOON COOK	Bing M.	10-7	10-7	off	10-7		off	10-7					off	10-7	off	
14		Vina D.	10-7	off	10-7			9-6	off	10-7	off	10-7	10-7	10-7	off	9-6	
15	RELIEF MANAGER	Sheri H.							-10-7 —								
16	RELIEF COOK	Fred G.	6-3	6-3		off	6-3		off	off	6-3				off	10-7	
17	Breakfast Cook Relief	Anita H.	6-3	6-3							6-3	6-3					
18																	

LEGEND

F----DINING ROOM & BUFFET TABLE
RP---REST PERIOD
SC---SHIFT CHANGE
PT---PART TIME

DR----DISH ROOM
K-----KITCHEN
SDR---SERVICE DINING ROOM

EXHIBIT VI-13

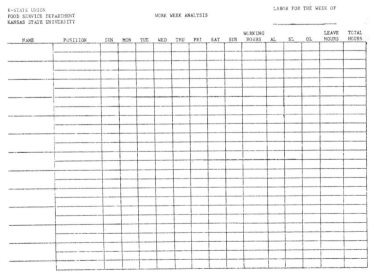

K-STATE UNION
FOOD SERVICE DEPARTMENT
KANSAS STATE UNIVERSITY

WORK WEEK ANALYSIS

LABOR FOR THE WEEK OF

NAME	POSITION	SUN	MON	TUE	WED	THU	FRI	SAT	SUN	WORKING HOURS	AL	SL	OL	LEAVE HOURS	TOTAL HOURS

AL = Annual Leave (Vacation_
SL = Sick Leave
OL = Other Leave

When it comes to wages for your regular employees, there are a number of factors which must be considered:

Area wages for similar occupations -- As with supervisors, the most important element in setting wages is to make them competitive with similar jobs in your area. You should be familiar with prevailing wage schedules of your local hotel and restaurant union, as well as the general scales paid in non-union food service operations. In making wage recommendations to your superiors, this information should always be included to provide a sound basis for comparison.

Wages of other non-classified employees on campus -- Unlike food service supervisors, who really have no one on campus to compare themselves with, your regular employees will most certainly compare their own salaries with that of the janitors, maids, and other maintenance workers on campus. Even though the food service industry is notoriously low-paid (and you cannot change that all by yourself), there should be some reasonable relationship between the hourly wages of a cook, for instance, when compared to those of a maid or janitor. Although you will be able to offer some special fringe benefits, such as free meals when working, these do not always make up for what may be significant wage differences between the two positions.

Minimum and maximum wages -- The federal and state governments have, during the past decade, taken the problem of minimum wages away from the individual operator, and have, for all practical purposes, made the decision for him. Chances are that your starting wages for any regular employee will be dictated by the area wage scale and the availability of labor at that prevailing wage scale. Your greater problem is likely to be that of excessive wages, caused by annual wage increases which may have been far greater than the increase in the cost of living. This is a special, and serious problem for many colleges and universities. If you don't watch out, you could find that after ten years of continuous wage increases, your kitchen employees are all earning 20%-33% above prevailing area wages. This is a natural set-up for a new food service director who can come in with a promise to save the college thousands of dollars in salaries merely by firing every kitchen employee and re-hiring a new staff at more reasonable wages.

It is appropriate and necessary to establish maximum wage rates for every position in your kitchen. It is equally appropriate to let everyone know just what these maximums are. If a salad worker, for example, has reached her maximum wage, then she knows that the only way she can earn more money is to be promoted to cook. Cost of living adjustments, of course, are not a part of these considerations, but must be continuously provided for, if you wish to retain your present staff.

Promotions -- As with raises for supervisors, pay raises for regular employees should normally occur just once a year, either on the anniversary date of employment or when everyone else on campus gets theirs. Regardless of how valuable a specific employee may be to your organization, you simply cannot cave in to individual wage demands by employees. You can, of course, suggest possible changes in status, or changes in work schedules, or anything else that may mollify a good employee who is asking for a raise. In fact, offering possible chances for promotion is really a much better way to upgrade an employee than merely paying him more money. Here are some natural promotion opportunities in your college food service unit:

- Porter or dishwasher to head porter
- Line worker to salad maker
- Breakfast cook to dinner cook
- Salad maker to head salad maker
- Dinner cook to head cook

In order to make such promotions more meaningful, and to be certain that those whom you promote are fully qualified to work at the next higher level, you might establish some formal, written criteria for each position. For example, how would you determine whether or not a breakfast cook is really able to assume the greater responsibilities of cooking the dinner meal? One solution would be to establish a test period of one week, during which the breakfast cook, with a minimum of skilled assistance from others would be asked to cook the unit's dinner meal. At the end of the week, both you and the cook would know whether or not he had passed the test. The same general idea can be followed with all other promotions; the better you structure each job, and each step-up, the fairer you will be perceived by your staff, and the higher will be their morale.

Merit versus step increases -- Those who favor merit increases will argue convincingly that employees who work hardest and are most productive should get an increase, while those who merely perform an average amount of work should not get one, or if they do, it should be a smaller increase. This is fine in theory and may work quite well in certain establishments, especially those which are privately owned. As a general rule, however, merit increases do not work well in institutional food service. They often cause more problems than they solve. In order for a merit system to work, the supervisor must be able to evaluate, clearly and objectively, the relative performance of each worker vis-a-vis the other workers. This is very difficult to do in a large kitchen, where a number of workers perform the same job at different times, and usually most, or all of them perform the job well. Sometimes you may find a significant difference in quality of work or in work attitude, or even in work performance between one employee and another. The question, however, is whether you are willing to risk alienation and disaffection of those employees who do not get the merit increase merely in order to show your gradritude to the superior worker. A kitchen staff is a closely-knit social group, and a system of merit increases may cause more divisiveness than you bargained for, and may actually harm your overall productivity.

As a general rule, it is wiser to stick to automatic step increases by classification of employee. By doing this, you are notifying your employees that if their work is satisfactory throughout the year, they will earn a raise at the beginning of next year. Obviously, you have the right to give somewhat larger raises to your cooks, for example, than to your porters, whose job demands less skill. Sometimes, your increases for each classification will be based on how the average wage in that group compares to the prevailing area wage. There may be other times when everyone in your food service operation will get the same amount of raise, either as a percentage of his salary (say 5%), or else as a fixed amount (say $.20 per hour).

Confidentiality of wage increases -- Any effort to keep salaries or wages confidential is doomed to failure; don't waste your time. While it is proper to make salary and wage notifications a private affair (between the supervisor and each individual worker), there is no way you can keep the employee from talking with another about his wages. Once you recognize this, you won't be tempted to make special "arrangements" with favorite employees, at the expense of the others. In fact, if you do decide on uniform increases for each classification, it is often better to be quite open about it, and let your people know what these increases are. Many schools have clearly defined job classifications and wage scales, and publish their wage schedules for everyone to see. Remember, anything you can do to build up a solid level of mutual trust between you and your staff will help you in your career, and wage administration is a good place to start.

Assessment of productivity -- It is difficult for a new manager to know how productive his workers should be. In the absence of experience on the job, and without such aids as time-and-motion studies, he cannot always tell whether or not an employee is overloaded with work, or is just performing less well than normal. An interesting case is the one of the "mayonnaise lady," a salad worker at the University of California at Davis who was fired for being too slow. Her employer claimed, among other things, that she did not spread the mayonnaise on sandwiches evenly and fast enough. She fought the dismissal in court. The University's Board of Regents decided to make the case a matter of principle, and carried the case all the way up to the State Supreme Court. The Regents lost. One of the reasons given was that their claims as to the worker's incompetence were vague, and that productivity standards for making sandwiches had not been clearly established.

Good labor cost control depends upon receiving high productivity from your workers. This being the case, it is essential that you know and can define for your staff just what this productivity is, and what you expect from them. Often, in college kitchens, the regular workers have been literally "spoiled" with student help, to the extent that when they are asked to do a normal day's work alone, they think they are being overworked. One of your priorities, therefore, should be the establishment of clear job specifications which will give in detail the work expected from each employee. Student workers should be assigned to help only when a clear need exists, and not merely to make things a little easier for your regular staff. Some sample job descriptions are shown in Exhibit VI-14.

As in the case of your supervisors, regular employees, too, need annual performance appraisals. These should be done by their immediate supervisor, and should be carried on in a relaxed, non-threatening manner. The appraisal should be an occasion where the two can talk with each other, where the employee can get some things off his chest, and where the supervisor can do some helpful job counselling. It is a grand opportunity for two-way communications. You are wise if you establish

EXHIBIT VI-14

MEMORIAL UNION AND STUDENT ACTIVITIES:
OREGON STATE UNIVERSITY, CORVALLIS, OREGON

Position Description: Food Service Aide, Salads
Responsible to: Food Service Supervisor, Production

General Description:
Assists in the overall preparation of attractive and appetizing salads; performs clean-up operations in work area and sets up salads on display areas on lines.

Specific Duties and Responsibilities:
1. Assists in the preparation of various types of attractive and apetizing salads and dressings.
2. Cleans and prepares all ingredients for salads.
3. Prepares all dressings for salads.
4. Sets up salads and dressings on serving lines.
5. Prepares salads for all luncheons, banquets and buffets.
6. Assists in the ordering of salad ingredients from storeroom clerk on proper stores requisition sheet.
7. Keeps refrigerators and salad area clean at all times.
8. Assists in training all new employees in the proper methods and procedures of salad preparation.
9. Other duties are assigned by food service supervisor, production.
10. Is constantly alert for new recipes and ideas for salad area.
11. Helps maintain highest satndards of safety and sanitation in assigned area.
12. Cooperates in establishing good relationships with all M. U. Food Service employees.

UNIVERSITY OF THE PACIFIC
FOOD SERVICE

Job Description: Cafeteria Line Worker

Job Summary:
Responsible for serving the hot food items and maintaining proper portion sizes. The line worker should also be responsible for keeping the serving area clean both during and after meal service. This person also should inform the inside runner of anticipated food needs. When not busy the server can replenish desserts or help in other areas of the ktichen as specified by the manager. The server plays an important role in promoting good public relations with the students: thus, friendliness is most necessary.

Responsibilities:
1. Serves the main entree and vegetable.
2. Uses proper portion sizes for serving food. Checks to see that food is hot.
3. Keeps area clean during the serving time as much as possible.
4. Replenishes desserts as needed.
5. Makes sure that plates are hot.
6. Other duties are assigned.

Clean-Up Responsibilities:
1. Cleans steam wells. Both the top of the steam table and the glass in front of it should be cleaned.
2. The dessert display area should be cleaned -- including all three shelves and glass.
3. Cleans tray line in front of serving line.
4. Removes ice cream from small freezer and wipes out freezer.
5. Wipes under steam wells where plates are kept.
6. Wipes out inside and outside of back-up warmers.
7. Cleans out sink behind the serving area.
8. Other duties as assigned.

establish such performance appraisals as a regular feature of your personnel program. A sample evaluation form is shown in Exhibit VI-15.

Getting high productivity out of the kitchen employee depends not only on the employee; there are many reasons for low productivity in the food service industry which are the fault of management, not the worker. Here are some for you to think about:

Frequent distractions -- A worker will produce at a maximum rate if he can attend to his job for sustained periods of time without being disturbed. An assembly-line worker, to use an extreme example, does the same job hour after hour and is interrupted only by the bell that calls him for the coffee break or for the lunch hour. A kitchen worker, in the middle of making salads, is interrupted dozens of times:

- May, they're out of coffee in the dining room; could you make some please?

- Ella, Jim needs a sack lunch, and he's in a hurry!

- Abbie, they need you on the line for a few minutes.

The pot washer, most abused of all in this connection, can never reduce the stack of pots and pans with constant interruptions like these:

- Jack, there's milk all over the receiving dock; would you just take a minute to clean it up?

- Reggie, would you give me a hand with this crate of lettuce?

- Jim, somebody spilled something in the dining room; please bring a mop right away!

These are examples of daily occurrences, and there is no way to prevent them. As a good manager, you should be aware of what they do to your workers' productivity and decide how you can best staff your kitchen with a minimum of work interruptions. Frequently a student "floater" who can perform all these little chores during the busy meal hours can be the answer.

Poor kitchen layout -- Another frequent cause of low productivity is poor layout of the kitchen. Good kitchens are efficient because they are designed by architects and consultants *in conjunction with* the food service managers. Cooks and salad workers need sinks and refrigerators near their work stations, not 15 feet away. Receiving areas need hot and cold water hose bibs and large floor drains right where the food is set down from the trucks. Coffee urn stations need cabinet space for the coffee and other urn equipment. These are all obvious examples, but many are forgotten in the planning of commercial kitchens. Some of the worst examples can be found in ultramodern institutional kitchens where the designer confused size with efficiency, and where all the workers take hundreds of unnecessary steps every day just to traverse the great distances between one department and another.

Poor personnel -- Some workers are just plain "slow-pokes"; they have just one speed, slow, and there is no way you can get them to shift into second or third gear. Normally, with firmness, fairness, and friendliness (the three F's in personnel handling) you can get most people to speed up their work. The nervousness of the first few

EXHIBIT VI-15

STANFORD UNIVERSITY PERFORMANCE RATING
FOR FOOD SERVICE EMPLOYEES

Employee's Name_____ Job Title_____
Date_____Rating Period Covered_____

Key for Rating: E (Excellent), G (Good), F (Fair), P (Poor)

ATTITUDE: RATING
1. Carries out assignment without constant supervision.   _____
2. Follows new mehtods willingly.   _____
3. Realizes importance of employees working as a team.   _____
   COMMENTS:

COOPERATION:
1. Keeps supervisor informed of important details.   _____
2. Offers practical suggestions.   _____
3. Willingly does his share and more when necessary.   _____
4. Accepts necessary changes readily.   _____
   COMMENTS:

WORKING ABILITY:
1. an be depended upon to follow instructions.   _____
2. Works with care; seldom makes mistakes.   _____
3. Takes pride in his work.   _____
4. Observes safety rules to avoid qccidents.   _____
   COMMENTS:

MAINTENANCE OF FOOD STANDARDS:
1. Shows interest in learning good food standards.   _____
2. Observes correct procedures in food preparation and
   handling.   _____
3. Has "Clean as you go" work habits.   _____
4. Follows cleaning routines diligently.   _____
   COMMENTS:

RELATION WITH CO-WORKERS AND STUDENTS:
1. Makes good impression on those he serves.   _____
2. Is alert and helpful to needs of others.   _____
3. Shows mature behavior; commands respect.   _____
4. Is willing to share his knowledge and experience.   _____
   COMMENTS:

PERSONAL APPEARANCE AND HABITS:
1. Is neatly groomed.   _____
2. Observes acceptable personal habits.   _____
3. Shows understanding of importance of correct personal
   habits in handling of food.   _____
   COMMENTS:

DEPENDABILITY:
1. Attendance: Punctual   _____
               Regular in attendance   _____
2. Leave privileges:
   Absences due to illness (dates)_____
   Absences for personal reasons (dates)_____
   Absences due to accidents at work (dates)_____
   COMMENTS:

Rater's Signature_____ Position_____ Date_____

Employee's Signature_____ Date_____

days disappears, and workers will usually gear their own production to that of their peers. If, however, you happen to hire one who simply cannot adjust to the normal pace, be sure to catch this during the probationary period while you can still let the employee go without cause and replace him or her with someone else who can do the job properly.

Poor training and supervision -- Unfortunately, the food service industry is notorious for its poor training methods. On-the-job training in many restaurants and institutions consists principally of telling the new employee, "Go over there and work with Catherine. She'll show you what to do!" Supervision similarly often leaves much to be desired. Sometimes it consists merely of the supervisor making sure that the new employee is physically there, and that someone has given him a job to do. Unless the manager is prepared to take some time and make certain that a new employee knows his job, knows exactly what is expected of him, and knows, also, that he is being supervised, it is probably that he will be less than fully productive in his job.

Lack of incentives -- One of the problems with any production job, in any industry, is that it often is monotonous, and that there is little specific incentive for the worker to produce at a faster rate. It is now commonly known that such benefits as higher wages, good working conditions, and friendly supervision are not, by themselves, sufficient to motivate the worker. On the other hand, praise, recognition, growth on the job, promotion and, most of all, the work itself are factors which strongly stimulate interest and production. Once you, as the manager, are aware of these basic principles of motivation, you can set an example for your supervisors by praising and recognizing the good things your people do, and giving everyone the greatest possible opportunity to grow and develop on the job.

Control of overtime -- If your basic staffing pattern is the first determinant of labor cost, then control of overtime is the second. Once you have decided how many workers to hire and how much to pay them, your only serious variable is the amount of overtime they work. Since overtime is normally paid at the rate of one-and-a-half times regular wages, it doesn't take long for the totals to add up. The key to the overtime problem is *tight control.* Overtime is not something you just allow to happen, nor is it a kind of fringe benefit that you give to your workers in lieu of pay. If you are properly staffed and have a realistic work schedule, overtime becomes necessary only in emergencies, and only if you or one of your managers thinks it necessary. There are three tools you can use to control overtime:

Time cards -- Most state laws provide that you must pay overtime for every 15 minutes worked beyond 8 hours per day or (in the restaurant industry) 48 hours per week. It is therefore important that your employees punch in and out exactly as instructed. Most experienced personnel managers advise that unless you have explicit written instructions governing time card procedures, it is better to pay the time shown on the employee's time card and then counsel the employee if he habitually punches out late, rather than arbitrarily deduct the extra few minutes from the time card. In the case of a conflict, state personnel boards may decide to go by the time shown on the worker's cards. You must make all this clear to your staff, and make it equally clear that anyone who frequently or carelessly punches his time card incorrectly is subject to dismissal from employment.

Overtime authorizations -- Don't make it too easy to get overtime. Make sure that every minute of overtime is formally authorized by the supervisor-on-duty, and is properly recorded in an overtime authorization for, listing the circumstances under which overtime became necessary and was approved by management. Two sample overtime authorization forms are shown in Exhibit VI-16.

Prohibition against all overtime -- In most food service operations, overtime occasionally becomes necessary. A late banquet, an accident in the kitchen, sudden thunder showers which cause everybody to eat later, all these are examples of circumstances beyond your control. Therefore, for special emergencies, each of your managers should have the right to authorize overtime if he deems it necessary. There are some special situations, however, where it may become necessary to prohibit all overtime, regardless of need. Such a situation could arise if you find yourself financially pinched toward the end of the year and your boss insists that you cut costs regardless of the results. At first you will think this impossible, and your entire food service staff will agree. Visions of dirty kitchens and hopeless confusion will be conjured up. When the dust settles, however, you'll discover that you can, in fact, work without overtime, that through judicious scheduling and possible rearrangement of work schedules, overtime can be eliminated at least for a time, from your operations. Once you have been through such an exercise, you will begin to ask yourself much more frequently whether all overtime is really necessary.

Maintenance of flexibility -- In a large food service operation, it is not always easy to employ the exact number of workers that you need. There is always a temptation on the part of the unit manager to hire just one extra person to take care of emergency illnesses, to serve as a spare relief worker or for other reasons. When a rash of colds or other illnesses hits your kitchen in November and again in the spring you want to be protected by having an adequate staff. This is understandable, but a luxury you cannot afford. Instead, you must have flexibility. If at all possible, develop a cadre of part-time or temporary substitutes, workers whom you can call in on short notice to pinch-hit in emergencies. It may actually be wise for you to fill one or two full-time jobs with several such part-time workers, who could expand their work to full-time when necessary. There are always student workers on whom you can call, giving you a tremendous advantage over a commercial operator, whose access to student labor is not as convenient. Nevertheless, there are some jobs in your kitchens which untrained students simply cannot perform adequately, and therefore you should try to develop a somewhat flexible staff from your regular employees.

Employee turnover -- One of the often overlooked factors contributing to high labor cost is employee turnover. It is a difficult factor to control. If you have too high a turnover, it is costly, but if no one ever leaves your employment, and you have a very low rate of turnover, it can also be costly.

EXHIBIT VI-16

NOTICE OF LEAVE OR OVERTIME
FORM SP-6   WASHINGTON STATE UNIVERSITY

| NAME OF EMPLOYEE | | | | | | | | | DATE | |

| EMPLOYING DEPARTMENT | EXPLANATORY COMMENTS |

TYPE OF LEAVE	FROM				TO				TOTAL HOURS
	HR.	MO.	DAY	YR.	HR.	MO.	DAY	YR.	
ANNUAL LEAVE									
COMPENSATORY TIME OFF DUTY									
SICK LEAVE									
MILITARY LEAVE									
LEAVE FOR CIVIL DUTY									
LEAVE WITHOUT PAY									
ABSENCE WITHOUT OFFICIAL LEAVE									

WHERE EXTENDED LEAVE WITHOUT PAY IS REQUESTED, GIVE THE REASONS FOR SUCH LEAVE. MEDICAL CERTIFICATES MUST ACCOMPANY ALL REQUESTS FOR SICK LEAVE IN EXCESS OF ONE WEEK. THE SPACE PROVIDED ON THE BACK OF THIS FORM MAY BE USED FOR THIS PURPOSE. CERTIFICATION OF SHORTER SICK LEAVE IS NOT REQUIRED.

APPROVAL – EMPLOYING DEPARTMENT

APPROVAL – STAFF PERSONNEL

OVERTIME WORK

OVERTIME AUTHORIZATION

Date _10/25/73_

Name _Mary Jones_   Unit _Quad_

Reason for Overtime _Worked 6th day_

Helped with banquet

Amount of Overtime: _6½_ Hrs.

Signature of Unit Manager

High employee turnover -- There is something wrong with an organization in which employees constantly come and go. It may be the wages paid, the personnel policies, the nature of the work, or a combination of reasons which cause such a turnover. In terms of labor productivity, however, the results can be terrible. First, the employer is trianing and, in effect, subsidizing the new employee until he has learned enough to do the job for which he was hired. In food service, this is usually a matter of a few days at least, and these few non-productive days add up when there is a frequent hiring of new employees. Second, there is a negative effect on the quality of the food operation while the new employee is learning the ropes; he makes mistakes often at the expense of the students who are eating what he has prepared. Third, the frequent departures of employees are bound to have an adverse effect on staff morale. When everyone else is leaving, those who remain wonder what is wrong with the place. Fourth, there is always the let-down which normally characterizes the work of a departing employee during his last week of work. Often his work is so poor that you wish he hadn't shown up at all. Finally, there is the direct cost of higher unemployment compensation rates which you will pay if you have a high rate of turnover. Even if some employees leave of their own accord, a high rate of turnover usually means also a high rate of dismissals, and these are a direct addition to your labor costs.

Low employee turnover -- Paradoxically, an unusually low turnover can be just as costly to you. A certain amount of staff change is normal and healthy. If you are managing a food service operation in a small town, for example, where your college may be one of the largest employers and other jobs are hard to get, then you will probably experience a relatively low rate of staff turnover. The following are some of the problems which this can cause you: First, you may be paying *excessively high wages.* If an employee has received a wage increase every year for ten years, then his wages may have crept up to a point beyond what is reasonable or common for the work being done. This point was covered earlier in the section under Wage Determination. Second, some long-term employees (admittedly, there are many exceptions) may *lose their initial enthusiasm* and ambition after many years in the same job, and little chance for a promotion or a change. Third, your *fringe benefits will go up,* as long-term employees earn more and more vacation and sick leave benefits. Finally, there is the real problem of *"in-breeding":* your operation will be characterized by a routineness, a monotony caused by absence of fresh ideas brought into your operations by new employees from their previous place of employment, employees who look at your operations from a more objective point of view.

There is not much you can do to increase your rate of turnover. A consistent retirement policy helps, however. An awareness of the problem helps also. Sometimes it may mean letting an old and trusted employee go, rather than making special concessions to keep him.

Control mechanisms -- The success in all your efforts to control labor costs and to keep these within budget lines depends on your ability to tell where you are and where you are heading at any point in time. An earlier portion of this chapter deals with the use of weekly reports, which show either the labor-cost-per-meal or the meals-served-per-labor-hour, or both these statistics on a weekly, monthly and year-to-date basis. It also stresses the importance of overtime authorization forms. There are other simple control tools. One is to simply add the cost of each payroll (preferably broken down into supervisory, regular, and student labor) to the previous one, in order to get a to date comparison of total payroll amounts expended so far. Another is to ask for, or prepare weekly reports for any labor (regular or student) which was used in excess of the standard staffing schedule. Labor cost percentages of total income are also easy to develop and helpful to you in analyzing whether or not you are still within your budget. Occasional audits of time cards by you or someone in your office are also effective controls. You have a choice of many tools with which to control your cost of labor. Be sure to use them regularly.

Some managers may find it helpful to calculate labor costs daily, as is the practice in large hotels. This procedure is especially helpful in cash operations with large catering activities, since it tells the manager immediately whether he is staffing his highly fluctuating operations properly. An example of such daily costing is found in Appendix 12.

Student Employees

It has been stated earlier that student workers are essential to your success. They provide flexibility in staffing, they are ambassadors of good will, they are generally intelligent, eager to please and a joy to have around. All this "joy" should not blind you, however, to the fact that even student labor costs money and must therefore be controlled. Remember also that student workers are your employees, not your clients, and should be treated as such. Most of your student workers will start as freshmen. Few will have had any prior meaningful work. Your responsibility for their training and character development is real and awesome. The habits and attitudes which your student workers develop while on your campus may well become the basis for their work habits the rest of their lives. Some food service managers do not fully understand this point. They feel that student employees must be treated in a special way, gently, condescendingly, with special empathy and understanding. Others feel that any student, worker or not, is a client of food service and must be treated like one. Most of your student employees neither want, nor expect special favors. They want to earn money, and they want to learn about life, and work, and above all, getting along with others. One of the most exciting aspects of your job is your role as teacher and character-builder. It requires firmness, along with fairness and friendliness. When you develop a staff of student employees, follow these basic principles:

Hire selectively -- As with other employees, you need not hire anyone who, in your judgment, would not be a good employee. In addition, be careful not to fall victim to the "halo" effect and let one impression influence you unduly.

Hire according to your needs -- You are running a food service operation, not a welfare department. If you have a formal agreement with your deans or student-aid officers to honor a certain number of special requests from their offices, you must, of course, honor them. Every college food service director should reserve a few slots, in fact, for especially needy students referred to him by such college officials. Aside from those, however, you have no obligations to help student-applicants through school. The fact that you are doing so for most of your student workers is, and must remain, coincidental. When hiring students, remember that you are a professional, operating a college food service as efficiently as possible. For a typical job application form, which includes some basic conditions of employment, see Exhibit VI-17.

There are always some exceptions which prove the rule. Obviously, if you have pleasant young men or women who have difficulty walking, you would try to find them a sedentary job (such as cashier or accounts clerk). Anything you can do for someone that does not adversely affect your operation is, of course, desirable.

Establish firm ground rules -- A student will respect you if, at the time he is hired, clear and explicit rules and regulations are explained. It is not enough to say, "Be sure to have a substitute, if you can't come in"; it is much better to say:

"We do not condone unexcused absences; your presence on the job is essential to the smooth operation of the entire food service. If you must be absent, therefore, obtain an approved substitute, and so notify us. Failure to do so once or twice will result in warnings; three such offenses will result in automatic dismissal."

The same need for firmness and clarity is required when it comes to such procedures as punching a time clock (e.g. should they punch out while eating?), eating food during work hours, dress requirements (do you allow them to come in with tank tops and sandals?) and many other details of the job.

Establish a training program -- Some college food service managers believe, either because students are usually eager and intelligent, or else because they are only, in effect, temporary help, that training for them is not really necessary. "Here is a ladle, serve the soup," is often the extent of someone's "training program." Experience will show that complaints about poor service are often a direct result of student workers' lack of courtesy, lack of training, and lack of concern for the customers. Student and regular workers are both your responsibility and you need to train them properly if they are to represent you properly.

Supervision -- Depending on the number of students involved, you may choose to hire a student supervisor or to leave all the workers, regular and student alike, under the general supervision of the unit manager. Most colleges and universities use student supervisors. The advantages and drawbacks of this practice have been described in Chapter IV. Suffice it to say that carefully recruited, well-guided student supervisors can be a real asset to you. Nevertheless, general, overall supervision should always come from your professional managers. The reason for this becomes clear when you observe students in action: they will respect and follow a good student supervisor -- most of the time. There are, however, crisis situations where the authority and credibility given to a student by management is simply not enough, and only the professional manager can solve the problem.

EXHIBIT VI-17

JOB APPLICATION - U.O.P. FOOD SERVICE

Semester _____ 19 ___

Name: _____
Campus Address: _____
Home Address: _____
Phone/Room Number: _____   Anderson _____
Year: Freshman __ Sophomore __ Junior __ Senior ___   Grace Covell _____
Social Security No. _____   Quad _____
Employed as _____   Date Hired _____

CLASS SCHEDULE

Hour	Department and Course No.	M	T	W	TH	F	S	Room
8								
9								
10								
11								
12								
1								
2								
3								
4								
Other								

Comments or Special Requests: _____
_____
_____
_____
_____

STATEMENT OF RESPONSIBILITIES

In accepting student employment in the U.O.P. food services for the coming semester, I acknowledge the following responsibilities:

1. I shall always report to work neatly groomed and neatly dressed.

2. I agree to have chest X-ray taken if and when instructed to do so.

3. If for any reason, I should not be able to report to work, it is my responsibility to find a qualified substitute. Failure to do so may be a cause for immediate dismissal.

4. I understand that I am accepting employment for the whole semester throughout the final examination period. I accept this responsibility and am aware that failure to work throughout all of the semester may disqualify me for any work in the university food service in the future.

_____
(Signature of Student)

Staffing -- When recruiting a staff of student workers, remember that you are staffing for your convenience, not theirs. It is easy to make special assignments that suit students' individual schedules. There are times, of course, when you have to do this. But generally, the situation should be the other way around. You should set the slots and time periods, and leave it up to the student applicant to find free time in which to work. Too often a student will say, "Oh, I can work from 11 to 2" and the manager will hire him for that time period, instead of hiring him for a shorter time, as he originally intended. There goes your cost control.

Always monitor the level of student staff; it changes with the seasons. If, for example, you are operating with the same number of student workers in the spring as in the fall, you should be feeding the same number of students. Chances are you are feeding fewer and should therefore have fewer workers. Sometimes the number of students needed depends on the quality of the student workers themselves: it may take two students to fill the shoes of one who has left. In this case, find a third one who can do the job alone.

Wage determination -- In most state-supported colleges and universities, the wages of student workers are clearly established by higher authorities. In some schools, however, the food service director must make the decision. In such an instance, the popular phrase: "Equal pay for equal work" does not always apply. Traditionally, the student worker has been paid less than the regular worker, even for doing the same type of work. In the judgment of most, this is not necessarily unfair. You must remember that it takes three to four students to produce the work equivalent of one regular employee. Jobs are given to students at times when it is convenient for the student to work. Often one full-time employee would be much more productive than three part-time student workers. Starting wages for new student employees should meet two criteria: they should be roughly equivalent to student wages in similar schools within your region, and they should comply with the state and federal minimum wage.

Try to keep wage differentials among student employees to an absolute minimum. The great advantage of student workers, as noted earlier, is their flexibility. If you create too many wage standards for different jobs, it becomes increasingly cumbersome to move students from one job to another. Ideally, all student workers except student managers should work for a uniform starting wage. In practice, there may well be certain jobs which, because of their extra responsibility, or perhaps because of their odiousness, deserve extra money. A pot washer has such a job; a student cashier also.

Promotions -- Even though you should not have too many different types of student jobs, it is helpful if a loyal student worker, after a year or two, can be promoted to a job with more responsibility and pay. Students are just like everyone else, they like the recognition and benefits which a promotion brings. On the other hand, for most student workers the job in food service is a means to an end, a way to earn some money while attending school, and so, perhaps, the matter of promotion is not as crucial to them as it is to regular employees. In the case of students, the matter of merit in considering promotions takes on special significance. What you were advised against when it came to regular employees (see Merit Versus Step Increases) will probably work very well with students. Since you may have only two or three promotion opportunities for some 50 to 100 student workers, you should pick out the ones who are clearly the best, the most responsible, the natural leaders. The other students will usually accept the promotion with grace, if you've made the right decision.

Assessment of productivity -- Ideally, student employees need, and deserve a performance evaluation in the same way that do regular employees. A periodic counselling session with each student employee by his food supervisor would do much to raise the standard of the student's performance as well as his morale. Working in food service is not normally an area of primary interest to the student worker. Nevertheless, the process of obtaining a job, performing well in it, improving his job performance, and being advised on how to do better, can be a very important part of his general education and growth. Food service directors are in error if they feel that student workers always should or prefer to be treated differently than regular employees. While exceptions are made for students when it comes to scheduling, few other exceptions from normal personnel procedures should be made.

Control of overtime -- In most states, time-and-a-half pay for any work over 8 hours per day is required by law; states differ regarding the 40-hour and 48-hour work week, but most require overtime payments to anyone working more than 48 hours in any one week. Overtime should not be a factor with student employees. With proper scheduling, no student should have to work more than eight hours per day. Since split shifts are no problem in the case of students living on campus, send them home for a few hours if you need them again later that night. Keep in mind that the student's principal reason for being there is to get a college education and not to work in food service. Schedule him for a reasonable amount of time (e.g. 15-20 hours per week) so that overtime does not even enter the picture.

Maintenance of flexibility -- The mere fact that student employees constitute a large pool of part-time workers, readily available, normally eager to work, and very adaptable to almost any kind of work assignment in itself provides the manager with great flexibility in work assignments. It is important, however, not to diminish this flexibility by too much rigidity in scheduling student workers. The following, for example, would be a mistake:

- Guaranteeing every student worker a minimum number of hours.
- Establishing strict job classifications for student workers, with complicated systems of transferring a student from one job to another.
- Assigning some jobs strictly on the basis of sex. Completely aside from the requirements of "Affirmative Action," it so happens that women make excellent dishroom workers as well as managers, just as do men!

Control mechanisms -- There are two principal tools with which to control the cost of student labor: one is the posted schedule, and the other is a close watch over the time cards. If each unit has posted, well in advance, a clear schedule which lists each student job, the hours to be worked, and the name of the student assigned to each job, then it is known in advance how many hours will be spent on student labor. The companion step, of course, is to make sure that the schedule is being followed. This can be done by closely monitoring all student time cards, and by calling into the office any student who has deviated without a supervisor's permission from the posted schedule. Particularly important, in this connection, is monitoring whether or not students are punched out while eating meals. Most employers follow the practice, in the case of regular employees, of merely adding 30 minutes to an hour to the employee's daily work schedule to take care of the meal time factor. Some, and these are in the minority in the food service industry, include the meals in the total 8-hour day. Few, if any, knowledgeable food service directors on college campuses permit their student help to eat on college time. This is a wholly unnecessary fringe benefit, one not generally asked for nor expected by the student. An exception to this general rule, however, is usually made in the case of served banquets or special events, when student waiters and waitresses are asked to wait, at the convenience of the manager, so that they can clear off the banquet dishes at the conclusion of the program. In such a case most managers will let the waiters eat their meal while waiting for the banquet to conclude.

Meals for student workers -- The question of whether or not to provide meals for student workers is a difficult one under even the best conditions. Being completely fair to one's institution, to the student living on campus who already has paid for a meal ticket, as well as to the off-campus student who needs to eat is always difficult. What makes the problem even harder is the fact that it is almost impossible to stop a hungry student who is working in food service from eating, regardless of whether or not he has paid for his food. Some colleges permit students to eat in lieu of pay (e.g. 2 hours per day entitles a student to eat). This practice is becoming less frequent. Other colleges let their student food service workers eat free meals, in addition to pay. This, in the eyes of most observers, is a needless and costly luxury, and elevates the effective earning of those students beyond an effective and realistic wage. Then there are colleges at the other extreme, which prohibit any eating by student workers while on duty, and make no provision for discounts or charge privileges for any student worker. Most college food service workers usually get charge privileges, whereas all other students may not. In cash operations, student workers often get a discount ranging from 33% to 50% off list price.

One problem that is difficult to control is that of an off-campus student who wishes to work in food service, but declines to buy meals while working, even at discounted prices. Most managers solve this problem by hiring only students who have meal tickets; others do it by insisting that students eat and pay for meals while on duty. Although this latter practice works, it may be illegal in some states. Yet another solution is to let the student have his way, with the understanding that he will be immediately dismissed if he is caught taking food without paying for it. But it is not pleasant to have to play policeman to your student workers. Be sure the system you devise is simple to control, and fair to everyone.

CONTROL OF FOOD COSTS

If the control of labor costs demands special human relations skills, then controlling food costs demands special detective skills. The profits in a food service operation can escape in many ways. Their disappearance has been compared to water leaking out of a dike; no sooner have you plugged a leak in one place than it pops up in another. The term "food cost control" is a broad one and had perhaps better be defined. Food cost controls are those activities in a food service operation which help management to keep the cost of food at a pre-determined level.

Because there are so many different places, and so many ways in which food can be wasted or lost, the good manager must keep on top of things at all times and be aware of possible food cost problems. For example:

- A delivery man leaving food at the receiving dock without someone there to check it in
- The storeroom door wide open
- The oven thermostat set at 400°F. or above
- Unusual amounts of leftovers on student plates
- An employee leaving the kitchen with a small package or paper bag, without a package slip

Any one of these, and dozens of other instances, alert the food service manager every day to the fact that food cost control is a continuing and important task, one which he can never fully delegate to others. There are three basic activities involved in the control process:

- Keep informed
- Compare
- Investigate

As long as you are on top of things, as long as your staff tells you of problems that arise, you are at least alerted to the dangers of unnecessary food losses and can take steps to halt or prevent them. As long as you know where you are going, know what food cost percentage or cost per meal served you should have, know in which group of foodstuffs the problems occur, know the proper portion sizes, cooking temperatures, utensils, etc., then you can compare what is proper and what was done in past periods with what is actually being done and take steps to change whatever needs changing. Then, if something occurs which you don't understand, you must investigate and discover the cause, before the problem gets worse. That's where your abilities as a detective come in, you must look for all kinds of clues and eliminate each suspect one by one until you've discovered the culprit that is causing you all the trouble.

A good way to conduct food inquiries is to follow the path of the food as it travels through your kitchen: from menu planning and purchasing to receiving, storing, issuing, preparing, and serving. In addition, you must check into possible over-production and theft (the two are sometimes connected) and, in case of cash operations, into the problems of cash control and setting the proper selling prices.

Menu Planning

Everything in a food service operation depends upon the menu. The cost of the raw food purchased, the number of employees needed to prepare and serve it, the popularity of the establishment, all these are determined by what is written on the menu. The proper balance between high cost and low cost entrees, the careful blending of labor-intensive with labor-saving production items, the optimum use of kitchen equipment, all this is accomplished by effective menu writing.

When it comes to food cost control, the menu is your most effective tool. Take advantage of seasonal offerings, price specials, and popular low-cost dishes to offset the higher-cost items. Cost out each menu and compare its cost with previous ones. Gauge possible fluctuations in volume, and insert short-order and easy-to-prepare items at times of uncertain volume.

The techniques of menu writing for residence hall and cash operations are discussed in Chapters IX and X. Remember that menu planning is a crucial step in food cost control.

Purchasing

Your best way to control the raw prices for the food you purchase is to follow the general principles about food purchasing outlined in Chapter V. Using the proper specifications, buying the grades appropriate to the use, placing orders well in advance and asking for as few deliveries as possible, those are the steps that will help you buy food at the lowest possible price. Another important area of concern in this connection is your decision whether or not to purchase pre-fabricated meats and convenience food entree items. These decisions, which are more fully covered in Chapter XI, can have a significant impact on your overall food cost picture and require knowledge, analysis, and careful checking before they are finally made.

Receiving

The receiving dock is a common place for food cost slippage. If the vendor has made a mistake or if the driver has short-changed you, that's the place to catch it. Watch out for invoices that don't match up against the purchase orders, or items marked "back-order" or "out-of-stock." If you have a central receiving place you will have a full-time receiving clerk who does all this for you. If, however, you are like most college food service managers, then your kitchen does its own receiving, and you never know who will be there to count and accept the merchandise. Weighing in all meats and other goods purchased by weight, rejecting unsatisfactory merchandise, taking appropriate credits when necessary, and catching vendor's errors, these are the food cost control steps needed at the receiving dock. It is especially important, therefore, that not everyone (certainly not every student employee) is authorized to receive and sign for merchandise. It is equally important that food deliveries are made at a mutually convenient time, and not only at a time of the vendor's choosing. An appropriate sign at the receiving dock, enforced by your staff, will help solve this problem.

Storage

If business managers, architects, and kitchen planners understood the importance of proper storeroom space in the cost control process, there would undoubtedly be better storerooms in college food services today. Unfortunately, they often don't. As a result, you are probably hampered by inadequate storage space, which prevents your buying as advantageously as you could, increases the problem of food spoilage, and complicates your inventory process. It is dangerous to generalize about minimum storage space requirements in a college food service operation. It is especially foolish to try and provide minimum square footages, based on number of meals served, since there are so many variations in the type of kitchen, style of service, menus, and types of institutions. Nevertheless, if you are working in a college which is isolated and runs the danger of being cut off during winter storms, you might follow these guidelines:

- You should have enough storage capacity on campus to enable you to purchase a six-month supply of canned goods that may be subject to shortages or serious inflationary pressures.

- In the absence of a central commissary, each kitchen should have enough dry storage capacity to operate without deliveries for a two-week period.

- Freezer capacity should be sufficient to allow the kitchen to operate without deliveries for a period of 2-4 weeks. If large amounts of frozen convenience foods are used, this capacity needs to be even larger.

- Walk-in refrigerator capacity should be large enough to enable you to operate for a one-week period witout deliveries. Separate facilities for produce, dairy products, and all other perishables should be available.

- Reach-in boxes and cabinets or shelving should be available at each production station sufficient to hold a day's supply of most essential items.

- Holding refrigerators, sufficient to hold the prepared food for each meal's requirements, should be installed near the serving lines.

Even if you are more fortunate, and your risk of being cut off from your normal sources of supply is less, the above storage capabilities would be ideal to have, and are worth including in a newly-planned college food service installation.

There are a few additional basic points to remember:

- Remove all delivered goods from the receiving dock into storage as quickly as possible. Refrigerate perishables immediately.

- Keep your storeroom locked throughout the day, and your refrigerators locked as soon as the cooks and salad makers leave. Be sure to have locks on all reach-in boxes also.

- Mark your incoming meats with the date of receipt, a description of the item, and the date of intended use. A sample form for this purpose is shown in Exhibit VI-18.

- Remove produce from crates, water, and sort out spoiled items as quickly as possible.

- Maintain, and constantly check proper refrigeration temperatures in all refrigerators and freezers.

EXHIBIT VI-18

Date Received_____

MEAT PLANNING TAG

Item_____

Meal   **Lunch**____   **Dinner**____

Day _____

Comments _____

Print this label on **Satin Label Crack 'n Peel** permanent adhesive so that it will adhere to all boxes and packages.

Issuing

Many college food service units do not have a formal checking-in and checking-out procedure. The cooks and salad workers go into the storeroom and refrigerators and take out whatever they need for the coming meal. It may, in fact, not be practical for you to employ someone as a storekeeper. If you keep the storeroom locked during the day, you can give your head cook and your head salad worker a key. Even walk-ins can be limited to use by those who must have access. Perhaps you can keep an informal sheet in the storeroom, which lists what was taken out and by whom each day. Remember the tighter control you have over the movement of food, the lower will be your food cost.

Finally, a key control feature regarding storeroom and refrigerators is inventory control. This matter has been covered thoroughly in Chapter VI, but deserves mention here also, since weekly inventories are one of the best tools available for controlling food cost.

Food Preparation

If every food service manager knew exactly how much food was being wasted right under his nose, in the preparation process, he would be tempted to install automatic controls on every oven and kettle, one-way mirrors at the cooks' stations, and hidden microphones everywhere where food was being prepared. If he knew for certain that for every 100 pounds of meat roasted, he could save $20 in shrinkage costs, he would be tempted to hire a "temperature watcher" just for the cooks. If he knew the exact value of the fat wasted because it was not properly filtered, or thrown out earlier than necessary, he would train one cook to handle specifically this area of the work. Finally, if he knew the total value of all the food ingredients that were not called for nor needed in the recipes, he would be tempted to do what some large kitchen operations have actually done, issue the food needed for each recipe in quantities pre-proportioned by the storeroom personnel.

Some of the loss caused by these various errors in food preparation can only be guessed at. However, your losses are probably more significant than you think, and are surely sufficient to require your constant attention. Here are some things for you to remember:

- Use standardized recipes. Place these in front of the cooks daily. Make certain that they are followed.
- Provide adequate control tools (numbered scoops, sized ladles, portioned scales by ounces and pounds, meat and oven thermometers, slicers, and sharp knives.)
- Check oven temperatures regularly; calibrate oven thermostats several times during the school year, insist on *low-temperature roasting* of meats. See Exhibit VI-19.
- Insist on utilizing all usable food items such as juice from canned fruits, the tops of celery, drippings from roasts, etc.
- Conduct continuous training programs in proper food preparation, stressing cost consciousness as well as preparation skills.

EXHIBIT VI-19

COOKS!

HELP US SAVE MEAT

The two most important factors affecting shrinkage can be controlled by the cooking method;

1. **Oven Temperatures:** The higher the oven temperature, the greater the shrinkage of the roast and the less the amount of meat to serve. Use low temperatures for roasting all meat 250 Deg. F. to 300 Deg. F. constant temperature.

2. **Degree of Doneness:** The degree of doneness to which a roast is cooked may influence its shrinkage as much as the temperature at which it is cooked. As the degree of doneness is increased, the shrinkage is increased. Use Meat Thermometers to remove the guess work.

Remember that the less the shrinkage during roasting, the greater the number of servings available and the less the cost per serving of meat.

Lois Ohms
Test Kitchen Dietitian
Stanford University Food Service

Serving of Food

Many colleges and universities use regular employees in the kitchen and student employees on the serving lines. This is poor public relations (students should be able to see those who are preparing the food), and poor food cost control. It makes little sense to follow all the necessary control steps right up to the serving process, and then permit the worst kind of food wastage on the cafeteria counter. It takes considerable effort, patience, and frequent repetition before line servers understand the need for strict portion control and practice it constantly and uniformly. The presence of regular workers alongside student servers will help assure that your portion instructions are being adhered to faithfully. While some students are conscientious and loyal workers, others are simply not that concerned or interested in food cost control practices at the cafeteria counter. The opposite attitude produces equally disturbing results: the servers are too strict, and actually serve the students less than they are supposed to receive. A similarly costly practice, both from the standpoint of food cost and also public relations, is to dish up the food in advance, before the individual student has reached the server. This may well be a faster way of serving, but it is destructively impersonal, allows the food to get cold, and does not allow for possible food cost savings on items not wanted by the student. If you ever noticed how many students decline either the potatoes or the vegetables as they pass through the line, you will understand this point even better. Follow these principles for good food cost control on the serving counter:

- Use exact portion specifications and train all serving personnel in their use. Consider preportioning roast meats on patty paper.
- Utilize numbered spoons, scoops, and ladles whenever possible.
- Maintain constant supervision over the serving counter during meal periods.

Overproduction

Of all the areas of possible food cost slippage, overproduction is one of the hardest to control. It is difficult because the serving of food in colleges always involves a certain amount of guesswork. The number of clients to be served is never constant, and the amount of food they will eat is never exactly the same. In residence halls, the number of meal ticket holders who are absent from meals always varies to some degree, and in cash operations such factors as weather, campus and town activities, menus and selling prices cause constant fluctuations in sales volume. Good record-keeping, and soundly-based forecasts of meals to be served are most helpful in minimizing the problem, but it nevertheless continues to plague every food service manager, as it will plague you.

Why is overproduction such a serious problem? If all leftovers are properly utilized, what is so wrong with having a little left over? Is it not better to prepare too much food than to prepare too little and run out of food in the middle of a meal? After all, a leftover roast of beef can always be used again during the next few days, but it is impossible to come up with additional servings of roast beef quickly if the demand exceeds expectations. These are all reasonable questions, asked constantly by responsible managers who have faced hordes of hungry students who expected, and sometimes demanded the item just depleted, and who would not gracefully accept a substitute.

The answers are complex. Normally, it is impossible to utilize 100% of all the food left over in a kitchen, and even less possible to utilize it at the same value as when originally produced. Some items, like roast beef, lend themselves to easy storage and re-use for a few days following cooking. Other items, such as a seafood Newburg cannot be heated, cooled, and re-heated for an infinite number of times without affecting quality and increasing the chance for food contamination. As a result, many items that are leftover one day and re-heated another day, will be thrown out by the cook after the second serving. This is good sanitation practice, but it is wasteful from the standpoint of food costs. Cooks do not always utilize even such leftovers as roast beef to their full potential value. Often it is used for cold beef sandwiches (a good way to use it), or re-heated at the occasion of another roast beef meal (still a good use, but the beef is subjected to additional shrinkage when cooked a second time). Occasionally, however, the cook will cut up a small piece of leftover roast beef for soup, or other casserole dishes. By doing that, he may be using an expensive cut of meat for a dish which would taste just as good with a less expensive cut. He may not have any other choice, and he is utilizing his leftovers, but nevertheless, he is wasting food dollars.

There are a number of ways in which you can minimize the problem of overproduction, even if you can never fully eliminate it:

Daily production sheet -- When it comes to food production, an institutional kitchen should be operated just like any other manufacturing plant: management should decide what is to be produced, and the production workers should follow the established production schedule. Sounds logical? Sounds simple? It may be logical, but it isn't simple. Not in most kitchens, anyway. Perhaps because the old-fashioned European Chef kept everything in his head, or perhaps because many cooks are also homemakers who gauge their food needs on the known appetites of their families, many college and university cooks even today do not have formal production sheets or, if they do have them, refuse to follow them. Kitchen supervisors must share some of the blame. They are pleased when cooks substitute their own personal judgment for what is written on the production sheets because often the cooks are right and the sheets are wrong. Nonetheless, if you want to operate an efficient kitchen and keep overproduction to a minimum, then you, and not the cooks, must decide how much of each item is to be produced. You must decide this two or three days in advance, you must be willing to spend a little time to dig up the pertinent facts. Here are some basic questions to be answered before the production sheet is drawn up:

- How many customers will we feed today? How many did we feed yesterday, and on the same day last week, and what, if anything, makes today different from the other days?

- If more than one entree is prepared, how many are we likely to serve of each? How many did we serve of each entree item the last time this combination of entrees was served, i.e. five weeks ago? How much of each was left over? How about the time before, what happened then?

- What variables may occur today which would affect our estimates? Weather? Campus events? Vacations? Special menus at other campus locations?

The good supervisor digs up the answers to these questions and then, before finishing his production sheet, discusses it with the cooks. Together they must arrive at the best possible estimate. Once that has taken place, and the production sheet has been drawn up, it should be as constant as the law. It must not be changed on a whim, or on a second guess by a kitchen worker.

The production sheet is more than merely a notice of what has been planned, what was produced, what was served and how much was left over. Therefore, the role of the cooks in completing the information on the sheet is as important as the role of the supervisor in drawing it up. Such sheets are not limited to entree items; whether it be an entree, a vegetable, a salad, or a dessert in the same manner. This is where you will be tempted to disagree:

> "Why bother making up production sheets for salads and sandwiches,
> when it is easy to make up more if you run out?"

You are right, in emergencies, it is much easier to prepare additional sandwiches or salads than it is to cook more entree items. You would also be right if you pointed out that vegetables, which should be cooked in small batches anyway, are easily and quickly cooked when needed. Nevertheless, none of this justifies the lack of a careful production plan. Such a plan will make you more cautious about the numbers to be produced of these easily-fixed items. Remember, also, that your production sheets affect not only your food cost, but also your labor cost. If you plan in advance to make more sandwiches in the middle of the lunch period, then you cannot, at the same time, plan to utilize the sandwich-maker on the serving line to help serve the food. Here there is a slight distinction between a residence hall kitchen and a kitchen in a cash operation. In the former, things are at their most efficient if, during the meal period, most of the production workers are used on the serving line. In the latter, where the choices are greater and production fluctuates more, things are most efficient if toward the end of the meal period most pre-prepared fast food items have been sold, and the remaining orders are filled as needed. Samples of typical production sheets in both residence hall and cash operations are shown in Exhibit VI-20.

Checking refrigerators -- More food is thrown out of refrigerators than from any other place in the kitchen. When cooks and managers get too busy, they merely shove the leftover food into the refrigerators, with the intention of utilizing it at the first suitable opportunity. Two weeks later, they will accidentally stumble over these leftovers, sheepishly wonder whether the food is still edible and then, with a bold stroke for good sanitation, proudly throw the food away. Unfortunately for you,

EXHIBIT VI-20

FOOD SERVICE - UNIVERSITY OF THE PACIFIC
Quad ___ DINING HALL - MENU & PRODUCTION SHEET

Cycle III   DATE Tuesday, Sep. 10, 19 7?

		Amount Planned	Amount Made	Amount L.O.	Amount Served
BREAKFAST					
Fruit Juice:	Canned Apricots	✓			
Fruit:	Malt-O-Meal				
Daily:	Assorted dry cereal Can.Bacon	75#	30#	—	35
Daily:	Hard or soft boiled eggs	✓	✓		
Daily:	Buttered toast syrup	✓	✓		
Entree:	1. Buckwheat or plain pancakes	✓	✓		
	2. Pineapple-filled coffeecake	✓	✓		
LUNCH	Verje:Grilled Cheese	30	30+5	—	35
Soup:	Tomato and Macaroni Soup	6 gal.	12 gal.	—	410
Entrees:	1. Gr. Cheese/Colombo Bourdough	500	410	—	410
	2. Spanish Noodles	6 pans	5	—	6 pans
Cold Plate:	Roast Beef Slice (dieters)	✓	✓		
Vegetable:	Spinach	2 cs	2 cs	—	2 cs
Salads:	1. Salad Bar	✓			
	2. Carlfruit Salad	✓			
	3. Fruited Strwb.Gelatin	✓			
	4. Fresh Fruit	✓			
Bread:	Molasses Cookies	✓			
Dessert:	1. Ice Cream Novelty	✓			
	2. Fruit	✓			
	3.				
DINNER	Verje:Spaghetti/ Mushroom Sauce	40 sv.	1 pan	1/4 pan	3/4 pan
	1. Spaghetti/Meat Sauce				
	2. Grilled Liver & Onions	30#	30#	—	120 v.
Potatoes:	Turkey Slice (Dieters)	✓	✓		
Vegetable:	Parsley butt.potatoes	90#	90#	—	90#
Salads:	1. Italian cut Green beans	2 cs.	2cs+9cans	—	
	2. Salad Bar	✓			
	3. Green Salad Bar	✓			
Bread:	Garlic bread	22 loaves	22	—	
Dessert:	1. Ice Cream Fresh Fruit	✓			
	2. Pudding Dutch Apple cheesecake	✓			
	3.				
	4.				

UNIVERSITY OF THE PACIFIC
UNIVERSITY CENTER FOOD PRODUCTION SHEET

Date Wed. Feb 7 1979

	Amount Left Over From Previous Day	TYPE OF BREAD	AMOUNT ORDERED	AMOUNT MADE	AMOUNT LEFT OVER 5 p.m.	AMOUNT SERVED
DONUTS						
COLD SANDWICHES						
American Cheese	1	White	2		1	
Bologna		White	2	✓		
Bologna & Cheese		White	2	✓	1	
Healthfood - Bacon		W. Berry	14	✓	1	
Healthfood Jack Cheese	8	W. Berry	1		3	
Healthfood Tuna	1	W. Berry	14	✓	1	
Deviled Egg	3	Wheat	2	✓	1	
Deviled Egg		White	8	✓	1	
Ham	3	Rye	1		1	
Ham	4	White	1	✓	1	
Ham & Cheese		White	8	✓	1	
Ham & Cheese		Rye	8	✓	1	
Poor Boys		Fr. Roll	16	✓	1	
Pastrami		Rye	10	✓	1	
Roast Beef		Wheat	10	✓	1	
Roast Beef		White	2	✓	1	
Salami Italian		Rye	2	✓	1	
Salami	2	White	2	✓	1	
Salami & Swiss Cheese	3	White	1		1	
Swiss Cheese		Rye	2	✓	1	
Swiss Cheese		White	2	✓	1	
Tuna Salad		Wheat	8	✓	1	
Tuna Salad		White	8	✓	1	
Turkey		White	4	✓		

your reach-ins, roll-ins, and walk-in refrigerators and freezers don't contain nuts and bolts, or cloth or stationary. They hold highly perishable commodities which must be inspected daily and must be utilized well before there is any possibility of spoilage. One of the first acts of every kitchen supervisor is to inspect the refrigerators. He should check to make sure that all food is properly covered, that all meats have been properly marked as to their date of receipt and their intended date of use (see Exhibit VI-18). He should inspect all leftover food and, if it is not marked, should check the menu and decide when it is to be used again. Sometimes, if it is left from the day before, he may decide to freeze it (how much better for that food, had it been frozen immediately after the dinner meal the night before).

If you want an effective, short, and clear-cut policy about leftover foods, you might do well to follow the example of Douglas Richie, who established the following policy at California State University/Long Beach:

Policy for Leftover Foods

There are three things to do with leftover
food within a 24-hour period:

1. Serve it
2. Freeze it
3. Throw it away

Checking freezers -- Freezers should not be immune from periodic inspections by the supervisor. In addition to the weekly freezer inventory, during which the manager decides what frozen foods should be utilized during the following week, it is good management to take a quick look into the freezers every day. A sloppy freezer means a sloppy crew of cooks. There is never any emergency so critical, that a cook has a right to pull a box of frozen food from the bottom of a pile and let everything else fall topsy-turvey on the floor; there is never an excuse to remove one popsicle from an ice cream freezer, while all the others in the box are allowed to spill out. It is wrong, furthermore, to assume that just because an item is in the freezer, it is usable indefinitely, regardless of how it is handled. Freezer burns will destroy the palatability of food, and food can get mangled and squashed in the freezer just as it can in the refrigerators.

Another important reason for checking the freezers daily is the need for defrosting certain food items in the walk-in refrigerators prior to use. This is often forgotten. There are many food items, such as pork chops, for example, which simply do not taste as good when cooked directly from the frozen state. Some items, such as frozen waffles, must be kept frozen until just before cooking and so the knowledge and judgment of the manager is important in this whole process.

Plan follow-up meals -- The problem of overproduction can be minimized if the unit manager has the authority to modify his existing menu in order to utilize his leftovers. If you are responsible for a number of food operations, give your various managers this privilege. On the other hand, leftover foods must be utilized judiciously, and you might lay down certain guidelines as to how this can be done without adversely affecting the quality of your menu. Obviously, substituting macaroni and cheese for a roast beef dinner is not a practice designed to win friends among your college students. However, adding some leftover pans of macaroni and cheese to the regular roast beef dinner menu or else using it as a hot luncheon entree, could make many students happy, especially the vegetarians. Remember, whenever possible, serve out leftovers, as they were originally prepared, at the next possible meal. Students are wary of "mystery meats" and the use of leftovers in a careless way could destroy confidence in a food service operation.

Theft

Earlier in this chapter it was stated that overproduction is one of the hardest items to control, but theft is even harder. Stealing goes on in just about every large kitchen in America today. Theft is generally understood to be the unauthorized and surreptitious taking of something of value by someone who has no right to do so. Technically, therefore, the cook who takes some stale bread home to feed his pigs (bread that could have been used to make breadcrumbs) is stealing. The porter who pours a little pot-washing soap into a small container for use at home or the salad worker who slips a tangerine into her purse for her little girl at home are also stealing. "Hold it a minute," you will say, "that is being very technical. Surely you don't expect me to fire my porter for a cup-full of soap or my salad girl for taking a tangerine?" Of course not. What is expected of you, however, is to devise a set of regulations and a system of oversight that makes stealing of any kind, large or small, difficult and unprofitable for the employees. You must approach the entire problem of theft with a certain sense of foreboding. The cup full of soap today may become a 5-gallon jar tomorrow. The tangerine may become a bag-full; the stale bread may become fresh bread and before you know it, more food seems to *leave* through the back door than comes into it!

It helps to realize that your kitchen workers have no criminal tendencies. They would not steal one penny from the bank teller, and would turn in the wallet full of money that they found on the street. Honesty is not merely a mode of behavior established in society, it is also a personal, subjective matter. If you are a low-paid salad worker and have six children at home, and you see that there is a pan of sweet rolls left over from that morning which will, in all probability be thrown away, the temptation to take some of these home to your children, especially if there is no one to see you do it, is almost irresistible.

Preventing theft-circumstances -- Your first step in theft prevention is to create a set of circumstances that makes it almost impossible for your kitchen workers to steal anything, or at least anything of value. Keeping the store-room locked during the day prevents access to it by anyone other than those who have a key. This keeps someone else from going in, taking a can of peaches, for instance, and putting it into his locker for removal that night. Locking up the walk-ins at night as soon as the cooks leave the kitchen is another prevention measure. Those who remain to clean up will have no access to the food. If you can install small locks on all the reach-in refrigerators and freezers, and bread and cake cabinets, you can remove another temptation.

Preventing theft - regulations -- Together with a good set of control mechanisms, you should also issue a clear set of rules and regulations concerning such matters as taking home leftovers, buying of food by the employees, and issuing packing slips. Some food service managers don't like to do this sort of thing. They consider it an insult to their employees if they broach this important subject in such a direct manner. If you, too, feel this way, change your attitude. It is a lot simpler, and less offensive, to issue clear rules before the theft than to discipline an employee after he has been caught stealing. The following are some suggested rules you should consider for your own operation:

Taking home leftovers -- Most well-run commercial and institutional kitchens prohibit the taking home of leftovers by food service personnel. Except in rare circumstances, such as a special dinner, or at Christmas, or when the unit manager feels that he must do something special to boost morale, this rule is applied firmly and without exceptions. Even though it is hard to explain to a needy worker why some food is better thrown out than given to him, this explanation must be made. "If kitchen workers are permitted to take food home," you should explain, "then somehow there will always be food left over and more and more food will be taken home -- and this is something we simply cannot afford!"

Buying of food by employees -- This is a practice that differs from one institution to another and depends on many variables which cannot be handled adequately in this book. If properly controlled, and if the manager feels that sale of food to employees is a fringe benefit which he would like to grant, then there is nothing objectionable to this practice. On the other hand, your kitchen is not a supermarket, and what may be a purchase one day may become a theft the next. In general, it is not a good idea to let employees purchase food from the kitchen as a regular practice. It is, however, much more acceptable to make such a privilege available occasionally as a special favor. In some isolated communities, for example, the food service manager might give his staff a chance to buy their Thanksgiving turkeys wholesale through food service. Candy purchases for the Christmas dinner could be extended to include orders from kitchen staff for their families. Sometimes, if an individual worker has a special problem at home; unexpected company, illness of family members, etc., and the manager feels that an exception is warranted, then the sale of food, at cost plus a small markup for overhead, (to discourage abuse of the practice) is quite appropriate. There are food service directors who disagree with this. In state institutions, especially, much stricter regulations apply than in private colleges and universities, where the relations between managers and staff are often less restricted, and are not governed by state regulations.

Package slips -- It is a good idea to insist that any employee taking a package out of the kitchen carry a dated package slip, signed by the supervisor which indicates the content of the package. Such a slip would apply to personal belongings as well as to items taken from the kitchen itself. This is a practice followed by most large department stores and other commercial establishments and is an effective theft-prevention measure. It formalizes the process of getting approval for taking anything out of the kitchen and thus increases the risk by the one who takes something without authorization. A sample of such a slip is shown in Exhibit VI-21.

EXHIBIT VI-21

UNIVERSITY OF THE PACIFIC
Stockton, California

PERSONAL PROPERTY PASS
FOOD SERVICE

This is to authorize

_____

to remove the item(s) listed below from

_____ kitchen

_____

_____

_____

_____   _____
Date   Food Supervisor

Preventing theft - oversight -- When it comes to theft prevention, managers cannot be like ostriches; they cannot stick their heads in the sand and hope that the problem will not exist. Instead, managers should be aware of the possibility of theft, and actively take steps to discourage it. If an employee carries a package on the way out, it is perfectly in order for the manager to ask, "Have you a package slip for this, Judy?" If a refrigerator door was left unlocked, it is important to reprimand the cook who forgot to do so. If an employee has been given permission to make a purchase from the kitchen, the charge slip should be made out right on the spot. Constant surveillance of these practices, a constant awareness of the possibility of theft, and an honest commitment to discourage any improper activities, no matter how small, these are the steps that are needed to minimize the problem. None of this means that you are to go around acting like a small town sheriff. Snooping, constant suspicious behavior, and insulting innuendoes are not part of your job, but an honest treatment of a serious potential problem is.

INTERDEPARTMENTAL TRANSFERS

When your spouse asks you for money, you probably reach into your pocket and hand it over. No accounting is kept, and none should be. When your fellow manager, your friend who is running the cafeteria on the other side of campus, urgently sends over for a case of butter, you probably will give it to him also. That is as it should be. But in this case, there is one important difference: a record and subsequent charge of this transaction is absolutely essential, if your costs and those of your friend are to have any meaning at all. Transfers of food, both raw and cooked, between various food service units on a campus are frequent, and often add up into the thousands. You must regard each unit as a separate operation, with its own set of books. These books can only be as accurate as those who keep them. Lack of record-keeping when inter-departmental transfers occur is not a sign of generosity, it is merely sloppy bookkeeping.

The problem is not as simple as it appears. Sometimes, unit managers refuse to cooperate with their colleagues, precisely because of the record-keeping requirements. Such a negative attitude, of course, is just as wrong as not charging for the item transferred. Your job is to put everything into proper perspective. Your policy should be clear:

- Unit managers are to cooperate with each other in every possible way when it comes to lending or selling food and supplies within the food service organization.
- A written record is to be kept of all such transfers, and appropriate charges, at cost, are to be made by the transferring unit.

EXPENSE ACCOUNTS - TRIPS - CONFERENCES

Most colleges and universities have established rules governing personal expenses accrued in connection with school business, and many also have policies or budget items governing the number of trips and confrences which can be attended by the professional staff. If your school is one of these, then your job is simple. Familiarize yourself with your school's policies, and make certain that they are followed by those who report to you.

If, on the other hand, the responsibility for establishing such policies falls to you, then you must prepare a clear set of instructions which lists your philosophy about expense accounts in general and which gives specific guidelines to the individual involved. Some business managers feel that a person travelling on school business should be allowed a flat, per-diem sum to cover his lodging and dining costs; others, instead of setting a maximum, prefer to have the traveller list every expense item and be reimbursed accordingly. There are others, yet, who establish guidelines for the traveller, but who will approve extraordinary out-of-pocket costs in addition to those covered in the guidelines. If you work in a state institution, you will probably have no voice in this matter at all. In other schools, a moderate approach to expense accounts seems the best course to follow. When you or your staff travel on school business, it is not an occasion to make extra money; neither should it require a personal financial sacrifice, as a result of expense policies which are too restrictive.

Attendance at regional and national conferences and meetings, as well as visits to other food service operations, is a very constructive and popular way to develop yourself and your staff professionally and it should be encouraged, rather than restricted. You, as the person in charge, should take a leadership role in getting approval for your staff to travel and in encouraging staff members to take advantage of the opportunities you create for them. Such opportunities, furthermore, should not be limited to supervisory staff only. There are benefits to be gained by taking your cooks and salad makers to a food service demonstration, or to visit another college or university. Equally constructive is sending your porters to a floor maintenance seminar, or your cooks to a 2-week course in professional food preparation, such as the one conducted annually by the Culinary Institute of America, Hyde Park, New York. The cost of such efforts is minimal, when weighed in terms of morale of the entire staff, and in the light of reduced personnel turnover. If you can get each traveller to give an oral and/or written report of each trip, then other members of your staff can enjoy the trip vicariously and also learn from the experience provided.

It is important in the budgetary process to provide a sufficient and reasonable sum for trips and conferences. Your professional staff (managers, supervisors) should be able to attend in-state conferences at least once or twice a year. As a reward for faithful service, an out-of-state trip every two or three years is also appropriate. Some schools, such as Washington State University in Pullman, are so isolated from population centers that they are usually liberal with out-of-state travel allowances for their food service managers, and consider this policy an important recruiting and retention tool.

Finally, in judging these matters, you must remember the real value of such trips to your overall food service operation. It is very easy, in the food service business, to get into a rut. New ideas, new experiments, new ways of doing things are the only way to keep from falling into such a rut. If each staff member comes back with only one good new idea, one new menu item, one cost-saving step, then chances are that the trip has paid for itself.

VII. BUILDING A FOOD SERVICE STAFF

One of the greatest satisfactions that comes to a food service manager is working with an able, dedicated, and loyal staff. It is a thrill to be at the head of a staff whose objectives are the same as yours, whose affections for the school and for its students are like yours, people who enjoy their jobs, enjoy being around students, and get special satisfaction out of making them happy.

Such conditions exist, believe it or not, in many colleges and universities today. They don't happen accidentally, though, they have to be created. A food service staff is like any other group of working people. They come to the job with personal needs that must be satisfied: a decent wage, good working conditions, friendly supervision. Beyond that, each member of the staff seeks other satisfactions -- praise, recognition, interesting work and, most important, a chance at self-fulfillment. The good manager recognizes all these needs, and does everything within his power to help his employees fulfill their personal job objectives. At the same time, he explains to them his own principal goals for food service and creates enough understanding so that everyone on the staff is pursuing the same goals.

Accomplishing the above is not as simple as it may sound. It takes more than being merely a "nice guy." It takes more than being technically competent in one's profession and more than mere loyalty to one's institution. It takes time, time for you to get to know each employee, and time for them to get to know you. This type of staff does not develop overnight. It also takes enthusiasm, your enthusiasm for the job to be done and their enthusiasm along with yours. It takes trust. You must trust them to do correctly all the things that need doing if your common goals are to be achieved, and they must trust you to tell them the right things, to keep your word, and to protect them against unfair criticism from others. It takes professional skill. Your employees want to learn how to do things correctly. If you can show them the right way, they'll go along. Finally, it takes affection. You must genuinely feel close to your employees in a personal, human way, and this feeling must be reciprocal. This doesn't mean, of course, that there will be no disagreements, disciplinary problems, or personnel crises. It does mean that the general relationship between you and your staff, and also between the employees themselves, should be sincere and harmonious.

The food service director by his example sets the tone for the entire food service staff. Similarly, the unit manager does it for his unit. If you walk into a kitchen where everyone is happy, smiling, and working hard, you can assume there is a manager who is also happy, smiling, and working hard. If everyone is grouchy, snappish, and unproductive, chances are the manager is at fault. You, the manager, set the standard for everyone else who is working with you -- a standard of honesty, enthusiasm, dedication, industriousness, personal appearance, and, very important, a standard of service to the students of your school. If you show that you care about each individual student, then your employees will also start to care. If you make a special trip to get a piece of lemon for the student requesting it for his tea, then either the lemons will be there in the future, or other employees will also fetch the lemon when asked. If you want your employees to be genuinely concerned about personal hygiene, you must yourself practice it.

To build a special staff, you yourself have to become a special type of manager. Setting an example is not enough. You must forego the temptation to show, or use your authority, in favor of a more democratic approach. You must be willing to solicit the opinions and advice of even the newest and least skilled of your employees, and to follow such advice if it makes sense.

There are some food service directors, especially on the larger campuses, who see themselves more as business managers than as personnel managers. They let their unit managers handle all personnel matters and, because there are so many food service employees working in their department, make little attempt to deal with any of them personally. They are misguided. Food service is a "people" business, and a good food service director must be people-oriented before he deals with any other matters. Regardless of the size of your staff, whether it is counted by the dozens or even by the hundreds, constant and continuing personal contact with your food service employees is a prerequisite to building a quality staff.

SUPERVISION

What is most important in a supervisor is his ability to relate to students and to employees in a friendly manner. All the other benefits, whether knowledge of dietetics and nutrition, knowledge of food preparation and sanitation, or knowledge of cost controls, are just fringe benefits. Here are some supervisor types you should avoid hiring:

- One who is afraid of students
- One who does not like to go into the dining room to chat with students
- One who thinks that all he has to do all day long is to visit with students
- One who is moody or temperamental
- One who yells at the employees
- One who does not follow through on sanitation

Here are some qualifications which are especially helpful in supervisors:

- A pleasant, friendly, outgoing personality
- A college degree in hotel, restaurant, or institutional management
- A degree in home economics or nutrition with completed internship in dietetics
- A good background in quantity food preparation, preferably with experience in high-quality establishments
- Supervisory experience at other colleges or universities
- Training and experience as a sanitarian

Training of Food Supervisors

It is unlikely that a newly-hired supervisor or unit manager can take over and do a good job for you within weeks or even months after being hired. Much more probable, he will take three to six months to become accustomed to the new college, to the new job, and to your way of doing things. The more time you can give a new supervisor to learn the ropes, the better it will be for your operations. Hiring him on August 15th, and expecting that he take charge of an entire unit by the time school opens is not only unfair, but unrealistic. At the same time, there is much you can do to train your new supervisors.

On-the-job training -- The most common method of training a new supervisor is to let him learn on the job, preferably by working with another, experienced manager. The opportunity to work with someone else for a few months is important. It makes learning easier and removes the pressure. Some food service directors don't like the idea of having a new supervisor with one of the older ones. They are afraid that he might learn bad habits, or they think it is a waste of money and time. Actually, if you have properly indoctrinated your new supervisor as to what your goals are and what you expect from him the chance that he might learn bad habits from a present supervisor is slim. Giving him an opportunity to learn from another manager is certainly not a waste of money and often turns out to be mutually beneficial.

Staff meetings -- There are many good reasons why a manger should have regular meetings with his staff. The opportunity to create effective two-way communications, the opportunity to set common goals, the opportunity to relate to one another in a regularly scheduled but relaxed setting are three such reasons. Another important one, however, is to use the staff meeting as a training device. There is much a new supervisor must learn, and you have little opportunity to teach him. Setting broad goals, and explaining your general philosophy is fine during the hiring interview, but not nearly enough once he begins his work. There are hundreds of situations that come up every day, where a supervisor must make decisions. The better he knows what you expect, the better he learns what his peers the other supervisors might do in each instance, the more effective he will become. A good staff meeting will include the following components:

- It will be scheduled on a regular basis, preferably daily or weekly.
- It will have a regular agenda.
- It will allow time for discussion of items not on the agenda.
- It will give everyone a chance to participate.
- It will not be too long.

Conferences and workshops -- As mentioned in Chapter VI, a good way to train any supervisor is to let him attend regional conferences and workshops on matters dealing with college and university food service, or to visit other food service operations. The opportunity to meet with other people who have similar problems and challenges is helpful. The learning that comes through hearing the programs and group discussions is another benefit. It also is a great boost to supervisors' morale to be sent to special places and gives them a chance to get to know other food service supervisors in a relaxed atmosphere.

Duties of a Supervisor

Food supervisors have different types of jobs in different institutions. In a large state university with residence hall kitchens feeding as many as 1,500 to 2,000 students each, his job may be that of a specialist. He may be in charge of food production, or of clean-up, or of dining hall supervision. In a small college, he may be the director's principal assistant, and be responsible for everything that goes on. In spite of this difference, there are certain common duties and work routines which most college food service supervisors are asked to follow. A typical manager of a residence hall kitchen which feeds 1,000 students would probably not be involved in the purchasing of food, the scheduling of catering functions, budget preparation, or financial oversight. What most supervisors handle

- Supervising regular and student personnel
- Receiving, storage, and preparation of food
- Serving of food and beverages
- Supervision of dining halls
- Direct, personal contact with students
- Bookkeeping and accounting matters concerning their units
- Recipe and menu development

A supervisor is the person in tactical charge of his food operation. He has an important job and often does several things at one time. Just when one of the cafeteria lines has run out of food, one of the cooks may have a major problem while, at the same time, there may be something happening in the dining hall that requires his attention. Each problem may be related to the others, and his ability to solve them quickly is essential to his success.

Because there are many different matters to be attended to daily it is wise to establish a certain routine in fulfilling daily tasks. In outlining the duties to your supervisors, you should suggest some type of morning routine, such as the following:

A GOOD SUPERVISOR SHOULD

- Greet everyone personally and cheerfully
- Make sure that every employee scheduled to work is actually there. If not call in substitutes
- Check the daily menu, then inspect freezers and refrigerators personally. Consider use of leftovers
- Consult with cooks and salad makers
- Check the production sheets for each meal. Make sure that recipes are being followed

- Check catering board for all catering functions. Make sure that these have been assigned to specific workers and are being handled
- Inspect the cafeteria line at least 5 minutes before it is due to open to
  a. Instruct the line servers on portions to be served
  b. Taste the food
  c. Check for hot dinner plates
  d. Check overhead lights, steam table thermostats, and the covers on steam table pans
- Inspect the dining room prior to opening to
  a. Make certain that all tables and chairs are clean and ready for the meal
  b. Make sure that floors, conveyor belts, and beverage counters are clean
  c. Check salad tables, condiment tables, and beverage stations to be certain they are completely set up
  d. Be certain that the entire menu is posted, written on the blackboard or marked at the proper places on the cafeteria line
  e. Make certain that the hostess/cashier is in place and that the dining room doors are unlocked exactly on time or, preferably, a few minutes prior to the scheduled opening. (College students are generally early when it comes to dining. A college food service unit should open at least five minutes prior to the scheduled opening time, and close at least five minutes after the scheduled closing time. Students' watches are not all synchronized, and nothing angers a student more than if he misses his meal because of a technicality)
- Visit with students and faculty during meal hours to
  a. Make sure that they get everything on the menu
  b. Take care of special requests
  c. Make note of contructive suggestions about food service
  d. Engage in conversation and get to know as many students as possible
- Follow up on all sanitation procedures to assure
  a. Proper handling of leftover food after meals
  b. Proper cleaning of dining room tables and floors
  c. Proper kitchen and dishroom sanitation after each meal
  d. Proper cleaning of all movable carts, receiving dock, and other food service areas
- Keep checking on the cafeteria line during the meal to
  a. Make certain that the lines are kept supplied with food, without too much food being cooked too far in advance. This applies especially to short order items like hamburgers and vegetables
  b. Select a suitable alternate in plenty of time if an item runs out so that the line is not delayed. Make certain that menu is changed to reflect the substitution
  c. Make certain that all the food served at the end of the meal period is as plentiful and attractive as that served at the beginning

    d. Check plate waste in the dishroom in order to evaluate food preparation and portioning

REGULAR PERMANENT EMPLOYEES

Some managers, especially if they are young and inexperienced, have a tendency to unfairly criticize the regular kitchen employees for whatever difficulties they might encounter on a new job. One can just hear them mutter, not too discreetly, "If I just had a decent staff to work with." This approach is doomed to failure. When you take over an existing staff of workers, accept them at face value. Assume, unless you find out otherwise, that each of your people is a fine person, a loyal and dependable employee, likeable and competent. Assume, furthermore, that any practices and procedures which are not in line with your own ideas are not necessarily their fault, but possibly the fault of your predecessor, or perhaps just a case of poor work habits which require changing. In other words, instead of making snap judgments about your new employees, accept them, trust them, and work with them in a positive state of mind. You will discover, in time, that most of them are good employees, that they are willing to learn new things, and that they are anxious to please you. Eventually, you will have to solve specific problems with specific individuals. In some cases intensive training may be needed, in others, re-assignment. In one or two cases, even layoff may become necessary. But, your general approach should be one of enthusiasm for your new staff, and willingness to share with them whatever fresh ideas you have brought with you.

Undoubtedly, there will be much to change. It seldom happens that a new manager becomes merely a caretaker, and continues everything that went on before his arrival without change. Chances are that you will have to engage in intensive staff training during the first year on your new job. Special training sessions may have to be scheduled from time to time so that your new staff understands your ideas about sanitation, safety, food preparation, relations with students, and quality in general. Don't try to do this all at once. Go slowly, and follow up closely after each change. Make yourself a list of important subject matters, in order of priority, and tackle them one at a time. Pursue each subject with patience and determination, like a school teacher who is teaching writing or arithmetic to his students. It will take repetition, reminders, and more repetition before everyone on your staff finally catches on.

Take a simple matter such as the pre-heating of dinner plates. Assume that you have plenty of heated dish dollies and plenty of dinner plates. It would seem that all you needed to do was to tell everyone that from now on you expected every dinner plate to be pre-heated prior to serving time. Actually, it will take you at least six months before every member of your staff understands, finally, that you really mean it and that you insist on the plates being hot. Even then, some will always foreget to plug in the dollies, or to keep the dishes hot; others will complain about burning their hands, or worry about the students burning theirs. Patience, perseverence, and persistence are the only solutions to such a problem.

Creating a Team Spirit

One of your greatest frustrations when starting a new management job will be the realization of how difficult it is to mold different individuals working in different kitchens, and coming from different backgrounds, into a cohesive team. Even though you see yourself as heading one food service organization, serving just one clientele, the college community, your employees don't see it that way. They visualize themselves as working in Kitchen "A", and their loyalty is to that kitchen and to the students eating in their dining hall. Even if everyone of your people works in just one kitchen, you will find an intense rivalry between the morning shift and the evening shift.

> "Why can't the evening crew clean some lettuce before they leave? After all, we have to help them with their stuff after lunch."

> "Let the morning cooks fix the lunch. I have to get ready for my dinner meal. I can't stop to make bacon, lettuce, and tomato sandwiches."

> "I cleaned all the morning pots. Let Jimmy do the dinner pots when he comes in!"

It takes time and diplomacy to make everyone forget their possessive attitude, and to make everyone realize that any problem in food service is everyone's problem. Mixing staff assignments is very helpful in this regard. During recess or vacation periods, or from one semester to the next, shift people around a little. Make everyone work in a different place sometime, in a different job even, under a different manager. After a while, some of this parochial attitude disappears, and is slowly replaced with an understanding that everyone must cooperate if peace and tranquility and, even more important, good results are to be achieved.

Another good method of making your staff see things from your perspective is to share with them some of the students' comments and criticism. Type up a list of the major things that the students like and dislike, and distribute copies to each of your employees. Everyone likes to be proud of his work, and it is often quite a revelation for a cook to read:

> "I would like music, while I die eating raw eggs."

> "Why don't you send your cooks for consultation with my mother?"

> "I like everything on the menu, Paul, but not here!"

Recruitment and Retention of Staff

Finding good replacements for those who have left your staff is often a frustrating experience. Even if the school's personnel department, carefully briefed by you, has screened out the worst of the applicants, you are still left with the task of picking someone who is able, willing to learn, willing to work, willing to stay for a long time, and someone who can get along well with the rest of your staff. That is quite an assignment, particularly since you have only a few moments for each interview. There are a few ideas that may help you, however.

One of these is to utilize the recommendations of your existing staff whenever possible. Even though it is not a good idea to employ members of the same family in the same kitchen, there is usually little problem about hiring someone's friend or acquaintance. You will discover that your employees are very careful about recommending anyone to work for you. More often than not, such a person will probably be a good candidate and a good worker.

Another helpful idea is to invite a member of your present staff to participate in the interviews. Not only is it good for morale, but often the employee's judgment about an applicant is better than your own, and your chances of picking the best candidate improve considerably.

Word of mouth referrals by anyone on the college staff are often better than merely culling candidates from the files of the personnel department. Advertisements in the local newspaper will also bring in additional candidates and thus give you a better group from which to choose.

Close adherence to affirmative action statutes, and careful observation of all laws dealing with equal opportunities are not only legally necessary but morally right.

Employee Training

In building a college food service staff, keep in mind that many new employees are relatively inexperienced and that there is a natural desire in everyone to learn and improve oneself. Given these two facts, it is obvious that you must engage in a serious effort to develop an effective, permanent training program, not only for the purpose of orienting new employees, but also to remind and improve the present staff. Such training programs differ of course, depending on the size of staff, the type of food service program, and other factors. Following, however, is a suggested series of training steps that can be adapted and modified to suit almost any college food service operation.

Training the new employee -- All too often, the training of a new employee consists of someone giving him an employee's handbook, an apron, and a time card. He is then placed at a work station where, either alone or with the help of a more experienced exmployee, he is expected to begin his new job. If you really want a new employee to become a member of your team, to work for the same overall objective, and to be productive and successful on his new job, then you must put forth much greater effort. A new employee must first learn something about your college or university, then about the food service organization he is about to join, and, last but not least, details about the technical or professional aspects of his job.

General information about the institution's personnel policies, fringe benefits, and other vital data should be provided the new employee by the personnel staff by means of a handbook with verbal explanations of the most important matters. If there is no one in personnel to perform this, then someone on your staff must do it. The introduction to the food service is your responsibility. Whether you do it personally or assign the job to an assistant, it is crucial that the new employee be taken around your various kitchens and introduced to some of the managers and food service staff. A new employee gets quite a different opinion of the food service organization and of his part in that organization if he can see how everything fits together: if he can see several kitchens, knows where the food is bought, where it is stored, and how the various units on campus work together. The technical part of the new employee's orientation can be done a number of different ways. In the larger universities, one sometimes finds a special training supervisor who will put him through a brief training program. With the use of brief training films, slide presentations, and video-tape, the employee gets a chance to learn about the most important aspects of his job. During the past few years, a number of excellent audio-visual training aids have been produced for the food service industry. A major producer of such training films is National Educational Media in Encino, California; the National Restaurant Association in Chicago also offers a series of helpful training aids. Some colleges and universities have also produced their own slide presentations. On smaller campuses, the food service manager must take responsibility for the initial training. Perhaps, before the new employee is sent to begin his work, you, or one of your supervisors, can spend an hour or two working directly with the new worker, answering his questions and explaining how and why you do things as you do. Then a few minutes of personal introduction to the experienced worker who is to explain and demonstrate the job are most helpful. Finally, there should be a period of several days during which the new employee does not yet have production responsibility of his own, but is working with an experienced employee who will be training him.

Unfortunately, that's not the way it usually happens. Many people have a low opinion of the skills it takes to be a potwasher or a saladmaker, or even a cook. Few recognize that it takes skill to be a good potwasher, that a modern dishmachine is a complicated, expensive piece of equipment, that very few kitchen janitors have ever been shown the way to clean a kitchen and dining room floor professionally and that even the wiping of tables can be done incorrectly. The more effort you put forth in training a new employee initially, the better a job he will perform for you later.

Training your regular staff -- Since many workers in college and university kitchens have been at their jobs for years, it is understandable that some food service directors consider the training of such employees to be quite unnecessary. In many cases, these long-term employees know more about certain aspects of their job than does the director himself, and don't feel the need for additional training. They have seen all the sanitation films you could find, they know all about food preparation, and they have heard everything you ever said about "being nice to the students." Don't you believe it. Every worker, no matter how experienced, can always learn something new, or be reminded of something he forgot. You can never do enough training on the subjects of sanitation and safety. After all, is it not true that you still have occasional problems with dirty kitchens, and that you still have industrial accidents in your kitchen every year? Is it not true that some of your employees are careless when it comes to using kitchen equipment, and that even the most knowledgeable employee once in a while fails to follow some principle of good sanitation when preparing food?

Continuous training of food service workers should be a solemn obligation of every food service manager. One of the simplest ways is to include brief training sessions in regular weekly meetings of the entire kitchen staff. A few minutes of each meeting can be set aside to cover a simple item such as how properly to use a kitchen knife, how to clean and cut a head of lettuce, or how to wipe a dining room table. Another effective method is to distribute magazine or newspaper articles of special interest, novel recipes, new ways of doing things, or anything else pertaining to food service which the employee might enjoy. Excellent sources for printed educational materials are the various trade associations, such as the Florida Citrus Commission, the National Dairy Council, and the Cling Peach Association.

A highly effective framework for continuous training of a food service staff is the formal training meeting. Such meetings must be carefully planned, must be full of interesting content, and must be held on a day which permits the attendance of most of the food service staff. This is quite an assignment, since there are few days when a college food service can shut down, even for half a day. The best time for most schools is some quiet day during the summer and a similarly slow day during a recess period in the winter. The meetings should not be too long; kitchen workers are not used to going to class. A half day meeting, which starts with coffee and doughnuts in the morning and ends with a relaxed, informal lunch is ideal.

There are many topics which lend themselves to this kind of meeting, so it will be difficult for you to choose from among them. Remember that variety and interest are important. You must produce a training session that will not only be educational, but stimulating and enjoyable. There are many different methods of presenting subject matter. Listed below are some of these, together with appropriate subjects.:

Informal Talks

"The Importance of Food Service in the Educational Process" (dean of students)

"Our Food Service Philosophy: Service to the College Community" (food service director)

"Safety: A Review of Food Service Accidents During the Past Several Years" (members of the food service safety committee)

"Sanitation - A Way of Life" (talk and film by local health department official)

"Review of Food Service Policies and Practices" (food service unit manager)

Practical Demonstrations and Food Exhibits

"List of Garnishes for Salad Plates, Banquet Plates, and Cafeteria Food Pans" (dietitian)

"How to Make Hors d'oeuvres and Canapes" (head salad worker)

"How to Wash Silverware Properly" (dishroom crew)

"How to Make Good Gravy" (cook)

"How to Mop a Floor" (kitchen porter)

Audience Participation Programs

"How to Use a Fire Extinguisher" (film, demonstration, and audience participation -- local fire marshall)

"Sanitation and Safety Quiz"

"Quiz on Existing Food Service Policies"

"Group Discussion: You and the Stude: ."

Skits and One-Act Plays

"Serving Students: the Wrong Way and the Right Way" (food service supervisors)

"Handling Customers' Complaints" (supervisors and staff)

Films

A whole variety of films on sanitation, safety, food preparation, courtesy, public relations, etc., is available from local and state health departments, and also from commercial companies such as National Educational Media.

In these training sessions it is important that everyone is completely relaxed and feels no pressures from management. Therefore, if you decide on using a quiz as part of the program, make sure that such a quiz is for the person's own use, does not have to be signed, returned, or graded.

Sometimes it may be wise to schedule an entire training session on one subject only. On one such occasion, at the University of the Pacific, the entire meeting was turned over to the chairman of the speech department who, together with two colleagues, conducted a human relations seminar for food service workers. The seminar consisted of a brief talk, audience participation, and discussion by small groups; then came reports to the entire audience by the group leaders and, finally, a wrap-up by the department chairman. Most of the food service staff had never been exposed to this type of a participatory training session, and came away feeling excited about the experience. A sample employee training program is shown in Appendix 6.

Personnel Policies

Whether you like it or not, much of your time during the first year or two on a new job will be spent setting policies for food service personnel. Since a policy is a rule or regulation which is relatively permanent and inflexible, it takes more than ordinary caution when a new policy is being established. Before setting new personnel policies, review in your mind a number of questions:

- Is it fair to the employees and to the college?
- Does it conflict with existing personnel policies?

- What is its impact in terms of cost efficiency and morale?
- Will it solve the problem at hand?
- Will it be suitable for future, similar occasions?

The number of policy decisions you are asked to make will stagger you. Decisions about layoffs during recess periods, use of seniority in work assignments, weekend work, hiring workers for a.m. and/or p.m. shifts, employee meals and meal hours, time cards, keys, uniforms, and many others.

Policies should be distinguished from ordinary management decisions by their permanence. Therefore, they should always be put in writing, and distributed to everyone concerned, so that no one can claim ignorance. Similarly, when an existing policy is changed or dropped, everyone should be properly informed. Normally, a notice above the time clock in each kitchen is sufficient. In cases of special importance, however, it is wise to address a copy of the new policy to each employee individually, to make certain that everyone is familiar with it.

Personal Interest in Employees

It would be inappropriate to end this chapter without stressing the special importance of a genuine personal interest in each employee. It was mentioned earlier that you must demonstrate an honest affection for your staff if you want to gain their trust and friendship in return. Some managers become very friendly with their employees on a personal basis, visit their homes, and spend time together socially. Sometimes this is fine, at other times it can be disruptive and create jealousies and disunity. Frequent praise for work well done is one good way to show affection; remember, people need praise like they need fresh air.

Visits to the hospital in case of illness are another way to show personal interest. When your employees are in trouble they look to you for assistance and sympathy. In case of a death in the family, nothing is more important than your presence at the funeral, not even the luncheon of your board of trustees! Sometimes you will have a chance to help your employees with personal matters that are beyond the scope of their work at your college. Perhaps you can refer them to a lawyer or marriage counsellor, doctor or psychiatrist. Perhaps you can just listen to their problems and respond in a friendly, personal way without actually giving advice. You must be careful, of course, that your advice is sought out, and that you do not meddle in someone else's personal affairs. An employee can handle such meddling if it comes from a fellow worker, but it becomes more difficult if it is the boss who is interfering. Nevertheless, you have knowledge and talents which can be useful to your employees, and if you help them more than they expect, you are laying the groundwork for lasting loyalty.

STUDENT EMPLOYEES

Much of what you need to know about the use of student workers in your college food service operation has been covered in Chapter VI. At this point, it is proper to ask whether or not students should have a prominent part in your food service organization and, if so, how big a part? Some schools have hardly any student employees in food service, while others depend upon students for more than 90% of their kitchen work force. You have read earlier that student workers are often ambassadors of good will, that they provide an intelligent and flexible work force, and that there should be two or three part-time student workers for every full-time employee.

To place disproportionate responsibility on the student work force is to make two mistakes. One, it is to overlook the fact that the students are in college to learn a profession. Unless their future profession is to be in food service, their interest in their job is necessarily secondary to their interest in studies and life on campus generally. The second mistake is to expect a student, by mere use of his or her intelligence, to learn the skills which your regular staff has developed over many years. It does take skill to cook and to make beautiful salads and desserts. Students can be most effective as assistants, but disasters as independent production workers.

On the other hand, students often bring with them an enthusiasm which infects the entire kitchen. Many of them take their work very seriously and become natural partners in your efforts to maintain high standards of food preparation and service. What you must do is to become their friend, teacher, and employer all at the same time. If you explain sanitation, through talks, films, and demonstrations, they will often become as dedicated as you are. If you show them how to decorate food they will come up with new ideas that are better than your old ones. If you point out the need for good public relations with customers, they will cooperate willingly.

Students like to learn new things. It is easy to instill in them pride in their food service, if you can convince them of your emphasis on quality and service, if you dress them in distinctive smocks or jackets, if you teach them new skills, and offer them your friendship. At the same time, you must meet them half-way when it comes to study-connected problems which interfere with your operations. In the weeks before and during finals, permit substitutes to work in their place. At the end of the semester, don't expect them to stay on campus just for the sake of food service. If you want them to come early in the fall, before the start of classes, compensate them properly for the inconvenience. Pay them enough to make it worthwhile.

In summary, although students have separate shifts, separate wage scales, and fewer fringe benefits, they are an essential part of your overall food service staff. A separate set of policies, and a special way of working with students is not only legitimate, but absolutely essential if overall harmony and staff cohesion is to be maintained.

VIII. MAINTAINING QUALITY IN FOOD PREPARATION

DOES YOUR FOOD SERVICE RATE "EXCELLENT?"

Every food service manager would like to run an excellent food service operation. Many do, some think they do, and others would like to know how to do it. To be really excellent, a food service operation should follow the practices of other places that produce high quality food and service.

The problem with many food service managers is that they have not been in enough of these "other places" to judge the difference between good and excellent. The food service director must develop a set of impeccably high standards for himself and his staff, and maintain these in the face of every-day temptations to lower them. The first task, then, is to recognize quality when you see it. A truly clean kitchen, for instance, smells, feels, and looks clean the minute you enter. A first-class cafeteria counter has a dozen tell-tale signs: overhead lamps, attractively garnished pans of food, smiling uniformed servers, heated plates, attractive menu signs, etc. Other things which suggest excellence are recipes and production sheets posted at the cook's station, aluminum or plastic wrap over all food containers in the walk-in refrigerators, mops hanging up neatly on the wall, a cafeteria worker cleaning tables as soon as they are vacated, and every kitchen worker in uniform with proper hair covering.

You can tell a poor operation just as quickly, When smoking is allowed in the kitchen, when food or dirt is on the floors, when garbage cans are overflowing because no one is bothering to empty them, when newspapers and other junk are allowed to grace the top of refrigerators and ranges, and when lukewarm food is slopped on cold plates by disinterested cafeteria servers, then you know that overall quality is missing.

A truly excellent food service can be defined as one:
- Where the food is of top quality and tastes delicious
- Where it is presented in clean surroundings in a sanitary way
- Where it is properly merchandised and served in a pleasant manner and in a gracious atmosphere
- Where the customers are convinced that this particular food service operation is better than most others of a similar nature
- Where there is a spirit of cooperation, of pride, and of joyful activity among the staff
- Where all of the above is accomplished in an efficient and economic manner

HIGH STANDARDS OF FOOD PURCHASING AND FOOD PREPARATION

It is an axiom of food service that whenever high quality food is properly prepared and served it will taste delicious. Thus, the first step toward quality is to purchase only high quality food products. While there may be general agreement with this statement there is much disagreement about just what constitutes truly high quality food. Here are some typical comments you will encounter:

"Why use No. 1 apples for Waldorf salad?"

"Why use turkey breast for turkey a la king?"

"What's wrong with canned soup?"

"I can buy canned pie filling that is better than we can make ourselves!"

"Why purchase U.S. Choice meat for pot roast?"

"Whipped topping holds up better than whipped cream!"

"The students prefer plain jello to jello with fruit in it!"

If you read the above carefully, you will note that there is truth in every comment. The problem is not with the facts behind every statement, but how they may be used (or abused) by the food service manager. There is nothing wrong in using a No. 2 apple for Waldorf salad, as long as the apples served to the customers as fresh fruit are cool, crisp No. 1's. It is quite acceptable to use turkey rolls in a cooked turkey dish where the gelatin in the roll dissolves, as long as these rolls are not used to make turkey sandwiches or as a turkey entree item. Students seethe when they bite into the gelatin and skin covering. Some canned soups, such as cream of tomato, are really better than most cooks can produce but, as a general rule, nothing beats a delicious home made soup, with natural stock and plenty of "goodies" in it. While canned pie fillings are getting better all the time, it is highly doubtful that they can beat the taste of your baker's own pie filling made with frozen fruit cooked the day the pie is being baked. There may not be a taste difference between a chuck roast that is graded "U.S. Good" and one graded "U.S. Choice" when used in an item such as a pot roast, but is the small price difference worth the cost of your not being able to say anymore: "All we use in this institution are U.S. Choice meats?" Whipped topping, which contains a stabilizer, will hold up much longer than whipped cream, but no one would argue which of the two tastes the better. Finally, it is true that mnay college students like their gelatin salads to be red and plain, but that is no reason to forget the many others who would delight in such salads with fruits, nuts, and other delightful ingredients.

Let us look into the various categories of food produced, then, and see how we can identify true excellence in their preparation:

Soups

There is no phrase sweeter to the American ear than "home-made soup." It is in fact, an American tradition and the wise food service manager will make certain that his cooks can make their own soup. Even if an old-fashioned stock pot, simmering on the range, is not always practical, there are many excellent quantity recipes for delicious home-made soups which use soup base as an ingredient. Another important quality aspect is the offering of a rich variety of soups: there are dozens of popular soups in the American family repertoire, ranging from corn chowder to mulligatawny, and the students usually like them all. A very important factor in serving soup is that it must be literally boiling hot. This is difficult to do in a steam table since the thermostats for the wells holding the other foods cannot usually be turned up all the way without burning the food from the bottom. Nevertheless, if a special effort is made to turn up the thermostat under the soup well all the way, to keep a cover on the well, or better yet, to place an electric soup well and heated soup bowls in the dining room where the students can help themselves after having gone through the serving line, then the soup will still be very hot when the students sit down to eat. One other quality factor is often forgotten in the serving of soup: the serving of toppings or special ingredients adds interest and zest to the soup. Preparing croutons, litle pieces of onion or garlic toast, fried sausage or hot dog slices is easy. Adding popcorn on top of tomato soup, for instance, is no trouble at all. More difficult, but exciting, is to top onion soup with a slice of cheese and bake it in the oven in individual casseroles. There are dozens of other ways in which an otherwise ordinary soup can be made into an excellent dish.

Salads and Salad Plates

Salads are a vital part of a college student's meal. As American families become more nutrition-conscious, children are given more and more salads to eat, so that by the time they attend college, they look forward to having salads with their meals. Dieting students (and this includes, at one time or another, most women and many men), are especially concerned about salads, since they often eat little else.

Twenty-five years ago, when residence hall food service was in its early growth stages, there were no such innovations as salad bars. All salads were individually dished up and placed on cafeteria counters. Seldom was there much choice, although cottage cheese has been an alternate salad selection for a long, long time. The coming of the "smorgy" buffet-type restaurants and the introduction at about the same time of self-service salad bars in residence hall dining rooms, brought a drastic improvement to college food service. Most residence hall dining rooms now feature salad bars with several types of salads, dressing, relishes, and condiments. The most common salad bar features green salad with several dressings, cottage cheese, and one other salad. Fancier salad bars also offer fruit salads, starch salads (e.g. potato salad), meat salads (e.g. chicken salad) and a variety of relishes and condiments. A sample salad bar of this type is shown in Exhibit VIII-1.

Quality in salads does not depend only on the variety offered. The care with which salads are prepared is even more important. The lettuce in green salads should be thoroughly washed, cool and crisp, and cut in bite-size pieces. Radishes, celery, and tomatoes make attractive ingredients. Onions and green peppers should also be used, although more sparingly. Bowls of cottage cheese, potato and macaroni salad, and other plain-looking dishes should always be garnished to make them look more attractive. The same care must be given to individual salads: lettuce underneath, croutons, pickle chips, sliced beets, or a multitude of other garnishes on top, make the difference between an ordinary salad and one that is excellent. Variety is another element of quality in salad preparation. While college students are generally wary of trying new and strange dishes, they are much less reluctant to try a new and interesting salad. The addition of unusual and novel salads to the standard repertoire goes far to heightening interest in the entire meal. Even a cracker, or a piece of Melba toast, or some small cubes of cheese can make the difference.

EXHIBIT VIII-1

UNIVERSITY OF THE PACIFIC

INGREDIENTS OF U.O.P. FOOD SERVICE
TYPICAL SALAD BAR

1. Tuna Salad
2. Cottage Cheese
3. Fruit SaladBowl (canned and fresh fruits mixed)
4. Tossed Green Salad (3 kinds of dressing including low-calorie)
5. Carrot Sticks
6. Olives
7. Pickles
8. Celery Sticks
9. Ham or Chicken Salad
10. Potato or Macaroni Salad
11. Devil Egg Salad (optional)
12. Mixed Bean Salad
13. Pickled Beets

The variety of dressings offered with the green salads is also an important quality factor. The average food service operation will limit itself to the usual French, 1000-island, and Italian dressing; sometimes blue cheese dressing is also served. The quality operation will offer some home-made dressings such as blue cheese dressings made with buttermilk and pieces of real blue cheese, will always offer low-calorie dressings for dieters, and always have cruets of vinegar and oil for those who like to help themselves. Some institutions such as the University of California at Santa Barbara have a whole table of exciting additional salad ingredients, such as alfalfa and bean sprouts, garbanzo beans, bacon bits, etc. For a list of garnishes, see Exhibit VIII-2. Other quality institutions, such as Rutgers University in New Brunswick, N.J., have special yogurt bars in addition to the salad bars, where plain yogurt is offered on an attractive cart with two or three different fruit toppings, plus honey and wheat germ to top things off.

Those institutions which do not offer salad bars in residence halls, and all campus cash operations, should make a specialty out of salad plates. More and more, these are coming into their own as a favorite luncheon dish for both men and women alike. The variety and interest that can be created is unlimited, and the extent of careful planning that goes into these creations makes the difference between an ordinary and a quality operation. In order to achieve a first-rate salad plate repertoire, it is essential to create a recipe file for these just as you do for entree items. A sample list of salad plates is shown in Exhibit VIII-3.

Good ideas for salads are not the exclusive domain of the food service director. A gift of an inexpensive, illustrated salad book, or a subscription to a food service or homemakers' magazine given to your head saladmaker, can produce amazing results. Food service mangers should make it a practice to read and clip out pictures and recipes of novel and attractive dishes.

Sandwiches

Few staples of the American diet have been more abused and neglected in food operations than the ordinary, everyday sandwich. Many managers believe that all it takes to make a sandwich is two pieces of bread, and something to put in between. Secure in this mistaken belief, they then leave the sandwich preparation to their cooks or saladmakers, without worrying about the way the sandwich looks or tastes. The following are standards that must be upheld in sandwich preparation:

Bread -- The bread should be fresh, and of various types (white, whole wheat, rye).

Spread -- Except in unusual circumstances, sandwiches should be spread with some sort of moistener, such as margarine, butter, or mayonnaise, and in some cases, with a little mustard. All these should be used sparingly, and should be spread evenly over the bread's entire surface to the four corners.

Filling -- A good sandwich should have at least one-and-a-half to two ounces of ingredients, whether meat, or cheese, or some sort of meat or fish mixture. When

EXHIBIT VIII-2

UNIVERSITY OF THE PACIFIC
FOOD SERVICE
LIST OF GARNISHES

YELLOW ORANGE
Cheese and Eggs:
Balls, Grated, Strips
Rosettes
Egg, Hard Cooked or Sections
Deviled Egg Halves
Riced Egg Yolk

Fruit:
Apricot Halves, Sections
Cantaloupe Balls
Lemon Sections, Slices
Orange Sections, Slices
Peach Slices
Peach Halves with Jelly
Spiced Peaches
Persimmons
Tangerines

Sweets:
Apricot Preserves
Orange Marmalade
Peach Conserve
Peanut Brittle, Crushed
Sugar, Yellow, Orange

Vegetables:
Carrots, Rings, Shredded, Strips

Miscellaneous:
Butter Balls
Coconut, Tinted
Gelatin Cubes
Mayonnaise

RED
Fruit:
Cherries
Cinnamon Apples
Cranberries
Plums
Pomegranate Seeds
Red Raspberries
Marachino Cherries
Strawberries
Watermelon Cubes, Balls

Sweets:
Red Jelly
  Apple, Cherry, Currant
  Loganberry, Raspberry
Cranberry Glace, Jelly
Gelatin Cubes
Red Sugar

Vegetables:
Beets--Pickled, Julienne

Beet Relish
Red Cabbage
Pepper, Red, Rings,
  Strips, Shredded
Pimiento, Chopped, Strips,
  Shapes
Radishes--Red, Sliced, Roses
Stuffed Olive, Slices
Catsup, Chili Sauce
Tomato Slices

Miscellaneous:
Paprika
Tinted Coconut
Cinnamon Drops

GREEN
Fruit:
Avocado
Cherries
Frosted Grapes
Green Plums
Honeydew Melon
Lime Wedges

Sweets:
Citren
Green Sugar
Gelatin Cubes
Mint Jelly
Mint Pineapple
Mints

Vegetables:
Endive
Green Pepper, Ring, Strips
Green Onions
Lettuce Cups
Lettuce, Shredded
Mint Leaves
Olives
Parsley, Sprig
Pickles
Spinach Leaves

Miscellaneous:
Coconut, Tinted
Mayonnaise, Tinted
Pistachios

WHITE
Apple Rings, Balls
Grapefruit Sections
Gingered Apple
White Raisin
Pear Balls, Sections

Vegetables:
Cauliflowerets
Celery Cabbage
Celery Curls
Cucumber Rings
Mashed Potato Rosettes
Onion Rings

Miscellaneous:
Cream Cheese Frosting
Sliced Hard Cooked White
Shredded Coconut
Marshmellows
Almonds
Mints
Whipped Cream
Powdered Sugar

BROWN, TAN
Bread, Croutens
Fritters
Noodle Rings
Toast Strips, Cubes

Miscellaneous:
Cinnamon
Dates
French Fried Cauliflower
French Fried Onion Rings
Mushrooms
Nutmeats
Nut Covered Cheese Balls
Potato Chips
Toasted Coconut

BLACK
Raisins
Shredded Chocolate
Ripe Olives
Prunes

MISCELLANEOUS LIST
Meal Roll-Up
Flowers
Holly, Cranberries
Pepper, Beet, Onion
Gelatin Shapes
Turnip Lillies
Baked Orange, Pears
Macaroni
Popcorn
Parmesan Cheese
Frankfurter Slice
Chopped Bacon
Pastry Cut Outs
Capers
Nuts

EXHIBIT VIII-3

COLD PLATE SUGGESTIONS

MEAT - Serve with crackers where needed

1. Boiled Ham (1), Swish and American Cheese (2). Bologna (1) with potato salad (#12) garnished with deviled egg half, radish rose, pickles and served on crisp lettuce.

2. Cold meats (3) with potato salad (#12) served on crisp lettuce with hard cooked egg halves (2) carrot, celery, pickle sticks and onion rings.

3. Chef's plate of julienne ham (5), turkey (5) and American cheese (5) garnished with hard cooked egg wedges (2), tomato wedges (2) and ripe olives (2), served on bed of assorted crisp greens.

4. Baked Ham (2) and Swiss cheese (1) with potato salad (#12) on crisp lettuce garnished with hard cooked egg halves (2) pickles, and radish roses.

5. Chef's Plate of julienne salami (5) Swiss cheese (5), asparagus spears (5) garnished with egg and tomato wedges and ripe olives. Served on bed of assorted greens.

6. Dutch Cold Plate Cold ham (2), caraway cheese (1), hard cooked egg halves (2), tomato slices (2) and potato salad (#12). Served on crisp lettuce.

7. Sliced Bologna (2) Cheese (1), lunch meat served on lettuce with macaroni salad (#12) garnished with pickled beets and green bean salad. Served on crisp lettuce or other greens.

8. Cold Meat Rolls (3) potato salad (#12), cole slaw (#12), on crisp lettuce garnished with carrot sticks, tomato wedges, and pickles.

9. Boiled Ham (2), vegetable cottage cheese, sliced tomatoes (2) deviled egg half (1) and ripe olives.

10. Tomato stuffed with ham salad (#12) garnished with green pepper and onion rings, pickles and ripe olives. Served with potato chips.

POULTRY - Served with crackers as needed

1. Cold sliced turkey (3 oz.), egg salad (#16) with tomato wedges, ripe olives and carrot sticks. Served on crisp lettuce with potato chips.

2. Avocado half (or slices) with chicken salad (#12) with ripe and green olives and served with potato chips.

3. Trice Salad - Chicken Salad (#16) with sweet pickle chips, cottage cheese (#16) with tomato wedges and jellied fruit salad. Served on crisp lettuce.

4. Chicken or Turkey Salad (#12) with tomato wedge served on crisp lettuce and garnished with deviled egg halves (2), ripe olives and carrot sticks.

5. Sliced Turkey (3 oz.), sour cream slaw served on lettuce with portion cup cranberry sauce (2½ oz.) garnished with radish roses and ripe olives.

6. Chicken Salad with toasted almonds (#12) jellied Bing cherry salad, cottage cheese (#16), and citrus sections.

7. Chicken Drumsticks (2), potato salad (#12), hard cooked egg halves, radish rose and pickles.

EXHIBIT VIII-3 (continued)

FISH - Crackers to be added as needed

1. Crabmeat Salad (#12) on crisp lettuce, garnished with hard cooked egg quarters (2), tomato wedges (2) carrot sticks, lemon wedges and ripeolives. Served with potato chips.

2. Chef's Plate with (7) shrimps, hard cooked egg quarters (3), tomato (3) and lemon wedges, ripe olives and carrot curls. Served on bed of assorted crisp greens.

3. Salmon Salad on crisp lettuce with tomato slices (2), deviled egg halves (2), lemon wedge and sweet pickles. Served with potato chips.

4. Tunafish Salad on crisp lettuce with sliced hard cooked egg (1), tomato wedges, pickles, ripe olives and lemon wedge. Serve with potato chips.

5. Chilled Shrimp (5) in lettuce cup with lemon wedge, served with portion cup of cocktail sauce (2½ oz.), potato salad (#12) and garnished with egg wedges, pickles and radish rose.

6. Danish Sardines (5), deviled egg halves (2) and pickles on crisp lettuce garnished with pimiento cheese stuffed celery and radish roses.

FRUIT - Served with crackers as needed

1. Center mount of cottage cheese on sherbet (#12) surrounded with peach half, pear half, jellied salad, and bunch of grapes.

2. Peach half with cottage cheese (#30), jellied salad, fresh apple slices, served with meat and cheese finger sandwiches (3).

3. Cottage cheese center surrounded with peach half, blushing pear, red apple slices, pineapple curl and served with blueberry muffin.

4. Patio Fruit Plate - Individual lime-cream cheese mold, garnished with mint or parsley and circled with diced cantaloupe, peach slices, red berries and bananas cut lengthwise.

5. Jellied Salad Square, peach half with cream cheese nut center, grape clusters and orange slices served with muffin.

many sandwiches are made, the efficient kitchen worker spot checks the fillings on a scale occasionally, to make sure that the proper portion standards are still being observed. Certain sandwiches in *a la carte* operations, such as hot meat sandwiches sold at "deli" counters, contain up to four ounces of meat, all thinly sliced and sell, of course, for considerably more than regular sandwiches.

Garnish -- Whenever sandwiches are served on a plate, or wrapped in a sack lunch, it is nice to add a garnish. This can be a pickle wedge, some gherkins or pickle chips, green or black olives, carrot sticks, etc. These must, of course, not be placed so as to make the bread soggy and, in case of wrapped sandwiches, must be wrapped separately.

Because of the popularity of sandwiches with college students, any interesting variation will probably be much appreciated by your clientele. A popular one is the "sandwich by the inch." This is simply a large French bread (2-3 feet long) sliced in half and filled, like a regular submarine sandwich, with bologna, salami, ham, cheese, lettuce and tomato. In a la carte operations, it is then literally sold "by the inch," with the bread board marked off for easy measuring. Those schools which have their own bakeries can try variations of even this idea: at the University of the Pacific, the bakers baked six-foot long French bread (it took three people to carry each loaf) which was then made into a huge submarine sandwich and placed on the cafeteria counter in the residence hall and offered to the students as the main luncheon entree. California State University/Long Beach uses 7-grain bread, and four different recipes with natural ingredients for their "sandwich by the inch."

Whenever the cafeteria layout permits it, as in the "scramble-type" cafeterias, you might experiment with made-to-order sandwiches. At California State University at Chico, such sandwiches are offered regularly in their popular health food and deli bars.

Finally, don't overlook the possibilities of sandwiches for fancy catered lunches. At Mills College in Oakland, for example, they prepare a fancy, multi-layered sandwich loaf with different layers of bread, egg and tuna salad, and other ingredients. They then remove the crust, top it with cream cheese, and serve a slice, together with fresh fruit and sherbet, to make a beautiful luncheon plate.

Meats and Other Entrees

The entree is the most important part of the meal, so maintaining quality here is crucial to your success. The quality of an entree item can be affected at any stage of food preparation and special vigilance and high standards are therefore essential at every step.

Purchasing -- Saving money in purchasing by lowering the quality of the meat is a sure invitation to disaster. Meat purveyors will always have specials, and the wise buyer avoids these most of the time. If you purchase a tenderized steak for "steak night" for example, you will have at least 30% of your students complaining about tough meat. With such a complaint ratio, you are better off to purchase only U.S. Choice steaks as a matter of basic policy. Ground beef, at half the price, is always available, but it may have been in the freezer for months! Don't use it! There is nothing wrong with serving a "flaked" or "moulded" veal pattie, but if you are putting on a special dinner, don't believe for a moment, that it tastes the same as a cutlet from a leg of veal. Caution is advisable even in more controversial matters, such as whether or not to add soybean additive to your ground beef. Many experts will tell you that it makes the meat moister, that it is more nutritious, and that you can save from 3% to 5% on your cost of ground beef. Be wise: your only criterion should be the product's acceptability by the students, whose standard is likely to be, "If you can't even make a decent hamburger on this campus, how can we trust you with anything else?"

One of the important characteristics of a quality purveyor is his delivery process. This includes not only his method of food packaging, but also the dress and personal hygiene of his delivery staff, and the type and condition of his vehicles. An important requirement for a frozen food distributor is that he makes his deliveries in refrigerated trucks. While such trucks are standard for all dairies, they are not uniformly used with frozen foods. If you agree to delivery in non-refrigerated trucks of any food that should be refrigerated or frozen, you are not only running the risk of possible food contamination but are also contributing to the lowered food quality of the delivered product.

Storing -- Many good entree items have been ruined through improper storage. Improperly wrapped meats will incur freezer burns, for example, which will affect their taste. Partial defrosting and refreezing of entrees, an all-too-common occurrence in many food service units also lowers quality. Freezing meats which normally have a two-week shelf life such as ribs, roasts, turkeys, also affects food quality.

Preparation -- The skill of your cooks in preparing the food is important to the success of your food operation. Even when the cooks are skilled and experienced, however, one often finds cooking practices which are continuously followed, even though they have adverse effect on the quality of the food served. Some of these are as follows:

Cooking too far in advance -- This is a universal trait among many institutional cooks. You will spend your entire professional life fighting this practice, and never quite conquer it. Cooks like to have everything ready in plenty of time. What this means in practice is that the beef roast for dinner is put in the oven at 11 a.m. when it should probably go into the oven in several batches, 30 minutes apart, and not before 12:00 or 1:00 p.m. It also means that 100 or more hamburger steaks are ready when the serving line opens at 4:30 p.m. or at 4:00 p.m. when the cooks have their dinner. The result? Dry and tasteless hamburgers for 40-50 students. What is worse, the problem does not stop there. Cooks who get into a habit of cooking too far in advance do so throughout the entire meal period, so that even students who get there at 6:00 p.m. will be served hamburgers cooked an hour before. All short order cooking should be done on a progressive basis, and, whenever possible, in full view of the students. All other cooking should take place in accordance with a clearly spelled out time schedule, which allows enough time for proper food preparation without adversely affecting the quality of the food.

Roasting of meat at high temperatures -- Although the principle of roasting meat at low temperatures has been established and proven for over 25 years, some cooks still roast their meats at too-high temperatures. Roasts cooked at 275° or 300° not only suffer less shrinkage (an important cost factor!) but are often juicier and more flavorful. Using oven thermometers to check the accuracy of your ovens, meat thermometers to make sure the meat comes out at the proper time, and close, personal supervision over cooking practices in the solution of this problem. High temperature roasting should not be tolerated. An instruction sheet on meat cookery is shown in Exhibit VIII-4.

Carelessness by cooks -- One reason why close supervision of cooks is necessary in institutional kitchens is that most cooks, at one time or another, get careless. If you specify that 8 oz. of product should be placed into a casserole for beef pot pie, you will always find a few casseroles that are either half empty or overflowing. If you want the tortillas heated before rolling them into enchiladas, you will find a cook rolling them directly from the box. If you ask that the syrup for pancakes be heated before service, you will discover the syrup bottles, cold, on the condiment table. Among the worst instances of carelessness are the chickens that are undercooked, the meat loaf that comes out pink, and the roast beef that comes out too rare. Students recoil from such food as from rattlesnakes, and it takes them a long time to forgive you for such disasters.

Serving -- If you have any sensitivity and talent for merchandising, the cafeteria serving line is where you should use it most. Imagine 50 pork cutlets dumped willy-nilly into a cafeteria pan and placed on the line. Now imagine the same pork cutlets, stacked neatly in two rows in the pan, with some stewed apple slices separating the two rows. For another example, think how much prettier a meat loaf looks if some parsley, or frozen mixed vegetables are sprinkled on top of the pan. Think of the bland appearance of a pan of stewed chicken and dumplings, and the world of difference that some peas, sliced carrots, or peaches would make in its appearance. Do you remember how much more attractive and appetizing chicken croquettes are when the egg sauce is placed on the dinner plate first, and the croquettes placed on top of the sauce? Why is it that your cooks failed to make gravy for the rice or potatoes, just because the main course is Polish sausage? Serving gravy with potatoes or rice should be as automatic as serving cranberry sauce with turkey, applesauce with pork, mint jelly with lamb, and tartar sauce with all fried fish.

Convenience foods (entrees)

Sometime in the mid-60's, convenience foods hit the institutional market. Frozen food manufacturers began cooking and freezing all types of meats and other entrees for schools and hospitals. Their salesmen, filled with a missionary zeal that had no limits, considered the food service manager who insisted on cooking his own food old fashioned and reactionary. Some large universities, such as the University of Maryland, were held up as examples of the modern college food service, because they converted to a 100% convenience food operation.

Fortunately for the University of Maryland as well as for many other schools, these experiments were short-lived. Most institutional food service managers found out very quickly that convenience entrees were too expensive for regular use, that

EXHIBIT VIII-4

INSTRUCTIONS FOR COOKING MEAT

Very rare   The meat has only a thin portion of cooked meat around the edge; red, almost bloody juices, exude from the meat. Under pressure of the finger, the meat is soft and jellylike inside.

Rare   The raw portion is thinner and the meat around it is now pink; there is a good brown outer surface. The meat has a full, plump appearance and still feels somewhat soft to pressure. The juices are red but not bloody.

Medium rare   The interior is a rich pink. The meat is still plump and the juices are pink. The depth of the gray outer surface has increased and the firmness to touch is more apparent.

Medium   The color of the interior is a modified rose. Pink juices are apparent but the quantity is less plentiful. The exterior is well browned and the surface does not appear as plump or full. When pressed, there is a definite resistance.

Medium well   The pink color has completely disappeared. Juiciness is still evident, but the juices are clear or gray, not pink. There is no longer a plump appearance, and the meat is firm to touch.

Well   The meat is completely gray inside. Little or no juice appears. The meat has a hard, flinty touch and a shrunken appearance. The surface is browned and dry.

Temperatures indicating doneness are:
Beef   Rare 140° F, medium 160° F, and well 170° F
Lamb   Medium 165° F, well 175° F
Pork, fresh   Well 165° to 175° F (always cook pork well; note that temperatures recommended for doneness in pork have been lowered)
Pork, cured   Well 155° F
Poultry   Well 180° F, medium 165° F
Veal   Well 170° F

Courtesy of Stanford University Food Service.

they could not effectuate a savings in labor equivalent to the extra cost of the food, and that often the food prepared by their own cooks was as good, or better, than that bought from the frozen food manufacturer. It would be a mistake, however, to conclude from all this that prepared, frozen entrees have no place in your food service operation. On the contrary, they represent an esential, though perhaps small part of your food offerings, and will prove very helpful to you in everyday operations. The following are some logical uses of prepared frozen entrees:

For banquets -- For all types of luncheons and dinners, convenience entrees such as stuffed chicken breasts, beef Bourguignonne or beef Stroganoff, veal Scalloppini, are the ideal fare. Often your regular kitchen crew simply cannot put out another entree, and you will welcome the chance to purchase the entree ready-made, especially since its cost can be reflected in your banquet price.

As a second item -- Some convenience food items such as macaroni and cheese, spaghetti and meat sauce are relatively inexpensive. They can often be used as a second choice on your residence hall menu, are easy to heat, taste well, and reduce rather than add to your food cost.

In cash operations -- Many cash operations are primarily short order and grill places, where hamburgers and toasted cheese sandwiches are king. In those places, it may be advantageous for you to feature a hot convenience entree item daily, to satisfy those who would like something more substantial. Such items as turkey with dressing, or meatballs with gravy, lend themselves ideally for such use.

For emergencies -- You never know when both cooks in a kitchen will report sick on the same day, when a strike will threaten your school, when a blizzard will close all the roads, or when an unexpected busload of visiting high school students will descend on your cafeteria. Thank God for convenience entrees! As a wise and prudent food service manager, you will always have some of these foods in your freezer, enough, if necessary, to feed your entire student body for at least two days.

Vegetables
When it comes to vegetables, you have one consolation: only *half* of your students will be mad at you. It will be either the half that likes their vegetables overcooked, like some mothers cook them at home, or the half that likes their vegetables undercooked (most of your vegetarians, health food fans, and students with cosmopolitan backgrounds). Naturally, you do have an obligation to teach students about nutrition, and to explain to them that the best way to cook vegetables is *al dente,* just a touch undercooked so that the full flavor and all the nutrients are retained. What if your students don't like vegetables that way? What if the vegetables, without any liquids, dry out or cool off in the steam table? What if you lack enough kitchen help to cook your vegetables in small batches, as they should be cooked?

Don't lose hope. Vegetables are not only a frustration, but also a challenge. Remain flexible, and try to meet your student needs as best as you possibly can. At the University of the Pacific, the students in one dining hall continually complained about cold, underdone vegetables until an electric soup tureen was placed in the dining hall and the vegetables kept hot in the tureen for self-service. After that, there were few complaints. In another dining hall, students complained about overcooked vegetables and there the dietitian made certain that the vegetables were cooked properly, in small batches, and served from the cafeteria line.

The best way to cook vegetables is in quick high pressure steamers. If these are not available, you should make sure that the cooks are using very little water in cooking. Equally important is that the line servers use slotted spoons and are careful to drain the vegetables before they place them on the plate.

Obviously, the quality of vegetables used is also of great importance. Whenever you can afford it, buy fresh vegetables, even if it means more work for your cooks. Most institutions can afford to serve fresh carrots once in a while, or beans, or asparagus, squash, and other vegetables in season. When you give the students such a treat, be sure to let them know, so that you can get full mileage from the extra cost and labor involved. Most of the time, in a quality food service operation, you will be using frozen vegetables when you cannot use fresh, and will be using canned vegetables only in emergencies or under special circumstances.

One final note: Don't get discouraged if, in spite of your best efforts, there is a large group of students unhappy with, or disinterested in your vegetables. Remember that many students never ate their vegetables when they were children at home, and you cannot expect miraculous changes as soon as they leave home.

An instruction sheet on vegetable cookery is shown in Exhibit VIII-5.

Breads

A quick way to determine whether a food service unit has high quality food is to check the kind of bread offered. The average operation will feature only breads available from the bread man: sandwich breads, buns, and other standard bread items. Furthermore, the breads may be limited to the cheapest ones in his line (white, whole wheat and rye), so that even the limited assortment of exciting breads that he has, such as diet bread, raisin bread, and pumpernickel, is not available to the student. Many unusual breads are available from commercial bakeries, if you make special effort to bring them to your campus:

Sour dough French	Roman Meal
Sweet French	Butter and egg
Dutch crunch	Old fashioned home style
Buttermilk	Stoneground
Honey or cracked wheat	Seeded twist
English muffin bread	Jewish rye

Pumpernickel

Should you be fortunate enough to have your own baker, the sky is the limit for the many, exciting varieties of bread you can serve to your students. Following are some of the breads from the bake shop of the University of the Pacific:

EXHIBIT VIII-5

FACTS TO REMEMBER ON FROZEN VEGETABLES

Storage: The temperature must be 0° F or less, to preserve flavor, texture, color and nutritional value.

Refreezing: Regard frozen foods which have thawed as perishable, for microorganisms in the food will cause spoilage if the conditions are right. However, if the food still feels cold, contains ice crystals and it has been thawed only a brief time - then you may safely refreeze. Still, some quality loss will occur due to thawing and refreezing.

Holding: Hold frozen foods on steam table or in warm ovens as short a time as possible. Long standing tends to lower quality by affecting color, flavor and texture. Avoid this by preparing smaller amounts frequently.

Cooking: Cooking in too much water - This will cause a loss of many of the water soluable nutriments, also loss of flavor.

Over cooking - Results in colorless, tasteless, mushy vegetables low in food value. Vegetables should be cooked slightly underdone if the method for holding during serving allows further cooking.

Generally, green vegetables should be cooked uncovered so that acids may escape in the steam. Cooking them uncovered also reduces the danger of overcooking.

Frozen vegetables should be cooked in their frozen state -except for spinach and other leaf greens. Also, frozen squash, which is fully cooked, may be partially thawed, preferably under refrigeration. Because of its high water content the squash is a solid block when frozen and will cook unevenly. In addition, all frozen vegetables should be broken into four or five pieces before removing from the carton. This allows the heat to penetrate rapidly and evenly.

Don't add baking soda to green vegetables (an alkali that intensifies color). The alkaline solution created destroys Vitamin A and makes the vegetables mushy in texture.

Don't cook in too large quantities. This will cause loss of food value, and flavor and appearance will be poor.

Don't mix newly cooked vegetables with vegetables cooked earlier. Colors and textures vary.

Color may be lost without accompanying nutrient loss if you cook in hard water. The addition of vinegar or lemon juice to the cooking water will stablize color. Use about one teaspoon for each two cups of water with greens.

Another method of preserving color without losing nutrients is to cook vegetables in milk.

As the addition of water is ruinous to the flavor of some frozen vegetables, steaming or pressure cooking on a rack over hot water, double boiler cooking or baking is recommended. This is especially true for cut corn or squash.

Frozen vegetables may be substituted in recipes calling for fresh vegetables, but shorten their cooking time.

Courtesy of Stanford University Food Service

Oatmeal						Honey orange

Ecology (natural flours)		Lemon dill

Sunflower seed				Cheese snack bread

Sally Lunn (Southern egg bread)

An exciting variation from your normal routine is to place large stacks of fresh French bread, with breadboards and bread knives on the condiment table, letting the students cut their own bread. If, for reasons of sanitation, this does not appeal to you, then assign a student worker to do this in the dining room. Another special treat is to purchase or bake individual loaves of bread and give each student his own loaf. If the extra cost of some of these items seems too high, remember that it is the overall cost of the meal that is important, not the individual parts. Try serving some of these specials for holidays and other festive dinners.

Desserts

There are three basic rules to follow, in planning desserts for college students:

- They must look attractive.
- They must taste good.
- They must last until the end of the meal.

Reflect on this paradox for a moment: on one hand, a good dessert can save an otherwise ordinary meal in the eyes of your students; on the other, desserts are really not important to them. Students delight in a surprise lemon meringue or chocolate cream pie, strawberry tart or, better yet, a chocolate eclair. They love fixing their own ice cream or yogurt sundaes, and would miss the ice cream novelties which they devour by the case at noontimes. On the other hand, you can go many nights with fresh fruit and ice cream for dessert without many complaints. This paradox can probably be explained by the growing consciousness of the American public about weight reduction and nutrition, which causes more households to serve fewer desserts at home. At the same time, desserts are still a special treat for college students who are just a year or two from having been high school children.

Attractive appearance -- Compare the appearance of desserts in a commercial cafeteria or restaurant with those of the average institutional food service. The commercial cafeteria must make desserts look attractive in order to sell them. Therefore, all puddings are decorated with whipped cream, cherries, coconut, fruit, or dozens of other garnishes. Cream pies usually have a scalloped edge of whipped topping; jello cubes always have some whipped topping; bread puddings usually have a lovely lemon sauce; a chocolate pudding cake is often topped with a rich custard sauce. Why is it, then, that the college food service manager thinks that he can do any less? What right has he to just ladle out butterscotch pudding from a can and slop it into a dessert dish? Who told him that a dry, unappetizing looking bread pudding is a good use of leftovers? Where is it written that using chocolate sauce on top of rice pudding causes a reckless increase in the cost of food?

Good taste -- High standards of quality can be achieved and maintained only if the food service director himself knows the difference between an ordinary and a high-quality product. The average restaurant, for instance, will purchase ready-made tart shells, fill them with canned cherry pie topping, and call this tasteless shell with its chemical-tasting filling a dessert. The expert baker will make his own flaky tartlet, place a thin layer of cake on the bottom, add a little vanilla custard, then add the cherry topping (home-made with frozen cherries) and finally cover it with a thin fruit glaze. Similarly some restaurants use pie dough mixes, fill such thick, tasteless pie shells with commercial, canned pie fillings and dare to call these "home-made pies." The knowledgeable food service director can tell the difference, and will insist on his desserts being of top quality at all times. Nothing is so frustrating to the student as to take a beautiful looking cream puff, then to find out that there is little or no pastry cream inside, and what there is doesn't taste good. Almost as bad is biting into a beautiful looking Washington apple, only to find that it is soft and mealy, or taking a lovely looking Oregon pear and almost breaking a tooth. There is no getting away from it, the responsibility for such unnecessary disappointments belongs to the manager of the unit who permitted such desserts to be served.

Running out of desserts -- The problem of running out of food in a residence hall cafeteria is so important that it is dealt with in greater detail in a subsequent chapter (see Chapter IX). At this point, you should be aware, however, that whenever you feature a popular or interesting dessert, you should make a special effort to have enough for everyone. When every student knows that "tonight there is Boston cream pie," the student who is given a couple of oatmeal cookies at 6:30 p.m. with the excuse, "Sorry, we ran out" will be very disappointed. There is no great shame about having leftover desserts; the students will be delighted to get them for lunch the next day, and don't even mind a repeat for dinner the next night, as long as you add it to the night's menu as an extra and don't substitute it for a regularly scheduled dessert.

Dessert variety -- A very effective way of pleasing students and saving money at the same time is to offer a large variety of desserts whenever possible. The University of Pennsylvania, for example, has a self-service ice cream and yogurt dessert bar. Students scoop their own ice cream, draw their own yogurt from machines, and have a choice of various toppings. In addition, fresh fruit is served at every meal, as well as a limited number of pies, cookies, cakes, puddings and gelatin desserts. Such a variety of desserts reduces the average dessert cost by several cents, and also makes the students happy.

Remember and enforce in your food service operation the generally acknowledged standards of high quality desserts: Freshly baked bakery products, moist cakes, flaky pie crusts, cooked (rather than instant) puddings, whipped cream mixed with whipped toppings, and plenty of fresh, juicy fruit. Remember also that there is nothing wrong with serving leftover puddings that have already been dished up on the following day, but not in the original dishes. The pudding has to be poured into a large bowl, whipped slightly, and then portioned once again into new dishes. A good test is to ask yourself this question: "Would I buy this dessert, if I went into a restaurant?" The answer had better be "Yes."

Beverages

When it comes to beverages, students are relatively easy to please. All it takes is an understanding of their basic drinking habits, and attention to a few details.

Coffee -- The rate of coffee consumption by students is relatively low, but it increases as the student gets older. Frequently, the amount of coffee used in a freshman residence hall of 600-700 students is less than 3 gallons (60 cups). A most important factor in making coffee for students is that the coffee must not be too strong. A first-class hotel will use 2 gallons of water per pound of coffee; an average is 2½ to 3 gallons. College students generally don't like coffee that strong, and most colleges use a formula of approximately 14 oz. of coffee per 3 gallons of water. The problem with this, of course, is that it draws complaints from older students and faculty, who are used to stronger coffee. Therefore, it might be wise to make regular, strong coffee in your *a la carte* operation, but to dilute the formula slightly in the residence halls.

Another problem with coffee is that it is often served lukewarm. Coffee has to be absolutely hot (i.e. just below boiling). The fact that a pot of coffee is steaming doesn't mean that it is hot, and many warm cups of coffee have been served at banquets from steaming coffee pots to the disappointment of the diners.

Often you will drink coffee in a college dining room, and upon asking for cream, you will be given a package of powdered non-dairy "creamer". That will tell you that the manager has reduced his operation to a picnic level. Packages of powdered coffee creamer are good for a picnic or field trip, but not as a regularly served item in a food service unit. The best item to serve is still "half-and-half." Non-milk coffee creamer in individual containers is second best.

One of the most frequently committed institutional sins is serving coffee that is too old. Restaurants usually make coffee in small batch brewers, or else their turnover is so large that the coffee doesn't get a chance to become stale. In institutions, however, the old-fashioned 6-gallon twin coffee urn is an invitation to criminal neglect. Because it is a 6-gallon urn, the cafeteria workers will make 6 gallons of coffee when only 3 are needed, and worse yet, they will make the coffee when they themselves are having breakfast, which is usually around 6 a.m. The result is coffee which is 3 hours old at 9 a.m., 6 hours old at 12 noon, and if, heaven forbid, the coffee urn is not drained in the afternoon, it is a sad bitter brew at 5:30 p.m. when the students come for dinner.

Proper coffee making, and proper urn maintenance are, therefore, important supervisory responsibilities, responsibilities which, incidentally, should be shared by the coffee salesman, who should feel free to report to you incidents of poor coffee preparation. Most coffee salesmen are as interested in serving good coffee as you are, and they are happy to help keep an eye on the coffee-making procedures in the units for which they supply the coffee.

Tea -- Students are getting more and more interested in various varieties of tea, and you would do well to offer some of these varieties in addition to the standard orange pekoe tea that everyone is used to. Some of these varieties are

- English breakfast
- Earl Grey
- Cinnamon stick
- Lemon and spice

One important ingredient of a good cup of tea is a slice of lemon, and lemon wedges, therefore, should always be available next to your coffee urn. While the English and Irish usually take milk or cream with their tea, many others prefer it with lemon, and it is amazing how often this important fact is forgotten or overlooked. The best way to serve tea is in a small, individual teapot, which will keep the water boiling hot until the actual time of use. If you cannot do this in your regular dining service, at least make it a point to serve tea in this manner at banquets.

Hot chocolate -- Hot chocolate is the major hot beverage consumed by college students in the United States. Yet professional food service managers sometimes neglect its importance. Running out of hot chocolate is regarded by such managers as no more important than running out of, for example, peanut butter. Only a small percentage of college students will use peanut butter for breakfast, but most of them will want hot chocolate, not tea, and not coffee, for that important first meal of the day.

The most common method of serving hot chocolate is through a dispenser which mixes chocolate powder and hot water and whips it as it is dispensed into the cup. There is a considerable difference in the quality of the various makers, and you should conduct a careful taste test before making your decision. It is not the free equipment, but rather the product itself which should be the basis for your final decision. If your dispenser pan is not connected to a drain, then the drip pan needs frequent attention by your cafeteria workers or else you will have a mess on that portion of the cafeteria counter.

Because hot chocolate dispensers frequently break down, it is wise to arrange for a spare dispenser on your campus for emergency purposes. If this is impossible, remember that you can mix the powder manually in a large pot, and dispense it through an insulated beverage container. When you do so, be sure to mark the container clearly with a sign saying "hot chocolate," since you cannot expect the sleepy-eyed student to know what is inside that strange new can sitting on the counter.

Orange juice and orange drinks -- Next to beer and milk, the drink that is universally acclaimed most popular on a college campus is orange juice. Students love it and, if they could, would drink it all day long. Since you are wise about nutrition, and realize what a marvellous source of Vitamin C orange juice represents, you probably welcome the opportunity to serve orange juice. In fact, if it were not so expensive, you would serve it three times daily, instead of just for breakfast, as you are probably doing now. As the price difference between orange juice and milk narrows, this may, in fact, become a reality.

Orange juice presents few real problems for you. Some college and university food service directors try to save money by serving some sort of instant, powdered orange juice which is reconstituted in their own kitchens. Others use an artificial whipped orange drink, often made with a base of egg whites, and having a chemical taste to it. Either of these approaches is foolish, time-wasting, and probably counter-productive. If you are going to serve orange juice, then serve real, frozen orange juice, and not some artificially flavored substitute. You have the option of purchasing frozen orange juice and reconstituting it in your kitchens manually, or else purchasing it together with orange juice dispensers furnished by the vendor and having it mixed automatically. There is no question that mixing it manually is somewhat cheaper. Many food service managers feel, however, that the small price difference involved in the use of automatic orange juice dispensers is worth paying, and this has become the most common method in dispensing orange juice. Naturally, these dispensers must be equipped with a lock, so that you can control the times when students in a residence hall dining room may drink orange juice.

Carbonated beverages -- Until early in the 1960's, few responsible and conscientious food service managers in colleges and universities would even consider serving carbonated beverages in residence hall dining rooms. All felt that it would be irresponsible, from a nutrition standpoint, to serve an item which added weight, had no nutritive value, and helped to cause tooth decay. Eventually, however, a few colleges experimented with the serving of these beverages and found, not too surprisingly, that college students were ecstatic about the idea. Soon almost everyone fell into line, and there are only a few holdouts these days.

Chances are that you will have to serve carbonated beverages everywhere, both in your a la carte, as well as your residence hall units. Try to have an attractive area set aside with syrup tanks away from the serving area, but easily reachable by your student help or by the soft drink route salesman when he comes to exchange tanks. Make sure you always have at least one diet drink in the dispenser.

If your local health department will allow it, try to set up the drink dispenser on top of or near a small ice dispenser, where the students can put ice in their glasses by means of a small stainless steel scoop, attached to a chain. If this is not permitted, consider the use of an automatic ice dispenser which dispenses ice by the glass. Continuous breakdowns and maintenance problems seem to have plagued this particular piece of equipment ever since it was introduced, however, and caution is advised when purchasing such a dispenser.

There is one other aspect of carbonated beverages with which you should be familiar: the difference between pre-mix and post-mix beverages. Most installations serve the post-mix type. This means that the syrup is delivered in separate tanks, as is the CO_2, and the two are then automatically mixed with the chilled water furnished on location. On the other hand, there are occasions when a source of water is not readily available, such as at dances in the gym, or picnics on the lawn. At such times, you can purchase pre-mix beverages, to be delivered in tanks containing the beverage already mixed, usually in combination with iced bins for cooling the beverage. The later drinks are, of course, considerably more costly than the post-mix kind.

Punch -- Non-carbonated beverages are an important feature on a college campus. The students are used to drinking it from their earlier days in elementary school and high school, on Little League baseball diamonds and at dances as well as at home. Although adults don't like it, find it too sweet, too tasteless, and too full of "empty calories," you still need to serve it to your students. It is inexpensive, they like it, and it is easy to prepare. If possible, purchase a punch base which has Vitamin C added to it.

Powdered punch base -- This punch comes in the form of crystals. It has an advantage in that it can be bought without sugar, and you can control the amount of sugar to be added. This makes the resulting beverage more tart and, consequently, more refreshing. It also gives you more flavors than you can get in the liquid kind. Pink lemonade, for instance, is hard to get in a liquid base. The disadvantage is that your workers have to mix it every time they need more product, and this is time consuming.

Liquid punch base -- This punch comes in No. 5 or No. 10 cans, or gallon bottles, includes sweetener, and is ready for use when opened. Usually your people still have to mix it with water on a 6:1 or 7:1 basis, but this is no trouble and takes little time. There are also punch-machine accessories, which enable you to serve punch from 5-gallon tanks through a continuous flow mixing mechanism. These have been troublesome and subject to frequent malfunction, however, and you should be wary of them. The trouble with most liquid punch bases is that they are much too sweet. Careful comparative taste tests, including student opinion, are therefore essential before you select one product over another.

Appearance -- Another aspect of quality beverages is the appearance of the beverage bar. When serving punch, for example, you should try to purchase a dispenser with two or three tanks, so that you can always have a colorful punch assortment. The punch machines should always be at least half full, since nothing looks less appetizing than an almost empty punch bowl, with rings of punch base adorning the inside of the tanks, and a circulating pump weakly circulating a stream of punch into an almost empty container. In addition to a colorful assortment and full punch dispensers, the tidyness of the beverage counter is also of prime importance. In a poorly operated unit, one can always find dozens of empty glasses or paper cups left on the beverage counter or on the tray rail. One finds punch spilled on the counter, without anyone coming to wipe it up; one finds syrup all around the soft drink dispensers, empty creamers and squeezed-out lemon wedges near the coffee urn. Maintaining an attractive looking beverage counter is a vital quality ingredient and one which calls for your continuous attention.

IX. RESIDENCE HALL FOOD SERVICE

Most of this book deals with matters which pertain to college food service management in general, regardless of whether the food is being served in a residence hall, in a cash cafeteria, or in fast food outlets of a student union building. This chapter, however, will cover matters that apply specifically to residence hall food service. From a student's viewpoint, there are a few basic differences between eating in a residence hall and eating anywhere else:

- In most colleges, *he is forced* to eat there if he lives in the residence halls.
- His choice of *what* to eat is limited, compared to other eating places.
- His choice of *when* to eat is limited to the established meal hours.
- His choice of *whom* to eat with is limited, in most colleges, to other meal ticket holders.

From the unit manager's viewpoint, there are also some unique features about residence hall food service:

- Variety of menu offerings is limited and, more often than not, decided by someone else.
- Whereas substitutions of menu items in cash cafeterias is normal procedure, it is more difficult in residence halls, where each student expects to get what everyone else is eating.
- The obligatory nature of his meal ticket makes the student more demanding than if he were free to eat elsewhere.
- Because of the limited menu, and the generally conservative taste of the average student, one must take special care before experimenting with new or unusual dishes.
- While the average student accepts menu monotony at home and is normally suspicious of unfamiliar menu items, he nevertheless gets bored with what he calls the "menu monotony" in the residence halls.
- The typical student has higher expectations of residence hall food service than he has of the food in his own home.

From the above it must be obvious that managing a residence hall food operation takes a special type of person, with special understanding, if he or she is to be successful. The relationship between the student and those who feed him must be personal, friendly, and based on mutual trust and respect. The food service manager cannot, and should not try to take the place of the student's mother when it comes to matters of dining. At the University of the Pacific, one of the questionnaires asked students to compare residence hall food with that of their mothers. The responses were hilarious: most students laughed at the comparisons ("You must be kidding!"), some were indignant, and one student wrote: "My mother is a lousy cook, but I am pretty good!" The food service manager must remember that eating, in the typical American home, involves a great deal more than just opening the door and hollering "Come and get it!" Students are used to asking their mothers, "Mom, when will you fix chicken and dumplings again?" and expect, within a reasonable time, that their request will be met. They are used to having their mother serve them directly, mindful and aware of their personal tastes and appetites. The whole dining experience in many homes is part of a family ritual, and the change from that ritual to eating every meal with hundreds of other students, most of them strangers, is traumatic for the student, especially the freshman.

One often hears a food supervisor say, "They never had it so good!" or "I bet he never got as much choice or as much food, as he's getting here!" These observations, whether true or not, miss the central point: what the student needs is personal attention and a genuine interest in himself, and he needs this much more than extra choices and double quantities. The good food service director sees to it that every student in his dining hall gets this personal attention, not only from the director, but also from the dining room hostess, from those in the serving line, from the cooks and salad makers, in fact from everyone involved in food service. With this type of an attitude, he overcomes the objection so often heard: "We can't do this. What would happen if everyone wanted this?" Instead, he will meet special requests, if they are reasonable, with this type of response: "Sure, we can give it to you, as long as we have it." The girl who wants an orange, when it is not on the menu, instead of her regular breakfast; the boy who wants some Worcestershire sauce; those who want honey, or spiced tea, or just plain vinegar and oil for their salad, can all be satisfied without causing mass confusion.

MENUS

Of all the various tasks faced by a food service manager, few are more important than planning a menu. A carefully planned, well-written menu can help you achieve many of your food service objectives:

Customer satisfaction -- A menu containing items popular with the students, items that meet their personal preferences, that look attractive together on the plate, and that also taste good together will satisfy your students.

Food cost control -- A menu that has been written with care and with costs of food in mind will be an effective tool in food cost control. It will contain a harmonious balance between costly and less costly items, and will take advantage of special purchases, seasonal products, and items in the freezer that should be utilized. It will have been carefully pre-costed and its cost compared with budget objectives.

Labor savings -- Some menu items such as sandwiches and pizza are labor-intensive, while others such as chili, roast beef, and macaroni and cheese require comparatively little labor. By analyzing a menu carefully in advance, you can spot "problem days," needing additional labor just to get the food cooked and served, and change the menu to minimize such problems.

Optimum use of equipment -- It frequently happens that a dinner menu will feature roast beef, baked potatoes, and perhaps a vegetable souffle or other baked item on the same menu. Each of these items requires oven space, and such space is usually at a premium in most institutional kitchens. When a menu is analyzed from an equipment standpoint in advance, one or two simple changes can often mean the difference between a peaceful meal and one full of panic and confusion.

Pleasant atmosphere in kitchen -- An experienced food service director can often tell the success of a meal by the atmosphere in the kitchen. When people go about their work calmly, have smiling faces, and seem easy and relaxed, it's a sure sign that everything is going well out in the dining room. A well-planned menu brings this peace of mind. Everyone knows well in advance what to cook; the menu items go well together; and the students are pleased with what they get. Everyone in the kitchen is affected positively.

Nutritional balance -- Most cafeteria menus, and especially those in college residence halls, offer enough food variety for the customer to easily exceed his daily nutritional requirements. Unfortunately, the typical college student is not as familiar with good nutrition as he or she should be, and you, the manager, therefore, have a special responsibility in this regard. It is all too easy to include a starchy vegetable such as corn or lima beans with a dinner featuring potatoes and, for example, macaroni and cheese casserole, or to offer chocolate cream pie, when a fresh fruit or fruit salad would be more appropriate. Special attention to good nutrition principles in menu writing is an absolute "must," and another strong argument for careful, advance menu planning.

Who Should Write the Menu

On many college campuses, the director of food service personally performs this important task. On other campuses, it is one of the dietitians, or someone with a good knowledge of nutrition who does the menu-writing. Sometimes it is the person who has the most experience and knows best what the students like or dislike. At still other schools, supervisors take turns in writing a menu, each one of five supervisors taking on one week of a five-week menu cycle, for example.

As a general rule, it seems best to assign this job to one individual, the one who has the time and is the most qualified to perform his job conscientiously, and effectively. It should be someone who knows the students' tastes, knows basic nutrition principles, knows and understands the importance of color and texture in food, and has the imagination and inventiveness to try new menus without upsetting the student customers. Review and suggestions from others on the management team are, of course, always desirable.

Master Index of Menu Items

Anyone who has ever had to write institutional menus for several weeks knows how fast one runs out of ideas. If you consider that lamb and fish are not as popular in the United States as elsewhere in the world, that veal is expensive, and that a pork item always requires a non-pork alternative, you realize quickly that you are left with beef, poultry, or non-meat entrees. If you eliminate Brussels sprouts, cauliflower, lima beans, red cabbage, beets, and sauerkraut, the number of vegetables that are popular often seems too small for the requirements of your menu.

Fortunately, menus allow for many variations on the same theme. A breaded veal patty, for example, can be served plain, with tomato sauce, with Parmesan cheese, a la Holstein (with fried egg), and many other ways. The same is true for most other dishes. What the menu writer needs is a list of all these various food items, and their variations, readily available, together with latest costs (and, in cash operations, their current selling prices). Such a list is commonly referred to as a Master Menu Index.

Cycle Menus

For more than twenty years there have been friendly differences of opinion among college and university food service directors about the length of menus for residence hall operations. There are some who firmly believe that a new menu should be written each week, others who believe that a three week menu "cycle," repeated (with modifications) about five times each semester, is ideal. Many food service managers have adopted the five-week cycle, which means that each menu set is repeated three times each semester. There is no "right" or "wrong" menu plan, the ultimate test lies in the quality of the menu itself. Those who do not believe in any menu cycle at all argue that a cycle forces a certain monotony on the diner who will know, in advance, that "on Mondays it's tomato soup and toasted cheese sandwiches." This happens if a cycle never changes. Normally, though, adjustments and changes to reflect current tastes and seasonal foods are always made before a cycle menu is repeated. Those who believe in a shorter cycle, such as three weeks, argue that by serving the most popular items more often, they come closer to meeting students' real food preferences, which tend toward a few familiar dishes rather than many unfamiliar ones. They also make a convincing argument that shorter cycles allow for closer cost controls, better production planning, and a closer evaluation of student preferences.

On the other hand, those who use five-week menus are aware of the basic questions that must be answered every time a new menu is written:

- How popular is the menu item?
- When was the last time it was served?
- What does it cost? Does it fit into the budget?
- Does it provide variety, e.g. how does it blend in with what was served the day before, or what will be served the day after?
- What effect does it have on production?
- How nutritious is it? Does it meet the needs of dieters, vegetarians, and other special groups of students?
- How does it blend in with the rest of the menu?
- Will it broaden the student's eating experience without antagonizing him?

With all these considerations to keep in mind every time a menu is written, it is very easy to overlook something and to make mistakes. It is for this reason that cycle menus are popular, and that so many use a five-week menu cycle. Written at leisure, usually before the beginning of each semester or quarter, each week in the cycle can be carefully studied, costed out, reviewed, and compared with the previous and following week of the cycle. Each item can be analyzed as to its frequency in the cycle, its cost impact, and its popularity.

Repetition of Menu Items

When writing a cycle menu, some items can be listed more than once in a cycle. Popular items like hamburgers certainly should be offered frequently. Many other items, such as roast beef, spaghetti and meatballs, and fried chicken should appear on the cycle more than once. Less popular items such as lamb patties and chicken croquettes, should appear perhaps only once. Then there are some less costly items, not terribly popular, but yet reasonably well accepted by the students. These make good "second choices" and can therefore be featured two or three times in a 5-week cycle: various types of fish, macaroni and cheese, and meat loaf are good examples. Finally, there are some items, such as liver, which are very popular with a few, and equally unpopular with many. These should be featured only in combination with a very popular entree such as chicken, chopped sirloin steak or a roast meat.

Menu Balance

A good residence hall menu has balance. Everything on the menu fits together harmoniously, not only in terms of cost, but also in terms of color consistency, production difficulty, and popularity. The number of "extender items" (entrees such as meat loaf, stew, casseroles) is carefully balanced with the number of "solid meat items" (roasts, chops, cutlets). The amount of fish served is carefully considered. The frequency of vegetarian items is pre-planned, and the colors of the vegetables are evaluated in the terms of the appearance of the rest of the plate. The food service director should give a set of general instructions to the staff person who is writing the menus which might be something like this:

Basic Instructions for Residence Hall Menu Pattern
Budgeted food cost per meal served: $.92
Budgeted meals served per labor hour: 9

1. **Breakfast**
   a. Number of times meat is served at breakfast per week: 4
   b. To be served daily: hot and cold cereals
                            orange juice
                            soft and hard boiled eggs
                            sweet rolls or donuts
   c. Fruit: if fresh fruit is served at lunch or dinner, serve canned fruit for breakfast. If not, serve fresh fruit.
   d. Milk: choice of skimmed and whole milk at each meal.

2. **Lunch**
   Soup: serve daily on weekdays.
   Sandwiches: one hot or cold sandwich daily on weekdays.
   Casseroles: at least three times weekly.
   Salad Bar: daily.
   Desserts: light baked dessert (cookies, etc.) 4 x weekly.
            ice cream novelties: 5 x weekly.
            fresh fruit: whenever it is not served at breakfast or dinner.

3. **Dinner** (Two entree choices daily except Sundays)
Solid meat items: 5 x weekly (Average cost: $.50-$.70).
Extender items: 4 x weekly (Average cost: $.40-$.60).
Fish entrees: 2 x weekly.
Non-meat entrees: 1 x weekly.
Vegetables: Daily.
Potatoes, rice, or noodles: Daily.
Gravy: Whenever potatoes or rice are served.
For a sample menu out of a five-week menu cycle, see Appendix 2.

Menu Changes

Just as some managers differ on whether or not to use menu cycles, they also differ about whether or not menus can, or should be changed once the cycle has been written. There are some who believe that a cycle should not be changed except in emergencies, but most managers are more flexible. They regard the menu cycle merely as a convenient tool. Students' tastes change, sometimes from year to year, and if certain items on a menu are not very successful, they should be removed in favor of some which are. When this is done, however, it is wise to stick to the basic outline of the menu, and to select replacement items that are similar in cost, color, and type to the original item. Replacing veal chops with tuna casserole can be troublesome. Pork chops or a breaded veal patty are more suitable substitutes.

The good supervisor keeps continuous notes about the popularity of each menu item as it is served. Then, before the same weekly menu appears again on the cycle, changes can easily be made. It is crucial, at this point, to review the rest of the cycle menu whenever a change is made. Failure to do so can cause unexpected repetitions, such as pork three days in a row, or two entree items with a red barbecue or tomato sauce, one right after the other.

No week in a menu cycle should be repeated exactly as it was served the previous time. There is always some item that needs changing, some item that has just come into season, some item left over in large quantities that is in the freezer and should be used up.

New Menu Items

Fortunately for you and for everyone else in the food service industry, there are always new and exciting menu items being developed for the institutional market. Food service magazines outdo each other in offering new and colorful recipes in their publications. Your meat purveyors will bring you new meat items and your frozen food distributor will bring you samples of newly manufactured convenience entrees and other food items. How should you introduce these to your students?

Never use a new menu item unless you taste it first -- There is no justification for serving food to your students with which you are not familiar. Every new item should be taste-tested at a staff meeting first. If that is impossible, make certain that you and some others taste it informally before making a decision. Your cooks and salad makers can be of great help in making such decisions, and their knowledge and advice should be solicited. Students are always willing to participate in a taste test or even to form a taste panel of their own. They enjoy it, and you have another opportunity to show that you really care.

Remember that new menu items should be properly introduced. Once a college food service director served *Vichysoisse* (a chilled cream soup made with potatoes and leeks) without first telling the students that this was a famous French delicacy. The result? Angry students who stormed into the kitchen complaining about getting *cold* soup! Little signs on the sneeze guard of the cafeteria counter, or little tents on the dining room tables are an effective way of telling everybody about your new menu item. A most effective technique was developed at Northern Illinois University by Robert Buchanan and Barbara Turner:

Basic Technique
1. A 5"x8" card is printed with information concerning the new food product.
2. Card is placed on each dining room table in a card holder at the meal preceding the one at which the new product will be served.
3. The meal checker hands out a short questionnaire to each student trying the new food product. The response to the questionnaire usually decides whether the new product will be served again.

Vegetable Program Technique
Each week a new vegetable is introduced to the students. On the day this new vegetable is served, descriptive flyers appear on each table. At the end of the school year, the students get a chance to list their preferences. For a sample of the introductory memo, as well as a typical descriptive flyer, see Exhibit IX-1.

Taken and summarized from NACUFS Food Service Techniques Committee Report.

Popularity of Menu Items
As you will read in Chapter XVII, questionnaires about food service are a most useful way to determine how the students feel about their meals, and what suggestions they might have for changes or improvements. One such type of questionnaire deals with menu items preferences. Although it is true that *some* changes in student tastes do occur from year to year, and equally true that certain items may be very popular one year and less popular the next, the basic food preferences of American college students remain fairly constant, particularly within a given geographic region of the country. It is helpful, therefore, to ask your students about their likes and dislikes, and to remember these when writing menus.

A comprehensive study, involving between 40% and 50% of all students in residence halls, was conducted by Robert C. Bailey at Washington State University a number of years ago. Because the results are still valid today, and in order to give you a basis for comparison, the following is a condensed summary of the above-mentioned study:

1. *Favorite Breakfast Meats* (in order of preference)
   Bacon, sausage, ham

2. *Favorite Lunch Meats*
   Hamburger, roast beef or French dip sandwich, cold cuts, hot dogs, ham, pizza

3. *Favorite Dinner Meats*
   Steak, roast beef, fried chicken, ham, pork roast or pork chop, turkey

EXHIBIT IX-1

Card Examples:

To:　　　Resident

From:　　Mr. Robert Buchanan and Mrs. Barbara Turner of
the Residence Hall Food Service

Subject:　"Gourmet Vegetables for You"

A grourmet eats vegetables because he wishes to experience a pleasurable taste sensation. We would like to introduce you to vegetables prepared for gourmets. We will try to make each new "Gourmet Vegetable" a special treat for you. They will be vegetables prepared with a new touch, a subtle seasoning or a gay garnish.

Beginning on November 23rd, we will start introducing the "Gourmet Vegetables". On the day of service, a flyer will be circulated giving you information on the "Gourmet Vegetable" to be served that evening at Dinner.

Please plan to try a sample of each "Gourmet Vegetable" served -this should be a taste treat for you. Do tell your Food Manager how you liked the "Gourmet Vegetable" served. If you have a favorite "Gourmet Vegetable" - tell us what it is and we will try to serve it.

NORTHERN ILLINOIS UNIVERSITY
"GOURMET VEGETABLES" FOR YOU
BAKED ACORN SQUASH
Monday, November 23

Squash - the fleshy fruit of several species of teh genes cucurbita of the gourd family. There is unmistakable evidence that all squashes originated in the New World many centuries before the arrival of Columbus.

Squash is a good source of Vitamin A and Riboflavin.

BAKED ACORN SQUASH - "Gourmet Vegetable" served with Dinner tonight.

Method of Preparation
Acorn squash is cut into quarters and the seeds are removed, each piece is seasoned with salt, cinnamon, butter, and brown sugar and baked until tender.

4. *Favorite Vegetables*
    Corn, green beans, peas, carrots, asparagus

5. *Favorite Salads*
    Tossed green, fruit, plain jello, cottage cheese (plain), jello or cottage cheese with fruit.

For a sample taste preference questionnaire, see Exhibit IX-2. For a sample procedure on how to plan and write menus, see Appendix 7.

MEAL PERIODS

Deciding on the ideal meal periods for residence hall dining is more important than might at first appear. The longer you keep a cafeteria line open, the greater your labor cost. At the same time, however, you spread out your customers more evenly, and thus reduce the waiting in line and the crowding in the dining rooms. Furthermore, classroom schedules and study habits are constantly changing, and with that, the eating habits and needs of the students change also. At one time, most colleges and universities scheduled no classes during the noon hour, and few classes after 4:00 p.m. Today, continuous class scheduling from 8:00 a.m. to 5:00 p.m. is normal, and many schools schedule lab and other special classes right through the dinner hour. You need to arrive at the ideal blend of serving hours which meets the needs of the students on one hand, and your need to control costs on the other.

Historical Development

It might be helpful to review the changes in meal periods that have occurred on college campuses during the past twenty-five years. The residence halls which were built prior to World War II were really built on the style of overgrown homes: the dining room had enough places to seat everyone at one sitting, and the meal periods were correspondingly brief, perhaps an hour for breakfast, an hour for lunch, and an hour-and-a-half for dinner. When new residence halls were built in response to the post-war needs, funds were inadequate for such luxuries. Instead of table service or family-style service, colleges instituted cafeteria service, and instead of having a seat for every resident, the dining rooms accommodated perhaps two-thirds of all the residents and, in many cases, just one half. The dining room hours were still very limited, but were at least expanded to suit the needs of the cafeteria system, a system where an average of only 8-10 students could go through the line each minute, and where longer meal periods were necessitated just to serve and seat everyone who wanted to eat.

In the mid-1960's, as classroom schedules began to encroach on the lunch periods and as students became less and less willing to stand in long waiting lines, many college food service directors began to experiment with extended serving hours. Breakfast hours were extended to 9:00 or 10:00 a.m., lunch was served at 11:00 a.m. and continued to perhaps 2:00 or 2:30 p.m., and dinner started at 4:30 p.m. and continued to 6:30 p.m. or later. Some colleges even experimented with

EXHIBIT IX-2

FOOD PREFERENCE SURVEY - 1968/69

Name: (Optional) _____ Male _____ Female _____

College: COP*____ Raymond____ Elbert Covell ____ Callison ____ Other_____

Class: Freshman _____ Sophomore _____ Junior _____ Senior _____ Other _____

The entire Food Service staff is interested in pleasing you during your stay at Pacific. We want to serve you appetizing meals, of the type that you like, prepared the way you like it, and served in a pleasant and personal way. We know that sometimes we may not achieve this - but hopefully most of the time we do. It would help a lot if we could get your constructive suggestions for improvement, and possibly some new ideas which we could incorporate into our food service program.

This year, instead of waiting until the middle of the year (when it's almost too late) we want to let you participate early in our menu planning. On the other side of this sheet you will find the 5-week menu cycle which we have developed for this current year. Except for some modifications, necessitated by such reasons as Special Dinners, price changes, etc., this is the menu we plan to follow. Each week, however, at our supervisors' meetings, we review the menu and, when necessary, change an item here and there. We would like you to help us in this process, by indicating your likes and dislikes of the menu items in our cycle in the following manner:

LIKES: If you especially like an item, please circle it.

DISLIKES: If you strongly dislike an item, please cross it out.

NEUTRAL: If you can "take it or leave it", or are neutral about an item - don't mark it at all.

In addition, we are always interested in your comments. Because food committee representatives are not always available, and because you may be reluctant to approach your dining hall supervisor or myself, we have two methods by which you can express yourself:

1. Put a note in the suggestion box. (All signed comments are answered!)

2. Suggest some additional entree items - your favorites, not contained on this sheet.

3. Make your comment, compliment, or criticism in the space provided below. (Please feel free to comment on anything pertaining to Food Service; if we can, we will follow any constructive suggestion made!)

Thanks for your cooperation.

Paul Fairbrook

Paul Fairbrook
Director of Housing and Food Service

COMMENTS: _____

_____

_____

_____

_____

_____

_____

PLEASE RETURN THIS QUESTIONNAIRE TO YOUR DINING ROOM CASHIER.

EXHIBIT IX-2 (continued)

PLEASE RETURN THIS QUESTIONNAIRE TO YOUR DINING ROOM CASHIER.

UNIVERSITY OF THE PACIFIC -- FOOD SERVICE
FINAL COPY - 1968 - MENU CYCLE

CYCLE No.		MONDAY	TUESDAY	WEDNESDAY	THURSDAY	FRIDAY	SATURDAY	SUNDAY
I	L	CHICKEN SALAD SANDWICH / ITALIAN SPAGHETTI	REUBEN SANDWICH / CHILI CON CARNE / CORNED BEEF/RYE	BACON/LETTUCE & TOMATO SANDWICH / MACARONI & CHEESE	CHEESEBURGER	TUNA FISH SANDWICH / PORK CHOP SUEY	BACON WRAPPED CHEESE FILLED HOT DOGS WITH OR PLAIN DOGS WITH BUNS	DEEP FRIED FRENCH TOAST/STRAWBERRIES / HAM OR BACON
	D	HAM STEAK, HAWAII / SWEDISH MEATBALLS	ROAST BEEF, AU JUS	SOUTHERN FRIED CHICKEN	SHOULDER LAMB CHOP / NEW ENGLAND BOILED DINNER	CAPTAIN'S PLATE / MEAT LOAF	OLD FASHIONED BEEF STEW	POT ROAST OF BEEF
II	L	HAM SANDWICH / HAMBURGER-MACARONI	HAMBURGERS / 2ND ITEM OPTIONAL	HOT TURKEY SANDWICH / COLD PLATE	ENCHILADAS / GRILLED CHEESE SANDWICH	HOT ROAST BEEF SANDWICH	POOR BOY SANDWICH	CREAMED BEEF/TOAST / FLUFFY OMELET / BACON
	D	OVEN ROAST CHICKEN / DRESSING	LONDON BROIL	BRAISED CUBE STEAK / PORK & NOODLE CASSEROLE	BAKED HAM / RAISIN SAUCE / STUFFED GREEN PEPPERS	CRUMB BAKED SWORD- FISH / CHICKEN ALMOND CASSEROLE	COUNTRY FRIED STEAK	ROAST TOM TURKEY / DRESSING
III	L	PIZZA W/BEEF, SALAMI & MUSHROOMS / CHICKEN A LA KING	HOT DOGS ON BUN / CHILI CON CARNE	CLUB SANDWICH	HOT SLICED BAR-B-QUE PORK/BUN / MGR. CHOICE	EGG SALAD SANDWICH / LASAGNA / FISH FILET	HAMBURGERS	CHEESE BLINTZES / SCRAMBLED EGGS / HAM
	D	CORNED BEEF & CABBAGE / RAVIOLI	SOUTHERN FRIED CHICKEN	ROAST PORK W/DRESS- ING / MEATBALL STEW (IND. CASS. DISHES)	CHOPPED SIRLOIN STEAK / FRENCH FRIED ONION RINGS	BAKED HADDOCK / NEWBURG SAUCE / BEEF POT PIE	SPAGHETTI & MEATBALLS	TOP ROUND OF BEEF / AU JUS / YORKSHIRE PUDDING
IV	L	FRENCH DIP SANDWICH	GRILLED HAM & CHEESE SANDWICH	HOT MEATLOAF SANDWICH / CORN FRITTER & BACON	PASTRAMI ON RYE / CHICKEN JAMBALAYA	GRILLED HAMBURGER / MACARONI & CHEESE	ENCHILADAS / MGR. CHOICE	FRENCH TOAST / SCRAMBLED EGGS / BACON
	D	VEAL SCALLOPINI / CHICKEN NOODLE CASSEROLE	ROAST TURKEY / DRESSING	SWISS STEAK / LIVER WITH BACON	YANKEE POT ROAST JARDINIERE / CARROTS, ONIONS, & PEAS	FRENCH FRIED SHRIMP / PORK CHOW MEIN	BEEF STROGANOFF ON NOODLES	BAKED HAM / FRUIT SAUCE / SWEET POTATOES
V	L	TACOS	HOT TURKEY SANDWICH / WEINER BEAN POT	CHEESEBURGER	BAR-B-QUE SANDWICH / KNOCKWURST & SAUERKRAUT	SUBMARINES / DEEP FRIED FISH	SLOPPY JOE/BUN	FRITTERS & SAUSAGE / SCRAMBLED EGGS
	D	GRILLED CUBE STEAK	PORK CHOPS / DRESSING / SPAGHETTI/MEATBALLS	BRAISED SIRLOIN TIPS	ARROZ CON POLLO / MGR. CHOICE	BAKED HALIBUT / PORK STEAKS	CHOPPED SIRLOIN STEAK / FRENCH FRIED ONIONS	DINNER STEAK / BAKED POTATOES / TURKEY TETRAZZINI

INSTRUCTIONS: If you like an item, circle it.
If you dislike an item, cross it out. ✗
If you don't care either way, leave it alone.

continuous serving hours: a dining hall might serve breakfast starting at 7:00 a.m. and continue until 10:30 a.m. when the menu would switch to luncheon items, until 4:30 p.m. when dinner would be served until closing time. Those who argued in favor of these new hours claimed several significant advantages:

- They reduced or eliminated waiting lines.
- They reduced the cost of labor since fewer lines were needed, and fewer servers per line.
- They improved food quality, since progressive cooking (an ideal for which every good food service manager should be striving) was now not only possible, but almost mandated by the demands of the new system.

Several years later, when the excitement died down, it was found by most of those who tried it that continuous serving was not practical. On most campuses there were certain periods (such as between 10:30 and 11:00 a.m. and 2:00 and 4:00 p.m.) when students did not want to eat in any great numbers; that labor cost reductions were a myth, since every hour a cafeteria line is open requires back-up personnel in the kitchen and dishroom; and finally, that progressive cooking could be achieved without extended meal periods. Extended serving hours, however, remain with us up to this day, though significantly trimmed and modified from their original version. Many colleges now serve breakfast until 10:00 or 10:30 a.m., and many serve lunch until long past 1:00 p.m. Neither was the practice during the 1950's.

As described earlier in Chapter VI, the advent of "free flow' systems, which enabled the students to use their meal tickets in other eating places, such as the student union, made extended serving hours in the residence halls less important and allowed a return to slightly more restricted meal periods.

Current Campus Meal Schedules

When setting meal hours for residence halls today, all the factors previously mentioned must be taken into consideration:

- Classroom schedules
- Students' study and eating habits
- Ratio of dining hall spaces to total customers
- Alternative dining possibilities
- Optimum use of personnel
- Quality of food and service

There is no perfect answer, equally applicable to all colleges. You will probably have to experiment, cautiously, for several years before you can settle on meal schedules that fit your particular situation. Even then, you will continuously have to evaluate and often modify the schedules of the previous year. In periods of rising costs, the absence of waiting lines at 12:00 noon and 5:30 p.m. may be a luxury that you simply cannot afford. You may have to sacrifice a certain degree of efficiency and speed for some real economies in staffing. Students unwilling to wait may have to change their eating times. There are always ways to soften the impact of a more restricted meal schedule: the student who goes to work at 7:00 a.m. should be permitted to eat with the cooks at 6:30 a.m., the basketball team which arrrives regularly at 7:00 p.m. should have some food set aside for them.

Whatever your meal periods, be sure that you are punctual. In fact, it is a good idea to open the dining halls 5-10 minutes earlier than announced, and to close them at least 5 minutes after the scheduled closing time. Students watches are not synchronized with yours, and they, themselves, are not always punctual. Nothing will anger a student more than to be denied a meal merely because he is 5 minutes late.

Here is a fairly representative meal schedule for residence halls on a campus where there is no free flow privilege:

Weekdays
Breakfast: 7:30 a.m. to 9:00 a.m.
Lunch: 11:30 a.m. to 1:00 p.m.
Dinner: 4:30 p.m. to 6:00 p.m.

Weekends
Continental Breakfast: 8:30 a.m. to 10:00 a.m.
Brunch: 11:00 a.m. to 1:00 p.m.
Dinner: 5:00 p.m. to 6:30 p.m.

Weekend Meals

On the schedule shown above, you will note the absence of a regular breakfast on weekends; instead, the schedule provides for a continental breakfast (juice, toast and sweet roll, cereal, beverages) early on Saturday and Sunday mornings, a brunch at noon, and a regular dinner meal at night. This may not be suitable for every institution of higher learning, but it seems to fit the needs of most students. Except for those few who regularly get up early, or who have things to do in the mornings, or who go to early church on Sundays, the campus does not really stir on weekends until about 10:00 or 11:00 a.m. It therefore meets the students' needs to offer continental breakfast on Saturday and Sunday mornings to satisfy the "early birds," then expand the breakfast into a brunch by adding a salad bar and perhaps some luncheon meats or a light luncheon casserole dish as an additional choice. As an alternative, you may want to skip the continental breakfast altogether and advance the brunch by an hour to take its place.

Don't be discouraged if you are criticized by a few who prefer to have their regular three meals daily. Chances are that they are a minority. Most important is not whether or not you serve a brunch, a lunch, or even Sunday dinner at noon. What is important is that you accurately gauge the real need on your particular campus, and establish a weekend meal schedule that most nearly fits that particular need.

Consolidation of Meal Service

An effective way of cutting costs without lowering quality is to consolidate meal service during quiet periods. Throughout a typical school year, there are many days, or portions of days, which are unusually quiet and which permit the selective closing of at least some of the dining operations. Some of these are

- The first day residence halls open, at the beginning of school or after recess periods
- The last meal prior to vacation or recess
- Thanksgiving recess
- Winter term
- Periods between quarters or semesters
- Memorial Day weekend

Unless distances between residence halls are long and weather conditions severe, students do not usually mind walking to a dining hall other than their own, especially if it is for a limited period of time, and if the reasons for the change are explained. On the contrary, they often actually welcome the opportunity to eat in another dining complex where they can meet other students and make new friends.

Meal consolidation is a logical procedure. On a college campus, however, not everything is done on the basis of logic. It is crucial that you prepare the groundwork for such consolidation by obtaining the approval or at least tacit consent of the student personnel deans and hall directors. They can help discuss the consolidation with hall residents. Sometimes, it becomes necessary to get student cooperation by means other than mere logic. If students feel that saving money is not enough reason, you may wish to share with them the savings realized from their sacrifice. A food service contribution to the social fund, a special dinner, or a dance in the dining rooms may be in order.

You can save money if you begin regularly to close down one or more kitchens during such periods of consolidation. Not only will you save on labor, water, utilities, and kitchen supplies but you can actually save money in food costs. Theoretically, the cost of food should not be affected, regardless of whether or not the food is prepared in one or several kitchens. In practice, however, you will find that the fewer kitchens you operate, the lower your food cost per meal served.

FREE FLOW FOOD SERVICE

In Chapter VI you read about the free flow system, which permits students to use their meal ticket in any dining hall on campus and in some instances in the various cash operations on campus. Obviously, the students enjoy this flexibility. But you also stand to gain from such an arrangement, if local campus conditions permit (As noted earlier, a campus on which all the classrooms and cash operations are located in the center of campus, and most of the residence halls on the periphery would have trouble instituting "free flow" during the weekday lunch period. Furthermore, a university which has two separate food service organizations on the same campus, could not operate a "free flow" system unless inter-departmental charges were mutually agreed to by both organizations).

The following are the advantages of a free flow system for the food service director:

- **Greater Student Satisfaction.** If they don't like the food in one place, they go to another.
- **More Efficient Meal Scheduling.** Students with early or late classes can always use their meal ticket in the student union or in the dining room that is kept open longer hours.
- **Possible Food Cost Savings.** Students who use their meal ticket in the cash operations often do not take all they're allowed, especially during breakfast.
- **Consolidation.** It is easy to close one or more dining halls on campus if students can use their meal tickets anywhere and anytime. Meal periods tend to stretch out -- many students will eat as late as 9:00 p.m. -- and kitchens are less busy during rush periods.
- **Improved Social Climate.** Since eating together is an effective way for people to meet one another, a free flow system contributes to a good social climate on a campus. Chances of meeting faculty members and administrators eating lunch in the student union are also much better than in residence hall dining rooms.
- **Profitable Cash Operations.** Although it is a case of "robbing Peter to pay Paul," your campus cash operations can use the extra business volume from meal ticket holders. Since usually only an average of 10%-15% of all dorm residents regularly eat somewhere other than in their own dorms, this impact is one which the residence halls can usually afford. In arranging a transfer of funds from the residence halls to the cash operations, keep in mind that the halls should normally get the benefit of any "missed meal" factor. In other words, if a student is entitled to purchase a breakfast of up to $1.50 on his meal ticket and only buys $.50 worth, the cash operations should only charge the residence hall $.50.

There are, however, some disadvantages inherent in the free flow system:

- **Production Planning Problems.** Even though food service managers will soon know how many students they must feed even under a free flow system, the chance is there for days when everyone, or no one decides to eat in his own dining hall. Therefore, easy transport between the several dining centers is essential if this system is to work.
- **Loss of Residence Hall Loyalty.** Students who choose regularly to eat elsewhere may not identify as closely with their own residence hall. Since identification is often one of the stated goals of the residence hall program, free flow may work against this.
- **Greater Possibilities for Cheating.** The more places there are for the student to eat, the more chances he has to cheat -- either by lending a meal

ticket to someone else, or by claiming loss of the original meal ticket, getting a duplicate, and using both sets of tickets.

- **More Bookwork.** Keeping track of food served to students from other units imposes considerably more bookkeeping for both the charging and paying unit.

- **Decreased Absenteeism.** By allowing students to eat not only *wherever* they want, but also *whenever* they want, you also allow them to take better advantage of their meal tickets. This advantage for them is, of course, a financial disadvantage for you, since it reduces absenteeism, the "missed meal factor" described earlier.

In general, it is safe to state that any change in policies or procedures which gives the student more freedom of choice, and greater personal satisfaction without adversely affecting the institution, is a good change. Free flow does all that, and also improves the social-educational climate which is so very important to his overall personal growth.

NUTRITION, DIETS, AND WEIGHT REDUCTION

In the early days of college food service, relatively few food service managers were concerned with nutrition or diets. Food service directors made certain their students got enough to eat, while nutritionists discovered and corrected dietary *deficiencies*. If a student had a special dietary problem, he could either "pick and choose" from the residence hall menu or move off-campus. Food service management in colleges was, after all, in its infancy, and the full measure of opportunities for actively contributing to better health was not fully realized.

All this has drastically changed. Studies of coronary heart disease, and with them the studies of the effect of fats on blood cholesterol caused a growing awareness of the importance of proper diets and good health. Overnutrition and increasingly sendentary lives with little motivation for exercise, have caused "a substantial prevalence of obesity at every age in both sexes" according to *Obesity and Health,* a Public Health Service Publication. For the college food service manager, the task of advising the students in weight reduction has become an increasingly important responsibility. The student who gains 10 to 15 pounds during the freshman year is an all-too-common phenomenon. Given the importance which Americans attach to a thin and shapely female form, this sudden weight gain can be particularly damaging to the self-image of the woman student, even though physiologically it is of course equally harmful to both men and women.

It is difficult to pin-point exactly the reason for this sudden weight gain by college freshmen in residence halls. Drs. Stare and McWilliams, in their excellent book *Living Nutrition** attribute poor nutrition of adolescents to the following socio-psychological influences:

Stare, Frederick J., and McWilliams, Margaret, *Living Nutrition,* John Wiley & Sons, New York, 1973, 467 pp.

1. **Desire for Independence.** When the child first leaves home, parental influence is no longer felt at mealtimes.

2. **Acceptance by Peer Group.** The desire to be accepted by peers will impel students to eat snacks with their friends at odd hours, and eat foods not previously part of their normal diet.

3. **Achievement of a Desirable Self-image.** Even though the adolescent and young adult is aware of the importance of good nutrition to his appearance, his knowledge of good nutrition is limited, and the task of learning to control his own eating habits is a new and difficult one.

4. **Societal Pressures.** Because of pressures of society, many adolescent boys are concerned about being underweight, while many girls worry about being overweight. This concern about body weight is often exaggerated, but causes young people to adopt poor dietary habits. One of the worst ones, a phenomenon which every college food service manager can affirm, is to skip breakfast. Paradoxically, the same students who skip breakfast to lose weight will also eat snacks or late-night pizza or drink beer just in order "to conform."

5. **Emotional Stress.** It is difficult to follow good eating habits in times of emotional stress. These stresses, such as homesickness, unhappy social relationships, fear of examinations, are particularly acute for the college freshman and normally diminish as the student gets more used to campus life.

Recognizing the above phenomena, college food service managers have changed from passive observers, whose main function it was to "get the food on the table" to active counsellors who are genuinely concerned not only with the physical, but also with the mental and social development of students, through nutrition counselling, and special diets.

Students with diabetes, low blood sugar (hypoglycemia), peptic ulcers, or other dietary problems will normally find a sympathetic and helpful friend in their college food service manager. While today, as thirty years ago, it is still not wise for a college food service manager to assume responsibility for supplying a student with a complicated therapeutic diet, he is at least willing to counsel him to the limit of his knowledge and experience, and to facilitate the student's pursuit of his special dietary needs.

Another important new role for the college food service manager is an understanding of, and familiarity with the basic weight-reducing diets prevalent in society. When students ask him about the Weight Watcher's Diet, or low-carbohydrate or high-protein diet, he can point out the values and shortcomings of each. If students discover the Drinking Man's Diet, the Zen Macrobiotic Diet, or the Grapefruit Diet, he can guide them away from such potentially harmful fad diets to a safer, more universally recommended diet. Ideally, college food service staffs should include a professional dietitian who is fully qualified to give such advice. In the absence of such a dietitian, however, each food service manager should be prepared to give some advice on nutrition and diets, if not as a professional, at least as a well-informed friend. Obviously caution and discretion are necessary in this entire process: referral to a personal doctor or to the campus physician in any but routine inquiries is still an absolute "must," and nothing stated above suggests that you, in misguided enthusiasm, should practice medicine without a license.

Nutrition

Do not worry if your educational background included little or no opportunity to learn about nutrition. It is not necessary to be a nutritionist or a dietitian to do a good job in college food service. It is essential, however, to learn some of the fundamentals. One of these is a knowledge about daily food patterns. Since it is impractical to calculate the nutrient content of each meal, the Federal Government makes recommendations for nutritionally adequate, varied, and satisfying meals. Foods are placed into four groups on the basis of their similarity in nutrient content. The four groups are

- The meat group
- The vegetable-fruit group
- The milk group
- The bread-cereal group

The "Basic Four" enable the average person to eat a relatively balanced diet which includes the essential, if not all the nutrients required for nutritional balance. A table showing a recommended daily food pattern is shown in Exhibit IX-3.

In addition to knowing about the Basic Four, you whould also be able to answer questions about desirable weights for young men and women. The Metropolitan Life Insurance Company has an excellent chart, which will help you do this (see Exhibit IX-4). Another formula for judging weight which some feel is even more helpful is one which states the following:

- **Women** may weigh 100 lbs. and 5 lbs. for every inch over 5 feet.
- **Men** may weigh 110 lbs. and 5 lbs. for every inch over 5 feet.

Another helpful bit of information to share with students is the amount of calories used per hour for various activities. Someone weighing 140 lbs. uses 98 calories per hour just sitting and writing at a desk. A table showing the energy used for some routine daily activities is shown in Appendix 8.

Another item of important information is the recommended daily dietary allowance for men and women (Appendix 8). The average young women, for example, needs approximately 2,000 calories daily (see Appendix 8). Finally, it is a good idea to keep several reference books about nutrition and weight reduction in your office, including one which lists the various calorie counts of the foods the students eat. Some lists, such as the list of selected beverages shown in Appendix 8 can be permanently posted next to your beverage counter in the dining room.

This chapter is not intended as a primer on nutrition. Neither should you assume that it is necessary to pass yourself off as an expert on nutrition. The study of nutrition and dietetics is a highly specialized field, just as is food service management,

EXHIBIT IX-3

THE BASIC FOUR FOR THE ENTIRE FAMILY

GROUPS	DAILY AMOUNTS

Milk Group
Milk
(Whole, skim, evaporated; instant non-fat dry; buttermilk), with cheese and ice cream as alternates

Adults: 2 cups
Children: 3-4 cups

For calcium:
1 oz. American cheese equals ¾ cup milk
½ cup cottage cheese equals ⅓ cup milk
½ cup ice cream equals ¼ cup milk

Meat Group
Meat, poultry, fish, eggs— with dry beans, dry peas and nuts as alternates

2 or more servings.
Count as a serving: 2 to 3 ounces of lean cooked meat, poultry or fish; 2 eggs; 1 cup cooked dried beans; 4 tablespoons of peanut butter

Vegetable– Fruit Group

4 or more servings. Include: a citrus fruit or other Vitamin C-rich fruit or vegetable daily. A dark leafy green or deep yellow vegetable for Vitamin A at least every other day. Other fruits and vegetables—including potatoes—at least 2 or 3 servings daily. Count as a serving: ½ cup of vegetable or fruit.

Bread-Cereal Group

4 or more servings. Whole grain or enriched. Count as a serving: 1 slice of bread, 1 ounce ready-to-eat cereal; ½ to ¾ cup cooked cereal, noodles, rice, etc.

Note: Fats, oils and sugars can be combined with many foods to enhance flavor, but should be used sparingly. Although water is not a nutrient, it is essential to proper body functioning.

Courtesy of the Metropolitan Life Insurance Company.

5

EXHIBIT IX-4

Weight in Pounds According to Frame (In Indoor Clothing)

	HEIGHT (with shoes on) 1-inch heels Feet Inches	SMALL FRAME	MEDIUM FRAME	LARGE FRAME
Men of Ages 25 and Over	5 2	112–120	118–129	126–141
	5 3	115–123	121–133	129–144
	5 4	118–126	124–136	132–148
	5 5	121–129	127–139	135–152
	5 6	124–133	130–143	138–156
	5 7	128–137	134–147	142–161
	5 8	132–141	138–152	147–166
	5 9	136–145	142–156	151–170
	5 10	140–150	146–160	155–174
	5 11	144–154	150–165	159–179
	6 0	148–158	154–170	164–184
	6 1	152–162	158–175	168–189
	6 2	156–167	162–180	173–194
	6 3	160–171	167–185	178–199
	6 4	164–175	172–190	182–204

	HEIGHT (with shoes on) 2-inch heels Feet Inches	SMALL FRAME	MEDIUM FRAME	LARGE FRAME
Women of Ages 25 and Over	4 10	92– 98	96–107	104–119
	4 11	94–101	98–110	106–122
	5 0	96–104	101–113	109–125
	5 1	99–107	104–116	112–128
	5 2	102–110	107–119	115–131
	5 3	105–113	110–122	118–134
	5 4	108–116	113–126	121–138
	5 5	111–119	116–130	125–142
	5 6	114–123	120–135	129–146
	5 7	118–127	124–139	133–150
	5 8	122–131	128–143	137–154
	5 9	126–135	132–147	141–158
	5 10	130–140	136–151	145–163
	5 11	134–144	140–155	149–168
	6 0	138–148	144–159	153–173

For girls between 18 and 25, subtract 1 pound for each year under 25.

Courtesy of the Metropolitan Life Insurance Company.

12

and some of your students will know more about it than you do. What is important is that you recognize the genuine interest in nutrition and diets and that you do whatever you can to help them satisfy this interest, and help them develop better and more nutritious eating habits.

Your commitment to good nutrition should go beyond merely answering inquiries by students: you should actively promote good nutrition through individual suggestions to students, through special nutrition newsletters, special displays during nutrition week, and anything else that will help get the message across in a positive, helpful way. An example of such a newsletter is shown in Appendix 9. Another way of helping the dieting student is to mark your menu with calorie counts or to identify with an asterisk the foods that may be eaten to maintain a low calorie diet. An example of such a menu is shown in Appendix 2.

Basically, there are two types of diets: therapeutic diets, and diets for weight control. Therapeutic diets are those, generally prescribed by a physician or dietitian, which are intended to help cure a specific illness. Most weight control diets are for the purpose of losing excess weight, although in some instances a person who is underweight may wish to add weight through proper nutrition.

Therapeutic Diets

Whenever a student comes to you with a therapeutic diet request, send him to your campus dietitian. If there is none on your campus, try and help the student as best you can. Ask the nature of his illness and ask for the doctor's instructions. Do not attempt to prescribe a diet yourself, but listen to the student's needs, and try to help him as much as possible. The most frequent requests will come from students who suffer from diabetes or hypoglycemia (low blood sugar). In both cases, students should bring you written diets prescribed by their physicians, and you can then go over each requirement together.

Occasionally you will encounter a student suffering from a peptic ulcer (stomach ulcer). Although treatment for ulcers is changing, the most common diet still being prescribed eliminates irritants such as alcohol and coffee, and spices such as pepper. Many doctors prescribe bland diets, with much milk, eggs, cream soups, soft cereal, and frequent feedings. Others prescribe frequent small feedings of protein snacks or skim milk, but not cream. A frequent inquiry will come to you from students suffering from acne. For a long time it was thought that the main cause of acne was an overindulgence in carbohydrates and foods with high fat content (such as candy, chocolate, soft drinks and fried foods). There is significant disagreement with this theory, however, and most doctors, in addition to prescribing for the condition directly, advise a generally well-balanced diet without excessive calories, skin cleanliness, rest, exercise, fresh air and sunlight. Since young people suffering from acne are usually very sensitive and unhappy about their condition, friendly understanding on your part is most important.

You will have noted, in this brief review of some of the most common requests for special diets, that following a doctor's prescription is not complicated, expensive, or troublesome. Most of the time, the student, with your help, can find whatever foods he needs from your regular menu, and can take with him whatever additional snacks his condition may require. Do not begrudge the student the extra crackers, the extra piece of cheese or fruit, or the extra serving of meat that he needs for his physical well-being. On the contrary, you should seek out the students who have problems to let it be known that you are there, willing and eager to provide special assistance. Other students will understand, and the dieting student will be grateful. Moreover, your entire kitchen staff is usually anxious and willing to help those with special problems. A good example is a student who has broken his jaw. For several weeks, while his jaw is wired shut, he will depend on someone to provide him with a liquid diet which he can drink with a straw. If you are indifferent to his problem, he will depend largely on canned, liquid, high protein meals. If you care, get a blender and have someone liquify the regular meals so that the unfortunate student can get through this difficult period without the diet monotony that canned drinks impose.

Reducing Diets

Chances are students will ask your opinion about all sorts of diets, some good, some harmless, and some actually dangerous. Fortunately, there is considerable information available to assist you in counselling the inquiring students. Among the best known diets is that of Weight Watchers International. Weight Watchers is a commercial enterprise, with franchises throughout the U.S.A. Its diet is based on 1,200 calories for women, and 1,600 calories for men, and its objective is a weight loss of 2 to 2½ pounds per week. Since the words "Weight Watchers" is a commercial trademark, you must be careful not to use it without permission to represent any other diet as being a Weight Watchers Diet. On the other hand, you can certainly help those students who are participating in a Weight Watchers program by making the proper foods and amounts available to them, by lending them a portion scale if they need it, and by encouraging them in every way possible. Furthermore, there are other good low-calorie diets which allow relatively large proportions of protein, no more than 30% fat (mostly unsaturated), and a minimum of carbohydrates. There are also low-carbohydrate and high protein diets, but most of these have some specific disadvantages of which the student should be made aware before starting. Again, with any diet other than one which advises merely to "eat less" of the four basic food groups, it is wise to have him get the advice of a physician or a dietitian. A Zen macro-biotic diet of brown rice and tea, for example, can cause severe malnutrition and anemia, regardless of the spiritual "lift" it might give its followers. Most of the diets which emphasize one food category at the expense of the others are equally suspect. Your job is to point these dangers out, and to direct the student's interest toward the more balanced and better accepted diet programs.

Outline of a Nutrition Education Program on Campus

Shelley Zylstra was the assistant food service manager of the residence halls on the campus of California State University, Sacramento. She is also a registered dietitian. Perceiving what she felt to be a need, she proceeded to develop a program of nutrition education and weight reduction counselling which can serve as a model for many others interested in doing the same thing.

Her first step was to set up a "Lucy and Linus Booth" in the middle of the dining hall. There, accompanied by a member of the resident staff, she set up shop for five consecutive lunch periods and developed a first-hand acquaintance with the real and imagined food service and the nutritional problems of the students. All the usual complaints, such as "too much grease in the bacon" and "too many starchy items" surfaced, together with some more thoughtful and real concerns. After analyzing these comments, Shelley developed an outline for a five-week nutrition interest group. This group met once a week, on a Thursday evening from 6:00 p.m. to 7:00 p.m. Out of a total residence hall population of about 900 students, 65 signed up for Shelley's class. The classes became exciting discussion groups, in which the students asked, and Shelley fielded all kinds of pertinent questions dealing with vegetarianism, carbohydrates, cholesterol, fibers in food, etc. As expected, toward the end of the class, the number of participants dropped. Remaining, however, were a band of some 25 to 30 students who were deeply interested in nutrition and weight control and who wanted to continue learning from Shelley. For these students, Shelley developed a special behavior modification program (see Appendix 10). While most of the students in that program were women interested in losing weight, there were also a few men, some of whom wanted to gain weight. Each student was asked to keep a "diet diary" and to record in this diary everything he ate and why he ate it. These diaries became the basis for group discussion during the evening sessions. An example of a diet diary form is shown in Appendix 10.

In addition to classes and group discussions, Shelley did much more. She sent for "food models" and other materials from the National Dairy Council (9570 Williams Street, Rosemont, Illinois 60018). These food model cards, which showed pictures of a food (e.g. a grapefruit) on one side and the nutrient and calorie content on the other, were then pasted on the glass sneezeguards of the cafeteria counter. Large calorie charts and other colorful nutrition material was pasted on the dining room walls. Soon it became evident that the eating and drinking habits of the students were changing. Skim milk consumption, for example, shot up drastically, as did the consumption of fresh fruit.

As a spin-off from the original nutrition education class, some of the resident assistants formed physical exercise groups in the dining hall at night.

The above is a vivid illustration of how much one dedicated person can achieve in the field of nutrition education and weight reduction counselling, if given the freedom to discover the students' needs, and the freedom to develop a program that will meet these needs.

VEGETARIANISM

Until the mid-1960's, vegetarianism was not a significant factor in college food service in America. To be sure, there were a few groups such as the Trappist monks and the Seventh Day Adventists which followed vegetarian diets as a matter of religious belief, but it was rare to find a student vegetarian. With increased interest in good nutrition, coupled with the fascination of many young people for the teachings of the East (Zen Buddhism, etc.) vegetarianism suddenly started to attract many new followers. Some were drawn to it out of love of animals, belief in non-violence, or simply a belief in vegetarianism as a healthy diet form. Others, especially some of the students from the youth counterculture, followed an often confused course. Some believed in organic foods grown without the use of chemical fertilizers and pesticides. At the University of California/Santa Cruz, students grew their own organic foods and insisted that the food service caterer use only these foods in the college cafeteria. At other campuses, college food service directors were virtually forced by their students to purchase organic foods (usually at a much higher cost) even though there was then, and still is now, serious question among nutritionists whether or not organic foods have any advantage over regular foods. Other students began to follow Zen macro-biotic diets which can cause serious malnutrition if followed strictly over long periods of time. Yet another large group of students merely became interested in natural foods or health foods and thus started a very positive and beneficial trend back to the use of natural, unrefined flours and sugar in cooking and baking, greater care in the proper cooking of vegetables, and use of granola, raisins and nuts in everyday diets.

By 1970, there was hardly a college food service in the United States that did not, in some manner, recognize the demands of some students for a vegetarian diet, even though those regularly following vegetarianism rarely numbered more than 10%-15% of the entire boarding population. Many schools added granola, raisins, nuts, honey, and wheat germ to their breakfast menu. Most expanded their salad bars to include vegetarian protein-laden foods such as cottage cheese and garbanzo beans. Yogurt became a campus favorite, and many managers, following the examples set in the school lunch programs, began to experiment with TVP (textured vegetable proteins), "soyburgers" and other vegetarian entrees. At the turn of the decade, vegetarianism on some campuses had taken such a strong hold that complete vegetarian menus were being prepared for some of the food operations. At other campuses, interest seemed to diminish, to the extent that many food service directors felt that vegetarianism, as a diet fad, had spent most of its force.

It is now clear that vegetarianism is here to stay. Increased emphasis on nutrition education in the public schools has produced a college student who is more aware of good diet principles, more interested in preserving his health through proper diet and convinced that eating more vegetables and less meat is good for him. At the University of Maine, a recent poll of residence hall students showed, surprisingly, that more than 50% were interested in eating vegetarian meals *some* of the time. From Maine to California, colleges are offering vegetarian alternatives to the regular menus, and the number of dedicated vegetarians often runs as high as 10%-15% of the student population. In view of this, it is essential that every college and university food service manager become acquainted with the benefits and shortcomings of vegetarianism, learn to differentiate between the various types of vegetarian diets, learn to counsel his students on the intelligent pursuit of such a diet, and learn to develop nutritious and tasty vegetarian recipes.

Types of Vegetarians

There are basically two types of vegetarians: those who do not eat the flesh of any animal (no meat, poultry, fish, and other seafood) but who eat everything else, such as eggs, milk and other dairy products. These are called *lacto-ovo vegetarians*. Then there are those who abstain from all foods of animal origin, for philosophical and health reasons. They are called *pure vegetarians* or *vegans,,* and will not eat meat, seafood, eggs, milk, or dairy products.

From a nutrition standpoint, the lacto-ovo vegetarians pose no problem for you. It is easy (some say even better) for lacto-ovo vegetarians to get their full complement of nutrients without eating meat, provided you see to it that the non-meat entree substitutes have an adequate protein content. Since cheese, nuts, soybeans and other legumes, fruits, and eggs provide such proteins, it is quite easy to offer a vegetarian menu to your students every day of the week. For a typical vegetarian entree cycle, see Exhibit IX-5. An offshot of the lacto-ovo vegetarians are those who will eat dairy products, but not eggs. These are called *lacto-vegetarians* and their diet, from a nutrition standpoint, is not too difficult to manage either.

The pure vegetarians or vegans, pose a different problem. Their diet, without any animal protein, will lack some of the B vitamins, and especially Vitamin B_{12}(cobalamin). A Vitamin B_{12} deficiency will cause a disease called "pernicious anemia", which is characterized by weakness, fatigue, sore and cracked lips, involvement of the central nervous system and a decrease in the amount of hydrochloric acid in the stomach. Treatment of pernicious anemia requires injections of Vitamin B_{12} on a regular basis for the rest of the patient's life. It is possible that the student who decides to follow a pure vegetarian diet is not aware of the risk of vitamin deficiency, and it therefore is essential that you, as the only one who can really observe his eating habits in college, counsel and warn him of the potentially catastrophic consequences of this diet.

CAFETERIA SERVICE IN RESIDENCE HALLS

In earlier years, residence halls in colleges had very few, if any, cafeterias. Their dining rooms followed the examples set by fraternities and sororities which, even today, use "hashers" (student waiters and waitresses) to serve the food, family style. This type of service, which requires one hasher for every 15-20 diners, is labor-intensive and, therefore, very costly. By contrast, a single cafeteria line, which can usually handle up to 300-350 students during a meal period, can be staffed with three servers and a "runner" who keeps supplying the line with food from the kitchen. With one or two additional students supplying the salad and beverage counters and wiping the tables in the dining rooms, there are still only 6 students serving 300 diners, or about one for every 50 students. It should be stated that this comparison does not take into account the fact that hashers usually sweep and mop the dining room and kitchen and also wash the dishes. Furthermore, the capacity of a cafeteria line is increased in direct proportion to the length of the serving period. A residence hall dining room equipped with two cafeteria lines can, therefore, easily handle a total of over 800 students, if the serving period extends over at least a two-hour period.

EXHIBIT IX-5

UNIVERSITY OF THE PACIFIC FOOD SERVICE
VEGETARIAN ENTREE CYCLE

	MONDAY	TUESDAY	WEDNESDAY	THURSDAY	FRIDAY	SATURDAY	SUNDAY
LUNCH:							
CYCLE I	Soybean Casserole	Vegie Sandwich	Baked Lentils w/Cheese	Cheese Souffle	Macaroni & Cheese		
CYCLE II	Grilled Cheese Sandwich	Cheese Noodle Bake	Fondue Monterey	Vegie Sandwich	Macaroni & Cheese Bake		
CYCLE III	Vegie Pasties	Vegie Deli Sandwich	Vegie Tacos	Avocado/Sprout Sandwich	Ind. Pizza		
CYCLE IV	Grilled Cheese Sandwich	Submarine Sandwich	Celery & Pecan Loaf	Vegie Sandwich	Macaroni/Broccoli/Cheese Casserole		
CYCLE V	Grilled Peanut Butter & Raisin Sandwich	Macaroni & Mushroom Casserole	Downsider Sandwich	Vegie Deli Sandwich	Sprout, Avocado, Cheese-Pita Bread		
DINNER:							
CYCLE I	Vegetable Quiche	Stuffed Squash	Savory Pecan Loaf/Cheese Sauce	Stuffed Tomatoes	Meatless Tostada	Walnut Patties/Mushroom Sauce	Nutty Eggplant Casserole
CYCLE II	Complimentary Pie	Mushroom Cutlets	Stuffed Peppers	Macaroni & Bean Pie	Cashew Loaf/Cheese Sauce	Lasagne	Mushroom Patties/Bechamel Sauce
CYCLE III	Mushroom Patties/Bechamel Sauce	Spaghetti/Mushroom Sauce	Potato & Cheese Casserole	Artichoke & Cheese Puff	Macaroni Loaf	Egg Foo Yung	Spinach Souffle
CYCLE IV	Meatless Enchiladas	Fresh Mushroom Quiche	Lentil Patties/Bechamel Sauce	Stuffed Bell Pepper/Cheese Sauce	Meatless Lasagne	Chili Rellenos	Stuffed Tomatoes
CYCLE V	Lentil Loaf/Cheese Sauce	Meatless Manicotti	Linguini/Mushroom Sauce	Pecan Loaf	Rice & Nut Loaf/Tomato Sauce	Italian Potato & Cheese Casserole	Mushroom Patties/Bechamel Sauce

It is for reasons of efficiency, therefore, that cafeteria service became the most prevalent type of service in residence dining halls. In types of service, therefore, college dining rooms have some things in common with commercial cafeterias. At the same time, there are differences. The newcomer to college food service often makes one of two incorrect assumptions:

- A residence hall is like a home. Therefore, a cafeteria line in a residence hall should be manned and operated in a loose, informal way similar to the way food is served in the students' homes.
- A residence hall cafeteria is just like a commercial cafeteria. Therefore, it should be run similar to commercial cafeterias, with respect to merchandising, portion control, and customer service.

Actually cafeteria service in college residence halls is unique, in that it fits neither assumption accurately, although elements of both are true. Certainly, personal attention and informality are essential if a pleasant and friendly atmosphere is to prevail, and if the student is really to feel at home in the residence hall. A student who would not expect to get "just a little taste of this," or "just a spoonful of that" in a commercial cafeteria should feel free to make such requests in his own residence hall, where, presumably people care about him. Similarly, servers can be friendly and, to some extent, even banter a little with their fellow students in the line, something which would never be allowed between servers and customers in a commercial cafeteria. On the other hand, one must always remember that a cafeteria line serving hundreds is not like a kitchen serving six, and a residence hall is not like a home. Basic principles of merchandising which spell the difference between success and failure in a commercial cafeteria are also applicable in a residence hall. Food must look attractive as well as taste good. Cafeteria pans, therefore, should be garnished colorfully. Desserts or salads should be tempting just by appearance alone. Servers should be neat and uniformed, and not appear as if they just left the volleyball court. Very important, and often forgotten, is the matter of signs and labels: food items should be labelled on the cafeteria sneezeguard, in addition to being listed on the menu. New items should be explained so as to be clear and inviting:

Sidewalk Sandwich: Pocket bread, spread with cream cheese, filled with sliced roast beef, green salad and sliced pitted Greek olives

One of the most difficult things for cafeteria line servers to learn is the trick of putting themselves in the place of the student who is on the other side of the counter:

- The sleepy student does not want to wait and does not want to talk.
- The exhausted athlete, just from scrimmage, does not want an argument about "rules."
- The worried student, right after finals, needs sympathy.
- The dieting student needs special attention.
- The crippled student needs help with his tray.
- The short student can't see what's in the steamtable pans.

There is no irreconcilable conflict between carrying out the necessary rules of food service and being friendly and considerate to the persons being served. All it takes is empathy, friendship, and a desire to be helpful.

Progressive Cooking

The greatest challenge to successful cafeteria operation is bringing food to the cafeteria counter freshly cooked, hot and appetizing. Unfortunately, it is a challenge often unmet. There are few dishes which get better the longer they cook on the stove. Most hot foods are at their best immediately after cooking. Some items like pot roasts and casseroles retain their flavor and appearance for a considerable time after cooking. Others, like hamburgers, cutlets, and omelettes, deteriorate rapidly after being cooked. Still others, like vegetables, lose their nutrients if cooked or even just heated for long periods. Since quality and appearance are affected by the cooking and heating process, one would think that even in cafeteria service food would generally be freshly cooked. Unfortunately, this is not the case. More often than not, food is prepared, *and completed,* prior to the beginning of the serving period, and then kept hot in kettles, ovens, carts, heated pass-throughs and steam tables for the entire meal period. Worse, it is timed for completion not at the beginning of the meal period, but rather a half hour earlier, when the cooks sit down to eat. Sometimes, to make matters worse still, food is cooked well before the meal period, so that the cook has ample time to do other things. What this means in actual practice is that roast beef, which ideally should come out of the oven in small amounts at 4:00 p.m., 4:30 p.m., 5:00 p.m. and 5:30 p.m., is often placed into the ovens at 10:30 a.m., removed from the ovens at 3:00 p.m., allowed to cool off until 4:00 p.m., and then served, in rapidly deteriorating condition, from 4:30 p.m. to 6:30 p.m., to students who, understandably, find the meat tough, overcooked, and unappetizing.

If entrees like roasts and chops suffer from being cooked too far in advance, imagine what happens to the hapless hamburger. Any item as fragile and susceptible to rapid deterioration as a hamburger or a fried egg needs to be served immediately upon being cooked. But how can you cook 700 hamburgers to order? The answer is: progressive cooking, staggering the cooking of hot entrees in such a way that relatively small amounts become ready for serving at progressive periods throughout the meal period. It is such an obvious solution to pre-cooking or over-cooking of food that one wonders why it seems so difficult to accomplish.

In practice, it is easy to do with such quickly cooked items as scrambled or fried eggs, French toast, and pancakes. When it comes to other items, however, cooks seem to balk. The average college cook is afraid to be caught short without food, feels insecure if his entree is not ready when the dinner is about to start. If none of these excuses is accepted, he will argue that there must be free time for last minute preparations such as cooking vegetables, potatoes, etc.

These arguments on the part of college cooks do make some sense, and it is easy, therefore, for the manager to be lulled into premature and unnecessary acquiescence. The price of such acquiescence, however, is mediocre food and an unhappy clientele. If quality is what you're after, then progressive cooking is the technique to follow. The temptation to cook food too early, or to cook too much in advance is so ingrained in the system, however, that it will take a firm commitment on your part, and continuous, close supervision to bring it about. It takes more than just instructing the cooks, more than merely explaining the reasons, more than listing the cooking times on the production sheets. You must make it clear that progressive cooking is an inviolate policy of your operation, and that every cook is expected to follow this policy in his food preparation practices. Then, to make certain, you must personally check on the food preparation, must check on the times roasts are put in the ovens, cube steaks are browned off, and fryers are turned on. You must do even more: if you find that some pans of hamburgers were cooked too early, or cooked in the oven instead of on the griddle, you may have to pull these off the serving line and hold up the line until new and more acceptable products are prepared. It takes a firm resolve, but the resulting fresh, appetizing food is well worth the effort.

Hot Food

One of the constant complaints of college students is that the food is not hot enough. Most of the time, the complaints are legitimate. If you just stop to think, for a moment, about what happens to the food from the moment it leaves the oven, you can quickly see the reason. Food is taken from the oven, kettle, or fryer steaming hot, then is placed in a cold steam table pan, where it cools off a little bit, then it is placed in a warming cart or oven, where the temperature is considerably lower than the oven or kettle, and it cools off some more. It might also be placed directly on the steam table, where the heat comes only from the bottom and sides, but escapes out the top. There is no way in which a steam table can keep an open pan of food hot for any length of time; its main value is psychological: it lulls everyone into thinking that the food is kept hot. After the food has had a chance to cool off on the steam table, it is then placed on a dinner plate which, in all likelihood, is either cold or lukewarm. Immediately, the china will syphon off whatever heat is required to equalize the temperature between the food and the plate. By this time, the student's food is really lukewarm. Then the student goes into the dining room, to help himself to all the "goodies" that are waiting for him there. By the time he takes his bread and butter, chooses from the salad bar, pours his coffee or other beverages, takes his cream and sugar, ice water, and sits down, the food is practically cold. It happens so frequently that, in a sense this phenomenon is an industry-wide scandal. The only reason why some students don't complain more frequently is that they are used to lukewarm food from their high school days and because some of them prefer it that way.

A quality-minded food service manager must not permit this to happen. There is a basic, unwritten law in food service which says: Hot food *hot,* and cold food *cold!* It is one law you must obey. There are a number of steps you can take to minimize the heat loss of cafeteria-served food

1. Food should come to the line directly from the ovens, kettles, or fryers just as it is ready for serving (progressive cooking).
2. Steam table pans should be pre-heated.

3. All steam table thermostats should be checked frequently for accuracy, and their setting should be checked by the supervisor *at each meal period*. Any pan containing liquids (soup, gravy) should be turned on "high."

4. Wet-dry steam tables should have some water in them, to permit setting the thermostats at a higher temperature.

5. Every steam table should be equipped with adjustable infra-red overhead lamps, which must be turned on whenever food is in the steam table.

6. Food in steam tables should be covered at all times, except when food is actually being served. This means that if there is a lull in the serving process, steam table covers are put back on the pans.

7. Ideal pan covers are "half-covers". When the server serves from one half of the pan, the other half is kept hot with a stainless steel cover. When one half of a pan is empty, the pan is turned around, and the empty half covered with the half-cover.

8. Some managers object to serving students plates which are too hot for them to handle. Students, however, don't object, especially if the line servers warn them to pick up the plates on the sides, with both hands. Unfortunately, plates are rarely hot enough to require such safety warnings.

9. Hot food on sheet pans (e.g. B-L-T Sandwiches, corn bread) should be covered with an inverted sheet pan, to which a handle has been attached.

10. Dinner plates should be stored in a *heated dish dolly*. The sides and top of the dish dolly are to be kept closed during the serving process, and a small stack of dishes taken out each time, so that the bulk of the dinner dishes stays hot. The plates should be so hot that the cafeteria workers need gloves in order to handle them.

11. Soups, gravies, and other liquid foods should be replaced with fresh food directly from the kettle if, upon tasting with a spoon, the taster does not slightly singe his tongue.

Cold Food

Often, when people eat in a first-class restaurant and order a chef's salad, they exclaim in delight and wonderment about how crisp the salad is. "What a delicious salad," they will say, and the restaurateur will beam with delight, in the knowledge that his efforts have paid off. What is it that he did to gain such praise? First, he probably had his lettuce cleaned and then stored whole in drained pans in the refrigerator. Second, he cut the lettuce just minutes prior to serving. Third, the lettuce was cut in large, bite-sized chunks. Fourth, it was placed into pre-chilled salad bowls, and, finally, it was topped with ice cold salad dressing.

There is no great secret to serving cold food cold. It takes some conscious effort, that's all. In a residence hall, it is impractical to cut the lettuce to order, but everything else the restaurateur does, can be done by the college food service manager. There are an increasing number of quality-conscious schools, in fact, which keep their salad bowls in a portable chiller right next to the salad counter. There is no special trick to keeping food cold on the salad counter: all it takes is many *small* bowls (instead of one big bowl) and a runner to replace the empty bowls with fresh ones right out of the refrigerator. It also takes shaved ice on top of the salad cart (even though some of the cafeteria workers may point to the refrigerated plate in the salad cart and suggest that ice isn't really necessary). Bowls of fresh fruit should be placed on the dessert counter *at the last minute,* instead of a half hour before the serving line opens, and other chilled desserts should be removed from the holding refrigerator one pan at a time.

Long Waiting Lines

Anyone who has every served in the armed forces knows that waiting in line is synonymous with military service. Whether you line up for chow, the issuance of gear, or routine innoculations, you have to wait your turn in line. One wonders, sometimes whether some of that thinking has rubbed off on college food service managers. Waiting in line is synonymous also, with college cafeterias. Some waiting is unavoidable; when most students choose to eat at the same time, a line will develop quite naturally. There may not be much that you, as food service manager, can do to prevent the line from forming, but once it is formed, you are the one who can make it move more quickly, and you are the one who can make waiting in line less onerous.

You can start by realizing that you don't like long lines. Assume therefore that students don't like waiting in line either. If some lines are unavoidable, you accept them as a necessary evil, but never assume that students don't mind waiting in line. A good manager can speed up long cafeteria lines and minimize the annoyance of those having to wait:

- Check the serving line to see if anything is holding up the line. If it is, help expedite the item.
- Open up a second line at the strategic moment, just before the big rush begins, or just before the line becomes so long that you never can catch up.
- Go toward the back of the line, and explain to everyone waiting why there is a delay, and how long it may be until everyone is served.
- Make a chart or line graph at the beginning of the year, showing the number of students fed in each 30-minute segment of the meal period. Students can then decide for themselves if they want to come during peak periods or to wait a little. (This will happen naturally toward the end of the year, but the graph will speed up its occurence).

Resist, if you can, the natural temptation to pitch in and help on the serving line. Chances are that there may be someone else in the kitchen who can help for a few minutes. Usually, the manager can be much more helpful by breaking up bottlenecks and talking with the students than he can merely using his two hands to help serve. This, of course, isn't always true. You should pitch in whenever and wherever you feel it is appropriate, but use your talent and lend assistance where it can do the most good.

A final word of caution: don't let your dislike of long waiting lines cause you to overreact. You probably cannot afford to staff the cafeteria in such a way that no one ever has to wait in line. It is not practical to add extra costs to your operations in order to eliminate all waiting. Whether it is in a residence hall cafeteria or in the student union, there will be people waiting in line at noon and at other popular eating times no matter what you do. If you can reduce this waiting at peak hours to an amount of time that is normally acceptable by those waiting (5-10 minutes, in most cases), that is all you can be expected to do.

Cafeteria Servers

Following is a typical set of instructions given to someone without previous experience who is assigned to work on a cafeteria line:

- Wash your hands, comb your hair, wear a hairnet.
- Put on an apron (jacket, duster).
- Be nice.

In some cases, the instructions are even less explicit, and the server is merely put in place with a serving spoon in his hand. Given the importance of the cafeteria server to the success of the entire meal, such lack of training is inexcusable. Remember the mistakes that are frequently made on the serving line:

- Working in dirty blue jeans, with dirty hands, uncombed and scraggly hair, unshaven
- Dishing up food in advance and placing plate on counter shelf
- Not smiling, not speaking, not asking what the customer would like
- Running out of an item, without getting more from the kitchen
- Informing the student that there is no more food without first checking with the supervisor
- Not listening to, or complying with a student's special request
- Asking the student to hurry up and make up his mind
- Serving portions that are either too large or too small
- Slopping the food on the plate, regardless of how it looks, or whether it spills over the side
- Using plastic-gloved hands to pick up the meat from the pan and putting it on the plate without using tongs or spatula

Except for the cashier, and a visiting supervisor in the dining room, the cafeteria servers are the only ones actively representing your food service to the students. What they do, and how they act, therefore, is vital to your image and success. In most residence hall kitchens, almost the entire production staff (cooks, salad makers, etc.) is used to serve the students. This is not only labor-efficient, but it also makes a great deal of sense: the ones who prepared the food should also serve it and see how well it is accepted. Most colleges also supplement this staff with part-time student workers. A mix of regular and student employees on the serving lines is probably the best -- the pride in their product and the maturity of the older employees blends well with the easy informality and relaxed friendliness of the student workers.

Maintaining a pleasant atmosphere behind the serving counter is probably the most important requirement for cafeteria servers. Taking a personal interest in each student as he or she passes through the line is another. A general appearance of order, neatness, and general cleanliness is a third (nothing puts students off like dirty, empty steam table pans stacked up behind the serving line). Last is a requirement that cafeteria line servers take their job seriously, care about doing it well, and pay attention to their work at all times.

These are not requirements that come naturally to eveyone; they need to be spelled out at the time the servers are hired, they need to be taught at training sessions and reinforced at staff meetings. For a sample job description for a line server, see Exhibit VI-14.

Cafeteria Runners

A busy cafeteria, especially one in which two lines are operating, usually requires a runner. The runner, usually a student, watches the supply of food on the line and makes sure that a new pan of food is place on the line just at the moment that the former pan is being emptied of its last serving. That job is not as easy as it sounds. Without a runner, or with an inexperienced one, the following is likely to happen in cafeteria service:

- The line will run out of a certain food item. Even if the item is one of the subsidiary items, such as the second choice entree or the potatoes, the entire line will be held up until it arrives. Somehow a cafeteria line depends on being fully supplied, and no one moves until the missing item is replaced.

- The runner arrives a few minutes too early. If this happens, he will often place the new pan into the line and literally "dump" the few remaining portions from the former pan on top of the new pan, a most unsightly and unesthetic procedure.

- The runner arrives a few minutes too late. Even if the line is held up only for a minute or two, the rushing and puffing involved in the line runner literally *running* across the kitchen with a hot food pan in his hand (a dangerous procedure, at best) is enough to unnerve even the most placid observer, and disturbs what is supposed to be a peaceful and pleasant atmosphere at the serving line.

- The runner grabs the wrong pan out of the oven. If proper progressive cooking methods are being followed, not every pan of food in the oven is ready at the same time. Without special care, the runner is likely to grab a pan of broccoli still half frozen, or a casserole not yet fully cooked.

When choosing your runners, therefore, you must choose conscientious and responsible students. Pick those who get along well with the cooks so that there is natural cooperation between them. There is always a question of how much independence a runner should have; it is worrisome to see a runner rush up to the steam kettle to fill up an empty pan with more beef stew, for example, while the cook stands by doing not much of anything important. Ideally, a runner should do the line-watching and transporting of food, while the cooks supply him with whatever he may need. A two-way intercom system similar to that used in supermarkets, between the lines and the cook's station is a big help in facilitating this process.

Heated Food Containers

For many years, knowledgeable managers and food service consultants felt that the best piece of equipment to assist a smooth funtioning of a cafeteria line was a heated food container. It might be a portable insulated cart, or an in-place pass-through cabinet, or even a heated roll-in box placed strategically behind the cafeteria line, directly next to the usual pass-through refrigerator. In view of the frequent, and almost universal misuse of such warming equipment, it is now not at all certain that such equipment is ideal for cafeteria service. If the hot food container is used only to hold one pan of each line item for a few minutes prior to use, then it can be very useful indeed and be of great help to the line runner and line servers. The runner will be under less pressure, and need only watch the warming cabinets instead of the cafeteria lines themselves. Unfortunately, that is not what normally happens. Normal procedure is to do one of two things, both wrong:

- Fill up the heating cabinets full of food at the start of the meal. Even the most modern, and highest quality cabinet, cannot stop the food from either cooling off or deteriorating in quality, when placed in the cabinet for long periods of time. It is always much better right out of the oven, kettle, or fryer.
- Disregard the warming cabinets altogether. This is a waste of expensive equipment and if the cabinets are turned on, a waste of energy.

The ideal cafeteria line is designed in such a way that, with or without warming cabinets, the cook's station is fairly close to the serving lines, so that the process of re-supply can occur quickly, smoothly, and without loss of heat or food quality.

RESIDENCE HALL DINING ROOMS

Formal dining rooms in residences were fairly standard at one time. Since table service was the norm, there was a seat provided for every hall resident, and the dining halls were usually large, formal, multi-purpose areas, used for dining, receptions, dances and other social activities. With the post-war building boom, however, architects outdid each other in experimenting with dining room design. Sometimes, such experiments were glorious successes. Just as often, however, there were disastrous failures. The successful ones were usually those in which dining was a pleasant and relaxing experience: the room was large enough to provide a good social mix of students (100 to 200 seats), and yet small enough to retain intimacy and relative quiet; it was divided by means of planters, room dividers, booths, or other harmonious room treatments; the tables seated 2, 4, 6, 8, and even 10 or 12 students (with a large number of round tables holding 6-8 students). The unsuccessful ones were often cavernous convention halls holding from upwards of 500 students, designed primarily for efficiency and not for student comfort. Other experiments of doubtful value were those in which a large number of very small dining rooms were built, so small as to prevent the natural social interaction which is important to students.

Another frequent error was to design dining and service areas without provision for salad and beverage bars. As a result, many residence hall dining rooms now look like cluttered bazaars, instead of gracious dining areas.

In spite of design problems, there is a great deal the food service manager can do to make the atmosphere in the dining room pleasant and to make the dining experience an enjoyable one for most students. He can open the dining room on time, he can have a friendly cashier at the door, he can write nice greetings on the menu board, he can keep the tables and floors shiny, the salad bar appetizing and the beverage counters free of sticky syrup. He can play the right kind of music (easier said than done), not too loud and not too soft, he can encourage faculty members' presence (also easier said than done), place flowers or plants on some of the tables, or in the room, and act as a friendly but inconspicuous host.

Dining Room Cashiers

Considering the tremendous impact which the dining room cashier can have on the atmosphere in the room and the attitude of the students, it is amazing how little importance often is given to the selection of personnel for this important job. Some food managers consider this position merely another slot to be filled by one of the applicants for student jobs. Actually, it is a key job. The entrance door is the place where the student expects a friendly greeting, a personal welcome that makes him feel glad he came. It is also the place where the college must enforce meal ticket controls. While some cafeteria managers place their cashiers at the end of the cafeteria line and permit anyone to enter the dining hall, this is not practical if unlimited food (e.g. salad bar) or beverages are offered in the dining hall itself. Controlling meal tickets by punching, stamping or checking is an impersonal task. Asking the student to present his I.D. card (when in the student's mind, he should be known by now) is another. The cashier therefore has the difficult job of minimizing his control function in the mind of the student by maximizing his friendly and personal approach to each student that enters.

You may feel, as you read this, that the easiest solution is to select a personable and friendly student for this job. In doing so, you may solve only half of your problems, however, since the control function is also very important. A careless cashier, or one who shows favoritism to certain friends, can cost food service thousands of dollars yearly in lost revenue or stolen food. This being the case, you may decide that only an older person, a regular employee of food service, can perform these duties. Here again you may be wrong, since his or her attitude may harden after a while, and the control functions will predominate while the important functions of greeting and welcoming slide into the background. There is no specific type of person, no specific age group, no clear-cut ideal personality for this job. It takes a special person, with a sense of responsibility to the food service, with a warm and ingratiating personality, and a great deal of natural affection for students of all types, someone who can explain food service regulations and policies to the students and at the same time can act a friendly ombudsman for them if they have problems that are unknown to the manager. It is a premium job, requiring a premium person and deserving premium pay.

The casher should have a small intercom unit at the desk in order to contact the manager's office and solve special problems that may occur at the entrance door quickly and inconspicuously.

The problem of admitting someone who has no meal ticket into a dining room where food and beverages are readily available has been mentioned before. It is one for which there is no ready solution. If someone wishes merely to visit for a couple of minutes, and if the cashier can keep an eye on the visitor, the request should be granted. All other requests should probably be denied, since the temptation to take some food or beverages without paying for the meal is simply too great to resist. If, on the other hand, your college administration feels strongly that everyone should be admitted into the dining room, then your only option is to remove the temptation by placing all salads and beverages in back of the cafeteria line, where their consumption can be controlled. Some colleges, particularly private colleges where intimate student-faculty contact is stressed, make exceptions in the case of faculty members, who are encouraged to enter the dining rooms even if they bring their own sack lunch. This presents no great problem to the food service manager and enhances, in fact, the dining room atmosphere. Students do enjoy seeing their teachers in an informal setting, and generally understand if some exceptions are made in such cases.

X. CASH OPERATIONS

It has been pointed out that in order to run a successful residence hall dining service you must possess a combination of special skills, among which the most important are the ability to understand the needs of resident students and the ability to establish a warm rapport with students and staff alike. Managing cash operations on a college campus requires, in addition, another set of special aptitudes: a flair for merchandising, a thorough understanding of cost accounting, competitive zeal, and flexibility.

At one time, managing of cash operations on a college campus was much easier than it is today. There was usually little competition, food and labor costs were fairly low, and colleges ran these operations primarily as a convenience and not for purposes of making a profit.

Today, the picture is different. The number of off-campus students has increased dramatically over the years, as have their expectations of the cash operations. While food and labor costs have risen dramatically, so have the profit expectations of college administrations, who have seen that well-run cash operations could contribute to the cost of operating student services. Food service management companies, drawing on their experience in commercial food service operations, often brought a new type of expertise to college campuses. Finally, the changes in American eating habits, and the trend towards fast foods and ethnic or other specialty foods have brought yet another type of competition.

The challenge of managing cash operations on college campuses goes beyond that faced by the manager of a commercial cafeteria somewhere in town: the expectations on a college campus from different constituencies are different, difficult, often conflicting, and often paradoxical. The administration expects a satisfied clientele and a profit margin somewhat comparable to commercial enterprises. Students expect a large variety of services and offerings, at periods from early morning to late at night, regardless of whether such serving periods are profitable. Faculty and staff join the students in expecting campus food to be less costly than the same food off-campus. Almost everyone considers low-cost food in campus cash operations to be a legitimate fringe benefit to which he is entitled, by virtue of being a member of the college community.

Perhaps the most difficult aspect of managing cash operations on a college or university campus is the limited time period available to produce maximum sales. Most schools do not have very active summer sessions, and few have enough traffic on weekends to justify cash operations all day Saturdays and Sundays throughout the year. This leaves only the weekdays during the school year, approximately 160 to 170 days total, to produce the needed revenue to cover all operating costs for the entire year. What is more, the only really *busy* meal is the weekday lunch period. All this adds up to a tremendous assignment for the food service manager: "Sell enough in half a year to cover all your costs for the entire year!" It is a process of continually adjusting serving hours to the existing demand, of keeping accurate records about check averages and about numbers of customers fed at each hour of the day.

Given such challenges, today's food service manager must possess patience, tact, and ingenuity. There are also proven techniques and procedures which will help him. These are discussed in the following chapter.

TYPES OF CASH OPERATIONS

At one time, cash operations on campuses consisted mainly of three basic types: there was the typical cafeteria, the snack bar, and the vending machine. Interior decor and food merchandising were often considered secondary in importance, since the main purpose of all these installations was to serve as a convenience to the campus community. With the changing eating patterns of Americans during the past twenty years, changes came also to the campuses. The rising popularity of various fast food outlets was reflected in the types of food counters being built in student centers. Instead of typical cafeteria lines, the new installations featured a series of fast food counters specializing in one or two popular food items. The food service at the student union of California State University/Long Beach serves as a good example. Around a central shopping square are located a series of food counters, each about twenty feet long and fifteen feet deep which specialize in specific fast food items. These are as follows:

- "The Natural Way": features a self-service salad bar, made to order sandwiches, and frozen yogurt
- "Soup and Sandwich": features several types of home-made soups, and hot, sliced meat sandwiches (such as French dip and pastrami)
- "El Canton": features Mexican fast food items, such as tacos, burritos, enchiladas, and home-made refried beans
- "The Grill": features hamburgers and hot dogs
- "The Pancakerie": features all types of eggs (cooked to order in individual frying pans), pancakes, waffles, French toast and all types of omelettes
- "The Sweet Shoppe": features ice cream varieties, milk shakes, pies, and natural food cookies
- "The Beverage Counter": features coffe, hot chocolate, several types of tea, milk, chocolate milk, orange juice and lemonades, punch, and several types of carbonated beverages

Other schools have installed different fast food operations. Stanford University has a retail bakery, San Diego State a natural food store, Cornell University a soup kitchen, the University of Arizona a delicatessen, and Humboldt State University a take-out pizza parlor. At California State/Sacramento and other colleges, customers make up their own sandwiches and pay for them by the ounce. Many other types of fast food and ethnic food counters are found in colleges and universities throughout the United States, serving such products as crepes and waffles, fish and chips, sausages, vegetable and fruit juices, and various types of ethnic specialties. A relatively recent development has been the installation of beer parlors on college campuses. In these, atmosphere and chilled draft beer are all-important, and food is often served principally as an accompaniment to the beverage.

Because so many of these fast food operations are in competition with similar commercial places in town, it was inevitable that colleges and universities would eventually invite some of these well-known franchise operations to come to the campus. Whether or not such an arrangement is of long-term benefit to the average college remains yet to be proven. It would appear that only a large university could successfully absorb a fast food franchise, and still provide the other variety of cash operations needed for a well-balanced food service program. Suffice it to say, that the customer interests and appetites lie in these directions, and that their wishes must be fulfilled if you want them to keep eating on campus.

Almost as important as the menu of food items to be served in these various food operations is the interior decor. There will always be some units which have as their sole purpose dispensing large amounts of food and beverages to the largest possible number of customers in the shortest amount of time. Such places are rapidly giving way, however, to food counters and specialty restaurants which have a distinctive atmosphere and a unique interior design. The Barn at Northern Illinois University, the Country Store at Oregon State University, and the Rathskeller at the University of the Pacific are examples of such design.

Although each installation has to be planned to fit the needs of an individual campus, there are certain basic facts about each type of unit that are worth remembering.

Hamburger and Hot Dog Grill

Most people in food service know how to cook a good hamburger: take a high quality ground beef patty, preferably a quarter-pound or larger, place in on a char-broiler or grooved griddle, butter a fresh hamburger bun (a yellow bun made with eggs preferred), grill the bun until it is toasty around the edges, then place fresh crisp lettuce, tomato, catsup, mustard, and a pickle chip on the hamburger, put the buns together, and serve immediately. The problem is that not everyone can do it that way. First of all, not everyone has a char-broiler or grooved griddle. Second, not everyone has enough griddle space to toast the buns on the griddle. At the Tressider Union at Stanford University the buns are toasted in a rotary toaster, for example. Some schools actually must pre-cook their hamburgers in advance, in order to handle the noon-time rush. They cook the hamburgers just half way through and place them in a pan with natural juices, then toast the buttered buns, cover them with a moist towel and place these in the warming cabinet. When the rush comes, both the patty and the buns are placed briefly on the griddle and then served.

You may wonder if this is a quality hamburger. It certainly is not as good a product as the hamburger described earlier. How then does one justify pre-cooking the patties and pre-toasting the buns, if quality of product is the most important single requirement of a successful food service operation? The answer lies in the nature of the fast food operation on campus. Students do not like to wait; they want quick service at fast food counters, and you must be geared up to provide it. This is where you balance *quality of food with quality of service* and provide both to the best of your ability.

Hot dogs can be cooked in a variety of ways: they are good when grilled, steamed, or even when heated in a microwave oven. The most effective combination of cooking and merchandising is to cook and display them in a rotating hot dog rotisserie right near the counter. Key points to remember about hamburger and hot dog grills are these

- Buns should be buttered and grilled or toasted.
- Hamburgers and hot dogs should be juicy and hot.
- Lettuce and tomatoes should be kept chilled in a refrigerated pan until used.
- Any pass-through window or holding pan should be heated with infra-red heat lamps to keep the product hot for the few seconds while it is waiting to be picked up for service.

Delicatessen

The University of California/Berkeley operates a large and efficient "deli" as part of their student union food service. Prominent in the deli are long display-type refrigerators where students can select the sausage, cheese or other ingredients for their sandwiches. Favorite sandwiches are chopped chicken liver and egg salad, lox and cream cheese on a bagel, roast beef, pastrami, corned beef, B-L-T, and Reuben sandwiches. Avocado, tomatoes, and bean sprouts are optional sandwich additions. Homemade potato salad, cole slaw, three-bean salad, marinated vegetable salads, and daily specials are some of the salads offered. All items can be purchased for take-out, and "speedy-to-go" telephone orders are accepted. The key points to remember in a delicatessen are these

- All meats and salads must be attractively displayed in display refrigerators or in refrigerated steam table pans.
- Bread and rolls must be oven fresh, of interesting varieties, and also appetizingly displayed. Jewish rye bread, Kaiser or French rolls and, if possible, pumpernickel, are absolute essentials.
- All sandwiches should be served with a dill pickle wedge.
- Combinations of sandwiches and a small salad (potato, cole slaw, sauerkraut) are particularly popular, and help to increase the check average.
- Every sandwich must be made-to-order and mustard or mayonnaise should be offered.

Hofbrau

The Hofbrau is an important luncheon facility at the University Center of the University of the Pacific. Hot beef sandwiches, sliced to order and served plain or "French dip" style (the bun is dipped in natural gravy) are the mainstay of the menu. In addition, there are hot corned beef and pastrami sandwiches, as well as other grill sandwiches. These are the key points in a hofbrau:

- Meats should be sliced to order, paper thin, and piled up on the sandwich, about 3-4 oz. of meat, depending on price.
- If possible, rolls should be heated or, on request, dipped in hot gravy. Bread or rolls must always be fresh.
- Dill pickle wedge or other garnish must accompany each sandwich.
- Natural gravy must be kept piping hot at all times.

Ice Cream Fountain

Many colleges have installed ice cream fountains or old-fashioned soda shops on their campuses. In some cases, these are partly financed by the ice cream purveyor. They can be installed in a very small area, require little food service equipment, and continue to be popular throughout the country. Some schools have taken small ice cream freezers, equipped them with wheels and colorful umbrellas, and sold ice cream outdoors in high traffic areas of the campus. Key points:

- Interior decor and colors are all-important.
- Ice cream should be of good quality, with many different varieties.
- Both regular and sugar cones should be provided.
- Use frozen strawberries mixed with syrup rather than canned strawberry topping, if you want to serve a quality product.
- Serve cookies or other baked items to increase check average.
- Serve beverages also.

Soup-and-Salad Bar

Both Cornell University in Ithaca, New York and California State University/ Chico have been highly successful with their respective soup kitchens. In both instances, these feature at least two home-made soups daily. At Chico, the soup is offered in combination with a tossed salad and French bread. The great attraction is that a soup and salad meal is nutritious, filling, and inexpensive. Individual soup tureens, attractive iron soup kettles and large salad bowls add to the decor and excitement. Key points:

- Prices for soup-and-salad combinations must be moderate.
- Soups should be home-made, and advertised accordingly.
- Constant variety of soups is essential.
- Salads must be fresh, crisp, and cut in bite-size chunks. A large variety of dressings (Italian, French, Russian, blue cheese, low calorie, and especially a house dressing) should be offered, together with various toppings, such as croutons, garbanzo beans, bacon bits, chopped eggs and sliced beets. Cruets of vinegar and oil should also be available for those who like to "mix their own."

Mexican Food Counter

Mexican food items, especially tacos and enchiladas, once popular primarily on the West Coast, are now being purchased across the country. California State/Long Beach has an especially enthusiastic clientele when it comes to such foods, and tacos are almost as popular as hamburgers. The secret of a good taco is its paper-thin tortilla shell, freshly deep fried in a high quality oil (preferably poly-unsaturated), the crispness of the chopped lettuce and tomato filling, the zest of the spicy sauce. An enchilada must have a tasty filling (cheese, chicken, beef, etc.) and a good sauce, and be served piping hot. Key points to remember are

- Thin corn tortillas
- Tacos freshly fried in good oil
- Lettuce crisp and cold

Health Food Bar

One of the most successful health food bars is located on the campus of California State/Chico. It is a small and simple counter, one of a series which forms part of a scramble-type cafeteria. similar to that described of California State/Long Beach earlier. What is unique about this health food bar is its colorful display of fresh fruits, salads, and vegetables, its interesting menu offerings, and the fact that all the health food sandwiches are made to order from natural, non-meat ingredients, served in an attractive and appetizing way. The sandwiches are made from natural grain breads. Three of the most popular varieties include an avocado sandwich (fresh avocadoes with cream cheese), a mushroom burger and a soy vegeburger with bean sprouts. In addition, sandwiches are made to order with such pre-prepared fillings as egg salad and cream cheese with olives, both of which are kept in bowls of ice for ready use. The key to such a successful unit is the imagination and quality written into the menu; a copy of one from the Natural Food Bar of California State/Chico is shown in Appendix 11.

One of the features of natural food bars is their interesting beverages. You will notice in the menu of Chico State's Natural Food Bar such concoctions as old smoothies, tiger milkshakes, and protein pick-ups. These drinks can contain any interesting combination of fresh fruit, soft ice cream, milk, yogurt, etc. Two very exciting drinks are featured in the health food bar at Humboldt State University. They are called a smoothie and a whizzie. These are rich, milk-shake type drinks which include yogurt and fresh fruit. They are extremely popular with all vegetarian and health food devotees. (See Exhibit X-1.) There is no limit to interesting drink combinations that you can create: soft ice cream with orange juice and vanilla syrup is called, at the University of the Pacific, a tiger shake. Apple juice with soft ice cream, or cranberry juice with raspberry sherbet are other good combinations. Among the most popular fountain drinks at Stanford University are fruit shakes which consist simply of frozen fruit (such as strawberries, blueberries, and boysenberries) mixed with soft ice cream and milk. Key points to remember with health food bars are these

- Aim menu at vegetarians, health food devotees, and diet-conscious office workers.

EXHIBIT X-1

HEALTH DRINK RECIPES

Smoothie
¼ cup Water
¼ cup Ice
½ tsp. Protein powder
¼ tsp. Lecithin
¼ tsp. Brewers yeast
1 T. Honey
¼ tsp. B-6 Complex (if desired)

Blend together and add 4 oz. of fruit: Banana, Apple, Pear, Peach, Pineapple

Blend Well. To make different types of smoothies substitute orange juice or grape juice for water.

Vitality Cocktail
Fresh Carrot Juice - Fill to bottom line on blender
Celery Stick - 3" long
½ tsp. Protein powder
¼ tsp. Lecithin
¼ tsp. Brewers Yeast
¼ tsp. B-6 Complex
1 T. Honey
¼ cup Crushed ice

Place all ingredients in blender. Blend well.

High Protein Malt
1 tsp. Protein powder
¼ tsp. Brewers yeast
½ tsp. Lecithin
3 tsp. Powdered milk (Sanalac)
3 tsp. Soy Powder
1 tsp. Honey
½ cup Ice
½ cup Water
Desired flavoring

Blend well

Yogurt Whiz
6 oz. Yogurt
¼ cup Papaya Concentrate - diluted 50%
1 cup Pineapple spear
¼ Apple
½ Banana
1 T. Honey

Blend Well.

Tutti-Fruity
Papaya Concentrate - Diluted 50%. Fill to bottom line on blender
½ tsp. Protein powder
¼ tsp. Lecithin
¼ tsp. Brewers yeast
Place ingredients in blender and stir.
Add 4 oz. of fruit desired or combination of fruits not to exceed 4 oz.
½ banana
4 oz. strawberries
4 oz. apple slices
4 oz. pear slices
¼ cup crushed ice

Blend well.

Recommended research reading
The uses of Juices
Live Food Juices
Adventures In Cooking with Health Foods
Drink Your Troubles Away
Let's Live Health Food Dictionary
Instant Health the Nature Way
Eat, Drink & Be Healthy
The Joy of Eating Natural Foods
The Natural Foods Cook Book
Grow It & Cook It
Back To Eden

Courtesy of California State University/Chico.

- Use only fresh fruit and vegetables, whole-grain, natural breads, and other popular health food ingredients (such as alfalfa and bean sprouts, nuts, raisins, and honey).
- Display the fresh fruit and vegetables, breads, and cheeses prominently near the front of the counter.
- Prepare salads and sandwiches to order, if possible.
- Create interesting combinations of soups (e.g., peanut butter cream soup), salads, and sandwiches.

Pizza Parlor

Many colleges and universities operate pizza parlors in their cash operations. These range from small pizza take-out counters to large pizzerias which offer everything the commercial places do, including beer and entertainment. Methods of preparing the pizza also vary, from preparing the pizza dough from scratch, to purchasing complete frozen pizzas and merely re-heating these in a pizza oven. Several suppliers now offer a complete line of frozen and canned ingredients (frozen dough rounds, frozen cheese and meats, and canned tomato sauce). Most colleges do try to put the pizzas together on location, because the pizzas are better, and students enjoy watching them made. Oregon State University makes a pizza from a soft dough crust. The dough is purchased in frozen 4 oz. balls from a local bakery, while partially frozen, it is stretched out and placed into cake pans. This makes a nice, thick, soft dough crust in 7-inch, 10-inch, and 13-inch sizes. An important fact to remember in pizza preparation is to put enough cheese and enough tomato sauce on the dough, and to cover the entire pizza with sufficient meats and mushrooms to please the customer. It is better to charge a little more for a well-made, generous pizza than to charge little for a poor quality product. Another big factor in successful pizzeria operations is the take-out business. Oregon State and the University of Maine are two examples of universities which have capitalized on the tremendous market for food that exists in the residence hall during the late evening hours. Pizza orders are taken by telephone and delivered right to the student's door.

One other factor to remember is the single student, who rarely can eat a pizza all by himself. Either an individual small pizza, or single large pizza slices should be made available to such students. At the University of the Pacific, students are permitted to pool their dinner meal tickets, so that several tickets together can purchase pizza, salads, and beverages for a complete and nutritious meal. Key points:

- Make pizzas on location, if at all possible.
- Use only a regular pizza oven for best results.
- Offer only high quality pizzas (plenty of toppings) and charge accordingly.
- Do not allow food cost to exceed 33% of the selling price.
- Offer green salads, milk, apple cider, and other nutritious beverages, in addition to pizzas.
- Charge extra for take-out paper supplies.
- Gear operating hours to existing demand as determined by actual sales.

Vending Carts

Some schools with large campuses use portable vending carts to provide food service in distant corners of their campus. The University of California/Berkeley in addition to motorized vending trucks called "Oskimobiles," uses a number of hand-drawn pushcarts on their campus. These carts are similar to those used to sell hot dogs on street corners of large cities. They have heated compartments for buns and hot dogs, and non-refrigerated space for cookies, candies, etc. Some also come equippped with a pre-mix setup for carbonated beverages, or with refrigerated space for salads, sandwiches, and even ice cream. California State University/Long Beach goes even further. They operate a number of "Forty-niner wagons" which resemble the Conestoga wagons from pioneering days, except that they are pulled with a tractor and are equipped with the most modern food service equipment, including microwave ovens for hamburgers and other hot sandwiches. These wagons are plugged into 110-volt outlets at campus locations which have a heavy outdoor traffic flow. The following are key points to remember:

- Vending carts are not profitable if they cannot produce enough sales to meet all costs. At the University of California/Berkeley, the minimum was found to be $300 per day.
- The cost per cart should be depreciable in a 3-year period.
- Do not serve foods that cannot in every way satisfy all sanitation requirements.
- It is too costly to operate vending carts as a service to the campus community if sales are not sufficient to make the carts profitable.
- Attractive decor, food merchandising, and sales personnel are as important with carts as they are in the restaurants.

Cafeterias

Standard, old-fashioned cafeterias which serve a variety of hot and cold food, typically several hot entrees and vegetables, individual salads and desserts, sandwiches made and wrapped in advance, and beverages at the end of the counter do not meet the real needs of the college community unless they complete the full range of nutritional food offerings which fast food items alone cannot do.

A graduate student at the University of Pennsylvania several years ago made a study of consumers' taste preferences and their evaluation of existing cash operations. He discovered that while most of the food on campus was sold at cafeteria counters, the preferred type of restaurant for lunch was a delicatessen, and for dinner a soup kitchen or a creperie. Chances are that similar results would be found in many present college cafeterias, if they have not already converted some to fast food outlets, as the University of Pennsylvania has done.

In spite of the changes in customers' tastes toward fast foods, the college food service director does have a responsibility to provide full, nourishing hot lunches and dinners to his off-campus students. Many eat most of their meals at college, and relatively few know how to purchase the right combination of fast foods in order to wind up with a well-balanced diet. Complete hot meals with meat, potatoes and vegetables are much more likely to give students the necessary combination of nutrients than hamburgers, French fries, and soft drinks.

A common solution is to serve complete hot meals in a modified cafeteria line, i.e. as part of a comprehensive food offering which includes fast foods as well. A return to the "blue plate special" which became famous in the United States in the thirties and forties seems like a good idea. These specials should be reasonably priced, and include items which are popular and familiar. Chopped hamburger steaks, meat loaf, spaghetti and meat balls, beef pot pie and vegetarian entrees are examples. Rice or a variety of potatoes and gravy are always popular, and so is sliced roast beef, ham, turkey, and chicken.

If you operate some sort of hot meal line it will be more feasible to sell meal tickets to off-campus students. Even though the students themselves may prefer fast food items, many parents continue to feel that their son or daughter should have access to a complete hot meal daily and will purchase a meal ticket in order to insure this. Meal tickets, like scrip books, help to increase sales volume and should be offered in those schools where such a need exists. Key points to remember:

- Offer daily innovative specials of complete, hot, meals.
- Keep the selling price moderate.
- Offer popular, familiar dishes in a variety of interesting ways.

Table Service Restaurants

Every college and university president has a dream. He dreams of an elegant table service restaurant on his campus, where he can entertain campus visitors in a quiet, gracious setting, meet with faculty and staff assistants over a relaxed lunch, and generally accomplish matters that require a special atmosphere. With the proliferation of new student union buildings in the sixties, many of these dreams became a reality, only to be shattered quickly by economic facts. Union directors discovered that such restaurants simply did not pay. With the absence of a significant, steady dinner and weekend trade, and a turnover of perhaps two, at most three settings at lunch, there was insufficient volume to cover expenses. They also found out that while administrators and some faculty members enjoyed such a restaurant-on-campus, most of the students and faculty preferred less formal surroundings and, more important, could not afford the luxury of a served lunch.

As a result, most schools modified their original idea. Some used these restaurants for a dual purpose: table service during weekday lunches, banquets and special parties at all other times. Others converted these units into self-service cafeterias. At the University of California/Berkeley, the Golden Bear is operated on a modified self-service basis: the customers help themselves to salads at the salad bar, but waiters and waitresses serve them everything else. At the University of the Pacific, customers choose from a buffet line, then sit down for service of French bread, beverages, and desserts. Both these operations serve as table service restaurants only on weekdays at lunch; at all other times the rooms are used for banquets or other special events. They are, of course, ideal for such affairs as dinner theatre and other functions requiring various types of food and banquet service.

Some colleges have capitalized on their restaurant by opening it to church-going families on Sunday noon. By offering a relatively low-cost Sunday brunch or limited menu they have managed to attract large crowds of families and senior citizens and have turned the Sunday dinner into a good public relations feature as well as a most profitable venture.

There are few college food service managers who would argue for the existence of campus table service restaurants on the basis of economics. Given the need for modest selling prices, the extra cost of table service, linen, and the preparation of special menu items, it is seldom a profitable venture. On the other hand, there are often benefits that are equally important. The college president's dreams are not wholly unjustified, even though students will often think so. Colleges and universities are like large business enterprises, and the chance to conduct important business over a quiet lunch on campus can be most helpful to the college administrator. The faculty member also benefits from being able to sit down with students or with his colleagues in a setting other than the noisy fast food or cafeteria dining area. When students are allowed to use their meal tickets to pay all or most of the cost of such a served lunch, the operation of a campus restaurant is even more justified. The following are key points to remember:

- Keep the menu as simple as possible. Serve one or two special entrees at most. Restrict "to order" items to sandwiches and other quick, easy to fix items. Serve what the customers want.

- Restrict the hours to weekday noons, unless special conditions exist on your campus that justify additional hours.

- Set prices so that your food and labor costs combined do not exceed 70% of sales.

- Use cost-saving steps such as placemats and partial self-service.

- Try to meet the needs of all segments of the campus community, to keep the restaurant from becoming a faculty club. Use every possible means and incentive to attract faculty, and students, as well as staff to this facility.

- Utilize the room as fully as possible at all other times, to justify its continued use as a restaurant at noon.

A menu from the California State University/Sacramento "Sequoia Room" is shown in Exhibit X-2.

TEN BASIC RULES FOR CASH OPERATIONS

John Milano, Director of Food Service at California State University/Chico, is one of the knowledgeable experts on campus cash operations in the United States. During a recent meeting of the National Association of College and University Food Services (NACUFS), he listed the following ten rules for successful campus cash operations:

EXHIBIT X-2

Sequoia Room Dinner Menu

All Dinners Include Salad Bar, Roll and Butter

Specialties

Quiche Lorraine - Tasty combination of Swiss Cheese, Bacon and
Seasonings baked in a flaky pastry and garnished with fruit. $2.45

Roast Beef Au Jus - Served with Baked Potato and Vegetable. $3.75

Sauted Liver and Onions - Served with Bacon, Onion Rings,
Baked Potato and Vegetable. $2.75

Broiled Pork Chop - Served with Apple Compote and your choice
of Potato or Vegetable. $3.65

From the Broiler

Chopped Sirloin Steak -
Served with Madeira Sauce,
Baked Potato and Vegetable. $2.85

Top Sirloin Steak Sandwich -
6oz. Steak broiled to your
order and served on a hard
roll with French Fries. $3.75

Rib Eye Steak -
6oz. Steak broiled to order.
Served with Baked Potato and
Vegetable. $4.25

Prince & Pauper Kabob -
Tender Beef and Poultry
skewered with Pineapple,
Pepper and Onions. Served
with Rice Pilaf and Vegetable. $3.25

From the Sea

Mahi-Mahi -
Broiled and basted with
Pineapple Juice. Served
with Rice Pilaf and
Vegetable. $2.65

Fishermans Platter -
Featuring Perch Fillet,
Fried Clams, Scallops
and Breaded Shrimp.
Served with Crispy Fries. $4.25

Scallops -
Deep Fried golden brown.
Served with Lemon and Tartar
or Hot Sauce, Baked or French
Fried Potato and Vegetable. $3.95

Appetizers

Fresh Fruit Cup .... $.65

Soup du Jour .... bowl $.55
                  cup $.45

Beverages

Coffee, Sanka .... $.30

Tea 25

Milk 35

Iced Tea or Soft Drink 35

EXHIBIT X-2 (continued)

Entrees

Prince & Pauper Kabob - Tender Beef and Poultry marinated and
skewered with pineapple chunks, green pepper, and pearl onions,
broiled to order and served on a bed of fluffy rice pilaf.
Salad bar, roll and butter $2.90

Quiche Lorraine - Tasty combination of swiss cheese, bacon
and seasonings baked in a flaky pastry and garnished with fruit.
Salad bar, roll and butter $2.45

Tostado - Flour tortilla with refried beans and Mexican beef
chili, chopped lettuce and tomatoes, shredded cheese and
sour cream $1.90

Steak Sandwich - 6oz. top sirloin steak grilled to your order
and served on a hard roll with french fries. Salad bar $3.75

Soup and Sandwich - Cup of homestyle soup of the day and a piled
high Hof Brau sandwich $1.95

Soup and Salad - Your choice from our salad bar and a bowl of
homestyle soup of the day served with an individual hot loaf
of bread $1.90

Salad Bar - For those who want to make a complete lunch from
our salad bar. Served with an individual hot loaf of bread $1.50

Chef Salad - (served on Monday, Wednesday & Friday only)
Mixed greens with Julienne cut roast beef, ham and cheese,
garnished with tomato wedges, hard cooked eggs, asparagus spears,
olives and beet and carrot strips. Roll and butter $2.50

Cold Plate - (Served on Tuesday & Thursday only) Our special
tuna salad, cottage cheese, potato salad, deviled eggs, fresh
fruit cup and muffin or roll $2.50

Menu from the Sequoia Room, California State University/Sacramento.

Rule 1. First create the menu. Each food service area should be planned according to a clear concept, of which the menu is the heart. Successful ideas from others are worth copying; do so without hesitancy.

Rule 2. Streamline the menu for cost control. Once the menu is written, check it for its impact on food and labor costs. Simplify it. Upgrade the menu (by offering it in combinations, by adding a garnish, etc.) to increase your check average.

Rule 3. Offer quality, but charge a fair price. A poor grade of hamburger at a low price will bring you just as many complaints as a good hamburger at too high a price.

Rule 4. Develop a system of production for each item. No item should be placed on a menu, unless you know exactly how it will be produced. If you offer a "bratwurst" for example, will it be steamed, grilled, or heated in a microwave oven? If you can't do it well, don't serve it.

Rule 5. Pre-plan the merchandising of each item. How will each item be presented? Will the bratwurst be served on a hot dog bun or a French roll, with pickle or potato chips? Will it have a garnish? How will it be arranged on the plate? How will it be packaged?

Rule 6. Set the mood with the appropriate atmosphere. Be creative, find out what the customers on your campus want. In a "deli", for example, hang sausages and place loaves of bread where they help to create atmosphere; in a natural food place, fresh fruits and vegetables, hanging plants, arrangements of various grains are suitable.

Rule 7. Don't neglect basics of cleanliness and order. Unless each area is spotless, and unless the various items of food and supplies are kept neat and orderly, customers will either shun the place, or complain.

Rule 8. Sell the total concept. Use exciting menu signs, descriptive phrasing, catchy titles and slogans. Train your line workers in merchandising and sales techniques.

Rule 9. Develop a total communications program. A cash operation is not visited automatically by everyone, not even by the majority, merely because it is there. You must let everyone know that he is wanted. Find out how best to reach your campus customers, then develop a regular, standard, procedure of accomplishing this. Flyers, posters, newspaper advertising -- whatever works. Let everyone know what you are doing -- and do it regularly.

Rule 10. Take time to train serving personnel. The key to a successful cash operation is your servers, how they look, what they say, and how they serve. What is their attitude? Train them to *smile,* to care, to know the menu, to know the prices, to give fast and courteous service, and to "sell up" (i.e. sell more than the customer originally planned to buy) by suggesting: "Would you like a bowl of soup?" "We have hot apple pie today!"

SETTING PROPER SELLING PRICES

It is not easy to set the right selling price for each item in your cash operations. When thinking of your customers, you will be tempted to set these as low as possible. When thinking of your financial statements, your inclination will be to do just the opposite. The campus community expects that prices in the campus cafeterias will always be lower than anywhere else. The administration, however, will compare your profit and loss statements with commercial operations, and expect you to be as efficient and profitable as they are. What should you do?

First, you should prepare a budget and determine in advance what profit margin you wish to achieve. A net operating profit of 3% to 5% is a normal budget objective for campus cash operations, depending on what overhead costs are paid by the college. Many places do not always achieve such results, and many are operating at a loss. Second, you should determine your food cost objective. If your costs of labor are averaging between 30% and 35% of sales, and your other costs somewhere between 15% and 20%, then your food cost obviously must remain somewhere between 40% and 45% of sales. The result of this mix is budgeted at a 40% overall food cost. Many cash operations aim at food costs lower than 40%. The Kansas State Union, for example, prices most items (except beverages) at 2.7 times food cost and arrives at an overall food cost of 38% of sales.

Let us assume that you have decided to aim for an overall food cost of 40% of sales. The inexperienced food service manager might take every item on the menu, multiply its food cost by two-and-a-half and sit back, sure in the knowledge that he will achieve his cost objective. Chances are that he will fail. There are some items on a menu which have a very high profit margin (such as carbonated beverages), and there are others where the profit is very low (such as bakery items purchased for resale). The key to proper pricing, therefore, is to establish different food cost percentages for each of several *groups* of items, and to blend these groups in such a way that your original food cost objective is achieved. The University of California/Berkeley, for example, uses the following food cost percentages as a general guide in setting selling prices in their cash operations:

Hot entrees and hot meat sandwiches	33%
Cold sandwiches and salads	40%
Items purchased for re-sale	50%-75%
All beverages	20%-25%

Setting food cost objectives is not enough, however. Each item on the menu has to be considered individually. Setting proper selling prices requires a knowledge of psychology, merchandising, and market research. There are four basic rules to remember when setting a selling price for an individual item in a cash operation:

- Know the food cost of each item.
- Know (or estimate) the labor cost to produce each item.
- Know what others in similar operations are charging.
- Know what the customer is willing to pay.

Obviously, you must know what each item is costing you. The cost of food is relatively easy to establish. The cost of labor is more difficult. Some might argue that the cost of labor is not important at this stage of the pricing process, since you are aiming for a food cost objective, and since labor cost is taken into consideration in the total budget process. This type of thinking has been debunked some time ago, notably by Harry Pope, a highly successful cafeteria operator in the Midwest, who was one of the first to espouse the principle of "prime costing" i.e., that all pricing should consider not only the raw cost of food, but also the cost of labor necessary to produce the item. Merrill Baker, at the State University of New York/Cortland, is also a great believer in this approach.

Knowledge of what your competition is charging is an important factor in your deliberations. But competitors may be wrong, and following their example could lead you astray. Some managers want to be independent and disregard what competitive establishments nearby are charging. On the other hand, a basic principle for success in a free economy is to be competitive, and a haughty disregard for what goes on around you could be fatal. On a college campus, it is especially important to conduct periodic price surveys of cafeteria and fast food prices in the area near the campus, as well as those on other nearby campuses. Students will accept your price schedules much more readily if you can prove to them, by showing them the results of your price comparisons, that your prices are, indeed, reasonable and competitive.

None of the above information is of any consequence, however, if the price that you must charge is more than the customer is willing to pay. This happens. Price resistance is a difficult thing to assess, and often has to be learned from actual experience. Will your students be willing, for example, to pay $3.00 for a steak sandwich? It may be a perfectly reasonable price, and may possibly be charged by restaurants very near campus, but it may be a complete flop when offered in your own grill on campus. If so, take it off the menu. How and when do you raise the price of a cup of coffee, in the face of rising coffee prices? Can you afford to accept a lower-than-normal markup, for example, in order to keep the good will of your clientele? If so, how long can you afford to keep this up? If you find that you cannot afford to sell an item at a price your customers are willing to pay, take it off the menu. Setting of a selling price requires a knowledge of psychology as well as merchandising. Obviously, the time to raise the price of a cup of coffee is when coffee prices are rising everywhere, and when the customers more or less expect such a move. It is equally clear that, in order to gain at least a grudging acceptance of a price increase, you should explain to your customers the reason for such an increase. This is especially important on a college campus, where every customer is a potential self-appointed expert, willing to argue with you at the slightest provocation. A good way to do this is to be frank, and to share information with your customers. Here is an example of how this can be done:

SORRY, EVERYBODY, THE TIME HAS COME!

The last time we raised the price of coffee on this campus was three years ago. Since then, our cost for coffee has literally tripled, and now we must ask you to share the cost with us. The following is a list of wholesale coffee prices during the recent past:

Date	Cost of coffee per lb. at Wholesale	Selling price 8 oz. cup of coffee
December 1975	1.98	$.10
December 1976	2.67	$.15
March 1977	3.80	$.20

We will continue to serve you the best coffee we know how to make, and thank you for your understanding.

Signed: Dick Jones, Cafeteria Manager

A lively argument occurs every time a food service manager who believes in "even pricing" meets another who believes in "odd-cents pricing." The former believes that customers do not like to bother with pennies, and are willing, in most instances, to pay an even amount (say, to the next highest nickel). He believes, also, that those extra pennies add up, and help in the overall food cost objective. The other feels that setting selling prices at odd amounts is better psychologically, that it is easier to increase selling prices with an odd-cents pricing system, since the customers are not as aware of each individual price as they would be with an even pricing system. Most food service operators usually stick to the even pricing method, because of the convenience for both the customers and the cashiers, and the speedier serving lines.

Some managers are so concerned with the speed of their lines that they go to special lengths to make things as easy as possible for the cashiers. They select certain sizes of salad bowls, with each size having the same selling price. They select certain glasses or paper cups, with each costing the same. They carefully select each container so that the cashiers, almost by looking at the glass or container, can quickly calculate the price of the item.

One final consideration in setting selling prices is the impact which a change in a selling price of a certain item will have on profits. There is little point, for example, in changing the price of a peanut-butter-and-jelly sandwich, if the total number of such sandwiches sold each day numbers less than ten. Price changes do not have to be major, nor do they have to be dramatic such as shown in the above example on coffee. *Price changes can, and should occur as soon as the need arises throughout the year,* whenever wholesale prices, food cost percentages, or other factors indicate that need. They should be selective, and they should make a difference in the profit picture. You should, therefore, periodically engage in an analysis of your sales, and assign someone for an entire day to keep track of *everything* that is sold in your operation: every cup of coffee, every coke, every piece of toast, sandwich, hot dish, . . . everything. Having done that, you can then evaluate each item in terms of its contribution to total profits, leaving the price as is, increasing it, or removing the item from the menu entirely because it does not sell. Such a sales analysis is shown in Exhibit X-3.

MERCHANDISING IN CASH OPERATIONS

The next time you visit a restaurant, take a look at their merchandising techniques. If the restaurant is successful, it is also doing a good job of merchandising. It is not enough merely to sell a food product, you have to promote it, brag about it, combine it with some other item, display it, describe it, have people taste it, offer it as a special bargain, and suggest it in every other conceivable manner. The eating process begins with our eyes. The appearance of the food on the plate, the odor and attractiveness of the garnish, and the packaging -- all these are essential features of the merchandising process. Your success depends on how much people buy and your job is to get them to buy as much as possible. In fast food operations, you don't

EXHIBIT X-3

SALES ANALYSIS FORM

Menu Items	# of Items Sold	Selling Price	Gross Sales	Cost of Individual Item			Total Cost Per Item			Gross Profit		% of Sales
				Food Cost	Paper Cost	Total Cost	Food Cost	Paper Cost	Total Cost	Individual Item	Total G.P. Per Item	
Hamburgers, 4 oz.	182	1.00	182.00	.42	.02	.44	76.44	3.64	80.08	.56	101.92	56.0%
Green Salad, large	6	.45	2.70	.12	.01	.13	.72	.06	.78	.32	1.92	71.1%
Green Salad, small	24	.25	6.00	.06	.01	.07	1.44	.24	1.68	.18	4.32	72.0%

have much time. Your customers are not sitting down for a leisurely meal, and you have no waiters or waitresses who can carry on an extended conversation about the menu. Look, sometime, at the ways in which fast food restaurants merchandise their products:

- Hot Apple Pie Today. . .a la Mode. . .
- While in Season: Fresh Strawberry Sundaes. . .
- Every Friday: Home Made Clam Chowder. . .
- Fish Fry Every Wednesday Nite -- All You Can Eat. . .

It is not only *what* you merchandise, but also *how* you get the message across. One of the worst ways is merely to add a message to your already existing menu board. Chances are that no one will see it there. The average restaurant customer gets into a kind of routine, and if you want to get his special attention, then make a *special* effort to accomplish this. This is not easy. The typical small luncheonette has so many pieces of hand-scribbled paper stuck on to the back bar, that the customer at the counter can hardly read them all. Worse, none of them makes a special impression. Even a large, attractive sign is sometimes overlooked, and table tents often greet the client after he has already made his purchase. Suggestive selling on the part of the sales staff is *always* an excellent approach, but you also need a picture, a good sign, or a sample product to entice the customer. A college campus, with its overabundance of signs which promote everything from rock concerts to gay liberation, is an especially difficult place for successful merchandising. If you want to be successful in your college cash operation, you will tackle this problem as if your job depended on it, which it probably does!

Combination Sales

A long established merchandise technique is to combine certain popular items, sometimes at a slight reduction in price, in order to increase the check average. "Hamburger de luxe, with lettuce, tomatoes and French fries" is a common example; roast beef sandwiches and potato salad, homemade soup with French bread and green salad, and pie with ice cream are also familiar combinations. In many cases, fast food operators do not give their customers a choice. An enchilada may be served only in combination with rich and refried beans, and deep fried fish will be priced only in combination with French fried potatoes. On a college campus, it is difficult to be quite so arbitrary; on the other hand, it is easy to suggest your combinations in such a manner that the customers will quite naturally order the combination, rather than a single item. San Diego State University, where there is a large commuting student body, excels at combination sales. Their secret: combination packaging. Instead of merely wrapping a sandwich, they will place it on a plate, together with an attractive carrot and raisin salad, cole slaw, or some tempting pieces of fresh fruit. The customer, whose original intention may have been only to buy a simple sandwich, has difficulty resisting that piece of fresh pineapple, or the pickles and olives which garnish or supplement the sandwich. The result? A higher check average.

Signs

Even though some customers rarely look at signs, they are still a necessary ingredient to good merchandising. To begin with, your regular, every day signs need to be clear, easily visible, and attractive. It is a mistake to use those little black signs which have a felt back and white plastic letters; they look uninteresting and like everyone else's sign. Equally ineffective are the white plastic illuminated signs, often donated by a beverage purveyor or dairy. Worst of all, perhaps, are hastily scribbled signs on odd pieces of paper; these are quite common in small restaurants, and may be effective in a campus operation, but only as long as they are the *exception* to the rule and thus draw everyone's attention. The successful fast food operator generally has two types of signs, carefully planned out in advance:

- **Regular menu signs.** These are always attractive, carefully designed and built, with large lettering and prices, often with an illustration of the item to be sold. They allow for price changes without a major sign change, and generally are an integral part of the interior decor.

- **Special signs.** These always look different, can be found in a special place such as on an easel, or hanging from the light fixture, or pasted on the cash register, and are clearly temporary in nature.

Both types of signs have something in common: they are planned and designed far in advance of their actual usage. The permanent menu signs in a successful fast food franchise are part of the architectural design. The temporary signs advertising sales specials are often the result of sales promotions planned months in advance in the company's headquarters. You can take a page out of the franchiser's leaf; advance planning is part of good merchandising, and advance preparation of effective signs is an integral part of this process.

Flyers

Every campus has its own communication system and you must find out, through experience, which method of merchandising works best on your campus. Flyers placed in faculty mail boxes and residence hall lobbies are not as effective as you might expect. People have become accustomed to discarding junk mail, and your flyer is probably one of many received in a mail box every day. At California State University/Long Beach, the food service managers hire students for the specific purpose of handing out flyers at the busy intersection of this sprawling campus. While this may displease the groundskeepers, it is an effective method of communication, since most recipients glance at the flyer while they are walking to the next trash can. You can add other ingredients and drama to this business of handing out flyers. Furnish the distributor with a funny hat or costume, give him a whistle, or have him accompanied by a small band of musicians, and you'll get everyone's attention.

Posters

Large cardboard posters are a simple and relatively inexpensive method of merchandising. They can be placed in many locations, and can remain there for one or several weeks; they can be easily disposed of when out of date. Unfortunately, there is a lot of competition. Unless the poster is very clever, very large, and very clear, no one will bother to read it. Some sort of picture or drawing is *almost always* necessary, if the poster is to draw the attention of the reader.

Uniforms and Costumes

Attractive uniforms are an essential ingredient of any good food operation. The cost of uniforms for food service workers is a vital cost of doing business, and the manager who does not provide for this expenditure is making a mistake. For the same cost, however, as a plain white uniform or jacket, you can obtain much more exciting garb: attractively striped dusters, denim shirts with colorful kerchiefs and hats, old-fashioned dresses and bonnets, etc. A clever merchandiser will change some aspect of the employees' uniform in order to draw the customers' attention to a special event. A straw hat for everyone, a fresh carnation, a special lapel button, or an unusually colored apron attract attention in a dramatic manner.

Newspaper Advertisements

College newspaper advertising is relatively inexpensive and usually quite successful in drawing attention from the campus community. The ad should be fairly large (at least a quarter of a page) and should include attractive art work in addition to the text. The message should be short and pithy. Sometimes, like other newspaper advertisers, you will find it effective to include a coupon as a special incentive to buy the advertised product.

Suggestive Selling

One of the most effective methods of merchandising is to sell by suggestion. It is hard to resist a friendly salesperson who asks, with an engaging smile: "How would you like our special today?, old fashioned strawberry shortcake?" It takes an experienced food service manager to get every member of the sales staff motivated to the extent tht they literally "sell" all the time they are serving the customers. It takes training, staff meetings, and setting an inspiring example, before the entire crew gets the message. On a college or university campus, where the circle of clients is relatively limited and where the salesperson and customer have frequent, regular contact, selling by suggestion has to be especially skilled and tactful, if it is to be effective. Sales suggestions should be made in the spirit of friendship, and should reflect a genuine concern for the tastes and preferences of the customer. They should never become so routine, that the question "Would you like some French fries with your sandwich?" is asked of a student who is known to be on a diet. Instead, they should take the form of interested concern, such as: "We're going to have banana cream pie tomorrow, shall I save you a piece? or: "How about some French fried onion rings today? They're delicious!"

Free Samples

Free samples are always popular with the customers. Your question must be "Will it help me in my merchandising efforts?" When you are introducing a new product you believe would sell if people only knew how good it tasted, then giving away a small sample during a special sales promotion is probably a wise idea. The Hickory Farms organization, for example, which operates a chain of cheese and sausage stores throughout the United States, gives away tiny cubes of their special summer sausage as a matter of policy. They will also slice a sliver of any bulk cheese the customer may wish to taste. There are other reasons, however, why you might like to give away free samples. Anytime you give anything away, you create a stir, a kind of excitement which, if nothing else, is an attention-getter. For this reason alone, it is wise occasionally, to give something away in your food operation. Such give-aways can take many forms. Here are a few examples

- Samples of homemade soup in 2 oz. souffle cups
- Free coffee (or free seconds) from 3-4 p.m. on the day before the start of a big sales promotion
- Two donuts for the price of one
- Free orange juice with every full breakfast during Good Nutrition Week
- A free meal for anyone getting a cash register receipt with four identical consecutive numbers (e.g. 09999)

Special Menu Items

One of the sure-fire ways of successful food merchandising is to introduce new, interesting, and popular menu items. Some of these items may win a permanent place on your menu, and others are practical only once in a while. The introduction of a 60 lb. "steamboat round" of beef on your hot sandwich counter is always a crowd-pleaser. Everyone likes a roast beef sandwich sliced to order from such a huge, tempting piece of meat. If you can sell several hundred such sandwiches, you could conceivably offer this every day. If not, you can still introduce it as a special merchandising special, and utilize the leftover beef in some other manner the next day. For the imaginative food service manager, there is no limit to the number of items that he can offer as specials. California State University/Sonoma sells grilled "vegeburgers." Vegetables such as mushrooms, carrots, sprouts, and beans are made into a patty with a batter of natural wheat flour and eggs, then grilled just like a chopped sirloin steak. Those who like meat have a choice between a 5 oz. or an 8 oz. hamburger, both served on a French roll, with ranch-style French fried potatoes. At Sonoma, as well as other colleges and universities, the "submarine sandwich by the inch" has become a very popular specialty item. These menu examples are food merchandising at its best: a quality product, unique enough to be attractive, and priced to allow a fair profit for the food service manager.

Day-old Sales (Bakery Items)

If you have your own bake shop on campus, you may wish to sell donuts, cookies, pies and cakes on a retail basis, in addition to serving these as restaurant items. Under such conditions, chances are that you will occasionally have left-over baked goods. Some managers will argue that you should throw these away, or use them up in bread pudding, rather than sell them as day-old merchandise. Others prefer to offer such baked goods at half-price, knowing that there are always some people wishing to take advantage of such an obvious bargain. It is important, however, that you never sell day-old baked goods without clearly marking them as such and that you always sell them, if at all, at a much lower price than the fresh goods. Nothing will turn a customer off as quickly as giving him a stale product when he is expecting a fresh one.

Promotion Calendars

If you are a typical college food service manager, you will have little spare time in a day. Chances are when you come home you would like to forget everything connected with work, and are too tired to think about merchandising or anything else, for that matter. It is unrealistic, therefore, to expect that under normal, everyday conditions, you will have the time, the peace of mind, and the imagination to develop a creative and successful merchandising program. The time to develop this is during the summer, during recess periods, or at a time when you can concentrate on this specific task. While it is perfectly all right, and, in fact, sometimes exciting, to do a promotion on the spur of the moment, it is also necessary to have a promotional calendar, which has been carefully planned in advance. Such a calendar can be planned a month, a quarter, a semester, or even a full year in advance. All the material, the skitches, drawing, and printing can be done well in advance, and your entire staff will be primed and ready to go long before the actual date of each event. A sample of such promotional planning is shown in Exhibit X-4.

OPERATING HOURS IN CASH OPERATIONS

Food service operations in newly opened student unions often lose money during the first few months because of overstaffing and unprofitable operating hours. Normally, the new student union features an enlarged food service program, one that often requires more staff than can be justified by the volume of business on campus. At the same time, the students, deans, or union directors, proud and excited with their new building, make service demands on the food service manager which prove to be unrealistic. Within six months, when the operating losses are tallied, expectations are lowered, the staff is reduced to reasonable numbers, the operating schedule is adjusted downward, and the food service begins to cut its losses.

Much has been spoken and written about the special responsibilities a college food service director has toward his students. You must be concerned with their loneliness, their nutrition, their weight gain, and their academic pressures. You should be less concerned, however, with operating cash units in the evenings or on weekends merely to satisfy a small number of students who wish to purchase food and beverages during those unprofitable periods. Even if the college is located in an isolated place, and no other restaurants are nearby, you should not keep a cash operation open if there are not enough customers to justify it. There are always vending machines, or room refrigerators, or residence hall dining rooms to prevent

EXHIBIT X-4

UNIVERSITY CENTER

presents

STRAWBERRY FESTIVAL

sponsored by Food Service

Monday, May 2nd   through   Friday, May 6th

FRESH STRAWBERRY SUNDAES
     topped with fresh STRAWBERRIES   .70

FRESH STRAWBERRY MILKSHAKES
     topped with fresh strawberry   .70

BOWL OF FRESH STRAWBERRIES
     served with powdered sugar   .50

Thursday, May 5th on the REDWOOD DECK 11:30 - 2:30

SUPER STRAWBERRY SPECIAL!

STRAWBERRY SHORTCAKES
     with fresh crushed STRAWBERRIES   .95
     and whipped cream

your students from starving. Do not embark on a too-ambitious schedule, and then close the operation after discovering your losses. Instead, embark on a modest realistic schedule, and then, by slow, careful experimentation, expand your operating hours.

It is a fact that most cash operations on American campuses are closed during the day on Saturdays and Sundays. Many close on Friday afternoon and remain closed throughout the weekend. Others operate only one shift daily (such as 7:30 to 3:30) and open a vending installation or perhaps a small snack bar for the dinner trade. Keep records of the sales experienced during various portions of each day. "Sales per man-hour" is a statistic that can be used to convince students and administrators that it does not pay to stay open at certain times.

Calculation of Required Sales Based on Labor Hours

Budget for Cash Operations		Budgeted Sales Based on Labor Hours	
Labor Cost:	30%	Average Labor Hour:	$4.00/hr.
Food Cost:	40%	Food Cost (4/3 of $4)	5.33
Other Costs:	20%	Other Costs (2/3 of $4)	2.66
Budget Net:	10%	Net: 1/3 of $4	1.33
		Required Sales per Budget:	$13.32/hr.

If closing your food service units during loss periods is politically unfeasible, at least do everything you can to cut your losses. Reduce your menu, cut your staff, close portions of your restaurant. Only after having done everything appropriate from a fiscal standpoint, can you attempt to build up your volume to the point where possibly, sometime in the future, you will be able to remain open even during such quiet hours.

STAFFING FOR CASH OPERATIONS

Labor cost controls, and statistical measurements such as meals-served-per-labor-hour or sales-per-labor-hour are essential to the food service manager, but they don't provide all the answers. On a Wednesday noon, for example, when the line of waiting customers extends half way around the block, the manager is not interested in looking at statistics. On a Saturday morning, when it appears everyone is asleep except for the manager and the three people operating his unit, he doesn't need statistics to know that he is losing money. He abhors waiting lines. He wants to give good, fast, friendly service. At the same time, it seems as if waiting lines are here to stay, and that there are always periods when he has either too many or too few employees.

It has been mentioned in Chapter VI that a flexible payroll, with an adequate number of part-time workers who can be called in or laid off, is a good tool for the control of labor costs. It was also mentioned that student employees are a natural pool of such labor. Appendix 12 illustrates how one student union food service manager maintains a daily control sheet, and adjusts his labor assignments accordingly. There are certain rush periods that must be adequately covered. Weekday lunch periods are the best example, Most of the volume in campus cash operations is generated as a result of the weekday lunch. If you don't make it then, you'll never make it. Consequently, you must take in all the money and make all the sales possible during this busy period. On the other hand, you cannot possibly eliminate all waiting lines at every moment during the day, without being overstaffed some of that time. There are certain rush periods when some of your clients may have to wait a few minutes despite your best efforts. A wait of 3 to 5 minutes in front of a food counter is not really excessive, as long as cutomers are willing to do so. Most people on a college campus are very understanding and cooperative. If the wait does become excessive, however, your potential clients will go to the competition (outside restaurants or brown bags from home) or, equally bad for you, they may not eat any lunch at all.

It is difficult to provide valid staffing guides in a book like this. Not only is every campus different, but people themselves are different. On some campuses, students and faculty put up with lines which, at another campus, would be unthinkable. In large cities, or at schools which are surrounded by nearby commercial fast food units, the service must of necessity be as quick as that in the competitive units. In rural areas, everyone learns to be a little more patient.

XI. VENDING ON CAMPUS

Vending machines are a common sight on most college and university campuses today. Many college food service managers, however, have not been directly involved in their operation. If you are among these, you may feel somewhat apprehensive about assuming responsibility for vending on your campus. Some food service managers are just plain scared of getting involved in a vending operation.

True, vending is a highly technical operation, but so is the operation of a campus bake shop. You don't have to be a skilled baker to properly manage your bake shop. Similarly, you don't have to be an outstanding vending technician in order to properly manage a vending operation. As a professional food service manager, you can deal with vending on your campus if you have a basic knowledge about college vending, and if you can ask the proper questions to guide you in your decision-making. This chapter will furnish you with the basic facts about college vending, and enable you to make the right decisions concerning vending on your campus.

THE NEED FOR VENDING ON CAMPUS

Each campus differs from others in size and shape. On many campuses, food service facilities are no longer centrally located, due to the growth and spread of campus populations. When this happens, it is difficult to provide adequate service for everyone on campus. Surveys have shown that students prefer some sort of food service located conveniently to their classes and their movement patterns. Food service areas must, therefore, be located near the centers of student population and pedestrian movement.

Since there are wide differences in the way various campus customers eat, how much money they spend, and how much time they devote to eating, the various types and locations of food services must take these differences into account. The problem of time and the need for convenience will usually dictate that some vending installations are needed to augment the other food service facilities.

Vending income, whether it originates from contractor's commissions or from net profit of a self-operated system, should always be a part of the campus food services. If you decide to operate your own vending machines, remember that vending should always be thought of as an extension of the manual food service, and develop an integrated master plan for your total campus food service. With proper planning, manual food services can often be cut back during slack periods, resulting in substantial labor savings.

SELF-OPERATED OR CONTRACT VENDING?

Whether or not a college should operate its own vending machines is a difficult decision. Circumstances differ on each campus, and the decision is not normally made by the food service director alone. Nevertheless, he should be involved in making the final decision since vending will be either an integral part of, or possibly a competitor with, the manual food service. Before any decision is made, the following points should be thoroughly evaluated:

Location of Your Campus

If your school is located in or near a metropolitan area, there are probably several vending machine companies able and willing to provide you with the services needed. Investigate each of these, and check on their reputation for providing good service. Service is the most important factor to consider in evaluating various vending companies. A promise of large commissions, modern machines, or other tempting offers will be of little value if your campus is not receiving adequate service from the contractor.

If your school is located in a small town far away from any large city, you may find that there are no vending companies large enough, or near enough to provide the vending services you require. Many schools are in this predicament, and thus have no real choice. The only way that they can provide vending on campus is through the existing campus food services.

Minimum Sales Volume

Some experts will tell you that an annual sales volume of $200,000 is a minimum requirement for self-operating a successful vending operation. In practice, this is not necessarily true. There are some very successful campus vending operations which gross sales of less than $100,000 per year.

Obviously, sales volume affects operating percentages. Fixed overhead costs will vary on each campus, but in no case should the vending operation be charged with a disproportionate amount of overhead. Product costs should be in the range of 45% to 50% of sales, in no case more than 55%. The cost of labor will vary according to prevailing area wage rates and the number of vending machines being serviced. It should range between 20% and 30% of sales, and should not exceed 35%.

Naturally, as volume increases, your operating percentages will go down. In order properly to determine in advance what your minimum sales volume must be, if you are to go into campus vending yourself, you should prepare a "pro forma." This is a projected operating statement, prepared on the basis of one or more assumptions. Your projected costs in the pro forma should be based on the following methods of obtaining vending equipment:

- Straight purchase agreement
- Straight lease agreement
- Lease-purchase agreement

In preparing pro formas, it is a good idea to work with the major vending machine manufacturers. They are interested in having you use their machines and will give you considerable help in determining the number, type, and capacity of machines needed for your operation. You should also seek help from other colleges. A sample vending operating statement is shown in Appendix 13.

Finding Qualified Staff

A successful campus vending operation requires the services of at least one qualified vending technician. Such a person should be able to service as well as maintain and repair all types of vending machines. How do you find such a person? There are relatively few individuals who qualify for this type of work. Some community colleges do offer courses in vending maintenance and operations. Chances are, however, that you will have to attract such a person from a vending company in a large city. Most likely, such a qualified individual will command an above-average salary. However, you must remember that a college or university job has some special advantages not often found in commercial jobs. Not only are there tuition and other special fringe benefits, but the location of many schools is also a frequent attraction for a potential campus employee.

Some of the desirable qualifications for a vending machine technician/operator are

- Good mechanical ability, and knowledge of basic electrical circuits
- Good personality, with the ability to placate irate customers when they have lost some coins
- Vending experience, including experience in repairing all types of vending machines
- Management or supervisory experience and capability
- Knowledge of vending products, and the ability to sense customer buying trends

VENDING EQUIPMENT

Basic Vending Equipment

When starting a new vending machine operation, first consideration should be given to candy/snack machines. They produce a fast turnover, are fairly easy to maintain and operate, and produce a good profit. Next come the cold drink machines. Cost studies show that low volume locations can more easily support canned drinks, since these machines are less expensive to buy, to maintain and to service. They also have a longer useful life. As volume increases, however, the cup units become more profitable, since the product cost is lower. Surveys taken on the campus of California State University, Chico indicate that students there clearly prefer the canned soda over the cup drink. Another point in favor of can drinks is that the suppliers of canned drinks will supply machines for your campus, thus reducing your total equipment investment.

After cold drink units, you should consider the hot cup drink units. It is best to get the multiple drink machines, that can serve coffee, tea or Sanka, hot soup and hot chocolate. These machines are costly, but good profit-makers.

Next for your consideration would be the cigarette and ice cream units. Cigarettes are a high cost item, but they do help to build sales volume. Close inventory control over cigarettes is essential if this item is to be profitable to you. Equally important is the need to be sensitive to some campus groups that may object to your cigarette vending as a matter of principle.

Last are the food machines. These machines are not normally profitable. They do, however, draw a lot of people to a vending area, and almost always result in additional sales from other machines dispensing drinks, snacks, etc. The refrigerated cold food machines which vend sandwiches, fresh fruit, puddings, milk, juices, yogurt, pickles and eggs, and many other foods which are all highly perishable require a high 'sales volume area to support them and to control waste.

Other specialty machines such as hot canned food units, milk units, and sundry merchandisers require substantial volume and are not normally profitable. These should be considered only as needs arise and finances permit. The best advice is to start slowly with the basic units and purchase additional machines as required.

Purchasing Vending Equipment

There are about half a dozen major manufacturers of vending machines. As stated earlier, equipment is available on a straight purchase, lease/purchase, or a straight lease basis. Most manufacturers also provide service training, as well as financing.

Good vending equipment, although more costly, is most economical in the long run. To give you an idea of the relative cost of these machines, the following is a list of price ranges prevalent in 1978:

Candy/Snack	from $ 500 to $1800
Canned Soda	from $ 800 to $1500
Cup Cold Drinks	from $1000 to $4000 (non-ice)--(8 ice flavors)
Hot Cup Drinks	from $ 850 to $3500
Ice Cream	from $1000 to $2900
Cigarettes	from $ 450 to $1500
Cold Food	from $1100 to $2900
Hot Food	from $1000 to $2900

Price spreads are accounted for by various options included and differences in capacities of various machines.

Repair Parts

There is no need to establish a huge spare parts inventory on your campus. Parts can be held to a minimum by following suggestions from suppliers regarding the most commonly needed parts. Your distance from a major city will influence the size of your inventory, but most manufacturers ship spare parts promptly. A wise procedure is for you to stock major equipment assemblies, such as coin acceptance units which can be replaced in the machine quickly and easily. Parts for these assemblies can then be ordered at leisure, and the broken assemblies reparied at a more convenient time, without having the machine out of service for very long.

SUPPORT EQUIPMENT

In order to repair vending machines, you will have to invest in some basic tools. You will also need access to a suitable truck or similar vehicle to move machines from one location to another. The big question is how to move *products* daily to fill each machine. The decision on just the right moving equipment depends on the distance between locations, the campus topography, as well as the number of route people required to service machines. On a very small campus, a push cart may work. Most campuses, however, need at least one or more vehicles. Small covered electrical vehicles are becoming more and more popular for use in vending, since they are quiet, inexpensive to operate, and dependable.

In addition to tools and trucks, you will need equipment to handle cash. An automatic coin sorter and counter is required for any vending operation. However, in some areas arrangements can be made with a local bank to perform this service. Change machines, both coin changers and combination coin and dollar bill changers do not produce income, and it is difficult to tell whether or not they help stimulate sales. Generally speaking, locations should generate $550 a week or more in sales to justify a change machine.

Finally, you need to decide whether or not to purchase a micro-wave oven. Like coin changers, these are expensive and it is difficult to tell just how much increased sales they account for. The need for a micro-wave oven is determined largely by the product served, the specific needs of a location, and by the sales volume in each location. Be prepared for the fact that micro-wave ovens will probably get a lot of use by people who heat food not purchased in your vending machines. This misuse often causes damage to micro-wave ovens.

PURCHASING OF VENDING PRODUCTS

Many vendors of products for vending machines have substantial minimum purchasing requirements. If you are on a small campus, and have difficulty meeting the minimum, investigate a national cooperative called Automatic Vendors of America (A.V.A.) which gives smaller vending operations the advantage of quantity price breaks as well as equipment financing. Another option is to join with a retail outlet or the campus bookstore outlet, to meet the minimum quantities. Not only are there price advantages in buying in larger quantities, but additional savings can be effected if you take full advantage of all discounts given.

As a general rule, it is wise to stay with name brands when selecting a product for vending. A good buy on an off-brand or unknown brand is not a bargain if the item does not sell or if it does not satisfy your customers.

During the hot summer months, be extremely careful not to load your vending machine with soft chocolates. Handling and storage of all candies must be in a well-ventilated, cool storeroom or walk-in refrigerator to prevent spoilage.

PRODUCT COSTS

The cost of most vending products is similar throughout the United States, although occasional regional price differences may occur. The following averages will give you an idea of the cost and markup of the basic vending products.

Cost of Vending Products: Stated as percent of sales.

Candy	major brands	50-51%
Chips	major brands or local	48-50%
Pastry	major brands or local	52-55%
Hot Beverages	coffee, etc.	38-42%
Cold Cup Beverages	major brands	23-30%
Canned Soda	major brands	45-55%
Cigarettes	about 20 major brands	55-62%
Ice Cream	local	40-45%
Milk	plus dairy products	50-57%
Sandwiches	or separate individual meats	50-75%

OTHER COSTS

In addition to the cost of labor, cost of equipment and product costs, there are other incidental costs incurred as part of a vending operation such as accounting or business office costs, sales taxes, vehicle upkeep and gasoline costs, physical plant expenses, and rental or cost of storage spaces.

VENDING COMMISSIONS

Whether or not you decide to operate your own vending on campus, the question of sharing commissions with others will probably come up. As a general rule, you should not be paying commissions to anyone. Vending, as has been stated earlier, should always be considered to be a part of the total campus food service, and any income should go toward helping to achieve food service's basic goal: to provide the best possible service and the highest quality food at the lowest prossible price. There are some situations, however, where it may be necessary or at least wise, to share voluntarily some of the vending income. In residence halls or fraternity houses, for example, a small portion of the net income or commissions (e.g. 5-10%) should perhaps go to the house social fund. These matters can usually be worked out through mutual agreement. The good will of the house residents is essential to the success of such a vending location.

A frequent error is to place units in too many locations. This usually results in excessive labor costs, insufficient sales to justify the depreciation costs, general inefficiency, or all three of the above. The ideal vending set-up is located in major traffic areas which can support a whole bank of various types of machines. Such a bank, in addition to creating greater sales volume, also has the advantage of better merchandising. It can also be made to look attractive, by having the machines built into a well-designed framework. If the sales volume is especially high during peak hours, a host or hostess can be assigned to assist customers.

It is good to keep in mind that some machines are more dependent on high traffic locations than others. While people may seek out a cigarette and to a lesser extent, perhaps a coffee or cold drink machine, they may not do so in the case of candy or snacks. These are impulse sales items, and unless these machines are placed in high traffic areas, sales volume can suffer.

Another important consideration in selecting vending locations is whether the location is inside or outside a building. As a general rule, inside locations are more desirable. Aside from greater convenience to the customer, there is also the weather to contend with. Extremes in humidity and temperature have often serious effects on the mechanical operation of vending machines.

Minimum Weekly Sales

In determining possible locations, keep in mind the sales amounts that must be generated by each machine in order to justify its placement in a given location. The following are suggested weekly sales figures, broken down into various types of machines:

Type of Unit	Free Standing	In a Vending Bank
Candy/Snack	$50.00	$35.00
Cup Cold Drinks	70.00	50.00
Cup Hot Beverage	70.00	50.00
Canned Drinks	45.00	30.00
Cigarettes	40.00	30.00
Ice Cream (seasonal)	30.00	20.00
Milk	30.00	20.00
Cold Food, etc.	60.00	40.00

Please note that the above figures are minimums, and will not produce significant profit. If locations regularly produce sales below these figures, they should be reevaluated. An analysis of sales averages by product categories is shown in Exhibit XI-1.

Factors in Selecting Locations

When selecting locations on campus, ask yourself the following questions:

- How many potential customers are in the area?
- Is an outside location or inside location best for this area?
- Should I choose a ground floor location, or an upper floor or basement location?
- How many machines can I use per location?
- What space and utilities are required?

EXHIBIT XI-1

1977 OPERATING RATIO REPORT
National Automatic Merchandising Association
Compiled by Price Waterhouse & Co.

ANALYSIS OF GROSS PROFIT AND SALES STATISTICS BY PRODUCT - 1977

	Composition of Sales At Retail			Average Sales Per Machine		
	1977	1976	1975	1977	1976	1975
Cigarettes	13.1%	13.9%	16.9%	$2,488	$2,424	$2,144
Candy, nuts, gum	11.6	7.3	7.9	1,697	1,591	1,210
Cold cup beverages	7.1	7.0	7.4	3,100	2,900	2,199
Hot cup beverages	16.9	11.1	11.8	3,748	3,433	2,958
Ice Cream	.4	.4	.5	1,082	1,033	1,041
Milk	3.0	3.3	3.4	2,615	2,694	1,963
Sandwiches, salads, entrees, etc.	4.8	4.8	5.1	3,633	3,462	2,945
Pastry and Snacks	4.7	4.5	4.4	2,210	1,999	1,536
Hot canned soups & food	1.3	1.3	1.5	1,715	1,565	1,291
Bottled and canned drinks	3.1	2.1	1.9	4,125	3,262	2,862
Misc. vending machine products	1.1	8.3	2.1	2,379	990	1,225
TOTAL or averages for above	67.1%	64.0%	62.9%	$2,677	$2,378	$1,971
Sales other than through machine	32.9	36.0	37.1			
TOTAL SALES	100.0%	100.0%	100.0%			

*Snacks included with candy prior to 1976.

PROFIT ANALYSIS FOR 1977
(based on reported sales volume categories)

	Less than $250,000	$250,000 to $750,000	$750,000 to $1,000,000	$2,000,000 to $9,999,999	$10,000,000 Or More
Sales at retail	100.0%	100.0%	100.0%	100.0%	100.0%
Cost of sales	51.4	52.1	51.1	51.6	45.9
Total operating expenses	42.1	43.7	45.0	43.8	49.3
OPERATING PROFIT	6.5%	4.2%	3.9%	4.6%	4.8%
Less interest expenses	1.1	1.1	.8	.7	.2
Other income or charges (net)	.8	.9	.7	.9	1.4
PROFIT Before Income Taxes	6.2%	4.0%	3.8%	4.8%	6.0%

Courtesy of National Automatic Merchandising Association.

1977 OPERATING RATIO REPORT
National Automatic Merchandising Association
Compiled by Price Waterhouse & Co.

COMPOSITE AVERAGE OF ALL OPERATORS REPORTING RELATED DATA FOR 1977, 1976, 1975

	1977	1976	1975
Sales at Retail	100.0%	100.0%	100.0%
Cost of Sales	46.9	48.4	48.3
GROSS PROFIT	53.1%	51.6%	51.7%
Total Operating Expenses	48.3	48.4	48.1
OPERATING PROFIT	4.8%	3.2%	3.6%
Other Income	.9	.6	.5
PROFIT BEFORE INCOME TAXES	5.7%	3.8%	4.1%

OPERATING EXPENSES
(as a percentage of sales)

Salaries, commissions to servicemen	9.9%	10.1%	9.6%
Machine Maintenance - labor costs	2.8	3.1	2.7
All other salaries, wages, etc.	9.4	8.6	9.0
TOTAL PAYROLL*	22.1%	21.8%	21.3%
Maintenance cost of vending machines	1.	1.3	1.2
Location rental payments (commisions)	8.0	8.3	8.5
Depreciation or rental for vending machines	4.3	4.3	4.7
Other depreciation (except buildings)	1.	.9	1.2
Truck and automobile expense	1.5	1.5	1.4
Sales tax	3.0	3.1	2.6
Taxes, other than sales, federal and state income taxes	.6	.6	.6
Insurance, all types	.5	.5	.4
Building and garage rental or expense	.5	.7	.5
Corporate overhead expense	2.	2.2	2.3
All other expenses	3.4	3.2	3.4
TOTAL OPERATING EXPENSES	48.3%	48.4%	48.1%

*Includes fringe benefits and payroll taxes.

Courtesy of National Automatic Merchandising Association.

- If utilities are not available, who will pay for the installation?
- Is a micro-wave oven needed, or a dollar bill changer?
- How do I get approval for the location? Who is it who has the authority to grant it to me?
- What about trash cans and clean-up around the area?
- How do I make the area look good?
- What is the access to the machines? How hard is it to get products to the location?
- How good is security in the area?
- How will I handle refunds in the area?
- Are tables and chairs needed? Are stand-up bars needed?

In most cases, it is not wise to have seating because of cleanup costs, equipment costs, space costs, and the problem of maintaining a clean and attractive area during all hours of operation.

There are times when campus administrators will request vending machines in a location which you may evaluate as a very poor location. How will you handle such requests? It is important to develop standard evaluation criteria, which can then be used to support your argument.

VENDING SERVICE AND MAINTENANCE

Vending machines must be in good working order to satisfy the demands of students. A poor vending operation reflects poorly on the total campus food service operation and when a machine is out of order or out of product, sales are lost. Malfunctioning machines are a major cause of customer complaints. Once a customer has lost money in a machine, that same customer may be reluctant to put money in any campus vending machine in the future. An effective service and maintenance program is essential to the overall profitability of the campus vending operation.

Most vending problems can be capsuled into three major categories:

- Mechanical breakdowns
- Quality of products
- Communications

The first category is the easiest to handle, because of the availability of manuals, training programs for service personnel set up by manufacturers, and maintenance and repair information in trade magazines. Machines can be repaired. If they remain inoperative, it is because someone has not resolved that they can be repaired immediately.

The second category can be improved by purchasing the same high quality of products you serve in the manual food service operations. The same high standards of sanitation and merchandising applies to vended food and beverages, and the strictest adherence to standards is advisable regardless of how these products are served or sold on campus.

The third category is the one that takes the most work. Repair of the machines and serving high quality vending products are not enough, unless good communications exist between yourself and the customers. Whenever a vending problem occurs, you must be able to

- Identify the problem.
- Make arrangements to correct it.
- Convince the customer that the problem has been corrected, and that you are anxious to be of service.

In order to identify a problem, a system must be set up to call to your attention immediately all machine breakdowns, poor quality of products, or any other cause for customer dissatisfaction. One way to do this is to place a small printed sign on each machine which indicates your desire to please, as well as phone numbers to call for reporting problems. A sample sign is shown below:

WE WANT TO GIVE YOU, OUR CUSTOMERS, THE BEST POSSIBLE SERVICE. HOWEVER, MACHINES, LIKE PEOPLE, ARE NOT ALWAYS PERFECT. IF ANY PROBLEMS SHOULD ARISE WITH THIS MACHINE, PLEASE CALL US AT THE NUMBERS BELOW FOR ASSISTANCE.

From 8 a.m. to 5 p.m. -- 752-2656

After 5 p.m. -- 753-4969

If a machine cannot be immediately repaired, it may be wise to have the repairman place an out-of-order sign on the machine (preferably over the coin slot) to prevent further customer frustration.

Finally, a permanent record should be kept of all machine service problems, so that you can objectively evaluate the overall efficiency of the vending operation and the functioning of each machine. A sample form, called a "Vending Service Log" is shown in Exhibit XI-2, and another, a "Machine Outage Report," is shown in Exhibit XI-3.

Meeting Your Customers

Good communications include the necessity of meeting at least some of your vending customers in person, and periodically discussing your service with them. It is important that they know something about your vending problems, and feel comfortable to call about mechanical and other problems. Normally, there is one individual in each location who is either in charge of the building or department, or who works in the area, such as a secretary or custodian, who will normally receive the complaint. If you can establish a good working relationship with such building representatives, they can give you valuable assistance in solving vending problems. A sample poster for residence halls is shown in Exhibit XI-4.

Preventive Maintenance

An effective vending maintenance program is built around regular preventive

EXHIBIT XI-2

VENDING SERVICE LOG

TIME	NAME & TELEPHONE	KIND OF MACHINE	LOCATION	PROBLEM			ACTION TAKEN	DATE	TIME
				REFUND	OUT OF PRODUCT	OTHER Breakdown			

EXHIBIT XI-3

WASHINGTON STATE UNIVERSITY
FOOD SERVICE -- VENDING SERVICES UNIT
"Vending Machine Outage Report"

Date_____
Time_____

Machine Location_____
   (building and area in building)

Machine Identification _____
   (type of machine, model and serial number)

Cause of Machine Outage: (circle one) Vandalism Malfunction
   (concise description of
   vandalism or malfunction)_____

_____

_____

Estimated Date machine will be back in operation _____

Estimated Cost of Repair $_____

Actual Cost (When known) $_____

Value of Money $_____

  and/or merchandise lost or stolen   _____

TOTAL   _____

Incident reported to campus police   (yes or no)_____
   (acts of vandalism shall be promptly
   reported to campus police)   (date and time)_____

_____
(Signature of Vending Services Manager or Represent)

INSTRUCTIONS: This form is to be completed and forwarded to the Food Service Building in each instance of vandalism and when a machine cannot be returned to service on the same date the outage occurs. Such procedure will be helpful in responding to calls concerning machines and in compiling maintenance histories.

EXHIBIT XI-4

RESIDENCE HALLS
VENDING MACHINES

Each residence hall is provided with vending machines for the convenience of the students therein. At the present time approximately 5 per cent of the gross sales is returned to the residence hall for use by the students. Consequently, it is in the best interests of the residents that vending machines not be tampered with or damaged in any way. Damage to the machines results in a reduction of the amount of commission returned to the hall and can lead to removal of the machines, so your cooperation in helping to reduce damage will improve service and insure continued availability of the machines. Canadian coins will "jam" the machines so please don't use them. If you put a coin in a machine and it doesn't function, write down the hall, the time, the date, the kind of machine (cold beverage, candy, etc.), the coins lost; go to the Housing and Food cashier, French Administration Building before the end of the month, and receive your refund. Please report malfunctioning machines by calling 335-7307.

We're proud to serve you!

W.S.U. Vending Services   335-7307

Courtesy of Washington State University, Pullman, Washington.

maintenance and firm cleaning schedules, plus well-trained routemen and women to prevent breakdowns of machines. Service manuals for each machine are available from the manufacturers, and should be used to train your staff. The most frequent problems with vending machines are

- Coin mechanism hang-up
- Machine out of product
- Product improperly filled
- Electrical problems
- Improper amount of change deposited by customer

There are a number of steps to be taken regularly, whenever a machine is filled by the vending staff and checked out for operation:

- Push buttons and try to obtain product without inserting a coin.
- Inspect the machine to be sure it is properly loaded with product.
- Check the coin mechanism for bent coins and foreign objects such as washers, slugs and snaplid can tops.
- Inspect the interior of the machine for possible malfunction.
- Test the machine for possible malfunction by inserting coins.
- Check the machine to see that it is clean.

If these steps are taken each time a machine is visited, many malfunctions can be avoided.

Service Philosophy

To create the right attitude and motivation among your vending staff, it is necessary to adopt, believe in and follow an honest service philosophy. You, yourself must be concerned when machines are dirty or inoperative, or sell poor products to the campus community. You must set an example by your own attitude and actions, and show an honest concern when your vending clients are not receiving the service and products to which they are entitled.

MANAGEMENT CONTROL AND ACCOUNTABILITY

Vital to any self-operated vending system is an effective control procedure, which assures that you are getting every dime deposited in the machines, and that you are receiving accurate sales information. There are four basic steps that need to be taken to insure such control: the proper collection and recording of cash, the accurate recording of merchandise issued to routemen and women, the reconciliation of merchandise sold with cash collected, and tight inventory control.

Collecting and Recording Cash

Cash should be collected from each vending machine at least once a week, but more often if sales volume so indicates. Normally, the money is placed in a separate bag for each machine. The person collecting the cash should fill out a small, three-part collection form which includes the following: date of collection, type of machine, machine number, and machine location. Two copies of this form are placed in a bag with the cash, and one is retained for the manager. The bags are then turned into the cash room for counting. After each bag has been counted, the total is recorded on the collection forms, one of which is returned to the vending manager as soon as possible. The other is kept by the cashier, to verify the sales reports and the bank deposits. This system assures the manager that no bag has been lost, and that every machine was collected on schedule. It also gives sales figures quickly, thus helping to pinpoint machine shortages. The sales from each machine, should also be recorded in a sales report as follows:

- By machine number: to provide a history of each machine, to help show particular problems that might develop over a period of time
- By location: to help you evaluate each location and determine when to move a machine, and when to add a machine of larger capacity or to add more machines
- By product category: to determine the percent of sales for each product category and thus help to spot trends or problems

A sample of both the collection form and the sales report form are shown in Exhibit XI-5.

Recording Merchandise Issued to Vending Staff

The second control element required for an effective control system is to record the merchandise issued to the individual vending attendant. In a small operation, with only one or two attendants, this step may not be practical. In such a case, machine inventories are compared with machine sales as a way to spot problems. At the end of each month, total machine sales are compared to product usage, as an additional check. In a large operation, however, a "Merchandise Issued" form should be used to record all items issued to vending attendants.

Reconciling Merchandise with Cash

The third step in the control system is to balance the merchandise with the cash collected. There are several methods that can be followed, each requiring considerable detail work. Since each campus is different, and each vending organization is different, there is no one procedure that fits every campus. Whatever system you determine, remember to keep it as simple as possible. A sample form for recording sales is shown in Exhibit XI-6.

Inventory Control

The fourth step in the vending control procedure is inventory control. Your merchandise inventory consists of three types:

- The merchandise in the storeroom
- The merchandise on route trucks
- The merchandise in the vending machines

EXHIBIT XI-5

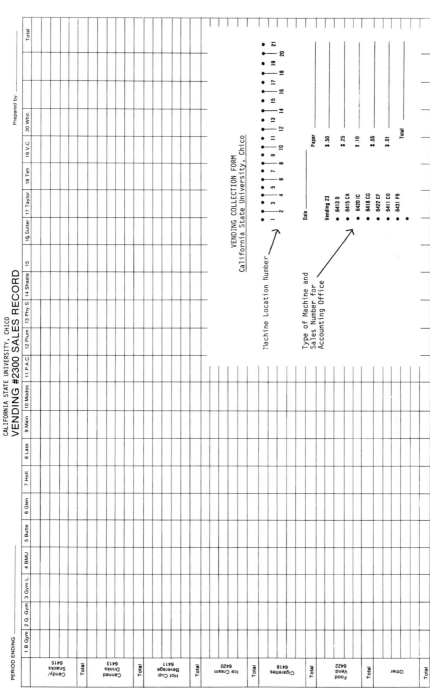

EXHIBIT XI-6

**WSU VENDING SERVICE
COLLECTION RECORD**

ROUTE NO. __04610__ COLLECTION DATE __1/15/79__

ROUTEMAN _____

NOTE: ALL ENTRIES MUST BE LEGIBLE AND ACCURATE

TRUCK MILEAGE

TRUCK NO.

ENDING

BEGINNING

	LOCATION	PRODUCT CODE	LOADS HI	LO	UNITS SPOILED	✓ IF NOT COLL.	TOTAL COLLECTIONS	
1	59-01	14	145	20	3⁰⁰	-1⁰⁰	35.	10
2	40-01	44	287	54	8¹⁰	-20	65	30
3	46-01		192	10	150	-7¹⁵	20	75
4	63-01		146	20		+1⁰⁵	38	25
5	89-01		143	20		+1¹⁴	37	40
6	55-01		293	80		+1⁰⁰	72	15
7	37-01	46	243	75		+1¹⁰	60	45
8								
9								
10								
11								
12						+424	308 ⁶⁵	
13								

PRODUCT CODES:
01-Candy 02-Hot Bev. 03-Cold Bev.
04-Hot Food 05-Pastries 06-Milk
07-Ice Cream 08-Sandwiches 09-Cigarettes

COUNTED AND RECONCILED BY   DATE   TOTAL

F-10-70

At the end of each weekly or monthly period, all three must be counted and added together by each category. This, combined with the recording of purchases by category, will allow for the calculation of "cost of goods sold" for each type of machine. The detailed inventory report, together with the cost of goods sold report provide the additional controls needed for a well-run campus vending operation. A sample form for keeping track of spoiled merchandise is shown in Exhibit XI-7.

CONTRACT VENDING ON CAMPUS

It may be, that for a variety of reasons you and your college administration decide that vending on your campus should be done by an outside vending contractor. As stated earlier, a major factor in this decision is the availability, the quality, and the resources of such contractors in your immediate vicinity. In such a situation, the administration will probably ask you, as their food service director, to become the liaison person and to make the necessary vending arrangements. There are a number of steps involved in performing this function:

- You must decide what your campus needs in the way of vending machines.
- You must clearly set this down in writing, in the form of bid specifications.
- You must select a successful bidder and agree with the bidder on final contract terms.
- You must have some means to coordinate, proctor and constantly evaluate the services provided to see that they meet the provisions of the contract.

Many vending companies have standard contract forms, which are tailored to the customs, laws and specific needs of their geographical area. For campus vending however, it is strongly recommended that a special contract, carefully drawn up to meet your needs, be prepared. One of the key mistakes made in the selection process is to emphasize the amount of commissions and to select the company which offers the largest commission rate. If, instead of commission percentages, you put extra stress on service, quality and equipment maintenance, the net result may be increased sales, a better total profit and a more successful vending program overall. A sample outline of specifications for a campus vending contract is shown in Appendix 14.

One final reminder: a contract is a mutual agreement between two parties. If it is to be successful and long-lasting, it must be beneficial to both parties, and must allow for some give and take by both the contractor and the institution.

EXHIBIT XI-7

WASHINGTON STATE UNIVERSITY
HOUSING AND FOOD SERVICE
VENDING SERVICES

SPOILAGE REPORT

DATE _____

Credit Merchandise Project 7001 $ _____

PRODUCT CODE	UNIT	VEND PRICE	QUANTITY	RETAIL PRICE	WHOLESALE VALUE	WHOLESALE PRICE
R1 Candy		$		$	$	$
R2 Hot Beverages						
R3 Cold Beverages						
R4 Hot Foods						
R5 Pastry						
R6 Milk						
R7 Ice Cream						
R8 Refrig. Food						
R9 Cigarettes						
Charge Spoilage Project 7100 Total				$	$	

Vending Services Manager

APPROVED: _____
Food Service Manager

XII. COMING TO GRIPS WITH SANITATION

In food service cleanliness *is* next to godliness. It is a pre-condition to success, so strict standards of sanitation must be established and enforced by the food service director at all times. State and local health departments are eager to furnish you with pamphlets, flyers, charts, and all kinds of material dealing with food poisoning and food infection. The National Restaurant Association in Chicago, as well as the Superintendent of Documents in Washington, D.C., is glad to make available a long bibliography on the subject. This chapter will give you an idea of how good sanitation works in actual practice, and how you, as food service manager, must take a leadership role to bring it about.

To begin with, you might ask yourself how you feel about sanitation in your kitchens. What exactly is your philosophy of cleanliness? Are you satisfied if your kitchens are generally clean, if the local health inspector gives you a passing grade? Are you anxious to have a clean kitchen, but not willing to spend more than the amount budgeted for clean-up in order to accomplish this? If so, it's not enough. Look around you. Every successful food service director is virtually a *fanatic* about sanitation. His objective is to be much cleaner than the health inspector requires. If the kitchens are dirty and he needs more personnel to clean up, he adjusts his budget rather than accept uncleanliness. He is acutely aware of the responsibility that he carries for the health of the hundreds of persons eating in his establishment. If he sees even one mouse in the kitchen, he does not set mouse traps, but calls the exterminators. One cockroach, and he has the entire kitchen fogged, even if it means that all the racks, pots, pans, and utensils have to be washed after the fogging. If there is a single weevil in the flour, the whole bag gets thrown out, and if there is any doubt in his mind about the acceptability or condition of any food item, he does not serve it. An atmosphere of strict cleanliness must be developed. A good food service manager insists that every violation of sanitation rules be corrected *on the spot, immediately,* and without undue concern about the feelings of the employee who may be responsible for the violation. Here are some examples of what such a food service manager expects from his staff:

- Instant pickup of food dropped on the floor
- Immediate washing of hands after such a pickup
- No tolerance of smoking anywhere in the kitchen
- Immediate reprimand if workers (including students) lack approved hair covering
- No mops in mop buckets; no dirty mop water in buckets
- No overflowing trash cans in kitchens
- No junk (newspapers, utensils, etc.) on top of refrigerators
- HOT food to be served piping hot, COLD food to be served cold

SOME BASIC FACTS ABOUT FOOD POISONING

In order properly to train your staff, many of whom are not familiar with food poisoning, a few basic facts should be clear in your own mind. These are the facts about which you must talk, explain, and instruct your entire professional life, so you might as well get them straight:

Types of Food Poisoning

There are four major types of foodborne illness. These are known as foodborne infections, foodborne intoxication, chemical poisoning, and poisonous plants and animals. More than three-fourths of all food poisoning comes from food infections, and almost one-fourth from food intoxication. Chemical poisoning and illness from poisonous plants or animals is rare.

Food Infections

Food infections occur when specific organisms contaminate the food and have the opportunity to grow and multiply to large numbers before the food is eaten. Unlike the illness caused by the presence of a toxin (see below), it is the organism itself that causes the illness. There are three basic types of foodborne infections: those caused by bacteria, by parasites, and by viruses. The most common bacteria are *salmonella, clostridium perfringens,* and *shigella.*

Food Intoxications

Food intoxication occurs when contaminating microorganisms have the opportunity to grow and produce chemical substances that are poisonous (toxic) to the person eating the food. These toxins do not usually change the flavor or appearance of the food, so they are particularly dangerous. Some toxins (such as that produced by the botulism organism) can be destroyed in a few minutes by boiling, whereas others (such as toxins produced by certain strains of *staphylococcus)* will withstand boiling temperatures for long periods of time and are virtually impossible to destroy by normal cooking methods. The most common toxins in food are caused by *staphylococcus* bacteria; occasionally, when you hear of people becoming ill or dying from eating home-canned food that was not properly boiled, the cause is a botulism infection *(clostridium botulinum).*

Chemical Poisoning

While this type of poisoning does not occur frequently, it is nevertheless one with which you must be familiar. Failure to properly rinse dishes or cooking utensils, for example, could cause illness; so could failure to properly wash the lettuce and other fresh fruits and vegetables that may have been sprayed with pesticide. Cadmium and zinc, used in making pots and pans, can cause metallic poisoning. Chemicals used for insect control, if accidentally mixed with food or drink, can also kill human beings.

Parasitic Infections

Infections caused by parasites are, fortunately, not common in the United States. Nevertheless, the two most common ones, *amoebic dysentery* and *trichinosis,* should be familiar to you. Amoebic dysentery occurs when moist, high protein foods (such as meat, eggs, poultry, and milk products) are contaminated with human feces from infected persons. Water contaminated with sewage is also frequently involved. Trichonosis, caused by a tiny worm that infects mostly hogs, can be easily prevented by properly cooking all pork or pork products.

Symptoms

The symptoms of various types of food poisoning are very similar and generally you will not know the cause of the outbreak until either a sample of the food or samples taken from the ill persons have been analyzed in a laboratory. Because the food service manager is often confronted with students claiming to have become ill from food, whereas actually their illness is non-food related, it may be helpful to know the symptoms arising from food poisoning.

- **Staphylococcus.** Illness 1 to 6 hours after eating; nausea, vomiting, diarrhea, and abdominal cramps
- **Botulism.** Illness 12 to 36 hours after eating; dizziness, double vision, muscular weakness, difficulty in swallowing, speaking, and breathing
- **Salmonella.** Illness normally in 12 to 24 hours; fever, abdominal pain, diarrhea, frequent vomiting and chills
- **Perfringens.** Illness 8 to 22 hours after eating; acute abdominal pain and diarrhea. Unlike salmonellosis, a clostridium perfringens infection will not usually cause nausea and vomiting. Also, fever, shivering, and headaches will be rare
- **Shigella.** Illness 2 - 3 days after consumption of food. Diarrhea, cramps, fever, and vomiting. In severe cases, the stool of the patient may contain blood

Methods by Which Bacteria are Spread

The two main ways in which microorganisms are spread are: 1) transmission through the food itself, and 2) transmission through utensils and equipment. Sometimes the food itself may enter your kitchen in a contaminated state; more often, it can become contaminated while being processed in your kitchen. The most common sources of such contamination are

- **Unclean Hands.** It is essential that all food service workers wash their hands frequently, and *always* after going to the bathroom. This requirement is so important, that special signs should be posted in the employee's bathrooms, reminding them of the importance of handwashing.
- **Carriers and Infected Persons.** It is easy for a kitchen worker to infect the food. It does not take "Typhoid Mary." Illness from influenza, hepatitis, or any other infectious illness, even a simple cold or cough, is

enough to cause food infection. Uncovered sores or cuts on the hands, or elsewhere on the body where the hands can touch, are also enough. Even if you need people for work, you are better off to send them home until they have fully recuperated from their illness.

- **Improperly Washed Fruits and Vegetables.** Even though fresh fruits and vegetables are rarely the cause of food contamination, they are full of pesticide sprays which, in themselves, are often toxic. Thorough washing of all such produce is essential to the health of everyone who consumes it.

- **Improperly Washed Utensils, Tableware, Kitchen Equipment.** One of the first places the health inspector checks is the dishmachine. If you do not have 180° rinse water, you are immediately cited. Since most bacteria are killed at temperatures between 150° and 180°, such hot rinse temperatures are a necessity. The problem arises with serving utensils, and kitchen equipment which cannot always be washed in the dishmachine and thus may not be properly sterilized. The blades of a meat slicer can do more damage than a dirty glass or plate, and your job is to see to it that every item which comes in touch with food is properly and completely sanitized.

- **Improper Handling and Storage of Food, Utensils, and Equipment.** If perishable food is kept at room temperatures, instead of being placed either in kettles or ovens for cooking, or in the refrigerator for chilling, then bacteria are allowed to spread. If utensils are not kept in clean drawers, and are not immediately sent to the wash sink after use, bacteria may spread. If equipment is not cleaned after each use and disinfected daily, bacteria may spread. Bacteria cannot live and multiply in very cold or very hot surroundings. They prosper at room temperatures, and in moist surroundings. A flyer describing proper temperatures for food, published by the National Restaurant Association, is shown in Exhibit XII-1.

Methods for the Protection of Food to Prevent Food Poisoning

The best way to prevent food contamination is to keep harmful bacteria out if possible, or to keep them from growing if they do get into the food. You do this by watching time, temperature and cleanliness.

- **Time.** Bacteria multiply geometrically, sometimes at a rate of 20 minutes per generation. Establish a basic rule: "No perishable food may remain more than *one hour* at room temperature."

- **Temperature.** Keep all chilled food refrigerated at 40°F. or lower until ready to be served. Keep all hot foods above 140°F., until served. Be especially careful with the following types of food:
  - Cream-filled or custard-filled pastries, cakes, puddings
  - Any dish made with a cream sauce
  - Meats, poultry, and fish
  - Dressing for poultry and meat
  - Sandwiches and sandwich filling

EXHIBIT XII-1

TEMPERATURES FOR FOOD SAFENESS

TABLEWARE AND UTENSIL SANITATION

FOOD HANDLING AND STORAGE
(TEMPERATURE OF FOOD)

Maximum temperature for mechanical rinse — 195°

Mechanical rinse at nozzle — 180°

Minimum rinse temperature at dish (mechanical or dip rinse) — 170°

165° Food cooked to this temperature—most harmful bacteria killed

Temperature for mechanical dishwashing — 150°

150° Minimum safe temperature of cooked food to kill bacteria

140°

Water temperature for hand dishwashing — 130° / 120°

Store or display hot cooked foods above this temperature (after cooking)

Temperature for scraping dishes — 110° / 100°

100°

Rapid Bacterial Growth

DANGER ZONE FOR FOOD SAFENESS
(Handling and Storage)

Normal Room Temp.

70°

45°
34°

Cold or chill food storage (slow bacterial growth)

Prepared by the NRA Public Health and Safety Committee

0°
-5°
-10°

Frozen food storage (not for freezing food)

Courtesy of the National Restaurant Association

- **Cleanliness.** Remember the following rules:
  1. Keep cold foods cold, hot foods hot. Don't let food stand at room temperatures.
  2 . Keep hands clean, and touch food with hands as little as possible.
  3 . Don't let anyone with a skin infection or a cold handle food.
  4 . Keep kitchens, dining rooms, and storage rooms free from rats, mice, and insects.
  5 . Protect food from sneezes, customer handling, and dust.
  6 . Be sure poisons are well labeled and kept away from food preparation areas.
  7 . Wash dishes, glasses, silver, and utensils by approved methods.

What To Do In Case of Food Poisoning

Compared to commercial establishments, the incidence of food poisoning in colleges and universities in very low. The level of sanitation in most institutions is high, and most food service managers have the professional knowledge necessary to prevent food contamination. Nevertheless, hardly a year passes without some student, or group of students, claiming they got sick from the food. The following procedures will help you in dealing with either a real, or imagined, case of food poisoning:

1. **Take each complaint seriously.** Even though an individual complaint is unlikely to have been caused by your food, don't ever dismiss it lightly. If it is, in fact, an isolated complaint, then it is relatively easy to convince the complainant that it could not have been the food service in your unit, since no one else has become ill, and since normally large numbers of students would have had similar symptoms. Nevertheless, take the time to listen carefully, and approach each complaint as if it were "the real thing."

2. **Save food samples immediately.** As soon as you hear of a possible problem, make certain that a sample of each food item served is placed in the refrigerator, for possible laboratory analysis. (In some large institutions, such samples are kept every day as a matter of policy).

3. **Get in touch with the campus physician.** You should always maintain a close and harmonious relationship with your campus doctor or health officer. He should know of your familiarity with food poisoning, of your every-day steps to prevent it, and of your genuine desire to track down every complaint in connection with your food. If he does, many possible complaints can be squashed by him. Often students suffering from influenza or virus infections imagine that they are suffering from food poisoning, and close collaboration with your campus doctor will nip such complaints in the bud. On the other hand, if ever you should have a real case of food contamination, his full knowledge of events and his

cooperation as a friend, not as an adversary, are crucial. Once it is determined that there was indeed a case of food contamination, the physician or health officer takes charge, and you take orders.

4. **Have food samples lab-tested.** Even if you are fairly certain that the complaint is not valid, you will be wise to confirm your own feelings by an independent lab report. This is especially true, if a number of students, for whatever cause, voice the same complaint. Your willingness, immediately stated, to undertake and pay for a lab analysis, will go a long way to satisfy the students involved.

5. **Pull the food off of the line.** If you have reason to believe that there may possibly be a legitimate complaint, do not take any further chances. Pull the suspected food off the serving line immediately, and, except for the sample, throw it away.

6. **Be available; communicate.** In potentially serious cases, make sure that you are available to answer any and all questions from the students, faculty, and staff of your college. Explain candidly what steps you have taken to investigate the situation, and share whatever knowledge you may have on the subject.

PERSONAL HYGIENE OF STAFF

The best way to make sure that your food service staff practices good personal hygiene is to hire the type of person who does this naturally. You can often detect someone with poor hygiene during the interview and usually during the probationary period. Don't try to teach such a person about good personal hygiene; you cannot take a chance in food service. On the other hand, when you detect problems of personal hygiene among your own employees, move in immediately and talk to the employee in a straight-forward manner. It may be embarrassing to tell someone that they have a problem with bad breath or body odor, but not nearly as much a problem as it is for your customers who come in contact with such a person. It may be difficult to tell a grown person that they must wash their hands after going to the bathroom, but not as difficult as visiting a student in the hospital, ill because of your reluctance to set your own house in order.

As the person in charge of a food service operation, everyone looks to you to set a standard, and to enforce some rules. Whether it is bandaging up a cut, wearing a hairnet, polishing your shoes, or coming in to work neatly dressed, nothing is too small and unimportant to escape your observation and, if necessary, comment. If someone touches his nose, his lips, his hair, or scratches himself anywhere on his body, make him wash his hands. If someone sneezes or coughs, make sure he has a handkerchief, and if someone looks sloppy or disheveled, admonish him about it.

SANITATION IN THE KITCHEN

Take a walk through your kitchen some day. Start at the receiving dock and end at the serving area. Look for sanitation problems, and jot them down. Such notes can become the basis for a regular cleaning schedule in your kitchens. Here are some ideas:

Receiving Areas

A clean receiving dock gets scrubbed down with hot water and a disinfectant at least once daily. All trash and garbage containers are covered. The mops and brooms are all clean, and are hanging up on the wall. The receiving scale is clean. Dirty linen is separated into separate bins for kitchen towels, table cloths and for uniforms. Any food received is put away almost immediately after being checked in. There are few flies, if any.

Storage Areas

A professional exterminator, on contract, makes certain that there are no silverfish, weevils, mice, or other pests in your storeroom. All bulk products (such as sugar, flour, and beans) are kept in tightly covered containers. Shelvings are sturdy,clean, and clearly marked. The floor is clean, and gets swept and mopped frequently. All food is brought in and taken out in accordance with the principle of "first in, first out."

Walk-In Refrigerators and Freezers

The walk-ins are painted with a non-toxic paint and are all equipped with thermometers. Food in the walk-in is covered with plastic wrap or aluminum foil, and marked as to contents where necessary. The walk-ins are straightened up daily, and inventoried at least once a week. The walls are washed, the light fixtures clean and without dust.

Employee Washrooms

Washrooms are cleaned by staff on a regular schedule. All uniforms and shoes are placed in lockers. The toilets and hand sinks are spotless; the soap container and the paper towel dispenser are both full. The mirror is clean, the lights are bright, and the floor is swept and mopped. The washroom is symbolic of the entire kitchen. Its cleanliness is important for morale, and also as an inspiration for better personal hygiene.

The Kitchen

A clean kitchen has a clean floor and clean shelving. The floor should always be spotless, even in the middle of a busy meal. Food that is dropped or spilled should be picked up, swept up, or mopped up immediately. Shelves should be kept straight, and no junk should be permitted to accumulate on the shelving, on top of refrigerators, or on ranges. Mops and brooms should be easily accessible, but stored in a neat, unobstrusive manner. Racks, carts, and other portable equipment should be clean. If dirty, they should be sent to the receiving dock or pot room for cleaning. Overhead and fire extinguishing pipes and high shelving, or tops of refrigerators should be checked for dust. Hand sinks should always be clean as should all food service equipment not in use. The doors to refrigerators and cabinets should be spotless, and the doors to the ice machine closed. The knife racks and cook's drawers should be checked for cleanliness. The undershelves under work tables should either be empty or orderly, and the floor sinks should be clean.

The Dish and Pot Washing Areas

In a sanitary kitchen, the floors in the dishroom and pot room are clean and reasonably dry. The silver is soaking in soapy hot water, the clean dishes, sheet pans, and pots are neatly stacked, while the dirty pots and utensils are in reasonable order on the drain board. The silverware is washed at least twice, the second time tumbled upside down in the containers. The walls and ceiling are clean, and the atmosphere is bright and cheerful.

The Cafeteria Serving Areas

Clean and shiny sneezeguards, spotless cafeteria counters and wells, dishes lined up neatly on serving shelves or in dish dollies, and utensils neatly arranged for service are marks of a sanitary serving area. Overhead lamps should be dust-free, and stainless steel pass-through doors should be without spots. Well-trained servers should use free moments to wipe their area, thus continuously keeping it clean and attractive looking. An important requirement for a clean cafeteria area is a stack of clean kitchen towels, neatly folded, ready to be used when pans of food are placed on the line. For a Self-Inspection Form for Restaurants, see Appendix 15.

SANITATION IN THE DINING ROOM

Keeping the dining rooms clean and attractive at all times is one of the toughest assignments in sanitation. There are so many tables, so many chairs, and so much spillage throughout the day that this seems a never-ending job. Some food service managers make a mistake by thinking that if the dining rooms are clean at the beginning of a meal period, they need not concern themselves with that area until the next meal. The student who comes in at the end of the meal, and finds tables dirty with crumbs, spilled beverages, dirty ash trays, and spilled sugar packets does not know, nor care that the dining room was spotless two hours earlier. The beverage counter needs constant attention if it is to look clean and appetizing to the late-coming student. The same applies to the salad bar or condiment counter. Continuous cleaning of the dining room is one of those essential labor costs you cannot do without.

A frequent problem is that college students do not know, and have not been shown, how properly to wipe tables clean. Often they take a moist sponge and spread the dirt evenly around the top of the dining room table. The proper method, of course, is to bring a cart to the table with two small bowls of hot water, one soapy, and one clean. One rag or sponge is used to wash the table top, the other to wipe it dry. A dining room table is clean only if there are no streaks left anywhere on the table top.

Dining room floors also need continuous care. There are some areas that cannot be left to the evening porters, but need to be swept or vacuumed or even mopped after every meal. Dining room chairs also need checking.

A frequent violation of good sanitation rules is placing dining room chairs on top of the tables. This brings the dirt from the floor directly on to the table tops and should never be permitted. Turning the chairs upside down on the tables is less objectionable, especially if the tables are wiped once again before the dining room is opened.

One constant concern in the dining room is the matter of cafeteria trays. No matter how much training and instruction you give to the dish crew, there will always be times when some trays are placed in the dining room which are still moist or even wet. When a student picks up a tray, he gets water all over his clothes. Sending all wet trays back to the dishroom will quickly teach the dish crew that you mean business.

XIII. ZEROING IN ON SAFETY!

An institutional kitchen is a dangerous place. Make no mistake about that. Accidents have happened in kitchens long before everyone was forcibly reminded of them by passage of the Occupational Health and Safety Act of 1970 (OSHA). Your concern for employees should be so great that the safety measures in your kitchen *exceed* those required under federal and state law. Stop and think. Isn't it true that most of the work-related injuries suffered by your employees during the past several years could have been prevented?

Most kitchen accidents fall into certain basic categories:

- Slips and falls
- Cuts
- Burns
- Bumps and bruises
- Electrical shock
- Overlifting

The reasons for these accidents are also fairly common. People slip because the floor is wet, and because they are either careless or in a hurry. Cuts are almost always the result of someone's carelessness, although a dull knife is also a frequent cause. Burns, one of the most frequent restaurant accidents, are often caused by someone taking a short cut (e.g. lifting a heavy roasting pan directly out of the oven instead of resting it first on the open door surface), or by insufficient training (an inexperienced employee should not operate a deep fat fryer without realizing the danger of splattering hot fat). Bumps and bruises occur most commonly when an employee runs instead of walks, when normal passageways are obstructed with cases of goods, or when someone pushes portable equipment around in a careless manner. Electric shocks are very often due to faulty maintenance, worn-out insulation in electric cords, ungrounded plugs, and wet hands. Overlifting is almost always due to an employee's inordinate haste or carelessness, or both.

Now that OSHA is here, safety in the kitchen is your legal responsibility. It has always, however, been a moral responsibility, one that many food service managers did not recognize. It takes a special awareness, a concentration on safety every bit as intense and dedicated as one's belief in cleanliness to meet this obligation. Safety, like sanitation, has to become a way of life, not only because of OSHA, but because of your own conscience. If one of your employees slips and suffers a permanent back injury, it may be your fault. If someone cuts a finger on the slicer, it may be your fault. If someone suffers serious burns, you are the one that might have prevented it. The buck stops at your door. You are the manager! A flyer on kitchen safety in general is shown in Exhibit XIII-1.

EXHIBIT XIII-1

KITCHEN SAFETY
Accidents don't happen. They are caused!

WHAT ARE THE COMMON ACCIDENTS?

1. Slips and Falls
2. Cuts
3. Burns
4. Bumps and Bruises
5. Electrical Shock
6. Overlifting

WHAT ARE THE CAUSES?

1. Inadequate Safety Instructions
2. Inadequate Maintenance
3. Carelessness
4. Haste
5. Employee Resistance to Training
6. Inadequate Equipment
7. Short Cuts
8. Improper Shoes

HOW CAN THEY BE PREVENTED?

1. Good Management Attitude
2. Proper Employee Training
3. Good Equipment
4. Proper Construction
5. Excellent Housekeeping
6. Correct Traffic Patterns

HAVE *FIRST-AID* FACILITIES AVAILABLE AND BE PREPARED TO PROVIDE AID

Courtesy of Public Health and Medical Services, Human Services Agency, County of Orange.

SLIPS AND FALLS

Most falls occur because the floor is wet. This may be due to the type of shoes worn (some neoprene soles are like skates on a wet surface) but most often due to someone walking or running too quickly over the wet surface. It is your job to train the staff so that any spillage, regardless of where and under what condition it occurs, is immediately wiped up. There is no waiting line so long, and no emergency so great, that a kitchen worker cannot take a moment to wipe up a spill and, if necessary, sprinkle salt on the floor to prevent slipping. There is no unwritten law that says that a dishroom floor always has to be wet, or that pots must be allowed to drip on the floor. Other causes of slips are unexpected obstructions, such as mops in buckets, ladders, carts, etc. Here is what you can do to prevent, or at least minimize slips and falls in your kitchen:

- Prohibit all running; stop it whenever you see it.
- Make certain your employees wear slip-proof shoes.
- Use small warning stands ("Caution: Wet Floor") whenever the floor is being mopped.
- Provide safe, sturdy, stepladders or stools.
- Remove obstructions in passageways whenever you notice them.

A pamphlet on how to avoid slips and falls is shown in Exhibit XIII-2.

CUTS

Most cuts are relatively minor, and occur because of careless use of knives. Employees don't look at what they're doing, the knife slips, or is dull and hangs up on the food. Some of the more serious cuts, however, occur when the employee is using kitchen equipment carelessly or without knowing how. No one should ever be permitted to operate a meat slicer without having been given adequate instruction. Using a glove or a towel to catch the sliced meat can be an invitation to disaster. Leaving an automatic slicer running while the operator is doing something else is equally dangerous. A sharp knife that sticks out over the table edge is just asking for the chance to cut the passerby. A buffalo chopper with its whirring rotating blades, can do serious damage in spite of its safety features. A knife falling on someone's sandalled, open toe can cut it off with ease (one of the reasons why proper footwear is an absolute requirement in a kitchen, even on a college campus). Here are some steps to prevent cuts:

- All knives should be regularly sharpened and placed in knife racks, not in drawers.
- No one should be permitted to use restaurant equipment without prior training.
- Cutting boards must be used whenever anything is to be cut, or sliced with a knife.

EXHIBIT XIII-2

5 STEPS to avoid SLIPS and FALLS

S-811

STATE OF CALIFORNIA
AGRICULTURE AND SERVICES AGENCY
DEPARTMENT OF INDUSTRIAL RELATIONS
DIVISION OF INDUSTRIAL SAFETY
455 Golden Gate Ave., San Francisco, California 9410
3460 Wilshire Boulevard, Los Angeles, California 9001u

1. LOOK FOR—
The unexpected when walking:

spilled liquid or food.
pencils
paper
paper clips
holes or broken places in walking area
freshly waxed areas
other people

2. REACH FOR
handrails—
when on steps or
escalators

3. REDUCE THE HAZARDS—
If you find anything in a walking area that shouldn't be there:
wipe it up...   pick it up...
AND IF YOU CAN'T DO THAT—
mark it   OR—
kick it out of the way to be picked up later
and Report anything needing maintenance or repair...

4. DONT... (WAIT!)
RUN on slippery floors! ....
But—

5. DO...
LOOK where you're walking and—
KEEP IN STEP WITH SAFETY FOR YOURSELF AND OTHERS.

- Everyone in the kitchen, student as well as regular worker, must wear closed top shoes (not sneakers) when working in a kitchen, Workers should be encouraged to wear shoes that are "slip proof."

BURNS

Over 90% of all burns are a result of carelessness. They happen so quickly that the mind cannot react fast enough to warn the careless person in time. A typical example is grabbing a hot sheet pan with one's bare hands. Since the pan is not red hot, there is no way for the person to receive a warning, unless he remembers that a pan in the oven is too hot to handle. Experienced chefs always leave a kitchen towel hanging on the handle of a hot oven. The deep fat fryer is a frequent source of burns, usually because the employee, pouring out the fat, forgets that it is super-hot fat, and not cold water he is pouring. Sometimes he is burned because his face is too close to the fat in the fryer, and he forgets that hot fat, under certain conditions, will splatter. Another frequent place for burns is the coffee urn. Often the short employee remembers too late that he cannot possibly reach the top of the rim with his gallon of hot water without using a stool or stepladder. Sometimes it is the manager's fault for not providing a solid and safe stepladder on which to step. Steamers are also danger spots. It takes experience and skill to operate a high-pressure steamer, and a student just named as a cafeteria runner should not be told to get the food out of the steamer. To minimize burns, do the following:

- Train your cooks to hang towels on handles of hot ovens.
- Have dry kitchen towels readily available near ovens, steamers, fryers, and steam kettles.
- Post warning signs ("Beware of Burns!") near cooking areas.
- Train your staff in proper handling of cooking equipment.
- When employees are rushing, slow them down.
- Make sure that there is an empty space opposite ovens, fryers, and steamers for hot food pans.

BUMPS AND BRUISES

There are really only two ways in which an individual can get a bump or a bruise: he either bumps against an object, or an object is bumped against him. Since this is obvious, it should be relatively simple to prevent such bumps and bruises. By insisting that every employee move in a normal manner, not rush or run, not hurry or get excited, you will probably prevent him from bumping into anything. At the same time, you may also stop someone who is pushing a cart or carrying something in his hands from carelessly bumping another person. Care should be taken that objects are not sticking out from corners or under shelves, so that the unaware passerby can hit his legs on them. Moving such objects back into place is only common sense, but it does take a special awareness on the part of the manager to prevent such unnecessary accidents.

- Prohibit all running or undue haste.
- Prohibit all horseplay, especially with racks and carts.
- Train employees to beware of protruding objects and to put these back in place.

ELECTRICAL SHOCK

Of all kitchen accidents, electric shocks are perhaps the most easily prevented. All it takes is a good campus electrician, an alert manager, and reasonable caution on the part of the employees. If you have a good electrician, he will make it a point to check all electrical cords periodically for worn spots. He will make certain that all plugs are grounded (as stipulated by OSHA), and he will mark all outlets properly and make it impossible, in fact, to plug a 110-volt plug into a 220-volt outlet. The manager, who is in the kitchen all the time, should also check electric cords and appliances for possible worn spots or defective plugs and, when he notices these, immediately take the piece of equipment out of action. All the employee has to do is to be as careful in the kitchen as he or she is at home: drying his hand before plugging in an appliance, not standing in water when working with an electric appliance, and keeping fingers out of light sockets. In spite of all these precautions, electric shocks will occur sometime, usually because some piece of electric equipment develops a short. Periodic preventative maintenance, testing each piece of electric equipment, can minimize such accidents.

- All electric cords should be checked periodically.
- All electric equipment should be tested for shorts or other defects.
- All 220-volt outlets should be clearly marked, or installed so that 110-volt plugs do not fit.
- Employees should be trained to dry their hands before plugging in electric equipment.

OVERLIFTING

People get hurt when they are in a hurry. Everyone knows his lifting capabilities; it is easy to find out before lifting a box or a meat roast whether or not it will be too heavy to handle. But when people are in a rush, they fail to take proper precautions. During an orientation session, show your staff how to carry certain items; demonstrate to them, for example, how two women can carry a crate of lettuce which might be too heavy for just one woman. Demonstrate the proper method of replacing a 5-gallon milk container and show your staff how, by improper lifting, one can develop a hernia.

- Demonstrate proper lifting in formal training sessions.
- Train employees to help each other with heavy objects.
- Keep heavy objects (e.g. 100 lb. bags) to a minimum.

A flyer on safety in handlifting is shown in Exhibit XIII-3.

FIRST AID

Although every kitchen normally has a first-aid kit of some sort, it is amazing how often these kits are badly depleted and do not contain the materials needed for effective first aid treatment. The State of California has a list of recommended first-aid supplies for firms with 16 to 199 employees, which is shown in Exhibit XIII-4.

In addition to a first-aid kit, it is wise to establish a formal first-aid procedure, and to make certain that each kitchen employee is familiar with the procedure.

- Train employees in the latest method of helping victims choking on food.
- Train employees in cardiac pulmonary resuscitation (CPR) techniques.
- Establish clear procedures of how and where to take an employee for further emergency treatment (college infirmary, hospital).
- Train employees in the latest method of treatment for burns.

OSHA

By now, most food service managers have become familiar with the requirements of the federal Occupational Safety and Health Act of 1970. In some states, like California, they have enacted similar legislation which is even stricter than the federal act. A number of colleges and universities have been fined because of OSHA violations in their food services. Citations were given both for substantive violations, as well as for minor infractions, such as not posting minutes of regularly scheduled safety meetings on the bulletin boards. You should have in your possession, applicable OSHA information, or if not, write to the U.S. Department of Labor. Following is an attempt to summarize the essential aspects of OSHA legislation:

- **Employer's Awareness.** The employer must be aware of his responsibility to provide a safe place of employment and to be familiar with mandatory OSHA standards.
- **Employee Awareness.** The employer must make sure that his employees know about OSHA.
- **Safety Precautions.** The employer must examine conditions for compliance with OSHA regulations, must equip his employees with safe tools and equipment, including personal protective gear, and must use color codes, posters, labels, or signs to warn employees of potential hazards. He must establish or update operating procedures and communicate these

EXHIBIT XIII-3

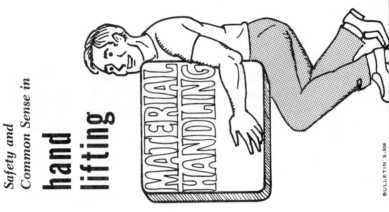

Safety and Common Sense in **hand lifting** — MATERIAL HANDLING

BULLETIN S-806

STATE OF CALIFORNIA
AGRICULTURE AND SERVICES AGENCY
DIVISION OF INDUSTRIAL SAFETY
455 Golden Gate Ave., San Francisco, Calif. 94102
3460 Wilshire Boulevard, Los Angeles, Calif. 90010

The question is not so much how to lift correctly but how, in this mechanical age, we can keep ourselves in physical condition so that we can do the work required in an emergency.

In other words, how can we keep our back muscles in good condition when we have little need for the use of muscular strength in our work?

The only solution is to do something that requires the use of muscles—such as calisthenics, active recreational games, swimming, body-building with weights, or strenuous work in the garden.

Whatever is done should be done regularly, at least three times a week, otherwise the muscles will continue to be sore and stiff.

The following exercises will help maintain good muscular condition, providing you have no back trouble. If you do have back trouble, consult your doctor about exercising.

FOUR EXERCISES

1. Stand with your feet apart, knees locked, and reach behind your heels, touching the floor with your fingers.

2. Lie on a rug or carpet, lift your feet and legs up, swinging them up over your head, and touch the floor with your feet. Then roll up to a sitting position with knees locked, and touch your toes with your hands.

3. Take a position lying face down on the floor, arch your back, and rock forward and back like a rocking chair.

4. With someone standing by to hold your feet down, lie face downward, placing the top of your hips at the forward edge of a strong bench, stool, or chair, and lift your head and trunk as high from the floor as possible by arching your back.

by CHARLES ALLEN PEASE

PRINTED IN CALIFORNIA OFFICE OF STATE PRINTING

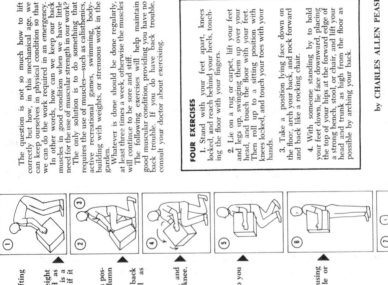

SEVEN POINTS

The main points to safe lifting are:

1. Get the center of the weight as high above the ground as possible. (Stand it up if it is a sack. Stand it on a corner if it is a box.)

2. Get the object as close to the supporting column (your backbone).

3. Set the feet, legs and back (back as nearly vertical as possible).

4. Lift with the arms first, and roll the object over your knee.

5. Pull the object as close to you as possible.

6. Stand up with the load, using the legs, thus placing little or no strain on the back.

7. Now turn your feet if your assignment requires turning, not your hips or shoulders.

EXHIBIT XIII-3 (continued)

LIFTING WITH SAFETY . . .

When we look at the complicated structure called the spinal column, with its 33 vertebrae, each with seven processes which seem to be sticking out in all directions, we realize that here is a mechanical structure which can get out of order.

Then, if we could see the mass of ligaments, discs, and muscles that hold this structure together and make it move, we would be amazed that it is ever in good working condition! But it does work, and it does give tremendous service over the years—if we take care of it!

We can compare our body to a derrick when we lift a weight from the ground. Our feet form the base upon which the platform (our hips and thighs) may turn; the spinal column is the boom from which our arms hang as the hoisting cable.

To operate a derrick, the engineer will turn the platform toward the object to be lifted. He will set the boom at the desired angle over the weight. He then will drop the cable and fasten it to the weight.

When everything is set, the engineer then takes up on the hoisting cable to lift the load. If any other movement of the load is desired, it is done after the cable has taken the load off the ground.

When a person desires to lift a load from the ground he must operate like the derrick.

First: set the feet.

Second: place the trunk of the body above the weight so that the arms will hang straight down to it.

Third: set the muscles of the legs, hips, and back ready to take the strain.

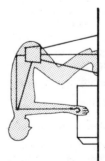

Fourth: lift the weight with the arms to get it off the ground, then straighten the legs and back.

This method of lifting will prevent back strain if everything is in good working order.

In this mechanical age, we either learn to care for a machine, or we employ someone to overhaul or remake it to keep it in perfect working order.

But we fail to keep our bodies, which are machines in a sense, in even fair working condition. But it does give tremendous service over the years—if we take care of it!

One needs only attend a luncheon club meeting to see examples of excellent machines "going to waist" from too much fuel and not enough good use of the equipment.

It is to this lack of physical condition that we can trace many of our back injuries.

If we could classify the type of individual who is most likely to have a back strain, we would pick the ex-athlete who has been sitting at a desk for about ten years, is 15 to 50 pounds overweight, and believes he is in just as good condition as he used to be.

This individual, when placed in an emergency situation, acts on the impulse—as he would have done ten years before when he was in top condition. He picks up the load; and in so doing, something "puts a kink in his back," and he is on the bench for two or three weeks or more.

A well-conditioned and trained back can enable one to lift unbelievable weights.

Paul Anderson, the world champion weightlifter, has pressed 407½ pounds over his head and has a total of 1129½ pounds in the three Olympic lifts. His best lift, unrecognized by officials, was 436½ pounds.

Our problem is not one of what is possible, but one of condition and training. Knowing how to lift can improve the performance as well as prevent injuries.

WEIGHTLIFTER'S TECHNIQUE

Let us see a weightlifter in action and analyze the action.

First: stand close to the weight with feet a walking step apart. Set the feet parallel to form a good base.

Second: bend the knees and hips to grasp the weight measuring the distance.

Third: when the distance is measured and position is comfortable, grasp the weight with hands more than shoulder width apart. Then set the muscles of the legs and back.

Fourth: from this "set" position, lift the weight off the floor with the arms, followed by extending the back and legs in that order. The height of the lift depends upon the amount of effort put into the flexion of the arms and the extension of the back and legs.

In the entire lifting process the weight is carried as close as possible to the supporting column. The spinal column is locked in a vertical position before the legs are fully extended.

APPLYING THE TECHNIQUE

How can we apply the weightlifter's technique when lifting something on the job or when working about the home?

In the first place, the weight should be about nine inches off the ground—so that it does not require a complete contraction of the legs and trunk.

When the legs and trunk are tightly contracted and a load must be lifted from that position, a much greater strain is placed on the back than if it were locked in a partially extended position.

So to follow the weightlifter's method, get the object as high off the ground as possible by standing it up, if it is a sack, or by standing it on one corner or edge if it is a box.

Next, move in close so that the object to be lifted is between the knees.

Set the muscles of the legs and trunk, and with the arms and hands, roll the object over the left knee (if you are right-handed), pull the object close to the trunk, then stand up with it.

With a little practice one will learn to roll the object over his knee, and there will be very little strain placed on the back.

EXHIBIT XIII-4

FIRST AID IN INDUSTRY -- Recommended Equipment and Supplies

III. FIRMS WITH 16 TO 199 EMPLOYEES

A. At least one centrally-located dustproof first-aid box, large enough so that each article therein is in plain view and easily accessible, and containing as a minimum:*

   1. An up-to-date advanced first-aid textbook or manual, such as that of the American Red Cross, or equivalent.
   2. Instruments consisting of:
      a. Bandage scissors,
      b. Assorted safety pins,
      c. Tongue depressors,
      d. Cotton-tipped applicators,
      e. Tweezers,
      f. Enamel basin,
      g. Thermometers,
      h. Flashlight.
   3. Drugs:
      No drugs, inhalant perles, skin antiseptic, or eye irrigation solutions should be included unless specifically ordered by a company-authorized licensed physician.
   4. Dressings, in adequate quantities, consisting at least of:
      a. Adhesive dressings, individually wrapped,
      b. Adhesive tape rolls, 1-inch wide,
      c. 1-inch gauze bandage rolls,
      d. Sterile gauze pads, 2-inch square,
      e. 2-inch gauze bandage rolls,
      f. Sterile gauze pads, 4-inch square,
      g. 4-inch gauze bandage rolls,
      h. Absorbent cotton packages,
      i. Triangular bandages,
      j. Splints of assorted sizes and splint padding,
      k. Sterile sugical pads, individually wrapped for dressings.

B. The first-aid box should be in charge of and maintained regularly by an employee who holds a current valid American Red Cross *Advanced* First-Aid and Emergency Care Certificate, or its equivalent, and who works in the immediate vicinity of the box.

C. The Red Cross or other certificate mentioned above should be prominently displayed in the vicinity of the main first-aid box.

D. Appropriate record forms should be kept.

E. Furnishings consisting at least of:
   1. A portable stretcher,
   2. Blanket, sheet and pillow.

F. Additional instruments, drugs, dressings, supplies, furnishings, and procedures as selected by a company-authorized licensed physician.

G. $See Appendix A.

*Tourniquet and carbolized petrolatum are also required by Section 2440, California Labor Code. Their use is no longer considered good first aid practice.

to his employees, so that they follow safety and health requirements of their own protection.

- **Record-keeping and Record-posting.** The employer must keep required OSHA records of work-related injuries and illnesses and post the annual summary during the entire month of February each year. He must report to OSHA each injury or health hazard that results in a fatality or hospitalization of five or more employees and must post the OSHA poster in a conspicuous place at work. He must also post any OSHA citations at the work site.

- **Employee Representatives.** The employer must designate or allow certain employees to confer with the OSHA compliance officer during an inspection, and not discriminate against employees who properly exercise their rights under the Act.

OSHA Inspections

An OSHA inspector will come whenever there is a fatal accident, or whenever he receives a complaint from an employee. He can also come if your place has been selected at random. The following are things he will look for (from "A Technical Bulletin about the Occupation Safety and Health Act," prepared by the National Restaurant Association, One IBM Plaza, Suite 2600, Chicago, Illinois, 60611):

- Fire extinguishers: location, application, and date tested
- Guards on floor openings, balcony storage areas, and receiving docks
- Proper and adequate hand railings on all stairs
- Guarding for machines and machine parts
- Electrical grounding of equipment and tools
- General housekeeping with areas clean and in good repair
- Passageways lighted and clear of obstruction
- Compliance with OSHA posting requirements
- Compliance with OSHA record-keeping
- Proper use of extension cords
- Exits marked and clear

OSHA Citations

In order to understand the seriousness of OSHA violations, it may be helpful to list some typical violations in food service establishments cited by CAL/OSHA, the OSHA agency in California:

- Failure to display OSHA poster, "Safety and Health Protection on the Job"
- Failure to keep emergency exits unobstructed
- Failure to provide guardrails on platforms, ramps, or working levels 30 inches or more above ground level

- Failure to display warning sign on automatic starting machine (e.g. freezer compressor)
- Failure to provide an exit door from the cold storage room which can be opened from the inside
- Failure to provide an illuminated switch and a fireman's type axe inside walk-in boxes
- Failure to provide walkways of not less than 24 inches wide in storeroom
- Failure to maintain hand tool (can opener) in good repair
- Failure to provide adequate first aid materials
- Failure to secure protective cover over disposal so that only authorized repairman may open it
- Failure to maintain soda and acid fire extinguisher in operable condition near vegetable department
- Failure to maintain work area free of slip hazards
- Failure to prohibit the use of flexible cord as a substitute for fixed wiring in a building (e.g. cord to cash register of excessive length)
- Failure to ground fixed equipment (e.g. refrigerator)
- Failure to ground exposed non-current-carrying metal parts of portable and/or cord and plug connected equipment (e.g. slicer, cash register, lamp, adding machine)
- Failure to identify all switches, circuit breakers, etc.
- Failure to provide 30 inches of unobstructed workspace in front of electrical control panels

These violations can be found in the pamphlet, *Restaurant Requirements,* by CAL/OSHA Division of Industrial Safety, State of California, 455 Golden Gate Avenue, San Francisco.

XIV. CATERING - THE KEY TO YOUR REPUTATION

In chapter IV, you read about the importance of catering in a college or university food service operation. When a college president, or a dean, or a faculty member arranges a served luncheon or dinner with campus food service he is, in fact, a host. If he were to invite guests to his home, he and his spouse would plan the menu carefully, have everything timed just right, and do everything possible to make the event a success. Therefore, if the same person arranges such a function with you, he is, in fact, *entrusting* these arrangements to you. He trusts you to care for the gastronomic welfare of his guests as well (or better) than he could do at home. This trust is important; the function is important. To you, it may be the fifteenth banquet in an already overcrowded week, but to the host, it may be a long-awaited occasion. When the English Department hosts a famous writer, or the Physics Department interviews a potential faculty member, or the fund raiser entertains a rich prospect for lunch, these events have an importance in the eyes of the hosts that you can only guess at. Your job, therefore, is to treat each catering function as if it were the most important event of your career and to make the host and his guests comfortable. The college shows its best side to the outside world when it caters an event. When important visitors are treated to a luncheon or dinner, when conference or symposium participants are guests at catered meals, when accreditation teams are hosted at cocktail parties or dinners, let the food service offer the best quality catering it can.

Once you recognize the importance of catering, you can develop a reputation for a fine catering service by establishing the highest possible standard of food preparation and service, and by making certain these standards are maintained by everyone in the food service organization. Personal involvement, clear-cut policies, efficient order-taking, good catering menus, top-notch food quality, and trained waiters and waitresses are the means by which you achieve and maintain such high standards.

PERSONAL INVOLVEMENT IN CATERING

The food service business is a people-oriented business, and there is no way in which a food service manager can be successful without getting personally involved with the people he serves. If this truism applies to serving students in residence halls or in cash operations, it applies even more in the catering field. Even on very large university campuses, where the food service director has dozens of managers and supervisors helping him, he will never cut himself off from all catering activities, if he values his job and his reputation. Even if his staff takes care of all the details, his personal presence at an important catering function assures the host that all is "under control." When the host is the college president, vice president, or a dean, such assurance is of course very important. Equally important, however, is the reaction of the faculty member, or the student officer when he sees, at a function important to him, the personal interest and personal appearance of the food service manager. There is an added advantage to such an approach: by being there when the banquet is served, you can see whether everything is done the way you want it. Any possible complaints later on can be handled by you from first-hand observation, rather than second-hand information.

CATERING POLICIES GOVERNING RELATIONS WITH CLIENTS

Chapter IV touched on the need for establishing policies dealing with different aspects of catering. Here we will deal with these in greater detail. Some policies, such as the type of functions that are permitted on your campus, or the service of alcoholic beverages on campus, are not made by you alone. The student personnel deans, vice presidents, and sometimes the president himself will have something to say about such matters. On other subjects, such as pricing policies, catering menus, locations of functions, and staffing of catering events, you will probably be the final authority. In any of these matters, it is wise to follow a clear-cut, written policy. You will encounter less confusion, less antagonism, and fewer misunderstandings if you can refer to these policies when arranging catering functions. You will encounter all types of catering clients: from the friendly dean who is delighted to leave all of the arrangements to you, to the overanxious host who wants to make sure that the color of the napkins matches that of the tablecloths. In between these extremes are the hundreds of clients whose requests, without clear-cut policies, would be difficult to handle. Here are some examples:

- "May I bring my own wine and serve it during dinner?"
- "May I take the leftover food home with me, since I paid for it?"
- "There will be some students with meal tickets. Do they have to pay also?"
- "I have made tentative arrangements with Ace Caterers to serve this dinner on campus. Have you any objections?"
- "We will be eating a little later than usual. Is 8:30 p.m. all right with you?"
- "Our count has dropped from 175 to 75."

Catering policies cover many subjects. They can be divided, for the sake of clarity, into policies which directly affect the customers, and those which affect operations. Following is a list of subjects which directly affect your customers:

- Catering prices
- Commercial caterers on your campus
- Use of residence hall dining rooms for catering functions
- Use of dining rooms for non-catering functions
- Alcoholic beverages at catering functions
- Pot luck meals
- Minimum guarantees

- College catering off-campus
- Wedding receptions
- Catering as unrelated business income

Catering Prices

Setting prices for catering functions in a college or university is a sensitive business. First, the food service manager is anxious to please his clients, who usually want catering services at the lowest possible cost. Second, catering involves a considerable amount of extra effort which should be properly compensated. Third, campus catering is frequently in direct competition with commercial caterers. Too low a catering price could cause justifiable resentment by caterers who will argue that you, as a tax-exempt institution, are competing unfairly against them, by charging unrealistically low prices. Such a claim is not without merit: while a dinner for resident students may not, in fact, be any real competition, a served dinner for the Junior Aid Society or a Boy Scouts Awards dinner may well be. Relations between a campus catering service and commercial caterers in town differ in different towns and cities. In larger cities, many colleges and universities may engage in healthy competition with local caterers, with each university department being free to engage either campus food service, or a commercial caterer. More often than not, however, the college food service retains exclusive catering rights on campus, rights often extended to off-campus groups which are potential clients of outside caterers. Under these circumstances, it seems the wisest course is not to engage in a price war with outside caterers, but instead to adopt prices which are similar to those charged off-campus. The above arguments, in fact, can be used to justify your catering prices to those on campus who argue for lower prices.

How to Calculate Catering Prices -- As a general rule of thumb, the profit on catering, after charging the cost of food, catering labor, and catering supplies, should be fifty percent of the combined cost of food and labor. In other words, if a banquet is estimated to cost $2.66 per person in food cost and catering labor, you should add one half of these combined costs for a total selling price of $4.00 per person. If your cost estimate is correct, your profit (after food and labor costs) will be $1.34 per person, or 33% of the selling price.

It is relatively easy to estimate the food cost of catering menus. The cost of most menu items remains relatively constant during the academic year. If you know the price per serving of one vegetable, you know the price of most. Once you know the cost of serving a green salad with tomato wedges, you have the cost of most salads at your fingertips. The same applies to most cakes, pies, and other desserts. Obviously, when you serve asparagus, or endive salads, or fresh strawberry tarts, your price per serving will be much higher, but none of this is difficult to calculate. When it comes to entree items, you need to have your meat and poultry prices close at hand. Here again, knowing the cost per cooked ounce of roast beef, for example, will give you a good idea of the cost of all types of roast meats, but such specialty items as Breast of Chicken Kiev, or Veal Cutlet Parmigiana might have to be looked up.

Estimating the cost of catering labor is also fairly simple. Some food service managers include the *total* labor cost in their calculations, i.e. they even include the pro-rated cost of cooks or dishwashers who could have been working at something else, such as serving the residents in a dormitory. This is probably the most accurate method of costing, but it may cause your prices to become too high. On the other hand, many food service managers include only the cost of "catering labor," i.e. that labor which was brought in specifically to help out with the banquet, such as extra cooks or dishwashers, overtime for regular staff, and of course, waiters and waitresses. That, too, is legitimate, and makes it a little easier for you to achieve your 33% net catering profit without charging exorbitantly high prices. After some experience, you will be able to estimate quite accurately how much it will cost in extra cooks' time and in overtime to put on a catering function. Your cost in waiters and waitresses is also fairly constant. You might actually establish a sliding scale ratio for manning banquet functions, such as the following:

Estimated number to be served	Type of Function	Number of Waiters of Waitresses
10 - 20	Served meal	1
21 - 40	Served meal	2
41 - 80	Served meal	3
81 - 120	Served meal	4
Above 120	Served meal	1 waiter or waitress for every 25-30 guests
41 - 80	Buffet	2
81 - 120	Buffet	3
Above 120	Buffet	1 waiter or waitress for every 40-50 guests

There are some catering functions which do not require individual costing for the purpose of setting a selling price. Coffee breaks, for example. Routine catering services should have a fixed price and should be handled in a routine manner. Doughnuts, sweet rolls, and cookies can be priced by the dozen, and beverages by the gallon. Standard charges can be established for such items as delivery service, table linen, and special services such as flowers, microphones, and set-ups for alcoholic beverages. Here is an example of how you can pre-cost a simple luncheon menu for 10 people using the cost of food and catering labor as the basis for a selling price:

Item to be Served	Estimated food cost per person
Chef's salad with tomato wedges, Italian dressing	.14
Breast of chicken	.95
Buttered green peas	.09
Rice pilaf	.07
Dinner rolls, butter	.08
Creme de Menthe sherbet, wafer	.09
Beverage	.08
Estimated cost of food	$1.50
Estimated cost of catering labor: 1 waiter X 2 hrs = $7.00 ÷ 10	.70
TOTAL	$2.20
Add 50%	$1.10
TOTAL SELLING PRICE	$3.30

A sample catering sheet, fully costed out, is shown in Exhibit XIV-1.

Pre-costed selling prices -- Prior to the start of each school year, you should prepare a list which shows basic price ranges for catered luncheons, dinners, and other events. Someone calling your office should be able to find out, for example, that an average served luncheon will cost between $3.00 and $4.00 per person, an average dinner between $6.00 and $8.00 per person, and a coffee break, $.25 per person for just coffee alone, or $.50 per person with doughnuts or sweet rolls. If these costs are based on minimum numbers (after all, a luncheon for four people, for example, is hardly ever profitable without a special surcharge) or certain meal times (a breakfast at 7:00 a.m. or a dinner at 8:00 p.m. can play havoc with your labor cost), this too should be determined in advance. Prices for deliveries, deposit requirements and other price data should all be established before the year begins.

Per-person versus total pricing -- There are some catering functions, the coffee break being a good example, which can be priced in two different ways. The price can be based on the number of persons participating or it can be based on the amount of food and beverages supplied. From the caterer's standpoint, the per person method is usually more profitable. Since it is more costly to the client, however, such pricing, at least for beverage breaks, is usually confined to outside groups or to special seminars and summer conference groups. Most schools post a basic charge per gallon for coffee, orange juice, or punch, per dozen for doughnuts and sweet rolls, and per sheet pan for coffee cakes and other cakes. The basic charge often includes cups and napkins, stirrers, sugar and cream, and sometimes even delivery. The charges should approximate those charged individually in your cash operations. Thus, if the price per cup of coffee in the snack bar is between $.20 and $.25 per cup, a gallon of coffee, which will serve 18-20 people, should be priced somewhere between $3.50 and $5.00 per gallon.

EXHIBIT XIV-1

UNIVERSITY OF THE PACIFIC
Stockton, California

Date 11-10-78

FOOD SERVICE CATERING SHEETS

Initials P.F.

Date of Event: FRI., DEC. 1, '78   Time: 12:00 NOON   Place: PATIO & TERRACE ROOM

Name of Organization: SOCIOLOGY   Price: $4.50

Function Ordered by: DR. MARY SMITH   Charge to: GENERAL FUND

Phone _____ Acct. No. _____

Preliminary Estimate 30-35   Minimum* Guarantee _____ By: _____   Set Up For _____

CHECKLIST

Service: Table	X	
Line		
Buffet		
Family Style		
Tables: Cloth	X	
Mats		
Paper rolls		
Napkins: Cloth	TANGERINE	
Paper		
Michrophone:		
Lectern:		
Blackboard:		
Screen:		
Decorations:		
Flowers		
Candles		
Other		
Ashtrays:	X	
Printing:		
Piano:		
Head Table		
Yes ___ No ___		
Set for _____		
Other Tables:		
ROUND TABLES OF 8		

TOSSED GREEN SALAD, GARNISHED   .15
BLEU CHEESE & ITALIAN DRESSINGS   .10

- -

STUFFED CHICKEN BREAST   1.25
   WINE SAUCE
RICE PILAF   .15
PARSLEY & LEMON GARNISH   .02

- -

HOT ROLLS - BUTTER   .15

- -

CREME DE MENTHE SHERBET   .125
FLORENTINE COOKIE   .125

- -

BEVERAGES   .15

     2.22

add 5% unproductive cost   .11

     2.33

Program After Meal:
   Yes ___ No ___
   Duration: ____

In accordance with Sec. 6363 (amen. 9-17-65) a 5% Sales Tax must be charged to all sales other than meals served to students.

* The University Food Service requires a guaranteed number at least 48 hours before a catering function. It will prepare 10% above the guarantee but cannot accept a reduction after the guarantee has been given.

Number served 34   Invoice No. 445   Invoice Date 12/9   Amount $153.00

EXHIBIT XIV-1 (continued)

CATERING ACCOUNTING SHEET

			Amount
Income			$ 153.00
Less:	Cost of Food	$79.22	
	Cost of Extra Labor	$11.60	
	Cost of Supplies etc	$ 5.76	
	Subtotal	$96.58	
	Overhead Costs (10%)	$ 9.65	
	Total Costs		$106.23
	Net (Income) or (Loss)		$ 46.77 31%

CATERING TIME SHEET

Name of Employee	Reg Hours	O.T. Hours	Amount	
Signe	2		5	80
Dillon	2		5.	80
Total			11	60

Cost-plus pricing -- It happens quite frequently that a special event requires unusual foods, services, or catering supplies. Whether these involve pineapples or orchids flown in from Hawaii, or special tablecloths, or a fountain for dispensing champagne, it is obvious that the food service manager will not always have the exact cost of these items at his fingertips. In some cases, he really will not know the exact costs until the function is over. In such an instance, especially if the client is part of the college community, and if he agrees, it is wise to quote the function on a cost-plus-profit basis, and to get the selling price after the function has taken place. The client is told that his price will consist of your total costs, plus a predetermined profit mark-up (e.g. 35% to 40%). Since this mark-up is based *on costs,* the net profit will usually be somewhat less than the 30% - 35% profit *on sales* which may be your profit objective on normal catering functions. It is often wise, however, to settle for a somewhat lower mark-up, in return for being certain that food service will not lose money on such unusual functions.

Late banquets, weekend banquets -- Occasionally a catering client will make special requests which will automatically cause you to incur extra costs. One such request, for example is to start the dinner at 7:30 or 8:00 p.m. instead of the usual 6:30 p.m. or at the latest, 7:00 p.m. dinner hour. Since most of your food preparation will ordinarily be handled by your regular kitchen staff, most of whom go home at about 7:00 p.m., such a late hour for dinner causes you special problems. You cannot always schedule a cook to come in late that day, and will probably have to pay overtime at time-and-a-half to keep the cooks for the additional one or two hours. The same problem could occur when you are asked to put on large catered meals on a weekend, when you normally would work with a reduced crew.

Even though a commercial caterer does not always incur special costs of this type (he often hires crews to suit each particular occasion), the fact that you have these costs must be taken into account when setting selling prices. Establish an extra charge for late dinners and weekend banquets. Southern Methodist University, for example, charges $1.50 to $2.50 extra for all weekend catered meals with a minimum requirement of 150 to 250 people and a special charge of $.75 per person for each half hour that a dinner starts after 7:00 p.m.

Catering prices and student meal tickets -- You will often receive requests for catering functions from student groups, in which some members will have meal tickets, and some will not. When such requests cover extra services like punch and cookies for social hours, there is usually no problem. Most residence hall groups have special social activity funds set up to cover such expenditures. When the request covers catering activities which take place in lieu of a regular meal, such as picnics, buffets, or served banquets, you face a different situation, however. The student will argue, with some logic, that those with meal tickets have already paid for their meal and any additional charge, therefore, should only cover your own extra out-of-pocket costs such as tablecloths, extra food costs, and the cost of banquet waiters or waitresses. You may agree with this argument, or you might try a different approach. You might point out that a meal ticket entitles the owner to a regularly served meal in the dining hall, and not to a specially-requested buffet or catered dinner. You can then offer meal ticket holders a credit equal to the meal ticket value for that particular meal. The difference between the two approaches is significant. To illustrate, let us assume that a student group requests a served steak dinner instead of their regular evening meal in the cafeteria, and that the extra cost of the food amounts to $3.00 per person, the tablecloths and napkins, $.25, and the waiter service, $.50, for a total extra cost of $3.75 per person. Assume, also, that the meal ticket value for an evening dinner is $2.25, and that your regular catering price for such a steak dinner is $7.00 per person.

Approach A: Charging Out-of-Pocket Costs
Meal Ticket Holders: $3.75 per person
All Others: $7.00 per person

Approach B: Crediting Meal Ticket Holders
Meal Ticket Holders:
$7.00 less $2.25 $4.75 per person
All Others: $7.00 per person

Many schools do not credit the students with the entire meal ticket value, but only with the actual *cost of the food.* In other words, instead of a credit of $2.25 in the above example, the credit might be only $1.10.

Your choice of approaches becomes further complicated by the fact that in most residence halls, students are treated to a special dinner on the average of once a month, and that such dinners often include tablecloths, candles, prime rib of beef or steak or some other expensive menu items. What if the students requesting a special banquet suggests that this banquet take the place of the regularly scheduled one? Furthermore, what if the student group represents only a small protion of the entire residence hall (e.g. a section or a corridor group)? What if the students are willing to accept the regular dinner menu, and all they want is tablecloths and waiter service?

It is difficult to establish pricing policies which fit every conceivable situation, but as a general rule it is wise to be accommodating and flexible if an entire dining room population is involved, and if the services requested do not cause significant disruptions in the overall food service. It is equally wise to establish reasonably high catering prices for smaller groups, or for special functions which cause a great deal of unscheduled effort and expenditures. Without such a policy, you could find yourself doing an inordinate amount of special function catering, without adequate staffing or compensation. A sample policy covering special dinners for campus residents is found in Exhibit XIV-2.

Steward's sales -- A "Steward's sale" in a hotel is a sale of food or beverage to a member of the hotel staff. The goods are usually priced at or near actual cost, and the sale is considered a courtesy or fringe benefit to the hotel staff. With some minor variation, a steward's sale on a college or university campus is the same thing. There will always be occasions when someone on campus will ask you to sell something to

EXHIBIT XIV-2

UNIVERSITY OF THE PACIFIC

February 12, 1978

POLICY REGARDING "SPECIAL GROUP DINNERS" FOR RESIDENCE HALL GROUPS

1. **PURPOSE:** The purpose of Special Group Dinners for students in residence halls is to enable our students to have a variety of dining experiences and to enjoy special, served dinners as a form of "monotony breakers."

2. **FREQUENCY:** Each living group (i.e., Quad residence hall, one or two Grace Covell "sections") is entitled to one Special Group Dinner per school year.

3. **COST:** "Special Group Dinners" are provided as a service by the University Food Service to its meal 'icket holders. The extra charge to the students will vary from $2.00 to $3.00 per person, depending on the entree selected and the location of the dinner. Food Service will pick up most of the cost of table service, linen, candles, etc.

   NOTE: Groups wishing to have special served meals in addition to their once-a-year "Special Group Dinners" may schedule these with the U.O.P. Catering Department at regular catering prices.

4. **LOCATION:** "Special Group Dinners" are restricted to the U.O.P. Center Redwood Room (Minimum number: 50), or to one of the rooms in the residence hall dining hall complexes.

5. **ALCOHOLIC BEVERAGES:** Existing University policy prohibits the service of alcoholic beverages (including wine and beer) at special dinners of this type.

them, and you cannot say no. It could be some bread or pastries from your bake shop. It could be a case of paper cups, or a box of sugar packets. It could also be prepared food which you might sell to a member of the faculty or staff whose spouse is ill and who, temporarily, needs some help with home-cooked meals.

For all such occasions, establishment of a steward's sale policy is the ideal solution. Since your college or university incurs costs other than the raw food cost, it is usually wise to add a percentage for overhead costs. This additional charge will also serve as a deterrent to those on your campus who might tend to take advantage of such a policy. Normally a mark-up of 15% to 20% over net costs is justified, and will be accepted without question by all your clients and campus associates.

A word of caution: A steward's sale policy is a necessary part of your pricing structure, but steward's sales should not be encouraged. You do not run a retail supermarket, and nothing in this chapter suggests that you should build up your volume by promoting such sales. Only for those special occasions when it is in your and the school's interest to charge as little as possible for food and services that must be provided by your department, is a steward's sale necessary and justified. Furthermore, the more you can charge such sales to college accounts, the less chance there is that you will have problems with income or sales taxes governing these transactions.

Commercial Caterers on Campus

On most campuses, the college or university food service is the exclusive and only caterer allowed. Just as a restaurant owner would not allow another caterer to serve a banquet in his restaurant, so a college food service director should have the same prerogative. There are some differences between the two, however. College food service directors do not *own* the college, and the college food service is merely a service organization for the college. Therefore, if you want to have the right to a catering monopoly on campus, you must be competitive with outside caterers. You must be able to offer the same basic services, the same or better quality, at approximately the same prices. If you are not able to do so, the many departments and organizations on campus which require catering services may have a legitimate right to ask others to perform such a service. On many larger campuses, and especially in some of the Ivy League schools, university departments are so powerful and so independent that the food service director cannot enforce a catering monopoly, even if he wanted to. Each department can choose whomever it wants to for catering purposes. In such a situation, the campus food service is truly in a competitive situation and simply has to be better than all other competitors if it wishes to retain this profitable business.

Often the issue is not so clear cut. On many campuses, the food services have the right of first refusal. If, for whatever reasons, it cannot handle a catering function, the university client is free to turn elsewhere. Many campus food services do not have a liquor license, whereas caterers frequently do. It is logical, therefore, to let such caterers handle cocktail parties and similar events. Often, when campus food service is shut down during recess, it would not be economical to open up a kitchen just for a small luncheon or dinner, and an outside caterer is a much better choice. Some days, such as homecoming, so overtax the campus food service that it is glad to share some of the alumni receptions and dinners with an outside caterer. Wedding receptions, if allowed on campus, are frequently beyond the capacity of a campus food service to handle. Thus, a somewhat flexible policy, with the food service director having a voice in the decision, seems to be the best policy for many schools.

If you should be in this category, it is important that you do not openly favor one caterer over another when recommending outside caterers to your campus clients. Such partiality, unless based on some pretty solid reasons, can have serious economic consequences for the less-favored caterer. It is far better to prepare a brief list of caterers who do quality work and make such a list available to anyone who needs such services. On the other hand, if certain caterers abuse their guest privilege on your campus, you then, of course, have the right to warn them or even to bar them from using campus facilities. In all these dealings, close liaison with the public relations people in your college or university is advisable, since they will often be the first ones to hear of any complaints or criticisms.

Use of residence hall dining rooms for catering functions -- Many schools, especially those with limited banquet facilities, must resort to residence hall dining rooms when scheduling banquets or special events. This practice presents no problem when the event includes members of the residence halls. It often presents a great problem, however, when the students are moved out of their regular dining room and fed elsewhere, so that the banquet can take place. The students get very upset if this happens often. This is where you, as campus food service director, must play the role of the firm, but tactful mediator. Fight strongly and courageously for the right of your residence hall students to eat in their dining halls without interruption. No department head or dean, no matter how influential, should be able to overrule you on that point, especially if alternate facilities can be made available. If necessary, solicit the aid of the vice president for student affairs to get the necessary leverage. Your students should know that under normal circumstances you defend their right to their own facilities, without intrusion by others. The principle that students are not normally displaced from their dining rooms should be a matter of stated policy, and included in your printed catering brochure.

There are times, however, when exceptions must be made. The annual awards dinner or the kick-off dinner for your college's million dollar fund-raising drive are important events. Your college president may personally intervene to make certain that these affairs come off successfully. If there is no other, or no better place than the residence halls, then some careful advance preparation, common courtesy, and tact will help you over potential trouble spots. First of all, discuss the problem with the student personnel deans and the residence hall staff. Second, after receiving their approval, make some suitable alternative arrangements for your residents. Third, place some large, appropriate signs on the dining room doors at least a day in advance, explaining when the dining room will be used by others, and for what reason. Students will accept a displacement occasionally if they know the reason why, and if they have been told in advance. Finally, treat the students especially well on the evening of the displacement. Wherever you feed them, have an especially good meal for them, and no "hassles."

Use of Dining Rooms for Non-Catering Functions

While it is bad enough to displace students in residence halls for catering functions, it is even worse to use dining rooms for non-catering functions. This is especially true in residence halls, but also, though perhaps to a lesser extent, for dining rooms in student union buildings or other such facilities. There are so many meeting rooms, classrooms, lounges and multi-purpose rooms on every campus, that the dining rooms should be the last places, not the first ones, to be used for non-catering events. Your college and university expects you to serve meals in these rooms in a clean and appetizing manner. You are expected to open these rooms for breakfast, lunch and dinner in sparkling shape, with tables and chairs wiped, the floors swept and mopped, the beverage counters clean, and with everything in place. If anyone who wants to have a meeting has a right to schedule the dining rooms, merely because he likes the room, such frequent use at odd hours will make it almost impossible for you to meet your responsibilities.

Here too, however, there is an area of flexibility and compromise. If the users are residence hall students, then you would want to allow them this privilege, provided they give you persuasive reasons (i.e., the admissions office has to give a test for 250 incoming freshmen and your dining room is the only place large enough for this). Needless to say, adequate cleaning arrangements by the users, at no expense to you, are a precondition for such use of dining rooms.

Alcoholic Beverages at Catering Functions

Policies regarding alcoholic beverages are as varied on college campuses as are the state laws governing the consumption of alcoholic beverages by young people. They vary from very permissive policies on campuses where Food Service is allowed to serve cocktails at almost any function, to restrictive policies on campuses where no alcoholic beverage is ever permitted. On this subject, you will have very little to say. Such policies are so sensitive that they are usually made by the top student affairs officer, or the president. Should your opinion be sought, however, consider these facts:

- On most campuses, students over the legal drinking age are permitted to consume alcohol in their room.
- Wine is becoming increasingly popular as an accompaniment to a catered dinner.
- Some festive occasions (e.g. weddings) absolutely require champagne.
- Catering cocktail parties, or even just charging for set-ups, can be a very profitable part of your catering.
- The serving of beer in student unions is becoming more and more popular throughout the United States.
- Careless or intentional violation of your state's alcoholic beverage laws is a misdemeanor, and could get you into legal difficulties.

Few campus food services have their own liquor license, and it is doubtful if this is normally advisable. From a food service manager's point of view, permission to serve beer in the student "hang-out" and wine with catered meals is all he needs in order to offer a complete service to the campus community and increase his profits.

Pot Luck Meals in Food Service Areas

Pot luck dinners are often a problem for the campus food service director. If people get food poisoning from food eaten on campus, it could easily become a problem for campus food services, even if none of the food was prepared on campus. If the pot luck meal is held in one of the dining areas, there is the problem of charging for the use of the facility (not always possible without loud complaints), for the use of dishes, silver, and glassware, and for clean-up after the meal. Ideally, each school should have some rooms other than campus dining halls where pot luck dinners can be held. In any case, you must establish clear-cut policies governing such affairs. These could include the following points:

- Pot luck meals on campus are permitted only for college-connected groups; e.g. at least one half of the group must be from the college community.
- Full responsibility for the meal rests with the sponsoring campus organization or group.
- Any use of campus food service facilities must be covered by a clean-up or damage deposit. Any clean-up necessary after the function will be charged against such a deposit.
- As a general rule, campus kitchens are not available for pot luck meals. If an exception is made, a regular member of the food service staff must be present throughout the event, and the salary must be paid by the user group.
- Pot luck meals are restricted to only specific areas.

Minimum Guarantees

Every hotel, restaurant, and commercial caterer insists on getting a firm minimum guarantee in advance for all banquets and other catered events. This is only natural, since such an event requires special staffing, special food purchasing, and other expenses incurred specifically in preparation for the event. Normally the caterer expects a firm guarantee within 48 hours of the event, and prepares for the possibility of a few last-minute guests over the guarantee. If the number of guests falls below the final number guaranteed, the client is billed for the guaranteed number; if above, he is billed for the actual number participating. Lack of firm guarantees makes catering physically impossible and economically unsound. Furthermore, on a college campus, any loss incurred as a result of faculty catering planning will probably come, indirectly or directly, out of the pockets of the students. This should never happen. Instead, to be certain of earning his desired 30% to 35% profit on catering events, the successful food service manager should follow a strict advance guarantee policy, and make such policy clear to any potential client. Moreover, the guarantee policy should be printed boldly on each catering or function sheet, so that no one is ever in doubt about it. (See Exhibit XIV-1).

How about exceptions? There are some college-connected functions such as a "Town-Gown Open House," when the entire campus is open to the local community where no one can give the required guarantee. There are other occasions, where the faculty member arranging for a special workshop or seminar, may prefer merely to let food service know of the special event rather than become responsible for a fixed guarantee. There are occasions, especially those sponsored by student organizations, where the guarantor turns out to be either unauthorized or without funds, and there is no way to collect the guaranteed amount. In addition to such exceptional cases, food service managers have to decide for themselves whether or not they wish to make additional exceptions. Many believe in always charging the full amount of the guarantee, regardless of circumstances. Others believe in giving the client a little leeway, such as perhaps 5% above or below the guarantee. Still others will split the difference between the number guaranteed and the number of guests they actually had. The reasoning for this latter approach is that clients always feel abused when charged for meals not eaten. Even though they may personally have given the guarantee, they never fully accept the idea of having to pay for services not rendered. Meeting them half-way, therefore, is sometimes a good policy, especially on a small campus where personal relationships are very close. On the other hand, some will argue that any compromise at all nibbles away at the basic principle of a minimum guarantee and should, therefore, be avoided at all costs.

College Catering Off-Campus

Almost every college and university food service director is asked occasionally to perform off-campus catering functions, at the president's house, in someone else's private residence, or a public meeting hall. These requests are usually a ticklish matter: telling a faculty department head that your catering service performs off-campus catering only for vice presidents and the president is just like waving a red flag in front of a bull. Many of the smaller schools are not even equipped to cater off-campus; even if you can cater large dinners in public places off-campus, you are almost certain to incur the wrath of other caterers who feel that you are unfair competition. Some schools, particularly those in larger cities, may not care about that. Most colleges and universities, however, bend over backward to live in harmony with their neighbors in town, and flagrant competition with commercial caterers is generally frowned upon.

It is essential that you establish some sort of clear policy that spells out what off-campus catering you can perform, when you can do it, and for whom. You might decide to do none at all, or to do light receptions only, or to cater only at the president's residence.

Wedding Receptions

Wedding receptions are very profitable, especially if your school has a beer and wine license. Many student unions depend on wedding affairs to help keep their food service in the black, and in some of the larger universities wedding receptions are "big business." Arranging such receptions, however, takes a great deal of advance preparation, and most of the smaller schools are not equipped to handle them. Those schools whose food services consist largely of residence halls plus small cash operations would not normally be staffed to handle large functions on weekends. Furthermore, the advance meetings with the prospective bride take an inordinate amount of time. Few schools, unless they have a large student union, have large dining rooms that are free on weekends, and can be used for wedding receptions without interfering with the students.

If you feel that you want to cater to wedding parties, make sure that, once again, you follow clear-cut written policies. Minimum guarantees, advance deposits, arrangements for champagne and other alcoholic beverages, the wedding cake, flowers and decorations, table arrangements and draperies, candles and silver service, loudspeakers, piano or other music -- all these are matters that have to be clearly understood by everyone if the affair is to be successful for all. Any policies should be defensible to the students, and the functions highly profitable for food service.

Catering as Unrelated Business Income

In recent years, colleges and universities have had to be more and more concerned with the question of just what constitutes "unrelated business income." The Internal Revenue Service, as part of the U.S. Government's overall tax reform activities, has questioned more closely all those activities engaged in by non-profit institutions, which are not directly related to the purpose for which the institution exists and for which it has been granted a tax exemption. Some institutions, therefore, like the University of Pennsylvania, have a policy of *serving only tax-exempt clients,* both on and off campus. Most colleges and universities have a more liberal policy, but require that the purpose of the catering function have a clear connection with university activities, or that it furthers the institution's goals and objectives.

Since no college and university would want to be put into a position where it would have to pay income taxes on catering, you should establish a clear-cut catering policy in this regard, and see that it is strictly enforced.

TAKING CATERING ORDERS

The first and most crucial step in conducting a successful catering function is taking the order. Everything must be absolutely clear to both parties if the catered event is to be mutually satisfying. To use a wedding reception as an example, the commercial caterer normally has several meetings with the bride, the mother of the bride, and anyone else who wants to participate in the planning. He lists such details as the bride's colors, whether the cake is to have sugar or whipped cream frosting, who supplies the cake knife, and whether or not the buffet table is to be skirted. On a college campus the problem is similar. There are many details that must be established for each catered luncheon or dinner. Some of these are

- The day, date, and time of the function
- The number of people expected and a deadline for final guarantee
- The price of the function, with or without sales tax
- The menu
- The style of service (served, buffet, modified service)

- Type of table cover (place mats, tablecloths, cloth or paper napkins)
- Flowers, candles or other decorations
- Microphones, or other audio-visual requirements
- Special dining room set-up (round tables, square tables)
- Head table requirements.

On a college or university campus, many of these catering orders are taken by telephone and details are often missed or confused. What is worse, the task of placing the order is often delegated to an assistant thus allowing for further potential misunderstanding between the client and the food service manager. Then, if the food service director or the catering manager assigns the job of taking catering orders to his or her own secretary, the potential for confusion and chaos is very high indeed. The more people who get involved in taking or giving the catering order, the greater the chance that mistakes or misunderstandings will occur. Often a client may be merely asking for information, while the secretary on the other end of the line may think she is being given a firm catering order. Conversely, the client may think that he has placed a firm order while the person at the other end believes that all he was doing was giving out preliminary information. *It is wise, therefore for the catering manager to take all "substantive" catering orders personally;* routine orders such as coffee breaks and box lunches can be handled by the staff. Some additional reasons for taking the order personally are

- The catering manager can better select the most suitable dining room.
- The catering manager has greater credibility with the client and can guide the latter to a better menu selection.
- The catering manager can better assess the impact on costs of special or unusual requests (such as a late dinner hour).
- The catering manager is more familiar with the specific production capabilities (and cooking talents) in each kitchen.
- The catering manager has more current data on the availability and price of different food items.

The Catering Calendar

Scheduling is a routine task, and most reservations for banquet rooms are taken on a first-come, first-served basis. The wise catering manager has a large calendar book in which all available dining rooms are listed on a separate page for each school day. Such a calendar book, which reserves a room for a client and lists the day and date, type of function, name of client, and number of people expected, can be maintained by the office staff. A sample of such a page is shown in Exhibit XIV-3. A note of caution here: some colleges and universities, especially those whose food service is operated by an outside caterer, have removed the scheduling function from the food service office. Instead, dining rooms are reserved by some other office (auxiliary services, dean of students, student union manager). This is inevitably a mistake! The selection of a dining room is as crucial to the catering manager as it is to the client, and both must choose the room best suited for the occasion.

EXHIBIT XIV-3

DAY __Wednesday__ DATE __February 21__ 19 __79__

R O O M	BREAKFAST	LUNCH	DINNER
P A C I F I C C L U B	Event _____ Time _____ Name _____ _____ Ordered by: _____ Phone _____ Est. No. _____ Remarks: _____ _____	Event _____ Time _____ Name _____ _____ Ordered by: _____ Phone _____ Est. No. _____ Remarks: _____ _____	Event _Served Dinner_ Time _6 PM_ Name _Taft Institute_ _____ Ordered by: _Dr. Jerry Briscoe_ Phone _____ Est. No. _30_ Remarks: _Will stay in club after_ _dinner_
R E D W O O D R O O M	Event _____ Time _____ Name _____ _____ Ordered by: _____ Phone _____ Est. No. _____ Remarks: _____	Event _____ Time _____ Name _____ _____ Ordered by: _____ Phone _____ Est. No. _____ Remarks: _____	Event _____ Time _730-9_ Name _Asian Alliance_ _____ Ordered by: _____ Phone _____ Est. No. _60_ Remarks: _Meeting only_
R E G E N T S D I N I N G R O O M	Event _____ Time _____ Name _____ _____ Ordered by: _____ Phone _____ Est.. No. _____ Remarks: _____	Event _Lunch_ Time _12⁰⁰Noon_ Name _U.O.P. Regents_ _Investment Committee_ Ordered by: _Mary Toy_ Phone _2345_ Est. No. _12-14_ Remarks: _____	Event _____ Time _____ Name _____ _____ Ordered by: _____ Phone _____ Est. No. _____ Remarks: _____
P A T I O	Event _____ Time _8 AM_ Name _U.O.P Credit Union_ Ordered by: _Dee Fillipone_ Phone _2171_ Est. No. _15_ Remarks: _Go thru line_	Event _____ Time _____ Name _____ Ordered by: _____ Phone _____ Est. No. _____ Remarks: _____	Event _____ Time _____ Name _____ Ordered by: _____ Phone _____ Est. No. _____ Remarks: _____
T E R R A C E	Event _____ Time _____ Name _____ _____ Ordered by: _____ Phone _____ Est. No. _____ Remarks: _____ _____	Event _____ Time _____ Name _____ _____ Ordered by: _____ Phone _____ Est. No. _____ Remarks: _____ _____	Event _____ Time _____ Name _____ _____ Ordered by: _____ Phone _____ Est. No. _____ Remarks: _____ _____

The Catering Function Sheet

The most crucial document in the catering process is the catering function sheet. Although each caterer has his own preferred form, the use of this sheet, and the information listed thereon, are generally similar. The sheet is so designed that all the important details listed earlier are easily noted, so that it serves as a checklist of things to remember. It is the uniform document governing the entire catering event, and is seen by the client, the unit managers or cooks, the baker, purchasing agent, audio-visual department, maintenance, and anyone else involved in the affair. *It is critically important, therefore, that a copy of the catering sheet, or a letter containing the information is sent to the client as soon as it is typed.* This not only places the final responsibility for any possible misunderstandings or errors directly upon the client, but also gives him an opportunity to make any necessary correction before it is too late. Equally important is the posting of each catering sheet on the kitchen wall or bulletin board during the week that it is to take place, preferably with the names of the staff members who will be involved in carrying out the assignment. This step shares the information with the entire kitchen staff, and thus relieves the unit manager from having to remember all the details connected with each function. A well-designed, completely filled out catering sheet, freely shared with whomever needs it, can go a long way toward simplifying the whole catering process. Catering must be a joint and cooperative effort between the client, the food service manager, and the kitchen staff, and everyone along the line must realize the importance of successful catering to the entire institution. The food service manager who regards banquets as a nuisance, or a secondary activity to his main job of feeding students, is making a serious mistake.

The catering sheet can serve as the basic costing document. A good catering manager will pre-cost a function as he takes the order. In other words, he will have calculated, before establishing a firm selling price, what the cost of the function will be, and how much he must add in order to gain the desired profit margin. This information, on his copy of the catering sheet, can later be compared with that written on the unit manager's copy, where the actual costs, both in food, labor, and other supplies are noted. A simple cost accounting form, printed on the back of the unit manager's copy is helpful in standardizing the cost and profit calculations of all catering functions. A sample form, both front and back, is shown in Exhibit XIV-1.

Decentralized Order-taking

Many food service directors have decentralized their operations. Unit managers are then asked or permitted to take their own catering orders. On large campuses where the volume of catered functions would stagger a central office, decentralization results in a better, more personal catering service. Even on a small campus, however, a certain amount of decentralization may be desirable. Coffee or other refreshment breaks, picnics or field trips, simple sit-down meals, and other simple functions involving residence hall groups can often be handled most easily, and with the least amount of red tape, by the unit manager. If the catered event is more complicated and involves special arrangements or unusual pricing problems, then such a function is often better handled by the food service director.

A general guideline: whenever unit managers can take a catering order which involves their own constituents (e.g. resident students) and which they can perform without undue difficulty, then such functions should be scheduled directly by them; any others should be scheduled centrally.

Collecting Payment for Catering Functions

Most commercial caterers have a policy of charging a down payment (usually a small percentage of the anticipated gross) at the time the catering event is booked and collecting for the balance immediately upon serving the meal. Colleges and universities have not adopted such policies because most of their catering is done with university clients and collection has not usually been a problem.

In the larger schools, however, where the relationship between client and caterer may be less close, where there may be decentralized billing, and where there is a possibility of payment problems later, collecting payment on the spot may be a preferred method. Down payments should also be considered when dealing with occasional and off-campus clients. The college food service cannot become a collection agency, but most adopt whatever policies are necessary to get payment for its services with the least amount of problems.

WRITING CATERING MENUS

A very special skill, acquired only through experience, is the ability to suggest the right menu to suit each client's special wishes. These wishes are many: some people are interested largely in price; others want international, esoteric, or gourmet type food; while others yet are interested strictly in meat and potatoes menus. Some clients prefer light lunches, such as salad plates and crepes, while others see the fulfillment of their dreams in a hot roast beef sandwich with mashed potatoes. Some callers accurately reflect the wishes of their superiors, while others, mistakenly, force their own individual tastes upon the catering manager. Woe to the college catering manager who agrees to serve oysters on the half shell as the first course, or sweetbreads as the main entree! It is a good idea to learn the personal likes and dislikes of the institution's top officials, and to make an extra effort to accommodate a client with special problems. Here is an example: Mr. Stringfellow Barr, noted author, wrote a book entitled *Purely Academic* which described a sumptious breakfast served to a university professor in a fancy hotel. When Mr. Barr visited the University of the Pacific, a photocopied page out of his book became the official menu, and the meal duplicated, in every respect, the breakfast described in the book. Needless to say, the meal was a great hit, and everyone, including the author, was enormously pleased.

Menu Selection by Clients

Most commercial caterers present the potential client with a catering menu. This is often a brochure containing sample menus of luncheons, dinners, receptions, wedding breakfasts and other meals. For any large catering organization, on or off-campus, this is a very practical tool. Even an untrained clerk can take catering orders, and inform the client about menu offerings, prices, guarantees, and any other special conditions applying to his function. Many colleges and universities use this approach, as can be seen by sample catering menus in Appendix 3. There are, as can be seen, many ways of setting up such a menu. Some schools offer banquet menus only in complete combinations; others do the opposite, and list all the various food items under their special categories in alphabetical order, and the client can put his own menu together. California State University, Sonoma, has established a base price for all the items that accompany the entree. The client can then choose the entree that most appeals to his taste and pocketbook. Some of the larger universities do a very large catering business and have, therefore, a series of catering menus and a number of people who take catering orders. At Brigham Young University in Provo, Utah, members of the faculty have the privilege of placing catering orders for personal use, and the university food service does a brisk take-out business in dinners for faculty families.

Menu Writing by Catering Managers

There are many college and university food service managers, however, who like to personalize the process of catering. They argue, quite logically, that since the faculty and administration often judge them on the basis of their catering excellence, they should become personally involved in planning, menu writing, and price setting as well as in supervising the catering event. Rather than present the potential client with a pre-printed menu, they prefer to write each catering menu to suit the client's individual perference. Such a procedure has several distinct advantages:

- The client feels that the menu is written especially for him.
- The food service manager can include items from the regular menu, thus simplifying the production process.
- The responsibility for the menu selection is thus removed from the client's secretary (who often is not knowledgeable on what to select for a successful catering function) to the food service manager, who is experienced and knowledgeable in this task.

Needless to say, the client in each case has the final word, and the right to change any menu item.

DEVELOPING A TRAINED CREW OF WAITERS AND WAITRESSES

When it comes to providing waiters and waitresses for catering functions, are you aware how lucky you are? Most commercial caterers would be in seventh heaven if they had access to an almost unlimited supply of attractive young men and women, living within a few blocks of the catered event, willing to come at almost a moment's notice and work for as many or as few hours as you may need them. On top of that, these young men and women are usually bright, cheerful, and eager to do a good job. Does this description apply to your help, or do you have trouble finding students willing to work, or to stay until after the program, or to dress properly for banquet service? Are they often clumsy, disinterested, and undependable?

If you have difficulty with student waiters and waitresses the problem lies either with you or with food service policies, and not with the students. Waiting on tables is a time-honored, part-time occupation for the college students on many campuses. Even on campuses which have difficulty recruiting students for regular student jobs, it is usually easier to find students for banquet service, because it is a pleasant job, takes only a few hours, and provides the off campus student with a delicious free meal and spending money. Treat banquet waiters and waitresses with importance, be selective in recruiting and careful in providing the necessary training.

Training Banquet Waiters and Waitresses

It does not take long to train a college student to be a good waiter or waitress. Students are learning all the time, and a short course in table service is merely another subject. Most students are eager to learn the proper methods of table service. Your example, your standards, and your instruction will set the tone. A well-trained waiter or waitress must know

- Proper dress and personal grooming
- How to set a table with silverware and dishes
- How to pour water and other beverages
- How to talk with guests
- How to carry plates
- How to serve and remove dishes from the table
- Whom to serve next
- When to stop serving
- When to eat, and when not to eat

Put these instructions into writing, and make sure that new student servers are properly informed about each of the points. A sample set of instructions is shown in Appendix 16.

Formal training sessions can consist of demonstrations, lectures on sanitation and personal hygiene, and special films, film strips, and training pamphlets on the correct way of serving are available through the State and National Restaurant Association. Informal training can occur in several ways. One good procedure is to call all the waiters and waitresses together a few minutes before the beginning of a banquet, and give everyone last-minute instructions on

- The nature of the group to be served
- The menu items to be served, and special instructions concerning them
- The order in which tables should be served, and the times when various items should be picked up off the tables
- Choices available to the guests
- Special time limitations imposed by the client
- Special assignments for selected servers

A brief orientation session is worth the time involved and enables the servers to do a better job.

Another good training method is to pair an inexperienced server with an experienced one, and let one teach the other.

Dress Code for Banquet Servers

While informality may be the dress norm on campus, it should not be permitted at a banquet which is generally a somewhat formal affair. The banquet manager has the duty to provide a type of service that blends in with the rest of the affair. While students generally do not like to dress up (there will be men students on campus who do not own a dress jacket, and women students who do not own a skirt), you have not only a right, but a duty to require that they do so when reporting for work in banquet service. Some schools actually furnish fancy waiter jackets and waitress uniforms to the students. Others furnish the usual white busboy coats and wrap-around smocks. Waiters may be asked to wear dark trousers, white shirts and ties, and the waitresses to wear dark skirts and white blouses. To compensate students for the extra cleaning costs involved, guarantee the service staff at least 2½ hours of work for a noon-time event, and 3 to 4 hours for an evening function. Service staff should wear proper dress shoes, and be neatly groomed when reporting for work. Hairnets required of food service production workers are not uniformly required for service personnel. Even the local health departments often permit waiters and waitresses with long hair to go without these, as long as the hair is confined in some other, acceptable manner. If you cannot supply your waiters or waitresses with uniforms, at least insist that they come dressed in dark pants or skirts, with white shirts and dark ties for the waiters, and white blouses for the waitresses. Supplying the waiters and waitresses with white gloves will fill two quality needs: it will enable them to pick up very hot plates without burning themselves, and it will also make an excellent impression on the guests at the banquet.

MAINTAINING QUALITY IN CATERING FUNCTIONS

Many of your clients will form an opinion about your food service on the basis of your catering service. Influential guests, such as trustees, regents, or important townspeople have little opportunity to judge your everyday efforts. They visit the campus for a day now and then and must therefore make their judgment as best as they can. Often their judgment is limited to dining experiences at catered functions. Some might argue that judgments from such outsiders are not as important as the opinions of the students who are the daily clients. Don't believe it. *Everybody's* opinion is important to you. In the case of students, you have the opportunity, at least, of explaining an occasional miscue, or of making up for a mediocre meal with an extraordinary one. In catering, you seldom get such second chances.

For these reasons, it is especially important that your quality standards be high, rigidly enforced, and continually upgraded. Menu items such as macaroni and cheese or turkey legs should never be served at a catered meal. Common or inexpensive entrees (e.g. fried chicken, meat loaf, lamb stew) should be avoided if at all possible. People can get these items at home often enough. When they attend a banquet in your dining hall, they are looking for something more festive, more exciting. For the same reason, you should avoid the use of paper plates or paper cups, or plastic utensils at catered affairs, except, of course, at large outdoor gatherings where they might be necessary.

Unless you are faced with rigid time limitations, you should not put the salad and dessert on the banquet table at the same time that people are eating their main dish. Every course should be served in order, and the plates for each course must be fully removed before the next course is served. At a quality banquet, this means that no dessert is placed on any table until every bread and butter dish, the bread baskets, and the salad dressings have first been removed. If you want to be absolutely correct, you would even remove the salt and pepper shakers before allowing the dessert to be served.

Insisting that every banquet plate is attractively garnished with a popular, edible garnish (parsley and crabapple rings are colorful but not very popular) is another important quality factor, as is the serving of tea and Sanka with individual pots of hot water, and the serving of lemon wedges whenever hot tea or ice tea is requested. In fact, the list of such little touches is endless. The important thing is that you are aware, that you care, and that you do not willingly agree to, permit, or contribute to the serving of a catering event of which you cannot be very proud.

CATERING POLICIES GOVERNING OPERATIONS

While it takes considerable skill to establish policies and office routines so that all catering requests are scheduled efficiently, equal skill is required to mesh such events into your regular kitchen production schedules, and to perform such catering without unduly interfering with everyday operations. Students are easily upset, if their dining room is closed for catering functions while they are asked to double up in another facility, with resultant long lines and other inconveniences.

The students are not your only concern when it comes to catering. Your regular kitchen people sometimes feel that their principal duty is to serve the campus community, and that you are imposing upon them if you ask them to prepare food for special catering events. This problem is not as prevalent in student unions, which depend on catering and do this regularly, as it is in residence halls, or in cash operations where catering is done only occasionally. Your job is not only to convince them otherwise, but to plan your catering activities so efficiently, that these can be meshed into your regular production without a tremendous kitchen upheaval. To do this is not as difficult as it sounds. The areas in your operations with which you must be concerned are largely those of purchasing, food production, the serving of food, dining room set-ups, types of service, and scheduling and feeding your crew of banquet waiters and waitresses.

Purchasing for Catering Functions

The key document for all catering activities, as mentioned earlier, is the catering function sheet. This sheet, which lists each menu item and the number of people to be fed, should serve as the basis for the kitchen manager's food requisitions. Unless a function is scheduled at the last minute, or a food item is especially hard to obtain, it is the kitchen manager's responsibility to have the necessary food on hand. Check with the manager before listing a specific food item. Sometimes you might actually order the item personally, and indicate this on the function sheet before it is sent to the kitchen. Communications between the catering office and the affected kitchen need to be close. A wise move is to phone the kitchen manager when a particularly large or troublesome function has been scheduled; another good procedure is to review all catering function sheets with all the managers at least one week prior to the scheduled dates.

Food Production for Catering Functions

A key to blending the catering food production with the regular work is to schedule enough personnel to do the work. The catering manager or food service director must know whether or not an extra cook, salad maker, or student worker is required to produce the additional food. When such extra help is needed and not provided, resentment builds up and the remaining kitchen crew feels that they are being overworked. On the other hand, scheduling is a prerogative of management, and every complaint of overwork is not necessarily legitimate.

Another important way to facilitate production for catering events is to inform the kitchen staff at least a day or two prior to the event. Post the banquet function sheets on the kitchen walls at the beginning of each week so that everyone can make adequate plans for the days ahead.

A way to ease catering production is to consolidate the menu whenever possible. There is no need to prepare two types of vegetables, potatoes, or even two types of desserts when, in fact, either the students or the banquet clients would be very happy to eat what the others are getting. This takes advance menu planning, knowledge of food costs and production capabilities, and authority to change menus if and when it is in the interest of the food service operation.

The Serving of Food for Catering Functions

Use of cafeteria counters for dishing up plates -- There are different ways in which the food can be dished up and served to banquet guests. The most common is to set up regular cafeteria lines and dish up the food when the guests are finishing their first course. In the case of small functions, say 100 people or less, this is often the simplest and most efficient way. Banquet plates can usually be dished up at the rate of about 10 plates per minute, so that each cafeteria line can dish up for 100 guests in 10 minutes or less, a very acceptable time period.

Heated plate carts -- If the number of guests gets up to 200 or more, however, cafeteria service becomes more difficult and more time-consuming. If banquet guests have to wait more than 15 or 20 minutes before the last person is served, you create an atmosphere of anxiety and unrest. Guests wonder why they have to wait so long, they worry if there is enough food, and the first ones served are finished before the last ones get their food. Therefore, unless you have additional serving lines available, consider pre-plating the main dish about 10-15 minutes prior to the start of the banquet, and placing these (with plate covers, stacked on top of one another) in pre-heated electric banquet carts. This is a procedure often used by commercial caterers in large banquets. Its advantage lies in the fact that, with each cart holding about 50-60 plates, you can have half of your dinner plates pre-dished prior to the start of serving. The disadvantage is that often the plates are too hot to handle, that sometimes the food has dried out and is not as fresh-looking as when served directly from the cafeteria counter. The way to overcome this problem is to dish up the main entree, potatoes and vegetable, but *not the gravy or garnish.* Then, when it is time to serve the meal, the plates are removed from the heated cart, the plate covers removed, the garnish and gravy added, the covers replaced and the plates then served. The advantage of filling the banquet carts prior to the meal is that, with an extra bowl of gravy and an extra pan of garnishes, you have actually created one additional serving area; in other words, two banquet carts loaded with 60 plates each, and one cafeteria line dishing up continuously, can probably serve 200 guests in less than 10 minutes.

Plate covers -- The key to both the cafeteria style service and the heated plate cart service is the careful timing (you cannot dish up food an hour in advance and expect it to look attractive) and the use of plate covers, without which the food quickly becomes cold. Many food service managers, unfortunately, feel that they can serve banquet plates without such plate covers and can do it quickly and efficiently, Most large hotels, however, have discovered that banquet plate covers are absolutely essential if the food service to guests is to remain piping hot between kitchen and dining room table. Follow their example and insist on banquet covers for every catering function.

Modified French service -- One of the most elegant methods of service at small parties (it is not practical with large groups) is to use a method of service which can be called, for want of a better term, "modified French service." In this method of serving, the catering manager or head waiter sets up a table in a corner of the dining room, to which platters and bowls of the entree, potato, gravy and garnish, and vegetable are brought. He then dishes up the plates in front of the guests and hands them to the waiters or waitresses who serve them to the guests. It is a very intimate and personalized way of dishing up food. If the platters used are attractive (silver platters are ideal, but even attractive china platters will do) and decorated before being sent into the dining room, this method will gain points with every guest.

Modified banquet service -- Occasionally you will encounter a group which either wants to save the money involved in full table service, or is in a hurry and cannot allow you the time it takes to serve a proper banquet. In such instances, you might suggest some sort of modification of regular service. The simplest modification, of course, is to place the first course and the salad, as well as the dessert on the table, and limit the waiter service to removing the salad plate, serving the main dish, and serving beverages. The main plate and dessert plates are then removed by the waiters or waitresses as they have the opportunity without, in any way, holding up the guests. Another successful modification is to set the tables with all the above items and have the guests come by a long table or cafeteria line where they pick up the main dish and then sit down at the banquet tables. In both instances you save serving time and reduce serving personnel.

Family-style service -- One of the oldest and friendliest methods of service is what is commonly called "family-style." This is a friendly and genial way of creating a relaxed atmosphere in the dining room. Food is placed on platters and in bowls, each enough to serve one table of 6-8 persons. Waiters place the bowls and platters on each table, and someone at each table acts as the host, or else the platters are passed from one to the other. This method is always successful with adult groups, but more difficult with students, who do not always limit their portions to a reasonable share. Furthermore, it is less formal, and more time-consuming than full banquet service. For that reason, it is not always popular with catering clients. Another possible disadvantage is that the use of serving bowls and platters almost inevitably invites requests for seconds, whereas regular banquet service generally precludes this possibility.

Unusual or fancy serving dishes -- The need for merchandising, so obvious to the restaurant owner, is often forgotten by the college or university caterer. Many believe that good and wholesome food is all that a guest expects. When it comes to catered functions, however, imaginative merchandising is as important on a college campus as it is in a fine restaurant. One way to make food look more interesting is to use some of the specialty dishes or serving platters available to hotels and restaurants. There are sizzling steak platters, special fish-shaped dishes for fish entrees, ceramic half shells for creamed seafood dishes, and wooden planks for serving steaks or cheese-and-fruit desserts. There are also casserole dishes for individual pot pies, shirred egg dishes for various breakfast and luncheon entrees, skewers for kabob entrees, and individual soup tureens for various types of soup. In addition, you can use champagne glasses for serving cold duck over raspberry sherbet, or creme de methe, Kahlua or Galliano over vanilla ice cream.

The "wave system" of serving -- When hotels or professional caterers serve large banquets, waiters and waitresses are normally assigned to specific stations. Each waiter has three to four tables assigned to him, and it is his responsibility to take care of his guests from the beginning to the end of the meal. This system works well when all the serving staff is experienced and dependable. In a college or university, the students are often not experienced, and assigning stations at a large banquet of several hundred people could mean that some table is forgotten or is not properly served.

For this reason, some food service managers use the wave system. Plates are served in order, beginning with the head table and gradually down to the other end of the dining room, somewhat similar to the way in which a wave washes on shore. Some prefer to serve the speakers *last,* so that when they start to speak, everyone else has eaten. The headwaiter or service supervisor stands near the head table next to some folding sidestands, while the waiters bring the trays of banquet plates. He then removes the banquet covers, while the rest of the waiters and waitresses serve the plates. As each row of tables is served, he moves the sidestands further down, and the process is repeated. While this is happening, several of the servers are assigned to start pouring coffee, or water.

It should be made clear that this system is not used to clear dirty dishes off the tables and not necessarily even for the serving of desserts, which is usually a much faster process. It is very practical for the serving of the main course, however, since it assures the supervisor that everyone gets served. It has an additional benefit in that it reassures the banquet guests, who see the wave of waiters and waitresses steadily moving towards them and thus know that they, too, will soon be served.

Decorating Dining Rooms and Tables

Decorating the dining rooms and the individual tables is normally left to the banquet host, who should assign someone on the host committee to perform this function. While there will be exceptions to this rule, the college or university food service is not ordinarily asked, nor should it be expected ot perform this function. Vases should be made available to the clients, as well as candlesticks and ashtrays.

Then there is the matter of table covers. At many luncheons, and even some informal dinenrs, paper placemats are quite acceptable, particularly if they are attractive ones showing the college seal, a college landscape or a prominent building. For formal banquets, only tablecloths and cloth napkins will do. White, gold, dark green, red, and checkered cloths are colors which most commercial laundries rent.

The host often wants to be permitted in the dining room several hours before the event in order to decorate the room and the tables, to hang banners and other decorations. Arranging to put the table cloths on the tables the night before or early in the morning, makes everything so much easier for the decorator who is trying to get a room ready for a luncheon banquet. Remember, that while the banquet involved may be merely one of a number that you have to take care of that particular week, it is of perhaps crucial importance to the host, and all the help and understanding that you can provide is needed and welcome.

Feeding Waiters and Waitresses

As obvious as it may appear, the feeding of banquet waiters and waitresses is not a clear-cut procedure and can cause you problems. First, there is the question of when to let them eat, then the question of what to feed them, and finally the question whether or not to pay them while they are eating.

Normally, it is a good idea to let the servers eat prior to the banquet. If waiters are hungry, they will often try to grab a bite here or there while serving the meal, whenever the supervisor is not looking. Needless to say, a chewing waiter or waitress makes a very poor impression on the guests and may interfere with the serving process. On a college campus, however, it is not always possible to get the students to appear an hour or more prior to the banquet, and so it is common to feed them afterwards.

When there is insufficient time for the servers to eat prior to the banquet, give them a sandwich or some small snack beforehand, to tide them over until after the banquet. Tender love and care for your serving crew will pay off in dividends of high morale, cheerfulness, and better service to the customers.

XV. SPECIAL EVENTS - THE MONOTONY BREAKERS

Once the excitement of leaving home has worn off, the doldrums set in. Students become homesick, worried about their studies, and bored with their food. Even if the food they get on campus is more varied and more plentiful than what they received at home, it just doesn't seem as good. After a while everything tastes the same and the students miss what they were eating at home. These feelings are particularly strong in late October and early spring, but the attitudes which they spawn, indifference or hostility toward the school in general, and toward food service specifically, can prevail throughout the school year. For this reason, food service directors came up with monotony breakers. These are events, both small and large, sprinkled into the food service program throughout the year to relieve the monotony of institutional food, impersonal service, sterile and often loud dining rooms, and all the other factors associated with large numbers and large institutions. There are different types of monotony breakers, and many ways of featuring each type. There are special dinners, unusual foods, birthday celebrations, special snacks, picnics, parties, and sometimes just changes from the everyday routine.

These special events are a standard element in college and university food service and are therefore a necessary and legitimate item in a college food service budget. Students rate their food service not only on the basis of good quality, but also on the basis of their general perception of the food services.

SPECIAL DINNERS

The most common form of monotony breaker is the special dinner which most residence halls plan at least once a month. Such a dinner should not be confused with the once-weekly steak dinner, which many contract caterers and some college-managed food services offer as part of their regular menu cycle. It is one thing to merely offer a steak on the dinner menu, but an entirely different thing to plan and provide a truly special dinner. Such a dinner, you see, is not merely one in which the menu is particularly popular. It is, rather, a very special effort on the part of the food service manager to make everything that happens during the dinner different and exciting. This includes the appearance of the dining room, the atmosphere (enhanced through music, different lighting, and the dress of the food service staff), the food itself, and at times, special entertainment and special gifts.

Nor is the special dinner reserved exclusively for students in residence halls. Various student groups, such as the Black students, Mexican-American students, Asian-American students, Jewish and foreign students all want and need a special event from time to time to enhance their sense of identity and support their campus activities. It is relatively easy for you to accommodate such requests. A soul food dinner is not difficult to prepare -- especially if you select those food items which are popular not only with black students, but also with the rest of the students. The same applies to Mexican food; since you know of the importance of Cinco de Mayo to the Mexican, you have all year to plan a special Mexican dinner on that particular day. Similarly, you should plan a Seder for the Jewish students during Passover: the addition of a few symbolic food items (such as a burnt lamb bone, a hard boiled egg, chopped seasoned apples, parsley and salt water) is not a difficult chore, and neither is the serving of Matzoh (unleavened bread) during the Passover holidays. Special dinners are a way in which you can show student groups you care for them.

Advance Planning

A successful special dinner is usually planned weeks, and sometimes months in advance. If the dinner is a normal holiday dinner (such as a Thanksgiving buffet or a Christmas dinner) menu planning is often simple and straight forward. The most popular entrees are still an old-fashioned steak, prime rib, or if the students ask for it, a turkey dinner at Thanksgiving. It is not too difficult to come up with a special first course, such as a cranberry shrub with cranberry juice and sherbet, or a fresh shrimp cocktail, an interesting vegetable such as peas with fresh mushrooms or broiled tomatoes, stuffed baked potato, and a popular or unusual dessert such as pumpkin pie, black bottom pie, or a chocolate whipped cream cake.

Planning the decorations, however, is more difficult. At the University of the Pacific, for example, dining hall managers plan such things months in advance. One summer the manager went up to the High Sierras to collect a carful of huge pine cones which, the following Christmas, were transformed into lovely gold and silver decorations. Another time, she gathered up large clusters of tumbleweed which, when sprayed and equipped with large pink paper ears, became Easter bunnies in the middle of each dining room. At yet another time, she gathered some student volunteers and made dozens of gilded angels out of paper mache. Wall decorations can be purchased months in advance in kits (there are Halloween, Thanksgiving, Christmas, Valentine's Day and Easter kits available), or they can be made by the staff (food service workers and resident assistants can make Christmas candles out of milk cartons, "stained glass" windows out of colored paper, etc.). In the case of international theme dinners, travel agencies, airlines, and the tourist information center of the various countries can be contacted for wall posters, menu covers and other printed material.

Advance planning includes also the early arrangements which must be made for entertainment, for special menus, dinner programs, and other souvenirs, as well as scheduling the event so it will fit in with the rest of the school calendar. Of particular importance is proper advance planning for publicity, so that everyone on campus, especially the students, knows when the event is to be held, and what is going to happen. For a list of steps taken at the University of Tennessee when planning a special event, see Exhibit XV-1.

Publicity, Menus, and Dinner Programs

Advance publicity can take many forms. It involves much more than merely placing the dinner on the campus calendar, or making up some announcements of the dinner. If the dinner is really going to be a super-extravaganza (such as an international or other special theme dinner) then you should consider placing an advertisement in the school newspaper. You might call the editor and ask for a reporter to

EXHIBIT XV-1

THE UNIVERSITY OF TENNESSEE
KNOXVILLE 37916
Food Services Department

SPECIAL EVENT PLANNING AND ARRANGEMENTS
By Jamesena M. Miller

I.   Planning
    A.   Selecting appropriate theme
    B.   Appoint and notify a committee
        1. Delineate duties and responsibilities
        2. Assign areas of coverage
    C.   Meeting with the committee
        1. State and define goals
        2. Decide on location, number anticipated, type of service, and menu

II. Coordinating and Arranging
    A.   Menu analyzed for authenticity and realism
    B.   Service method and area outlined and diagramed
    C.   Speed of service and time limits if any
    D.   Number of employees needed
    E.   Special equipment required and availability
    F.   Decor and special effects specifications, i.e., entertainment, workers' costumes, sound effects, and lighting
    G.   Budget structure
    H.   Outline other "special arrangements, i.e. security, crowd control, transportation, etc.
    I.   If necessary devise alternate plan, i.e. cookout rain plan.

III. Committee Meetings
    A.   Plan to meet with the committee as often as necessary, possibly three weeks before actual date of function and again one week before.
    B.   Meet with individual committee members as necessary to review each area.
    C.   Final meeting the day before the function - cover potential problems and cover each area for completion progress report.

IV. Actual Function Date
    A.   Observe each area and make notes of things that should be changed for future reference.
    B.   Observe clean up for time allotted, proper removal and storage of all equipment and debris and safety procedures used.

V.   Follow up
    A.   Evaluation of each area and the total function with committee members.
    B.   Completion of all financial arrangements
    C.   Thank you letters to those involved.

come and see you, so that you can share your advance preparations. Knowing that students appreciate souvenirs of special occasions, you should consider printing special menus for the event. One of your staunchest allies in this effort should be your school librarian. Most librarians will be happy to assist you in your preliminary search for photographs, art work, or recipes for your special occasions. Another ally is your campus director of information or public relations. The earlier you tell him what you are planning, the more publicity you will get, and the more successful will be your event. Your greatest allies in the effort to get good advance publicity are the students themselves. Two examples will illustrate this point:

- Several years ago, the University of the Pacific planned a special Latin-American dinner in honor of its many students from that part of the world. In preparation for this event, the school contacted Latin-American consulate offices in San Francisco and, approximately three weeks before the big dinner, drove approximately two dozen student representatives from the various Latin-American countries to meet their respective consuls in person and to hand them an engraved invitation to the upcoming dinner. In each case, the campus photographer took their pictures with the consul. These photographs were subsequently mailed not only to the consulates, but also to the two leading newspapers in that consulate's country. While in San Francisco, the students were treated to a special luncheon in a fine Mexican restaurant. They returned to campus full of excitement and enthusiasm, which they passed on to the rest of the student body. Many of the invited consuls attended the dinner which, as a result of this advance activity, turned out to be a huge success, and an effective recruiting aid for the university.

- One year, when there was an unusually large number of Hawaiian students in the freshman class, it was decided to plan a Hawaiian Luau as the theme dinner for that year. All Hawaiian students were invited to serve on a special Luau Committee, which met once a month for eight months to plan the event. The students suggested that the Luau be held outdoors, in May; that the college build a special stage, and that they, themselves, plan the entertainment. They then divided up the various tasks among them: one took charge of obtaining native plants for the outdoor stage, and baby orchids for all women on campus; another found a source of fresh pineapples, ordered directly from Hawaii; a third assumed the task of cooking the ceremonial pig in an underground pit. Others took charge of the entertainment, an exciting hour-long show, including dozens of Hawaiian men and women dressed in native costumes, doing Hawaiian dances; comedy relief, in the form of mainland students trying the hula on the stage for the first time, and a flaming sword dancer. Thousands of students and faculty members, attended the event. That evening, a special sense of belonging together united the entire campus community.

When planning an international dinner, it is a good idea to go a little beyond merely printing a dinner menu. The event should be an educational as well as a recreational experience, and you should make a point of educating the students about the customs and meal traditions of the country involved. Such information is readily available: American recipes are found in books such as the *American Heritage Cookbook,* foreign recipes in such volumes as the *Time/Life Foods of the World* series*. Examples of program notes are shown in Appendix 17.

Appearance of Dining Room

A cardinal rule for a special dinner: the dining room must *look different* than usual. College students are not always aware of what is going on around them, and you want to be certain that when you have gone to the trouble of planning a special dinner, that everyone entering the dining room is immediately aware that something special is going on. One way to do this is to decorate the walls and tables. Tablecloths are recommended and, if possible, the tables should be pre-set as at a banquet. In those dining rooms where each seat is turned over two or three times during a meal, extra students can be hired for the occasion to re-set each place. It is a good idea to change the table arrangement. For example, if many of the dining room tables are rectangular, these can be arranged in long lines of tables facing toward the middle (as spokes in a wheel), with the middle being a large round table on which are placed the special desserts, or the ice carving, punch fountain, or whatever. Each table should be decorated, with such items as candles, crepe paper streamers, special holiday napkins, berries, leaves, flowers from the garden, etc. In the case of a special theme dinner, some item or items depicting such a theme can be borrowed and placed in the dining room. In case of an indoor Western barbecue, for instance, a bale of hay, an Indian tepee, or a small tractor are ideal room decorations. In case of a New England dinner, a small sailboat and some netting and driftwood can make a nice central dining room decoration. Bright lights should be dimmed, whenever possible.

Special Dress and Costumes

One of the most effective ways to create a festive atmosphere is to get everyone to dress up. Costumes can be displayed at a contest sponsored by the food services and judged by the college president, the dean of students, or some other popular campus personality. Judging can take place in the middle of the meal period, be based on the volume of student applause, and be an informal, happy event. Prizes can consist of steaks, pizzas in the student union, or extra meal passes for guests.

At Halloween and other occasions students will dress up if they get a little urging from people they like. The same applies to your food service staff. While you cannot *insist* that your ladies wear long skirts when you have an old-fashioned American meal, the chances are that they will if you ask them. They will certainly wear kerchiefs for a Western hoe-down, or straw hats which you can give them for the occasion. You can purchase inexpensive caps, hats, paper aprons, and similar regalia to help create the right atmosphere. Suggest that your staff wear these uniforms or costumes the day before, to raise student participation.

**Foods of the World,* Time/Life Books, New York, 1969.

Needless to say, you set the example. You cannot expect others to get into the spirit of the meal, unless you are willing to do so. Exude an atmosphere of friendly relaxation and joy, if that is how you want others to feel. Be the first to put on a costume, or a funny hat. Everyone should know that you're going to have fun that night, and that all others are welcome to join you.

Special Food

The chief ingredient to a successful special dinner will always be the quality, interest, and variety of the food served. The trick is not only to select unusual dishes, but also those which college students will enjoy. While raw fish, poi, and pig's feet are undoubtedly genuine menu items in Japan, Hawaii, and Georgia, they are not items that will please college students at a special dinner. There are few willing to taste one of these unusual dishes. The criteria for menu item selection

- The item should be popular; if new, it should be well-accepted.
- The item should be different from those served in the regular menu cycle.
- Variety in the menu should be expanded.
- Food cost per meal served should be greater than usual.

It is difficult to come up with a special menu a day or two before the event. Plan these dinners months before they happen, and give others on your staff time to come up with some interesting menu suggestions. Trade magazines, cook books and recipes in daily newspapers are potentially good sources for such menus. If the recipe is given in small quantities, let someone experiment with it in larger quantities. If student workers help you in the preliminary tasting of unusual food items, you will spread good publicity throughout the campus.

Here are just a few examples of exciting and different foods:

- First course: fresh pineapple, shrimp, crab or seafood cocktail, antipasto platters, hors d'oeuvres
- Salad course: hearts of palm, hearts of celery, artichoke hearts, marinated asparagus, avocado, fresh orange slices
- Main entree: steak, prime rib of beef, shish kabobs, Cornish game hens, fresh crab, scampi, salmon
- Vegetables: fresh asparagus tips, fresh mushrooms, broiled stuffed tomatoes
- Potato: baked, stuffed, sweet potato patty with duchess potato ring, au gratin topped with bacon
- Dessert: ice cream pie, French pastries, individual fruit tarts, baked Alaska, fancy cheeses with crackers and fruit

Entertainment

If you are planning a special dinner, consider yourself more than just a food planner. Think of yourself, instead, as a composer trying to write a symphony and having to orchestrate all the parts. If you look at it this way, you won't feel as some do: "Entertainment is not my business," or "Let the students worry about that."

The right entertainment frequently makes dinner successful. Convince your music majors to perform at different events; you can have honky-tonk piano players, German bands, barber shop quartets, jazz bands, Christmas carollers, string quartets, or rock and roll groups (preferably reserved for outdoor picnics). Conservatory students like to perform in public, especially with a little encouragement (a small cash stipend, free meal passes).

If you are planning a special theme dinner, try to suit the entertainment to the occasion. If you have a Japanese dinner, for instance, you need a Japanese dancer or a Koto player, or two men who can demonstrate the art of Judo. If you have a Mexican dinner, you need a Mariachi band; if it is an American dinner, you may bring in some old-fashioned square dancers. Sometimes it is enough merely to provide the proper kind of recorded music and play it in all the dining halls. Dressing a student in a Santa Claus or Easter bunny outfit and having such a student give out candies or jelly beans to everyone is sure-fire entertainment. Having the food supervisors or faculty and administrators actually serve the students is equally entertaining.

Richard Gillis at the University of Arkansas has developed a special evening which he calls "Night at the Movies." He selects a simple but popular menu, similar to what students might buy when going to the movies, such as hot dogs, cheeseburgers, chocolate shakes, and banana splits, and then shows movies in the dining hall during the dinner meal. Short-reel comedies and cartoons lend themselves best to such a plan.

Handouts and Special Gifts

While it is easy to justify the expenditure of food service funds for such non-food items as decorations, menus, and within reason, even entertainment, it becomes more difficult when purchasing small gifts or other non-food items. Nevertheless, you should not hesitate to make modest expenditures necessary for the success of the meal. Chopsticks for a Chinese or Japanese meal, for instance, small flags for a Latin-American dinner, paper masks for a Halloween dinner, or Valentine cards for a Valentine's dinner are all appropriate and necessary.

With a little imagination, you can obtain small gifts or commercial handouts. The Florida Citrus Commission, for example, has given small fountain pens, the Sunkist Organization orange peelers, and other trade associations key rings, pencils, small notebooks, notebook covers, pamphlets on dieting and weight control, and similar goodies. If you give each student a small gift as he enters the door, it helps create the right mood. Give credit on your printed menu to everyone who has contributed something to the success of your dinner.

SNACKS AND MISCELLANEOUS MONOTONY BREAKERS

Not all monotony breakers need be super-extravaganzas like some of those just described. Some modest and simple surprises can reap the greatest joy. Having an open house in your bake shop is one example. Let everyone on campus come into your bake shop one morning to watch the bakers make bread and donuts. Give everyone a couple of free donuts. Invite the students the day before Valentine's day to come into the dining room in the afternoon and help decorate Valentine cookies, which they can then hang on a white tree in the middle of the dining room. Place whole loaves of freshly baked bread on the condiment counter, with cutting boards and bread knives, and let the students cut their own slices.

Snacks During Finals

The week preceding final examinations is probably the most difficult week for your students in the entire semester. Tension is great. Students often study all night through. They are worried and on edge. This is the time for you to make an extra effort. Not only should your regular menus be planned with special care, but extra snacks and beverages in the late evenings are a necessity. Open the dining halls from 9:00 p.m. to 11:00 p.m. the week before finals, and each night serve something slightly different in the way of light snacks and beverages, such as

- Hot donuts and sweet rolls
- Cookies, cakes, pies
- Popcorn, caramel corn
- Fresh fruit
- Make-your-own ice cream sundae
- Ready-made sandwiches, make-your-own-sandwiches
- Hamburgers, cheeseburgers
- Pizza
- Hot dogs
- Milk shakes, root beer floats
- Lemonade, punch
- Coffe, tea, hot chocolate

Snacks at Other Times

There are other times during the year when you can provide a special treat. If your football team comes back dejected from a game which they lost, why not have someone meet them at the airport at 1 a.m. in the morning with 10 gallons of hot chocolate and 12 dozen cookies? When your band leaves to play at a professional football game early on Sunday morning, why not open the dining hall for a continental breakfast or send a box full of sweet rolls and half-pints of milk with the bus? If your students have to line up for registration or for housing, or for any other purpose, why not be there with some goodies to show, again, that you care?

Birthday Celebrations

In recent years, companies have been formed which specialize in sending birthday cakes to students in colleges and universities. They pitch their sales toward the parents, many of whom eagerly embrace the opportunity to show their child that they love him and that they remember his birthday. A birthday is still an important event to someone of college age, and the food service manager should acknowledge this. It is impossible, of course, to celebrate everyone's birthday. You would have such celebrations daily. There are a number of things you can do, however, to let your students know that you understand the importance of their birthdays:

- Princeton University has, for years, celebrated its students' birthdays by having a fancy dinner party once a month. Everyone who has a birthday during that month is sent a special invitation. The affair is strictly dress-up, the dinner is elegant, and the students love it.

- A number of colleges and universities have their bake shops prepare and freeze small birthday cakes. Whenever someone has a birthday, he is presented with a cake. Some schools, which cannot afford to give such cakes away, have them available for purchase, and the student's friends are then encouraged to buy them at a very low price.

- The University of the Pacific, once a month, bakes a huge birthday cake in honor of everyone having a birthday during that month. The cake, which is composed of four 18" x 26" sheets, two layers thick, feeds over 500 students. It is decorated and inscribed with the words "Happy Birthday," followed by the appropriate sign of the zodiac. Even though the cake takes the place of the regular evening dessert, it gives everyone a good feeling and is therefore an effective monotony breaker.

Unusual Foods

Anytime you can come up with a new way of serving an old favorite, or an unusual food item you are creating a monotony breaker. The University of Tennesse, for example, once built a cherry pie seven feet in diameter; other schools have baked six foot long submarine sandwiches or roasted half a steer on an open spit. Students love such events, and you will enjoy the fun along with them.

Miscellaneous

There is no limit to the interesting things you can do to provide variety and spice to your food service program.

At Cornell University in Ithaca, Art Jaeger, the Director of Dining Services, has introduced a novel twist for Special Dinners: Each month he features a menu item from one of the prestigious restaurants in the United States. He works in close cooperation with the restaurant involved, uses their recipes, and tries to duplicate the item as faithfully as he can. Whenever possible, the owner or chef of the restaurant even comes up to lend a hand. Thus the restaurant gets good publicity, and so does Cornell University, whose students are thrilled with the excitement and the variety occasioned by these unusual meals.

While the monotony breakers discussed here are primarily for residence halls, they are by no means limited to that type of food service operation. The manager of a cash operation must be just as conscious of the need to diversify his offerings and create excitement if he wishes to retain his campus clientele. Here are a few more examples of successful monotony breakers:

- Good Nutrition Week: Send for hand-out pamphlets of weight control and nutrition from the U.S. Department of Agriculture. Set up a scale in the dining room, and let your campus physician or dietitian weigh each student who comes in the door (voluntary, of course!). Give everyone who is within the proper weight limit a big red apple. Have a table display of low-calorie and vegetarian dishes.
- Ice Cream Feed: Serve ice cream cones on a sunny afternoon on your patio or lawn.
- "Love Your Hashers Week": The week during Valentine's Day, give your hashers on the serving line special buttons and large name tags to promote friendship between the hashers and the students.
- Surprise Breakfast Buffet: Without advance notice, surprise your students some morning by having a lavish buffet instead of the usual breakfast.

For additional monotony breakers, see the list in Appendix 18 which was prepared by the Food Services Techniques Committee of the National Association of College and University Food Services.

THOROUGH ADVANCE PLANNING

Nothing fails as dismally, or destroys morale more than an extravaganza that fails to come off. If you have ever put on a reception which almost no one attended, you will understand. If you have sponsored a special food promotion item which no one bought, you will understand. If you every planned a campus-wide picnic, and only twenty-percent of your students showed up, you will understand. Regardless of how you may rationalize such disasters, the real reason for failure, more often than not, is lack of proper planning.

Good advance planning includes many factors. One is the *timing* of the event. Few students will voluntarily come to a 9:00 a.m. breakfast on a weekend, and fewer still will want to attend a costume ball during finals week. Faculty members usually guard their weekends zealously, and campus support personnel don't like to stay for any event after normal working hours. Another planning factor is the *popularity* of the event. String quartets will turn off many students, just as loud rock music disturbs most faculty members. You can plan the nicest Christmas dinner for your food service employees, but if they have to cook it first, chances are they will not enjoy it. A third factor is *client involvement*. The more clients you can get involved in the preliminary planning, the better your chances for ultimate success. Often your most successful events are thought up by students in a particular residence hall, modified or expanded by you, and then joined in by the rest of the campus community. A crucial element in advance planning is *publicity*. Your duty is to make certain that everyone who might want to know about your planned event is notified. This involves much more than merely printing up posters; it involves *taking whatever steps are needed to make sure that proper dissemination of information takes place!* Another advance planning factor is proper *budgeting* for special events. The extra and unusual costs of special events can often be compensated for by judicious menu planning prior to and following the event. Often student governments, residence hall social funds, funds from academic departments with special interest in the event being planned, and even the president's special fund can be tapped for financial assistance. Here are some specific examples of fund sources:

- The student government might sponsor a band to play at an all-campus barbecue.

- The residence hall social fund might help underwrite a "big brother" or "big sister" day, where students in the halls host disadvantaged children for a dinner or party.

- The modern languages or ethnic studies departments might share some of the costs of printing or similar expenses for special theme dinners involving their academic discipline. Similarly, the department of athletics may be convinced to contribute to a campus-wide tail-gate party prior to an important football game, or the political science department can fund the costs of hosting some local politicians at a town-and-gown function.

- For unusual expenditures, which would benefit the campus as a whole, but for which funds cannot be found anywhere else, the president's special fund is a sure bet. If you can get a governor, or a cabinet officer to visit the campus for a special event, the president is sure to fund the related costs. If you have a truckload of food for emergency relief in case of a natural catastrophe, paid for by the students, and you need to cover the costs of a truck to send the food, see the president.

XVI. PUBLIC RELATIONS - FORMULA FOR SUCCESS

Earlier in this book, you read about the importance of creating a favorable image among the campus community from the moment you arrive. You learned the importance of developing an outgoing, friendly personality. Most important, perhaps, you learned that the success of your food service operation depends not only on the quality of the food or the cost-effectiveness of your operations; it depends equally on how others on campus perceive the campus food service, and how they perceive you. These are truisms often not recognized by food service managers. If they were recognized, more attention would be paid to good public relations, and college food service directors would enjoy greater recognition.

Good public relations do not "just happen;" they have to be planned, created, and nourished. A professional P.R. man is much sought after in industry, and possesses skills which include an ability to understand the needs and wishes of others, a sensitivity to other people's feelings, and an ability to get along with them. On a college or university campus, these skills include a knowledge of campus politics: recognizing where the authority for decision-making is vested and who possesses the ability to influence the opinion of others.

Influencing the opinion of others is a key aspect in any public relations effort. In college and university food service, acceptable performance is not merely serving wholesome, nutritious, and tasty food, but also doing it in a manner that is pleasing to the majority of students and faculty. An increase in the board rate in a time of inflation does not necessarily have to be viewed as bad news, if the announcement is handled professionally so that students and their parents understand that an increase is necessary.

Another important public relations skill is the ability to predict what will create favorable publicity for campus food services, and to plan thoroughly in advance. Steps to assure maximum public relations impact should include

- Early involvement of campus P.R. officers
- Early publicity (through campus newspaper, posters, flyers) to campus community
- News releases to local news media; where appropriate, invitations or free tickets sent to media representatives
- Use of campus print shop for advance notices, menus, programs, tickets, etc.
- Invitations to appropriate campus officials (student, faculty, and administration leaders)
- Involvement of many people in the event itself
- Creation of photo opportunities for future use in slide shows, articles, alumni newsletters, etc.

THOROUGH ADVANCE PLANNING

There are four basic steps in public relations: 1) fact finding or research, 2) planning, 3) communications, 4) evaluation. Whatever you wish to do in food service, make certain that you have all your facts. Student tastes vary from year to year, as do their attitudes. The value of periodic questionnaires lies not only in showing your students that you are interested in their opinions, but also in determining what it is that they really want. There is no specific form, or set of questions that is better than all others. You can change your questionnaires every year. You can prepare "mini-questionnaires" with only one question. You can have someone go around and talk with students about specific matters. The important thing is not how you prepare a questionnaire, but that you get accurate, honest feedback from your students and that they learn from you what you are planning to do with such information.

Your second step, planning, follows fact-finding. Any special activity, whether it is a dinner, a new menu selection in your cash operations, or even the implementation of a new policy requires careful public relations planning. Certain questions are natural in the process of such planning:

- Is this what the students really want?
- If not, how can we best explain why it is necessary?
- Is this the right time?
- Is this the best way?
- What will be the general reaction?
- How can we do it so that it will be accepted by the majority?

Once the basic research and planning has been done, your job will then be communicating with your campus clientele and, after everything is over, evaluating your activities to see if they produced the proper results. A sample student questionnaire is shown in Exhibit IX-2, and a sample response letter is shown in Exhibit XVI-1.

INVOLVING THE CAMPUS PUBLIC RELATIONS OFFICERS

The public relations department of a college or university is a service department, ready to assist anyone on campus who has a public relations problem or opportunity. But it is astounding how often this fact is forgotten by professors who invite interesting speakers, students who perform social services in the community, or maintenance men who invent labor-saving devices. Among those who miss opportunities for public relations assistance is the food service director. He often believes that the campus P.R. officer exists primarily to edit the college catalog, put out the alumni newsletter, and place an occasional article about the college in the local newspaper. Actually, your public relations officer can be of significant help to you whenever you are planning a special event. He knows whether an event will be newsworthy and has personal contacts with media representatives. Your P.R. officer also has the technical skills which can aid you in the preparation of publicity

EXHIBIT XVI-1

UNIVERSITY OF THE PACIFIC
Stockton, California 95211

January 30, 1975

Letter to All U.O.P. Students
From: Paul Fairbrook

Hi!

Welcome back from your winter term! I spent part of this month reading and reacting to your questionnaires which, contrary to popular belief, do get our most careful attention and are generally very helpful. We have adopted a number of excellent suggestions and have responded to some valid complaints about the food service. We have intituted such things as:

1. Asked our line servers to pay more attention to your requests.
2. Improved the pizza recipe in the dining halls.
3. Added Root Beer in Callison.
4. Expanded the Rathskeller menu both at night and at noon.
5. Sped up the lines (we hope) in the Mall.
6. Re-hired Gary Verzani for next year.
7. Added second toasters in Grace Covell (Callison will soon follow).
8. Purchased diet salad dressing for the dining halls.
9. Revised your vegetarian menus, including the health food sandwiches in the Mall.
10. Margarine patties will be offered in addition to butter.
11. Soup is added to some dinner menus.
12. Arranged for finals snacks for Conservatory students.
13. Set up both lines at every lunch and dinner.

As you probably know by now, we also had to raise the board rates by 7% ($50-$60) to keep up with the spiraling food prices this past fall, especially canned goods and staples, which rose an average of approximately 20%. It does appear that the spiral has now levelled off, at least temporarily, and we are hoping that food prices may stay that way for awhile.

A week ago we opened the Redwood Room in the University Center for lunch, Monday through Friday. This is intended to be a quiet, somewhat fancier eating place than any other place on campus. You can use your meal ticket there, but will have to supplement it by $.65 cash. I think you will enjoy the different atmosphere and the waitress service available to you there. Your two free guest passes, incidentally are fully valid in the Redwood Room.

If, after all this, you still have to wait in line in the Mall, or find that we sometimes run out of a certain food in the dining room, or out of room to sit in the Rathskeller, *please don't get too angry!* Just keep letting us know your problems and we'll try to straighten them out to the best of our ability.

Sincerely,

Paul Fairbrook

material. He can show you how to get maximum mileage out of your special event.

PUBLICITY TO CAMPUS COMMUNITY

It is hard to get the attention of a college student. It is even harder to interest a faculty member. Bombarded with a variety of cultural and recreational offerings day after day, they become almost immune to even the most exciting event on campus. Posters, unless dragged by airplane or strung across roadways, barely attract attention. Tent cards on dining room tables are slightly better, because at least they are read between bites of food. Spot announcements on the campus radio station can be very effective, especially in the evening, when the students are listening. Best of all, however, is an early start to a publicity campaign, followed by repeated announcements right up to the day of the event. You must create a desire to participate in the event. Once having done that, you must remind people that the date of the event is approaching and finally that the day itself has arrived.

RELEASES TO NEWS MEDIA

Deciding what information should be given to the news media, how it is to be presented, and to whom it is to be given is no job for an amateur. Knowledge of the specific needs and interests of a newspaper or a radio station requires technical training and professional expertise. The ability to evaluate each story in terms of its possible publicty effect for the institution comes only after long experience. So does knowing which of several stories is the most important, and how often the media can use a story from your college. Any story or release should be cleared with your campus P.R. people.

A P.R. specialist does not have a corner of good ideas, however, nor should anyone stop you from establishing direct contacts with media representatives. If you are going to be a credible source of interesting information, reporters and editors should know you personally, and appreciate the special knowledge you bring to your job as food service manager. Whenever the society editor is interested in a special dinner event, the foods and nutrition editor is interested in a recipe, or a news reporter is interested in rising food prices, the person to be contacted should be you, and not the public relations representative.

There is nothing wrong in sending media representatives free passes for one of your special dinners, or suggesting to the campus newspaper editor that your innovations for the coming year would make a good story. The trick is to make certain that the publicity is not only good for campus food services, but also for the institution itself.

Learn to recognize material for a good human interest story or an article for a trade magazine. If one of your cooks is particularly good with vegetarian entrees, for example, the foods editor of your local newspaper might be interested. If another is an expert at making quilts or collecting butterflies, the society editor might be interested.

You can see from the above, that dealing with the news media, while a very important part of your public relations effort, is not a simple task. By developing a close and harmonious relationship with your public relations department, you can obtain maximum publicity mileage for your efforts without stumbling unnecessarily in the process.

USING THE CAMPUS PRINT SHOP

One of your allies in public relations efforts is the manager of the campus print shop. Considering the cost-effectiveness of printed material for food services, it is amazing that more food service managers are not taking full advantage of this opportunity. You can get special menus printed for pennies, and yet the effect of such a menu on parents and relatives of your students can be of inestimable value. When you spend thousands of dollars on expensive steaks, you can afford to spend a hundred on publicizing the meal. The list of materials that can be printed for you on your own campus is endless, but here are some examples

- Business cards
- Meal passes
- Menus, special dinner programs
- Tent cards, flyers
- Posters, signs
- Reprints of articles, newspaper stories
- Recipes, food service newsletters
- Food service handbooks

As long as you are going to have something interesting printed, why not print an extra thousand copies, and hand these out to parents, prospective students, and other campus visitors? Better yet, why not establish a special information section with a special bookshelf displaying these hand-outs? You would be amazed at how many printed items of interest to campus visitors can come out of a campus food service office each year. Furthermore, most of these items are of interest indefinitely, so you can get them re-printed when you have handed out the first batch. After a few years you will have a collection which is impressive not only to your staff, but also to those campus visitors who will come away from your office with pages of information about your campus food service.

The material you publish need not be limited to re-prints of special menus, or favorable newspaper articles. A letter to your students about good nutrition, a food service questionnaire, a list of garnishes, salad plate combinations, recommended portion sizes, and even memos to your staff about sanitation, handwashing, and personal hygiene are suitable subjects for handouts to visitors. True, some of those last mentioned might be reserved for food service visitors from other colleges, but many of them are of genuine interest to the layman. In every case, a visitor who has been given a handful of printed materials about your food service will come away favorably impressed with your operation. Samples of such reprints are shown as exhibits throughout this book as well as in Appendix 19.

INVITING CAMPUS OFFICIALS AND OTHERS

Did you every hear a fisherman tell the story of the big fish that got away? If the story is true, his chagrin lies not only in the fact that the fish got away, but that there was no one in sight to see the fish as it was being hooked. Many food service managers feel the same way when they successfully stage a special dinner which is attended exclusively by students. At such special occasions, it is gratifying for the entire food service staff if some of the important campus officials also come and enjoy the dinner. They will come -- usually with great pleasure -- if you ask them. The wrong attitude is "They know what's happening, let them come on their own." The right one is: "I would really like them to come, so I'm going to invite them." The matter of who is going to pay for the dinners of these officials should not stand in the way of your invitation. On many campuses, you will have the right to invite, on behalf of the students, selected members of the faculty and administration. You can work with student officers and let them make the invitation. On some campuses, particularly in state-supported colleges and universities, you may not have the right to pay for such invited guests out of food service funds. No matter. Invite them anyway, and if necessary, tell them it is "Dutch treat." At the very least, give your faculty and administration members an opportunity to come on their own by properly informing them of the upcoming event. What applies to faculty and administration also applies to student leaders. Often student government presidents or members of the student senate do not live in the residence halls and would therefore not participate in a special food service event. It is in your interest, and in the interest of good public relations, that they attend these functions. Here again, the question of who will pay for the dinner should not stand in the way of the invitation.

What applies to campus officials, also applies, from time to time, to outside guests such as community leaders, newspaper editors and reporters, and others. In all of these cases, your public relations officer can advise you who to invite, and just how an invitation should be tendered.

INVOLVING MANY PEOPLE IN THE EVENT

It is axiomatic in public relations that the more people you can get involved in an affair before it actually happens, the better your chance for success in the event itself. This applies as much to a special campus dinner as it does to homecoming. One group of people who should get excited about what is being planned are the food managers and supervisors, who will have to oversee everything. Food service workers, who will have to prepare the food and student food service employees, who will not only help with the preparation, but who will also be effective publicists for the event should also be involved. Students eating in the dining rooms, who will come if the event excites them, and finally the general campus community, whose curiosity and enthusiasm will assure a successful participation, need to be drawn in by publicity.

Involving all these groups in advance is not difficult. In your advance planning, you have probably shared the original concepts with all the food supervisors, and may even have assigned the planning job to a small committee. When you come up with unusual recipes, some of your food service employees will probably make up sample batches for tasting. If you call in some students to help you taste these interesting dishes, you will, in all probability, have some more boosters. Finally, if you take your Scandinavian cookie sample, your novel Hawaiian pineapple dessert or your Filipino "lumpia" to some of the campus offices and let faculty and staff members taste them, you will have created an advance rooting section that will assure you good and enthusiastic participation.

CREATION OF PHOTO OPPORTUNITIES

No amount of words can reproduce the sight of one of your students, dressed up in diapers and being pushed around in a shopping cart, or dressed like one of the creatures from *Star Wars,* or of the cook dressed as a Christmas present, Jack and his beanstalk, or Little Bo-Peep. Nor can you every adequately describe the beautiful ice carving or gingerbread house made by your cook for the Christmas dinner, or the Valentine Cookie Tree, or the colorful Easter Egg Mold prepared for your special dinners. The only way to describe them adequately is to take color photographs of the event. Unless you are very public-relations conscious, you may not think of this beforehand. More likely, you will berate yourself later, saying: "I wish I had had a camera."

The last person who should have the job of taking photographs is yourself. Not only have you many other things to do and to supervise, you will look a little ridiculous taking pictures to commemorate your own extravaganzas. Much better that you request the campus photographer, or hire a student photographer, to do this for you. A couple of complimentary dinner tickets, and your willingness to pay for film and developing will do wonders. If no photographer is available, ask one of your assistants to bring a camera.

These photographs can be used later to make slides for an impressive presentation. You and your staff will have dozens of opportunities to show these slides and to give talks about the campus food services. In fact, a set of 80 well-taken slides, illustrating all aspects of your campus food service, makes an ideal basis for talks to various community and civic groups, for recruiting, fund-raising, and other public relations purposes. If the quality of the slides is good enough, they can also be used as transparencies to illustrate articles in trade magazines and other publications. If not, it is often wise to take black and white photographs for this specific purpose (as well as for use by newspapers), in addition to the color slides. Color prints are a permanent record of your special events. They can be used in recruiting new food service personnel, or for on-the-job training of new employees.

FREE FOOD AND FREE PASSES

There are food service managers who feel that there should be no limit on how freely they dispense meal passes or donuts and coffee, as long as these contribute to good feelings about campus food service. There are others who believe that a food service manager is a trustee of student funds and that no one has the right to give such food away. The answer, as happens so often, lies somewhere in the middle. Certainly it is true that the food service manager has no right to dispense food indiscriminately. Especially on state-supported campuses, where rules are often much stricter than in private colleges and universities, discretion is advisable. But the ability of the food service manager to extend meal invitations, or to invite someone for coffee and donuts is a powerful public relations tool and should not be overlooked. Wise college officials recognize this fact, and allow the food service managers a reasonable leeway. For those who are especially budget-conscious, free food or free passes dispensed by the food service manager can be included in an item marked "promotion" or "public relations." However it is handled, the total cost of such favors is an insignificant part of the entire food service budget. But look at the favorable return you get from such an investment. A free pass will

- Help to mollify an angry student who may have been wrongly treated in the dining halls
- Please and impress parents visiting their children on campus (in private preparatory schools, such invitations to visiting parents are done as a matter of course)
- Make possible the quiet and relaxed atmosphere often necessary for the discussion of problems with other members of the campus community
- Establish a better relationship with salesmen, who normally expect to take their clients out to lunch, instead of being invited themselves

Giving out free donuts and coffee cake occasionally will have similar beneficial effects. Among these are

- Greater readiness on the part of maintenance personnel to respond quickly to emergencies in the food service areas
- A warm feeling of appreciation on the part of secretarial and other support personnel at the unexpected treat
- Greater appreciation of food service by students, who may be treated to such goodies unexpectedly while holding a meeting or other activity

Wholesale or indiscriminate giving is not being suggested. Instead, a carefully planned and reasonable program involving such favors is recommended as part of an overall public relations effort by campus food services. Those who already believe in giving out free passes and free food to their campus constituents should be warned: nothing above suggests that you do this recklessly, irresponsibly, and in any manner that could cause censure or other problems for your food service organization. The best approach is for the food service director to lay out a carefully planned program, with a specific budgeted dollar amount, have it approved by his superiors, and then have this implemented by his managers in accordance with clear and defensible guidelines.

DEALING WITH NEW STUDENTS AND THEIR PARENTS

During the past decade, the process of introducing new students and their parents to the campus has been developed into a fine art. Whether this process is condensed into an afternoon or even a single day, or whether it becomes a two- or three-day affair, the objectives are similar: to orient the students to their new surroundings, to inform them and their parents about major aspects of their new life, and to accomplish some of the preliminary activities such as registration and payment of fees before classes begin. Usually the orientation program is organized by the student personnel department, and food service personnel are given a minimal part in such proceedings. Somehow, the reasoning goes, students and parents will find the dining rooms, and anything they might want to know about food service can be explained there.

Such reasoning is as unfortunate, as it is erroneous. Concern about campus food service ranks very high on the list of worries that students and their parents bring with them to campus. Many mothers are accustomed to expressing love for their children by the food they prepare and are thus especially anxious about the food on campus. Many of the students wonder if what they have heard about institutional food service is really true. Others have real or imaginary dietary problems and wonder if their special needs can be satisfied. For these reasons, it is essential that the food service director have an important part in any orientation program.

In this context, it should be noted that new students, if addressed without their parents, require a different approach than do their parents. New freshmen retain very little, if anything, of what they learn during orientation. The absorb the endless mass of facts being poured over them like a sponge absorbs water. Unfortunately, most of it is squeezed out shortly after it is absorbed. Students make little attempt to remember anything for very long, and assuage their conscience by telling themselves that they can always learn about it later. For this reason, it is wise not to confuse them with too many facts. Introduce them to the food managers with whom they will come in contact, let them know where and how they can make wishes heard, and give them a "lift" -- a feeling that they will be taken care of well, by people who are anxious to please. If you get these points across, you will be successful in any orientation.

Parents of new students, however, require much more than that. Their curiosity goes much deeper, and their interest span is wider. When talking with parents, share the good features of your food service operation. Tell them about the flexibility in meal hours and dining areas, your menu patterns, vegetarian program, salad bars, special dinners, birthday celebrations, etc. Do this not in a somber, didactic way, but with joy and self-confidence, with some humor sprinkled in and with a slight self-deprecation that tells the listeners that you, as they, are only human. Be sure, also, to give the parents something to take home: sample menus, interesting recipes, reprints of articles about your food service, etc. Whatever you give them, they will read it. Parents of new students are a willing audience, so make the most of this one-time opportunity.

RELATIONS WITH OTHER FOOD SERVICE PROFESSIONALS

It has been suggested earlier that active participation in professional organizations such as the National Association of College and University Food Services can increase your knowledge of food service management. It can also establish valuable contacts, which can be sources of information and assistance when you need it. Most professionals are generous with their time and assistance, whenever a colleague needs them. Establishing personal friendships with other food service managers can also help you in your public relations efforts. It is important that your peers in other institutions know about you and your work. What others in your field think about you can have a tremendous impact on your reputation. Remember that other food service managers have children of their own, and that many of these are friends and relatives of your students. Remember, furthermore, that a food service reputation good or bad, is quickly disseminated among college commmunities. Students or faculty who visit your campus will almost certainly report their food experiences to the food service director of their own campus.

For these reasons you should make a special effort to cultivate the friendship of other food service professionals in your area. Visit them, invite them to the campus, take trips together, phone each other, and generally keep in touch. Everyone benefits from such contacts.

BLOWING YOUR OWN HORN

Most people are afraid to point out their accomplishments. They feel, with some justification, that when a person is really good he does not need to praise himself, since others will do it for him. Modesty is an acknowledged virtue. To some it comes naturally, while others force themselves to at least give an appearance of modesty. The client's perception of the food service depends only partly on the taste and the quality of the food. An equally important factor is his feeling about the food service operation and the people who staff it. It is to this latter perception that you must address yourself by consciously and actively reinforcing the positive impressions your food service gives.

Start by developing a healthy self-confidence. If you feel good about yourself, about what you do, about your staff and your whole operation, it is much easier to show pride in it. Recognize that if you don't tell others about all the good things being done in your operation, they will never know. Assuming you are subtle in the way you go about it, there is nothing wrong with disseminating positive information about your food service. Some readers may feel that it is all right to boast about a food service operation, and the people who work in it, but that it is poor taste to praise yourself. Not always. Americans identify a food service operation with a particular person. Perhaps this is a holdover from the old inns, where the innkeeper was the central figure. In any case, many of the successful restaurants carry the name of their owner (DiMaggio's, Henrici's). Capitalize on this by helping your clients identify *you* with your food service operation.

Be visible, and vocal in your expression of confidence for your food service operation. Make a personal appearance, however brief, at all important catering functions. Even if you have delegated the supervision to others, it is reassuring for the clients to see the manager at their function. Pay frequent visits to the dining halls and other food service areas, and talk informally with the students and faculty. Fill in at different places in the food service operation (cashier, counter, bus boy) to show everyone that you like to set a good example for your staff. This is particularly helpful during rush periods, when your intervention for a few minutes can help break a logjam. Personalize your leadership by signing important memos, notices, letters to students, etc. with your own name rather than "University Food Service," or with no name whatever.

This chapter would not be complete without a reminder that the most effective way to impress others with your own accomplishments is to point out those of your assistants, whose loyalty and performance make everything possible. Remember always that praise given to them also reflects on you, and that the better they look, the better you look.

XVII. RELATIONS WITH FACULTY AND STAFF

Ask anyone on your campus why he prefers to work at a college rather than in business or industry. The answer is usually the same: "I like the atmosphere on campus." Just what is meant by that, and how does it affect you?

When someone talks about the special atmosphere on campus, he means that there is a spirit of friendship and cooperation, of intellectual and professional communion, found on a college or university campus which is rarely found elsewhere. While no one should minimize the bickering and jockeying for position and favor which occurs whenever large numbers of people work within an organization, the work atmosphere on a campus is significantly different than in business and industry. The main reason for this is the difference in objectives: in business and industry, the principal objective is to make a profit, preferably a bigger profit than was made the previous year. At a college or university, the principal objective is to educate young people in the best possible manner and to do so, if possible, within a balanced budget. This difference is one of the main reasons why those working at a college or university prefer to remain there. It may be one of the reasons why you are working on a campus.

Anyone who wants to be successful in his dealings with faculty and campus staff must thoroughly understand and be in basic agreement with such an attitude. It affects everything that goes on, and the way people work with and relate to each other. In industry, for example, the person in authority generally has the last, and sometimes the only, word. He gives orders, and others obey. On a college campus, it doesn't always work that way. A tenured faculty member can publicly disagree with the college president, and still be sure of keeping his job. Rank and position, though important, are not automatic indicators of either ability and authority. The emphasis is on harmony and cooperation, even at the expense, occasionally, of efficiency and logic.

You may not agree with the above. In fact, you may easily point to examples on your own campus which disprove some of it. Nevertheless, it is generally true. You must be aware of it, and let this awareness guide your relationships with others. The line between academic and social activities, for example, is hard to draw. The concern of a teacher for what the students eat is as legitimate as your concern about what they may be doing in class or after hours. A dean's interest in the appearance of the dining hall is as natural as your own interest in the students' living situation. Successful food service managers, therefore, see themselves as part of a campus community, and are guided accordingly in their dealings with others on campus.

Specifically, this means that friendships with members of the faculty should be cultivated. Faculty should be as interested and familiar with what you are trying to achieve in college food services, as you should be with some of their own academic objectives and accomplishments. New faculty members should be encouraged to eat with the students as often as possible. Food problems in connection with field trips or other events should be quickly and pleasantly solved. Faculty criticisms of your food service should be given the same concern and attention as criticisms from administrators or students. Members of the support staff deserve equal attention. The gardener who brings you flowers for the dining room, the plumber who fixes your leaks, and the departmental secretary who calls in catering orders -- these too are people on whose good will you depend, and who look to you for friendship.

On the other side of the coin, you must regard yourself as an equal to others on campus. You are neither the head cook nor the local hamburger king. You are one of many professionals, and as food service manager, the most qualified on campus to solve food service problems.

In past years, on many campuses, expectations of the food service manager were sometimes not as high as they should have been. Consequently, the perceptions of these managers of their own role on campus may also have been faulty. This has changed. The college and university food service manager is now a highly trained individual, with many years of experience in a complex and technical field of specialization. His or her role in the process of helping the student to grow, to mature, and to learn is crucial.

This new role must be recognized by all food service managers if they are to have the status commensurate with their responsibilities and if they are to be successful in their assigned tasks.

XVIII. RELATIONS WITH STUDENTS

It is hard to fully understand the frustrations, uncertainty, lack of self-confidence and rebelliousness which characterize the age between puberty and adulthood. It is difficult to deal with young people who at one moment want to be accepted as adults (when they criticize your food) but at another, crave a more personal concern (when they confess to being lonely and homesick). An understanding of, and sympathy for the problems of your students are essential requirements for successful job performance.

Take the matter of honesty, for example. Students should have been taught honesty at home and by the time they get to college, they should know that it pays to be honest. The problem is that what may seem dishonest to you may appear to the students to be only a minor infraction of a rule. "Ripping off" food, for example, is a time-honored, sacred sport. Faculty laugh about it, students revel in it, and only you and your staff consider it stealing. Your job, therefore, is to regard yourself as an educator with potential impact on the character development of a student rather than a disciplinarian, whose prime emphasis is on enforcing the rules. When students yell obscenities at you, they are exhibiting symptoms of problems with which they have not learned to cope. Your yelling back won't help solve them. When students climb through the window into the kitchen at night, the act is not criminal but foolish. When they throw food at each other, your food is not really the problem. When they make a major issue out of some minor matter, they are merely exhibiting a characteristic of their age.

What matters is not only your conception of your students or even their parents' conception, but also how the students view themselves. College students regard themselves as fully grown young adults. Accept them as such.

The best relationship you can have with college students, however, is that of a friend. When you are friends, age differences don't matter. When you are friends, problems are easily solved. In fact, when you are friends, problems usually are resolved before they become serious. It is easy to become friends with students. Start by getting to know them by name. Nothing sounds sweeter than the sound of one's own name, so make it a point to know as many names as possible. Remembering names is not an inherited talent, it is hard work, a result of a concentrated and conscientious effort. It must be a primary step in your development of friendly, personal relations with students. Another way to establish friendships is to show your interest in some special way. Your football players like to see you at the games, and have you talk about them the next day. Your music students expect you to attend some of their recitals, and your sorority girls want you to buy something at their cookie sale. Individual attention is a good way to promote friendship. Giving a dieting student an apple in lieu of dessert is not nearly as much of a problem as some people make it out to be. Buying some raisins and bean sprouts for vegetarians, or some wheat germ for health food devotees is not either. Sitting down and talking with them during mealtimes, especially if they are sitting alone, is probably the best of all prescriptions for friendship. Don't listen to those who might counsel you: "Students do not want to be disturbed; if they want friends, they don't want you," or "You're not getting paid to sit down and just talk." Such advice may be true at one time or another, but as a general rule of conduct for a food service manager it is wrong.

There are times, of course, when your desire for friendship must take a back seat. These are the times when you have overriding responsibilities as a college official, such as when destruction or theft of college property is concerned. It is hard to change roles suddenly, and students are often incredulous when the friend turns into a disciplinarian. You will find, however, that students are basically fair-minded and will in the long run understand your sometimes conflicting responsibilities. "Fair, Firm, and Friendly" is a good motto to remember in such difficult situations. It is an approach that will carry you safely over the roughest spots.

CONCLUSION

Having read this book, you will have noticed that much of it deals with ways of being of service to others: service to students, faculty, staff, and administration of the college. The pleasure that you get from helping others is great indeed, but the desire to serve cannot come from a book -- it must be within you from the start. To be successful in college food service work, you must enjoy your work and the fact that because of your work others live a happier life. The word "service" in food service is a key word: if you remember what it stands for, and what you and your staff must do to live up to it, you will be successful.

This book is going into print at a time when major changes are around the corner in college and university food service. Apartments are rapidly replacing residence halls as the favorite place for students on campus. Women students are becoming more diet-conscious and therefore eat less while attending college. Both men and women are taking greater interest in vegetarianism and health foods. Skipping breakfast and eating dinner late in the evening are developing fads. Most important, perhaps, is the constanly rising cost of attending college and the view of many college business officers that food service, like laundry, is really not a proper function of their administration. If this view should become more popular on college campuses, then the college and university food service director may have to plan and direct a drastic change from the traditional college dining service: a change towards a completely self-sustaining, commercial type food operation, with limited or no contract feeding, a la carte food selections, and complete freedom of choice for the students. Such a change would enable the school to offer food service without requiring it, and to reduce the cash outlay of parents by eliminating food service from its fee schedule altogether. Since present food service systems at many colleges and universities are closely tied in with long-term financing plans for residence halls and student union buildings, drastic refinancing schemes might become necessary to permit the splitting off of food service from other auxiliary enterprises.

If you should become involved in such changes, do not see these as a threat to your job or to your profession. Regard them, instead, as a challenge to your imagination and administrative ability. As long as students attend school, they will need to be fed, and someone like yourself must be there to supervise. If you approach this challenge with a sense of purpose and dedication, with a self-confidence that comes from professional knowledge, from ability, and from a genuine affection for your students, then you will always be happy that you have chosen college food service management as a career.

APPENDIX 1

FOOD SERVICE PAMPHLET

*ood
service
at
Pacific*

University OF THE PACIFIC
STOCKTON, CALIFORNIA 95211

CALIFORNIA'S FIRST CHARTERED INSTITUTION OF HIGHER EDUCATION

A BRIEF, INFORMATIVE GUIDE TO THE
UNIVERSITY'S FOOD SERVICE DEPARTMENT

1978-1979

YOUR FOOD SUPERVISORS
Director, Auxiliary Services: Paul Fairbrook, Anderson Hall
Director, University Food Service: Mary Heacock, Anderson Hall
Manager, Grace Covell Dining Hall: Robert Woodward
Manager, Quad Dining Hall: Eddie Lang
Manager, University Center: Gary Verzani
Dietitian: Sheri Henderson
Assistant Manager, Quad Dining Hall: Carlos Cartaya

UNIVERSITY OF THE PACIFIC
FOOD SERVICE
1978/1979

We would like our new students to have a small preview of our Food Service. Listed are some items we are sure you and your parents will find of interest.

1. **MEALS** (Hours subject to change)
   A. **RESIDENCE HALLS**

WEEKDAYS

	Breakfast	Lunch	Dinner
Grace Covell	7:15-10:00	11:15- 1:30	4:30-6:30
Quad	7:15- 9:00	11:15-12:30	4:30-6:30
Raymond-Callison and Elbert Covell	CLOSED	11:30-12:30	5:00-6:15*

*Closed Friday Dinner

SATURDAYS AND SUNDAYS

	Continental Breakfast	Lunch	Dinner
Grace Covell	8:30-10:00	11:00- 1:00	4:30-6:30
Quad	8:30-9:30	11:00- 1:00	4:30-6:30
Raymond-Callison and Elbert Covell	CLOSED	CLOSED	CLOSED

   B. **UNIVERSITY CENTER**

UOP Mall	Monday through Thursday	7:30 a.m.- 4:30 p.m.
	Friday	7:30 a.m.- 3:30 p.m.
	Sunday	CLOSED
Redwood Room	Monday through Friday	11:30 a.m.- 1:30 p.m.
Rathskeller	Monday through Friday	8:30 a.m.- 2:00 p.m. & 5:30 p.m.-10:00 p.m.
	Saturday	9:00 a.m.-11:00 p.m.*
	Sunday	5:30 p.m.-11:00 p.m.

*Meal tickets valid till 9:00 p.m. Food Service ends at 10:00 p.m.

2. **FREE FLOW EXCHANGE**
   Students can use their meal ticket anywhere on campus (i.e., Grace Covell, Quad, Raymond-Callison, Elbert Covell, or the University Center).

3. **VARIABLE MEAL PLANS**

   On-campus students have the option of choosing from one of the following meal plans:

	COST	
	SEMESTER	PHARMACY TERM
21 Meals: This plan consists of three (3) meals daily, with breakfast on Saturdays and Sundays being Continental Breakfast and the noon meal being brunch.	$678	$565
15 Meals: This plan is a combination of the 14- and 15-meal plans offered in past years. It allows the student to have any fifteen meals per week, starting Mondays.	$635	$529
10 Meals: This plan allows the student any 10 meals per week, starting Mondays.	$565	$471
Off-campus students have one additional plan available:		
5 Meals: This plan allows any five(5) meals per week, starting Mondays. Does not include Winter Term.	$195	——

4. **CASH RATES**
   Cash prices in the residence hall dining rooms are as follows:
   BREAKFAST - $1.90   LUNCH - $2.25   DINNER - $3.00

5. **A LA CARTE SERVICE**
   Meal Ticket holders may use their Meal Tickets for "a la carte" purchases of food in the University Center and on weekday lunches in Raymond-Callison. No "seconds" are allowed on a la carte operations, and no refunds are given for allowances not used. In 1977/78, meal ticket values are as follows:
   BREAKFAST - $1.65   LUNCH - $1.85   DINNER - $2.40

6. **SCRIP BOOKS**
   Off-campus students wishing to eat in the residence halls may purchase special scrip books in the Finance Center. These cost $19 for Breakfast, $25 for Lunch, and $30 for Dinner and carry discounts of from 7-9%.
   Scrip Books for the University Center are also available at $25 each. All Scrip Books can be charged to student's accounts, if these are maintained in good standing.

7. MENUS

Menus at the University are prepared by the dietitian and reviewed by the entire supervisory staff at weekly meetings. Basically, we follow a five-week menu cycle, which is revised periodically to fit the season or to better reflect the menu preference of the students. Our typical menu pattern follows:

BREAKFAST: Choice of two juices (one is orange juice)
cold or hot cereal
one fruit
eggs, pancakes, or waffles
meat, four times a week
milk, skimmed milk, tea, coffee, or hot chocolate

LUNCH: Choice of three salads (one green)
hot soup
Choice of one (1) hot entree or one (1) sandwich
one vegetable
Fresh fruit, ice cream or one bakery item
milk, skimmed milk, soft drinks, tea, or coffee
hot chocolate

DINNER: Choice of three salads (one green)
two (2) hot entrees
one vegetable
one starch item
ice cream, fruit, or bakery item
milk, skimmed milk, soft drinks, tea, coffee,
or hot chocolate

SPECIAL DINNER: ONCE A MONTH DURING A WEEKDAY EVENING.

8. SALAD BARS

During weekdays, the Grace Covell, Quad and Elbert Covell Dining Halls feature smorgasbord-type salad bars which usually contain 4 to 5 different salad bowls (e.g., Green Salad, Cottage Cheese, Potato Salad, Green Bean Salad, and Fruit Salad), as well as pickles, olives, and other relishes. These are included in the price of the meal, and are available to every diner.

9. SPECIAL DIETS

Our menus are specially marked to help dieting students and often we have a low calorie entree just for dieters. All those interested should consult with our Dietitian, Miss Sheri Henderson.

10. FRESH FRUIT

Fresh fruit is served on the average of at least once a day, for either lunch or dinner. Fruit salad is, of course, available at every lunch.

11. HEALTH AND VEGETARIAN FOODS

The University operates a Health Food and Vegetarian Program consisting of the following:
BREAKFAST: Granola, with raisins, brown sugar, and honey is available in all dining halls. Hot cereals (including Cream of Wheat, Oatmeal and Ralston) are served daily.
LUNCH: In addition to the salad bar items, students who are vegetarians may request Cheese or Yogurt instead of the regular entree. Often, but not always, a special vegetarian item is offered at lunch.
DINNER: A vegetarian entree item is prepared each night at the Quad Dining Hall. We normally prepare only about 150 servings of this entree, and it is served on a first-come, first-served basis.

12. NUTRITION EDUCATION AND WEIGHT REDUCTION PROGRAM

For those students who are interested, Sheri Henderson, our dietitian, will conduct special programs dealing with nutrition and weight reduction beginning early in the fall semester. If you are interested, contact Sheri in her office in the Quad kitchen.

13. UOP BAKE SHOP

The University operates its own Bake Shop (adjacent to the Quad Dining Room) and students are encouraged to ask to be shown around. We bake fresh Sweet Rolls, Coffee Cakes, or Doughnuts six days a week, and also bake a variety of Specialty and Health food-type rolls and breads, including our popular ''Ecology Bread'' which is made with natural grain flours. We bake cookies for lunch 3 to 4 times a week and pies and cakes for dinner as well.

14. SPECIAL DINNERS

Throughout the year, Food Service prepares Special Dinners for holidays and other occasions. These include Outdoor Barbecues, Steak Dinners and International Gourmet Dinners. During normal years these are scheduled to take place monthly, but this year the total number will be limited.

15. SNACKS AT FINALS

During finals week, a late snack is provided to the students with the compliments of Food Service.

16. STUDENT EMPLOYMENT

The University Food Service employs over 200 students during the regular school year. Jobs vary from washing dishes to helping on the serving line, waiting on tables and many other duties. The average student works two hours a day. It is important, when choosing your classes, that you keep two hours free during the same period each day.

At the start of each year, student jobs are given out on the basis of the time of application and thus students should apply as soon as they come on campus. Former employees are, of course, given first preference. Dorm residents are given second preference for all jobs and are, therefore, encouraged to apply for student jobs in the dining hall where they eat. Off-campus students are hired whenever there are not sufficient applicants from the residence halls, and their meals deducted from their paychecks. Student Food Service workers are subject to special dress regulations while on duty. These are important, since neatly and appropriately dressed workers contribute to the overall satisfaction of the diner.

17. GUESTS

Ours is one campus where you do not have to sneak guests into the dining hall. If you have a meal ticket, we are glad to give you a couple of free guest meal passes each semester, if you pick them up, during regular office hours (8:30 a.m.-4:30 p.m.) in our office located in Anderson Hall. You are limited to two passes per semester.

18. MORE DINING

In addition to the Dining Halls we have already told you about, the University Center, the newest addition to our campus, houses the Redwood Room and the Rathskeller along with the Mall. The Redwood Room features an attractive buffet lunch in an elegant dining room with waitress service, Monday through Friday.

The Rathskeller is open for Continental Breakfast, Mondays through Fridays from 8:30 a.m. on. At lunch, it features Hofbrau-type hot sandwiches and health food items. At night, it has music and entertainment and serves pizza and various grill items.

Meal ticket holders can use their meal tickets (up to the maximum values for each meal) anywhere in the University Center. Breakfast tickets are good until 10:30 a.m. - lunch tickets until 4:00 p.m. - Dinner tickets (in the Rathskeller) until 9:00 p.m.

19. SICK TRAYS

Students who are sick but whose illness doesn't require them to stay in the Infirmary may have a sick tray brought to them by a roommate during the period of the illness. The sick student's meal ticket must be presented to the cashier.

20. SACK LUNCHES

We will provide sack lunches to meal ticket holders under the following conditions: A) If absence from the dining hall is necessitated by reason of classes (must have a note from faculty member). B) If a group of 8 or more students or a regular student organization is planning an off-campus affair.

Requests must be made to the Dining Room Manager at least 24 hours in advance.

Taking meals outside: Students may take their meals outside to eat them, but to insure the return of the trays their meal ticket must be left with the cashier. Upon return of the tray, the cashier will give back the meal ticket.

21. TAKING FOOD AND DISHES OUT OF THE DINING HALL

With the exception of sack lunches, all food served to contract students must be consumed in the dining halls. The reasons are obvious: the dorm rooms are no place to eat - the food itself should only go to students who have actually paid for it. As for the taking of dishes or silverware - this only creates shortages in the dining rooms which then inconveniences the rest of the students.

22. SELF-BUSSING

In all cafeteria dining halls, you are requested to take your tray to the dish window, conveyor belt, or bus cart when you've finished your meal. Self-bussing makes for savings we can spend on food rather than on labor. Furthermore, it enables other students who follow you to sit down at a clean table. The food supervisors and cafeteria personnel will remind you of the self-bussing rule, and we ask that you cooperate. At special dinners when tables are set, this rule does not apply and cafeteria personnel clear the dishes after the meal.

23. STUDENT COMMUNICATIONS

Because we serve more than 1500 students in four dining halls, it will take us a while to get to know you - and even longer to get to know your tastes and food preferences. We are interested, nevertheless, in your comments or criticism. The following are the channels by which you can express your ideas: 1) Suggestion Boxes. These are located in each dining hall. If you sign your suggestion, you will receive a personal note from your food supervisor. 2) Dining Hall Food Committee. At the beginning of the year, each dining hall or cluster college selects a small committee (three is an ideal number) to whom constructive suggestions or complaints should be made. This committee will evaluate all such thoughts and, if found to have merit, will pass these on to their food supervisor at periodic intervals. 3) Annual Questionnaires. During each school year, students are asked to fill out a food preference survey form in which they can express their complaints and compliments. These forms are then carefully studied by the Food Service staff and often become a basis for changes to be made in the following year. (Summaries of the most recent survey are available upon request in the Food Service Office, Anderson Hall.) 4) Direct contact with Food Supervisors. Last, but perhaps the most important, of all avenues open to you for expressing your individual food preferences is the direct contact with your food supervisor. The supervisor is always present during the serving hour - either in the kitchen, cafeteria line, or in the dining room. You are encouraged to approach him (at a mutually convenient time) and share your ideas with him. If you wish, you can also make an appointment with the Director of Food Service, Anderson Hall - Ext. 2532.

APPENDIX 2

RESIDENCE HALL MENU, FOOTNOTED FOR DIETERS

UNIVERSITY OF THE PACIFIC
NUTRITION WEEK 1978
CYCLE I

WHY NOT GO FIRST CLASS? EAT A BALANCED DIET EVERY DAY.

ORANGE & GRAPEFRUIT JUICES DAILY: 75
HARD & SOFT COOKED EGGS DAILY: 80
ASSORTED COLD CEREALS DAILY: 75

MONDAY, MARCH 5	TUESDAY, MARCH 6	WEDNESDAY, MARCH 7	THURSDAY, MARCH 8	FRIDAY, MARCH 9	SATURDAY, MARCH 10	SUNDAY, MARCH 11
BANANA 100	APPLE 90	TOMATO JUICE 90	LARGE ORANGE 75	PEAR NECTAR 95	FRESH FRUIT 75	APPLESAUCE 115
CREAM OF WHEAT 90	OATMEAL 60	CREAM OF RICE 95	FARINA 70	MALT-O-MEAL 70	COLD CEREALS 75	COLD CEREALS 75
FRIED EGG 115	POACHED EGG 80	BUCKWHEAT PANCAKES(2) 200	FRENCH TOAST (1) 180	HAM OMELET 210		
SAUSAGE LINKS (2) 120	ENGLISH MUFFIN 65	MAPLE SYRUP 75	MAPLE SYRUP 75	HASH BROWNS 145		
	BACON (2) 85	CHIVE OR PLAIN SCRAMBLED EGGS 140	SAUSAGE LINKS (2) 120		SKIM MILK 85	SKIM MILK 65
SKIM MILK 85	SKIM MILK 85	SKIM MILK 85	SKIM MILK 85	SKIM MILK 85	TOAST 65	TOAST 85
TOAST 65	TOAST 65	TOAST 65	TOAST 65	TOAST 65	RAISED DONUT 205	CHERRY MUFFIN 110
BUTTERMILK BAR 230	CHERRY FILLED COFFEECAKE 230	CAKE DONUT 180	SOUR CREAM COFFEECAKE 215	APPLE STREUDAL 245	FROZEN MIXED FRUIT 75	BANANA 100
VEGETABLE SOUP 80	TOMATO SOUP 75	BEEF NOODLE SOUP 60	FRENCH ONION SOUP 50	FISH CHOWDER 155	RAISIN OR PLAIN PANCAKES (2) 200	EGGS BENEDICT 260
TUNA BURGER ON KILPATRICK BUN 260	BEEF FRENCH DIP 365	PIG IN A BLANKET 215	HAMBURGER ON KILPATRICK BUN 290	HOT TURKEY SANDWICH 350	MAPLE SYRUP 75	HASH BROWNS 145
HAM & ASPARAGUS CREPE 240	ROAST BEEF SLICE 200	BEEF CROQUETTE(1) 205	FRENCH FRIES 130	MACARONI & CHEESE 225	SCRAMBLED EGGS 140	HOT FRUIT COMPOTE 110
SPINACH 15	CHICKEN A LA KING 140	WAX BEANS 30	CHILI CON CARNE 215	TURKEY SLICE 200	BACON STRIPS (2) 85	
	RICE		HAMBURGER PATTY 200	SCANDINAVIAN VEG. 55		COTTAGE CHEESE 90
	ZUCCHINI CREOLE 60		MIXED VEGETABLES 60		COTTAGE CHEESE 90	TOSSED SALAD
SALAD BAR	SALAD BAR	SALAD BAR	SALAD BAR	SALAD BAR	TOSSED SALAD	EGG SALAD 150
PEACH HALF/CREAM CHEESE 100	BROCCOLI SPEARS/ 50 CURRY SAUCE	BLUSHED BANANAS 50	PINEAPPLE SLICE 60	HARD COOKED EGG 80	TUNA SALAD 170	
FRUIT COCKTAIL MOLD 140	MOLDED CRANBERRY MOLD 140	JUBILEE GELATIN 140	DOUBLE STRAWBERRY MOLD 140	MANDARIN ORANGE/OR.MOLD 140		
SKIM MILK 85	SKIM MILK 85	SKIM MILK 85	SKIM MILK 85	SKIM MILK 85	SKIM MILK 85	SKIM MILK 85
FRESH FRUIT 75	FRESH FRUIT 75	FRESH FRUIT 75	FRESH FRUIT 75	FRESH FRUIT 75		
ICE CREAM NOVELTY 160	ICE CREAM NOVELTY 160	ICE CREAM NOVELTY 160	ICE CREAM NOVELTY 160	ICE CREAM NOVELTY 160	FRUIT DANISH 190	FRUIT MARBLE COFFEECAKE 230
CHOC. CHIP COOKIE 105	ICE CREAM 105	SUGAR COOKIE 75	BLONDE BROWNIE 125			
VEGIE:CHEESE & ASPARAGUS CREPES 225	VEGIE:CHEESE NOODLE BAKE 275	VEGIE:VEGIE SANDWICH 200	VEGIE: CHILI CON QUESO/ BROWN RICE 260	VEGIE:MACARONI & CHEESE 225		
TOSTADA 390	**Italian Nite+++	DEEP FRIED CHICKEN 300	GRILLED CHEESE STEAK 265	BREADED PORK CHOP 365	BBQ BEEF BRISKET 400	V-8 JUICE 35
SOLE/VELOUTE SAUCE 200	LENGUINI - 330 CHOICE OF MEAT, MUSHROOM, CLAM SCE.	BAKED CHICKEN 160	MEATLOAF 265	BAKED COD/LEMON 165	PORK CHOW MEIN/ 250	ROAST BEEF 225
BAKED SOLE 165	VEAL SCALLOPINE 350	OMELET GARGAMELLE 240	GRAVY 80	TARTAR SAUCE 95	CHOW MEIN NOODLES 110	WHIPPED POTATOES 95
BUTTERED RICE 100	VEAL 275	FRENCH ONION OR PLAIN POTATOES 95	BAKED POTATO 95	CANDIED SWEET POTATOES 165	RICE PILAFF 95	GRAVY 80
PEAS & MUSHROOMS 70	F.F. EGGPLANT 150	GRAVY 80	CHUCKWAGON CORN 75	BROCCOLI SPEARS 25 / FRENCH CUT GREEN BEANS 30		PEAS 65
SALAD BAR	SALAD BAR	CARROT COINS 25	SALAD BAR	SALAD BAR	CARROT RAISIN SALAD 150	AVOCADO-SPINACH SALAD 70
APPLE WALDORF 185	ANTIPASTO TRAYS 75	SALAD BAR	STUFFED CELERY/PEANUT BUTTER 75	APPLESAUCE 115	SALAD BAR	EGG BREAD 100
CHEESE BISCUIT 105	GARLIC BREAD 180	COLESLAW 70			WHOLEWHEAT BREAD 100	
	PANETTONE 105	DINNER ROLL 90	BUTTERMILK BREAD 100	COLOMBO SOURDOUGH BREAD 100		FRESH FRUIT 75
FRESH FRUIT 75	FRESH FRUIT 75	FRESH FRUIT 75	FRESH FRUIT 75	FRESH FRUIT 75	FRUIT 75	ICE CREAM 140
ICE CREAM 140	SPUMONI ICE CREAM 140	ICE CREAM 140	ICE CREAM 140	ICE CREAM 140	ICE CREAM 140	BANANA CREAM PIE 250
CHERRY COBBLER CAKE 215	ITALIAN RUM CAKE 350	JELLO CUBES/TOPPING 115	LEMON CRUNCH PIE 270	RAISIN CREAM PIE 320	TAPIOCA PUDDING 165	WHITE CAKE/COCONUT ICING 285
MARSHMELLOW DELIGHT(S.) 90			DOUBLE DRIBBLE MARBLE CAKE 235	ORANGE KISS ME CAKE 230		
VEGIE: TOSTADA 275	VEGIE:SPAGHETTI/ MUSHROOM SAUCE 330	VEGIE:OMELET GARGAMELLE 240	VEGIE:CHEESE NUT LOAF 210	VEGIE: LENTIL LOAF/ CHEESE SAUCE 295	VEGIE: CHOW MAINE 210	VEGIE: WALNUT PATTIES 180

THESE CALORIE COUNTS ARE APPROXIMATIONS DEPENDING ON PREPARATION AND SERVING SIZE.

APPENDIX 3

CATERING PAMPHLET, K-STATE UNION

This booklet contains many facts, menu suggestions and policies about the K-State Union Food Service. It is designed to be used as a guide when planning events including catered food.

We feel that our Food Service can provide quality food in comfortable surroundings and good service.

As "the center for people" on the KSU campus, our facilities are here to serve not only the campus community, but residents in and around Manhattan as well as the rest of the state.

We hope you'll contact us soon.

Walter D. Smith
Union Director

Terry R. Adams
Food Service Director

Scheduling

Catered Food Service is available only Monday through Saturday. Dinners should be scheduled for not later than 6:30 p.m. Refreshment orders are available on Sunday.

There are several steps necessary to make arrangements for a special event, including catering:

1. As soon as possible: reserve the date and room with the Scheduling Clerk in the Director's Office of the K-State Union, 532-6591.

2. No later than ten days before: plan the menu with the Union Food Service, 532-6580 at least ten weekdays before the function.

3. Two working days before: confirm with the Food Service Office a guaranteed number of persons to be served. (See below.)

Due to seating capacity of different dining areas, the Food Service needs close cooperation in estimating the number to be in attendance.

Guarantees and Cancellations

After a guaranteed number is given to the Food Service Office, the organization sponsoring the event is financially responsible for 95 per cent of that number.

The Union Food Service will be prepared to serve an additional five (5) per cent more than the guaranteed number.

Should it be necessary to cancel the event, the K-State Union requires a minimum of 24 hours notice before the date requested. If cancellation occurs after this time, the organization will be responsible for all costs incurred in preparing the banquet.

Decorations

The Union Food Service has a large assortment of colored linens which may be used with any catered meal. No other provisions are made to decorate banquet tables or rooms; this is left to the organization. However we ask that any such plans be coordinated with the Food Service Office.

Receptions and Special Services

For small receptions held in the Key or Bluemont Rooms a service charge of 15 cents per person for approved student organizations and 25 cents per person for non-student groups is made for setup and cleanup of the room. This charge is in lieu of a room rental.

Service charges for delivery, set-up and clean-up of items in other buildings on campus will normally be $5.00.

These charges are in addition to the cost of food items requested.

Billing

Bills are payable to the Business Office, K-State Union, KSU, Manhattan, KS 66506. All purchases are subject to Kansas sales tax of 3 per cent and are to be paid within thirty (30) days after the event.

A service charge may be added to accounts not paid within that time. A refund cannot be given for unused food.

| policies |
| breakfasts |
| luncheons |
| dinners |
| picnics / supplies |
| refreshments |
| ordering guide |
| price list |

| policies |
| breakfasts |
| luncheons |
| dinners |
| picnics / supplies |
| refreshments |
| ordering guide |
| price list |

Courtesy of K-State Union, Kansas State University Manhattan, Ka.

breakfast suggestions

A. Continental Breakfast
Choice of two chilled juices
Donuts or Danish pastry
Fresh fruit
Coffee — Tea — Milk

B. Scrambled Eggs and Hash Brown Potatoes

choice of:	choice of:
Orange Juice	Four crisp bacon strips
Tomato juice	Four link sausages
Grape juice	Three-ounce grilled ham slice
Apple juice	

Muffins or toast
Jelly — Butter
Coffee — Tea — Milk

C. Blueberry-filled Hotcakes with whipped cream and syrup
or
Apple-filled Hotcakes with whipped cream and syrup

choice of:	choice of:
Orange juice	Four crisp bacon strips
Apple juice	Four link sausages
Grape juice	Three-ounce grilled ham slice
Tomato juice	

Coffee — Tea — Milk

D. Scrambled Eggs and Hash Browns
or
French Toast with syrup

choice of:	choice of:
Orange juice	Four crisp bacon strips
Tomato juice	Four tiny link sausages
Apple juice	Three-ounce grilled ham slice
Grape juice	
Apricot nectar	
Fruit in season	

Homemade sticky rolls or Coffee cake
Muffins or toast
Butter — Jelly
Coffee — Tea — Milk

E. Special Brunch Breakfast
Scrambled Eggs with chives
Fruit-filled Hotcakes or Grilled French Toast
Tiny Link Sausages or Grilled Ham Slice
Fresh fruit (in season)
Mixed fancy fruit salad
Chilled orange juice and chilled V-8 juice with lemon
Homemade sticky rolls and muffins
Butter — Preserves
Coffee — Tea —

All breakfasts served with paper place mats and linen napkins. Full linen service available at additional cost.

breakfasts
luncheons
dinners
picnics / supplies
refreshments
ordering guide
price list

luncheon suggestions entrees

A. Baked Lasagna with parmesan cheese
Grilled Salisbury Steak with spicy tomato sauce
Stuffed Green Peppers with spicy tomato sauce
Beef Stroganoff with steamed rice
Swedish Meatballs over buttered noodles
Breaded Chicken Breasts with country gravy
Ground Pepper Steak with rich brown gravy
Hot Chicken Salad

B. Chicken Fried Steak with country cream gravy
Baked Swiss Steak with tomato sauce
Roast Breast of Turkey with cornbread dressing
Baked Ham Slices with fruit sauce

C. Stuffed Chicken Breast
Pot Roast of Beef with fresh garden vegetables

D. Chicken Cordon Bleu
Julienne of Beef Teriyaki over steamed rice

Choice of one of each of the following with above entrees:

Salad or chilled juice appetizer:	Potato:
Tossed green salad	Au gratin
Cottage cheese with fruit	Escalloped
Fruit salad	Whipped
Gelatin salad	French fried
Tomato juice	Sweet potatoes
Peach nectar	Baked
Apricot nectar	Rice
V-8 juice	Noodles

Vegetable:	Bread:
French cut green beans	Crown rolls
Peas	Homemade breads
Carrots	Hard rolls
Mixed vegetables	Soft dinner rolls
Whole kernel corn	Muffins

Dessert:
Gelatin parfaits
Puddings
Cake

Coffee — Tea —

All luncheons served with paper place mats and linen napkins. Full linen service available at additional cost.

luncheons
dinners
picnics / supplies
refreshments
ordering guide
price list

cold salad plates

A. **Maurice Salad Bowl:** Julienne of Ham, Turkey and Cheese over a bed of crisp lettuce, surrounded by egg and tomato wedges. Served with salad dressing of your choice.

B. **Fresh Fruit Plate:** Fresh Fruits in Season — melons, strawberries, grapes, etc. — on a bed of lettuce leaves with scoop of sherbert (In season only.) Served with banana nut, date nut and cheese bread slices with butter.

C. **Stuffed Tomato Salad:** Ripe Tomato stuffed with Creamy Tuna or Chicken Salad, garnished with carrot curls, asparagus spears, assorted olives, pickled watermelon rind, deviled egg halves and potato salad.

D. **Shrimp Salad Bowl:** Whole Shrimp Meat over crisp lettuce, egg and tomato wedges, asparagus spears, ripe olives and choice of dressing.

E. **Spring Salad Bowl:** Chicken Salad on crisp lettuce leaf, glazed banana and ham roll, cheese and salami stix, fruit salad, peach half with Jamaica relish and Ritz crackers.

Choice of one of each of the following with above:

Appetizer:

Cup of hot soup or Glass of chilled juice

Bread:	**Dessert:**
Homemade breads	Gelatin parfaits
Crown rolls	Custard
Muffins	Cake slice
Hard rolls	Pudding with whipped cream

Coffee — Tea — Milk

sandwiches

COLD SANDWICHES

A. Sliced Breast of Turkey with crisp lettuce on toasted whole wheat bread
Cold Baked Hickory-Smoked Ham with Swiss cheese on pumpernickel bread
Cold Roast Beef on buttered white or whole grain bread
Thinly Sliced Pastrami on rye bread
Open-faced Chicken Salad with crisp lettuce

Choice of one:

Chilled potato salad
Gelatin mold
Creamy cole slaw
Sliced tomato
Crisp potato chips

All cold sandwiches garnished wth dill pickle (See soup and dessert choices below)

HOT SANDWICHES

B. Open-faced Hot Beef with brown gravy
Hot Roast Turkey with giblet gravy
Hot Pastrami on rye bread with kosher dill wedge
Baked Ham on pumpernickel bread with kosher dill wedge

C. French Dip Sandwich Au Jus with kosher dill wedge

All hot sandwiches served with garnishes and choice of whipped or French fried potatoes

Choice of each of the following with the above hot or cold sandwiches:

Appetizer:

Cup of soup or chilled juice

Dessert:

Gelatin parfait, Pudding with whipped cream, Cake slice

Coffee — Tea —

All luncheons served with paper place mats and linen napkins. Full linen service available at additional cost.

buffet luncheons
(50 or more persons)

salad buffet

Chilled relishes
Tossed green salad with choice of dressings
Potato salad or Macaroni salad
Marinated bean salad or Vegetable cole slaw
Gelatin molds
Cottage cheese and fruit
Assorted cheese tray — Swiss, American and cheddar
Tomato and cucumber tray
Assorted cold meat platter — ham, salami and turkey
Assorted breads and butter
Assorted cracker and bread stick basket

Dessert (choice of one):

Gelatin parfait
Custard

special luncheon buffet

Chilled relishes

Salads

Tossed green salad with choice of dressings
Potato salad or Macaroni salad
Marinated bean salad or Vegetable cole slaw
Gelatin molds or Fruited cottage cheese

Vegetable of your choice

Entree (choice of one):

Gourmet Casserole
Swedish Meatballs
Baked Ham Slice
Beef Cutlets
Salisbury Steak
Baked Macaroni and Cheese
Chicken a la King
Sweet and Sour Pork
Deep Fried Chicken

Bread (choice of one):

Homemade breads
Hot rolls
Hard rolls
Crown rolls

Dessert (choice of one):

Gelatin parfaits
Custard
Pudding
Cake slice

Coffee — Tea —

All luncheons served with paper place mats and linen napkins. Full linen service available at additional cost.

dinners

picnics / supplies

refreshments

ordering guide

price list

dinners

picnics / supplies

refreshments

ordering guide

price list

dinner suggestions

entrees

A. German Pot Roast with rich beef and vegetable sauce
Roast Top Round of Beef with au jus
Baked Ham Slice with fruit sauce
Roast Young Tom Turkey with cornbread stuffing and giblet gravy
Breaded Veal Steak Parmesan with strained tomato sauce
Grilled Salisbury Steak with vegetable gravy and fried onion rings
Choice Round Steak, Swiss Style

B. Broiled Steak Diane with mushroom butter sauce
Chicken Cordon Bleu, Stuffed Chicken Breasts, or
Chicken a la Kiev

C. Veal Scallopini

D. Top Sirloin Steak — 10 ounce

E. New York Steak — 12 ounce

Choice of one of each of the following with above:

Salad or Chilled Juice Appetizer:	Potato:
Tossed green	Whipped
Cole slaw	Baked
Fruit salad	Steamed rice
Vegetable:	Rice pilaf
French cut green beans	Buttered noodles
Peas	Escalloped
Carrots	Au gratin
Mixed vegetables	Duchess
Whole kernel corn	
Dessert:	**Bread:**
Assorted fruit pies	Homemade bread
Tarts	Crown rolls
Parfaits	Hard or soft dinner rolls
Sliced cake	
Coffee — Tea — —	— —

gourmet entrees

A. Roast Leg of Spring Lamb with minted Bartlett pear halves
Baked Stuffed Boneless Pork Chops with hot spiced applesauce
Braised Choice Beef Tips with tomato, mushrooms, green pepper, onion
en brochette
Roasted Quail with blended wild rice stuffing, glazed with orange sauce
Baked Grouse with cranberry mornay sauce
Roasted Whole Cornish Game Hen with blended rice stuffing, glazed
with polvrade sauce and served with red currant jelly

B. Lobster Thermidor

C. Broiled Filet Mignon Bernaise
Roast Prime Rib of Beef Au Jus
New York Roast Loin of Beef
Broiled New York Sirloin Steak with mushroom buttons
Roast Choice Tenderloin of Beef Marchand du Vin

Choice of one of each of the following with above:

Appetizer:	Salad:
Cranberry cocktail	Tossed green
V-8 juice	Fruit salad
Apricot nectar	Individual gelatin mold
Peach nectar	Potato or Potato Substitute:
Vegetable:	Whipped
French cut green beans	Duchess
Peas	Baked
Carrots	Escalloped
Mixed vegetables	Au gratin
Whole kernel corn	Almondine
Bread:	Steamed rice
Individual loaves	Rice pilaf
Homemade breads	Wild rice
Hard rolls	Seasoned noodles
Soft rolls	**Dessert:**
Crown rolls	Fruit pies
Coffee — Tea —	Assorted tarts
	Parfaits
	Sliced cake

dinners

picnics / supplies

refreshments

ordering guide

price list

buffet dinner one

(50 or more persons)

Entree No. 1 (choice of one):
Beef Stroganoff over Rice
Sweet and Sour Pork
Hungarian Goulash
Swedish Meatballs

Entree No. 2
Seafood Platter
which includes:
Clam Crisps
Shrimp Puffs
Batter Dipped Cod

Entree No. 3 (choice of One):
Deep Fried Chicken
Roast Sliced Turkey
Baked Swiss Steak
Baked Ham Slices with fruit
Veal Parmesan

Salads and Appetizers
Iced relish tray
Green salad bowl with choice of four dressings
Molded gelatin salad with mayonnaise dressing
Vegetable macaroni and cheese salad bowl
Deviled egg platter
choice of one:
Marinated bean salad
Garden cole slaw
Carrot and raisin salad
Fruit salad with whipped cream

Potato (choice of one):	Bread (choice of one):
Hot German Potato salad	Soft dinner rolls
Escalloped	Hard rolls
Au gratin	Homemade breads
Seasoned rice	Crowns
Buttered noodles	

Pudding with whipped cream
Cake slice
Coffee — Tea — Milk

buffet dinner two

(50 or more persons)

Entrees
Sweet and Sour Pork
Baron of Beef — carved to order

Vegetables
French cut green beans and mushroom casserole
Au gratin cauliflower or Hot German potato salad

Salads and Appetizers
Assorted chilled vegetable relish tray
Chef's salad bowl with choice of four dressings
Assorted chilled pickle tray
Deviled egg halves
Potato salad
Special gelatin salad mold
Special marinated bean salad or fruited cole slaw
Fruit salad with whipped cream or frozen fruit salad

Bread (choice of one):
Homemade breads
Hot rolls
Individual loaves
Hard rolls
Crown rolls

Dessert (choice of one):
Custards
Fruit pies
Apple crisp
Fruit cup
Cake with icing
Angel food cake with lemon icing
Boston cream pie
Rice pudding
Dessert of the month

Coffee — Tea —

picnics / supplies

refreshments

ordering guide

price list

gourmet dinner buffet
(50 or more persons)

Appetizers
Ice relish trays — artichoke hearts, pickled melon, okra, carrot, celery
  sticks, radishes, cauliflower buds, green pepper slices with horseradish
  sauce
Fresh pineapple boats with chicken salad
Assorted cheese platter — American, Swiss, roquefort, cheddar
Jumbo shrimp on ice with hot cocktail sauce
Assorted fish platter — smoked oysters, sardines, pickled herring
Apple halves with maraschino cherries

Salads
Green salad bowl with bleu cheese
Fresh fruit basket
Potato and shrimp salad mold
Old fashioned cole slaw
Individual strawberry gelatin molds
Special marinated bean salad
Deviled egg platter with anchovies
Special relishes — Corn — Jamaica

Vegetables
Fresh vegetable casserole
Blended wild rice or Hot German potato salad

Entrees
Baron of Beef — carved to order
Gourmet Prawns and Clam Crisps

Breads
Individual loaves of homemade bread
Butter — orange marmalade

Desserts
Fruit pies
Cheese cake with fruit topping
Fresh fruit tarts or Eclairs

Coffee — Tea —

All dinners served with full linen service.

picnics

A. **Picnic Menu One**
  Charcoal Broiled Hamburger Steak
  Au gratin potatoes
  Fruit salad
  Tossed green salad
  Chilled relishes
  Hard dinner rolls and butter
  Dessert — ice cream bars
  Punch

B. **Picnic Menu Two**
  Barbecued Beef or Ham
  Sesame buns
  Potato salad
  Gelatin salad
  Dessert — ice cream bars
  Choice of beverage

C. **Picnic Menu Three**
  Charcoal Broiled New York Steak
  Au gratin potatoes
  Chilled relishes
  Fruit salad
  Tossed green salad with three dressings
  Garlic buttered French bread
  Dessert — strawberry tarts
  Choice of beverage

supplies
Styro cups (6 ounce)
Paper cold cups (10 ounce)
Paper cold cups (16 ounce)
Paper tea napkins
Paper dinner napkins (two ply)
Paper plates (6" inexpensive)
Paper plates (6" expensive)
Paper plates (10¼")
Paper tablecloths (54" x 54")
Heavy weight plastic forks, spoons, knives
Plastic tip and toss cups (8 ounce)

picnics / supplies
refreshments
ordering guide
price list

picnics / supplies
refreshments
ordering guide
price list

refreshments

Beverages
Coffee (sugar and cream included)
Tea
Hot chocolate
Fruit punch
Hot apple cider
Breakfast orange juice
Brownies, Cakes, Cookies & Donuts
Pan brownies (sheet pan)
Frosted sheet cake
Decorated sheet cake
Assorted cookies
Tea cookies
Cake donuts (plain or sugared)
Raised donuts (plain round)
Cake donuts (buttermilk)
Maple bars or twists
Petit-fours

special orders

K-State Crown
Rings
Plain Bread
Vienna Bread
Cinnamon Bread
Whole Wheat Bread
Light and Dark Rye

refreshments

ordering guide

price list

ordering guide

This ordering guide is included to help you plan for working with the Union Food Service. For more information contact the Food Service Office, first floor Union or call 532-6580.

Date _____ | MENU _____

Dining Room _____ _____

Time (on ticket) _____ _____

(Begin Service) _____ _____

Organization _____ _____

_____ _____

Estimated No. _____ _____

Guaranteed No. _____ _____

Price _____ + Tax _____ _____

Service Plan _____ _____

Head Table _____ _____
　　　　　on risers

Table Arrangement:

ordering guide

price list

370 College and University Food Service Manual

- Many food items are available other than those listed in this guide. Please consult the Union Food Service Office, 532-6580 for more information.
- The prices listed are subject to change. Please confirm prices with the Union Banquet Manager.
- Student organizations are eligible for a reduction on breakfasts, luncheons and dinners.

BREAKFAST SUGGESTIONS:
A $1.50
B   2.25
C   2.75
D   3.25
E   3.75

LUNCHEON SUGGESTIONS
Entrees
Group A $3.10
Group B   3.50
Group C   3.75
Group D   4.75

Cold Salad Plates:
A $3.00
B   3.00
C   3.10
D   3.75
E   3.50

Sandwiches:
Group A $2.75
Group B   2.75
Group C   3.25

Buffet Luncheons:
Salad Buffet $2.75
Special luncheon buffet   3.00

DINNER SUGGESTIONS:
Entrees
A $4.25
B   5.50
C   6.00
D   6.50
E   7.00

Gourmet Entrees
A $6.25
B   6.75
C   7.75

Buffet Dinner One
$5.00

Buffet Dinner Two
$6.00

Gourmet Dinner Buffet
$8.00

PICNICS:
A $3.25
B   3.25
C   6.50

SUPPLIES:
Quotes upon request

REFRESHMENTS:

Beverages (gallons)	paper	china
Coffee (sugar & cream)	$3.50	$4.00
Tea: cold	2.00	2.50
Tea: hot	2.00	2.50
Hot Chocolate	4.50	5.00
Fruit punch	3.50	4.00
Hot apple cider	4.00	4.50
Breakfast orange juice	4.25	4.75

(continued on reverse side)

price list

APPENDIX 4

UNIVERSITY OF THE PACIFIC
STOCKTON, CALIFORNIA

MEAT AND POULTRY SPECIFICATIONS
1978-79

Please Note:

1. All quotations MUST be phoned, mailed in, or delivered to the Food Service Office by *4:00 p.m. on Monday of each week.*

2. All prices must be firm for any deliveries requested Monday through Saturday of the *following* week.

3. Failure to comply with U.O.P. specifications may result in your being dropped from bidder's list.

4. On portioned meats there shall be no more than ½ oz. + or − tolerance.

5. When portioned meats are ordered in the frozen state, this means that they are to be *flash frozen* and packaged with heavy paper between layers and enclosed in a plastic bag. *Cartons of portioned meats must not exceed 25 lbs. in weight.*

6. All products shall be purchased at *net weight* only, and cartons are to be marked accordingly.

7. All products shall be only from plants which are completely U.S. Government inspected.

8. All meat and poultry items are to be bid on the basis of "fresh" or "frozen" *as per directions of the U.O.P. buyer.* Where a quotation is specifically for a *frozen* state, bidder must so indicate.

9. All references to MBG Specs. refer to the detailed specifications described in the *Meat Buyers Guides* published by the National Association of Meat Purveyors.

10. Cartons and boxes must never exceed 25 lbs. in weight - unless specifically stated, in advance, by the purveyor. All cartons must be clearly marked on the outside as to weight and content.

11. ALL GRADES TO BE *U.S. CHOICE.* BIDDERS MAY ALSO BID ON *U.S. GOOD,* BUT WHENEVER DOING SO, MUST INDICATE THIS *IN WRITING* ON THEIR BID FORM.

Return Bid to:

Mary T. Heacock, Director, Food Service
University of the Pacific
Stockton, California
946-2531

ALL MEAT AND POULTRY ORDERS WILL BE GIVEN OUT BY COLLEGE PHONE CALL ON TUESDAY MORNINGS.

Item Specification

BEEF

1. TOP ROUND (INSIDE), U.S. CHOICE, cut in accordance with MBG Specs. No. 168. Max. fat cover 1". Weight Range: 18-20 lbs. Minimum Age: 10 days.

2. CHUCK ROLL, Boneless. Cut in accordance with MBG Specs. No. 116A except that all the "finger meat" (i.e. all the fatty meat adjacent to the eye) is to be removed.

3. R.R. RIBS, Cut in accordance with MBG Specs. No. 109A. Weight Range: 18-20 lbs. Minimum Age: 2 weeks.

4. BOTTOM SIRLOIN FLAP, Defatted. Cut in accordance with MBG Specs. No. 185A.

5. CUBE STEAKS, Cut from flank steaks, defatted, cubed twice. 5-5½ oz. each.

6. TOP SIRLOIN STEAK, Boneless. Max. fat cover: ½". Min. Age: 2 weeks. Weight specified upon order - allowing ½ oz. tolerance each way. Cut in accordance with MBG Specs. No. 184.

7. STEW MEAT, Boneless, cut in 1" to 1½" cubes. Free of membrane and gristle. Supply in 10 lb. packages. Cut in accordance with MBG Specs. No. 135A, except Max. fat cover: 1/8".

8. KABOB CUBES, Cut from Sirloin Flap into 1 oz. cubes. Completely defatted. Min. Age: 2 weeks.

9. SHORT RIBS, 3-Rib cut, 2 inches wide. *Kosher Style.* Heavy fat covering removed down to red mat. Use only rib nos. 6, 7, and 8.

10. HAMBURGER PATTIES, Thoroughly blended. Grind twice, with final 1/8". Max. fat content: 18-20% by chemical analysis. When purchased frozen, must be frozen immediately after grinding and not frozen longer than 10 days before delivery.

11. HAMBURGER STEAKS, SAME AS 10 ABOVE except to weight 7 *oz.*

12. GROUND BEEF, SAME AS 10 ABOVE. Supply in 10# packages.

LAMB

13. LEG, Boneless, roast, tied in accordance with MBG Specs. No. 234A. Domestic lamb only.

14. FRANKFURTERS, All meat, skinless, no skim milk or other filler added. 10 per lb., 10# bulk pack. Specify Brand.

15. SAUSAGE LINKS, Skinless, pure, pork, milk spice. 16 per lb. Farmer Johns brand or approved equal.

16. LAMB SHANKS, NEW ZEALAND, 8-9 oz.

17. LAMB SHOULDER CHOP.

18. DELI HAM, Boneless, water added. Bidder to list brand.

Item Specification

PORK

19. HAM, Smoked, boneless, shank meat included, fully cooked, USDA inspected, no imitation hams, defatted to ¼", 10-12 lbs. Bidder to list brand.

20. "BREAKFAST HAM", Boned, rolled, tied, metal tip ends, AC casing, round, water added. 10-12 lbs.

21. FRESH HAM, Boned, rolled, tied, defatted to ½", 5-8 lbs. per roast. Cut in accordance with MBG Specs. No. 402B.

22. PORK CHOPS, Center cut, bone in, 6 oz. each, cut from 12-14 lb. loins. Cut in accordance with MBG Specs. No. 1412. No blade bone.

23. PORK STEW, Max. 1" cubes, free from membrane and gristle, cut from Boston Butt.

24. HAM, PICNIC, IMPORTED PULLMAN, Canned, cooked, whole 8-12 lbs., max. of 12% gelatin, but not over ½" fat at any one point. 4" x 4".

25. CANADIAN BACON, 6-12 lbs., fully cooked, buck eye off. Rose Brand, or approved equal.

26. BACON, Platter style, center cut, 18-22 slice count. Bidder to specify brand.

27. BOSTON BUTT STEAKS, Bone in, cut in accordance with MBG Spec. No. 1406. 7 oz. with ½ oz. tolerance, as lean as possible.

28. PORK SPARERIBS, Cut wing off, send split and cut into approximate portion of 6 oz.

29. ROUND (STEAMSHIP), Rump and Shank off. Cut in accordance with MBG Specs. No. 164.

30. BEEF BACK RIBS.

31. BONELESS BEEF BRISKET, Deckle off. Cut in accordance with MBG Specs. No. 120.

32. CORNED BEEF, Spiced, Deckle off, Kosher Style, Raw, Cut in accordance with MBG Specs. No. 120.

33. PASTRAMI - BRISKET PASTRAMI

34. BEEF LIVER, Skinned and Devained, sliced, 4 oz.

35. LIVERWURST.

POULTRY

36. CHICKEN, fresh, quartered, from 2½-3 lbs. fryers, eviscerated neck and giblets out, 9-11 oz., quartered, tail removed, bid price on delivered net weight. Chickens to be iced.

37. CHICKEN, fresh, whole fryers, 2½-3 lbs., eviscerated neck and giblets out, bid price on delivered net weight.

38. TURKEY, eviscerated, broad-breasted toms, Grade A, frozen 26-28 lbs.

39. TURKEY ROLLS, cooked, mixed, white meat (60%), dark meat (40%), no skin or other unusable meat, bidder to specify brand and weight. Frozen.

APPENDIX 5

COUPON MEAL TICKET PLAN, KENT STATE UNIVERSITY

Kent State University's Residence Halls Food Service (RHFS) staff is committed to providing the people who live, work and study on our campus with the highest quality food service at the most reasonable possible cost.

In line with this objective, we have refined the coupon board plan introduced last year under which all RHFS facilities sold food items on an a la carte basis (you pay for individually-priced items you select). But in order to fully understand the plan, and the many advantages it offers, a little background on institutional board plans might be helpful.

Basically there are two kinds of board plans widely used by colleges and universities in Ohio—the "unlimited" plan and the "coupon" plan.

THE UNLIMITED PLAN

Under the "unlimited" plan, which is used by the vast majority of Ohio colleges and universities, participants pay one flat fee per quarter for the use of the school's dining facilities and they can eat as much or as little as they please. Unfortunately, there are a number of inequities and disadvantages inherent in this system such as:

● Because everyone pays the same amount of money, light eaters are in essence, subsidizing heavy eaters.
● When you miss any of the scheduled meals the value of that meal has been lost.
● A great deal of food is often consumed by persons not on the board plan driving up the cost of the plan for participants.
● There is no incentive to curb waste. It's easier for participants to take more food than they can eat initially than to go through the line a second time.
● The only way to control costs is to cut back on the quality of food or service.

● Food Service facilities are normally only available to customers at breakfast, lunch and dinner.

The "coupon" plan, on the other hand, is specifically designed to offset many, if not all of these deficiencies by enabling participants to tailor our food service plan to meet their individual needs.

THE COUPON PLAN

Here's how it works. At the beginning of fall quarter, participants enter into a food service contract for the entire academic year in which they agree to pay a quarterly fee of $190.00. Fifty per cent of this fee ($95.00) pays for the overhead or fixed costs of operating the dining facilities. For this portion of the payment, you will receive a photo I.D. card identifying you as a program participant. This card must be presented to cashiers when making coupon food purchases for personal consumption.

The remaining $95.00 of the quarterly payment pays for $190.00 worth of coupons which can be used to buy individually-priced items at campus dining facilities (RHFS and Kent Student Center) in much the same way you would buy food at a public cafeteria. So in essence, for every one dollar spent on coupons, you're getting two dollars worth of purchasing power at all RHFS facilities.

WHY $190.00?

We selected the $190.00 minimum payment because our records show that this reflects the average spending level of our "Average Resident Student." This figure also takes into account the fact that we know the "Average Resident Student" will use our facilities for about twelve meals per week, eat off-campus occasionally, and leave the campus on a number of weekends during the year.

Courtesy of Kent State University, Kent, Ohio.

Naturally, we know some participants will eat more than $190.00 worth of food and some will eat less. So we've designed additional flexibility into the system to make the plan as equitable as possible for both these groups.

ADDED FLEXIBILITY

If you are a hearty eater you may purchase all the extra coupons you need from the Residence Services Business Office in Korb Hall on a two-for-one basis. This means a coupon book that costs you $23.75 will actually buy you $47.50 worth of food at campus dining facilities. And conversely, if you are a light eater and don't use up all the coupons purchased in your initial quarterly payment, we'll buy them back from you at their cash value ($23.75 per unused book).

Naturally you are the only one who can accurately estimate how much food and consequently how many coupon books you'll need each quarter. But to give you a rough idea of what you can expect, see the chart below:

Light eaters—
9-11 meals per week/2-3 books
Medium eaters—
10-15 meals per week/4-5 books
Heavy eaters—
16-18 meals per week/6-7 books

This system offers a number of advantages over "unlimited" plans used in the past including:

- Light eaters no longer must subsidize heartier eaters.
- The value of missed meals is not lost as coupons can be used at any time, at campus dining facilities.
- The plan provides financial incentives for curbing food waste and discouraging consumption of food by persons not participating in the plan.

- It's possible to offer a much wider variety of items on the menu.

In addition to breakfast, lunch and dinner, the plan may be used in continuous service available on campus from morning through evening (see enclosed operation schedules).

COST EFFICIENCY

In addition, this new coupon plan is extremely cost efficient in comparison with food service plans at other Ohio colleges and universities. For example, the chart below shows the comparative costs (using 1978 rates) of the food plans at some other State Universities.

WHO'S ELIGIBLE?

The RHFS a la carte coupon board plan is open to all Kent State University students (including non-resident and commuter students), faculty and staff members who regularly use RHFS facilities.

FOR MORE INFORMATION

For further information on KSU's food service program, contact the Residence Halls Food Service staff at Korb Hall or call 672-7000. Also feel free to make any suggestions as to how we can further improve the food service program here at Kent State University.

k.s.u.
residence
services

"people helping people
in a community that cares"

APPENDIX 6

The University of Tennesse
FOOD SERVICES WORKSHOP
For
Professional Employees
Tuesday and Wednesday, March 18 & 19

PROGRAM

Tuesday, March 18

8:00- 8:30 a.m.	University Center Registration Coffee, Donuts	Tennessee Auditorium
8:30 a.m.	"Welcome"	Mr. Norman Hill
9:30-11:30 a.m.	*Bakers & Helpers, Cooks & Helpers, Pantry* Home Economics Building "Proper Use of the Standard Recipe"	Room 104-6 Mrs. Anne Cook
9:30-11:30 a.m.	*Porters, Dishwashers, Receiving* University Center "Your Health and Your Job" Randy Dewitt, Health Educator Knox County Public Health Department	
12:00- 1:00 p.m.	Luncheon University Center	Hermitage Room
1:00- 2:00 p.m.	University Center "An Outbreak of Salmonella" COKE BREAK	Tennessee Auditorium
2:30	University Center Tennessee Auditorium "Pride" — Presented by the Society for the Preservation and Promotion of Me, Myself and I General Discussion	

Wednesday, March 19

8:00- 8:30 a.m.	University Center Coffee and Donuts	Smokey's Palace
8:30-11:00 a.m.	Agricultural College Campus "Science in the Food Service Industry" (Board Buses Outside Rafters Entrance to Center)	
11:00- 1:00 p.m.	Presidential Court Dining Hall "Putting Together a Buffet — Cookout"	
1:00- 4:30	*Cooks and Helpers* Tour of East Tennessee Packing Company (Board Buses, Main Entrance Frances Ave.)	
1:00- 4:30	*Porters, Dishwashers, Receiving* Presidential Court Dining Hall "Dishroom Sanitation Mr. Boyd Dudley COKE BREAK	
1:00- 4:00 p.m.	*Pantry and Bakers* Tour of Automatic Retailers of America Vending Operations (Board Transportation from Loading dock)	

APPENDIX 7

SAMPLE PROCEDURE FOR MENU PLANNING

1. The responsibility for writing the menus should be delegated to one person. This does not mean however that an interchange of ideas should not be sought by this one person among his colleagues and subordinates. The purchasing agent and chef or cook are two valuable sources of advice that should be looked for, along with others you have around you, throughout the menu-writing process. This should also bring about increased co-operation and interest in the food service operation in general.

2. Plan your menus at least one week in advance. This does not mean you won't have occasional changes to take advantage of good buys or to use foods that are on hand. But planning menus in advance gives worthwhile results in many ways; among them are:
   1) Better use of your food dollar
   2) More efficient purchasing
   3) More attractive and varied menus
   4) Less chance of repetition
   5) Time and labor saved in planning and preparing meals
   6) It eliminates the worry of what to serve for the next meal

3. Follow a basic menu pattern on a planning sheet that provides ample space for writing three meals a day for the number of days you serve.

4. Write menus in a quiet place where it is possible to concentrate and where there is space to keep recipe books, recipe files, previous menus, and other aids convenient for reference. (Try to set aside a certain time one day each week for this.)

5. Always check the inventory on hand for food products that should be considered before planning the week's menu.

6. Write information directly on the menu that might be useful to the cooks, salad makers, or other employees.

7. If you rotate your weekly menus, creating cycle menus, it is best not to do so over less than a five-week period. With cycle menus too, seasonal changes and other variations must continually be made or else the ones fed will know exactly what is coming on a certain day.

8. Try to include a new menu item every week.

9. Anticipate the preparation and service problems of your menus and discuss them with your employees.

10. Your menu should be balanced to your staff and to your equipment. Full use of the capability and talents of your production staff should be strived for. Also the work load should be spread over all of the equipment available with special care taken not to have too many items on the grill or in the fryer, etc., for any one meal thus leaving other expensive equipment standing idle.

*This Appendix is part of a report by the Recipe and Menu Committee of NACUFS, prepared by Tom McDonough, University of Cincinnati.

HOW BROAD SHOULD YOUR MENU REALLY BE?

Your own circumstances are the critical factors of course in determining the broadness of your menu, so take a look at them. Do you have the proper layout and equipment and number and type of employees to adequately prepare and serve five, six, or more entrees at one meal? Even if you do, is it really necessary in most of our cases?

Exactly what are the food needs of your customers? Don't you agree that they expect and deserve a wholesome, nutritious and tasty meal; served pleasantly and efficiently when they come to your dining room. To do this, a lot of thought must go into the kinds and types of food that you're going to serve. And even more thought when you consider that these same customers are coming back, tomorrow and tomorrow and tomorrow -- therefore one perfect menu, if there is such a thing, is not sufficient! We must vary our bill of fare greatly day after day to comply with the eating habits of these people who are the means of our livelihood!

Let's take a look at the advantages of the somewhat limited menu. More variety is possible. The same food items do not appear so often, which can be boring the customers. Of course old standbys you couldn't delete, such as hamburgers or grilled cheese. But you couldn't serve 6 or more entrees at a meal without repetition. Regular restaurants offer a broader menu -- but they offer the same menu every day, changed only by a few specials. Their customers change, while most of ours are the same -- day in, day out.

Some type of pattern should be followed to insure complete variety. Price must be considered too, as well as texture, form, and appearance of the dishes. Three kinds of pie are not variety, any more than three beef dishes or three kinds of green vegetable. We must look for a deeper variety. Try to serve distinctly different types, such as a roast, a stew or ground meat item, and a meat substitute or extended meat item. In the dessert line we might have a cake, a cobbler, and a pudding. Wise variation of menu items keeps the customer from feeling that the same food is being offered from day to day.

A limited menu has other advantages too, such as production planning. It is much easier to cook a lot of three entrees than to cook a smaller amount of six or more entrees. Production records will be easier and more accurate resulting in better control of costs and leftovers.

At the same time storage and inventory problems will be less involved. Fewer items have to be on hand, and they can be used faster and stay fresher. Stocking for broader menus means smaller amounts of more items and the greater possibility that something will not be ordered when needed.

Caution must be used always in writing menus to be certain that they're not over simplified. A limited menu is by no means an answer to inefficient or poor food production or service. A limited menu is a means for us to better serve our customers, to give them more recognizable variety, and to give them better quality and service in general.

AN APPROACH TO WRITING MENUS

Usually, in about any project we undertake, a system of some sort works best. This holds very true in planning menus. Any sort of hit-and-miss manner of putting the menu item in its place will fall short of your goals. Here is the kind of system being referred to; breaking down the menu writing process into several steps.

Step #1. Use a large table or desk where you can spread out your reference material; previous menus, especially the previous week's; your master menu index; recipe files; notes and suggestions you've taken or received; an, any other reference books that you may want to use.

Step #2. The best place to start is with the entrees. Write them in for the entire week -- breakfast, luncheon, dinner. (If you are writing cycle menus, spread out blank forms for the number of weeks being written and proceed in the same manner.) After the second step, the luncheon section of your menu might look something like this.

MONDAY	TUESDAY	WEDNESDAY
Hot Roast Beef Sandwich	Delux Hamburgers w/Sliced Tomatoes	Braised Shortribs of Beef
Chicken ala King on Toast	Braised Chicken Livers on Rice	Grilled Sausage Patty w/Scalloped Apples
Stuffed Green Peppers with Tomato Sauce	Grilled Ham Steak	Fried Fillet of Sole

With this mental picture of your counter each week, it is easy to check and double check each item. Weekly variety is not difficult to achieve as well as daily variety that is so essential.

Step #3. In this step add the soup or appetizer and the potato. Care should be taken here to fit them as closely as possible with the entrees. Your menu is progressing as follows.

MONDAY	TUESDAY	WEDNESDAY
French Onion Soup with Croutons	Home Style Vegetable Soup	Old Fashioned Bean Soup
Tomato Juice	Pink Lemonade	Fruit Punch
Hot Roast Beef Sandwich	Delux Hamburger on Bun w/Sliced Tomatoes	Braised Shortribs of Beef with Fresh Vegetables
Chicken ala King on Toast	Braised Chicken Livers on Rice	Grilled Sausage Patty w/Scalloped Apples
Stuffed Green Peppers w/Tomato Sauce	Grilled Ham Steak	Fried Fillet of Sole
Mashed Potatoes	French Fried Potatoes	Hash Brown Potatoes

Step #4. Now insert the vegetables and salads. Try to avoid repeating any vegetable that has been used in the entree or soup. Of course, this is sometimes impossible when trying to match a vegetable with three entrees; but, be on the lookout for obvious duplications or clashes. An example of such a duplication would be stewed tomatoes on the Tuesday when vegetable soup is offered and there are sliced tomatoes with the delux hamburger. Here is the menu so far:

MONDAY	TUESDAY	WEDNESDAY
French Onion Soup with Croutons	Home Style Vegetable Soup	Old Fashioned Bean Soup
Tomato Juice	Pink Lemonade	Fruit Punch
Hot Roast Beef Sandwich	Delux Hamburger on Bun w/Sliced Tomatoes	Braised Shortribs of Beef w/Fresh Vegetables
Chicken ala King on Toast	Braised Chicken Livers on Rice	Griled Sausage Patty w/Scalloped Apples
Stuffed Green Peppers w/Tomato Sauce	Grilled Ham Steak	Fried Filled of Sole
Mashed Potatoes	French Fried Potatoes	Hash Brown Potatoes
Buttered Broccoli	Buttered Peas	Stewed Tomatoes
Glazed Carrots	Cream Style Corn	Buttered Asparagus
Molded Cranberry Salad	Coleslaw	Pineapple Cottage Salad
Tossed Green Salad	Fruit Salad	Relishes

Step #5. Add the desserts and the menus are completed; that is, if you do not see any improvements that can be made the next time you look them over.

APPENDIX 8

Energy Used for Some Routine Daily Activities (excluding basal metabolism and influence of food)[a]

Activity	cal. per kg per hr	Activity	cal. per kg per hr
Bicycling (century run)	7.6	Piano playing (Beethoven's *Appassionata*)	1.4
Bicycling (moderate speed)	2.5		
Bookbinding	0.8	Piano playing (Liszt's *Tarantella*)	2.0
Boxing	11.4		
Carpentry (heavy)	2.3	Reading aloud	0.4
Cello playing	1.3	Rowing in race	16.0
Crocheting	0.4	Running	7.0
Dancing, foxtrot	3.8	Sawing wood	5.7
Dancing, waltz	3.0	Sewing, hand	0.4
Dishwashing	1.0	Sewing, motor driven machine	0.4
Dressing and undressing	0.7	Shoemaking	1.0
Driving automobile	0.9	Singing in loud voice	0.8
Eating	0.4	Sitting quietly	0.4
Exercise		Skating	3.5
Very light	0.9	Skiing (moderate speed)	10.3
Light	1.4	Standing relaxed	0.5
Moderate	3.1	Stone masonry	4.7
Severe	5.4	Sweeping with broom, bare floor	1.4
Very severe	7.6	Sweeping with carpet sweeper	1.6
Fencing	7.3	Sweeping with vacuum sweeper	2.7
Horseback riding, walk	1.4	Swimming (2 mph)	7.9
Horseback riding, trot	4.3	Tailoring	0.9
Horseback riding, gallop	6.7	Typewriting rapidly	
Ironing (5 lb iron)	1.0	(standard typewriter)	1.0
Knitting sweater	0.7	(electric typewriter)	0.5
Laundry, light	1.3	Violin playing	0.6
Lying still, awake	0.1	Walking (3 mph)	2.0
Organ playing (1/3 hand work)	1.5	Walking rapidly (4 mph)	3.4
Painting furniture	1.5	Walking at high speed (5.3 mph)	8.3
Paring potatoes	0.6	Walking down stairs	b
Playing ping pong	4.4	Walking up stairs	c
Piano playing (Mendelssohn's *Song without Words*)	0.8	Washing floors	1.2
		Writing	0.4

[a] Adapted with permission of The Macmillan Company from **Foundations of Nutrition,** 6th ed., by Taylor and Pye. © The Macmillan Company, 1967.

[b] Allow 0.012 calorie per kilogram for an ordinary staircase with 15 steps, without regard to time.

[c] Allow 0.036 calorie per kilogram for an ordinary staircase with 15 steps, without regard to time.

Reprinted from *Living Nutrition,* Stare and McWilliams, with permission from John Wiley & Sons, N.Y.

Recommended Daily Dietary Allowances, Revised 1974[a]
(Designed for the maintenance of good nutrition of practically all healthy people in the U.S.A.)

	Age (years)	Weight (kg)	Weight (lbs)	Height (cm)	Height (in)	Energy (kcal)[b]	Protein (g)	Vitamin A Activity (RE)[c]	Vitamin A (IU)	Vitamin D (IU)	Vitamin E Activity[e] (IU)	Ascorbic Acid (mg)	Folacin[f] (μg)	Niacin[g] (mg)	Riboflavin (B₂) (mg)	Thiamin (B₁) (mg)	Vitamin B₆ (mg)	Vitamin B₁₂ (μg)	Calcium (mg)	Phosphorus (mg)	Iodine (μg)	Iron (mg)	Magnesium (mg)	Zinc (mg)
Infants	0.0–0.5	6	14	60	24	kg × 117	kg × 2.2	420[d]	1,400	400	4	35	50	5	0.4	0.3	0.3	0.3	360	240	35	10	60	3
	0.5–1.0	9	20	71	28	kg × 108	kg × 2.0	400	2,000	400	5	35	50	8	0.6	0.5	0.4	0.3	540	400	45	15	70	5
Children	1–3	13	28	86	34	1300	23	400	2,000	400	7	40	100	9	0.8	0.7	0.6	1.0	800	800	60	15	150	10
	4–6	20	44	110	44	1800	30	500	2,500	400	9	40	200	12	1.1	0.9	0.9	1.5	800	800	80	10	200	10
	7–10	30	66	135	54	2400	36	700	3,300	400	10	40	300	16	1.2	1.2	1.2	2.0	800	800	110	10	250	10
Males	11–14	44	97	158	63	2800	44	1,000	5,000	400	12	45	400	18	1.5	1.4	1.6	3.0	1200	1200	130	18	350	15
	15–18	51	134	172	69	3000	54	1,000	5,000	400	15	45	400	20	1.8	1.5	2.0	3.0	1200	1200	150	18	400	15
	19–22	67	147	172	69	3000	54	1,000	5,000	400	15	45	400	20	1.8	1.5	2.0	3.0	800	800	140	10	350	15
	23–50	70	154	172	69	2700	56	1,000	5,000		15	45	400	18	1.6	1.4	2.0	3.0	800	800	130	10	350	15
	51+	70	154	172	69	2400	56	1,000	5,000		15	45	400	16	1.5	1.2	2.0	3.0	800	800	110	10	350	15
Females	11–14	44	97	155	62	2400	44	800	4,000	400	12	45	400	16	1.3	1.2	1.6	3.0	1200	1200	115	18	300	15
	15–18	54	119	162	65	2100	48	800	4,000	400	12	45	400	14	1.4	1.1	2.0	3.0	1200	1200	115	18	300	15
	19–22	58	128	162	65	2100	46	800	4,000	400	12	45	400	14	1.4	1.1	2.0	3.0	800	800	100	18	300	15
	23–50	58	128	162	65	2000	46	800	4,000		12	45	400	13	1.2	1.0	2.0	3.0	800	800	100	18	300	15
	51+	58	128	162	65	1800	46	800	4,000		12	45	400	12	1.1	1.0	2.0	3.0	800	800	80	10	300	15
Pregnant						+300	+30	1,000	5,000	400	15	60	800	+2	+0.3	+0.3	2.5	4.0	1200	1200	125	18+[h]	450	20
Lactating						+500	+20	1,200	6,000	400	15	80	600	+4	+0.5	+0.3	2.5	4.0	1200	1200	150	18	450	25

a Reproduced by permission of the Food and Nutrition Board, National Academy of Sciences—National Research Council. The allowances are intended to provide for individual variations among most normal persons as they live in the United States under usual environmental stresses. Diets should be based on a variety of common foods in order to provide other nutrients for which human requirements have been less well defined. See text for more detailed discussion of allowances and of nutrients not tabulated.

b Kilojoules (kJ) = 4.2 × kcal.

c Retinol equivalents.

d Assumed to be all as retinol in milk during the first six months of life. All subsequent intakes are assumed to be half as retinol and half as β-carotene when calculated from international units. As retinol equivalents, three fourths are as retinol and one fourth as β-carotene.

e Total vitamin E activity, estimated to be 80 percent as α-tocopherol and 20 percent other tocopherols.

f The folacin allowances refer to dietary sources as determined by Lactobacillus casei assay. Pure forms of folacin may be effective in doses less than one fourth of the recommended dietary allowance.

g Although allowances are expressed as niacin, it is recognized that on the average 1 mg of niacin is derived from each 60 mg of dietary tryptophan.

h This increased requirement cannot be met by ordinary diets; therefore, the use of supplemental iron is recommended.

Reprinted from Living Nutrition, Stare and McWilliams, with permission from John Wiley & Sons, N.Y.

Estimated Daily Calorie Requirement for a Female
18 Years Old (body surface = 1.5 square meters, wt. 50 kilograms)

Calculations	kcal (24 hr)
Basal metabolism 35.8 × 1.5 × 24 = 1289 kcal kcal/sq m/hr age 18 female = 35.8[a] Surface area (5'3") = 1.5[b] Hours = 24	1289
Activity Time (hr) kcal/hr[c] (kg) kcal[d] Dressing 1 × 0.7 × 50 = 35 Eating 1 × 0.4 × 50 = 20 Driving 2 × 0.9 × 50 = 90 Studying 8 × 0.4 × 50 = 160 Walking 2 × 2.0 × 50 = 200 Watching TV 2 × 0.4 × 50 = 40 Sleeping _8_ 24 545 kcal	545
Specific dynamic action Basal metabolism 1289 Activity _545_ 1834 kcal 1834 × 10% = 183	183
Total	2017

[a] From Table 4.4.
[b] From Figure 4.1.
[c] From Table 4.6.
[d] Time × kcal/hr × (kg) = kcal required.

Weight Control and Energy Needs   chapter four

Reprinted from *Living Nutrition,* Stare and McWilliams, with permission from John Wiley & Sons, N.Y.

Caloric Content of Selected
Beverages in Amounts Commonly Served[a]

	Measure	kcal
Milk type		
Whole milk	1 cup	160
Skim milk	1 cup	90
Fortified low-fat milk	1 cup	145
Buttermilk	1 cup	90
Eggnog (nonalcoholic)	1 cup	235
Malted milkshake	1 cup	330
Fruit juice type		
Orange juice	1/2 cup	60
Lemonade	1 cup	100
Carbonated		
Colas	8 oz	96
Ginger ale	8 oz	70
Sodas, fruit flavored	8 oz	112
Alcoholic		
Beer	12 oz	151
Wine, table	3 1/2 oz	85
Daiquiri	3 1/2 oz	120
Manhattan	3 1/2 oz	165
Martini	3 1/2 oz	220
Whiskey (86 proof)	2 oz	140
Gin (90 proof)	2 oz	150
Coffee, black	5 oz	2-5
Tea, unsweetened	5 oz	2

[a] Data compiled and adapted from *Composition of Foods—Raw, Processed, Prepared.* Agriculture Handbook No. 8, U.S.D.A., 1963; *Nutritive Value of American Foods,* Agriculture Handbook No. 456, U.S.D.A., 1975.

Reprinted from *Living Nutrition,* Stare and McWilliams, with permission from John Wiley & Sons, N.Y.

APPENDIX 9

NUTRITION NEWSLETTER TO OUR STUDENTS

Hi Everyone!   3/8/76

National Nutrition Week starts on Monday, March 8th. At a recent lecture we listened to a renowned nutritionist, Dr. Z. I. Sabry from Toronto. We think you'll be interested in a summary of what he had to say:

1. **The American Diet.** The average American eats too much *salt, fat,* and too much *sugar* (some of which converts to fat!). This problem has to be solved when the person is *young,* not when he approaches middle age.

2. **The Average American College Student.** A study of 50 U.S. colleges showed the following difference between *actual* and the *ideal* food intake of college students:

		ACTUAL	IDEAL*
a.	Percent of **Protein** in total calories	14%	10-15%
b.	Percent of **Fats** in total calories	42%	30%
c.	Percent of **Carbohydrates** in total calories	44%**	43-48%
d.	Ratio of Poly-unsaturated to saturated fats	.39:1.0	1.0:1.0
e.	Level of Cholesterol - Men	482 mgm/day	300 mgm/day
	Level of Cholesterol - Women	325 mgm/day	300 mgm/day

In the choices made by the students . . .

   f. ⅓ of college meals were deficient in Vitamin "D"
   g. ¾ of college meals were deficient in Folic Acid and Vitamin B-6

3. **Nutritional Deficiencies.** The following are some of the most prevalent deficiencies in the average American's diet:
   a. **Iron.** Iron in the blood carries oxygen to all parts of the body. Without it, you become anemic (tire easily, etc.). The average woman needs 15 mgm. daily, and has to consume at least 2,500 calories to get that much iron. The average man would have to get 2,000 calories daily. *One out of four women is low in iron!* Eat liver, meat and eggs.
   b. **Calcium.** We get 80% of calcium from milk. The more phosphates we consume (in processed foods), the more calcium we need. *You must drink milk,* but non-fat or 2% milk is much better for you (in whole milk, 50% of the calories are from fat; in 2% milk, only 30% of the calories are fat). Cheeses are OK also.
   c. **Folic Acid (Vitamin B-2 Complex).** Found in green, leafy vegetables. Deficiency causes a type of anemia and probably lowers resistance to some illnesses. Eat your lettuce!

4. **Cholesterol.** Obesity and cardio-vascular disease are the most prevalent problems caused by poor nutrition in America today. If more than half of your fat consumption is in saturated fats (e.g., the fat in meat, milk products, coconut oil), you're headed in the wrong direction! Poly-unsaturated fats (soft margarine, soybean or most other vegetable oils) are better for you -- they are more easily broken down in the body and do not retain cholesterol as saturated fats.

*Statistics taken from lecture notes; not verified
**Doesn't indicate how much is in the form of starches or refined sugar.

5. **Trace Minerals.** Only in recent years have we learned that Man needs a small amount of trace minerals to live. These are minerals from the Earth's crust (like zinc, silicone, arsenic, etc.). *Meats* are a good source of such trace minerals. To have good metabolism, these are necessary in small amounts.

6. **Vegetarianism.** For young adults above the age of about 20-22 years, modified vegetarian diets or non-meat diets, are O.K., since the need for trace minerals and various other nutrients (50 in all!) drops when you've reached full physical development. *A vegetarian diet before that age is unwise, and can easily be harmful.* In all ages, however, we must have milk or cheese for calcium!

   However: Meat is not "the staff of life" and we must reduce the amount of meat eaten in America. *WE EAT TOO MUCH MEAT!*

7. **Health Foods.** "Wholesome" (i.e., unrefined foods) are fine, but even white bread is better than donuts (empty calorie food). "Organic" foods are foods that are fertilized with manure rather than artificial fertilizers. *Note:* A plant does not *eat* manure, it takes the nitrogen out of the nitrate regardless of its source. There is no difference, nutritionally, between organically grown and other foods. Regarding the use of pesticides and insecticides: "it is either us or the insects which get the food first!" (Sabry). We must control the insects through insecticides and pesticides, but we must also wash the food carefully before eating.

CONCLUSION

It takes a long time to develop good eating habits. As a student, one should learn more about good nutrition, from "nutrition clubs" on campus, and become more aware of special and economic issues which effect the food system.

Your Food Service Director and his professional staff members are all concerned with these important issues, and are willing to help you in your quest for Nutrition Education.

Yours, for better nutrition,

Paul Fairbrook
Director, Auxiliary Services

PF:sth

HELPFUL NUTRITION HINTS TAKEN FROM
NATIONAL NUTRITION WEEK MARCH 6-12, 1977
PROPER DIET

Merely improving nutrition could be one of the best preventive health measures people could take, the Senate Select Committee on Nutrition and Human Needs said in a report, "Dietary Goals for the United States".

Committee Chairman, George McGovern (D-S.D.), noted at hearing on the report in early February that six of the 10 leading causes of death in the United States has been tied to eating and drinking habits; heart disease, cancer, stroke and hypertension, diabetes, arteriosclerosis and cirrhossis of the liver.

Diets too high in fats and cholesteral appear definitely related to cardiovascular disease, which affects the heart and blood vessels. More Americxns die from this disease than any other.

Eating too much sugar can lead to tooth decay, diabetes and obesity, while high salt intake contributes to hypertension. Most Americans do not realize the amount of sugar they consume, since much of it comes from processed foods and soft drinks. The "hidden" sugar we eat in such foods has more than tripled in the past 60 years. *Cutting down on soft drinks and baked goods was the report's principal recommendation on sugar intake.*

If your eating habits are typically American, here are some changes the Committee report said would result in less obesity and better health:

Eat more carbohydrates, so that they amount to 55-60% of your total calories consumed. Most of them should be complex carbohydrates (fruits, vegetables, grains) rather than sugar.

Reduce fat consumption to 30% of calories eaten, from the existing 40% average level. Saturated fats should account for only 10% of total calories. Butter is composed of 50% saturated fat, while other cooking oils and margarines, such as safflower, soybean and corn, are much lower in saturated fat.

Cut cholesterol intake to 300 milligrams a day, from the current 600 milligrams a day.

Eat less sugar. It should provide no more than 15% of caloric intake, down from the average 24%.

Reduce salt consumption to three grams a day (3/5th of a teaspoon). Americans now eat between 6 and 18 grams a day.

McGovern was quick to say, "We don't want war with the food industry and the agricultural producers; we need their cooperation." Nevertheless, those groups are bound to oppose some of his recommendations.

Excerpt from Congressional Quarterly by Mary Link as it appeared in the Palo Alto Times, Tuesday, February 22, 1977.

March 1977

WANT TO LOSE WEIGHT ON THE CAMPUS MENU????

1.   Eat three meals a day, using smaller portions.

2.   Avoid extras -- sauces, whipped toppings, gravies. Ask for plain meat or plain vegetables. Skip the mushroom gravy and cheese sauce.

3.   Cut down on salt usage. Drink plenty of water.

4.   Eat slowly.

5.   Do not eat between meals and *never* after dinner.

6.   Try to jog around the field or play basketball in the gym; effective weight loss includes exercise *and* a decrease in caloric intake.

7.   Use skim milk, and omit butter and ice cream, all baked desserts, soft drinks, and limit other carbohydrates.

Sample suggestions:

Soft cooked egg on dry toast, juice, and skim milk . . . for breakfast

Lean meat or half sandwich, vegetables, fruit, and skim milk . . . for lunch

Lean meat, vegetables, fruit, and 1 slice wholewheat bread . . .

Remember, what you eat in private, shows in public!

APPENDIX 10

BEHAVIOR MODIFICATION FOR WEIGHT REDUCTION

WEEK ONE: Pre-Therapy Evaluation and Introduction
1. Greeting weigh in (private)
2. Eating history analysis (our own)
3. Ideal body weight - calorie expenditure
4. Eating is behavior to change
Discuss:
   a. Existing behavior
   b. Modification of existing behavior breifly
   c. Practicing and rewarding new behavior
Weekly Task: Keep record of diet, exercise, time and place eaten, and associated feelings. (Especially important if diet is not maintained.)

WEEK TWO:
1. Weigh in and discuss diary
2. Practice and reward new behavior
3. Discuss four food groups and necessity of having some of each every day.
4. Discuss nutrients
5. Discuss snacking
Behavior Task: Find a way to eat slower. Increase awareness and appreciation of food. Gain a sense of control:
   a. Wait a full minute before starting to eat
   b. Lay down utensils several times
   c. Don't be afraid to leave some food on plate
   d. Use a small plate
Nutritional Task: Decrease refined sugar. Be sure to eat fruits as outlined on your diet.

WEEK THREE:
1. Weigh in and discuss diet diary
2. Discuss places as cues to stimulate eating
3. Discuss importance of bulk in good nutrition
Behavior Task: Decrease food availability:
   a. Containerize foods
   b. Fresh vegetables as snacks - strips
   c. Food which requires lengthy preparation
Nutritional Task Review: Nutrients
   a. Stress low calories and nutrients in vegetables
   b. Watch portions

WEEK FOUR:
1. Weigh in and discuss diet diary
2. Review task compliance
3. Discuss protein requirements and sources (nutritianist and patient)
Behavior Task: Decrease high risk situations - friends, T.V., etc.
Nutritional Task: Eat 6 oz. meat (or meat equivalents) per day.

WEEK FIVE:
1. Weigh in, nutritional review. Discuss diet diary.
2. Discuss carbohydrate sources and associated nutrients.
3. Check on exercise program
Nutritional Task:
    a. Find a way to make food more attractive
    b. Bring in low - cal recipes
    c. Review nutrients
Behavior Task: Get feed-back for individual task

WEEK SIX:
1. Weigh in, discuss diet diary - feed back nutrients
2. Measure success
3. Compare behavioral and nutritional change
4. Make commitment for future program

	Breakfast	**Lunch**	**Dinner**

6 oz. Meat (70 Cal. per oz.). . . . . . .420 Cal.
chicken, turkey, lamb, liver, pork, veal,
fish, beef, hot dogs, cold cuts, cheese,
cottage cheese, eggs

16 ox. Lowfat Milk (125 per glass). 250 Cal.

Breads - 4 or more servings (70 each). . . . .
. . . . .280 Cal.

1 slice bread	1½" sq. cornbread
1 small roll	1 small muffin
1 tortilla	2 sq. graham
5 soda crackers	crackers
½ cup cereal	5 vanilla wafers
½ cup noodles	½ cup sherbet
½ cup macaroni	1½" sq. angel food
	cake (uniced)

Fruits - 3 servings (40 Cal. per ½ cup). . . .
. . . . .120 Cal.

Apple	Grapefruit	Peach
Applesauce	Fruit Cocktail	Pear
Apricots	Grapes	Pineapple
Banana	Melons	Plums
Berries	Orange	

Vegetable - 4 or more servings. . .110 Cal.
eat as desired - 0-20 Cal. per ½ cup

Asparagas	Mushrooms	Clear Broth
Broccoli	Radishes	Coffee
Brussel Sprouts	Rubarb	Diet
Cabbage	Sour Pickles	Dressing
Cauliflower	Spinach	Diet
Celery	String Beans	Gelatin
Cranberries	Summer	Diet Soda
Eggplant	Squash	Lemon
Leafy Greens	Tomato Juice	Tea
		Vinegar

veg. - 40 Cal. per ½ cup

Beets	Onions	Winter
Carrots	Peas	Squash

veg. - 70 Cal. per ½ cup

Potatoes	Rice

veg. - 70 Cal. per ½ cup

Baked Beans	Lima Beans	Yams
Corn	Sweet Potatoes	

Fats - 1½ servings (45 Cal. each). .70 Cal.

1 tsp. Margarine	1 Tbsp. French Dress.
1 tsp. Mayonnaise	1 Tbsp. Cr. Cheese
1 tsp. Oil	⅓ Avacado
3 oz. Nuts	2 slices bacon

TOTAL CALORIES 1250

Did anything cause a special eating problem today?_____

ACTIVITIES - What activity did I do today?_____

APPENDIX 11

HEALTH FOOD BAR MENU
CALIFORNIA STATE UNIVERSITY, CHICO

THE GARDEN

The Vegetable Basket
Juice Bar and Health Salads

THE HEALTH NUT............$ .75
Goblet of yogurt with toasted Sun
flower seeds and raisins.

CRISP VEGETABLE SALAD.....$ .75
with sprouts and mushrooms.

MIXED BEAN SALAD...........$ .50

LOW-CAL COTTAGE CHEESE...$ .40

CARROT & RAISIN SALAD......$ .50

Apple Cider..................$ .40

Old Fashioned Apple Juice......$ .55

Kifer ....$ .60

Natural Bottle Juices...........$ .55

THE GREAT, GREAT HONEY YOGURT
SHAKE $1.25
Yogurt, with 1 whole egg, honey, wheat
germ and non-fat milk, blended
together with loving care.

THE FRESH FRUIT BOWL - Cup..$ .85
Cool and refreshing.

HEALTH BAR BLENDER DRINKS$ .85
*Protein Pick-up   *Old Smoothie
*Mixed Fruit   *Tiger Milkshake
FRUIT YOGURT SHAKE SPECIAL$ .85
Your choice of flavor blended with non-
fat milk.

Fresh Whole Fruit.............$ .25

Raw Carrot & Celery Stixs.......$ .25

Hard Boiled Egg...............$ .25

Continental Yogurt............$ .60

THE GARDEN

The Vegetable Basket
Natural Foods

THE SUNFLOWER............$1.30
Cream cheese topped with toasted
Sunflower seeds, raisins, & sprouts on
Wheat Berry bread.

SOY VEGEBURGER & SPROUTS.$ .90
On Wheat Berry
  with cheese...............$1.00

THE AVOCADO SANDWICH....$1.35
Served with sprouts and cucumbers
with cheese.................$1.45

THE MUSHROOM BURGER.....$1.25
Fresh mushrooms & Jack Cheese
grilled on Wheat bread with sprouts
and cucumbers.

THE SUPER PEANUT BUTTER
RAISIN ....$ .95
Chunky peanut butter covered with
raisins, diced celery, shredded carrots,
and sprouts on Wheat or Rye bread.

THE VEGETABLE QUICHE......$1.35
Cheese custard pie blended with
garden vegetables and served with
fresh fruit.

CUCUMBER & EGG SALAD.....$1.10
with sprouts.

NATURAL SWISS OR
JACK CHEESE...............$ .95
and sprouts.

GRILLED EGG SALAD..........$1.25
with fresh mushrooms.

BROWN RICE & VEGETABLES..$ .60
  with cheese...............$ .70

SPANISH GAZPACHO . . Mug...$ .85
A vegetable tomato soup served chilled
or served hot.

APPENDIX 12

DAILY LABOR REPORT

1. The purpose of the Daily Labor Report is to give the food service management an account of the Daily Labor Expense as compared to Daily Income.

2. This report will enable management to forecast its labor needs more effectively, and in conjunction with the income generated.

3. The Administrative rate will include all Supervisors, Dietitions and the Food Service Director, their wages will be divided by the number of working days in that pay period.

4. The classified monthly will be the office secretaries, their monthly wages will be divided by the number of working days in that pay period.

5. The classified hourly will include all classified employees, placed in their proper dollar rate column.
   a. The hours to be totaled in each horizontal line.
   b. The total hours times their respective rates will give a subtotal of wages for that horizontal line.
   c. Add the total of horizontal lines under the classified hourly.

6. Under total regular salaries, add the Administrative, Classified Monthly and Classified Hourly.

7. The student hourly will include all student employees placed in their proper dollar rate.
   a. The hours to be totaled in each horizontal line.
   b. The total hours times their respective rates will give a subtotal of wages for that horizontal line.
   c. Add the total of horizontal lines under the student hourly.

8. Under total salaries add total regular salaries and total student salaries.

9. To find the Fringe Benefit Factor, take the total salaries times accumulative % to date.

10. To find the total Labor Expense today, add total salaries and Fringe Benefit Factor.

11. Accumulative Labor Expense Brought Forward is from the preceding day.

12. Total Accumulative Labor Expense is adding together the total Labor Expense Today and the Accumulative Labor Expense Brought Forward started over a month.

13. Catering Salaries are designated to help in the forecast for both caterings and the stateroom operations.

14. Catering Administrative refers to 100% of the Managers Salary and 30% of the Food Service Director's Salary.

15. Classified Monthly refers to 30% of office secretaries.

16. Classified Hourly refers to the total dollars spent during the operational day.

17. Student hourly refers to the total dollars spent during the operational day.

18. Total Catering Salaries is the summation of Administrative, Classified Monthly, Classified Hourly and Student Hourly.

19. Fringe Benefit factor is computed by multiplying total Catering Salaries times accumulative % to date.

20. Total Catering Labor Expense is the summation of total Catering Salaries plus the Fringe Benefit Factor.

21. The following areas will be maintained to show daily and accumulative totals.
    a. Customers
    b. Sales
    c. Labor
    d. % Labor/Sales

Courtesy of K-State Union, Kansas State University, Manhattan, Kansas.

K-STATE UNION
FOOD SERVICE DEPARTMENT
KANSAS STATE UNIVERSITY

DAILY LABOR COST
5-6-77
DATE
Friday

PAY PERIOD ENDING

	TOTAL HOURS	RATE	TOTAL HOURS	% OF INCOME
ADMINISTRATIVE	NA	NA	188.13	
CLASSIFIED MONTHLY	NA	NA	44.09	
CLASSIFIED HOURLY CODE SHEET			232.22	

8.0	8.2	6.9	6.0	8c	7.9	7.9	7.9	7.8	5.5	7.6	8.1	6.4	10.6	4.3	6.3	117.4	2.42	284.10
8.0	5.9															13.9	2.52	35.02
8.0	4.5	7.9														20.4	2.63	53.65
7.8																7.8	2.74	21.37
4.5	5.0	4.5	7.5	8.0												29.5	2.86	84.37
8.0	7.8															15.8	2.98	47.08
8.0	7.9	8.0	5.8	8.0												37.7	3.11	117.24
6.7	8.3	6.9	7.8													29.7	3.25	96.52
5.6	8.2															13.8	3.39	46.78
7.9																7.9	3.69	29.15
8.0	8.0															16.0	3.85	61.60
8.0	8.2															16.2	4.04	65.44

		TOTAL HOURS		TOTAL
TOTAL CLASSIFIED HOURLY SALARIES		326.1		942.32
TOTAL REGULAR SALARIES				1,174.54

STUDENT HOURLY

4.8	2.8	6.4	3.1	2.5	3.1	2.1	2.5	2.5	.9	4.5	2.9	2.8	4.1	4.1			
3.2	5.9	3.2	3.11	7.0	3.7	5.7	2.1	2.7	1.8	5.6	3.2	1.6			97.9	2.30	225.17
															3.4	2.40	81.60
															3.9	2.50	9.75

		TOTAL HOURS		TOTAL
TOTAL STUDENT SALARIES		105.2		316.52

	TOTAL HOURS		TOTAL
TOTAL SALARIES	431.3		1,491.06
FRINGE BENEFIT FACTOR %			298.21
TOTAL LABOR COST TODAY			1,789.27
ACCUMULATIVE LABOR COST BROUGHT FORWARD			23,121.02
TOTAL ACCUMULATIVE LABOR COST			24,910.29

CATERING SALARIES

			TOTAL
ADMINISTRATIVE			58.25
CLASSIFIED MONTHLY			13.22
CLASSIFIED HOURLY	35.1		96.96
STUDENT HOURLY	48.8		112.24
TOTAL CATERING SALARIES			280.67
FRINGE BENEFIT FACTOR %			56.13
TOTAL CATERING LABOR COST			336.80

	TODAY	ACCUM	TODAY	ACCUM	TODAY	ACCUM	TODAY	ACCUM
STATEROOM	4624	30,565	2564.17	11,430.80	1,452.47	23,992.48	56.6	
CATERING	444	1,847	1483.56	4,349.79	336.80	917.81	22.7	
TOTAL	5068	32,412	4,047.73	15,780.59	1,789.27	24,910.29	44.2	
	CUSTOMERS		SALES		LABOR		%LABOR/SALES	

— = Regular Food Service Personnel
— = Banquet Personnel

APPENDIX 13

CALIFORNIA STATE UNIVERSITY, CHICO

#2300 VENDING OPERATING REPORT

Period Ending _____

Prepared by: _____
Approved by: _____

	Candy	Can Drink	Coffee	Ice Cream	Cigarettes	Food Vend.	Pin Ball	Other	TOTALS
TOTAL SALES FOR PERIOD (1)									
Total Purchases (from VIR)									
Plus: Beginning Inventory									
Sub-Total									
Less: Ending Inventory									
Cost of Sale (6)									
Cost of Sale %									

OPERATING REPORT	%		DIRECT EXPENSES		INDIRECT EXPENSES		REMARKS:
Total Sale (Line 1)	100%		Auto & Truck		Acct.		
Cost of Sale (Line 6)			Advertising		G.M.		
Gross Profit			Repair & Maint.		Insurance		
			Office Supplies		Depreciation		
Payroll - Reg. Staff			Other		Other		
Payroll - Indirect							
Payroll - Students							
Sub-Total							
Taxes							
Retirement							
Health Insurance							
Total Labor Costs							
Direct Expenses							Average Sale per-hour worked $
Indirect Expenses							
							LABOR HOURS AND OVERTIME
							Hours Worked - Reg. Staff
Total Expenses							Hours Worked - Student
							Total Hours Worked
							No. Full Time _____ No. Students
Operating Profit or (loss)							Over-time Hours
							Over-time Costs $

APPENDIX 14

OUTLINE OF SPECIFICATIONS FOR
CAMPUS VENDING BID

1.) **General Terms**
   a.) Definition of terms
   b.) Period of agreement, i.e., number of years
   c.) Method of communication, i.e., student committee
   d.) When and how to adjust terms
   e.) How to resolve disputes
   f.) Unusual occurances, i.e., calamity, war, etc.
   g.) Insurance requirements
   h.) Responsibility for permits and licenses
   i.) What contractor will provide
   j.) What campus will provide
   k.) Campus right of inspection

2.) **Vending Price, Minimum Portions and Product Specifications**
   This section would cover labeling, coding of perishable foods, brand names preferences, etc. It must also provide a procedure for adjusting individual specifications.

3.) **Personnel, Employment Practices and Staffing**
   This section is critical in terms of providing quality service throughout the day and throughout the year.

4.) **Equipment, Utilities, Supplies and Space Use**
   a.) List of initally desired equipment, with provision to adjust as service needs change
   b.) Minimum age of equipment to be used plus other design requirements
   c.) Method for replacing equipment or adding equipment
   d.) Location requirements
   e.) Utilities and storage space provided by campus
   f.) The use of microwave ovens and change making equipment
   g.) The need for condiment stands, tables and chairs, etc.

5.) **Maintenance of Equipment and Facilities -- Replacement and Sanitation**
   a.) Stipulation of a preventive maintenance program
   b.) When and how repairs will be made
   c.) Minimum service requirements for delivery of products to machines
   d.) Regular replacement of worn equipment
   e.) Cleaning of vending areas

6.) **Commissions, Accounting and Payments**
   a.) The basis for commissions to be computed
   b.) In some cases a minimum guarantee total commission is included
   c.) Accounting procedures and reports to campus
   d.) Refund system
   e.) Sales tax
   f.) When payments will be made

7.) **Contract Termination**
   a.) Cancellation clause
   b.) Breach by either party
   c.) Damages for breach or cancellation

8.) **Bid Submittal Forms**
   The actual forms to bid on

APPENDIX 15

SELF INSPECTION FORM FOR RESTAURANTS

THE WAY I SEE IT

INSPECTOR FOR THE DAY:

_____

ESTABLISHMENT_____

LOCATED AT_____

_____

IF IMPROVEMENT IS NEEDED, MARK ☐

1. **FLOORS**
   ☐ Clean   ☐ Easily cleaned   ☐ Safe, good repair
   ☐ Clean under equipment   ☐ Dustless "cleaning" methods

2. **WALLS AND CEILINGS**
   ☐ Clean   ☐ Washable, easily cleaned   ☐ Clean behind equipment

3. **DOORS AND WINDOWS**
   ☐ Clean   ☐ Screened   ☐ Tight fitting   ☐ Fly Fans Operating

4. **VENTILATION**
   ☐ Hood Clean   ☐ Filters Clean   ☐ No Smokey Appearance
   ☐ Reasonable Employee Comfort

5. **LIGHTING**
   ☐ Adequate to see if dishes and glasses are clean
   ☐ Sufficient light on work surfaces
   ☐ Sufficient to see cleanup operations

6. **TOILETS**
   ☐ Clean throughout   ☐ Floors and walls washable and waterproof
   ☐ Ventilated to outside air   ☐ Enough toilets provided   ☐ Flyproof
   ☐ Doors self-closing   ☐ Paper in holder

7. **HANDWASHING**
   ☐ Employee hands clean   ☐ Soap in dispenser
   ☐ Convenient to wash hands before returning to work from toilets
   ☐ Single Service towels in dispenser   ☐ Lavatory clean
   ☐ Handwashing signs posted   ☐ Hot and cold water

8. **DISHWASHING**
   ☐ Dishes are clean   ☐ Dishes are pre-scraped
   ☐ Dishes are properly racked for machine
   ☐ Dishes are machine washed at 160° F.
   ☐ Sinks set up for wash-clear rinse-sanitize

9. **SANITIZING** (either method)
   ☐ Final rinse with water at 180° F.
   ☐ Approved chemical sanitizer used according to directions with operator
   knowing amount of water in sink and measuring sanitizer

10. **EQUIPMENT AND UTENSILS**
    ☐ Clean   ☐ Free of chips, seams and cracks
    ☐ Cutlery, saws, etc., cleaned frequently
    ☐ Easily disassembled for cleaning with responsible person knowing how to
    disassemble

11. **UTENSIL STORAGE**
    ☐ Protected from rust, dirt, mop splash, etc.   ☐ Protected from sneezes
    ☐ Silver stored so handles only can be grasped
    ☐ Paper service handled correctly ☐ Shelves and draws washable and clean

12. REFRIGERATON
☐ Neat and clean   ☐ Thermometer present   ☐ Temperature below 40°
☐ Flat containers for perishables
☐ Produce, egg cartons, packaged foods stored on bottom shelves.

13. FOOD STORAGE
☐ Protected from dust, dirt, mop splash, sneezes, etc.
☐ Protected from rodents, insects   ☐ Protected from overhead leakage
☐ Bacterial growth prevented by keeping perishables above 140°/below 40°
☐ Original contents only stored in tin cans   ☐ Older foods used first

14. FOOD WORKERS
☐ Clean washable outer garments used for no other activities   ☐ Sober
☐ Free from colds, open sores, communicable disease   ☐ No smoking
☐ Hair confined   ☐ "No Smoking" signs posted

15. WASTE DISPOSAL
☐ Premises clean   ☐ Containers washable and clean
☐ Fly tight, rodent proof refuse containers ☐ Removed at least twice weekly
☐ Sewage properly disposed

16. RODENT AND INSECT CONTROL
☐ Pests present (specify)_____
☐ Entrances and breeding places hunted out and eliminated
☐ All possible food and attractants eliminated
☐ Poisons properly labeled, stored and used so as not to contaminate food and utensils
☐ All openings more than ¼ inch into or under buildings sealed with rodent proof material.

IF YOU WOULD LIKE ASSISTANCE in improving the sanitation of your restaurant, the sanitarian in your district will be glad to assist you.

DIVISION OF ENVIRONMENTAL SANITATION
ORANGE COUNTRY HEALTH DEPARTMENT
8th and North Ross Streets
Santa Ana, California

APPENDIX 16

RULES FOR SUPERVISORS · U.O.P. BANQUET SERVICE

1. SILVERWARE:
   a. Please check all silver, especially knives, for cleanliness and water spots. If necessary, have someone go over them with wet cloth.
   b. Put two forks on every place setting always. If the dessert requires a fork, and if there is enough silver use three forks. If there is not enough silver, send a clean fork in with the dessert.

2. REUSABLE FOODS:
   a. Butter: Place two (2) pats per person in each bowl; three (3) if there is baked potato. Ice on bottom and top of the butter.
   b. All reusable foods (butter, bread, salad dressing) should be cleared off the tables before the dishes, and brought back directly to the serving counter (where the salad women have to put it away).
   c. When milk pitchers are used, these should be returned to the kitchen for use by the cooks.

3. ICE WATER:
   a. Glasses should be half full with ice at the start of the banquet.
   b. Ice water pitchers should be at least ⅓ full with ice.
   c. On all served banquets, water pitchers are to be readied before the banquet and placed on side tables for use by the waiters during the meal. Whenever possible, there should be one pitcher per waiter.
   d. When there is a lengthy program, each table should be provided with a full pitcher of ice water just as the program starts. If possible, these pitchers should be filled ahead of time.
   e. Waiters must see to it that people always have full glasses of water throughout their meal. It is often wise to assign one or two waiters just for this purpose, as soon as the main course has been served.
   f. Waiters are not to pick up the glass, but pour directly from pitcher to the glass on the table *without asking the guest if he wishes more water*. Pitchers should never be more than ¾ full.

4. ROLLS:
   a. Waiters should place roll baskets on tables either just *before* or, (if the rolls are hot) right *after* the main dish has been served. If there is a shortage of rolls, serving it after the main course is better. Supervisors are to make sure, though, that rolls are not entirely forgotten. Waiters should also be on the lookout for empty roll baskets, and ask if more rolls are desired by the particular table. Usually, a basket needs to be refilled only half full.

5.   BEVERAGES:
      a.   At breakfasts, coffee should be served immediately, and then again as
            often as necessary until everyone has had the right to refuse coffee.
      b.   At lunches and dinners coffee should be served right after the main
            course and then again after the dessert. The serving of coffee should be
            interrupted when the main dishes are cleared, and again when desserts
            are served so that every waiter can be used for this important activity.
      c.   Coffee pitchers should not be filled more than ¾ full. Inexperienced
            waiters or waitresses must take the cup and saucer and *step back* from
            the table to avoid any possibility of burning the guest. Cups should be
            filled only ¾ full.
      d.   Sanka and Tea must be ready at all times, and the hot water for these
            should be served in a small pre-heated stainless steel pot.
      e.   Milk and Ice Tea should be served, if requested, in a glass, on a small
            plate.
            NOTE: Saucers are needed for glasses and small pots at all times, except
            if the table seems overcrowded. Lemon is always to be served with tea or
            ice tea, and some wedges should be readied in advance.

6.   CLEARING DISHES:
      a.   Salad plates may be cleared off either before the main course or right
            afterwards. Often waiters would do better to clear their salad plates than
            to gang up at the serving counter waiting for their entree plates.
            When salads are cleared with the entree plates, *never* allow waiters to
            place these plates on top of the entree plate in front of the guest. The
            table is not a garbage dump!
      b.   At most banquets, there is inadequate preparation for the clearing of dir-
            ty dishes. The proper way to prepare for this crucial activity is as follows:
            (1) Enough sidestands are placed aroung the room, and covered with
                 sheet pans as a base for the gray bus tubs.
            (2) If possible, each side stand should have at least 2-3 *clean* tubs placed
                 beside it (one on top, 2 on the floor).
            (3) Where available, small buscarts (with 3 tubs) should also be placed in
                 the dining room (at the far end of the room). Tubs should be carried by
                 busboys at all times.
            (4) The dishroom should be notified as soon as these buckets start to
                 come in, and should be instructed to empty *and* run these through
                 right away and return them to the waiters as quickly as possible.
            (5) Waiters should not be permitted to stack dishes in these tubs, but
                 rather to place them in there just as they come out of their hands
                 (gently, if possible!)
            (6) If at all possible, dessert dishes and coffee cups should be cleared
                 before the program starts. The headwaiter or supervisor may discuss
                 this with the program chairman and, possibly, give him a sign when
                 these dishes are all cleared.
            (7) Breakfast entree plates, or lunch and dinner dessert plates are always
                 to be cleared before the program starts - unless the chairman of the
                 program specifically requests otherwise.

7.   TABLE SERVICE:

   a.   The standard method of table service at U.O.P. is the "Wave System".
         This method calls for all waiters and waitresses to follow each other from
         one end of the dining room to the other end to complete the serving of
         each item as a team.

         The wave always starts at the tables nearest to the head tables and then
         moves toward the other end of the dining room.

         The wave system applies only to the serving of food, and not to the clear-
         ing of dishes or the serving of beverages. These latter activities are done
         by waiters individually, who fan out throughout the dining room to take
         care of these functions. It is the duty of the headwaiter or supervisor to
         see no table is forgotten in this process.

APPENDIX 17

MENUS AND MENU NOTES FROM INTERNATIONAL DINNERS AT U.O.P.

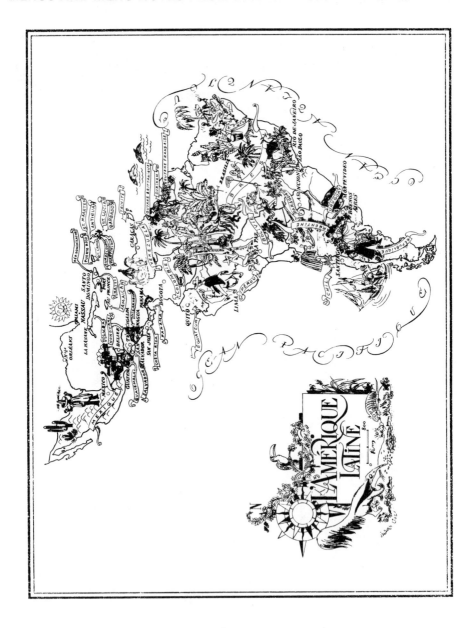

Description of Menu Items

CREAMED CHICKEN AND POTATO SOUP WITH AVOCADO AND CAPERS
Ajiaco Bogotano
(Colombia)

The highest and coolest mountain valleys of Colombia, especially the 8,500 foot one where Bogota is located, produce good white potatoes, and many traditional Bogota dishes feature these. In Colombia, as in many other Latin American countries, corn is another easily available and popular starch. The *Ajiaco Bogotano*, therefore, utilizes two popular foods and, by combining these with avocados and local spices, becomes a truly indigenous, as well as very tasty, dish.

STEAK WITH SPICED PARSLEY SAUCE
Carne a la Chimichurri
(Argentina)

In Argentina, more than any other Latin American country perhaps, beef is the staff of life. Many people eat it at every meal - and they sometimes eat little else. Beef and other meats are commonly broiled or roasted. The *chimichurri* sauce is a traditional sauce made with vinegar, oil, chopped parsley, and other spices, and adds an unusual aroma to an already exciting entree.

BEEF DUMPLINGS IN TOMATO SAUCE
Bollos Pelones
(Venezuela)

The main starch among the poorer people of Colombia and Venezuela is the *arepa*, a primitive sort of cornbread of Indian origin. Bollos Pelones is a sophisticated dish, made by stuffing balls of *arepa* dough with a mixture of seasoned finely diced meat, and then simmered in soup or fried in deep fat, until the crust is golden brown.

PORK STEW WITH SWEET RED PEPPERS
El Seco de Chivo
(Ecuador)

"Chivo" means goat in Spanish, and goat meat is sometimes used in Ecuador in preparing delicate dishes. In this instance, we have substituted pork for goatmeat - but in every other way, the dish is authentic. Coriander, the parsley-like, pungent herb adds a distinctive flavor of its own.

RICE WITH TOMATOES AND ONION
Arroz Brazileira
(Brazil)

No Latin American admires the way North Americans generally cook rice; plain, and white, with the grains stuck together. Rice is one of Brazil's basic foods, and the consumers insist that it be *glorified*. The most popular is to fry it with thinly sliced onions in lard or oil and to stir in a cut-up tomato.

CRANBERRY BEANS WITH SQUASH AND CORN
Porotos Granados
(Chile)

Chile is not a cattle country, and beef is comparatively scarce. So popular chilean dishes feature seafood, beans, and meat in moderate quantities. The leading national dish is *porotos granados*, a delightful way of preparing beans. It is almost certainly of Indian origin since it contains the three most typical indian foodstuffs: beans, corn and squash.

CARAMEL MILK PUDDING
Natillas Piuranas
(Peru)

A pleasant ingredient of many desserts is *manjar blanco*, a specialty of Peru. Essentially, it is milk boiled down with sugar and vanilla until it becomes a thick, golden-brown paste with a light caramel flavor. *Natillas Piuranas* is a single but delectable form of this dessert and is popular throughout Latin America.

UNIVERSITY OF THE PACIFIC
Stockton, California

February 17, 1971 All-Campus Latin American Dinner

in honor of Elbert Covell, founder of Elbert Covell College

Menu

Hors d' Oeuvres

BAKED MEAT TURNOVERS
Empanadas al Horno
(Argentina)

BANANA CHIPS
Chifles
(Ecuador)

AVOCADO DIP WITH TOSTADO CHIPS
Guacamole
(Mexico)

Soup

CREAMED CHICKEN AND POTATO SOUP WITH AVOCADO AND CAPERS
Ajiaco Bogotano
(Colombia)

Entrees

STEAK WITH SPICED PARSLEY SAUCE
Carne a la Chimichurri
(Argentina)

BEEF DUMPLING IN TOMATO SAUCE
Bollos Pelones
(Venezuela)

PORK STEW WITH SWEET RED PEPPERS
El Seco de Chivo
(Ecuador)

Vegetables

RICE WITH TOMATOES AND ONION
Arroz Brasileiro
(Brazil)

PARAGUAYAN CORNBREAD
Sopa Paraguaya
(Paraguay)

CRANBERRY BEANS WITH SQUASH AND CORN
Porotos Granados
(Chile)

Desserts

CARAMEL MILK PUDDING
Natillas Piuranas
(Peru)

CARAMEL-FILLED COCONUT COOKIES
Alfajores de Maicena
(Argentina)

Beverage

COFFEE
Cafe
(Colombia)

Pacific Luau 1974

In the late 1800's, King Kalakaua's revival of the hula and early meles began a musical renaissance still underway, and many hula songs of recent years follows styles and rhythm patterns dating back to Hawaii's earliest tradition.

* * * * *

DANCERS

Aiona, Duke
Alalima, Charles
Anderson, Betsy
Anderson, Cathie
Ashford, Frank
Ashford, Joan
Bartley, Sue
Bernhardt, Caroline
Bautista, Ricky
Bickel, Cindy
Cafferty, Pat
Chow, Chris
Coonley, Nancy

Dillingham, Peggy
Fong, Mele
Hager, Shannon
Hess, Leslie
Higashi, Kay
Jasper, Jeananne
Kekuewa, Rusty
Lo, Pauline
Runyan, Jim
Sakai, Sharon
Taira, Laurene
Unupe, Chandra

MUSICIANS

Aiona, Duke
Anamizu, Ed
Cafferty, Pat

Miyashiro, Bruce
Tsukazaki, Jon

Luau Cover by Betsy Anderson

* * * * *

Plenty Mahalo to the Hawaii folk who helped with the decorations.

HAWAII NO KA OI!!!

ALOHA! UOP's 60 Hawaiian students and our food service welcomes you to this year's special dinner, a feast from Hawaii, called a LUAU.

LUAU MENU

HAWAIIAN PUNCH
MACADAMIA NUTS

ROAST SUCKLING PIG
TERIYAKI CHICKEN
LOMI LOMI

FRIED RICE
SWEET POTATOES

FRESH PINEAPPLE AND PAPAYA
HAUPIA
KONA COFFEE

* * * * *

Hawaiian punch - a blend of native juices capped with a vanda orchid flown in from Kalei florists in Honolulu.

Macadamia nuts - a Hawaiian snack is termed *pupu* and we've chosen the nut that grows on the "Big Island, Hawaii." Almost all of the world's commercial production of macadamia nuts is Hawaiian.

Roast suckling pig - Cooking of *kalua* pig is generally done in an *imu* or underground oven. The Pig is cooked until it literally falls off the bone. The pig was prepared by Charlie Alailima and Vai Nuusa and Tafale Ainu.

Teriyaki Chicken - a sugar and soy sauce marinade which came to Hawaii from the Japanese. It is the most popular way of preparing meat in Hawaii today.

Lomi Lomi - Lomi means massage in Hawaiian. The raw thin salted salmon fillets have been massaged and washed to remove the salt. Onions and tomatoes are added to provide one of the great taste treats of Hawaii.

Fried Rice - provides one of the staples of the Hawaiian diet.

Sweet potatoes - In Hawaii, the taro root is used for *poi*, but for our dinner, we've chosen the sweet potato.

Fresh pineapple and papaya - These were flown in from Hawaii just for our luau. Pineapple is Hawaii's second largest crop. More than 1/3 of the world's supply of pineapples comes from Hawaii.

Haupia - this is a sweet sticky pudding made with coconut milk and cornstarch. The coconut milk was flown in from Honolulu.

Kona Coffee - The coffee grows on the island of Hawaii, mostly on small family farms.

PROGRAM

Aia la o Pele
Kawika
Hawaiian War Chant
Wahine Hololio
Ulupalakua
Kawohikukapulani
Laupahoehoe
Papalina Lahilahi
Waikiki
Honolulu I am Coming Back

* * * * *

A Brief History of the Hula

The origin of the hula dates back to Hawaiian legend. Various legends of the hula tell of the gods and goddesses who brought these beautiful dances to the people of Hawaii.

The hula was originally danced only by men. As time went on and the Island civilization became more complex, wars and governing duties kept the men too busy for the years of rigid training necessary. Women were then allowed to assume some of the ritual.

Some of the ancient hula chants were intricately worded, and held several meanings beyond the obvious word-for-word one--an occasionally ribald double meaning, a mythological, historical or topographical import, and sometimes a secret meaning hidden in a use of the language known only to the royalty or the initiated.

The hula gradually expanded into the "opera" of old Hawaii, with dancers and singers combining to tell history and folk tales. Meles or songs for the hula accompaniment touched on almost every aspect of daily or historical life.

The songs were composed by specially skilled poets, called haku mele, highly honored in the ancient hierarchy. Their works were passed down by word of mouth, and it is only through these sagas that any Hawaiian history has been preserved from the days before the coming of European civilization and a written language. In addition, much Island religious philosophy was incorporated into the chanted poetry.

日本食の夕べ

昭和四十三年 二月二十七日

御 献 立

あ ら れ

豆腐 の 吸物

牛肉 す きやき

海老 と 茄子 の 天婦羅

鶏肉 照焼

御 飯 · 漬菜

羊 羹 · 蜜柑

緑 茶

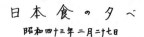

Menu

All Campus   Japanese Dinner   Tuesday, February 27, 1968

Shirakiku Rice Cakes

Bean Curd Soup

Pickled Cabbage

Steamed Kokuho Rice

Deep Fried Shrimp Tempura
with sliced eggplant

Beef Sukiyaki

Barbecued Chicken Teriyaki

Yokan (Sweet Bean Cake)

Japanese Tangerines

Japanese Green Tea

Please note: A Japanese host and hostess will be in each dining hall during the dinner. They will be happy to answer any questions about Japanese food or customs that you may wish to ask them.

YOU DON'T HAVE TO RIKE THEM ALL, BUT BE SURE TO TLY THEM ALL.

Japanese cuisine, refined product of the artistic culture of many thousand years, is characteristic and unique in that its picturesque arrangement of the food is just as important to our eyes as its delicate taste is to our tongue, and also in that the seasoning is limited to the minimum so that the original flavor of each fresh material should not be killed by strong seasoning. Japan is a rather small country, but its great length of 2000 miles gives a great variety of regional climates, and each material of each region in each season makes cooking of almost any kind possible on the Japanese dinner table. It is also important that each material be very fresh and be cooked in separate pots and be served on separate dishes so that the flavor of and the fragrance of each material should not be transferred to another. At a traditionally Japanese dinner, each guest has his own small table with more than twenty small dishes, each of which has a specific use for a specific item. In Japan, completely surrounded by sea, no authentically Japanese dish can be conceived of without fresh marine products and fresh vegetables and fruits so abundant in the country.

Our efforts to make this genuine Japanese dinner an exciting, educational experience have been greatly helped by the generous assistance of Mr. Yoshio Shida, owner of the Chiyo Restaurant in San Francisco (he serves many of our students and faculty at the Dental School), who has come personally to our campus with his family to supervise our preparations; also by the fine cooperation of Mr. Kazuaki Kuwada, Vice President of Japan Food Corporation, who has helped us in obtaining the right foods and decorations for this event. If you have any further questions about this meal or about Japanese customs generally, feel free to direct them to the Japanese host in your dining hall.

(Y. Kawarabayashi - Director, Language Laboratory)

Soup: There are largely two types of soup in Japanese cooking, one being clear consommé and the other creamy bean soup. The one served tonight is a clear consommé with bean curd.

Rice: This is not the famous "Flied lice," but it is the steamed Japanese rice, which is to the Japanese people what potatoes and bread are to the Westerners.

Pickle: Japanese dinner is always accompanied by lightly pickled vegetables such as radish, cabbage, melon, cucumber, eggplant, etc. You are served cabbage lightly pickled in salt water.

Tempura: Almost any fresh marine product and vegetable can be fried into tempura, some of the most popular ones being shrimps and eggplants, which you are tasting tonight.

Teriyaki: Teriyaki is barbecued meat, after having been marinated in soysauce, sugar, wine, etc. Any meat from the sea, land and the sky can be used, and tonight chicken has been selected for you.

Sukiyaki: You must all know the famous song, "Sukiyaki." The translation of the word means "As you like it," and this is one of the few Japanese dishes in which many different materials are cooked and served together. It has one type of meat (beef, chicken, pork, etc.) and fresh vegetables cooked in soysauce, wine, sugar, etc. Beef Sukiyaki has been prepared especially for you tonight.

Dessert: Two types of typically Japanese dessert are usually served: fresh fruit and preserved sweet cake. Tonight you will have Japanese tangerines and yokan (sweet bean cake).

Japanese green tea: Japanese green tea is harvested from the very same tea plants as the Western Black tea, but the former is steamed and dried directly while the latter is steamed and fermented before being dried. Thus the Japanese green tea which you are having tonight has a very fresh fragrance.

Menu

THE EAST Grace Covell	MIDWEST/SOUTHWEST Callison	THE SOUTH Anderson	WEST/HAWAII/ALASKA Elbert Covell
New Jersey Cranberry Juice Cocktail	*Kansas Apple Cider*	*Florida Orange Juice*	*California Oranges*
New England Clam Chowder	*Beef BBQ Ribs*	*Maryland Fried Chicken with Cream Gravy*	*Washington Apples*
Pennsylvania Dutch "Schnitz & Kneppe"	*Iowa Corn-on-the-Cob*	*Kentucky Fried Peach Half*	*Oregon Pears*
	Pickled Beans & Beet Salad	*Louisiana Jambalaya*	*Hawaiian Pineapples*
Boston Baked Beans	*Michigan-Wisconsin Cheese Tray*	*Virginian Sally Lunn*	*Alaskan "Aqutuk" (Ice Milk & Blueberries)*
Boston Brown Bread	*Hot Homemade Bread*	*Black-eyed Peas*	*Oatmeal Cookies Toll-House Cookies Old-Fashioned Farm Cookies*

UNIVERSITY OF THE PACIFIC ALL-CAMPUS "DISCOVER AMERICA" DINNER　　　*FEBRUARY 21, 1972*

DESCRIPTION OF MENU ITEMS

The East

New Jersey Cranberry Cocktail Juice

After a few hard and lean winters, the Pilgrims had learned to utilize the food in the New World. In addition to using maize, turkeys, and various kinds of seafood, they also started to raise apples and pears, and to use the fruit in the cranberry bogs.

Cranberries are now raised in Massachusetts, New Jersey, Wisconsin, Washington, and Oregon, and the pamphlet in your Travel Kit will tell you more about this delicious fruit.

New England Clam Chowder

A Pilgrim minister once wrote: "Bad dinners go hand-in-hand with depravity. A man properly fed is already half saved". In New England, the sea provided an abundance of fish and shell-fish for chowders. Every cottage had its herb garden: Parsley, thyme, marjoram and savory grew in fragrance beside the kitchen doorway. No wonder then, that clam chowder is now such a renowned New England specialty!

Pennsylvania Dutch "Schnitz und Knepp"

The Pennsylvania Dutch are not Dutch at all, but descendants from the early German Moravians from the Palatinate along the Rhine. They followed William Penn into the wilderness, and have changed little with the times. The harsh winters account for their early attempts to dehydrate food - most notably "Schnitz" - which are apples, cut into slices and dried, that were stored in the attic and used throughout the winter. "Schnitz und Knepp" are dried apple slices, simmered in water with ham and tiny yellow dumplings. When eating this dish, do follow the old Pennsylvania Dutch Saying: "Fill yourself up, clean your plate!".

Boston Baked Beans

Baked beans is another traditional New England recipe. The Puritan housewife cooked her beans all day Saturday, served them for dinner on Saturday night, and again as leftover warmed over the following Sunday noon. It was prepared differently in every section of New England. Here are a few variations:

Massachusetts: Use molasses.
New Hampshire and Vermont: Maple syrup instead of molasses.
Main: Put a peeled onion in the pot.
Connecticut: Add an onion and tomato catsup or chili sauce.

Boston Brown Bread

To fully utilize the heat of the oven, brown bread was cooked alongside the beans in the New England oven, and served hot

and steamed as a regular accompaniment. One of its prime ingredients, rye flour, was milled from a grain that grew well in the cool climate.

The South

Florida Orange Juice

Even though Californians are properly proud of their delicious oranges, it is nevertheless a fact that most of the frozen orange juice sold in the U.S.A. today comes from Florida oranges. Under the guidance of the Florida Citrus Commission, growers are busy to constantly improve the taste and durability of their juice. The latest item under development is a new type of "freeze-dried" process, which will open new world-wide markets for this "all-American"drink.

Maryland Fried Chicken with Cream Gravy

Chicken is one of America's most controversial foods. Every Southern cook had her own way of preparing it - some dipping the pieces in batter, some in buttermilk, some in nothing at all; some frying them in deep fat, some in only a little fat, some in oil.

In Maryland, traditionally the bird is seasoned and floured before frying, and it is served with gravy made from the pandrippings. Old-fashioned Marylanders never cover the chicken while it is frying. They say: "It is only people who don't want to scrub the stove afterward who use a lid for cooking fried chicken".

Kentucky Fried Peaches

What can one say about lovely cling peaches, cooked in butter and sugar, and basted with genuine Kentucky Bourbon? To your health!

Jambalaya

The food of the earliest French settlers in Louisiana consisted primarily of smoked meat, potatoes, and stewed alligators. The first improvement in cooking began with the arrival of French girls shipped over as brides for the lone male colonists. They were of two kinds: Loose women of the Paris jails, and poverty-stricken orphan girls. Creole cooking today is a beautiful blend of French, Spanish, Anglo-Saxon, and Indian influences - a cuisine that utilizes local ingredients, crabs, shrimp, oysters, crawfish, and mixes with it the wild spices and Indian herbs of the Western World. Jambalaya is a Creole-Cajun dish, a mosaic of highly flavored rice, ham, shrimp, and tomatoes, derived from the Spanish paella.

Virginia Sally Lunn

Many of the famous Southern breads are made of corn meal - to this day affectionately called "pone" (a word derived from "appone", the Indian word for cake). This includes such popular breads as cornmeal bread, spoon bread, hush puppies, hoe cakes, corn sticks, and cracklin' bread. We are serving you today another popular Southern bread - derived from an English recipe, using flour and lots of eggs.

Black-Eyed Peas

The term "soul food" is only a relatively recent one, but the cooking it stands for goes back a long way. It is a basic element of "soul" - a black life-style that disdains the hidebound puritanical Anglo-Saxon culture and instead emphasizes directness, spontaneity, an uninhibited feeling. The food originated as the food of the poor South - the greens, the corn and beans, and pork. It includes catfish, black-eyed peas, beans, sweet potatoes, as well as molasses and a variety of African spices.

The MidWest/SouthWest

Kansas Apple Cider

Even though some of the best apples are grown in Michigan, our extensive search for a Midwestern cider ended in Kansas. While we cannot explain this phenomenon at the time this is written, it is nevertheless true that 75 gallons of cider are being shipped from Kansas for your enjoyment this evening!

Barbecued Beef Ribs

"Barbecue", wrote an early journalist, "is any four-footed animal - be it a mouse or mastodon - whose dressed carcass is roasted, whole. At its best, it is a fat steer which must be eaten within an hour, for if ever the sun rises upon Barbecue, it becomes cold, baked beef - staler in the chill dawn than illicit love". The average American now consumes more than 176 pounds of meat - and in the Southwest, especially, a "barbecue" continues to be a feast of gigantic proportions. Short ribs are the narrow ends of what is popularly known as the "Prime Rib of Beef"; it is a highly underrated cut which, if eaten in patience and with the fatty layers removed, is truly an American delicacy.

Iowa Corn on the Cob

The U.S. leads the world in corn production, growing some 114 million tons a year. While the Midwest is the leading producer of field corn, Florida leads in the production of sweet corn, followed by California and New York.

Most people overcook corn. The best way is to drop it in boiling water and milk, bring the water to a boil again, and leave the corn there for no longer than five minutes. A pinch of sugar may be added, but do not add salt - it will toughen the kernels!

Pickled Beets and Bean Salad

The United States, perhaps more than any other country, loves salads. In the Midwest, the combination of beets, green beans, and wax beans, when mixed with vinegar, and spices makes a tart and tasty mixture which is a popular specialty of that part of our country.

Michigan and Wisconsin Cheese Tray

Americans are consuming more cheese than ever. The average American now eats over nine pounds a year, and the U.S. has become the world's largest producer of this protein-laden food. In 1801, when Jefferson was inaugurated, he was presented with a 1,600 pound cheese. Among the oldest of our domestic natural cheeses is the ever-popular Cheddar - as produced in New York, Vermont, and Wisconsin. We are also serving Frankenmuth cheese made in central Michigan.

Hot Homemade Bread

There is nothing more truly American than a hot loaf of wheat bread, served fresh out of the oven. To remind you of these vanishing memorabilia, we are recreating this experience for you today.

The West / Hawaii / Alaska

California Oranges

Few of us are aware how much the flavor of the American kitchen are a carryover from the Mexican. Canned chili peppers, frijoles, garbanzos, tortillas, as well as such items as the avocado and the artichoke - all these items have become accepted in our American West - even though they originated from Mexico. Surprisingly, perhaps, many of California's most popular fruits also came from Mexico, planted here by the Mission fathers. Surpassing the lemon, date, and fig, the orange ranks as the most popular of these transplanted fruits.

Oranges are always ready for picking in California. Valencias (the variety that grows near Ventura) ripen in spring and summer; naval oranges, the state's other leading orange, ripen in the fall and winter.

Washington Apples

The rich soil and abundant rain in the Pacific Northwest produce some of the finest berries, fruits, and vegetables in the United States. The Washington Delicious apple is probably the finest apple in the world. Many of them are grown in the Wenatchee Valley. The apple is easily recognized by its bright red color, tapering body, and five knobs at the blossom end.

Oregon Pears

The greatest pear country in the Pacific Northwest is in Oregon's Rogue River Valley. A good way to travel in the summer is to visit Ashland's Shakespeare Festival, and drive on to Medford to visit the orchards of Harry and Davids, a huge fruit mail-order business. Bartlett pears are the best known, but Comice, Anjous, and Russet Boscs are also fine eating pears.

Hawaiian Pineapples

Whether or not the average American college student is more interested in beautiful Hawaiian natives in the sarongs, or in luscious, fresh, juicy pineapples is a matter open to debate and depends, perhaps, to other factors such as his or her sex, the time of the year, and the availability of either.

In any case, the pineapples you are enjoying today were picked about ten days ago, flown across the Pacific through the courtesy of UNITED AIRLINES, ripened to perfection during the past week, and are ready today for your complete enjoyment. In addition to our debt to United Airlines, we must thank Mr. William E. Douglass, Manager of the Mid-Pacific Country Club in Kailua, Hawaii, and Mr. Ed Segarini for the special assistance given us in obtaining these classic American fruits in the perfect state in which we are serving them to you today.

Alaskan "Agutuk" (Blueberries and Ice Milk)

For all their many berries, Oregon and Washington suffer in comparison with Alaska, the true berry kingdom of the United States. In Alaska, most of the berries grow not only bigger, but better. A favorite Eskimo dish is to take fresh snow and top it with wild blueberries. We have substituted ice milk for the fresh snow - and we cannot guarantee that the blueberries actually came from Alaska - but we ask your indulgence and a little imagination.

Toll House, Oatmeal, and Old-Fashioned Farm Cookies

The classic after-school snack eaten by generations of American children consists of cookies and milk. Today we are serving the three most classic popular of all - the oatmeal cookie, the toll house cookie, and the old-fashioned farm cookie.

Menu

Appetizer

KALTER AUFSCHNITT
Cold Cuts

PUMPERNICKEL   *ROGGENBROT*
Pumpernickel   Rye Bread
Served with "Near-Beer"

Soup

LINSENSUPPE AUF SALZBURGER ART
Lentil Soup, Salzburg Style

Entrees

SAUERBRATEN   *KONIGSBERGER KLOPSE*
Marinated Pot Roast in Sweet & Sour Sauce   Poached Meatballs in Lemon & Caper Sauce

Vegetables

ROTKOHL MIT ÄPFELN   *SPINAT VOM RHEIN*
Red Cabbage with Apples   Spinach from the Rhineland
KARTOFFELKLÖSSE
Potato Dumplings

Salad

SELLERIESALAT
Celery Root Salad

Bread

WEISSBROT MIT KÜMMEL
White Bread with Caraway Seeds

Dessert

OBSTTORTE   *SCHWEINSOHREN*
Fruit Tart   Pigs Ears

Beverage

KAFFEE

MENU NOTES

German cooking is far more suitable to the average American taste than that of some other European nations. The German emphasis on "meat and potatoes", their love of sausages and beer, of butter and sweet desserts, suit Americans to a "T".

Meat is the cornerstone of German cooking and the *Braten* (or roast) is Germany's national dish. Like our American roasts, the *Braten* may be cooked in an oven; it may also be cooked with a little liquid in a tightly covered pot on top of the stove. Among the smaller meats, the most famous is the *Schnitzel* (cutlet) and the *Klops* (meatball). One of the most unique ways of German cooking is the *Eintopfgericht* (one-pot meal) which combines meat or fish with vegetables and potatoes into a long and slow-simmering stew. Easy and economical!

German sausage *(wurst)* fall basically into four basic types: *Rohwurst* is curved and smoked by the butcher; and then eaten as it is without further cooking; *Brühwurst* is both smoked and scalded by the butcher; it may be eaten as it is or heated by simmering; *Kochwurst* (i.e. like our cold cuts) may be smoked and is always well cooked by the butcher; and *Bratwurst* is sold raw by the butcher and must be pan-fried before eating.

The Germans eat not *three* square meals a day but *five;* traditionally, they eat Breakfast, Second Breakfast (like our lunch), Dinner (at noon), Coffee (usually coffee and pastries or sandwiches) and Supper.

Geographically, German cooking stems from three basic regions:
1. The Northern coastal plains (cabbage and bacon, pickled and smoked meats, roast duck and goose, halibut, flounder, eel and herring).
2. The central rolling hills (ham, pumpernickel, Pork, apples, plums, sausages and potatoes).
3. The mountainous south (game birds, venison, wine, sausages, pancakes, mushrooms and beer).

Today's dishes have been selected from all three of the regions mentioned above.

DESCRIPTION OF MENU ITEMS

KALTER AUFSCHNITT (Cold Cuts) The Germans like cold cuts even more than Americans, and especially when these consist of the various types of home made sausages which are world famous. Today we are serving the following types: Braunschweiger, Thueringer and Leberwurst (liver sausage).

PUMPERNICKEL The course dark bread made from unsifted rye flour, is a bread that cries out for butter and cold cuts and cheese. Good pumpernickel must leaven for 24 hours, then bake slowly for another 24 hours so that the natural sugar in the rye flour will darken and sweeten the bread evenly.

ROGGENBROT (Rye Bread) Until the modern science of nutrition made dark breads fashionable, white bread was a status symbol. In early Germany, the rich ate white bread when they could; generally speaking, the poor ate dark rye-bread.

LINSENSUPPE (Lentil Soup) Germany's thick soups, made from potatoes, dried peas or lentils, robustly flavored with sausage and onions, are famous throughout the world. In former days, lentil or pea soup with sausage or smoked pork would often constitute the main course for a modest income family. Today, everyone appreciates this hearty and delicious dish.

SAUERBRATEN (Marinated Pot Roast in Sweet and Sour Sauce) Pot roast marinated in wine is one of the most popular, truly German roasts, and originated in the Rhine country. The meat is left in the marinade (which includes onions, peppercorns, berries and bayleaf) for 2-3 days and then browned, and simmered for several hours. The sauce includes gingersnap crumbs or honey.

KÖNIGSBERGER KLOPSE (Poached Meatballs in Lemon and Caper Sauce) Königsberger Klopse differ from other meatballs in being poached. They always contain pork and at least one other kind of meat, very finely ground and combined with seasoning, eggs and bread crumbs. Dropped into boiling liquid, they are cooked like dumplings.

ROTKOHL MIT APFELN (Red Cabbage with Apples) From the early days, cabbage and turnips have been staples of the German's winter diet, and they invented many interesting variations on how best to cook it. This cabbage contains apples, onions, red wine and seasonings.

APPENDIX 18

NATIONAL ASSOCIATION OF COLLEGE AND UNIVERSITY FOOD SERVICES

Food Service Techniques Committee Report

WHAT ARE SOME OF THE EXTRA "LITTLE THINGS" YOU DO FOR THE STUDENTS THAT MAY RELIEVE THE MONOTONY OF THE DAY-AFTER-DAY OF SERVING "3 SQUARE MEALS"?

FOOD
Birthday cakes each month
All coffee they want each Sunday
Gold fish crackers w/special soup
Carve Ship Round or 30# hams on the line
Serve juice in lobby
"Sick Baskets" to hospitalized students
Unlimited relishes on lazy susan
Surprise dessert
Help students w/diet problems
Punch and hors d'oeuvres at special dinner
A la mode dessert
Fruit pancakes w/appropriate syrup
Homemade bread
Nut cups
Surprise menu - charcoal grilled steaks
Ice cream and salad bar
Hot cross buns during Lent
Make your own banana splits
Non-alcoholic cocktails and hors d'oeuvres in the lounge before buffet dinner
Seconds on coffee during meal hours

EXAM TIME
Music in dining room
Dessert buffet 9:30 p.m.-11:00 p.m.

Snacks
Snack bar open 17 hours -
$.10 hot dog -
$3.50 lobster tail
Free coffee
Special meal of popular foods
Snack bags
Care packages
Late snack parties
Steak for breakfast on 1st day of exams
Midnight snacks
All night operations w/hourly specials of: Thermos of coffee
Make your own sundae
Full bushels of popcorn
Suvival lunch and desperation dinner at special prices on "Dead" day

UNUSUAL MEALS
Special meal for each holiday
Thursday special steak
Foreign meals (Italian dinner, etc.)
Week-end specials:
Steak nights
Picnics - cookouts
Pizza nights

Continental breakfast on Sunday
Outdoor barbecues
Smorgasbord

UNUSUAL MEALS - con't.
Informal picnic - no limit
Salmon bake
White dinners or breakfast
Honorary meals for officials of
University or outside guests

ENTERTAINMENT
Music during exam time
Dinner dances
After-dinner movies on Friday
Christmas dinner dance and Buffet
Clothesline art show w/beverage and
goody stands and red-checked
tablecloths
Teenage "Hootenanny" of campus
talent in grill area on slow
afternoons
T.V. in food service area for World
Series, etc.

DECORATIONS
Decoration to suit the holiday
Candlelight
Employees wear costumes for
special occasions
Tablecloths

Plastic flowers on serving line
Fresh flowers on table on special
days and they may take them
Special napkins for a holiday
Decoration in dining room
National Cherry Week
Edible center pieces (Halloween)
Candy cane with silverware
at Christmas
Gold, pink, aqua tablecloths,
matching aprons and head bands
for servers

SERVICE
Formal buffet and formal banquet
each year
Student plan menu
Waiter service in women's halls
Exchange dinners between halls
Beverage bars and relishes in
dining room
Toasters, soup and vegetables in
dining room
Family style dinner
Furnish newspaper early
morning guests

ANY SUGGESTIONS FOR DISPLAYING AND POSTING THE NEXT DAY'S MENU?
Those Posting Menus Use the Following Methods and Ideas:
Make 500 copies weekly and ask for comments on new recipes through suggestion box
Decorate effect on posted menus during holidays
Post in all places possible on campus
Have special board outside entrance to cafeteria with pictures of "today" and "tomorrows" menu
Use strip type menu board
Publish in daily campus newspaper
Big sign with "We are serving"
Special 5 x 6 cards posted in front of counter
Have listed on posted menu, "Subject to Change"

DO YOU HAVE A SPECIAL PLACE TO SERVE "SPECIAL" FOOD THAT THE STUDENTS PARTICULARLY LIKE? HO DO YOU MERCHANDISE IT?
Serve potato pancakes in night coffee shop form 9:30-12:00 midnight
Have special bake sales
Serve pizza in the snack bar
One line for salads at noon; use it for hot selection at night
Snack bar serving pizza and submarine sandwiches
German Rathskeller in the planning stage
Special "speed line"
One-quarter hamburger, char-broiled to order in full view of customer
Special cafeteria area next to grill fountain section, serving Mexican Foods - tacos, tamales, enchiladas, burros, from 11:00 a.m. to 6:30 p.m.

WHAT IS THE ONE OUTSTANDING DINNER OR FEATURE YOU HAVE DONE THIS PAST YEAR?

INTERNATIONAL DINNERS

Madrigal Dinner - Old English Tradition: University of Nevada
Main Center Attraction - Boar's head
Menu:
Holly-read Mead - Tomato juice
Boef Dissh-metes - Prime Rib
Ofen-baken Pome - Oven-browned potato
Cremed Crop and Rote - Creamed carrots and peas
Gene Herbe with Cranberrys-frut - Fine herbs with cranberry fruit
Garden Fodes - Combination salad
Butterhornes Loves - Dinner rolls
Plum and Hony Confiture - Plum pudding
Festliche Drynke - Festival drink (choice of punch)
Wassail Cuppe - Coffee
Melk - Milk

Smorgasbord - Pacific Luthern University
Decorations:
"Bountiful Harvest" - Baskets filled with fruit, vegetables, cones, wheat, autumn leaves on tables.
Cornhusks, pumpkins and fall greenery in large containers against the walls of the dining room.
Napkins were tied with colored twine with an autumn leaf just above the bow.
Menu:
Baron of Beef carved by two male students
½ Cornish Rock hen w/Meringo Sauce
French fried prawns
Sweedish meat balls w/brown gravy
Baked and decorated whole Salmon (cooked w/head and tail on)
Sliced cold turkey
Sliced cold ham
Wild rice, whole green beans w/toasted slivered almonds and mushrooms
Assorted cheese trays - Swiss, cheddar, etc.
East India salad - served in large wooden bowls
Romaine, Endive & lettuce
Watermelon balls
Cantaloupe wedges
Green grapes
Grapefruit sections, pink
Wedges of red apples
Pomegranate seeds to garnish top
Salad dressings - Blue cheese, Sour cream w/mayonnaise
French honey w/celery seed dressing
Shrimp and macaroni shell salad, garnished with deep purple cabbage leaves

Fruit tray:
    Fresh fingers of pineapple
    Assorted wedges of melon - honeydew, watermelon and cantaloupe
    Sliced oranges dusted with powdered sugar
    Bunches of grapes - green, purple and tokay
    Pear halves - pale green, minted - pale pink, cinnamon
Lazy Susan:
    Cottage cheese with chives
    Cottage cheese with fruit
    Herring in wine
    Pickled herring
    Ripe olives
    Stuffed olives
    Spiced crab apple
    Sliced dill pickles
    Sliced sweet pickles
    Sweet gherkins
Lazy Susan - Relishes:
    Whole pickled beets
    Sliced onions
    Radish roses
    Celery sticks
    Carrot sticks
    Green pepper rings
Tray:
    Sliced tomatoes
    Stuffed ½ egg - kippered salmon & egg yolks,
    garnished with parsley
Molded Salads:
    Lime - mandarin oranges, grapefruit sections
    Red - apple sauce, crushed pineapple
    Orange - Thompson grapes and pecans
Waitresses moved through the dining room with food carts at desesrt time and offered the guests the following desserts:
    Parfait with cookie
    Pumpkin pie
    Mocha angel food cake

Dessert Smorgasbord - Northern Illinois
    Dessert Smorgasbord is served one night during the final exams.
    Menu:
    Cloud top cherry pie, fudge cake with fudge icing, peach princess pudding, fruit cup and jello cubes with topping.
    These are made available in each dining room, rather than at the serving counter. Each student is permitted to eat as many desserts as he desires.

Italian Dinner - Ball State Teachers College
    The Italian dinner menu is very popular and by request this year, was repeated three times. Our dining rooms look very much like an Italian restaurant when we light the stubby candles stuck in old bottles, highlighting the clever Italian placemats and serve the following menu:

Menu:
Grape Juice
Italian Meat Balls
Long Spaghetti with Meat Sauce and Parmesan Cheese
All Green Salad w/Italian Dressing
Garlic French Bread
Spumoni Ice Cream w/Sugar Cookie
Coffee - Tea - Milk

CHRISTMAS DINNERS

Buffet: University of California at Davis
Elaborate display tables, complete with traditional suckling pig, decorated turkeys, hams, lobsters, gelatin salad molds, fruits, plus quite an array of food on the buffet table.

Dinner: California State College at Hayward
Special Hour (Lobby)
ʼHot Wassail bowl with Flaming lady apples
Dinner:
Breast of Chicken Cordon Bleu
Whole spiced apricot garnish
Parsley potato balls in herb butter
Cranberry and orange salad
Parker house rolls - butter curls
Post Social Hour (Lobby)
Demitasse - christmas cakes, cookies

FORMAL DINNER DANCE - Harvey Mudd College

Price: $2.00 per couple
Locally Popular Band
Coat - check girl
Menu:
Passion fruit cocktail
Caesar salad (no anchovies)
Grilled 9 oz. New York Steak, melted butter
Buttered peas
Baked potato with sour cream
Hot dinner rolls with butter
Creame de menthe sundae
Coffee

SPECIAL HOLIDAY DINNERS: - University of Oklahoma

Special Holiday Each Month:

February: On Lincoln's Birthday, the traditional Lincoln Log is served. On Valentine's Day appropriate foods and decorations are used. Cherry Washington cake is served on Washington's Birthday. The ladies serving on the lines wear red paper hatchets as name plates.

March: In observance of Saint Patrick's Day, the engineers celebrate "The Shaving of the Beards". The campus newspaper is printed in green and green bulbs are used in the campus street lamps. Each unit serves Irish foods and decorates the dining froom and linen accordingly.

West Liberty State College

Ash Wednesday
Decorations: Jonquils
Menu:
Fruit cup
Seafood Plate: scallops, shrimp, fillet of sole
French fried potatoes
Tomato garnish
Orange raisin rolls
Pecan mint ice cream with chocolate syrup

BARBECUES AND PICNICS: - University of California at Los Angeles

Hobo's Holiday

A combo was secured to play music throughout the dinner meal (5:00 - 7:00 p.m.). The tables were arranged in such a way as to allow plenty of dance space. Buffet dinner was served, featuring ranch style foods - foot long hot dogs, baked beans, etc. Students provided and set up the dining room decorations in accord with the theme.

Ball State Teachers College

Chuck Wagon Dinner

You won't want to miss the Chuck Wagon Supper, Thursday, January 21, at the D.S. Ranch - and the residents didn't.

Residents were informed that the meal would be served on the D.S. Ranch, where the vittles would be served from the chuck wagon. Upon entering the dining room they were directed to the chuck wagon, by a cow poke where ladies in sun bonnets and colored aprons served up the vittles. Kerosene lamps, crocks and granite coffee pots accentuated the western atmosphere. An *original chuck wagon* menu usually consisted of beef, boiled potatoes in jackets, pinto beans, stewed dried fruit - pickled in barrels, biscuits, wild honey and boiled coffee. *The chuck wagon* vittles we served was roast beef, new potatoes cooked in jackets, green beans, spiced peach half, stewed fruit compote, assorted pickles, biscuits, honey, butter, and apple pie with cheese wedge, coffe and milk.

Each hall's music committee arranged to have special western type music played for the evening. Residents were invited to wear western type clothes and bring their ukes if they liked.

University of Tennessee

L.B.J. Barbecue

When President Johnson visited the campus, "L.B.J. Barbecue" special in the cafeteria, "Him N Her" Hot Dog Special - "two for the price of one" and Texas Burger Plate were served in the grill.

Kent State University

Down on the Farm

Once each month a special dinner is served without advance notice to the students so that it comes as a surprise to them. This type of idea is very well received by the students and everyone enjoys it. These special dinners started several years ago at Kent State University. This year, to start things off, an all-university event was planned for the first weekend after the students arrived for the Fall quarter. On this beautiful sunshiny afternoon, during a victorious football game, what could happen but the aroma from a barbecue pit started to float in the direction of the stadium. This attracted 7500 students and guests, who came wandering into the barbecue area. A pleasing and breath-taking sight of 168 feet of flaming pit, just loaded with four tons of golden browning chicken awaited them. A corral-type entrance to the barbecue area with bright colored flags, plus straw hats and bandana kerchiefs donned by the "farm hands", added to the atmosphere in this "Down on the Farm Affair".

Duke University

Election Night Dinner
Red, white and blue decorations - flags, campaign pictures, Uncle Sam hats for college girl employees, red, white and blue balloons and candles. Recipes from Mrs. Goldwater and Mrs. Johnson, and cakes decorated with L.B.J. and Barry.

North Park College and Theo. Seminary

"Nite on the Town"
I served a "Nite on the Town", converting the entire dining room (seats 432) into a restaurant. Linen tablecloths, linen napkins, floral centerpiece, my banquet china, silver and glassware were used. Hosts seated the students and presented a menu; waiters took the orders and filled them. I also arranged for student entertainment on a very casual basis; a piano player, a duo, a soloist, etc. All performed intermittently.

    Menu:
    Chilled fruit juice
    Choice of one: Fried chichen, Roast sirloin of beef, Seafood plate -
      shrimp and/or scallop
    Baked potato or mashed potato and gravy
    Choice of two: Broccoli with hollandaise sauce
      Buttered fresh corn
      Peas amandine
    Frozen fruit salad or head lettuce with dressing
      Green goddess dressing
      French dressing
      Italian dressing
    Our own homemade rolls - oatmeal - herb - cheese
    Desserts - choice of one:
      Mocha Torte, strawberry shortcake, chocolate eclair, ice cream
      sundaes: chocolate, strawberry, butterscotch, or wild blackberry,
      or orange sherbet
    Beverages: Milk - coffee ala Henrici - tea

APPENDIX 19
SAMPLE HANDOUTS FROM "PROPAGANDA ROOM"

FOOD SERVICE
AT PACIFIC

A time and a place for every taste!

AT THE UNIVERSITY CENTER

THE REDWOOD ROOM

MONDAY TO FRIDAY
11:30 A.M.—1:30 P.M.

*Featuring: an Elegant Buffet
or a Light Lunch in a Relaxed
Atmosphere.*

SAMPLE MENU

Entrees	Roast Beef Au Jus	**$3.25**
	Lasagne	
Soup	Clam Chowder	
Salad	Tossed Salad	Fruit Salad
Buffet	Jello Salad	Potato Salad
	Assorted Relishes	Cottage Cheese
	Carrot or Cole Slaw	
	Fresh French Bread	
Desserts	Ice Cream or Pudding	Beverages

Light Lunch
Soup or (1) Salad **$1.85**
Sandwich of the Day
Beverage

MEAL TICKETS HONORED
VALUE $1.85

THE MALL

Monday-
Thursday   7:30 A.M.—4:30 P.M.
Friday   7:30 A.M.—3:30 P.M.
Closed Saturdays & Sundays

*Featuring: Quick-Service Type
Foods, Ready-Made Sandwiches
and Salads, Fountain Items,
Beverages and Desserts.*

SPECIAL BREAKFAST
Two (2) Eggs, fried or scrambled
Hash Browns, Toast   1.10
With Ham, Bacon or Sausages   1.70

LUNCHEON MENU

Hamburger	1.00	Hot Dog	.65
Cheeseburger	1.10	Hot Dog W/Chili	.75
UOP Special		Hot Soup	.50
W/Chips	1.10	Chili W/Crackers	.65
		French Fries	.50

Plus assorted Salads, Sandwiches and Desserts

MEAL TICKETS HONORED
B'FAST   TILL 10:30:   1.65
Value: LUNCH   TILL 4:00:   1.85
DINNER   TILL CLOSING: 2.40

THE RATHSKELLER

Mon.—Fri. 8:30 AM—2:00 PM; 5:30 PM—10:00 PM
Sat. 9:00 AM—2:00 PM—Sun. 5:30 PM—10:00 PM

Continental Breakfast
8:30 to 10:30 AM

LUNCH 11AM—2PM
HOFBRAU
Hot Roast Beef Sandwich 1.85
w/salad, pickle on french roll

Assorted Cold Sandwiches	1.05	Soup	.50
Salad	.30-.50	Hot Chili	.65

GRILL

Hot Dog	.65	Grilled Cheese	.70
Hamburger	1.00	Grilled Cheese W/Ham	1.05
		French Fries	.50

HEALTH FOOD BAR
Sample Sandwich: Avocado,
Cheese, Alfalfa Sprouts, tomatoes 1.00
Sample Drink: "Whizzie"
Yogurt, Honey, Fresh Fruit   .85
Health Food Salad 75

NIGHTS
Food Served 5:30 PM—9:30 PM — Bar till 10:00 PM

Pizzas: Plain	2.00	2.95	3.75	
1 Item	2.30	3.60	4.30	Tossed Salad
				large bowl 1.05
Chicken Dinner			2.40	individual .55
Trailmaster Steak Sandwich		1.25	French Fries	.50
Diet Plate			1.20	Popcorn .30

Plus other grilled sandwiches
WITH MUSIC AND ENTERTAINMENT

AT THE RESIDENCE HALLS

GRACE COVELL DINING HALL

Weekdays: B'fast 7:15 AM—10:00 AM
Sat. and Sun.: Cont'l B'fast 8:30 AM—10 AM
Lunch 11:15 AM—1:30PM
Brunch 11:00 AM—1:00 PM
Dinner 4:30 PM—6:30 PM

*Grace Covell has a large, cheerful dining
hall with two serving lines for speedy
service and two private dining rooms where
small groups can eat in privacy.*

ELBERT COVELL DINING HALL

Weekdays: B'fast: Closed
Sat. and Sun.: Closed
Lunch 11:30 AM—12:30 PM
Dinner 5:00 PM—6:15 PM

*Elbert Covell is a friendly dining room
where you can practice your Spanish with
the "Covellianos" and where rice and hot
gravy or special casserole dishes are served
everyday for lunch.*

RAYMOND DINING HALL

Weekdays: B'fast: Closed
Sat. and Sun.: Closed
Lunch 11:30 AM—12:30 PM
Dinner 5:00 PM—6:15 PM

QUAD DINING HALL

Weekdays: B'fast 7:15 AM—9:00 AM
Sat. and Sun.: Cont'l B'fast 8:30 AM—9:30 AM
Lunch 11:15 AM—12:30 PM
Brunch 11:00 AM—1:00 PM
Dinner 4:30 PM—6:30 PM

*In addition to meeting interesting students and faculty who
have been in Asia, you will also like Quad if you are
vegetarian. While all dining rooms serve suitable foods for
vegetarians during breakfast and lunch, only Quad serves
specially-cooked vegetarian entrees at all meals. Be sure to
come early — they usually go fast!*

SELF-INSPECTION CHECKLIST FOR COLLEGE FOOD SUPERVISORS

A.   DINING ROOM
  1. Are the dining room doors open on time?
  2. Are the dining room hours clearly posted?
  3. Is the menu posted near the entrance?
  4. Is the cashier/checker friendly?
  5. Is the dining room atmosphere (decor) cheerful?
  6. Are there plenty of napkins, trays, silverware?
  7. Are the trays dry?

B.   SERVING LINE
  1. Are the servers *neat* and friendly?
  2. Are the servers wearing smocks or uniforms?
  3. How well is unusual food described or marked?
  4. Is "hot food" really kept "hot"?
  5. Can I come back or my ice cream when I'm ready for it?
  6. Are the dinner plates heated?
  7. Are any food pans decorated or garnished?

C.   BEVERAGE COUNTER
  1. Are there saucers for the coffee cups?
  2. Is plain ice water available and clearly marked?
  3. How can you tell which milk dispenser is full?
  4. Is ther *always* non-fat milk?
  5. Is there sticky coke syrup all around the soft drink dispenser?
  6. Is there Sanka, tea (with lemon), and hot chocolate?

D.   CONDIMENT AND SALAD COUNTER
  1. Are there at least two (2) kinds of salad dressing?
  2. Is every salad decorated, even cottage cheese?
  3. Does the fruit cocktail contain some fresh fruit (e.g. apples, bananas, grapes)?
  4. Is there *always*:
     a. Cranberry sauce with turkey?
     b. Apple sauce with pork?
     c. Tartar sauce with fried fish?
     d. Mint jelly with lamb?
  5. Is there always plain oil and vinegar?
  6. Is the salad bar kept wiped clean throughout the meal period?
  7. Is the salad bar as appetizing at 6:30 as it is at 5:00 p.m.?
  8. Are there any rings (at 5:00) or dried-up residue inside the containers for the mayonnaise, mustard, catsup, or dressings?

E.   RECEIVING AREA, AND JANITORS MOP AREA
  1. Is there loose garbage?
  2. Is there water on the floor?
  3. Could a thief steal food or supplies from the receiving area?
  4. Are all the mops and brooms hung up?
  5. Are any mop buckets full of dirty water?
  6. Are the mops white or dark grey?
  7. Is the required OSHA poster somewhere in an obvious place?
  8. Is there a "No Smoking" sign posted in the kitchen?
  9. Is there color (or wall decorations) on the kitchen wall?
  10. Are there hand washing signs in every washroom?

F.   KITCHEN
  1. Is there a lot of "junk" (aluminum foil, hot pads, etc.) on the cook's work tables? On top of the refrigerator?
  2. Is any piece of cooking equipment turned on without being used?
  3. Is the hand sink clean? Equipped with soap and towels?
  4. Are all the cooks knives stored in knife racks?
  5. Are all items stored in the salad refrigerator *tightly covered*?
  6. Are plent of *clean* kitchen towels readily available in the salad prep area?
  7. Are the drain troughs and floor mats clean and sanitary?

G.   PERSONAL APPEARANCE
  1. Is hair clean, contained, and properly worn?
  2. Is make-up, if any, appropriate?
  3. Are clothes (or uniform) clean and pressed?
  4. Are hands and fingernails clean?
  5. Are shoes appropriate (no sandals or sneakers) and shined?

F-4   Sunday, Sept. 23, 1973   Stockton (Calif.) Record

ONE TO A CUSTOMER, PLEASE
Greg Robinson, Chuck Knutson Aren't Phased

ALL THE MILK YOU CAN DRINK
Linebacker Carter Corey Can Have His Fill

MEAT'S STILL BIG ON MENU
This Night It's Roast Pork

It's Real Family-Style Cooking

Go Easy on the Meat and Clear Your Plate

With 2,200 mouths to feed on a budget already shot by rocketing food prices, the University-of the Pacific is cutting down.

Its main economies? No "seconds" on main dishes and a party only every month and a half instead of every month. (The first was a steak barbecue Wednesday.)

This may sound like fairly elegant thrift in most families, but for Pacific food services director Paul Fairbrook any curtailment in meals is hard to decree.

In the past several years Pacific's food department has gained a reputation as a rather sophisticated purveyor of meals—preparing dishes with the spices and condiments most institution kitchens ignore, offering a more varied bill of fare than many restaurants, catering to the latest student tastes (Pacific's ovens turn out "ecology bread" for those who prefer "natural foods" and cooks put together special meatless meals every day for 150 vegetarians on campus) and, in

general, acting as if food services ought to suit the students instead of vice versa.

Adding glamor to this prescription for contented customers the party-throwing techniques of an administrator who sees himself as a host.

The fiscal facts of life closed in on Fairbrook immediately after he returned from his summer vacation. Costs no accountant could foresee when the budget for 1973-74 was set early this year already plainly spelled out a $125,000 increase in expenses with bills coming

in anywhere from 25 per cent to 129 per cent above spring totals. Among the super shocks: bacon, from 69 to $1.30 a pound; chicken, from 41 to 94 a pound; salad oil, from $9.25 to $19.10 a case; top round, from $1.18 to $1.43.

Fairchild did not—does not —want to see the tab for board and room raised although an $80 boost would have done the trick. He says "at $1,400 a year we are among the top four in the 10 colleges with which we compare ourselves."

He opted instead for trying

for a $50,000 reduction in the deficit through day-to-day economies, aiming for savings approximating 25 cents per student per day. He admits this kind of cutback isn't easy and says the college may have to consider upping the board bill in February or later next year.

The first change he made was in his "all you can eat" approach. Students now are limited to single servings of meat, baked goods, fresh fruits and bacon and eggs. (The daily dinner menu continues to feature two entrees,

Please turn to F-15

UOP BAKES ITS OWN GOODIES
And Asks Students To Eat Wisely

BUT DIETERS AND VEGETARIANS ARE NOT FORGOTTEN
'Ecology Bread,' Yogurt Are Campus Favorites

however, and the second one is not limited.)

The second was to reduce the number of times he serves high-cost items. And the third was to exercise better control over portions served. This means the right-sized serving implement in the right dish and the placement of the expensive items—roast beef slices—on patty papers. "It's not aesthetic," Fairbrook sighs, "but it's fair."

Fairbrook thinks dining, even en masse, should be exciting and he's been pleased that Pacific has been willing to spend $100 to $200 more per student for food than other colleges.

He informed every student of his dilemma, and its resolution, by letter and has thus far had no complaints. "Students are basically fair-minded."

If students do have gripes, he expects to hear them. This is no back-of-the-kitchen food administrator. He's "out front" much of the time with the "customers," and when

he's at his desk, the door is open. Because he wants to meet and know students, he refuses to mail free guest tickets to students as some colleges do. He insists on meeting guests personally, showing them around, and finding out what they think of operations.

Tuned in to students, his department decreed that students who wanted short orders could use their meal tickets at the campus hamburger stand, the End Zone, and could share their tickets there with

friends. And during finals week, the department puts out complimentary late night snacks for crammers.

In a final economy, Fairbrook has decided to give only six parties instead of nine in 1973-1974. In the past these events have covered the globe in cuisine and atmosphere and even incuded what may be the largest progressive party in area history—a walking-eating party early this year that took students from dining hall to dining hall and from one fa-

mous American dish to another. Does he have any advice for the family trying to make ends meet? "Make creative casseroles, and cook thick soups. Crisp small pieces of sausage and add them to soups as you would croutons. This helps make a soup a meal."

He ends inthe interview on a happy prediction: meal. "Prices will come down."

INDEX

A